# MARTIN HEIDEGGER:

# BIBLIOGRAPHY AND GLOSSARY

# BIBLIOGRAPHIES OF FAMOUS PHILOSOPHERS

The Philosophy Documentation Center is publishing a series of "Bibliographies of Famous Philosophers," Richard H. Lineback, general editor. Published bibliographies include **HENRI BERGSON: A BIBLIOGRAPHY, JEAN-PAUL SARTRE AND HIS CRITICS: AN INTERNATIONAL BIBLIOGRAPHY (1938-1975), ALFRED NORTH WHITEHEAD: A PRIMARY-SECONDARY BIBLIOGRAPHY, EDMUND HUSSERL AND HIS CRITICS: AN INTERNATIONAL BIBLIOGRAPHY (1894-1979), JEAN-PAUL SARTRE AND HIS CRITICS: AN INTERNATIONAL BIBLIOGRAPHY (1938-1980), Second Edition,** and **MARTIN HEIDEGGER: BIBLIOGRAPHY AND GLOSSARY**. Forthcoming bibliographies include works on Thomas Hobbes and George Santayana.

# MARTIN HEIDEGGER:

# BIBLIOGRAPHY AND GLOSSARY

**Hans-Martin Sass**

Published by

**PHILOSOPHY DOCUMENTATION CENTER**
**BOWLING GREEN STATE UNIVERSITY**
**BOWLING GREEN, OHIO 43403**
**U.S.A.**

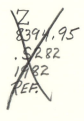

Library of Congress Card Number: 81-86346

ISBN 0-912632-48-8

# CONTENTS

# PART I
# INTRODUCTION

Martin Heidegger's *Thought* is a part of Western philosophy, nevertheless his influence, still increasing, outgrows the limits of Western tradition. His philosophy addresses some of the most crucial and most essential issues in contemporary intellectual orientation of mankind. The overemphasis on critical and rationalistic analysis since the Age of Reason has laid grounds for the contemporary world of a global civilization, more and more based on Technology and Science and on the concept of Open Society. As a result of these processes of emancipation out of factual or pretended ideational and political dominations, Truth has been reduced to the verification or falsification of scientific datas, while Freedom is understood as a result of social contracting which finally establishes legal systems and civil rights. Heidegger's response to these developments is not simply a refusive one. On the contrary, his questioning Being reaches for deeper founding and then for turning of what he would call "seinsvergessende" narrowed concepts of Truth and Freedom.

In understanding Truth as taking things out of concealment, letting them be seen in their unconcealment, and in understanding Freedom as letting beings be, Heidegger re-opens the dialogue with the early Greek understanding of hermeneutics of Dasein and the being's relationship to logos. In questioning the individual being's relationship to Being Heidegger also bridges the gap between Eastern and Western tradition offering dialogues to positions like Taoism and Zen-Buddhism. The Bibliography covers Heidegger's intense dedication to the hermeneutics of Western philosophical texts, to philosophically interpret what is going on in modern technology, and to increasingly developing dialogues between Eastern and Western thought.

Starting within the phenomenological movement in "Sein und Zeit" (1927) he surveyed the fields of Ek-Sistense-ontology influencing existentialist thought, terminology, and lifestyle immensely. He himself, however, did not consider "Being and Time" to be a contribution to "existentialism". On the contrary, it was the very first step of phenomenologically unconcealing the elusive nature of Being, followed by his Marburg lectures on "Logic" (1927) and "Fundamental Problems of Phenomenology" (1928), using the method of phenomenological reduction in his very own way: (1) interpreting Dasein on the ground of temporarily and explicating Time as the transcendental horizon for the question of Being; (2) deconstructing the history of Western ontology by eagerly questioning prime texts on the being's relationship to Being, which turned out not to be at the human being's command, "nicht verfuegbar". However the "growing originality of the opening up (wachsende Urspruenglichkeit der Erschliessung)" finally necessarily forced the method which opened up to go out of date (Grundprobleme der Phaenomenologie, 1975, p. 467) Heidegger's serving struggle (dienender Kampf) with the phenomena transformed the method of phenomenology, previously understood to be a scientific one, into more adequate postphenomenological approaches to unhiding Being and bring the thinker closer to the Being's shining.

Among those paths are (1) the importance of being silent, of exericising the power of listening, of overcoming the encrusted every-day behavior, of preparing oneself to let the unhiding happen ("Letter on Humanism", 1974); (2) the extending of the dialogue with ontological tradition to the poets, Hoelerlin became his favorite partner in discourse but also contemporaries like Paul Celan and Rene Char were included in those dialogues ("Elucidations of Hoelderlin's Poetry" 1944); (3) the questioning of language, eagerly searching for the interrelationship between logic, language and truth, understanding language as a dwelling place of Being (e.g., "On the Way of Language" 1959); (4) the analysis of technology, as demanding and challenging (herausforded) ontologically, clearing away concealing hedges and walls, releasing ("The Question concerning Technology" 1954); (5) the crafting of Thoughts ("Gedachtes", 1971), a kind of poetry, heavy and with heavy words, unusual connections, correspondences and intercourses, comparable to the fragments of Heraclitus or Hoelderlin, which might allow unconcealing to happen; bridging Dichten und Denken, to create and to think. Heidegger himself called it Turn (die Kehre) what happened to his approach to Being and to the paths he pursued: "Through Phenomenology to Thought."

This is not the place to enumerate all the fields of Heidegger's influence in philosophy, culture and science, as well as his unexpected and still growing influence outside Europe, in the Americas and in contemporary Eastern thought. The immense widespread of topics and the quantity of entries itself, as presented in the Bibliography, are self-explanatory.

In putting the Bibliography together I enjoyed the cooperation of many colleagues, too numerous to mention. The help and the advice I received is not only a deep personal satisfaction but also a fine example of international communication in a highly specialized field of academic research. Tadashi Kouzuma and T. Kakihara (Tokyo) contributed all Japanese entries, while Krzysztof Michalsky (Warsaw), Eduard Landolt (Catania), Orlando Pugliese (Buenos Aires, Berlin) and Todor Oiserman (Moskau) as well as Keith Hoeller (Seattle) and John Sallis (Pittsburgh) provided, together with many other colleague and friends, information in their particular field of Polish, Italian, Iberoamerican, Soviet and American literature. I am especially grateful to the wisdom and knowledge of Otto Poeggeler (Bochum) Joseph Kockelmann (Penn State) and Koichi Tsujimura (Tokyo).

Bibliographical essays written by Pelegri, Pereboom, Kouzuma and Lapointe have been used as well as reviews of my two previously with Hain Verlag, Meisenheim am Glan, Bundesrepublik Deutschland, published bibliographies on Heidegger (1968, 1972). The Philosophers Index's on-line-service was also examined; it might be worthwhile to note that as a result of a different type of selection, out of 1165 entries in the on-line-service available in spring of 1979 only 770 are represented here, the remaining just mentioning Heidegger, would not be understood as genuine secondary sources on Heidegger.

The Table of Contents does not need elaborate explanation. The works by Heidegger are represented in chronological order with cross-references wherever necessary or helpful. It would not have made sense to present the works by Heidegger along the lines of the so-called Gesamtausgabe, because this edition--unfortunately the only one which has access to Heidegger's unpublished papers--does not meet generally accepted standards of historico-critical editions (see; *Allegemeine Zeitschrift fuer Philosophie,* 3, 1977, 70-74, and *The New York Review of Books,* Dec. 4, 1980, 39-41).

There will be translations of many volumes of the Gesamtausgabe, especially of its Section II: *Lectures,* which might hopefully be able to improve the texts, at least in its translations. In the United States some volumes will be published in translation by Indiana University Press and by Pennsylvania State University Press, while Sobunsha Publishing House in Tokyo under the chief editorship of Koichi Jsujimura and Harmut Buchner will publish most of the volumes in a Japanese Gesamtausgabe called *Haideya Zenshu.*

Among the Indexes are those for Names and Subjects. Between the two alternatives of preparing a Subject Index, either in a rather small or a widely layed out and interpreting manner, the first alternative had been chosen. The "Index of Translations" presents alphabetical lists referring to "Works by Heidegger", while the "Index of Reviews of Works by Heidegger" refers to "Works concerning Heidegger". However, as the distinction between a review and an article in general quite often is difficult to be made, this is even more true for the literature on Heidegger. The lists of papers given at the fifteen Heidegger Conferences held so far in the United States and Canada may serve as one example among others, important enough to document the rich and lasting influence of Heidegger's thought worldwide, this time on the North American continent.

Hans-Martin Sass
Ruhr-Universitaet, Bochum
Georgetown University, Washington D.C.
Fall 1981

# PART II
# WORKS BY HEIDEGGER

### 1912

1      "Das Realitätsproblem in der modernen Philosophie." *Jahrbuch* (Fulda), 25, 1912, 353-363. Rpt. in *Frühe Schriften.* (Gesamtausgabe, Abt. 1: Veröffentlichte Schriften 1914-1970, Bd. I). Ed. Fr. W. von Herrman. Frankfurt: Klostermann, 1978, 1-15. *See* 181.

**Translation**

Italian: "Il problema della realita." In *Scritti Filosofici,* by Martin Heidegger. Ed. and trans. A. Babolin. Padova, 1972, 131-148.

2      "Neuere Forschungen über Logik." *Literarische Rundschau für das katholische Deutschland* (Freiburg), vol. 38, 1912, 465-472, 517-524, 565-570. Rpt. in *Frühe Schriften.* (Gesamtausgabe, Abt. 1: Veröffentlichte Schriften 1914-1970, Bd. I). Ed. Fr. W. von Herrmann. Frankfurt: Klostermann, 1978, 17-43. *See* 181.

**Translation**

Italian: "Recenti reicerche sulla logica." In *Scritti Filosofici,* by Martin Heidegger. Ed. and trans. A. Babolin. Padova, 1972, 149-179.

### 1913

3      Rev. of "Kants Briefe in Auswahl." Ed. and comment by F. Ohmann. Leizig, 1911. *Literarische Rundschau für das katholische Deutschland* (Freiburg), vol. 39, 1913, 74.

**Translation**

Italian: "Recensioni 1913-1914." In *Scritti Filosofici,* by Martin Heidegger. Ed. and trans. A. Babolin. Padova, 1972, 180-209.

4      Rev. of "Zeitlichkeit und Zeitlosigkeit. Ein grundlegender theoretisch-philosophischer Gegensatz in seinen typischek Ausgestaltungen und in seiner Bedeutung für die modernen philosopischen Theorien," by N. v. Bubnoff. Heidelberg, 1911. *Literarische Rundschau für das katholische Deutschland* (Freiburg), vol. 39, 1913, 178-179.

**Translation**

Italian: "Recensioni 1913-1914." In *Scritti Filosofici,* by Martin Heidegger. Ed. and trans. A. Babolin. Padova, 1972, 180-209.

5      "Curriculum Vitae." In *Die Lehre vom Urteil im Psychologismus. Ein kriisch-positiver Beitrag zur Logik.* Leipzig, 1914, 111.

**Translation**

English: "Curriculum Vitae." Trans. T. Schrynemakers. *Listening. Journal of Religion and Culture,* vol. 12, no. 3, 1977, 110. Rpt. in *Martin Heidegger,* by J. Kockelmanns. Pittsburg: DuQuesne Univ. Press, 1965, 1-2.

## 1914

6    *Die Lehre vom Urteil im Psychologismus. Ein kritisch-positiver Beitrag zur
Logik.* [Meinen Eltern] Leipzig, 1914, VIII, 110. [Phil. Diss. Freiburg 1914]
Rpt. in *Frühe Schriften.* (Gesamtausgabe. Abt. 1: Veröffentlichte Schriften
1914-1970. Bd. I). Ed. Fr. W. Herrmann. Frankfurt: Klostermann, 1978,
59-188. Excerpts in *Zeitschrift für Philosophie und philosophische Kritik*
(Leipzig), vol. 155, 1914, 148-172, 156. Leipzig, 1915.

**Translation**

Italian: *La dottrina del giudizio nello psicologismo.* Ed. A. Babolin. Padova:
La Garangola, 1972, 167 p.

7    Rev. of *Von der Klassifikation psychischer Phänomene. Neue, durch Nachträge
stark vermehrte Ausgabe der betreffenden Kapitel der Psychologie vom
empirischen Standpunkt,* by F. Brentano. Leipzig, 1911. *Literarische
Rundschau für das katholische Deutschland* (Freiburg), vol. 40, 1914,
233-234.

**Translation**

Italian: "Recensioni 1913-1914." In *Scritti Filosofici,* by Martin Heidegger. Ed.
and trans. A. Babolin. Padova, 1972, 180-209.

8    Rev. of *Kant and Aristoteles. Ins Deutsche übertragen von L. Heinrichs,* by C.
Sentroul. Kempten/München, 1911. *Literarische Rundschau für das
katholische Deutschland* (Freiburg), vol. 40, 1914, 330-332.

**Translation**

Italian: "Recensioni 1913-1914." In *Scritti Filosofici,* by Martin Heidegger. Ed.
and trans. A. Babolin. Padova, 1972, 180-209.

9    Rev. of *Kant-Lainenbrevier. Eine Darstellung der kantischen Welt- und
Lebensanschauung für den ungelehrten Gebildeten aus Kants Schriften,
Briefen und mündlichen Äusserungen.* Compiled by Dr. F. Gross. Zweite
verbesserte Auflage München, 1912. *Literarische Rundschau für das
Katholische Deutschland* (Freiburg), vol. 40, 1914, 376-377.

10   "Besprechungen, 1913/1914." In *Frühe Schriften.* (Gesamtausgabe, Abt. 1:
Veröffentlichte Schriften 1914-1970, Bd. I). Ed. Fr. W. von Herrmann.
Frankfurt: Klostermann, 1978, 45-54.

[Contains reviews of "Kants Briefe in Auswahl," "Bubnoff...,"
"Brentano...," "Sentroul...". *See* 3, 4, 7, 8.]

## 1916

11   *Die Kategorien und Bedeutungslehre des Duns Scotus.* Heinrich Rickert in
dankbarster Verehrung. Tübingen: J. C. B. Mohr, 1916, 265. [Habilitation
thesis presented to the Philosophiche Facultalt, Univ. of Freiburg, Spring
Term 1915.] Rpt. in *Frühe Schriften.* (Gesamtausgabe, Abt. 1:

Veröffentlichte Schriften 1914-1970, Bd. I). Ed. Fr. W. von Herrmann. Frankfurt: Klostermann, 1978, 189-411.

[As a photocopy: Ann Arbor, Michigan: Xerox University Microfilms, 1974.]

**Translations**

French: *Traité des categories et de la signification chez Duns Scot.* Trans. and intr. F. Gaboriau. Paris, 1970, 240.

Italian: *La dottrina delle categorie e del significatio in Duns Scoto.* Ed. A. Babolin. (Piccolo biblioteca filosofica Laterza, 92). Roma-Bari: Laterza, 1974, XXVI-261.

12      "Der Zeitbegriff in der Geschichtswissenschaft." *Zeitschrift für Philosophie und Philosophische Kritik* (Leipzig), vol. 161, 1916, 173-188. Rpt. in *Frühe Schriften.* (Gesamtausgabe, Abt. 1: Veröffentlichte Schriften 1914-1970, Bd. I). Ed. Fr. W. von Herrmann. Frankfurt: Klostermann, 1978, 413-433. *See* 181.

**Translations**

English: "The Concept of Time in the Science of History." Trans. H. S. Taylor and H. W. Uffelmann. *The Journal of the British Society for Phenomenology* (Manchester), vol. 9, 1978, 3-10.

Italian: "Il concetto di tempo nella scienza della storia." In *Scritti Filosofici 1912-1917,* by Martin Heidegger. Ed. and trans. A. Babolin. Padova, 1972, 210-231.

13      "Abendgang auf der Reichenau." *Das Bodenseebuch 1917. Ein Buch für Land und Leute* (Konstanz), vol. 4, 1916, 152.

**Translation**

Italian: "Passagiata serale a Reichenau." In *Scritti Filosofici 1912-1917,* by Martin Heidegger. Ed. and trans. A. Babolin. Padova, 1972, 232.

### 1917

14      "Selbstanzeige. Die Kategorien und Bedeutungslehre des Duns Scotus." *Kantstudien* (Berlin), vol. 21, 1917, 467-468. Rpt. in *Frühe Schriften.* (Gesamtausgabe, Abt. 1: Veröffentlichte Schriften 1914-1970, Bd. I). Ed. Fr. W. von Herrmann. Frankfurt: Klostermann, 1978, 412. *See* 181.

**Translation**

Italian: "Autopresentazione." In *Scritti Filosofici 1912-1917,* by Martin Heidegger. Ed. and trans. A. Babolin. Padova, 1972, 234 ff.

15      "Anmerkungen zu Karl Jaspers 'Philosophie der Weltanschauungen' (1919/21)." In *Wegmarken.* (Gesamtausgabe, Abt. 1: Veröffentlichte Schriften 1914-1970, Bd. I). Ed. Fr. W. von Herrmann. Frankfurt: Klostermann, 1976, 1-44. *See* 165.

[This is an unaltered text with marginal notes of the author.]

## 1925

["Kant und das Problem der Metaphysik." Lecture series. Marburg, Fall Term 1925/26. Also presented at the Herderinstitut in Riga, September 1928, and at the Davos Hochschulkurse, March 1929. *See* 22.]

["Geschichte des Zeitbegriffs." Lecture series. Marburg, Spring Term 1925. *See* 189.]

["Logik. Die Frage nach der Wahrheit." Lecture series. Marburg, Fall Term 1925/26. *See* 171.]

## 1926

["Grundbegriffe der antiken Philosophie." Lecture series. Marburg, Spring Term 1926.]

["Geschichte der Philosophie von Thomas v. Aquin bis Kant." Lecture series. Marburg, Fall Term 1926/27.]

## 1927

16 *Sein und Zeit,* Erste Hälfte. [Edmund Husserl in Verehrung und Freundschaft zugeeignet. Todtnauberg i. Bad. Schwarzwald zum 8. April 1926.] *Jahrbuch für Phänomenologie und phänomenologische Forschung* (Halle), vol. 8, 1927, XI-438. 2nd ed. Halle, 1929. 3rd. ed. Halle, 1929. 4th ed. Halle, 1935. 5th ed. Without the dedication to Husserl, Halle, 1941, VII-438. 6th ed. Tübingen: Niemeyer, 1949. 7th ed. Tübingen, 1953, XI-437. 8th ed. Tübingen, 1957. 9th ed. Tübingen, 1961. 10th ed. Tübingen, 1963. 14th ed. With marginal notes by the author, Tübingen, 1977. [For alterations in Heidegger's text *See* R. A. Bast and H. P. Delfosse. *Handbuch zum Teststudium von M. Heidegger's "Sein und Zeit."* 2 vol. Stuttgart, 1980/81.] Rpt. in (Gesamtausgabe, Abt. 1: Veröffentlichte Schriften 1914-1970, Bd. II). Ed. Fr. W. von Herrmann. Frankfurt: Klostermann, 1976, XIV-586. *See* 169. Excerpts in "Die Weltlichkeit der Welt. Ein Kapital aus 'Sein und Zeit'." Intr. H. Mörchen. Frankfurt: Texte für den Philosophieunterricht, 1959, 40. 2nd ed. Frankfurt: 1964. "Verstehen und Auslegung." Section 32, 33. *Hermeneutische Philosophie.* Ed. O. Pöggeler. München, 1972, 87-99.

**Translations**

English: *Being and Time.* Trans. of the 7th German. Ed. J. Macquarris and E. Robinson. New York, 1962, 589 p. 2nd ed. Oxford, 1967.

French: *L'Être et le temps.* Trans. R. Boehm and A. de Waelhens. Paris, 1964, 325 p.

Italian: *Essere e tempo.* Trans. P. Chiodi. Milano, 1953, 457 p.

*Essere e tempo. L'essenza del fondamento.* Trans. P. Chiodi. Torino, 1969, 700 p.

Japanese: *Sonzai to Jikan.* Trans. S. Terajima. Tôkyô, 1929/39.

*Sonzai to Jikan.* Trans. K. Matsuo. Tôkyô, 1960, 467 p. 2nd ed. 1966.

*Sonzai to Jikan.* Trans. T. Kuwaki. Tôkyô, 1960. 2nd ed. 1963.

*Sonzai to Jikan.* Trans. S. Hosoya, Y. Kamei and H. Funabashi. Tôkyô, 1963.

*U yo Toki.* Trans. K. Tsujimura, with the aid of H. Buchner. Tôkyô, 1967.

Korean: *Chonjaewa sigan.* Trans. I. Kyuho. *Seoul, 1972.*

Spanish: *El ser y el tiempo.* Trans. J. Gaos. Mexico, 1951, LII-510 p. 2nd ed. 1962, 479 p. 5th ed. 1977.

**Translations of Parts**

English: "Being and Time, Introduction Section 1-8." *Basic Writings.* Ed. D. F. Krell. New York: Harper and Row, 1977. London: Routledge and Kegan Paul, 1977.

Chinese: Trans. of Section 4, 6, 9, 14, 16, 26, 27, 28, 40, 41, 53, 65, 74, by Wei Hsiung. Peking, 1963. "Being and Time, SS (1-10)." *Mou Zongsan, Zhi de zhijue yu zhongguo zhexue* (Intellektuelle Anschauung and Chinese Philosophy. Trans. M. Zonsan. Taibei: Shanwu yin shu guan, 1971.

Czech: "Vábor z dila Sein und Zeit." Trans. S. Vitek. *Antologie existencialsmu* (Praha), vol. 1, 1967, 25-135.

French: *Qu'est-ce que le métaphysique?* Trans., intr. and editorial notes by H. Corbin. 10th ed. Paris, 1951, 115-208. 1st ed. 1938.

Japanese: "Kaishakugakuteki Junkan no Mondai." (Section 32-33. Trans. from "Hermeneutische Philosophie." Ed. O. Pöggeler. 1972). Trans. K. Mizoguchi. *Kaishakugaku no konponmondai.* Kyôto: Kôyôshobô, 1977, 119-139.

Korean: *Chonjaewa sigan.* Trans. C. Myonga, et al. Seoul, 1972.

Polish: Section 4, 9, 44, 45-62. *Antologia filosfici egzystencjalnej.* Trans. J. Polomski and L. Kolakowski. Warszawa, 1965.

Spanish: "Qué no es y qué debe ser la persona." *Revista Cubana de Filosofia.* Trans. H. Pinera Llera. La Habanna, 1951. Selection taken from *Sein und Zeit.*

Yougoslav: *Ekspozicija vprasanja o smislu biti, Uvod k "Bit in cas."* Trans. into the Slovene by I. Urbancic. 1968.

17     "Zur Geschichte des Philosophischen Lehrstuhls seit 1866." In *Die Philipps-Universität zu Marburg. 1527-1927.* Marburg, 1927, 680-687.

18     "Letter to E. Husserl (1927)." In *Phänomenologische Psychologie,* by E. Husserl. Ed. W. Biemel. (Husserliana, 9). Den Haag, 1962, 237ff, 517 ff, 599 ff.

**Translations**

English: "The Idea of Phenomenology." Trans. J. N. Deely and J. A. Novak. *New Scholas,* vol. 44, 1970, 325-344. (Sum., 1970).

"The Idea of Phenomenology, With a Letter to Edmund Husserl (1927)."
Trans. T. J. Sheehan. *Listening. Journal of Religion and Culture* (River
Forest), vol. 12, no. 3, 1977, 11-21.

["Die Grundprobleme der Phänomenologie." Lecture series. Marburg, Spring
Term 1927. *See* 168.]

["Phänomenologische Interpretation von Kants Kritik der reinen Vernunft."
Lecture series. Marburg, Fall Term 1927/28. *See* 176.]

["Phänomenologie und Theologie." Lecture series. Tübingen, 9 October 1927.
Repeated in Marburg, 14 February 1928. *See* 152.]

19  "Einleitung:" to Edmund Husserl Vorlesungen zur Phänomenologie des
inneren Bewusstseins." Ed. M. Heidegger. *Jahrbuch fur Phänomenologie
und phänomenologische Forschung* (Halle), vol. 9, 1928, 367-368.

20  Rev. of *Philosophie der symbolischen Formen,* by E. Cassirer. 2 Teil: Das
mythische Denken. Berlin, 1925. *Deutsche Literaturzeitung* (Berlin), N.F.
5, 1928, 1000-1012.

**Translation**

English: "Book Review of Ernst Cassirers Mythical Thought." *M. Heidegger:
The Piety of Thinking Essays.* Trans. J. G. Hart and J. C. Maraldo. Indiana
Univ. Press, 1976.

["Logik (Leibnitz)." Last lecture in Marburg, Spring Term 1928. *See* 182.]

## 1929

21  *Was ist Metaphysik?* Bonn, 1929, 29 p. [Inaugural lecture Freiburg, delivered
24 July 1929.] 2nd ed. Bonn, 1930. 3rd ed. Bonn, 1931. 4th ed. With an
epilog. Frankfurt: Klostermann, 1943, 31 p. 5th enlarged ed. Frankfurt:
Klostermann, 1949, 47 p. *See* 55. 7th ed. Frankfurt: Klostermann, 1955,
51 p. 8th ed. Frankfurt: Klostermann, 1965. 10th ed. Frankfurt:
Klostermann, 1969. 11th ed. Frankfurt: Klostermann, 1975. Rpt. in
*Wegmarken.* Frankfurt: Klostermann, 1967, 1-19. 2nd rev. and enlarged
ed. Frankfurt: Kostermann, 1978. *See* 130. Rpt. in *Wegmarken.*
(Gesamtausgabe, Abt. 1: Veröffentlichte Schriften 1914-1970, Bd. IX).
[Unaltered text with marginal notes of the author] Ed. Fr. W. von
Herrmann. Frankfurt: Klostermann, 1976, 103-122. *See* 172. Excerpts in
*Panorama des zeitgenössischen Denkens.* Ed. G. Picon and H. Scheffel.

**Translations**

English: "What is Metaphysiks?" Trans. R. F. C. Hull and A. Crick. In
*Existence and Being,* by Martin Heidegger. London, 1949. 2nd ed. 1956,
353-392. 3rd ed. Chicago, 1965, 292-324.

"What is Metaphysics?" In *Basic Writings,* by Martin Heidegger. Ed. D.
F. Krell. New York: Harper and Row, 1977; London: Routledge and Kegan
Paul, 1977, 95-116.

Chinese: Chinese trans. Wei Hsiung. Peking, 1964.

Croation: *Was ist Metaphysik?* 1929; *Vom Wesen der Wahrheit,* 1943; *Brief uber den Humanismus,* 1947; *Der Ursprung des Kunstwerks,* 1950; *Was ist das die Philosophie?* 1956. Trans. I. Urbancic. Ljubljana, 1967, 413 p.

Czech: "Co je metafyzika?" *Listy pro umeni a filosofii* (Praha), [Blätter für Kunst und Philosophie], vol. 7, 1946, 377-392.

"Co je metafyzika?" Trans. B. Baumann. *Listy pro umeni a filosofii* (Czechoslovakia), vol. 1, no. 3, 1946/47, 413 p.

Dutch: *Wat is metafysica?* Intr., commentary, and supplements by J. M. M. Aler. Trans. M. S. G. K. Van Nierop. Nederlandse Heidegger-Bibliotek 2, Tielt/Ultrecht, 1970, 184 p.

French: "Qu'est-ce la metaphysique?" With excerpts from *Sein und Zeit* and a lecture on Hölderlin. Trans., intr. and annotations by H. Corbin. *Les essais.* 1st ed. Paris, VII, 1938, 21-44, 254 p. 10th ed. Paris, 1951.

*Questions I:* Qu'est-ce que la métaphysique?, Ce qui fait l'être-essentiel d'un fondement ou "raison." De l'essence de la vérité. Contribution a la question de l'être. Identité et différence. Trans. and ed. H. Corbin, R. Munier, Al de Waelhens, W. Biemel, et al. Paris, 1968, 47-52.

"Qu'est-ce que la métaphysique?" Trans. R. Munier. *Le nouveau commerce* (Paris), Cahier 14, 1969, 57 ff.

[The translation contains a letter of Heidegger addressed to R. Munier, with explanations on the edited text. *See* 141.]

Italian: *Che cos' è la metafisica?* Trans., intr. and annotations by A. Carlini. Firenze, 1953, XI-143. 2nd ed. Firenze, 1959.

[With excerpts from "Letter on Humanism."]

Spanish: "Qué es metafisica?" Trans. X. Zurbiri. *Cruz y Raya. Revista de Afirmación.* Madrid, 1933, 85-115. Mexico, 1941, 59 p. Buenos Aires, 1955. 1967, 112 p.

*Que es metafisica?* Trans. X. Zubiri. Cruz del Sur, Mexico, 1963, 74 p.

"Qué es metafisica?" Trans. E. G. Belsunce. *Revista de Filosofia* (La Plata), vol. 14, 1964, 74-82.

*Qué es metafisica?* Trans. X. Zubiri. Buenos Aires, 1967, 120 p.

Japanese: *Keijijôgaku towa Nan zoya.* Trans. Seinosuke Yuasa. Tôkyô, 1930. *Keijijôgaku towa Nani ka.* Trans. Seishiro Ôe. Tôkyô, 1952.

Polish: "Co to jest Metafizyka?" Trans. W. Strozewski and St. Grygiel. *Znak* (Warszawa), vol. 127, 1962.

Portugese: *"Que é metafisica?"* Trans. and intr. E. Stein. Sao Paulo, 1969, 82 p.

**Translations of Parts**

French: Excerpts in *Panorama des Idées Contemporaires.* Ed. R. Bertele. Paris: Gallimard, 1957.

Indian: Indian trans. 1952.

Korean: *Sinûn chugôssda.* Trans. C. Tonghui. Seoul, 1959.

*Humaenisûtûeui p'yônji.* Trans. S. Kwanghui. Seoul, 1960.

Spanish: "Was ist Metaphysik?" Einleitung zur 5. Auflage. Introduction a la 5a. edicion de "Que es metafisica?." *El retroceso al fundamento de la metafísica.* Trans. L. Piossek-Prebisch. Argentina, 1962.

**Other Translations**

*See* 55.

22   *Kant und das Problem der Metaphysik.* [Max Scheler zum Gedächtnis] Bonn, 1929, XII-236. [Lecture series delivered in the Fall Term 1925/26.] 2nd ed. With an intr. Frankfurt: Klostermann, 1951, 222 p. 3rd ed. Frankfurt: Klostermann, 1965. 4th rev. ed. Frankfurt: Klostermann, 1973, 268 p.

**Translations**

English: *Kant and the Problem of Metaphysics.* Trans. J. S. Churchill. Intr. T. Langan. Bloomington, 1962, XXV-255. 2nd ed. 1966.

French: *Kant et le problème de la métaphysique.* Trans. and intr. A. de Waelhens and W. Biemel. Paris, 1953, 312 p.

Japanese: *Kanto to Keijijogaku.* Trans. Keijo Sato. Tôkyô, 1938.

*Kanto to Keijijogaku no Mondai.* Trans. R. Teruoka. Tôkyô, 1959.

Spanish: *Kant y el problema de la metafísica.* Trans. G. I. Roth. Rev. by E. C. Frost. Mexico: Fondo de Cultura Económica, 1954, 212 p.

Italian: *Kant e il problema della metafisicy.* Trans. M. E. Reina. Intr. E. M. Forni. Milano, 1963, 327 p.

**Translations of Parts**

French: *Kant et le probleme de la metaphysique: Qu'est-ce que la metaphysique?* Trans., intr. and annotations by H. Corbin. Paris, 1938. 10th ed. Paris, 1951, 221-230.

Polish: "Kant und das Problem der Metaphysik," 41-44. Trans. M. Skwiecinski. In *Filosofia i Socjologia XX Wieku.* Warszawa, 1965.

23   "Edmund Husserl zum 70. Geburtstag." *Akademische Mitteilungen. Organ für die gesamten Interessen der Studentenschaft an der Albert-Ludwigs-Universität in Freiburg* (Freiburg), vol. 9. Semester, 4, no. 3, Thursday, 14 May 1929, 46-47.

24   "Vom Wesen des Grundes." *Jahrbuch für Philosophie und phänomenologische Kritik.* (Ergänzungsband. Festschrift, Edmund Husserl zum 70. Geburtstag gewidmet). Halle, 1929, 71-100. 2nd ed. Halle, 1931. 3rd ed. Complemented with an intr. Frankfurt: Klostermann, 1949, 50 p. 4th ed. Frankfurt: Klostermann, 1955. 5th ed. 1967. 6th ed. 1973, 54 p. Rpt. in *Wegmarken.* Frankfurt: Klostermann, 1967, 21-71. *See* 130. (Gesamtausgabe, Abt. 1: Veröffentlichte Schriften 1914-1970, Bd. IX). Frankfurt: Klostermann, 1976. *See* 172.

**Translations**

English: *The Essence of Reasons.* [Bi-lingual edition: English and German.] Ed. and trans. T. Malick. Evanston, Illinois, 1969, 144 p.

French: "Ce qui fait l'être-essentiel d'un fondement ou 'raison'. Qu'est-ce que la métaphysique." Trans., intr. and annotations by H. Corbin. 10th ed. Paris, 1951, 47-111. 1st ed. 1939. Rpt. in *Questions, I:* Qu'est-ce que la métaphysique? Ce qui fait l'être-essentiel d'un fondement ou "raison." De l'essence de la vérité. Contribution a la question de l'être. Identité et différence. Ed. and trans. H. Corbin, R. Munier, A. de Waelhens and W. Biemel, et al. Paris, 1968, 315 p.

Italian: *Essere e tempo. L'essenza del fondamento.* Trans. P. Chiodi. Torino, 1969, 700 p.

Portugese: *Sobre a essencia do fundamento.* Trans. and intr. E. Stein. Sao Paulo, 1971, 27-80.

[Edition with translation of "Aus der letzten Marburger Vorlesung" and of "Hegel und die Griechen."]

Japanese: *Konkyo no Honshitsu.* Trans. S. Saito. Tôkyô, 1939.

**Translation of Parts**

English: *Philosophy-What is it? The Search for Being. Essays From Kierkegaard to Satre on the Problem of Existence.* Ed. and trans. J. T. Wilde and W. B. Kimmel. New York, 1962, 507-520. 3rd ed. 1969.

25 "Arbeitsgemeinschaft Cassirer-Heidegger." [Report written by O. F. Bollnow and J. Ritter.] In *Ergänzungen zu einer Heidegger-Bibliographie,* by G. Schneeberger. Bern, 1960, 17-27. Supplement no. 4.

[Report on a seminar at the 2. Davos Hochschulkurse, 17 March-6 April 1929. *See* 163.]

**Translations**

French: "Heidegger et Cassierer interprètes de Kant." Trans. and comments by H. Decleve. *Revue Philosophique de Louvain* (Louvain), vol. 67, 1969, 517-545.

*Colloque Cassirer-Heidegger.* Davos, printemps 1929. Rédaction Dr. O. F. Bollnow and Dr. J. Ritter. *Débat sur le Kantisme et la Philosophie,* by E. Cassirer and M. Heidegger. Ed. and trans. P. Aubenque. Paris, 1972, 28-51. *See* 163.

Spanish: "Debate de Davos." *Ideas y Valores* (Bogata), 48-49, 1977, 87-103.

["Einleitung in die Philosophie." Lecture series. Freiburg, Fall Term 1928/29.]

["Der Deutsche Idealismus (Fichte, Hegel, Schelling) und die philosophische Problemlage der Gegenwart." Lecture series. Freiburg, Spring Term 1929.]

["Einführung in das akademische Studium." Lecture series. Freiburg, Spring Term 1929.]

["Die Grundbegriffe der Metaphysik. Der Weltbegriff." Lecture series. Freiburg, Fall Term 1928-30.]

## 1930

["Vom Wesen der Wahrheit." Public lecture. Bremen/Marburg/Freiburg, Fall and Winter Term 1930. Dresden, Summer 1932. Lecture series. Freiburg, Fall Term 1931/32. *See* 43.]

["Über das Wesen der menschlichen Freiheit." Lecture series. Freiburg, Spring Term 1930.]

["Hegels Phänomenologie des Geistes." Lecture series. Freiburg, Fall Term 1930/31.]

## 1931

["Aristoteles: Metaphysik IX." Lecture series. Freiburg, Spring Term 1931.]

["Vom Wesen der Wahrheit." Lecture series. Freiburg, Fall Term 1931/32. *See* 42.]

## 1932

["Vom Anfang der abendländischen Philosophie (Anaximander und Parmenides)." Lecture series. Freiburg, Spring Term 1932. *See* 58, 78.]

## 1933

26     "Schlageter." *Freiburger Studentenzeitung* (Freiburg), 7th Semester (XIV), 1933, 1. Rpt. in *Nachlese zu Heidegger,* by G. Schneeberger. Bern, 1962, 48 ff.

**Translation**

French: "In Memoriam A. L. Schlageter." In "M. Heidegger, Discours et proclamations." Trans. J. P. Faye. *Méditations* (Paris), 3, 1961, 149-150.

27     "Arbeitsdienst und Universität." *Freiburger Studentenzeitung* (Freiburg), 7th Semester (XIV), no. 4, 30 June 1933, 1. Rpt. in *Nachlese zu Heidegger,* by G. Schneeberger. Bern, 1962, 63 ff.

**Translation**

English: "Labor Service and the University." In *German Existentialism,* by Martin Heidegger. Trans. and intr. D. D. Runes. New York, 1965, 21-22.

28     "Deutsche Studenten." *Freiburger Studentenzeitung* (Freiburg), 8th Semester (XV), no. 1, 3 November 1933, 1. Rpt. in *Nachlese zu Heidegger,* by G. Schneeberger. Bern, 1962, 135 ff.

**Translations**

English: "German Students." In *German Existentialism,* by Martin Heidegger. Trans. and intr. D. D. Runes. New York, 1965, 27-28.

French: "Etudiants allemands " In "M. Heidegger, Discours et proclamations." Trans. J. P. Faye. *Méditations* (Paris), no. 3, 1961, 139.

29    "Deutsche Männer und Frauen " *Freiburger Studentenzeitung* (Freiburg), 8th
      Semester (XV), [Wahlausgabe], 10 November 1933, 1. Rpt. in *Nachlese zu
      Heidegger,* by G. Schneeberger. Bern, 1962, 144-146.
      **Translation**
      French: "Allemands et Allemendes " In "M. Heidegger, Discours et
      proclamations." Trans. J. P. Faye. *Méditations* (Paris), no. 3, 1961, 140-141.

30    "Deutsche Lehrer und Kameraden Deutsche Volksgenossen und
      Genossinnen." Bekenntnis der Professoren an den deutschen Universitäten
      und Hochschulen zu Adolf Hitler und dem nationalsozialistischen Staat.
      Überreicht vom Nationalsozialistischen Lehrerbund. Dresden, 1933, 13-14.
      [Article in document by the Nationalsocialist Teachers Association, in
      which they declared themselves for Adolf Hitler.] Rpt. in *Nachlese zu
      Heidegger,* by G. Schneeberger. Bern, 1962, 148-150; as "Complement II"
      in *Ergänzungen zu einer Heidegger-Bibliographie,* by G. Schneeberger. With
      4 Complements and a picture print. Bern, 1959, 13-15.
      **Translations**
      English: "Avowal to Adolf Hitler and the National State." In *German
      Existentialism,* by Martin Heidegger. Trans. an intr. D. D. Runes. New
      York, 1965, 29-33.

      French: "Professeurs et camerades allemands. Compagnons du peuple." In
      "M. Heidegger, Discours et proclamations." Trans. J. P. Faye. *Méditations*
      (Paris), no. 3, 1961, 142-145.

31    "Die Selbstbehauptung der Universität." [Speech delivered at the inaugural
      ceremony when succeeding to the Rectorship at Freiburg Univ., 27 May
      1933.] Breslau, 1933. 4-6 thousands, 1934. Excerpts in "Die drei
      Bindungen." *Völkischer Beobachter, Kampfblatt der nationalsozialistischen
      Bewegung Grossdeutschlands* (München), Süddeutsche Ausgabe, 46 Jg.,
      201. Ausgabe, 30 July 1934, supplement.
      **Translations**
      French: "L'autoaffirmation de l'université allemande. Discours de Rectorat,
      27 mai 1933." In "M. Heidegger, Discours et proclamations." Trans. J. P.
      Faye. *Méditations* (Paris), no. 3, 1961, 149.

      Japanese: *Doitsudaigaku no Jikosucho.* Trans. Jokiyi Araki. Tôkyô, 1934.

      Spanish: "Discusso rectoral de 1933." Trans. B. B. Edy. *Revista de Filosofía
      de la Universidad Costa Rica* (San Jose), vol. 10, 1961, 183-188.

      ["Die Grundfragen der Philosophie." Lecture series. Freiburg, Spring Term
      1933.]

      ["Vom Wesen der Wahrheit." Lecture series. Freiburg, Fall Term 1933/34.
      *See* 42.]

## 1934

32    "Der Ruf zum Arbeitsdienst." *Freiburger Studentenzeitung* (Freiburg), 8th
      Semester (XV), no. 5, 23 January 1934, 1. Rpt. in *Nachlese zu Heidegger,*
      by G. Schneeberger. Bern, 1962, 180 ff.
      **Translations**
      English: "The Call to Labor Service." In *German Existentialism,* by Martin
      Heidegger. Trans. and intr. D. D. Runes. New York, 1965, 34-36.

      French: "L'appel du service du travail." In "M. Heidegger, Discours et
      proclamations." Trans. J. P. Faye. *Méditations* (Paris), no. 3, 1961, 141-142.

33    "Das Geleitwort der Universität." *150 Jahre Freiburger Zeitung* (Freiburg),
      6 January 1934, 10. Rpt. in *Nachlese zu Heidegger,* by G. Schneeberger.
      Berlin, 1962, 171.

34    "Nationalsozialistische Wissensschulung." [Rede zu erwerbslosen Arbeitern
      im grössten Hörsaal der Albert-Ludwigs-Univ. am 22. Januar 1934.] In *Der
      Alemanne. Kampfblatt der Nationalsozialisten Oberbadens, Folge 33.*
      Abendausgabe vom I. Februar 1934, 9. Rpt. in *Nachlese zu Heidegger,* by
      G. Schneeberger. Bern, 1962, 192-202.
      **Translation**
      English: "Follow the Führer." In *German Existentialism,* by Martin
      Heidegger. Trans. and intr. D. D. Runes. New York, 1965, 37-42.

35    "Schöpferische Landschaft: Warum bleiben wir in der Provinz." In *Der
      Alemanne Kampfblatt der Nationalsozialisten Oberbadens.* Folge 67a: Zu
      neuen Ufern. Die wöchentlich erscheinende Kulturbeilage des Alemannen,
      Folge 9. Freiburg, 1934, 1. Rpt. in *Nachlese zu Heidegger,* by G.
      Schneeberger. Bern, 1962, 216-218.
      **Translations**
      English: "Why do I Stay in the Provinces? (1934)." Trans. Thomas J. Sheehan.
      *Listening. Journal of Religion and Culture* (River Forest), vol. 12, no. 3,
      III, 1977, 122-125.

      Japanese: "Naze Warera wa Inaka ni todomaruka?" Trans. A. Yashiro. In
      *1930 Nendai no Kiki to Tetsugaku* (Crisis in the Nineteenth-Thirties and
      Philosophy). Tôkyô: Iza rashobo, 1976, 105-112.

      Spanish: "Por que permanecemos en la provincia?" *Eco.* (Bogotá, Columbia),
      Bd. 6, 35, 1963, 472-476.

36    "An den Reichsführer der deutschen Studentenschaft am 6. Februar 1934"
      (Letter to the "Reichsführer" of the German Students' Association, dated
      from 6 February 1934). Rpt in *Nachlese zu Heidegger,* by G. Schneeberger.
      Bern, 1962, 205 ff.

      ["Über Logik als Frage nach der Sprache." Lecture series. Freiburg, Spring
      Term 1924.]

      [Hölderlins Hymen "Germanien" und "Der Rhein." Lecture series. Freiburg,
      Fall Term 1934/35. *See* 185.]

## 1935

["Der Ursprung des Kunstwerks." In its primary drafting the theme of a lecture, delivered on 13 June 1935 at the "Kunstwissenschaftliche Gesellschaft" in Freiburg. This lecture was repeated in Zürich, following an invitation of the Students' Association. The 1950 edition contains 3 lectures delivered at the "Freies Deutsches Hochschulstift" in Frankfurt on 17, 24 November and 4 December 1936. *See* 58, 105.]

[*Die Frage nach dem Ding, 1962.* Text of the lecture series, under the title "Grundfragen der Metaphysik" in Freiburg, Fall Term 1935/36. *See* 66.]

["Einführung in die Metaphysik." Lecture series. Freiburg, Spring Term 1935. *See* 69.]

## 1936

37          "Hölderlin und das Wesen der Dichtung." *Das Innere Reich* (München), vol. 3, 1936, 1065-1078. [Speech delivered in Rome on the 2 March 1936.] Off-print, München, 1937, 19 p. Rpt. in *Erläuterungen zu Hölderlins Dichtung.* Frankfurt, 1944, 50 p. *See* 46. 2nd enlarged ed. Frankfurt, 1951, 31-46. Rpt. in *Hölderlin. Beiträge zu Seinem Verständnis in unserem Jahrhundert.* Ed. A. Kelletat. Tübingen, 1961, 131-143.

**Translations**

English: "Hölderlin an the Essence of Poetry." Trans. D. Scott. In *Existence and Being,* by Martin Heidegger. London, 1949. 2nd ed. London, 1956, 291-315.

Chinese: "He Deling yu shi zhi benzhi." Trans. C. Meili. In *Cai Meili Cunzaizhuyi dashi-Hai Dege* (Heidegger-Master of Existentialism). Tabai: Daxue Congkan, 15, 1970.

Czech: "Hölderlin a podstats básnictvî. Trans. V. Bohmova-Linhardtova and J. Patoocka. *Tvár* (Praha), vol. 1, 1965, 18-23.

French: "Hölderlin et l'essence de la poesie." In *Qu'est-ce que la métaphysique?* Trans., intr. and annotations by H. Corbin. Paris, 1938. 10th ed. Paris, 1951, 233-252.

Italian: *Hölderlin a l'essence della poesia.* Trans. C. Antoni. Firenze: Studi Germanici, 2, 1937.

Japanese: *Herudarin to Shi no Honshitsu.* Trans. S. Saito. Tôkyô, 1938.

*Herudarin to Bungaku no Honshitsu.* Trans. U. Sato. Tôkyô, 1943.

Korean: In *Humaenisûtûeûi p'yônji.* Trans. S. Kwanghûi. Seoul, 1960. Rpt. in *Chilliran muôsinga* (What is Truth). Ed. Y. Sahae Kwahak. Seoul, 1960. [Trans. of Parts.]

Spanish: "Hölderlin y la esencia de la poesia." Trans. G. F. *Escorial* (Madrid), vol. 10, 1943, 180-193.

*Hölderlin y la esencia de la poesia.* Trans. J. D. Bacca. Mexico, 1944.

"Hölderlin y la esencia de la poesia." Trans. J. D. Bacca. *Revista National de Cultura* (Caracas), vol. 109, 1955, 163-174.

"Hölderlin y la esencia de la poesia." In *M. Heidegger Arte y poesia.* Ed. and trans. S. Ramos. Mexico, 1958, 115 p.

*Hölderlin y la esencia de la poesia.* Trans. and commentary by J. D. Bacca. Merida, Venezuela: Univ. de los Andes, Facultad de humanidades y educación, Escuela de letras, 1968, 87 p.

[1936-1940: 5 semesters of lecture series on Nietzsche, Univ. of Freiburg. *See* 58, 107.]

["Schelling: Über das Wesen der menschlichen Freiheit." Lecture series. Freiburg, Spring Term 1936. *See* 159.]

["Nietzsche: Der Wille zur Macht als Kunst." Lecture series. Freiburg Fall Term 1936/37. *See* 106.]

38    "Lettre de M. Heidegger, Response a M. J. Wahl." (Société française de Philosophie, seance du 4 décembre 1937). *Bulletin de la Société française de Philosophie* (Paris), vol. 37, 1937, 193. Rpt. in *Existence humaine et trancendance,* by J. Wahl. Neuchatel, 1944, 134-135.

[French trans. of a still unpublished original written in German.]

39    "Wege zur Aussprache." In *Alemannenband. Ein Buch von Volkstum und Sendung.* Für die Stadt Freiburg. Ed. Dr. F. Kerber. Stuttgart, 1937, 135-139. Rpt. in *Nachlese zu Heidegger,* by G. Schneeberger. Bern, 1962, 258-262.

["Nietzsches metaphysische Grundstellung im abendländischen Denken: Die Lehre von der ewigen Wiederkehr des Gleichen." Lecture series. Freiburg, Spring Term 1937. *See* 107.]

["Grundfragen der Philosophie." Lecture series. Freiburg, Fall Term 1937/38.]

## 1938

40    "Author's Prologue." *Qu'est-ce que la métaphysique?,* by Martin Heidegger. Ed. and trans. H. Corbin. Paris, 1938, 7-8.

[Followed by excerpts from "Sein und Zeit" and from a conference on Hölderlin.]

[Lecture delivered on 9 June 1938 entitled "Die Begründung des neuzeitlichen Weltbildes durch die Metaphysik." This was the last lecture of a series arranged by the "Kunstwissenschaftliche-Naturforschende and Medizinische Gesellschaft zu Freiburg." *See* 57.]

["Einleitung in die Philosophie." Lecture series. Freiburg, Fall Term 1938/39.]

## 1939

["Lecture on Hölderlin." Repeated in 1939 and 1940. *See* 41.]

["Nietzsches Lehre vom Willen zur Macht als Erkenntnis." Lecture series. Freiburg, Spring Term 1939. *See* 106.]

["Kunst und Technik." Lecture series. Freiburg, Fall Term 1939/40. *See* 75.]

## 1940

["Nietzsche: Der Wille zur Macht. Der europäische Nihilismus." Lecture series. 1st trimester of 1940. *See* 107.]

["Grundfragen der Philosophie." Lecture series. Freiburg, Fall Term 1940/41.]

## 1941

41     *Hölderlins Hymne "Wie wenn am Feiertage..."* Halle, 1941, 32 p. Rpt. in *Erläuterungen zu Hölderlins Dichtung.* 2nd enlarged ed. Frankfurt, 1951, 47-74. *See* 62.

**Translations**

Korean: *Humaenisûtûenûi p'yonji.* Trans. S. Kwanghui. Seoul, 1960.

["Grundbegriffe." Lecture series. Freiburg, Spring Term 1941.]

["Nietzsches Metaphysik." Lecture series. Freiburg, Fall Term 1941/42. *See* 107.]

## 1942

42     "Platons Lehre von der Wahrheit." *Geistige Überlieferung* (Berlin), vol. 2, 1942, 96-124. [Written in 1940 for a private lecture.] 2nd ed. Bern, 1947. *Platons Lehre von der Wahrheit. Mit einen Brief über den Humanismus.* 119 p. 3rd ed. 1954. *See* 52. Rpt. in *Wegmarken.* Frankfurt, 1967, 109-144. *See* 130. Rpt. in *Wegmarken.* (Gesamtausgabe, Abt. 1: Veröffentlichte Schriften 1914-1970, Bd. IX). [Unaltered text with marginal notes of the author.] Ed. Fr. W. von Herrmann. Frankfurt: Klostermann, 1976, 203-238. *See* 172.

**Translations**

*See* 52.

[Seminars on Hegel's "Phänomenologie des Geistes" and on Aristotle's "Metaphysics" (Bks. IV and X) 1942/43. *See* 58.]

[Hölderlins "Andenken." Lecture series. Spring Term 1942.]

["Parmenides." Lecture series. Fall Term 1942/43.]

## 1943

43     *Vom Wesen der Wahrheit.* Frankfurt: Klostermann, 1943, 28 p. 2nd ed. With epilog. Frankfurt: Klostermann, 1949, 27 p. *See* 53. 3rd ed. Frankfurt: Klostermann, 1954. 4th ed. Frankfurt: Klostermann, 1961. 5th ed. 1967. 6th ed. 1976, 28 p. Rpt. in *Wegmarken.* Frankfurt: Klostermann, 1967, 73-97. 2nd rev. and enlarged ed. 1978. *See* 130. Rpt. in *Wegmarken.* (Gesamtausgabe, Abt. 1: Veröffentlichte Schriften 1914-1970, Bd. IX). [Unaltered text with marginal nates by the author.] Ed. Fr.W. von Herrmann. Frankfurt: Klostermann, 1976, 177-202. *See* 172.

**Translations**

English: "On the Essence of Truth." Trans. R. F. C. Hull and A. Crick. In *Existence and Being,* by Martin Heidegger. London, 1949. 2nd ed. 1956, 317-351. Chicago, 1965, 292-324. Rpt. in *Basic Writings.* Ed. D. F. Krell. New York: Harper and Row, 1977. Trans. J. Sallis. London: Routledge and Kegan Paul, 1977, 117-141.

Arabic: Trans. A. G. Mikkawy. 1977.

Croatian: *Was ist Metaphysik?* 1929; *Vom Wesen der Wahrheit,* 1943; *Brief über den Humanismus,* 1947; *Der Ursprung des Kunstwerks,* 1950; *Was ist das die Philosophie?* 1956. Trans. I. Urbancic. Llubljana, 1967, 413 p.

Czech: *O bytostném urceni pravdy.* Trans. J. Nemec. Praha, 1970, 136

*O Pravde a Byti.* [Bi-lingual ed.] Trans. J. Nemec. Praha, 1970, 82 p.

French: *De l'essence de la vérité.* Trans. and intr. A. de Waelhens and W. Biemel. Louvain/Paris, 1948, 108 p. Rpt. in *Questions I:* Qu'est-ce que la métaphysique? Ce qui fait l'être-essentiel d'un fondement ou "raison." De l'essence de la vérité. Contribution à la question de l'être. Identite et différence. Ed. and trans. H. Corbin, R. Munier, A. de Waelhens, W. Biemel, et al. Paris, 1968, 315 p.

Italian: *Dell'essenza della veritá.* Trans. and comments by A. Carlini. Milano, 1952.

*Sull'essenza della verità.* Trans., intr. and annotations by U. Galimberti. (Il pensiero). Brescia: La Scuola, 1973, LIX-50.

Japanese: In *Shinri no Honshitsu nitsuite. Puraton no Shinri-Ron.* Trans. S. Kiba. Tôkyô, 1961.

Korean: In *Chilliran mûosinga* (What is Truth?) Ed. and trans. S. Kwahak. Seoul, 1960.

Norwegian: *Dei filosofiske vilkar for sanning. Vom Wesen der Wahrheit. Ei tolking av Martin Heidegger sanningslaere.* [Bi-lingual ed.] Trans. G. Skirbekk. Oslo, 1966, 166 p.

Portuguese: *Da esencia da verdade.* [With a prologue by the author.] Intr. and annotations by D. F. de la Vega and R. Pineiro. Vigo, 1956, 81 p.

*Sobre a essencia da verdade.* Trans. and intr. E. Stein. Sao Paulo, 1970, 15-50.

[Includes a trans. of "Kants These über das Sein."]

Spanish: "De la esencia de la verdad." Trans. C. Astrada. *Cuadernos de Filosofia* (Buenos Aires), vol. 1, 1948.

"De la esencia de la verdad." *Cuadernos de Filosofia* (Buenos Aires), vol. 1, 1949.

"De la esencia de la verdad." Trans. H. P. Llera. *Revista Cubana de Filosofia* (Haban), vol. 10, 1952, 5-22.

"De la esencia de la verdad." Trans. E. G. Belsunce. In *Ser, Verdad y Fundamento,* by Martin Heidegger. Caracas, 1968, 61-83.

44    *Was ist Metaphysik?* 4th enlarged ed. With an epilogue. Frankfurt: Klostermann, 1943, 31. 1st ed. 1929. *See* 21. Epilogue also in *Wegmarken.* Frankfurt: Klostermann, 1967, 99-108. *See* 130. Rpt. in *Wegmarken.* (Gesamtausgabe, Abt 1: Veröffentlichte Schriften 1914-1970, Bd. IX). [Unaltered text with marginal notes by the author.] Ed. Fr. W. von Herrmann. Frankfurt: Klostermann, 1967, 303-312. *See* 172.

45    "Andenken." *Hölderlin. Gedenkschriften zu seinem 100. Todestag.* Ed. P. Kluckhohn. Tübingen, 1943, 267-324. Rpt. in *Erläuterungen zu Hölderlin Dichtung.* 2nd enlarged ed. Frankfurt: Klostermann, 1951, 75-143. *See* 62. 4th enlarged ed. Frankfurt: Klostermann, 1971.

**Translations**

English: "Remembrance of the Poet." Trans. D. Scott. In *Existence and Being,* by Martin Heidegger. London, 1949. 2nd ed. 1956, 251-290.

["Heimkunft," "An die Verwandten." Speech at the Univ. of Freiburg, 6 June 1943, in remembrance of Hölderlin during the celebration of the 100th recurrence of the day of his death. *See* 46, 159.]

["Heraklit." Lecture series. Freiburg, Spring Term 1943. *See* 74, 183.]

46    "Nietzsche's Wort 'Gott ist tot'." *Holzwege.* Frankfurt: Klostermann, 1950, 193-247.

[Publicly and privately lectured in 1943.]

**Translations**

*See* 58.

## 1944

47    *Erläuterungen zu Hölderlins Dichtung.* Frankfurt: Klostermann, 1944, 50 p. [Contains "Heimkunft/An die Verwandten" and "Hölderlin und das Wesen der Dichtung."] 2nd enlarged ed. Frankfurt: Klostermann, 1951, 144 p. *See* 62. 3rd ed. 1963. 4th enlarged ed. Frankfurt: Klostermann, 1971, 196 p.

**Translations**

Japanese: *Heruderurin no Hika "Kikyô" ni tsuite.* Trans. T. Tezuka. Tôkyô, 1949.

Korean: In *Siwa ch'orhak* (Poetry and Philosophy). Trans. S. Kwanghui. Seoul, 1972.

[Trans. of parts.]

Trans. of "Heimkunft." In *Chilliran muosinga* (What is Truth?) Ed. Y. Sahae Kwahak. Seoul, 1960.

["Logos." In *Festschrift für H. Jantzen* (1951). Taken from the lecture on logics Spring Term 1944. *See* 65.]

["Logik (Heraklits Lehre vom Logos)." Lecture series. Freiburg, Spring Term 1944. *See* 183.]

["Denken und Dichten." Lecture series. Freiburg, Fall Term 1944/45.]

## 1945

48 "Brief Heideggers an das Rektorat der Albert-Ludwigs-Universität in Freiburg vom 4. Nov. 1945." [Excerpts from a letter addressed to the rectorat of the Univ. of Freiburg.] Trans. A. De Towarnicki. Visite Martin Heidegger. *Les Temps modernes* (Paris), vol. 1, 1945/46, 717-724.

## 1946

49 "Wozu Dichter?" *Holzwege.* Frankfurt: Klostermann, 1950, 258-295.

[Lectured in a private circle in remembrance of Rilke's death on 29 December 1926.]

**Translations**

*See* 58.

50 *Über den Humanismus.* Frankfurt: Klostermann, 1949, 47 p. 6th ed. 1967. Rpt. 1975.

[Revised and enlarged version of a letter written in Fall 1946 to Jean Beaufret and first published in 1947. *See* 52.]

**Translations**

*See* 52.

51 "Der Spruch des Anaximander." In *Holzwege.* Frankfurt: Klostermann, 1950, 296-343. 5th ed. Frankfurt: Klostermann, 1972. Rpt. in *Holzwege.* (Gesamtausgabe, Abt. 1: Veröffentlichte Schriften 1914-1970, Bd. V). Frankfurt: Klostermann, 1977. *See* 58.

**Translations**

English: "Martin Heidegger: The Anaximander Fragment." Ed. and trans. D. F. Krell. *Arion: A Journal of Humanities and the Classics,* New Series I, no. 4, Winter 1974, 576-626. Rpt. in *Early Greek Thinking.* Trans. D. F. Krell and F. A. Capuzzi. New York: Harper and Row, 1975.

Japanese: *Anakushimandorosu no Kotoba.* Trans. M. Tanaka. Tôkyô, 1957; 1973.

## 1947

52 *Platons Lehre von der Wahrheit. Mit einen Brief über den Humanismus.*
[Sammlung: überlieferung und Auftrag.] Ed. E. Grassi with W. Szilasi.
Bern: Reihe Probleme und Hinweise, 1947, 120 p. 2nd ed. Bern, 1954. 3rd
ed. Bern, 1975. [Contains "Platons Lehre von der Wahrheit." 1st ed. Berlin,
1942, 5-52. *See* 42. "Über den Humanismus." Letter to Jean Beaufret, Paris,
53-119. *See* 50.] Rpt. in *Wegmarken.* Frankfurt: Klostermann, 1967,
109-144, 145-194; *Wegmarken.* (Gesamtausgabe, Abt. 1: Veröffentliche
Schriften 1914-1970, Bd. IX). [Unaltered text with marginal notes by the
author.] Ed. Fr. W. von Herrmann. Frankfurt: Klostermann, 1976,
203-238, 313-364. *See* 172.

**Translations**

English: "Plato's Doctrine of Truth. Letter on Humanism." Trans. J. Barlow
and E. Lohner. In *Philosophy in the 20th Century.* Ed. W. Barnett and H.
Aiken. New York, 1962, 251-270, 270-302.

Arabic: Trans. A. G. Mikkawy. 1977.

[Trans. includes "Aletheia" and "Vom Wesen der Wahrheit."]

Italian: "La Dottrina politica della verità." In *Il Pensare Poetante,* by Martin
Heidegger. Ed. and trans. E. Mirri. Perugia, 1971.

*La dottrina di Platone sulla verità. Lettera sull 'umanesimo.* Ed. A. Bixio
and G. Vattimo. (I libri del filosofi). Torino: Società editrice internazionale,
1975, 159 p.

Spanish: *Doctrina de la verdad según Platón y Carta sobre el humanismo.* Univ.
of Chili, 234 p.

**Translations of "Platons Lehre von der Wahrheit"**

French: *Questions II:* Qu'est-ce la philosophie? Hegel et les Grecs. La Thèse
de Kant sur l'être. La doctrine de Platon sur la vérité. Ce qu'est et comment
de détermine la physics. Ed. and trans. K. Axelos, J. Beaufret, D. Janicaud,
L. Braun, et. al. Paris, 1968, 280 p.

Japanese: *Shinri no Honshitsu nitsuite. Puraton no Schinri-Ron.* Trans. S. Kiba.
Tôkyô, 1961.

Korean: *Chilliran muôsinga* (What is Truth?) Ed. Y. Sahae Kwahak. Seoul,
1960.

Spanish: "La doctrina de Platon acerca de la verdad." Trans. N. V. Silvetti.
*Cuadernos de Filosofia* (Buenos Aires), vol. 10-12, 1952/53, 35-57.

"La doctrina de Platon acerca de la verdad." *Revista dominicana de
Filosofia,* vol. 5, 1959, 58-89.

**Translations of "Letters on Humanism"**

English: *Basic Writings.* Ed. D. F. Krell. New York: Harper and Row, 1977;
London: Routledge and Kegan Paul, 1977.

Chinese: Trans. Wei Hsiung. Peking, 1963.

Croation: *Über den Humanismus.* Trans. D. Pejovic. Yougoslavia, 1978. *Was ist Metaphysik?* 1929; *Vom Wesen der Wahrheit,* 1943; *Brief über den Humanismus,* 1947; *Vom Ursprung des Kunstwerks,* 1950; *Was ist das die Philosophie?* 1956. Trans. I. Urbanic. Llubljana, 1967, 413 p.

Czech: "Co je clovek? Myslensky Martina Heideggera." Trans. J. Nemec. *Tvár* (Czechoslovakia), vol. 2, no. 6, 1965, 28-29.

[Trans. of parts.]

Dutch: *Brief over het humanismo.* Trans. G. H. Buyssen. Intr. and commentary by J. J. G. A. Kockelmans. (Nederlandse Heidegger-Bibliotheck). Tielt/Ultrecht, 1973, 128 p.

French: "Lettre sur l'humanisme I-II." Trans. R. Munier. *Cahiers du Sud* (Paris), vol. 40, no. 319, 1953, 384 ff; no. 320, 68-88.

*Lettre sur l'humanisme.* Trans. and intr. R. Munier. Paris, 1957, 192 p. 2nd rev. ed. Paris, 1964, 188 p.

In *Questions III:* Le chemin de campagne. L'experience de la pensee. Hebel Lettre sur l'humanisme. Sérénité. Trans. A Preau, J. Hervier and R. Munier. Paris, 1966, 232 p. 2nd ed. 1980, 225 p.

Italian: *Su l' "umanismo. Che cos' è la metafisica?* Trans., intr. and annotations by A. Carlini. Firenze, 1953, 93-137.

Japanese: *Hyûmanizumu ni tsuite.* Trans. T. Kuwaki. Tôkyô, 1958.

Korean: In *Hûmaenisutûeui p'yonji.* Trans. S. Kwanghui. Seoul, 1960.

In *Humaenisûmnon* (On Humanism). Trans. C. Chaehûi. Seoul, 1961.

Portuguese: *Carta sobre o humanismo.* Ed. and trans. C. Leao. Rio de Janeiro, 1967.

Spanish: "Carte sobre el humanismo." Trans. A. W. De Reyna. *Realidad* (Buenos Aires), 7-9, 1948.

In *Culturales.* Santiago: Univ. de Chile, 1955.

*Existencialismo y humanismo.* Buenos Aires, 1963, 63-121.

*Carta sobre el humanismo.* Trans. R. G. Giradot. Madrid, 1970, 71 p.

["Aus der Erfahrung des Denkens." Written in 1947, published in 1954. *See* 72.]

## 1949

53      *Vom Wesen der Wahrheit.* 2nd enlarged ed. With an epilog. Frankfurt: Klostermann, 1949, 21 p. 1st ed. Frankfurt: Klostermann, 1943. *See* 43.

54      *Vom Wesen des Grundes.* 3rd enlarged ed. With an intr. Frankfurt: Klostermann, 1949, 50 p. 1st ed. Halle, 1929. *See* 43.

55      *Was ist Metaphysik?* (Hans Carossa zum 70. Geburtstag). 5th enlarged ed. With an intr. and a revised epilog. Frankfurt: Klostermann, 1949. 1st ed. Bonn, 1929. *See* 21. Intr. rpt. in *Wegmarken.* Frankfurt: Klostermann, 1967, 195-211. *See* 130. Intr. rpt. in *Wegmarken.* (Gesamtausgabe, Abt. 1:

Veröffentlichte Schriften 1914-1970, Bd. IX). [Unaltered text with marginal notes by the author.] Ed. Fr. W. von Herrmann. Frankfurt: Klostermann, 1976, 365-383. *See* 172.

**Translations of the "Introduction"**

English: "Introduction to the 5th edition, 1949." Trans. W. Kaufmann. In *Existentialism From Dostojiwski to Satre.* New York, 1957, 207-221.

French: "La remontée au fondement de la métaphysique." Trans. J. Rovan. *Fontaine* (Paris), vol. 58, 1957, 888-898.

"Le retour au fondement de la métaphysique." Trans. R. Munier. *Revue des Sciences Philosophiques et Theologiques* (Le Saulchoin), vol. 43, 1959, 401-433.

Polish: "Wprowadzenie do 'Co to jest metafizyka'." Trans. K. Wolicka. *Znak,* 6, 1974, and 2, 1977.

Spanish: "El retorno al fundamanto de la Metafisica." Trans. R. G. Giradot. *Ideas y Valores* (Bogota), 3-4, 1952, 203-220.

**Other Translations**

*See* 21.

56   "Der Zuspruch des Feldweges." *Sonntagsblatt* (Hamburg), vol. 2, no. 43, 23 October 1949, 5. Also entitled: "Der Feldweg." *Wort und Wahrheit* (Wien), vol. 5, 1950, 267-269. *See* 60. Separate ed. *Der Feldweg.* Frankfurt: Klostermann, 1953, 7 p. 2nd ed. Frankfurt: Klostermann, 1955. 3rd ed. Frankfurt: Klostermann, 1962. 5th ed. Frankfurt: Klostermann, 1975.

**Translations**

English: "The Pathway." Trans. T. F. O'Meara. *Listening. Journal of Religion and Culture* (River Forest), vol. 2, 1967, 88-91.

Czech: "Poini cesta." *Arch. I* (Czechoslovakia), I, 1969, 17-19.

"Polni cesta." Trans. A. Geuss. *Orientace* (Czechoslovakia), vol. 3, no. 4, 1968, 87-88.

French: "Le chemin de campagne." *Questions III.* Trans. A. Preau, J. Hervier, and R. Munier. Paris, 1966, 232 p. 2nd ed. 1980, 225 p.

Italian: "Il sentiero." Trans. E. Castelli. *Archivio de Filosofia* (Roma), vol. 19, 1950, 18-21.

"Der Feldweg - Il sentiero de campagna." [Bi-lingual ed.] Trans. and annotations by E. Landolt. *Toeresi* (Catania), vol. 16, 1961, 3-27.

Japanese: *No no Michi. Hêberu-Ie no Tomo.* Trans. M. Kosaka and K. Tsujimura. Tôkyô, 1960.

Norwegian: *Der Zuspruch des Feldweges.* Trans. E. Wyller. 1973.

Portuguese: *O caminho do campo.* Trans. and intr. E. Stein. [Ed. with a trans. of "Zur Seinsfrage."] Sao Paulo, 1969, 65-72.

Romanian: *Drum de câmp.* Trans. I. Alexandru. 1968.

Spanish: "La voz del camino." *Cuadernos Hispano-americanos* (Madrid), vol. 5, 1950, 18-21.

"La voz del camino." *Notas y Estudios de Filosofia* (Tucamán), vol. 2, 1951, 1-4.

"La voz del camino." Trans. A. Fuentes. *Universidad de Antioquia* (Medellin), vol. 31, 1955, 307-310.

[4 lectures in the Club of Bremen entitled "Einblick in das was ist," December 1949. Repeated, Bühlerhöhe, Spring 1950, "Das Ding Das Gestell. Die Gefahr. Die Kehre." "Das Ding" was published in a revised version in 1950. *See* 66. "Das Gestell," in an enlarged version in 1953, entitled "Die Frage nach der Technik." *Die Künste im technischen Zeitalter. Dritte Folge des Jahrbuchs "Gestalt und Gedanke."* Ed. Bayrische Akademie der Schönen Künste. München, 1954, 70-108. *See* 75, 78. "Die Gefahr," still is unpublished. "Die Kehre," is published in *Die Technik und die Kehre.* 1962. *See* 115.]

**1950**

57    "Die Zeit des Weltbildes." *Holzwege.* Frankfurt: Klostermann, 1950, 69-104. *See* 58.

58    *Holzwege.* Frankfurt: Klostermann, 1950, 345 p.

Contains:

"Der Ursprung des Kunstwerks," 7-68. *See* 105.

"Die Zeit des Weltbildes," 69-104. *See* 57.

"Hegels Begriff der Erfahrung," 105-192. *See* 59.

"Nietsches Wort 'Gott ist tot'," 193-247. *See* 46.

"Wozu Dichter," 248-295. *See* 49.

"Der Spruch des Anaximander," 296-343. *See* 51.

3rd ed. Frankfurt: Kostermann, 1957. 4th ed. Frankfurt: Klostermann, 1963. 5th ed. Frankfurt: Klostermann, 1972. *Holzwege.* (Gesamtausgabe, Abt. 1: Veröffentlichte Schriften 1914-1970). [Unaltered text with marginal notes by the author.] Ed. Fr. W. von Herrmann. Frankfurt: Klostermann, 1977, 382. *See* 179. Separate print: *Der Ursprung des Kunstwerks.* [Theodor Hetzer zum Gedächtnis.] Intr. H.-G. Gadamer. Stuttgart, 1960, 126.

**Translations**

Chinese: Trans. of parts by Wei Hsiung. Peking, 1964.

French: *Chemins qui ne ménent nulle part.* Trans. W. Brokmeier and F. Periers. Paris, 1962, 320. 2nd ed. 1980, 461.

Italian: *Sentieri interrotti.* Ed. and trans. P. Chiodi. Firenze, 1968, 354.

Spanish: *Sendas perdidas.* Trans. J. R. Armengol. Buenos Aires, 1960, 316.

**Translations of "Der Ursprung des Kunstwerks"**

English: "The Origin of a Work of Art." Trans. A. Hofstädter. *Philosophies of Art and Beauty.* New York, 1965, 647-701.

"The Origin of the Work of Art." Trans. and intr. A. Hofstädter. In *Poetry, Language, Thought.* New York: Harper and Row, 1975, 15-87. Rpt. in *Basic Writings.* Ed. D. F. Krell. New York: Harper and Row, 1977; London: Routlege and Kegan Paul, 1977.

Croatian: *Was ist Metaphysik?* 1929; *Vom Wesen der Wahrheit,* 1943; *Brief über den Humanismus,* 1947; *Vom Ursprung des Kunstwerks,* 1950; *Was ist das-die Philosophie?* 1956. Trans. I. Urbancic. Llubljana, 1967, 413.

*Der Ursprung des Kunstwerks.* Trans. D. Pejovic. 1959.

Czech: "Zrozeni umeleckého dila." Trans. I. Michnakova. *Orientace* (Czechoslovakia), vol. 3, no. 5, 1968, 53-62; no. 6, 75-83; vol. 4, no. 1, 84-94.

Japanese: *Geijutsusakuhin no Hajimari.* Trans. E. Kikuchi. Tôkyô, 1962.

Spanish: "El origen de la obra de arte." *Cuadernos Hispano-americanos* (Madrid), vol. 9, 1952, 3-29, 339-357.

"El origen de la obra de arte." Trans. F. Soler Grima. In *El origen de la obra de arte y la verdad en Heidegger.* Bogota: Univ. National de Columbia, 1953, 27-81.

**Translations of "Die Zeit des Weltbildes"**

English: "The Age of the World View." Trans. M. Grene. *Measure,* vol. 2, 1951, 269-284. Rpt. in *Martin Heidegger and the Question of Literature.* Ed. W. V. Spanos. Bloomington: Indiana Univ. Press, 1979, 1-15.

"The Age of the World Picture." In *The Questions Concerning Technology,* by Martin Heidegger. Ed., intr., and trans. W. Lovitt. New York: Harper and Row, 1977, 115-154.

Czech: "Doba, kdy svet je obrazem." Trans. S. Vitek. *Antologie existencialismu* (Praha), vol. 1, 1967, 137-159.

Japanese: *Sekaizô no Jidai.* Trans. T. Kuwaki. Tôkyô, 1962.

Polish: "Czas swiatoobrazu." Trans. K. Wolika. *Odra,* vol. 9, 1974, and vol. 2, 1978.

**Translations of "Hegels Begriff der Erfahrung"**

English: *Hegel's Concept of Experience.* [With a section from Hegel's *Phenomenology of Spirit.*] Trans. K. Dove. New York, 1970, 155.

*Hegel's Concept of Experience.* Trans. G. Gray and F. D. Wieck. New York: Harper and Row, 1970.

Japanese: *Hêgeru no 'Keiken' Gainen.* Trans. S. Hosaya. Tôkyô, 1954.

**Translations of "Nietzsches Wort 'Gott ist tot'"**

English: "The World of Nietzsche: God is Dead." In *The Question Concerning Technology,* by Martin Heidegger. Ed., trans, and intr. W. Lovitt. New York: Harper and Row, 1977, 53-112.

Japanese: *Nîche no Kotaba "Kami wa Shiseri."* Trans. S. Hosaya. Tôkyô, 1954.

Korean: In *Sinûn Chugossda.* Trans. C. Tonghui. Seoul, 1959.

**Translations of "Wozu Dichter?"**

English: "What are the Poets for?" In *Poetry, Language, Thought.* Trans. and intr. A. Hofstädter. New York, 1975, 91-142.

Japanese: *Toboshiki Jidai no Shijin.* Trans. T. Tezuka and H. Takahashi. Tôkyô, 1958.

Korean: In *Siwa ch'orhak* (Poetry and Philosophy). Trans. S. Kwanghui. Seoul, 1972.

Spanish: "Por qué el poeta?" Trans. H. P. Llena. *Revista Cubana de Filosofia* (La Habana), vol. 6, 1950, 66 p.

**Translations of "Der Spruch des Anaximander"**

English: "Martin Heidegger: The Anaximander Fragment." Ed. and trans. D. F. Krell. *Arion: A Journal of Humanities and Classics,* New Series I, vol. 4, Winter 1974, 576-626.

Japanese: *Anakushimandorosu no Kotaba.* Trans. M. Tanaka. Tôkyô, 1957.

60   "Der Feldweg." *Wort und Wahrheit* (Wien), vol. 5, 1950, 267-296. 1st published entitled "Der Zuspruch des Feldweges." 1949. *See* 56.

["Das Ding." Public lecture, delivered on 6 June 1950 in München at the Prinz-Carl-Palais, following an invitation from the Bayrische Akademie der Schönen Künste. This lecture was a revised and enlarged version of the lecture given in 1949. *See* 66.]

["Die Sprache." Public lecture delivered in memoriam of Max Kommerell 7 October 1950 at the Bühlerhöhe. Repeated lecture 14 February 1951, Stuttgart at the Würrtembergische Bibliotheksgesellschaft. *See* 99.]

## 1951

61   *Kant und das Problem der Metaphysik.* (Max Scheler zum Gedächtnis). 2nd ed. With a new intr. Frankfurt: Klostermann, 1951, 222 p. 1st ed. 1929. *See* 22.

**Translations**

*See* 22.

62   *Erläuterunten zu Hölderlins Dichtung.* 2nd enlarged ed. Frankfurt: Klostermann, 1951, 144 p. 1st ed. *See* 47. Added texts: "Wie wenn am Feiertage..." 1st ed. Halle, 1941, 47-74. *See* 41; and "Andenken." Tubingen, 1943, 75-143. *See* 45.

**Translations**

English: Trans. of "Heimkunft. An die Verwandten" and "Hölderlin und das Wesen der Dichtung." In *Existence and Being.* Ed. and intr. W. Brock. Chicago: Henry Regnery Company, 1949.

French: *Approche de Hölderlin.* Trans. H. Corbin, M. Deguy, F. Fedier, and J. Launay. Paris, 1962, 194 p.

Contains:

"Heimkunft" (Retour). Trans. M. Deguy. 11-38,

"Hölderlin und das Wesen der Dichtung" (Hölderlin et l'essence de la poésie). Trans. H. Corbin. 39-61.

"Wie wenn am Feiertage..." (Comme un jour de fête). Trans. M. Deguy and F. Fédier. 63-98.

"Andenken" (Souvenirs). Trans. J. Launay. 99-194.

Japanese: *Herudârin no Shi Kaimei.* Trans. T. Tezuka, S. Saito, S. Tsushida, T. Takeuchi. Tôkyô, 1955.

**Translations of Parts**

*See* 41, 45, 47.

63　　"Brief an Emil Staiger." In "Emil Staiger: Zu einen Vers von Mörike. Ein Briefwechsel mit Martin Beidegger." *Trivium* (Zürich), vol. 9, 1951, 1-16. Separate print: Zürich, 1951, 1-16. Rpt. in *Emil Staiger, Die Kunst der Interpretation.* Zürich, 1955, 34-39.

64　　"Selbstverlassenheit und Irrniss." In *Ernst Barlach. Dramatiker Bildhauer, Zeichner.* [Published by the municipal administrative authorities for culture of Darmstadt and the National Theatre Darmstdt, 1951], 5-12. Rpt. in "Überwindung der Metaphysik." *Vorträgte und Aufsätze.* 1954, 71-99. *See* 78.

[Written between 1936 and 1946.]

65　　"Logos." In *Festschrift für Hans Jantzen.* Ed. K. Bauch. Berlin, 1951, 7-18. Rpt. in *Vorträge und Aufsätze.* Pfullingen: Neske, 1954, 207-229. *See* 78. 2nd ed. Pfullingen: Neske, 1959. 3rd ed. Pfullingen: Neske, 1967. 4th ed. Pfullingen: Neske, 1978.

[Compilation from a lecture delivered in the Spring Term 1944, and a public lecture held in 1951, with particular focus on the fragment B 50.]

**Translations**

English: "Logos." In *Early Greek Thinking.* Trans. D. F. Krell and F. A. Capuzzi. [English trans. of 4 essays] New York: Harper and Row, 1975.

French: "Logos." Trans. J. Lacan. *La Psychoanalyse* (Sur la Parole et la Language), vol. 1, 1956, 59 ff; 1953; 1955.

Japanese: "Rogos." Trans. Y. Utsunomiya. *Risô* (Tôkyô), vol. 514, 1976, 172-184; *Risô* (Tôkyâ, vol. 513, 1976, 164-176.

66　　"Das Ding." *Gestalt und Gedanke. Jahrbuch.* Ed. Bayrische Akademie der Schönen Künste. München, 1951, 128-148. Rpt. in *Vorträge und Aufsätze.* Pfullingen: Neske, 1954, 163-181. [With an epilog: "Nachwort: Ein Brief an einen jungen Studenten." 182-185.] *See* 78. 2nd ed. Pfullingen: Neske, 1959. 3rd ed. Pfullingen: Neske, 1967. 4th ed. Pfullingen: Neske, 1978.

**Translations**

English: *What is a Thing?* Trans. W. B. Bartin, jr. and V. Deutsch. Commentary by E. J. Gendlin. Chicago, 1968.

"The Thing." Trans. and intr. A. Hofstädter. In *Poetry, Language, Thought.* New York: Harper and Row, 1975, 163-186. 1st ed. 1971.

Spanish: "La cosa." Trans. R. Gutierrez Giradot. *Ideas y Valores* (Bogotá), 7-8, 1952/53, 661-677.

"La cosa." Trans. R. Gutierrez Giradot. *Cuadernos Hispano-americanos* (Madrid), vol. 15, 1953, 3-20.

"La cosa." Trans. V. Sanchez de Zavela. *Cuadernos Hispano-americanos* (Madrid), vol. 33, 1958, 133-158.

["Bauen, Wohnen, Denken." Public lecture delivered 5 August 1951 in the course of the Darmstadt Colloqium 2 on "Mensch und Raum." *See* 78.]

["...dichterisch wohnet der Mensch..." Public lecture delivered 6 October 1951 at the Bühlerhöhe. *See* 73, 78.]

["Was heisst Denken?" Lecture Series. Univ. of Freiburg, Fall Term 1951/52, and Spring Term 1952. *See* 78, 79.]

### 1952

67     *Bauen Wohnen Denken. Mensch und Raum. Darmstädter Colloquy 2.* Ed. on behalf of the magistrate of the City of Darmstadt and the Committee "Darmstädter Gespräch 1951" by O. Bartning. Darmstadt, 1952, 72-84. [Lecture delivered in 1951.] Rpt. in *Vorträge und Aufsätze.* Pfullingen: Neske, 1954, 145-162. 4th ed. Pfullingen: Neske, 1978. *See*

**Translations**

English: "Building Dwelling Thinking." In *Basic Writings.* Ed. D. F. Krell. New York: Harper and Row, 1977; London: Routledge and Kegan Paul, 1977, 319-339.

"Building, Dwelling, Thinking." In *Poetry, Language, Thought.* Trans. and intr. A. Hofstädter. New York: Harper and Row, 1975, 145-161. 1st ed. 1971.

Polish: "Budowaá, mieszkaá, mysleá." Trans. K. Michalski. *Teksty,* vol. 4, 1974, and vol. 2, 1977.

*Budowaá, mieszkaá, myáleá. Eseje wybrane.* Selected essays. Ed. K. Michalski. Warszawa, 1977.

Spanish: "Construir, habitar, pensar." Trans. F. Soler. *Teoria* (Santiago de Chile), vol. 5-6, 1975, 150-162.

68     "Was heisst Denken?" *Merkur* (München), vol. 6, 1952, 601-611. [Lecture broadcasted in Bavaria, May 1952.] Rpt. in *Vorträge und Aufsätze.* Pfullingen: Neske, 1954, 129-143. 4th ed. Pfullingen: Neske, 1978. *See* 78. *Was heisst Denken?* Tübingen: Niemeyer, 1961. *See* 79.

**Translation**

*See* 79.

## 1953

69 *Einführung in die Metaphysik.* Tübingen: Niemeyer, 1953, 156 p. 2nd ed. Tübingen: Niemeyer, 1958, 156 p. 3rd ed. Tübingen: Niemeyer, 1967. 4th ed. Tübingen: Niemeyer, 1976.

**Translations**

English: *Introduction to Metaphysics.* Trans. R. Manheim. New Haven, Oxford, 1959; New York, 1961, 182 p.

*An Introduction to Metaphysics.* Trans. R. Manheim. Yale, 1974.

Czech: *Myslenky M. Heideggera* (What is a Human Being - The World of M. Heidegger). Trans. and intr. J. Nemec. *Tvár* (Praha), vol. 6, 1965.

French: *Introduction à la métaphysique.* Ed. and trans. G. Kahn. Paris, 1958, 244 p.

Italian: *Introduzione alla metafisica.* Ed. and trans. G. Vattimo and G. Masi. Milano, 1968, 211 p.

Japanese: *Keijijogaku-Nyumon.* Trans. E. Kawahar. Tôkyô, 1960.

Portuguese: *Introducao à Metafisica.* Trans. C. Leao. Rio de Janeiro, 1966.

Spanish: *Introducción a la metafisica.* Trans. and with prologue: "El problema metafisica en las ultimas obras de Heidegger," by E. Estiu. Buenos Aires, 1956. 2nd ed. 1959, 247 p.

70 "Georg Trakl. Eine Erörterung seines Gedichtes." *Merkur* (München), vol. 7, 1953, 226-258. Rpt. in *Unterwegs zur Sprache.* Pfullingen: Neske, 1959, 35-82.

[Here, the work is entitled "Die Sprache im Gedicht. Eine Erörterung von Georg Trakls Gedichte." *See* 99.]

**Translations**

French: "Georg Trakl." Nouvelle revue francaise, vol. 6, 61/62. Paris, 1958, 52-75, 213, 236.

Spanish: "Georg Trakl, una localización de su poesia." Trans. H. Zucchi. Buenos Aires: Editorial Carmina, 1956, 56 p.

71 "Heidegger über Heidegger, [A letter to the editor, on Ch. E. Lewalter's 'Wie liest man 1953 Sätze von 1935'," *Die Zeit* (Hamburg), vol. 8, 33, 13 August 1953, 6], *Die Zeit* (Hamburg), vol. 8, 39, 24 September 1953, 18.

["Wissenschaft und Besinnung." Lecture delivered 15 May 1953 on the occasion of the conference of the "Arbeitsgemeinschft wissenschaftlicher Sortimenter" at the "Schauinsland" near Freiburg and 4 August 1953 as a preparatory lecture for a conference on "Die Künste in technischen Zeitalter." Arranged by the Bayrische Akademie der Schönen Künste. *See* 76.]

"Wer ist Nietzsches Zarathustra?" Lecture delivered in the Club of Bremen on 8 May 1953. *See* 78.]

["Die Frage nach der Technik." Lecture delivered on 18 November 1953 at the conference on "Die Künste im technischen Zeitalter." Arranged by the

Bayrische Akademie der Schönen Künste; an enlarged and revised version of a lecture delivered in 1949 entitled "Das Gestell." *See* 75.]

## 1954

72  *Aus der Erfahrung des Denkens.* Pfullingen: Neske, 1954, 27 p. [Written, 1947] 2nd ed. Pfullingen: Neske, 1965. 3rd ed. Pfullingen: Neske, 1976.
**Translations**

English: "The Thinker as the Poet." In *Poetry, Language, Thought.* Trans. and intr. A. Hofstädter. New York: Harper and Row, 1971, 1-14. 2nd ed. New York: Harper and Row, 1975.

French: *Questions III:* Le chemin de Campagne. L'expérience de la pensée. Hebel. Lettre sur L'Humanisme. Sérénité. Trans. A. Preau, J. Hervier, and R. Munier. Paris, 1966, 232 p. 2nd ed. 1980, 225 p.

Italian: "Dall'esperienza del pensare." In *Il Pensare Poetante,* by Martin Heidegger. Perugia, 1971.

"Dall'esperienza del pensare." Trans. F. Favino. *Filosfia* (Torino), 1957, 373-378.

"Aus der Erfahrung des Denkens." *Teoresi* (Catania), vol. 20, 1965, 3-28. [Bi-lingual ed.]

Japanese: *Shii no Keiken yori.* Trans. K. Tsujimura. Tôkyô, 1960.

Norwegian: *Aus der Erfahrung des Denkens.* Trans. E. A. Wyller. 1964; 1973.

Portuguese: *Da experiencia do pensar.* Ed. and trans. M. C. T. Miranda. Porto Alegre, 1969, 54 p.

Spanish: "De la experiencia del pensar." Trans. J. M. Valverde. *Cuadernos Hispano-americanos* (Madrid), vol. 20, 1954, 173-180.

"De la experiencia del pensar." Trans. J. M. Valverde. *Annario de Arte Literatura* (Buenos Aires), 1961/62.

73  "...Dichterisch wohnt der Mensch..." *Akzente Zeitschrift für Dichtung* (München), vol. 1, 1954, 57-71. Rpt. in *Vorträge und Aufsätze.* Pfullingen: Neske, 1978. *See* 78.
**Translations**

English: "...Poetically Man Dwells..." In *Poetry, Language, Thought.* Trans. and intr. A. Hofstädter. New York: Harper and Row, 1975, 211-229.

French: "L'homme habite en poète." Trans. A. Preau. *Cahiers du Sud* (Paris), vol. 44, no. 344, 1958, 49-66.

Spanish: "Poéticamente habita el hombre." Trans. F. de Walker. *Humanitas* (Brescia), 1960, 13-27. Rpt. in *Humboldt 4-14* (Hamburg), 1963, 29-36.

"En poema habita el hombre." Trans. and intr. R. Gutierrez Giradot. *Revista National de Cultura* (Caracas), vol. 110, 1955, 145-158. Rpt. in *Revista de Filosofia* (Santiago de Chile), vol. 7, 1960, 77-91.

74 "Heraklit." In *Festschrift zur Feier des 350jährigen Bestehens des Heinrich-Suso-Gymnasiums in Konstanz.* Konstanz, 1954, 60-76. Rpt. in *Vorträge und Aufsätze.* Pfullingen: Neske, 1978. *See* 78.

**Translations**

*See* 78.

75 "Die Frage nach der Technik." In *Die Künste im technischen Zeitalter. Dritte Folge des Jahrbuchs 'Gestalt und Gedanke'.* Ed. Bayrische Akademie der schönen Künste. München, 1954, 70-108. Rpt. in *Vorträge und Aufsätze.* Pfullingen: Neske, 1954, 13-44. 4th ed. Pfullingen: Neske, 1978. *See* 78.

*Die Technik und die Kehre.* (Opuscula aus Wissenschaft und Dichtung). Pfullingen: Neske, 1962. 3rd ed. Pfullingen: Neske, 1976. *See* 115.

**Translations**

English: *The Question Concerning Technology and Other Essays.* Ed., intr., and trans. W. Lovitt. New York: Harper and Row, 1977.

Contains:

"The Questions Concerning Technology," 3-35.

"Science and Reflection," 155-182.

"The Question Concerning Technology." In *Basic Writings.* Ed. and intr. to each selection by D. F. Krell. New York: Harper and Row, 1977; London: Routledge and Kegan Paul, 1977, 283-318.

76 "Wissenschaft und Besinnung." *Börsenblatt für den Deutschen Buchhandel* (Frankfurt), vol. 10, no. 29, 13 April 1954, 321-330. Rpt. in *Vorträge und Aufsätze.* Pfullingen: Neske, 1954, 45-70. 4th ed. Pfullingen: Neske, 1978. *See* 78.

77 "Anmerkungen über die Metaphysik." In *Im Umkreis der Kunst.* Eine Festschrift für Emil Preetorius. Ed. F. Hollwich. Wiesbaden, 1954, 117-136. [Witten between 1936-1946.] Identical in part to "Überwindung der Metaphysik." In *Vorträge und Aufsätze.* Pfullingen: Neske, 1978. *See* 78.

78 *Vorträge und Aufsätze.* [Dem einzigen Bruder] Pfullingen: Neske, 1954, 283 p.

Contains:

I. "Die Frage nach der Technik." 1949. Lecture entitled "Das Gestell;" delivered in an enlarged version, 1954, 13-44. *See* 75.

"Wissenschaft und Besinnung." Separate publication, 1954. *See* 76.

"Überwindung der Metaphysik." 1936-1946 notes; partially published in separate editions "Seinsverlassenheit und Irrnis," 1951 and "Anmerkungen über die Metaphysik." 1954, 71-99. *See* 64, 77.

"Wer ist Nietzsches Zarathustra?" 1953 lecture, 101-126.

II. "Was heisst Denken?" 1952 lecture. 1st print, 1952, 129-143. *See* 68.

"Bauen Wohnen Denken." 1951 lecture. 1st print, 1952, 145-162. *See* 67.

"Das Ding." 1st print, 1951. *See* 66. With an epilog "Ein Brief an einen jungen Studenten," 163-185.

"..Dichterisch wohnet der Mensch..." 1951 lecture; separate publication, 1954, 187-204. *See* 73.

III. "Logos." [Heraklit. Fragment 50] 1951, 207-229.

"Moira." [Parmendes. Fragment VIII, 34-41] Taken from a lecture series entitled "Was heisst Denken," delivered 1951/52, and 1952, 231-256.

"Aletheia." [Heraklit. Fragment 16] 1954, 257-282. *See* 74. 2nd ed. Pfullingen: Neske, 1959. Rpt. in separate volumes: Vol. I: 3rd ed. 1967, 119 p.; Vol. II: 3rd ed. 1967, 79 p.; Vol. III: 3rd ed. 1967, 79 p.; 4th ed. Pfullingen: Neske, 1978.

**Translations**

French: *Essais et conférences.* Trans. A. Preau. With a prologue entitled "Les Essais" by J. Beaufret. Paris, 1958, 350 p.

Italian: *Saggi e discorsi.* Ed. G. Vattimo. (Bibliotace di filosofia. Testi, 9). Milano: Mursia, 1976, XVIII-194.

**Translations of "Wer ist Nietzsches Zarathustra?"**

English: "Who is Nietzsche's Zarathustra?" *Review of Metaphysics* (Haverford), vol. 20, 1966/67, 411-431.

Japanese: "Nîchie no Tsuaratosutora we dare ka." Trans. S. Arai. *Risô* (Tôkyô), vol. 524, 1977, 180-191; *Risô* (Tôkyô), 1977, 150-162.

Spanish: "Quien es el Zaratustra de Nietzsche?" Trans. L. G. Suarez-Llanos. *Cuadernos Hispano-americanos* (Madrid), vol. 50, 1962, 321-340.

**Translation of "Moria"**

Japanese: "Moria." Trans. Y. Utsunomiya. *Risô* (Tôkyô), vol. 514, 1976, 143-155; *Risô* (Tôkyô), vol. 515, 1976, 147-160.

**Translations of "Aletheia"**

Arabic: Trans. A.-G. Mikkawy. 1977.

Japanese: "Arêtheia." Trans. Y. Utsunomiya. *Risô* (Tôkyô), vol. 516, 1976, 202-214; *Risô* (Tôkyô), vol. 515, 1976, 106-120.

**Translation of "Wissenschaft und Besinnung"**

Japanese: "Kagaku to Chinshi." Trans. S. Arai. *Risô* (Tôkyô), vol. 518, 1976, 129-140; *Risô* (Tôkyô), vol. 519, 1976, 134-144.

**Translations of "Überwindung der Metaphysik"**

English: In *The End of Philosophy.* Trans. J. Stanbaugh. New York: Harper and Row, 1973.

Japanese: "Keijijogaku no Chokoku." Trans. S. Arai. *Risô* (Tôkyô), vol. 522, 1976, 151-165; *Risô* (Tôkyô), vol. 523, 1976, 143-155.

**Other Translations**

*See* 65, 66, 67, 68, 73, 75.

79  *Was heisst Denken?* (Der treuen Gefährtin zum 60. Geburtstag). Tübingen, 1954, 174 p. [Text of the lecture series delivered in the Fall Term 1951/52 and in the Spring Term 1952.] 2nd ed. Tübingen: Niemeyer, 1961. 3rd ed. 1971. *See* 68.

**Translations**

English: *What is Called Thinking?* Trans. and intr. J. G. Gray. New York, 1968, XXVII-244.

*What is Called Thinking?* Trans. F. D. Wieck and J. G. Gray. New York: Harper and Row, 1972, 252 p. Rpt. in "What Calls for Thinking?" In *Basic Writings,* by Martin Heidegger. Ed. D. F. Krell. New York: Harper and Row, 1977, 345-367.

French: *Qu'appelle-t-on penser?* Trans. A. Becker and G. Granel. Paris, 1967, 272 p.

Italian: "Che significa Pensare?" In *Il Pensare Poetante,* by Martin Heidegger. Ed. and trans. E. Mirri. Perugia, 1971.

Spanish: "Qué significa pensar?" Trans. H. Zucchi. *Sur* (Buenos Aires), 215-216, 1952.

"Qué significa pensar?" Trans. H. Kahnemann. Buenos Aires, 1956, (1958), 234 p. 2nd ed. Buenos Aires, 1964.

80   "Über 'die Linie'." In *Freundschaftliche Begegnungen. Festschrift zum 60.* (Geburtstag, Frankfurt, 1955). 9-45. [As entitled "Zur Seinsfrage." Frankfurt, 1956. *See* 82.] Rpt. in *Wegmarken.* 1967, 213-253.

80a  "Die Spache Johann Peter Hebels." *Der Lichtgang* (Freiburg), vol. 5, no. 7, 1955, 3-4. (Nachrichtenblatt der öffentlichen Kulturen und Heimatpflege im Regierungsbezirk Südbaden, with a supplement).

[*Gelassenheit* (1955). Speech on the occasion of the 175th recurrence of the birthday of Conradin Kreutzer, the composer, held on 30 October in Messkirch.]

[*Was ist das-die Philosophie?* 1956. Lecture in Cerisyla-Salle/Normandie, 1955. *See* 81.]

[*Der Satz vom Grund.* 1957. Lecture series. Fall Term 1955/56. *See* 83.]

81   *Was ist das-die Philosophie?* Pfullingen: Neske, 1956, 46 p. 3rd ed. Pfullingen: Neske, 1963. 6th ed. Pfullingen: Neske, 1976, 28 p.

**Translations**

English: *What is Philosophy?* [Bi-lingual ed.] Trans. W. Kluback and J. T. Wilde. New York, 1958, 97 p.

Chinese: "He wei zhexue." Trans. C. Meili. In *Cai Meili Cunzaizhuyi dashi-Hai Dege* (Heidegger - Master of Existentialism). Taibei: Daxue Congkan, 1970, 15.

"Zhexue shi shenmo." Trans. S. Yicheng, C. Zhengyun, and Y. Bozxin, Zhexue yu wenhua yuekan. *Universitas: Monthly Review of Philosophy and Culture* (Taibei), vol. II, no. 9, 1975.

Croation: *Was ist Metaphysik?* 1929; *Vom Wesen der Wahrheit,* 1943; *Brief über den Humanismus,* 1947; *Vom Ursprung des Kunstwerks,* 1950; *Was ist das-die Philosophie,* 1956. Trans. I. Urbancic. Llubljana, 1967, 413 p.

Dutch: *Was ist dat-Filosofie?* Intr. and commentary by J. Kockelsman. Trans. G. H. Buijssen. Tielt/Ultrecht, 1970, 64 p.

French: *Qu'est-ce que la philosophie?* Trans. K. Axelos and J. Beaufret. Paris, 1957, 50 p.

"Qu'est-ce que la philosophi." In *Questions II.* Ed. and trans. K. Axelos, J. Beaufret, D. Janicaud, L. Braun, et al. Paris, 1968, 280 p.

Italian: "Cos è la filosofia." In *Il Pensare Poetante,* by Martin Heidegger. Ed. and trans. E. Mirro. Perugia, 1977.

Japanese: *Tetsugaku to wa Nanika.* Trans. T. Hara. Tôkyô, 1960.

Korean: *Cilliran muosinga* (What is Truth?) Ed. Y. Saheae Kwahak. Seoul, 1960.

Portuguese: *Que e isto-a filosofia?* Trans. and intr. E. Stein. [Ed. includes a trans. of "Identität und Differenze."] Sao Paulo, 1971, 15-42.

Spanish: *Qué es esto, la filosofia?* Trans. V. Li Carillo. [Includes a letter by Heidegger addressed to Carillo] Lima: Univ. Major de San Marcos, 1958, 59 p.

*Qué es eso de filosofia?* Trans. A. P. Carpio. Buenos Aires, 1960, 75 p.

*Qué es filosofia?* Trans. J. L. Molinuevo. (Collection Bitácora, 64). Madrid: Narcea, 1978, 144 p. 2nd ed. 1978, 134 p.

82    *Zur Seinsfrage.* Frankfurt: Klostermann, 1956, 43 p. [First publication entitled "Die Linie." 1955.] *See* 80. 2nd ed. Frankfurt: Klostermann, 1959. 3rd ed. Frankfurt: Klostermann, 1967. 4th rev. ed. Frankfurt: Klostermann, 1977, 48 p. Rpt. in *Wegmarken.* Frankfurt: Klostermann, 1967, 13-253. *See* 130.

*Wegmarken.* (Gesamtausgabe, Abt. 1: Veröffentlichte Schriften 1914-1970, Bd. XI). [Unaltered text with marginal notes by the author.] Ed. Fr. W. von Herrmann. Frankfurt: Klostermann, 1976, 385-426. *See* 172.

**Translations**

English: *The Question of Being.* [Bi-lingual ed.] Trans. W. Kluback and J. T. Wilde. New York, 1958, 109 p.

French: *Questions I:* Qu'est-ce que la métaphysique? Ce qui fait l'être essentiel d'un fondement ou "raison." De l'essence de la vérité. Contribution à la question de l'être. Identité et différence. Ed. and trans. H. Corbin, R. Munier, A. Waelhens, W. Biemel, et al. Paris, 1968, 315 p.

Japanese: *U no Toi e.* Trans. T. Kakihara. Tôkyô, 1970.

Portuguese: *Sobre o problema do ser.* Trans. and intr. E. Stein. [Includes a trans. of "Der Feldweg."] Sao Paulo, 1969, 11-63.

Spanish: *Sobre la question des ser.* Trans. G. Bleiberg. Madrid, 1958, 77 p.

83    "Der Satz vom Grund." *Wissenschaft und Weltbild* (Wien), vol. 9, 1956, 241-250. [1956 lecture] Rpt. in *Der Satz vom Grund.* Pfullingen: Neske, 1957, 189-211. 5th ed. Pfullingen: Neske, 1978. *See* 86.

84 "Gespräch mit Hebel beim 'Schatzkästlein' zum Hebeltag 1956." Lörrach: Schriftenreihe des Hebelbundes, 1956, 4. Rpt. in *Hebeldank. Bekenntnis zum alemannischen Geist in sieben Reden beim "Schatzkästlein."* Ed. H. Ubl. Freiburg, 1964, 51-64.

85 "Encuentros con Ortega y Gasset. Ortega y Heidegger en Alemania." *Clavileno* (Madrid), vol. 7, no. 39, 1956, 1-2.

["Der Satz vom Grund." 1956. Public lecture delivered at the Club of Bremen on 25 May 1956 and on 24 October 1956 at the Auditorium Maximum at the Univ. of Vienna. *See* 83, 86.]

[Seminar on Hegel's "Wissenschaft der Logik." Fall Term 1956/57. Parts included in "Die onto-theo-logische Verfassung der Metaphysik" and *Identität und Differenz,* 1957. *See* 88.]

**1957**

86 *Der Satz vom Grund.* Pfullingen: Neske, 1957, 212 p. Contains Lecture series. Fall Term 1955/56, 11-188. Public lecture 1956. 1st publication 1956, 189-211. *See* 83. 2nd ed. 1958. 3rd ed. 1965. 4th ed. 1971. 5th ed. Pfullingen: Neske, 1978.

**Translations**

English: "The Principle of Ground." Trans. K. Hoeller. *Man and World* (The Hague), vol. 7, 1974, 207-222.

[Trans. of 83.]

French: *Le principe de raison.* Ed. and trans. A. Preau. Prologue by J. Beaufret. Paris, 1962, 270 p.

Japanese: *Konkyoritsu.* Trans. K. Tsujimura and H. Buchner. Tôkyô, 1962.

87 "Der Satz der Identität." In *Die Albert-Ludwigs-Universität Freiburg 1457-1957.* Die Festvorträge der Jubiläumsfeier. Freiburg, 1957, 69-79. Rpt. in *Identität und Differenz.* Pfullingen: Neske, 1957, 11034. *See* 87.

88 *Identität und Differenz.* Pfullingen: Neske, 1957, 76 p.

Contains:

"Der Satz der Identität." In *Die Festvorträge bei der Jubiläumsfeier.* Freiburg, 1957, 69-79. *See* 87.

"Die onto-theo-logische Verfassung der Metaphysik." Public lecture, 1957, 35-73. 2nd ed. Pfullingen: Neske, 1957. 4th ed. 1967. 5th rev. ed. Pfullingen: Neske, 1976.

**Translations**

English: *Essays in Metaphysics. Identity and Difference.* Trans. K. F. Leidecker. New York, 1960, 82 p.

*Identity and Difference.* Trans. and intr. J. Stambaugh. New York: Harper and Row, 1969, 146 p. 2nd ed. New York: Harper and Row, 1969, 146 p. 2nd ed. New York: Harper and Row, 1974.

*Identity and Difference.* London, 1970, 160 p.

*Identity and Difference.* Ed. J. G. Gray. Trans. J. Stambaugh. London, 1975.

French: *Questions I:* Qu'est-ce que la métaphysique? Ce qui fait l'être-essentiel d'un fondement ou "raison." De l'essence de la vérité. Contribution à la question de l'être. Identité et différence. Ed. and trans. H. Corbin, R. Munier, A. De Waelhens, W. Biemel, et al. Paris, 1968, 315 p.

"Le principe d'identité." Trans. G. Kahn. *Arguments* (Paris), vol. 7, 1968.

[Trans. of parts: "Der Satz der Identität."]

Italian: "Identità e differenzie." Trans. E. Landolt. *Teoresi* (Catania), vol. 21, 1966, 3-22.

"Identità e differenzia II: La concezione onto-theo-logica della metafisica." Trans. E. Landolt and M. Cristaldi. *Teoresi* (Catania), vol. 22, 1967, 213-235.

Japanese: *Doichisei to Saisei.* Trans. S. Oe. Tôkyô, 1960.

Portuguese: *Identidade e diferenca.* Trans. and intr. E. Stein. [Ed. includes a trans. of "Was ist das-die Philosophie?"] Sao Paulo, 1971, 43-104.

89     *Hebel der Hausfreund.* Pfullingen: Neske, 1957, 39 p. [Enlarged version of *Gespräch mit Hebel.*] *See* 84. 3rd ed. Pfullingen: Neske, 1965. 4th ed. Pfullingen: Neske, 1977.

**Translations**

French: *Questions III:* Le chemin de campagne. L'expérience de la pensée. Hebel. Lettre sur l'Humanisme. Sérénité. Trans. A. Preau, J. Hervier and R. Munier. Paris, 1966, 232 p. 2nd ed. 1980, 225 p.

Japanese: *No no michi. Heberu-Je no Tomo.* Trans. M. Kosoka and K. Tsujimura. Tôkyô, 1960.

## 1958

90     "Vom Wesen und Begriff der Physis. Aristoteles Physik B 1." *Il Pensiero* (Milano), vol. 3, 1958, 131-156, 265-290. Off-print in *Testi Filosofi: Biblioteca "Il Pensier."* 1960. Rpt. in *Wegmarken.* Frankfurt: Klostermann, 1967, 309-371. *See* 130.

*Wegmarken.* (Gesamtausgabe, Abt. 1: Veröffentlichte Schriften 1914-1970, Bd. IX). [Unaltered text with marginal notes by the author.] Ed. Fr. W. von Herrmann. Frankfurt: Klostermann, 1976, 239-301. *See* 172.

**Translations**

English: "On the Being and Conception of Physics. Aristotele's Physics B, 1." Trans. T. J. Sheehan. *Man and World* (The Hague), vol. 9, 1976,

French: *Questions II:* Qu'est-ce que la philosophie? Hegel et les Grecs. La thèse de Kant sur l'être. La doctrine de Platon sur la vérité. Ce qu'est et comment se détermine la physics. Ed. and trans. K. Axelos, J. Beaufret, D. Janicaud, L. Braun, et al. Paris, 1968, 280 p.

Italian: "Dell'essere e del concetto dells Physis, Aristoteles Fisica B 1." Trans. G. Guzzoni. In *Il Pensiero*. Milano/Varese, 1958, 235-260, 372-395.

*Vom Wesen und Begriff der Physis. Aristotoles Physik B 1.* Trans. G. Guzzoni. Milano/Varese, 1960, 112 p.

["Das Wort." Public lecture at a matinee in the Burgtheater of Vienna, delivered on 11 May 1958 and entitled "Dichten und Denken. On Stefan George's poem 'Das Wort'." *See* 99.]

["Hegel et les Grecs." Public lecture at the Nouvelle faculté in Aix-en-Provence on 20 March 1958. Repeated at the general conference of the Akademie der Wissenschaften of Heidelberg on 26 June 1958.]

91     "Grundsätze des Denkens." *Jahrbuch für Psychologie und Psychotherapie* (Freiburg/München), vol. 6, 1958, 33-41. [V. E. Freiherrn von Gebsattel zum 75. Geburtstag.]

**Translations**

English: "Principles of Thinking." In *M. Heidegger. The Piety of Thinking Essays.* Trans. K. Hoeller, J. M. Hart and J. J. C. Maraldo. Indiana Univ. Press, 1976.

French: "Principes de la pensée." *Arguments* (Paris), vol. 4, no. 20, 1960, 27-33.

Japanese: *Shii no Knopon-Meidai.* Trans. A. Takeichi. Kyôto, 1959.

92     "Brief an Victor Li Carillo." In *Que'es esto la filosofia.* Trans. V. Li Carillo. [Con una costa de Heidegger al traductor.] Lima, 1958. *See* 81.

93     "Gelassenheit. Bodenständigkeit im Atomzeitalter." In *Ethik und Gegenwart,* vol. 7. Trans. K. Tsujimura. Tôkyô, 1958.

[Speech on the occasion of the 175th recurrence of the birthday of Conradin Kreutzer, the composer held 30 October 1955.]

## 1959

94     *Gelassenheit.* Pfullingen: Neske, 1959, 73 p.

Contains:

"Gelassenheit." 9-28. *See* 93.

"Zur Erörterung der Gelassenheit. Aus einem Feldweggespräch über das Denken." 1944/45, 29-73. 2nd ed. Pfullingen: Neske, 1960. 3rd ed. 1967. [1st published in Japanese, 1958. *See* 93.] Rpt. in *Gelassenheit.* (Zum Atomzeitalter). Ed. H. Buchner and T. Kakihara. Tôkyô, 1962. [Identical with the Neske ed., 1959; with an epilog by Buchner and Kakihara, and annotations. The text is an exercise designed for the German instruction of Japanese students.]

**Translations**

English: *Discourse on Thinking.* Trans. J. M. Anderson and E. H. Freund. Intr. J. M. Anderson. New York, 1966, 93 p.

French: *Questions III:* Le chemin de compagne. L'expérience de la Pensée. Hebel. Lettre sur l'humanisme. Sérénité. Trans. A. Preau, J. Hervier and R. Munier. Paris, 1966, 232 p. 2nd ed. 1980, 225 p.

Italian: "Rilassamento." In *Il Pensare Poetante,* by Martin Heidegger. Ed. and trans. Mirri. Perugia, 1971.

"Rilassamento, I." Trans. e. Landolt. *Teoresi* (Catania), vol. 24, 1969, 3-17.

"Rilassamento, II." Trans. E. Landolt. *Teoresi* (Catania), vol. 27, 1972, 3-35.

Japanese: "Gelassenheit. Bodenständigkeit im Atomzeitalter." In *Ethik und Gegenwart, 7.* Trans. K. Tsujimura. Tôkyô, 1958. *See* 93.

*Hoge.* Trans. K. Tsujimura. Tôkyô, 1958.

Netherlands: *Gelatenheid.* Ed., trans. and commentary by E. van Doosselere. Tielt/Amsterdam/Lannoo, 1979, 138 p.

95      "Antrittsrede." In *Jahreshefte der Heidelberger Akademie der Wissenschaften 1957/58.* Heidelberg, 1959, 20-21.

**Translation**

English: "A Recollection." Trans. H. Seigfried. *Man and World,* vol. 3, 1970, 3-4.

96      "Der Weg zur Sprache." In *Die Sprache. Jahrbuch. Gestalt und Gedanke.* 5th ed. Bayrische Akademie der Schönen Künste. München, 1959, 137-170. [Public lecture, 1959; revised version *See* 99.] Rpt. in "Sprache und Wirklichkeit." In *Essays.* Ed. C. G. Podewils. München, 1967, 44-69. [Revised and enlarged text.]

97      "Hegel et les Grecs." Trans. J. Beaufret and P.-P. Sagave. *Cahiers du Sud* (Paris), vol. 45, no. 349, 1959, 355-368. [Public lecture, 1958. 1st German publication: *Hegel und die Griechen.* 1960. *See* 104.] Rpt. in *Wegmarken.* Frankfurt: Klostermann, 1967, 255-272. *See* 130, 172.

98      "Aufzeichnungen aus der Werkstatt." *Neue Züricher Zeitung* (Zürich), vol. 180, 27 September 1959; (Zürich), Fernausgabe 264, 26 September 1959.

99      *Unterwegs zur Sprache.* Pfullingen: Neske, 1959, 270 p.

Contains:

"Die Sprache." Public lecture. 1960, 9-33.

"Sprache im Gedicht. Eine Erörterung von Georg Trakls Gedicht." [1st publication entitled "Georg Trakl. Eine Erörterung seines Gedichts." 1953], 35-82. *See* 70.

"Aus einem Gespräch von der Sprache. Zwischen einem Japaner und einem Fragenden." (Dating from 1953/54, 83-155). *See* 122.

"Das Wesen der Sprache." Public lectures. 1957 and 1958, 157-216.

"Das Wort." Public lecture. 1958, 217-238.

"Der Weg zur Sprache," 239-268. *See* 96. 2nd ed. Pfullingen: Neske, 1960. 4th ed. Pfullingen: Neske, 1971. 5th ed. Pfullingen: Neske, 1975, 269 p.

**Translations**

English: *On the Way to Language.* Ed. and trans. P. D. Hertz and J. Stambaugh. New York, 1971, 200 p.

Trans. of "Die Sprache." 1950: "Language." In *Poetry, Language, Thought.* Trans. and intr. A. Hofstädter. New York: Harper and Row, 1975, 189-210. 1st ed. 1971. "Sprache-Language." Trans. T. J. Sheehan. *Philosophy Today* (Celina, Ohio), vol. 20, 1976, 291 ff.

French: *Acheminement vers la parole.* Trans. J. Beaufret, W. Brockmeier, and F. Fédier. (Classiques de la Philosophie). Paris: Gallimard, 1976, 264

Italian: *In camino verso il linguaggio.* Ed. A. Caracciolo. Trans. A. Caracciolo an M. Perotti Caracciolo. (Biblioteca di filosofia, Testi 5). Milana: U. Murcia, 1973, 217 p.

Japanese: *Shi Kotaba.* Trans. M. Miki. Tôkyô, 1963.

["Der Weg zur Sprache." Lecture to the Bayrische Akademie der Schönen Künste, 19-23 January 1959. Univ. of München, 26-30 January 1959, Reuter-Haus in Berlin.]

["Hölderlins Erde und Himmel." Lecture delivered at the conference of the Hölderlin Society on 6 June 1959 at the Cuvillié - Theater der Residenz in München. Repeated on 14 July 1959 to the Bibliotheksgesellschaft Stuttgart at the Liederhalle, and on 18 January 1960 at the Univ. of Heidelberg. *See* 100.]

["Dank an die Messkircher Heimat." Speech delivered on the occasion of his being appointed an honorary citizen of the city of Messkirch, 27 September 1959. *See* 108.]

## 1960

100      "Hölderlins Erde und Himmel." *Hölderlin Jahrbuch.* [1958-1960] vol. 11. Tübingen, 1960, 17-39. [1959 lecture.]

101      "Sprache und Heimat." *Hebbel-Jahrbuch 1960.* Ed. in commission of the Hebbel Society by L. Koopmann, with the assistance of E. Trunz. (Heide i. Holstein). 1960, 27-50.

     [Lecture delivered on 2 July 1960 in Wesselburen; abridged version in Dauer im Wandel. Festschrift zum 70. Geburtstag von C. J. Burckhardt. München, 1961, 174-193. Rpt. in *Johann Peter Hebel,* by Th. Heuss, C. J. Burckhardt, W. Hausenstein, B. Reifenberg, R. Minder, W. Bergengruen, and M. Heidegger. Tübingen, 1964, 99-124.]

102      "Dank bei der Verleihung des Staatlichen Hebel-Gedenkpreises." In *Hebel-Feier. Reden zum 200. Geburtstag des Dichters.* Karlsruhe, 1960, 27-29.

103      *Ansprache.* [Dedicated to Ludwig Ficker in remembrance of his 80th birthday.] (Nürnberg o.J. [private publication], 1960), 19-20.

104     "Hegel und die Griechen." In *Die Gegenwart der Griechen im neueren Denken.*
Festschrift für Hans-Georg Gadamer zum 60. Geburtstag. (Comemorative
publication on the occasion of H. G. Gadamer's 60th birthday). Tübingen,
1960, 43-57. [1958 lecture. 1st publication in French: "Hegel et les Grecs."
1958.] *See* 97. Rpt. in *Wegmarken.* Frankfurt: Klostermann, 1967, 255-272.
2nd rev. and enlarged ed. Frankfurt: Klostermann, 1978. *See* 130.

*Wegmarken.* (Gesamtausgabe, Abt. 1: Veröffentlichte Schriften 1914-1970,
Bd. IX). [Unaltered text with marginal notes of the author.] Ed. Fr. W. von
Herrmann. Frankfurt: Klostermann, 1976, 427-444. *See* 172.

**Translations**

French: *Questions III:* Qu'est-ce que la philosophie? Hegel et les Grecs. La
thèse de Kant sur l'être. La doctrine de Platon sur la vérité. Ce qu'est et
comment se détermine la physics. Ed. and trans. K. Axelos, J. Beaufret,
D. Janicaud, L. Bran, et. al. Paris, 1968, 280 p.

Japanese: "Hegeru to Girishajin." Trans. A. Takeichi and K. Nagasawa. In
*Benshoho no Konvonmondai.* Kyôto: Kôyôshobô, 1978, 1-24.

Portuguese: *Hegel e os gregos.* Trans. and intr. E. Stein. [Ed. includes the trans.
of "Vom Wesen des Grundes" and "Aus der Retzten Marburger
Vorlesung."] Sao Paulo, 1971, 107-125.

Spanish: "Hegel y los griegos." *Eco.* (Bogota), vol. 1, 1960.

105     *Der Ursprung des Kunstwerks.* [Theodor Hetzer zum Gedächtnis.] Intr. H. G.
Gadamer. Stuttgart, 1960, 126 p. 2nd ed. 1967. First in *Holzwege.*
Frankfurt: Klostermann, 1950, 7-68. *See* 58, 179.

## 1961

106     *Nietzsche, Vol. I.* Pfullingen: Neske, 1961, 662 p. 3rd ed. Pfullingen: Neske,
1976, 661 p.

Contains:

"Der Wille zur Macht als Kunst." 1936/37, 11-254.

"Die ewige Wiederkehr des Gleichen." 1937, 255-472.

"Die Wille zur Macht als Erkenntnis." 1939, 473-658.

**Translations**

English: *Nietzsche, Vol. I, 1 sec.: Will to Power as Art.* Ed., trans, with an
analysis by D. F. Krell. New York: Harper and Row, 1979.

*Nietzsche, Vol. I, 2 sec.: The Eternal Recurrence of the Same.* Ed. with an
analysis by D. F. Krell. New York: Harper and Row, 1981. [Forthcoming]

*Nietzsche, Vol. I, 3 sec.: Will to Power as Metaphysics.* Ed with an analysis
by D. F. Krell. New York: Harper and Row, 1982. [Forthcoming]

French: *Nietzsche, Vol. I.* Ed. and trans. P. Klossowski. Paris, 1971, 514 p.

107     *Nietzsche, Vol. II.* Pfullingen: Neske, 1961, 494 p. 3rd ed. Pfullingen: Neske,
1976, 481 p.

Contains:

"Die ewige Wiederkehr des Gleichen und der Wille zur Macht." 1939, 7-29.

"Der europäische Nihilismus." 1940, 31-256. [Rpt. in Darmstadt: Wissenschaftliche Buchgesellschaft, 1980, 106-123.]

"Nietzsches Metaphysik." 1940, 257-333.

"Die seinsgeschichtliche Bestimmung des Nihilismus." 1944-1946, 335-398.

"Die Metaphysik als Geschichte des Seins." 1941, 399-457.

"Entwürfe zur Geschichte des Seins." 1941, 458-480.

"Die Erinnerung in die Metaphysik." 1941, 481-490.

[Rpt. in parts in *Der europäische Nihilismus.* 1967. *See* 132.]

**Translations**

English: *Nietzsche, Vol. II: Nihilism.* Ed. with an analysis by D. F. Krell. New York: Harper and Row, 1980. [Forthcoming]

*Nietzsche, Vol. II: The End of Philosophy.* Trans. J. Stambaugh. New York, 1973.

French: *Nietzsche, Vol. II.* Ed. and trans. P. Klossowski. Paris, 1971, 407 p.

Italian: "Momenti di storia della metafisica." (Nietzsche II, 129-203). In *Il Pensare Poetante,* by Martin Heidegger. Ed. and trans. E. Mirri. Perugia, 1971.

Japanese: *Niche. Vols. I, II, III.* Trans. M. Sonoda. Tôkyô: Hakusuishi, 1976, 502, 480 p.; 1977, 300 p.

108   "Dank an die Messkircher Heimat." [Speech delivered by Professor Martin Heidegger on the occasion of his being appointed an honorary citizen of the City of Messkirch 24 September 1959.] *Messkirch gestern und heute.* Heimatbuch zum 700-jährigen Stadtjubiläum 1961. Ed. Stadt Messkirch. 1961, 84-86. Rpt. in *See* 147.

109   "Sprache und Heimat." In *Dauer in Wandel. Festschrift zum 70. Geburtstag von Carl Jacob Burckhardt.* Ed. H. Rinn and M. Rychner. München, 1961, 174-193. [An abridged version of the text published in 1960.] *See* 101.

110   "Hölderlin und das Wesen der Dichtung." In *Hölderlin.* Beiträge zu seinem Verständnis in unserem Jahrhundert. Ed. A. Kelletat. Tübingen, 1961, 131-143. [1st publication, 1936. *See* 37.]

111   "Brief an D. Carvallo-20.3.1952." In *Die ontische Struktur,* by D. Carvallo. Pfullinger: Neske, 1961, 20-21.

112   *Der Feldweg. Hebel-der Hausfreund.* Ed. and annotations by H. Buchner. Tokyo, 1961, 98 p. [This text is an exercise designed for the German instruction of Japanese students; the texts were first published in 1949 and 1956.] *See* 56, 89.

[Ansprache zum Heimatabend am 22. Juli 1961. 1962. Speech delivered at the "Heimatabend" on 2 July 1961. *See* 118.]

113   *Die Frage nach dem Ding. Zu Kants Lehre von den transzendentalen Grundsätzen.* Tübingen: Niemeyer, 1962, vii-189. 2nd ed. Tübingen: Niemeyer, 1975.

[1935/36 lecture series.]

**Translations**

English: *What is a Thing?* Ed. and trans. W. B. Barton and V. Deutsche. Analysis by E. T. Gendlin. Chicago: Henry Regnery Co., 1968, 310 p.

French: *Qu'est-ce qu'une chose?* Ed. and trans. J. Reboul and J. Taminiaux. Paris, 1971, 254 p.

Japanese: *Mono e no Toi.* Trans. K. Arifuka. Kyôto: Kôyôshobô, 1978, 342 p.

Spanish: *La pregunta por la cosa.* Buenos Aires, 1964, 231 p.

*La pregunta por la cosa.* (Collection Carbela). Buenos Aires: Alfa, 1975, 212 p.

114 "Kants These über das Sein." *Existenz und Ordnung.* Festschrift für Erich Wolf zum 60. Geburtstag. Ed. T. Würtenberger, W. Maihofer, and A. Hollerbach. Frankfurt, 1962, 217-245. Also separate: *Kants These über das Sein.* Frankfurt: Klostermann, 1963, 36 p. *See* 119. Rpt. in *Wegmarken.* Frankfurt: Klostermann, 1967, 272-307. *See* 130.

*Wegmarken.* (Gesamtausgabe, Abt. 1: Veröffentlichte Schriften 1914-1970, Bd. IX). [Unaltered text with marginal notes by the author.] Ed. Fr. W. von Herrmann. Frankfurt: Klostermann, 1976, 445-480. *See* 172.

**Translations**

English: "Kant's Thesis About Being." Trans. T. Klein and W. Pohl. *The Southwestern Journal of Philosophy* (Norman), vol. 4, no. 3, 1973, 7-33.

French: *Questions II:* Qu'est-ce que la philosophie? Hegel et les Grecs. La Thèse de Kant sur l'être. La doctrine de Platon sur la vérité. Ce qu'est et se détermine la physics. Ed. and trans. K. Axelos, J. Beaufret, D. Janicaud, L. Braun, et al. Paris, 1968, 280 p.

Italian: "La tesi kantiana sull'essere." *Studi Urbinati di Storia, Filosofia e Letteratura* (Urbino), vol. 42, 1968, 4-67.

[Also comprises the German text.]

Japanese: *U ni suite no Kanto ne Teze.* Trans. K. Tsujimura. Kyôto, April/July 1964.

*U ni suite no Kanto ne Teze.* Trans. K. Tsujimura and A. Takeichi. Tôkyô, 1967; 1972.

Portuguese: *A tese de Kant sobre o ser.* Trans. and intr. E. Stein. [Ed. includes a trans. of "Vom Wesen der Wahrheit."] Sao Paulo, 1970, 51-96.

Spanish: "La tesis de Kant sobre el ser." In *Ser, Verdad y Fundamento,* by Martin Heidegger. Caracas, 1968, 87-119.

115 *Die Technik und die Kehre.* (Opuscula aus Wissenschaft und Dichtung 1). Pfullingen: Neske, 1962, 47 p. 2nd ed. Pfullingen: Neske, 1967. 3rd ed. Pfullingen: Neske, 1976.

Contains:

"Die Frage nach de Technik." Public lecture. 1949, 5-36. An enlarged version 1953. First published 1954. *See* 75, 78.

"Die Kehre." Public lecture, 1949, 37-47.

**Translations**

English: "The Turning." In *The Question Concerning Technology and Other Essays,* by Martin Heidegger. Ed., intr. and trans. W. Lovitt. New York: Harper and Row, 1977, 36-49.

Dutch: *De techniek en de omekeer.* Trans, intr. and commentary by H. M. Berghs. (Nederlandse Heidegger-Bibliotheek). Tielt: Lannoo, 1973, 136 p.

*De Techniek en de omekeer.* Trans. J. Aler. 1973.

French: *Questons, IV:* Temps et être; a fin de la philosophie et la tâche de la pensée. Le tournant. La phénoménologie et la pensée de l'être. Les séminaires de Zähringen. Trans. J. Beaufret, F. Fedier, J. Lauxerois, and C. Roels. (Classiques de la philosophie). Paris: Gallimard, 1976, 339 p.

Japanese: *Gijutso-Ron.* Trans. T. Kojima and L. Armbruster. Tôkyô, 1965.

**Other Translations**

*See* 75, 78.

116    "Aus einer Erörterung der Wahrheitsfrage." In *Zehn Jahre Neske Verlag.* Pfullingen: Neske, 1962, 19-23.

117    *Nachlese zu Heidegger.* Ed. G. Schneeberger. Bern, 1962, 288.

Contains:

"Schlageter." 1933, 48 ff. *See* 26.

"Arbeitsdienst und Universität." 1933, 63 ff. *See* 27.

"Deutsche Studenten." 1933, 135 ff. *See* 28.

"Deutsche Männer und Frauen." 1933, 144-146. *See* 29.

"Deutsche Lehrer und Kameraden? Deutsche Volksgenossen und Genossinnen?" 1933, 148-150. *See* 30.

"Das Geleitwort der Universität." 1934, 171. *See* 33.

"Der Ruf zum Arbeitsdienst." 1934, 180 ff. *See* 32.

"Nationalsozialistische der Deutschen Studentenschaft." 1934, 205 ff. *See* 36.

"An den Reichsführer der Deutschen Studentenschaft." 1934, 205 ff. *See* 36.

"Schöpferische Landschaft: Warum blieben wir in der Provinz." 1934, 216-218. *See* 35.

"Wege zur Aussprache." 1937, 258-262. *See* 39.

118    "Ansprache zum Heimatabend am 22. Juni 1961." *700 Jahre Stadt Messkirch.* (Festansprachen zum 700-jährigen Messkircher Stadtjubiläum vom 22. -30. Juli 1961). Messkirch, 1962, 7-16.

[*Zeit und Sein.* Lecture delivered at the Auditorium Maximum at the Univ. of Freiburg, 31 January 1962. *See* 135, 139.]

**1963**

119    *Kants These über das Sein.* Frankfurt: Klostermann, 1963, 36 p.

      [First published in *Existenz und Ordnung.* Festschrift für Erik Wolf. 1962.] *See* 114.

120    "Mein Weg in die Phänomenologie." *Hermann Niemeyer zum 80. Geburtstag am 16. April 1963.* [Private publication honoring th 80th birthday of Hermann Niemeyer, the publisher.] Rpt. in *Zur Sache des Denkens.* Tübingen: Niemeyer, 1969, 81-90.

   **Translation**

     English: "My Way to Phenomenology." In *On Time and Being,* by Martin Heidegger. Trans. and intr. J. Stambaugh. New York: Harper and Row, 1972, 74-82.

121    "Ein Vorwort. Brief an P. William J. Richardson." [Written in April 1962 in Freiburg as a prologue for the text indicated.] Trans. W. J. Richardson. In *Heidegger. Through Phenomenology to Thought.* The Hague, 1963, Viii-XXIII. [German original and English trans.] Rpt. in *Philosophisches Jahrbuch* (Fulda), vol. 72, 1965, 397-402.

   **Translation**

     English: "A Letter From Heidegger, With a Commentary by W. J. Richardson, S.J." In *Heidegger and the Quest for Truth.* Ed. M. S. Frings. Chicago: Quadrangle Books, 1968, 17-27.

122    *Listening to Heidegger and Hisamatsu.* Kyôto: Bokubi Press, 1963, 88 p.

      [Tri-lingual, in English, German, and Japanese. A discussion between Heidegger and Hisamatsu, 18 May 1958 at Freiburg on "Art and Thinking." Minutes taken by A.Guzzoni. The limited ed. of 800 copies also contains a letter of Heidegger to the Japanese artist L. Alcopley and paintings of Alcopley done during the Heidegger-Hisamatsu discussion. The paintings are entitled "Structures."]

**1964**

123    "Aus der letzten Marburger Vorlesung [Leibniz]." In *Zeit und Geschichte. Dankesgabe an Rudolf Bultmann zum 80. Geburtstag im Auftrag der Alten Marburger.* Ed. E. Dinkler and Hartwig Thyen. Tübingen: Niemeyer, 1964, 491-507. Rpt. in *Wegmarken.* Frankfurt: Klostermann, 1967, 373-398. *See* 130.

      *Wegmarken.* (Gesamtausgabe, Abt. 1: Veröffentlichte Schriften 1914-1970, Bd. IX). [Unaltered text with marginal notes by the author.] Ed. Fr. W. von Herrmann. Frankfurt: Klostermann, 1976. *See* 172.

**Translation**

Portuguese: *A determinacao do ser ente segundo Leibniz.* Trans. and intr. E.
Stein. Ed. includes trans. of "Vom Wesen des Grundes" and "Hegel und
die Griechen."] Sao Paulo, 1971, 81-105.

124    *Über Abraham a Santa Clara.* Ed. City of Messkirch. 1964, 16 p. *See* 147, 148.
**Translation**

Dutch: "Martin Heidegger Over Abraham a Santa Clara." Ed. and intr. S.
Ijesseiling. *Streven* (Amsterdam), vol. 20, 1967, 743-753.

125    "Brief an Bernhard Heiliger." *Katalog der Bernhard-Heiliger-Ausstellung.*
Galerie im Erker/St. Gallen/Schweiz, 3 October-7 November 1964, 18.

126    "Brief an René Char zum Andenken an den Grossen Freund George Braque."
(Freiburg, 6 September 1963). In *Hommage a George Braque: "Derrier le
mirior."* Paris: Maeght Editeur, May 1964, 144-146.


### 1965

127    "Brief an T. Kojima." (Freiburg, 18 August 1963). *Begegnung.* Zeitschrift für
Literatur, bildende Kunst Musik und Wissenschaft. Ed. D. Larese. vol. 1,
no. 4, [9 Jg. der Internationalen Bodenseezeitschrift.] (Amriswil o.J., 1965),
4-7.


### 1966

128    "Leserbrief." [Letter to the editor on "Mitternacht einer Weltnacht." *Der
Spiegel* (Hamburg), vol. 20, no. 7, 7 February 1966, 110-113.] *Der Spiegel*
(Hamburg), vol. 20, no. 11, 3 March 1966, 12.

129    "Das Ende der Philosophie und die Aufgabe des Denkens." *Kierkegaard
vivant.* Ed. J. Beaufret and J. Fedier. [In a French trans. entitled "La fin
de la philosophie et la tâche de la pensée." Paris, 1966, 165-204.]
[Lecture by Heidegger delivered at Unesco Coloquium in Paris, April 1966.
First German publication 1969 in *Zur Sache des Denkens. See* 139.]
**Translations**

*See* 139.

[Heraklit, Seminar at the Univ. of Freiburg, together with Eugen Fink. 1st
publication, 1970. *See* 154.]

[Seminaires at Le Thor, 1966, 1968, a, d, 1969. *See* 138.]


### 1967

130    *Wegmarken.* Frankfurt: Klostermann, 1967, VIII-398. Rev. and enlarged ed.
Frankfurt: Klostermann, 1978. *See* 172.
Contains:
"Vorbemerkung." VII-VIII.

"Was ist Metaphysik." 1st publication, 1929, 21-72. *See* 24, 54.

"Vom Wesen des Grundes." 1st publication, 1929, 21-72. *See* 24, 54.

"Vom Wesen der Wahrheit." 1st publication, 1943. 2nd ed. 1949, 73-97. *See* 43, 53.

"Nachwort zu 'Was ist Metaphysik?'" 1st publication, 1943, 98-108. *See* 44.

"Platons Lehre von der Wahreit." 1st publication, 1942, 109-144. *See* 42, 52.

"Brief über den 'Humanismus'." 1st publication, 1947, 145-194. *See* 50, 52.

"Einleitung zu 'Was ist Metphysik?' Der Rückgang in den Grund der Metaphysik." 5th ed. 195-211. *See* 55.

"Zur Seinsfrage." Entitled "Über'die Linie'." 1st published, 1955, 213-253. *See* 80.

"Hegel und die Griechen." 1st publication, 1959 as "Hegel et les Grecs." 1st German publication, 1960, 255-272. *See* 97, 104.

"Kants These über das Sein." 1st publication, 1962, 272, 307. *See*

"Vom Wesen und Begriff der Physis. Aristoteles' Physik B, 1." 1st publication, 1958, 309-371. *See* 90.

"Aus der letzten Marburger Vorlesung." 1st publication, 1964, 373-395. *See* 123. Rpt. in *Wegmarken*. (Gesamtausgabe, Abt. 1: Veröffentliche Schriften 1914-1970, Bd. IX). [Unaltered text with marginal notes of the author.] Ed. Fr. W. von Herrmann. Frankfurt: Klostermann, 1976, X-490. *See* 172.

**Translations**

*See* under first publications.

131    "Brief an Max Kommerell vom 4, 8. 1942 aus Todtnauberg." In *M. Kommerell, Briefe und Aufzeichnungen 1919-1944*. Ed. I. Jens. Freiburg, 1967, 404-405.

    [Pre-published in *Frankfurter Allgemeine Zeitung,* 3-4 April 1967.]

132    *Der europäische Nihilismus.* Pfullingen, 1967, 269 p.

    Contains:

    "Der europäische Nihilismus." 1st published in *Nietzsche, Vol. II.* 1961.

    "Die seinsgeschichtliche Bestimmung des Nihilismus." 1st published in *Nietzsche, Vol. II.* 1961. *See* 107.

133    "Der Weg zur Sprache." *Sprache und Wirklichkeit.* Ed. C. G. Podewills. München, 1967, 44-69.

    [Public lecture dating from 1959. *See* 99. This text is revised and enlarged.]

134    "Hans Jantzen, dem Freunde zum Andenken." In *Erinnerung an Hans Jantzen. Worte der Freunde zum Freund.* Freiburg: Univ. lung, 1967, 19-22.

## 1968

135 "Zeit und Sein." In *L'endurance de la pensée.* Festschrift für J. Beaufret. Paris, 1968, 12-71.

[Public lecture delivered on 31 January 1962 in the course of the Studium Generale, supervised by Eugen Fink, Freiburg, with a French trans. *See* 139.
**Translations**
*See* 139.

136 "Brief an Francois Bondy." (29 January 1968). Published by F. Bondy. Trans. F. Fédier. *Critique* (Paris), vol. 24, 1968, 433-435.

137 "Brief an Manfred S. Frings." (20 October 1966). In *Heidegger and the Quest for Truth.* Ed. and intr. M. S. Frings. Trans. W. J. Richardson. Chicago: Quadrangle Books, 1968, 17-19.

[German original and English trans. with a commentary by W. J. Richardson. 21-27.]

138 *Das Gedicht.* In honor of Friedrich Georg Jünger's 70th birthday, Amriswil, 25 August 1968.

[Publicly published in 1971 in "Erläuterungen zu Hölderlin's Dichtung." *See* 158.]

## 1969

139 *Zur Sache des Denkens.* Tübingen: Niemeyer, 1969, 92 p. 2nd ed. Tübingen: Niemeyer, 1976.

Contains:

"Zeit und Sein." 1-25. 1st published in *L'endurance de la pensée.* Paris, 1968, 12-71. *See* 135.

"Seminar Protokoll zu Heidegger's Vorlesung 'Zeit und Sein'," 27-58. Written by A. Guzzoni and rev. and complimented by Martin Heidegger.

"Index of the Aspects Discussed in the Seminar on 'Ziet und Sein'," 59-60.

"Das Ende der Philosophie und die Aufgabe des Denkens," 61-80. 1st publication in French in *Kierkegaard vivant.* Paris, 1966, 165-204. *See* 129.

"Mein Weg in die Phänomenologie," 81-90. 1st private publication in "Hermann Niemeyer zum 80, Geburtstag am 16." April 1963. *See* 120.
**Translations**
English: *On Time and Being.* Trans. and intr. J. Stambaugh. New York: Harper and Row, 1972, 84 p. Paperback, 1977.

Japanese: *Shisaku no Kotogara e.* Trans. K. Tsujimura, et al. Tôkyô, 1970.

*Shisaku no Kotogara e.* Trans. K. Tsujimura and H. Buchner. Tôkyô: Chikumashobo, 1973, 224 p.
**Translations of "Zeit und Sein"**
French: "Temps et être." In *L'endurance de la pensée.* Festschrift für J. Beaufret. Paris, 1968, 16-71.

*Questions I:* Temps et être. La fin de la philosophie et la tâche de la pensée. Le tournant. La phenomenologie et la pensée de lêtre. Les seminaires du Thor. Le séminaire de Zähringen. Trans. J. Beaufret, F. Fedier, J. Lauxerois and C. Roëls. (Classiques de la philosophie). Paris: Gallimard, 1976, 339 p.

**Translations of "Das Ende der Philosophie"**

English: In *Basic Writings,* by Martin Heidegger. Ed. D. F. Krell. New York: Harper and Row, 1977; London: Routledge and Kegan-Paul, 1977.

French: "La fin de la philosophie et la tâche de la pensée." Trans. J. Beaufret and F. Fédier. *Kierkegaard vivant.* Paris: Gallimard, 1966, 167-204.

*Questions IV:* Temps et être. La fin de la philosophie et la tâche de la pensée. Le tournant. La phénoménologie et la pensée de l'être. Les séminaires du Thor. Le Séminaires de Zähringen. Trans. J. Beaufret, F. Fédier, J. Lauxerois and C. Roëls. (Classiques de la philosophie). Paris: Gallimard, 1976, 339 p.

Italian: "La fine della filosofia e il compiti del pensare." In *Il Pensare Poetante,* by Martin Heidegger. Ed. and trans. E. Mirri. Perugia, 1971.

Polish: "Koniec filozofii i zadanie myálenia." Trans. K. Michalski. *Teksty,* vol. 4, no. 5, 1977.

Portuguese: *O fim da filosofia ou A questäo do pensomento.* Trans. and intr. E. Stein. Sao Paulo, 1972, 111 p.

Spanish: "El fin de la filosofia y la tarea del penamiento." Trans. A. P. Sanchez Pascual. *Kierkegaard vivant.* Madrid, 1968, 142 ff.

140 "Theologie et Philosophie." *Archives de Philosophie* (Paris), vol. 32, 1969, 355-415.

Contains:

"Phänomenologie und Theologie," 356-395. See 152. [With a French trans. by the editors and M. Méry entitled "Phénomenologie et Théologie." Text is based on a public lecture delivered in Tübingen on 9 July 1927 at the Evangelische Theologenschaft.]

[Some remarks on "Das Problem eines nichtobjektivierenden Denkens und Sprechens in der heutigen Theologie," 396-415. With a French trans. by the editors and M. Méry entitled "Quelques indications sur des points de vue principaux du colloque théologique consacré au 'Problème d'une pensée et d'un language non-ob-jectivants dans la Théologie d'aujourd'hui'." Freiburg, 1 March 1964.]

**Translations**

*See* 152.

141 "Lettre a Roger Munier." (31 July 1969). *Le nouveau commerce* (Paris), vol. 14, 1969, 57-59. [Preamble to *Qu'est-ce que la métaphysique?,* by Martin Heidegger. Trans. R. Munier.] Rpt. in *Martin Heidegger, Vier Seminare.* Trans. from the original French version [*Questions IV.* Paris: Gallimard,

1976.] by Kurt Ochwadt, 144-146. (Quotations of a letter to R. Munier, dated 16 April 1973. *Ibid,* 146-147). *See* 177.

142 "Fragen nach dem Aufenthalt des Menschen." Dankrede an der Geburtstagsfeier in Amrisinl am 28 September 1969. *Neue Zürcher Zeitung.* No. 606 [Fernausgabe 273], 5 October 1969, 451. Rpt. in *Duitse Kroniek,* vol. 21, 1969.

143 "Zeichen." *Neu Zürcher Zeitung,* 579 [Fernausgabe 260], 21 September 1969, 51.

144 *Die Kunst und der Raum.* St. Gallen, 1969. Text carved in stone by Martin Heidegger. 7 Litho-Colloages by E. Chillida.

[Exhibition on the genesis of the works: 12 October-15 November 1969. Vernissage by E. Kästner in the presence of M. Heidegger and E. Chillida on 12 October 1969. Limited ed., 150 copies. The book is supplemented by a printed copy of the German text as well as by a French trans. by J. Beaufret and F. Fédier. Also enclosed is a record, recorded by the author himself. The text entitled "Die Kunst und der Raum" is based on a lecture delivered by Heidegger on 3 October 1964 in the art gallery "Im Erker" in St. Gallen, on the occasion of an exhibition ("plastic") by B. Heiliger. The lecture then had the title "Raum. Mensch und Sprache."]

Simultaneous publication *Die Kunst und der Raum.* In *L'art et l'espace.* St. Gallen: Erker-Verlag, 26p.

**Translations**

English: "Art and Space." Trans. C. H. Seibert. *Man and World* (The Hague), vol. 6, 1973, 3-8.

French: "L'art et l'espace." Trans. J. Beaufret and F. Fédier. In *Die Kunst und der Raum,* by Martin Heidegger. St. Gallen: Erker Verlag, 1969.

[Supplement to the limited ed.]

Japanese: "Geijutsu to Kukan." Trans. A. Takeichi. In *Geijutsutetsugaku no Konponmondai.* Kyôto: Koyoshobo, 1978, 282-294.

Romanian: *Arta si spatiu.* Trans. I. Alexandru. 1970.

145 "Dankansprache von Professor Martin Heidegger." In *Ansprachen zum 80. Geburtstag 1969 in Messkirch.* Private publication by Heuberg Druckerei. Messkirch: F. G. Acker, 1969, 33-36.

[For reports on the celebration of Heidegger's 80th birthday in Messkirch, refer to "Schwäbische Zeitung. Messkircher Anzeiger." (9 September 1969). On the occasion in Ariswil, "Südkurier." (29 September 1969).]

146 "Vom Geheimnis des Glockenturms." 1956. In *Martin Heidegger zum 80. Geburstag von Seiner Heimatstadt Messkirch.* Frankfurt: Klostermann, 1969, 7-10. *See* 148.

147 *Über Abraham a Santa Clara.* Messkirch: F. G. Acker, 1969.

[Private publication by the City of Messkirch of a speech delivered in 1964.] *See* 124, 148.

148 *Martin Heidegger. Zum 80. Geburtstag von seiner Heimatstadt Messkirch.* Frankfurt: Klostermann, 1969, 64 p.

Contains:

"Vom Geheimnis des Glockenturms." 1956, 7-10. *See* 146.

"Der Feldweg," 11-15. 1st publication. Frankfurt: Klostermann, 1949. *See* 57.

"Gelassenheit," 16-30. [Speech on the occasion of the 175th recurrence of the birthday of Conradin Kreutzer, the composer, held on 30 October 1955, in Messkirch. Rpt. in parts in "Gelassenheit." Pfullingen, 1959.] *See* 94.

"Ein Wort des Dankes," 31-35. [Speech on the occasion of his being appointed an honorary citizen of the City of Messkirch. *See* 108. Private publication, 1959.]

"Über Abraham a Santa Clara," 46-57. [1964 speech, private publication by the City of Messkirch. *See* 124. Printed by Heuberg-Druckerei. Messkirch: F. G. Acker, 1969. *See* 147. This ed. also contains 5 photographs of Heidegger and other illustrations.]

149 "Auszüge aus Briefen Heideggers an Karl Löwith 1921-29." In *Zu Heideggers Seinsfrage: Die Natur des Menschen und die Welt der Natur. Zu Heideggers 80. Geburtstag,* by K. Löwith. (Heidelberg, 1969). [Minutes of the Akademie der Wissenschaften, Heidelberg, 1969. Excerpts from Heideggers letter to Karl Löwith, 1921-29.] Rpt. in *Aufsätze und Vorträge 1930-1970,* by K. Löwith. Stuttgart, 1971, 189-203.

150 Seminaire tenu au Thor en septembre 1969 par le Professeur Martin Heidegger.

[Minutes of the seminar. Chairman of the seminar was René Char; participants included: Martin Heidegger, J. Beaufret, R. Munier, et al. The seminar took place 2-11 September 1969. 1st German publication, 1977. *See* 175, 177.

**1970**

151 "Letter to the Editor." *Der Spiegel* (Hamburg), vol. 24, 19 January 1970, 14.

[In the editorial of the news magazine *Der Spiegel* (3 November 1969, no. 23, 5) as well as in Heidegger's letter to the editor, the authenticity of a certain interview with M. Heidegger in the French Magazine *L'Express* is disputed. The editorial quotes from a letter in which Heidegger expressively affirms that any such interview has never taken place. This is repeatedly confirmed in Heidegger's letter to the editor. The interview in question was published as "L'entretien que Martin Heidegger a bien voulu accorder à notre collaborateur." The interviewers were Frédéric de Tarwanicki and J.-M. Palmie. It was published in *L'Express* on 20 October 1969. *L'Express* (Paris), vol. 954, 1969, 78-85.]

152 *Phänomenologie und Theologie.* Frankfurt: Klostermann, 1970, 47 p.

Contains:

"Phänomenologie und Theologie," 13-33. [Lecture delivered in Tübingen, 9 March 1927, and repeated in Marburg, 14 February 1928.] 1st published in *Archives de Philosophie* (Paris), vol. XXXII, 1969, 396-415, (With a French trans.). *See* 140.

"Einige Hinweise auf Hauptgesichtspunkte für das theologische Gespräch über 'Das Problem eines nichtobjektivierenden Denkens und Spechens in der heutigen Theologie'," 37-46. [1st publication in *Archives de Philosophie* (Paris), vol. XXXII, 1969, 396-415.] *See* 140.

**Translations**

English: "Phenomenology and Theology." In *The Piety of Thinking,* by Martin Heidegger. Trans. K. Hoeller, J. G. Hart, and J. C. Maraldo. Indiana Univ. Press, 1976.

Croatian: *Filozofija i teologija.* Trans. B. Despot. Yougoslavia, 1972.

French: "Theologie et philosopie." In *M. Heidegger: Debat sur la Kantisme et la Philosophie,* by E. Cassirer. Ed. P. Aubenque. Paris, 1972, 101-131.

Italian: *Fenomenologia e teologia.* Ed. and trans. N. M. de Feo. (Dimensioni, 31). Firenze: La Nuova Italia, 1974, XXV-51.

Polish: "Fenomenologie i teologia." Trans. J. Tischner. *Znak,* vol. 1, no. 2, 1979.

153    "Martin Heidegger im Gespräch." In *Martin Heidegger im Gespräch.* Ed. R. Wisser. München, 1970, 67-77.

[Minutes of the disputation between M. Heidegger and R. Wisser, published as a written documentation on the television broadcasted on the occasion of Heidegger's 80th birthday 26 September 1969. The programme was aired on 24 September 1969.]

**Translations**

French: "L'être a besoin des hommes." (Interview with M. Heidegger by R. Wisser). *Magazine Litéraire* (Paris), vol. 117, 1976, 22-23.

Japanese: "Haidegga wa Kataru." Trans. E. Kawahara. *Risosha* (Tôkyô), 1973, 94 p.

Spanish: "Martin Heidegger dialoga; entrevista Heidegger-R. Wisser." Trans. R. A. Herra. *Revista de Filosofia de la Univ. de Costa Rica* (Costa Rica), vol. 7, 1969, 129-139.

154    *Heraklit. Martin Heidegger-Eugen Fink. Seminar 1966/67.* Frankfurt: Klostermann, 1970, 264 p.

[Text based on the minutes of a seminar on Heraklit, held at the Univ. of Freiburg, Fall Term 1966/67. Not identical to 183.]

**Translation**

English: *Heraclitus Seminar, 1966-1967,* by Martin Heidegger and Eugen Fink. Trans. Charles H. Seibert. Univ. Alabama: Univ. of Alabama Press, 1979. 169 p.

French: *M. Heidegger-E. Fing. Heraclite.* Trans. J. Launay and P. Levy. Paris: Gallimard, 1973, 222 p.

155     "Letter to A. H. Schrynemaker." [For the Heidegger Conference, Duquesne Univ., 15-16 October 1966.] In *Heidegger and the Path of Thinking.* Ed. J. Sallis. Pittsburgh: Duquesne Univ. Press, 1970, 10-11.

[Bi-lingual]

156     "Letter to A. Borgmann." [For the conference on "Heidegger and the Eastern Thought." Univ. of Honolulu, 17-21 November 1969.] Trans. A. Borgmann. *Philosophy East and West* (Honolulu), vol. 20, 1970, 221.

[Bi-lingual]

157     "Antworten an Zygmunt Adamczewski" ("On the Way to Being Reflections on Conversations With M. Heidegger.") In *Heidegger and the Path of Thinking.* Ed. J. Sallis. Pittsburgh: Duquesne Univ. Press, 1970, 12-36.

[Report on a 3 day conversation with Martin Heidegger in Todtnauberg and Freiberg, October 1968.]

## 1971

158     *Erläuterungen zu Hölderlins Dichtung.* 4th englarged ed. Frankfurt: Klostermann, 1971, 192 p.

Contains:

"Vorwort. Heimkunft/ An die Verwandten," 9-31. 1st publication, 1944. *See 46.*

"Hölderlin und das Wesen der Dichtung." 1st ed. München: Langen und Müller, 1937. Rpt. in 1944 with the above mentioned speech as "Erläuterungen zu Hölderlins Dichtung." Frankfurt: Klostermann, 33-48. *See 46.*

"Wie wenn am Feiertage..." 1st ed. München: Langen und Müller, 1937. Rpt. with the above mentioned speech as "Erläuterungen zu Hölderlins Dichtung." Frankfurt: Klostermann, 1944, 49-77. *See 46.*

"Andenken." 1st ed. *Hölderlin-Gedenkschrift.* 1943, 79-151. *See 45.*

"Hölderlins Erde und Himmel." [Lecture delivered at the conference of the Hölderlin-Society, 6 June 1959, in Munich. 1st publication in *Hölderlin-Jahrbuch,* vol. 11, 1958/59, 152-181. *See 100.*

"Das Gedicht." [Rev. text based on a lecture delivered on the occasion of the 70th birthday of Fr. G. Jünger. Armiswil, 25 August 1968, 182-192.] *See 138.*

159     *Schellings Abhandlung über das Wesen der menschlichen Freiheit (1809).* Ed. H. Feick. Tübingen, 1971, 236 p.

[Text based on a lecture delivered at the Univ. of Freiburg, Spring Term 1939. The appendix comprises selections from the minutes of an advanced seminar on Schelling, added by H. Feick and M. Heidegger.]

**Translations**

English: *Schelling on Human Freedom.* Trans. J. Stambaugh. New York, 1978.

French: *Schelling: le traité de la liberté humaine.* Ed. H. Feick. Trans. J.-P. Courtine. (Classiques de la philosophie). Paris: Gallimard, 1977, 349 p.

[Letter to H. G. Gadamer, 2 December 1971. *See* 165.]

### 1972

160    *Frühe Schriften.* Ed. Fr. W. von Herrmann. Frankfurt: Klostermann, 1972, 386 p. Enlarged ed., *See* 181.

Contains:

"Vorwort von M. Heidegger." IX-XI.

"Die Lehre von Urteil im Psychologismus. Ein Kritisch-positiver Beitrag zur Logik." Phil. Diss. Freiburg 1914 1-129. *See* 6.

"Die Kategorien-und Bedeutungslehre des Duns Scotus," 130-353. *See* 11.

"Selbstanzeige der Habilitation," 354. *See* 14.

"Der Zeitbegriff in der Geschichtswissenschaft," 355-375. *See* 12.

161    "Hölderlins Hymnen 'Germania' und 'der Rhein'." [Quotations from a still unpublished lecture, Fall Term 1934/35.] In *Philosophie und Politik bei Heidegger,* by O. Pöggeler. Freiburg/München, 1972, 20-21, 28-29; annotations: 108-109. 1st complete publication, 1979. *See* 185.

162    "Pensivement-Gedachtes. Für René Char in freundschaftlichem Gedenken." *L'Herne* [Hommage à René Char] (Paris), vol. 15, 1972, 170-187.

Contains:

"Zeit," "Wege," "Winke," "Ortschaft," "Cézanne," "Vorspiel," "Dank." [All with a French trans. by J. Beaufret and F. Fédier.]

**Translations**

English: "Thoughts for René Char in Friendly Remembrance." Trans. K. Hoeller. *Philosophy Today* (Celina, Ohio), vol. 20, 1976, 286-290.

French: "Pensivement." *L'Herne* (Paris), vol. 15, 1972, 170-187.

163    "Colloque Cassirer-Heidegger." [Davos, Spring 1929; Rédaction Dr. O. F. Boolnow and Dr. J. Ritter.] *Ernst Cassirer Martin Heidegger. Débat sur le Kantisme et la Philosophie (Davos, March 1929) et autres textes de 1929-1931.* Ed. P. Aubenque. Trans. from the German by P. Aubenque, J.-M. Fataud and P. Quillet. Paris: Beauchesne, 1972, 28-51.

Contains:

Intr. by P. Aubenque. Trans. of Heidegger's lectures on Kant's "Kritik der reinen Vernunft" and "Aufgabe einer Grundlegung der Metaphysik," 21-24. 1st publication in *Davoser Revue* (Davos), vol. 4, no.7, 1929, 194-196.

Martin Heidegger. Rev. of *Philosophie der symbolischen Formen,* by E. Cassirer. 85-100. *See* 20.

*Theologie und Philosophy,* by Martin Heidegger. 101-131. *See* 140. [The publication of the German text by K. F. Gründer is announced.]

[Letter to H. G. Gadamer, 29 February 1972. *See* 165.]

[Letter to H. Mongis, written on 7 June 1972, in Freiburg. 1st publication, 1976. *See* 174.]

## 1973

164 "Statt einer Rede [Zur Einweihungsfeier für das Gymnasium in Messkirch am 14. Juli 1973.]" *Festschrift zur Einweihung des neuen Gymnasiums in Messkirch am 14. Juli 1973.* Published by the City of Messkirch, 1973, 3 p.

[Speech delivered on the occasion of the inauguraton of the new Messkirch High School, 14 July 1973.]

165 "Dalla Lettera di M. Heidegger del 2. Dicembre 1971 a H. G. Gadamer" and "Dala Lettera di M. Heidegger del 29. Februaraio 1972." In *H. G. Gadamer La Dialettica di Hegel.* Trans. and annotated by R. Dottori. Torino: Marietti, 1973, 148-151.

## 1973

166 *Frau Doktor Hildegard Feick. Der langjährigen Getreuen Mitarbeiterin zum Gedächtnis/Martin Heidegger.* Frankfurt: Klostermann, 1974, 10 p.

[The same text in Heidegger's handwriting inserted.]

## 1975

167 "Andenken an Max Scheler." Ed. P. Good. In *Max Scheler im Gegenwartsgeschehen der Philosophie.* Bern/München: A. Francke AG Verlag, 1975, 9-10.

[Originally delivered on 21 May 1928 as the opening of a seminar in the Spring Term 1928, eulogizing Scheler's death, 19 May 1928.]

168 *Die Grundprobleme der Phänomenologie.* (Gesamtausgabe, Abt. 2 Vorlesungen 1923-1944). Ed. Fr. W. von Herrmann. Frankfurt: Klostermann, 1975, X-473.

**Translation**

English: *Fundamental Problem of Phenomenology.* Trans. A. Hofstädter. Bloomington: Indiana Univ. Press, 1981. [Forthcoming]

169 *Sein und Zeit.* (Gesamtausgabe, Abt. 1: Veröffentlichte Schriften 1914-1970, Bd. II). Ed. Fr. W. von Herrmann. Frankfurt: Klostermann, 1976. *See* 16.

[Text revised by Fr. W. von Herrmann.]

170 "Nur noch ein Gott kann uns retten." [Interview with M. Heidegger by R. Augstein and G. Wolff.] *Der Spiegel* (Hamburg), vol. 30, no. 23, 31 May 1976, 1, 193-219. [This interview was recorded 23 September 1966.]

**Translations**

English: "Only a God Can Save Us." [*Der Spiegel: Interview with Martin Heidegger.* Trans. M. P. Alter and J. D. Caputo. *Philosophy Today* (Celina, Ohio), vol. 20, 1976, 267-284.

"Only a God Can Save Us Now." [An interview with Martin Heidegger.] Trans. D. Schendler. *Graduate Faculty Philosophy Journal* (New York), vol. 6, 1977, 5-27.

Dutch: "Der Spiegel in gesprek met Martin Heidegger. Alleen nog een God kan ons redden." Trans. P. Beers. [Interview with Martin Heidegger by R. Augstein and G. Wolff. (23 September 1966).] *Wijsgerig Perspectief op Maatschappij en Wetenschap* (Amsterdam), vol. 17, 1976/77, 309-337.

French: *Réponses et questions sur l'histoire et la politique. Martin Heidegger interroge par "Der Spiegel."* Trans. J. Launy. Paris: Mercure de France, 1977, 81 p.

Japanese: "Haideggâ no Benmei. Haideggâ/Shupî geru Taidan." [Heidegger's Apology/Heidegger-Spiegel Dialogue.] Trans. E. Kawahara. *Risô* (Tôkyô), vol. 520, 1976, 2-38.

Polish: "Tylko Bóg mógby nas uratowaá." Trans. of the interview with Martin Heidegger by *Der Spiegel. Teksty,* vol. 3, 1977.

Spanish: "Sole un Dios puede salvaruos todavia." [Interview with Martin Heidegger by R. Augstein and G. Wolff. (23 September 1966). *Revista de Occidente* (Madrid), vol. 3, no. 14, 1976, 4-15.

171    *Logik. Die Frage nach der Wahrheit.* (Gesamtausgabe, Abt. 2: Vorlesungen 1923-1944. Vol. XXI). Ed. W. Biemel. Frankfurt: Klostermann, 1976, VII-418.

172    *Wegmarken.* (Gesamtausgabe Atb. 1: Veröffentlichte Schriften 1914-1970. Bd. IX). [Unaltered text with marginal notes by the author.] Ed. Fr. W. von Herrmann. Frankfurt: Klostermann, 1978, X-490. *See* 130.

Contains:

"Anmerkungen zu Karl Jaspers 'Psychologie der Weltanschauungen'." 1919-21, 1-44. *See* 15.

"Phänomenologie und Theologie." 1927, 45-78. *See* 152.

"Aus der letzten Marburger Vorlesung." 1928, 79-101. *See* 123, 130.

"Was ist Metaphysik." 1929, 103-122. *See* 21, 44, 55, 130.

"Vom Wesen des Grundes." 1929, 123-175. *See* 24, 54, 130.

"Vom Wesen der Wahrheit." 1930, 177-202. *See* 43, 53, 130.

"Platons Lehre von der Wahrheit." 1931/32; 1942, 203-238. *See* 42, 52, 130.

"Vom Wesen und Begriff der Physis. Aristoteles, Physik B 1." 1939, 239-301. *See* 90, 130.

"Nachwort zu 'Was ist Metaphysik?'" 1949, 303-312. *See* 44, 130.

"Brief über den Humanismus." 1946, 313-364. *See* 50, 52, 130.

"Einleitung zu 'Was ist Metaphysik?'" 1949, 365-383. *See* 55, 130.

"Zur Seinsfrage." 1955, 385-426. *See* 80, 130.

"Hegel und die Griechen." 1958, 427-444. *See* 97, 104, 130.

"Kants These über das Sein." 1961, 445-480. *See* 114, 130.

**Translations**

*See* earlier separate editions.

173      "Preface." In *Wiplinger, Fridolin: Metaphysik. Grundfragen ihres Ursprungs und ihrer Vollendung.* Ed. P. Kampits. Freiburg: Alber, 1976, 312 p.

174      "Letter to Henri Mongis." (Freiburg, 7 June 1972). In *Heidegger et la critique de la notion de valeur,* by Henri Mongis. La destruction de la fondation métaphysique. The Hague, 1976, XVI-XX.

[Heidegger's letter is a kind of pre-published review of Mongis' book on the concept of value.]

**Translation**

French: *Letter-preface to Mongis. Henri, Heidegger et la critique de la notion de valeur. La destruction de la fondation métaphysique.* (Phänomenologica, 74). The Hague: Nijhoff, 1976, VI-XI.

175      *Questions IV:* Temps et être. La fin de la philosophie et la tâche de la pensée. Le tournant. La phenomenologie et la pensée de l'être. Les séminaires du Thor. Le séminaire de Zähringen. Trans. J. Beaufret, F. Fédier, J. Lauxerois and C. Roëls. (Classiques de la philosophie). Paris: Gallimard, 1976, 339 p.

[Hand-out papers of the courses given at the Thor and Zähringen had been copied privately in 1966, 1968, 1969, and 1973. *See* 150, 177.]

### 1977

176      *Phänomenologische Interpretation von Kants Kritik der Reinen Vernunft.* Marburger Vorlesung, Wintersemester 1927/28. (Gesamtausgabe, Bd. XXV). Ed. I. Goerland. Frankfurt: Klostermann, 1977, XII-436.

177      *Vier Seminare.* Le Thor, 1966, 1968, 1969; Zähringen, 1973. Trans. C. Ochwadt. Frankfurt: Klostermann, 1977, 151 p.

[Trans. by C. Ochwadt from the original French minutes of the Seminaires held at Le Thor, 1966, 1968, and at Zähringen 1973, enlarged by an epilogue by C. Ochwadt, 139-151. The epilogue contains the original German version of the "Lettre à R. Munier." *See* 141. Published in French in 1969. For private publications of the 3 seminaires at Le Thor, *See* 150, 175.]

178      "Neuzeitliche Naturwissenschaft und Technik." *Research in Phenomenology.* Vol. VII. (Heidegger Memorial Issue). New York: Humanities Press, 1977, 1-4.

[A letter to the participants of the tenth Heidegger Colloqium, 14-16 May 1976 in Chicago, dated 11 April 1976; appears in German and English trans.]

179     *Holzwege.* (Gesamtausgabe, Abt. 1: Veröffentlichte Schriften 1914-1970, Bd.
        V). [Text of the 1960 ed. with marginal notes by the author.] Ed. Fr. W.
        von Herrmann. Frankfurt: Klostermann, 1977, 382 p.
        Contains:
        "Der Ursprung des Kunstwerks." 1935/36, 1-14. *See* 58, 105.
        "Die Zeit des Weltbildes." 1938, 75-114. *See* 57, 58.
        "Hegels Begriff der Erfahrung." 1942/43, 115-208. *See* 58, 59.
        "Nietzsches Wort 'Gott ist tot'." 1943, 209-268. *See* 46, 58.
        "Wozu Dichter?" 1946, 269-320. *See* 49, 58.
        "Der Spruch des Anaximander." 1946, 321-374. *See* 51, 58.

179a    *Ein Wort des Dankes.* Annotated by T. Kakihara. Tôkyô, Dogakusha-Verlag,
        1977, 33 p. [Copyright Klostermann Verlag, Frankfurt.]

180     "Zollikon Seminar. Randbemerkungen." In *Zollikoner Seminare. Erinnerung
        on M. Heidegger,* by M. Boss. Pfullingen: Neske, 1977, 31-45.
        **Translation**
        English: "M. Heidegger's Zollikon Seminars." Trans. B. Kenny. *Review of
        Existential Psychology and Psychiatry,* vol. 16, 1978/79, 7-21.

## 1978

181     *Frühe Schriften.* (Gesamtausgabe, Abt. 1: Veröffentlichte Schriften 1914-1970.
        Bd I). Ed. Fr. W. von Herrmann. Frankfurt: Klostermann, 1978, xii-454.
        [In part, identical with 160.]
        Contains:
        "Das Realitäts problem in der modernen Philosophie." 1912, 1-15. *See* 1.
        "Neuere Forschungen über Logik." 1912, 17-43. *See* 2.
        "Besprechungen." 1913/14, 45-54. *See* 10.
        "Die Lehre vom Urteil im Psychologismus." 1914, 59-188. *See* 6, 160.
        "Die Kategorien-und Bedeutungslehre des Duns Scotus." 1916, 189-411.
        *See* 11, 160.
        "Selbstanzeige." 1917, 412. *See* 14, 160.
        "Der Zeitbegriff in der Geschichtswissenschaft." 1916, 413-433. *See* 12,
        160.

182     *Metaphysische Anfangsgründe der Logik im Ausgang von Leibniz.*
        (Gesamtausgabe. Abt. 2: Vorlesungen 1923-1944, Bd. XXVI). Ed. K. Held.
        Frankfurt: Klostermann, 1978, VI-291.

## 1979

183     *Heraklit.* 1. Der Anfang des abendländischen Denkens: 2. Logik. Heraklits
        Lehre vom Logos. (Gesamtaugabe. Abt. 2: Vorlesungen von 1923-1944, Bd.
        IX). Ed. M. S. Frings. Frankfurt: Klostermann, 1979, 408 p.

184    *Prolegomena zur Geschichte des Zeitbegriffs.* (Gesamtausgabe. Abt. 2: Vorlesungen. Bd. XX). Ed. P. Jäger. Frankfurt: Klostermann, 1979, 448 p.

185    *Hölderlins Hymnen 'Germanien' und 'Der Rhein'.* (Gesamtausgabe. Abt. 2: Vorlesungen. Bd. XXXIX). Ed. S. Ziegler. Frankfurt: Klostermann, 1979, XI-296. *See* 161.

### 1980

186    "Seminaire de Zurich." (6 November 1951). Trans. de l'allemand et pres. par F. Fédier. *Po & Sie* vol. 13. Paris: Libraire Classique E. Belin, 1980, 52-62.

    [French trans. of the still unpublished original German version.]

187    "Letter to Martin Grabmann." ["Heidegger schreibt an Grabmann."] Ed. and commentary by Hermann Köstler. *Philosophisches Jahrbuch,* vol. 87, 1980, 96-109. [A letter to Martin Grabmann, dated 5 January 1917.]

188    *Hegels Phänomenologie des Geistes,* by Martin Heidegger. (Gesamtausgabe. Abt. 2: Vorlesungen 1923-1944. Bd XXXII). Ed. Ingtraud Görland. Frankfurt: Klostermann, 1980, vii-221 p.

# PART III
# LIST OF TRANSLATIONS

## Translations Into English

"The Age of the World View." *See* 58.

"The Anaximander Fragment." *See* 51, 58.

*Art and Space. See* 144.

"Avowal to Adolf Hitler and the National State." *See* 30.

*Basic Writing* [Translations of: The End of Philosophy and the Task of Thinking; What is a Thing?; Building, Dwelling, Thinking; The Origin of the Work of Art; On the Essence of Truth; Letter on Humanism; What is Called Thinking; What is Metaphysics?; Being and Time (Introduction)]. *See* 139, 113, 67, 58, 43, 52, 68, 21, 16.

*Basic Problems of Phenomenology. See* 168.

*Being and Time. See* 16.

"Book Review of Ernst Cassirer's Mythical Thought." *See* 20.

"Building, Dwelling, Thinking." *See* 67.

"The Call to Labour Service." *See* 32.

"The Concept of Time in the Science of History." *See* 12.

*Discourse on Thinking. See* 94, 139.

*Early Greek Thinking* (Translations of: The Anaximander Fragment; Logos). *See* 51, 58, 65.

*The End of Philosophy and the Task of Thinking. See* 139.

*The Essence of Reasons. See* 24.

*Existence and Being. See* 37, 45.

"Follow the Führer." *See* 34.

"German Students." *See* 28.

"Hegel's Concept of Experience." *See* 58.

*Heidegger Memorial Issue* (Neuzeitliche Naturwissenschaft - bi-ling). *See* 178.

"Hölderlin and the Essence of Poetry." *See* 37.

"The Idea of Phenomenology." *See* 18.

*Identity and Difference. See* 88.

*Introduction to Metaphysics. See* 69.

"Introduction to the 5. Edition of 'What is Metaphysics?'." *See* 55.

*Kant and the Problem of Metaphysics. See* 22.

"Kant's Thesis About Being." *See* 114, 119.

"Labour Service and the University." *See* 27.

"Language." *See* 99.

*Letter on Humanism. See* 52.

"Letter to A. Borgmann." *See* 149, 156.

"Letter to Manfred Frings." *See* 137.

"Letter to P. Richardson." *See* 155.

"Letter to A. H. Schrynemaker." *See* 155.

*Listening to Heidegger and Hisamatsu. See* 122.

"Logos." *See* 65.

*Nietzsche (Vols. I, II). See* 106, 107.

"Only a God Can Save Us." *See* 170.

"On the Being and Conception of Physics in Aristotle's Physics, B 1." *See* 172.

*On the Essence of Truth. See* 43.

*On the Way to Being. See* 157.

*On the Way to Language. See* 99.

*On Time and Being. See* 139.

"The Origin of the Work of Art." *See* 58.

"The Pathway." *See* 56.

"Phenomenology and Theology." *See* 152.

*Philosophy - What is it? See* 81.

*The Piety of Thinking* [Translations of: On the Being and Conception of Physics in Aristotle's Physics, B 1; Principles of Thinking; Book Review; Phenomenology and Theology]. *See* 172, 91, 20, 152.

"Plato's Doctrine of Truth." *See* 52.

"Poetically Man Dwells..." *See* 73.

*Poetry, Language, Thought* (Translations of: Language; Building, Dwelling, Thinking; The Think; Poetically Man Dwells). *See* 99, 67, 66, 73.

"The Principle of Ground." *See* 86.

*Principles of Thinking. See* 91.

"The Question Concerning Technology." *See* 75, 78.

*The Question of Being. See* 82.

"A Recollection." *See* 95.

"Remembrance of the Poet." *See* 45.

*Schelling on Human Freedom. See* 159.

"Summary of a Seminar on the Lecture 'Time and Being'." *See* 139.

"The Thinker as Poet." *See* 72.

"Thoughts." *See* 162.
"My Way to Phenomenology." *See* 120.
"What are Poets for?" *See* 58.
*What is a Thing? See* 66, 113.
*What is Called Thinking? See* 68, 79.
*What is Metaphysics? See* 21.
*What is Philosophy? See* 81.
"Who is Nietzsche's Zarathustra?" *See* 78.
"Why do I Stay in the Provinces?" *See* 35.

## Translation Into Arabic

*Aletheia. See* 74, 78.
*Über den Humanismus. See* 52.
*Vom Wesen der Wahrheit. See* 43.

## Translations Into Chinese

*Brief über den Humanismus. See* 52.
*He deling yu shi zhi benzhi. See* 37.
*He wei zhexue. See* 81.
*Holzwege. See* 58.
*Neuere Forschungen über Logik. See* 2.
*Sein und Zeit. See* 16.
*Was ist Metaphysik? See* 21.
*Zhexue shi shenmo. See* 81.

## Translations Into Croatian

*Grief über den Humanismus. See* 52.
*Ekspozicija vprasanja o smislu biti, uvod k "Bit in cas." See* 16.
*Filozofija i Teologija. See* 140.
*Vom Ursprung des Kunstwerks. See* 58.
*Vom Wesen der Wahrheit. See* 43.

*Was ist das-die Philosophie?* *See* 81.
*Was ist Metaphysik?* *See* 21.

## Translations Into Czechoslovakian

*Co je clovek? Myslenky Martina Heideggera.* *See* 52.
*Co je metafyzika?* *See* 21.
*Doba, kdy svet je obrazem.* *See* 58.
*Hölderlin a podstata basnictvi.* *See* 37.
*Myslenky Martina Heideggera.* *See* 69.
*O bytostnem urceni pravdy.* *See* 43.
*O pravae a Byti.* *See* 43.
*Polni cesta.* *See* 56.
*Vybor z dila Sein und Zeit.* *See* 16.
*Zrozeni umeleckeho dila.* *See* 58.

## Translations Into Dutch

*Alleen nog een God kan ons redden.* *See* 169.
*Brief over het humanisme.* *See* 52.
*De techniek en de omekeer.* *See* 115.
*Der Spiegel in Gesprek met Martin Heidegger.* *See* 169.
*Gelatenheid.* *See* 94.
*Martin Heidegger over Abraham a Santa Clara.* *See* 124.
*Wat is dat - Filsofie?* *See* 81.
*Wat is metafysica?* *See* 21.

## Translations Into French

*Acheminement vers la Parole.* *See* 99.
"Allemands et Allemandes " *See* 29.
*Approche de Hölderlin.* *See* 62.
"Ce qu'est et comment se détermine la physic." *See* 91.
"Ce qui fait l'être-essentiel d'un fondement ou 'raison'." *See* 24.

"Le chemin de Campagne." *See* 56.

*Chemins qui ne mènent nulle part. See* 58.

*Colloque Cassirer-Heidegger. See* 164.

"Comme un jour de fête." *See* 62.

"Contribution à la Question de l'être." *See* 82.

*De l'essence de la vérité. See* 43.

"La Doctrine de Platon sur la Vérité." *See* 52.

*Essais et conférences. See* 78.

*L'etre et le temps. See* 16.

"Etudiants allemands " *See* 28.

"La Fin de la philosophie et le Tâche da la pensée." *See* 129, 139.

"Georg Trakl." *See* 70.

"Hebel." *See* 89.

"Hegel et les Grecs." *See* 97, 130, 104.

"Heidegger et Cassirer interprètes de Kant." *See* 25.

"Heidegger et la Critique de la Notion de Valeur." *See* 174.

*Héraclite (Heidegger/Fink). See* 154.

"Hölderlin et l'essence de la poésie." *See* 37, 62.

*Identité et Différence. See* 88.

"In memoriam A. L. Schlageter." *See* 26.

*Introduction à la Métaphysique. See* 69.

*Kant et le Problème de la Métaphysique. See* 22.

"L'Appel du service du Travail." *See* 32.

"L'Art et l'Espace." *See* 144.

"L'Autoaffirmation de l'université Allemande." *See* 31.

"L'Être a besoin des Hommes." *See* 153.

*L'Être et le Temps. See* 16.

"L'Expérience de la Pensée." *See* 72.

"L'Homme habite en Poète." *See* 73.

"Lettre à Jean Beaufret." *See* 49.

"Lettre à François Bondy." *See* 136.

"Lettre à Roger Munier." *See* 141, 177.

"Lettre à Jean Wahl." *See* 38, 47.

*Lettre sur l'Humanisme. See* 52.

"Logos." *See* 65.

*Nietzsche. See* 106, 107.

"Pensivement." *See* 162.

"Le Principe d'Identité." *See* 88.

"Le Principe de Raison." *See* 86.

"Principes de la Pensée." *See* 91.

"Professeurs et Camerades Allemands " *See* 30.

*Qu'appele-t-on penser? See* 79.

"Qu'est-ce que la Métaphysique?" *See* 21, 40.

*Qu'est-ce que la Philosophie? See* 81.

*Qu'est-ce qu'une Chose? See* 113.

*Questions I* [Qu'est-ce que la métaphysique?; Ce qui fait l'être-essentiel d'un fondement ou "raison;" De l'essence de la vérité; Contribution à la question de l'être; Identité et différence.] *See* 21, 24, 40, 43, 82, 88.

*Questions II* [Qu'est-ce que la philosophie? Hegel et les Grecs; La thèse de Kant sur l'être; La doctrine de Platon sur la vérité; Ce qu'est et se détermine la physics.] *See* 81, 104, 114, 52, 91.

*Questions III* [Le chemin de campagne; l'expérience de la pensée; Hebel; Lettre sur l'Humanisme; Sérénité.] *See* 57, 72, 89, 52, 94.

*Questions IV* [Temps et être; La fin de la philosohie et la tâche de la pensée; Le tourant; La phenoménologie et la pensée de l'être; Les séminaires du Thor; Le séminaire de Zähringen.] *See* 139, 129, 115, 175, 177.

"La Remontée au Fondement de la Metaphysique." *See* 55.

"Résponse à M. J. Wahl." *See* 38.

"Résponses et Questions sur l'Histoire et la Politique. Heidegger interrogé par le 'Spiegel'." *See* 170.

"Retour." *See* 62.

"Le Retour au Fondement de la Métaphysique." *See* 55.

*Schelling: le Traité de la Liberté Humaine. See* 159.

*Séminaire de Thor. See* 138, 144, 150, 177.

*Séminaire de Zähringen. See* 177.

"Séminaire de Zurich." *See* 186.

"Sérénité." *See* 94.

"Souvenirs." *See* 62.

"Temps et être." *See* 139.

"Théologie et philosophie." *See* 140, 152.

"La Thèse de Kant sur l'Etre." *See* 114.

"Le tourant." *See* 115.

*Traité des Catégories et de la Signification chez Duns Scot. See* 11.

## Translations Into German

"Abendgang auf der Reichenau." *See* 13.

"An den Reichsführer der deutschen Studentenschaft am 6. Februar 1934." *See* 36.

"Andenken," *Hölderlin. Gedenkschriften zu seinem 100. Todestag. See* 45.

"Andenken an Max Scheler." *See* 167.

"Anmerkungen über die Metaphysik." *See* 77.

"Anmerkungen zu Karl Jaspers 'Philosophie der Weltanschauungen' (1919/21)." *See* 15.

"Ansprache [Dedicated to Ludwig Ficker in remembrance of his 80th birthday.]" *See* 103.

"Ansprache zum Heimatabend am 22. Juni 1961." *See* 118.

"Antrittsrede." *See* 95.

"Antworten an Zygmunt Adamczewski." *See* 157.

"Arbeitsdienst und Universität." *See* 27.

"Arbeitsgemeinschaft Cassirer - Heidegger." *See* 25.

"Aufzeichnungen aus der Werkstatt." *See* 98.

*Aus der Erfahrung des Denkens. See* 72.

"Aus der Letzten Marburger Vorlesung [Leibniz]." *See* 123.

"Aus einer Erörterung der Wahrheitsfrage." *See* 116.

"Auszüge aus Briefen Heideggers an Karl Löwith 1921-29." *See* 149.

"Author's prologue." *See* 40.

"Bauen Wohnen Denken. Mensch und Raum. Darmstädter Colloquy 2." *See* 67.

"Besprechungen, 1913/1914." *See* 10.

"Brief an J. Beaufret." *See* 50, 52.

"Brief an Fr. Bondy." *See* 136.

"Brief an A. Borgmann." *See* 149.

"Brief an D. Carvallo." *See* 111.

"Brief an R. Char." *See* 126.

"Brief an M. Frings." *See* 137.

"Brief an H. G. Gadamer." *See* 165.

"Brief an M. Grabmann." *See* 187.

"Brief an B. Heiliger." *See* 125.

"Brief an E. Husserl." *See* 18.

"Brief an T. Kojima." *See* 127.

"Brief an M. Kommerell." *See* 131.

"Nationalsozialistische Wissensschulung." *See* 34.

"Neuere Forschungen über Logik." *See* 2.

"Neuzeitliche Naturwissenschaft und Technik." *See* 178.

*Nietzsche, Vol. I. See* 106.

*Nietzsche, Vol. II. See* 107.

"Nietzsche's Wort 'Gott ist tot'." *See* 46.

"Nur noch ein Gott kann uns retten." *See* 170.

"Pensivement - Gedachtes. Für René Char in freundschaftlichem Gedenken." *See* 162.

*Phänomenologie und Theologie. See* 152.

*Phänomenologische Interpretation von Kants Kritik der reinen Vernunft. See* 176.

"Platons Lehre von der Wahrheit." *See* 42.

*Platons Lehre von der Wahrheit. Mit einem Brief über den Humanismus. See* 52.

*Prolegomena zur Geschichte des Zeitbegriffs. See* 184.

"Das Realitätsproblem in der Modernen Philosophie." *See* 1.

Rezension: C. Sentroul, *Kant und Aristoteles. See* 8.

Rezension: E. Cassirer, *Philosophie der symbolischen Formen. See* 20.

Rezension: F. Brentano. *Von der Klassifikation psychischer Phänomene. See* 7.

Rezension: "Kants Briefe in Auswahl." *See* 3.

Rezension: *Kant-Laienbrevier. See* 9.

Rezension: Karl Jaspers, *Psychologie der Weltanschauungen (1919). See* 165.

Rezension: N. v. Bubnoff, *Zeitlichkeit und Zeitlosigkeit. See* 4.

"Der Rufzum Arbeitsdienst." *See* 32.

"Der Satz der Identität." *See* 87.

"Der Satz vom Grund." *See* 86.

"Der Spruch des Anaximander." *See* 51.

*Schellings Abhandlung über das Wesen der Menschlichen Freiheit (1809). See* 159.

"Schlageter." *See* 26.

*Sein und Zeit. See* 169.

"Schöpferische Landschaft: Warum bleiben wir in der Provinz." *See* 35.

*Sein und Zeit. See* 16.

*Die Selbstbehauptung der Universität. See* 31.

"Selbstanzeige." *See* 14.

"Selbstverlassenheit und Irrniss." *See* 64.

"Seminaire de Zurich (6. nov. 1951)." *See* 186.

*Seminaire tenu au Thor. See* 150.

"Die Spache Johann Peter Hebels." *See* 80a.

"Sprache und Heimat." *See* 101, 109.

"Statt einer Rede." *See* 164.

*Die Technik und die Kehre. See* 115.

*Über Abraham a Santa Clara. See* 124.

"Über 'die Linie'." *See* 80.

*Unterwegs zur Sprache. See* 99.

*Der Ursprung des Kunstwerks. See* 105.

*Vier Seminare. See* 177.

"Vom Geheimnis des Glockenturms." *See* 146.

*Vom Wesen der Wahrheit. See* 43, 53.

*Vom Wesen des Grundes. See* 24, 54.

"Vom Wesen und Begriff der Physis. Aristoteles Physik B 1." *See* 90.

*Vorträge und Aufsätze. See* 78.

"Vorwort." In: Fr. Wiplinger, *Metaphysik. See* 173.

"Was heisst Denken?" *See* 68, 79.

*Was ist das - die Philosophie? See* 81.

*Was ist Metaphysik? See* 21, 44, 55.

"Der Weg zur Sprache." *See* 96, 133.

"Wege zur Aussprache." *See* 39.

*Wegmarken. See* 130, 172.

"Wissenschaft und Besinnung." *See* 76.

"Wozu Dichter?" *See* 49.

"Zeichen." *See* 143.

"Die Zeit des Weltbildes." *See* 57.

"Zeit und Sein." *See* 135.

"Der Zeitbegriff in der Geschichtswissenschaft." *See* 12.

"Zur Geschichte des philosophischen Lehrstuhls seit 1866." *See* 17.

*Zur Sache des Denkens. See* 139.

*Zur Seinsfrage. See* 82.

"Zollikon Seminar. Randbemerkungen." *See* 180.

## Translation Into Indian

*Was ist Metaphysik. See* 21.

## Translations Into Italian

"Autopresentazione." *See* 14.

*Che cos' è la Metafisica? See* 21.

*Che significa Pensare? See* 79.

"Il Concetto di Tempo nella Scienza della Storia." *See* 12.

"Dall'Esperienzia del Pensare." *See* 72.

*Dell'Essenza della Verità. See* 43.

"Dell'Essere e del Concetto della Physis." *See* 90.

"La Dottrina del Giudizio nello Psicologismo." *See* 6.

*La Dottrina delle Categorie e del Significatio in Duns Scoto. See* 11.

*La Dottrina di Platone sulla Verità. See* 52.

*Essere e Tempo. See* 16.

*Essere e Tempo. L'Essenza del Fondamento. See* 16, 24.

*Fenomenologia e Teologia. See* 152.

"La Fine della Filosofia e il Compito del Pensare." *See* 139.

*Hölderlin e l'Essenza della Poesia. See* 37.

"Identatà e Differenzia." *See* 88.

*In Cammino verso il Linguggio. See* 99.

*Introduzione alla Metafisica. See* 22.

*Kant e il Problema della Metafisica. See* 22.

"Momenti di Storia della Metafisica." *See* 107.

"Passagiata Serale a Reichenau." *See* 13.

*Il Pensare Poetante. See* 52, 72, 79, 81, 94, 107, 139.

"Il Problema della Realità nella Filosofia Moderna." *See* 1.

"Recenti Ricerchi sulla Logica." *See* 2.

"Recensioni 1913-1914." *See* 3, 4, 7, 8.

"Rilassamento." *See* 94.

*Saggi e Discorsi. See* 78.

*Scritti Filosofici. See* 1, 2, 3, 4, 7, 8, 12, 13, 14.

*Sentieri Interrotti. See* 58.

"Il Sentiero." *See* 56.

"Il Sentiero di Campagna." *See* 56.

*Su l'"Umanismo". Che cos' è la Metafisica? See* 52.

"La Tesi kantiana sull'Essere." *See* 114.

## Translations Into Japanese

*Anakushimandorosu no Kotoba. See* 51, 58.

"Arêtheia." *See* 78.

*Doichisei to Saisei. See* 88.

*Doitsudaigaku no Jikoshucho. See* 31.

*Geijutsusakuhin no Hajimari. See* 58.

"Geijutsu Kukan." *See* 144.

*Gijutso-Ron. See* 115.

*Haideggâ to Hisamatsu. See* 122.

"Haideggâ no Benmei. Haideggâ - Shupîgeru Taidan." *See* 170.

"Haideggâ - Shupîgeru Taidan." *See* 170.

*Haideggâ wa kataru. See* 153.

*Hêgeru no "Keiken" Gainen. See* 58.

"Hêgeru to Girishajin." *See* 104.

*Herudârin to Shi no Honshitsu. See* 37.

*Herudârin no Shi Kaimei. See* 62.

*Heruderurin no Hika "Kikyô" ni tsuite. See* 47.

*Hôge. See* 93, 94.

*Hyûmanizumu ni tsuite. See* 52.

"Kaishakugakuteki Junkan no Mondai." *See* 16.

"Kagaku to Chinshi." *See* 78.

*Kanto to Keijijôgaku. See* 22.

*Kanto to Keijijôgaku no Mondai. See* 22.

"Keijijôgaku no Chôkoku." *See* 78.

*Keijijôgaku-Nyûmon. See* 69.

*Keijijôgaku towa Nan zoya. See* 21.

*Konkyo no Honshitsu. See* 24.

*Konkyoritsu. See* 86.

"Moira." *See* 78.

*Mono e no Toi. See* 113.

"Naze Warera wa Inaka ni todomaruka." *See* 35.

*Nîche (Vols. I - II). See* 107.

*Nîche no Kotoba "Kami wa Shiseri." See* 58.

"Nîchie no Tsuaratosutora wa dare ka." *See* 78.

*No no Michi. Heberu - Je no tomo. See* 56, 89.

"Rogos." *See* 65.

*Sekaizô ni Jidai. See* 58.

*Shii no Keiken yori. See* 72.

*Shii no Konpon-Meidai. See* 91.

*Shi Kotoba. See* 99.

*Shinri no Honshitsu nitsuite. Puraton no Shinri-Ron. See* 43, 52.

*Shisaku no Kotogara e. See* 139.

*Shiyui no Keikenyori. See* 72.

*Sonzai to Jikan. See* 16.

*Tetsugaku to wa Nanika. See* 81.

*Toboshiki Jidai no Shijin. See* 58.

*U ni suite no Kanto ne Teze. See* 114.

*U no Toi e. See* 82.

*U to Toki. See* 16.

## Translations Into Korean

*Chilliran mûosinga* [Hölderlin und das Wesen der Dichtung; Vom Wesen der Wahrheit; Erläuterungen zu Hölderlins Dichtung; Platons Lehre von der Wahrheit; Was ist das-die Philosophie.] *See* 37, 43, 46, 52, 81.

*Chonjaewa sigan. See* 16.

*Humaenisumnon. See* 52.

*Humaenisûtûeui p'yônji. See* 37, 41, 52, 21.

*Sinûn Chugossda.* [Was ist Metaphysik?; Holzwege.] *See* 21, 58.

*Siwa ch'orhak.* [Erläuterungen zu Hölderlins Dichtung; Holzwege.] *See* 47, 58.

## Translations Into Norwegian

*Aus der Erfahrung des Denkens. See* 72.
*Dei Filosofiske Vilkar for Sanning. See* 43.
*Der Zuspruch des Feldweges. See* 56.

## Translations Into Polish

"Budowaá, mieszkaá, myálá." *See* 67.
"Co to jest Metafizyka?" *See* 21.
"Czas áwiatoobrazu." *See* 58.
"Fenomenologia i Telogia." *See* 152.
"Kant und das Problem der Metaphysik." *See* 22.
"Koniec filozofii i zadanie myálenia." *See* 139.
"Sein und Zeit - Pars. 4, 9, 44, 45-52." *See* 16.
"Tylko Bóg móglby nas uratowaá." *See* 170.
"Wprowadzenie do 'Co to jest metafizyka'?" *See* 21.

## Translations Into Portuguese

*Carta sôbre o Humanismo. See* 52.
"Da Esencia da Verdade." *See* 43, 114.
*Da Experiência do Pensar. See* 72.
*A Determinacao do Ser entre segundo Leibniz. See* 123.
*Hegel e os Gregos. See* 104, 123.
*Identidade e Diferenca. See* 88.
*Intorducao à Metafisica. See* 69.
*O Caminho do Campo. See* 56.
*O Fim da Filisofia ou A Questao do Pensomento. See* 139.
*Que e isto - a Filosofia? See* 81, 88.
*Que e Metafisica? See* 21.
*Sobre a Essência da Verdade. See* 43.
*Sobre a Essência da Fundamento. See* 24.
*Sobre o Problema do Ser. See* 82.

*A Tese de Kant sobre o Ser. See* 114.

## Translations Into Romanian

*Arta si spatiu. See* 144.
*Drum de câmp. See* 56.

## Translations Into Spanish

*Carta sobre el Humanismo. See* 52.
"Construir, Habitar, Pensar." *See* 67.
"La Cosa." *See* 66.
"Debate de Davos." *See* 25.
"De la Essencia de la Verdad." *See* 43.
"De la Experiencia del Pensar." *See* 72.
"Dicusso rectoral de 1933." *See* 31.
"La Doctrina de Platón acerca de la Verdad." *See* 52.
*Doctrina de la Verdad según Platón y Carta sobre el Humanismo. See* 52.
"Encuentros con Ortega y Gasset. Ortega y Heidegger en Alemania." *See* 85.
"En Poema Habita el Hombre." *See* 73.
"Esencia del Fundamento." *See* 24.
"El Fin de la Filosofia y la Farea del Penamiento." *See* 139.
*Georg Trakl, una Localización de su Poesia. See* 70.
"Hegel y los Griegos." *See* 104.
*Heidegger: Ser, Verdad y Fundamento. See* 24.
"Hölderlin y la Esencia de la Poesia." *See* 32.
*Introducción a la Metafísica. See* 22.
*Kant y el Problema de la Metafísica. See* 22.
"Martin Heidegger dialoga; entrevista Heidegger-R. Wisser." *See* 153.
"El Origen de la Obra de Arte." *See* 58.
"Poéticamente Habita el Hombre." *See* 73.
"Por qué el Poeta?" *See* 38.
"Por qué permanecemos en la Provincia?" *See* 35.
*La Pregunta por la Cosa. See* 113.

# PART IV
# WORKS ON HEIDEGGER

1000     Aalders, W. I. "De Circel van Heidegger." *Nieu theologische Studien* (Groningen), vol. 14, 1931, 237-245.

1001     Abbagnano, N. "Outline of a Philosophy of Existence." *Philosophy and Phenomenological Research* (Buffalo, New York), vol. 9, 1948/49, 200-211.

1002     Abbagnano, N. *Philosophie des menschlichen Konflikts.* Hamburg, 1957.

1003     Abbagnano, N. *Introducción al Existencialismo.* (Fondo de Cult. Econ.), Mexico, 1958.

1004     Abbagnano, N. Forward to P. Chiodi, *L'esistentialismo di Heidegger. Con una appendice sulla Einführung in die Metaphysik.* 3rd ed. Torino, 1965.

1005     Abbagnano, N. *Critical Existentialism.* Trans. and intr. N. Langiulli. New York, 1969, ix-247 p.

1006     Abe, Kazunari. "Haideggâ no 'Sein und Zeit' ni mirareru 'Dasein' ni tsuite" (The Meaning of 'There-Being' in 'Sein und Zeit'). *Tetsugaku Nenshi, 1, Taishô Daigaku Tetsugakukai,* (Tokyo), 1963, 50-56.

1007     Abe, Masao. "Zen and Western Thought." *International Philosophical Quarterly,* vol. 10, December 1970, 501-541.

1008     Abeille, Jean. "Remarques sur la cohérence de l'oeuvre de Martin Heidegger." *Foi et Vie* (Paris), vol. 72, no. 5-6, 1973, 17-28.

1009     Abellán, J. L. "Nuestra sociedad en el 'existencialismo'." *Diagnóstico* (Indice), no. 140, 1960, 4-5.

1010     Acevedo, Jorge. "La técnica en Heidegger." *Revista de Filosofía* (Santiago), vol. 15, 1977, 93-107.

1011     Acham, Karl. "Zum Problem des Historismus bei Wilhelm Dilthey und Martin Heidegger." Phil. Diss. Graz 1964.

1012     Achard Abell, M. "Heidegger et la poésie de Saint-John Perse. Un rapprochement." *Revue de Métaphysique et de Morale* (Paris), vol. 71, 1966, 292-306.

1013     Aáin, J. "Being, Thinking, Speaking." (In Serbocroat). *Delo* (Beograd), vol. 23, no. 10, 1977, 17-30.

1014     Adachi, Kazuhiro. "'Imi' no Genshogaku: Fussaru to Haideggâ o megutte" (The Phenomenology of the Significance: On Husserl and Heidegger). *Jôkyô* (Tôkyô), 1975, 141-169.

1015     Adachi, Kazuhiro. "Haidegga no Koe" (The "Voice" of Heidegger). *Episutêmê* (Tôkyô), vol. 8 and 9, 1976, 309-315.

1016     Adachi, Kazuhiro. "'Imi' no Genshôgaku" (The Phenomenology of the Meaning: Husserl, Heidegger, Merleau-Ponty). Junbun-Gakuhô, *Tôkyô Toritsu Daigaku* (Tôkyô), vol. 110, 1976, 3-69.

1016a    Adamczwesski, Zygmunt. "Questions in Heidegger's Thought About Being." *The Question of Being.* Ed. M. Sprung. Univ. Park, 1978, 55-66.

1017    Acker, L. van. Rev. of *Introduction à la métaphysique,* by Martin Heidegger. *Revista Brasileira de Filosofia,* vol. 9, 1959, 261.

1018    Adamczewski, Zygmunt. "Martin Heidegger and Man's Way to Be." *Man and World* (Pittsburgh), vol. 1, 1968, 363-379.

1019    Adamczewski, Zygmunt. "On the Way to Being." In *Heidegger and the Path of Thinking.* Ed. J. Sallis . Pittsburgh, 1970, 12-36.

1020    Adamczewski, Z. "Commentary on Calvin O. Schrag's 'Heidegger on Repetition and Historical Understanding'." *Philosophy East and West* (Honolulu), vol. 20, 1970, 297-301.

1021    Adler-Vonessen, H. "Angst in der Sicht von S. Kierkegaard, S. Freud und M. Heidegger." *Psyche* (Heidelberg), vol. 25, 1971, 692-715.

1022    Adkins, A. W. H. "Heidegger and Language." *Philosophy* (London), vol. 37, 1962, 229-237.

1023    Adorno, Theodor W. "Jargon der Eigentlichkeit." *Neue Rundschau,* vol. 74, 1964, 371-385.

1024    Adorno, Theodor W. *Jargon der Eigentlichkeit. Zur deutschen Ideologie.* Frankfurt, 1964, 139 p.

1025    Adorno, Theodor W. *Negative Dialektik.* Frankfurt, 1966, 406 p., (specifically pages 102-134).

1026    Adorno, Theodor W. "Metacritique of Epistemology." *Telos,* vol. 38, Winter 1978/79, 77-103.

1027    Adriani, M. "Review: *Heidegger, Holzwege.*" *Giornale di metafisica* (Torino), vol. 7, 1952, 362-363.

1028    Aghemo, Alberto. "Essere e origine nella parola poetica: Heidegger lettore di Hölderlin." *Il Cannocchiale* (Roma), no. 1-3, 1976, 13-31.

1029    Aguilar, F. "'Esse' tomista y 'Sein' heideggeriano." *Cuadernos de Filosofia* (Rosario), 1950, 35-63.

1030    Ahlers, Rolf. "Is Technology Repressive?" *Tijdschrift voor Filosofia* (Leuven), vol. 32, 1970, 651-700.

1031    Ahlers, R. "Technologie und Wissenschaft bei Heidegger und Marcuse." *Zeitschrift für Philosophische Forschung* (Meisenheim/Glan), vol. 25, 1971, 575-589.

1032    Ahlers, Rolf. "Technologie und Wissenschaft bei Heidegger und Marcuse." *Zeitschrift für Philosophische Forschung* (Meisenheim/Glan), vol. 25, 1971, 575-590.

1033    Aichinger, I. Versuch. *Martin Heidegger zum 70. Geburtstag. Festschrift.* Pfullingen, 1959, 291-298.

1034    Akanuma, Ichirô. "Haideggâ no Kagakuron o megutte - Bungaku to Wareware no Tachiba" (On Heidegger's "Science": Fiction and Our Point of View). *Nagoya Daigaku Kyôyôbu kiyô* (Nagoya), vol. 11, 1967, 40-51.

1035 Akanuma, Ichirô. "Shohyô 'Bissâ(hen), Haideggâ wa Katura" (Book Review: *Thus Spoke Heidegger*). Ed. R. Wisser. *Jitsuzonshugi* (Tôkyô), vol. 64, 1973, 62-63.

1036 Akanuma, Ichirô. "Kagaku no Haigo ni Arumono: Haideggâ ni okeru "Besinnung" ni tsuite" (Behind the Science: On Heidegger's "Besinnung"). *Denkitsûshin Daigaku Gakuhô* (Tokyo), vol. 25, no. 1, 1974, 161-172.

1037 Akisawa, Shûji. "Sonzai to Busshitsu: Haideggâ oyobi Hêgeru ni okeru 'Sonzai to Mu' ni kanren shite" (Being and Subject-Matter: 'Being and Nothing' in Heidegger and Hegel). *Yuibutsuron - Kenkyû* (Tokyo), vol. 25, 25, 1934, 1935, 25-28, 53-68.

1038 Albizu, Edgardo. Rev. of *Martin Heidegger im Gespräch.*" Ed. Richard Wisser. *Cuadernos de Filosofia* (Buenos Aires), vol. 11, 1971, 249-252.

1039 Albizu, Edgardo. "Heidegger, pensador de la historia, I." *Cuadernos de Filosofía* (Buenos Aires), vol. 11, no. 15-16, 1971, 137-153.

1039a Albizu, Edgardo L. "Hegel y Heidegger. El camino del pensar contemporáneo." *Revista de la Facultad de Filosofía y Letras de la Universidad de Morón* (Morón), no. 3, 1972, 9-76.

1040 Albrecht, H. *Deutsche Philosophie heute. Probleme. Texte. Denker.* Bremen, 1969, 427 p.

1041 Alcorta, J. S. "Existencia, libertad y opción en el existencialismo." *Revista de estudios politicos,* vol. 41, 1952, 127-132.

1042 Alcorta, J. I. "El humanismo en Heidegger." *Sapientia, Revista Tomista de Filosofia* (La Plata), vol. 15, 1960, 7-17, 107-119.

1043 Alcorta, J. I. "Constitutivo ontologico existencialismo." *Revista de Filosofia* (Madrid), vol. 15, 1956, 5-53.

1044 Alcorta y Echevarria, J. I. De. *El realismo transcendental.* Madrid, 1969, 270 p.

1045 Alcorta, Jose Ignacio. "Sentido de la nueva vision de la filosofia." *Convivium,* vol. 37, 1972, 65-84.

1046 Aldermann, Harold G. "Heidegger and the Overthrow of Philosophy." Phil. Diss. Tulane Univ. 1968. (Of 01057) *Dissertation Abstracts International,* vol. 29, 1968, 105-107, 1561.

1047 Alderman, Harold G. "Heidegger's Critique of Science." *The Personalist* (Los Angeles), vol. 50, 1969, 549-558.

1048 Alderman, Harold G. "Heidegger: The Necessity and Structure of the Question of Being." *Philosophy Today* (Celina, Ohio), vol. 14, 1970, 141-147.

1049 Alderman, Harold G. "Heidegger: Technology as Phenomenon." *The Personalist* (Los Angeles), vol. 51, 1970, 535-545.

1050 Alderman, Harold G. "Heidegger on Being Human." *Philosophy Today* (Celina, Ohio), vol. 15, 1971, 16-29.

1051    Alderman, Harold G. "Heidegger on the Nature of Metaphysics." *The Journal of the British Society for Phenomenology* (Manchester), vol. 3, 1971, 12-22.

1052    Alderman, Harold. "Heidegger on the Nature of Metaphysics." *The Journal of the British Society for Phenomenology* (Manchester), vol. 2, 1971, 12-22.

1053    Alderman, Harold G. "The Work of Art and Other Things." In *Martin Heidegger: In Europe and America.* Eds. Edward Goodwin Ballard and Charles E. Scott. The Hague: Martinus Nijhoff, 1973, 157-169.

1054    Alderman, Harold G. "The Very Idea of a University." *Tulane Studies in Philosophy* (New Orleans), XXII, 1973.

1055    Alderman, Harold G. *Nietzsche's Gift.* Athens, Ohio: Univ. Press, 1977.

1056    Alderman, Harold G. "The Place of Comedy." *Man and World* (The Hague), vol. 10, no. 2, 1977.

1057    Alderman, Harold. *Heidegger and the Overthrow of Philosophy.* Phil. Diss. Tulane Univ. 1968. Ann Arbor, Michigan: University Microfilms, 1977, vi-352 p.

1058    Alderman, Harold G. "The Dreamer and the World." *Soundings,* vol. 60, no. 3, 1977.

1059    Alderman, Harold G. "Heidegger's Critique of Science and Technology." In *Heidegger and Modern Philosophy: Critical Essays.* Ed. Michael Murray. New Haven (Connecticut): Yale Univ. Press, 1971, 35-50.

1060    Aler, J. "De taal bij Martin Heidegger." *Algemeen Nederlands Tijdschrift voor Wijsbegeerte en Psychologie* (Assen, vol. 53, 1960/61, 241-260.

1062    Aler, J. "Van metafysica tot zignsdenken. Inleiding tot Heidegger's gedachtenwereld." *Duitse Kroniek,* vol. 21, no. 3, 1969, 84-99.

1063    Aler, J. "Einleitung und Kommentar zur niederländischen Übersetzung von 'Was ist Metaphysik?'." In *Wat is Metafysica,* by Martin Heidegger. Tielt/Utrecht, 1970.

1064    Aler, J. "Heidegger's Conception of Language in Being and Time." In *On Heidegger and Language.* Ed. J. J. Kockelmans. Evanston, Illinois, 1972, 33-62.

1065    Aleu, J. "El concepto de fe cristiana en Heidegger." *Espiritu* (Barcelona), vol. 6, 1957, 142-149.

1066    Aliotta, A. *Critica dell'esistenzialismo.* Roma, 1951, (specifically pages 43-51).

1067    Allemann, B. Rev. of *Einführung in die Metaphysik,"* by Martin Heidegger. *Die Weltwoche* (Zürich), vol. 14, no. 8, 1953, 5.

1068    Allemann, B. *Hölderlin und Heidegger, Zürich.* Freiburg, 1954. 2nd ed. 1956, 224 p.

        [Contains also: B. Allemann, "Heidegger und die Literaturwissenschaft." French trans.: Paris, 1959, 290 p.]

1069    Allemann, B. "Der Ort war aber die Wüste." In *Martin Heidegger zum 70. Geburtstag. Festschrift.* Pfullingen, 1959, 204-216.

1070 Alleman, B. "Martin Heidegger und die Politik." *Merkur Jg. 21* (Stuttgart), Heft 10, no. 235, 962-976. Rpt. in *Heidegger.* Ed. O. Pöggeler. Köln/Berlin, 1969, 246-260.

1071 Allen, Jeffner. "Husserl's Philosophical Anthropology." *Philosophy Today* (Celina, Ohio), vol. 21, 1977, 347-355.

1072 Allen, Jeffner. "Madness and the Poet." *Review of Existential Psychology and Psychiatry* (Northwestern Univ., Evanston, Illinois), vol. 16, no. 1-2-3, 1978-1979.

1073 Allers, Rudolf. "On Darkness, Silence, and the Nought." *Thomist,* vol. 9, October 1946, 515-572.

1074 Allers, Rudolf. "Les ténèbres, le silence et le néant." *Revue de Métaphysique et de Morale* (Paris), vol. 61, 1956, 131-154.

1075 Allers, Rudolf. "Ontoanalysis: A New Trend in Psychiatry." *Proceedings of the American Catholic Philosophical Association,* vol. 35, 1961, 78-88.

1076 Allers, Rudolf. "Heidegger on the Principle of Sufficient Reason." *Philosophy and Phenomenological Research* (Buffalo, New York), vol. 20, 1959/1960, 365-373.

1076a Allers, Rudolf. "The Meaning of Heidegger." *New Scholas,* vol. 36, 1962, 445-474.

1076b Allers, Rudolf. Rev. of *Being and Time,* by Martin Heidegger. *The New Scholasticism,* vol. 38, 1964, 244-297.

1076c Almazán, Ramón. "En Torno a la polaridad libertad-verdad en et pensamiento de K. Jaspers y de M. Heidegger." *Estudies de Metaphisica,* vol. 2, Valencia 1971-72, 219-227.

1076d Almeida, Roberto de Amorin. *Natur und Geschichte Martin Heidegger und Karl Loewith.* Meisenbeim 1976, 163.

1077 Alphéus, K. "Was ist der Mensch?" (Nach Kant und Heidegger). *Kant-Studien* (Köln), vol. 59, 1968, 187-198.

1078 Alquié, F. "Existentialisme et philosophie chez Heidegger." *La revue internationale* (Paris), vol. 10, 1946, 224-252, 333-342.

1079 Alvarez, Arroyo Jesus. "El humanismo de Heidegger." *Logos* (Mexico City), vol. 2, 1974, 399-447.

1079a Alvarez Arroyo, Jesus. "Un humanismo en Heidegger." *Libro Anual* (Mexico), 6, 1977, 229-274.

1080 Alvrez-Bolado, J. "Exégesis ontológica de la primitiva caracterización del 'Dasein'." (Sein und Zeit). *Convivium* (Barcelona), vol. 1, no. 2, 1956, 73-114.

1081 Alvarez-Bolado, A. "Boletin heideggeriano." *Pensamiento* (Madrid), vol. 20, 1964, 307-318. Rev. of these Heidegger Works:

[*Die Frage nach dem Ding.* Tübingen, 1962.]

[*Nietzsche.* Bd I-II. Pfullingen, 1961.]

[*Kants These über das Sein.* Frankfurt, 1963.]

[*Vom Wesen und Begriff der Pysis.* Mailand-Varese, 1960.]

1082	Alvarez-Bolado, J. "Heidegger y la escatologicidad de la Metafisica." *Convivium* (Barcelona), no. 17-18, 1964, 107-125.

1083	Alvarez Gómez, A. "El sentido del 'cogito' cartesiano, según Heidegger." *Revista de Filosofia* (Madrid), vol. 27, 1968, 91-115.

1084	Amann, B. "Existentialphilosophie und Ganzheitslehre." *Ständisches Leben, Blätter für organische Gesellschafts- und Wirtschaftslehre* (Berlin/Wien), vol. 5, 1935, 433-450.

1085	Amar, A. "La logique et l'ontologie. Dans lesillage d'Heidegger. La difference fondamentale entre la rechereche scientifique et la meditation." *Science* (Paris), vol. 36, 1965, 9-19.

1086	Amar, A. "Lecture selon Heidegger et lecture selon la tradition juive." *Rencontre* (Paris), vol. 13, no. 60, 1979, 80-87.

1087	Améry, J. "Martin Heidegger: Der Magus aus Blut und Boden." *Liberale Beiträge zur Entwicklung einer freiheitlichen Ordnung* (Neuwied), vol. 12, 1970, no. 3, 174-186.

1088	Améry, Jean. "Die Gefahr der Verklärung. Zum Tode von Martin Heidegger." *Die Zeit* (Hamburg), vol. 24, 04.06. 1976, 39.

1089	Amorim Almeida, Robertu de. "Natur und Geschichte: Zur Frage nach der ursprünglichen Dimension abendländischen Denkens vor dem Hintergrund der Auseinandersetzung zwischen Martin Heidegger und Karl Löwith." Phil. Diss. München 1973; Meisenheim 1976. *Monographien zur Philosophischen Forschung,* 130.

1090	Amoroso, Leonardo. "Il discorso come struttura esistenziale e la dimensione pragmatica della comunicazione glosse al Section 34 di *Sein und Zeit* di M. Heidegger." *Annali della Scuola normale superiore di Pisa* (Lettere, Storia e Filosofia) (Pisa), vol. 6, no. 4, 1976, 1263-1275.

1091	Anders, Günter. Rev. of *Was heisst Denken?,"* by Martin Heidegger. Tübingen, 1954. *Rundfunkvortrag* (UKW: "Der Bücherhich"), vol. 24, no. 9, 1954.

1092	Anders, G. "Nihilismus und Existenz." *Die neue Rundschau* (Stockholm), Oktober 1946, 48-76. (Die Stockholmer neue Rundschau. Auswahl). Berlin/Frankfurt, 1949, 96-124. Rpt. in *Nachlese zu Heidegger,* by G. Schneeberger. Bern, 1962, 265-267.

1093	Andersen, W. *Der Existenzbegriff und das existentielle Denken in der neueren Philosophie und Theoloàie.* Gütersloh, 1940, (specifically pages 78-84, passim).

1094	Anderson, James F. "Bergson, Aquinas, and Heidegger on the Notion of Nothingness." *Proceedings of the American Catholic Philosophical Association,* vol. 41, 1967, 143-148.

1095	Anderson, James F. *The Bond of Being. An Essay on Analogy and Existence.* New York, 1969, 341 p. (Nachdruck v. J. 1949)

1096 Anderson, John M. "On Heidegger's *Gelassenheit:* A Study in the Nature of Thought." *The Journal of Existentialism* (New York), vol. 5, 1964-1965, 339-351.

1097 Anderson, John M. "Truth, Process, and Creature in Heidegger's Thought." In *Heidegger and the Quest for Truth.* Ed. M. S. Frings. Chicago, 1968, 28-61.

1098 Anderson, John M. "... Since the Time We are a Dialogue and Able to Hear From One Another." *Man and World* (The Hague), vol. 10, no. 2, 1977, 115-136.

1099 Anderson, Thomas C. "The Rationalism of Absurdity. Sartre and Heidegger." *Philosophy Today* (Celina, Ohio), vol. 21, no. 3, 1977, 263-272.

1100 Anders-Stern, Guenther. "On the Pseudo-Concreteness of Heidegger's Philosophy." *Philosophy and Phenomenological Research,* vol. 8, March 1948, 337-371.

1101 Andô, Takatsura. *Keijijôgaku* (Metaphysics). Tôkyô, 1962, 211-247.

1102 Andô, Takatsura. "Haideggâ no Sonzairon (1)" (Heidegger's Theory of Being). *Ritsumeikan-Bungaku* (Kyoto), vol. 340, 341, 342, 1973, 115-221.

1103 Andô, Takatsura. "Haideggâ no Sonzairon" (Heidegger's Theory of Being). In *Koronsha* (Tôkyô), 1975. 259 p.

1104 Andô, Takatsura. "Haideggâ Tetsugaku no Igi" (The Significance of Heidegger's Philosophy). *Tetsugaku* (Tokyo), vol. 27, 1977, 71-82.

1105 André, H. "Nachdenkliches zu Heideggers neuesten fundamentalontologischen Betrachtungen." *Neue Ordnung* (Köln), vol. 4, 1950, 427-433.

1106 Angelino, C. "Heidegger interprete di Hegel." In *Indicenza di Hegel. Studi raccolit in occasione del secondo centenario della nascita della filosofo.* Ed. F. Tessitere. Napoli, 1970, 987-1014.

1107 Angelloz, J. F. "Martin Heidegger." *Mercure de France* (Paris), vol. 299, 1947, 37-42.

1108 Aniákowicz, M. Rev. of *Budowaá, myáleá. Eseje mieszkaá, wybrane,* by Martin Heidegger. (Bauen, Wohnen, Denken. Ausgewählte Essays). Ed. Krzysztof Michalski. Warszawa, 1977. *Kierunki,* vol. 39, 1977.

1109 Aniz, Canido. "La Significtion Estructural De 'En Termino De Un Dia' En Calderon." *Estudios Filosoficos,* vol. 22, September-December 1973, 415-424.

1110 Anon. "Nonnescius heom. - Physiologus alter." *Bestiarum philosophicum* (Bonn), 1976. (Heidegger: 90-91)

1111 Anquin, N. de. "Heidegger, filosofo del ser." *Estudios teológicos y filosóficos* (Buenos Aires), vol. 2, 1960, 135-145.

1112 Anteile. *Martin Heidegger zum 60 Geburtstag.* Frankfurt, 1950, 284 p.

1113 Antoni, C. *L'exitenzialismo di M. Heidegger. A cura di Michele Biscione.* Neapel, 1972, 278 p.

1114    Antunes, M. "Heidegger renovador da filosofia." *Brotéria* (Lisboa), vol. 103, no. 1, 1976, 3-15.

1115    Anz, Wilhelm. "Die Stellung der Sprache bie Heidegger." In *Das Problem der Sprache. Achter deutscher Kongress für Philosophie.* Ed. H.-G. Gadamer. Heidelberg, 1966; München, 1967, 469-482. Rpt. in *Heidegger.* Ed. O. Pöggeler. Köln/Berlin, 1969, 305-320.

1116    Aoki, Shigeru. "Kotai to Choetsu: Haideggâ ni okeru 'Jijitsusei' no bunseki" (Individual and Transcendence: Analysis of 'Facticity'). In *Heidegger. Tokyo Joshi Daigaku 50 Shunen Kinen Ronbunshu* (Tokyo), 1968, 27-67.

1117    Akoi, Shigeru. "Haideggâ no Kant kaishaku" (Heidegger's Interpretation on Kant). *Jitsuzonshugi* (Tôkyô), no. 69, 1974, 38-48.

1118    Apel, Karl Otto. "Dasein und Erkennen. Eine erkenntnistheoretische Interpretation der Philosophie Martin Heideggers." Phil. Diss. Bonn 1950 VI and 246.

1119    Apel, Karl Otto. "Wittgenstein und Heidegger. Die Frage nach dem Sinn von Sein und der Sinnlosigkeitsverdacht gegen alle Metaphysik." *Philosophisches Jahrbuch* (Freiburg), vol. 75, 1 Halbband, 1967, 56-94. Rpt. in *Heidegger.* Ed. Otto Pöggelo. Berlin, 1969, 258-296.

1120    Apel, Karl Otto. "Wittgenstein y Heidegger: la pregunta por el sentido der ser y la sospecha de falta de sentido contra toda metafisica." *Dianoia* (Mexico), vol. 13, 1967, 111-148.

1121    Apel, Karl Otto. "Heideggers philosophische Radikalisierung der 'Hermeneutik' und die Frage nach dem 'Sinnkriterium' der Sprache." *Die hermeneutische Frage in der Theologie.* Eds. O. Loretz and W. Strolz. Freiburg/Barcelona/Dr-Es-Salaam/New York, Sao Paulo/Tokio, 1968, 86-152.

1122    Apel, Karl Otto. "Wissenschaft als Emanzipation?" *Zeitschrift für allgemeine Wissenschaftstheorie* (Düsseldorf), vol. 1, 1970, 173-195.

1123    Arai, A. T. "Le metafisica de Heidegger." *Letras de México* (Mexico), vol. 3, no. 17, 1939.

1124    Arai, Keijû. "Haideggâ" (Heidegger: Man and Thought). Century Books, Bd. 35. Tôkyô: Shimizushoin, 1970, 193 p.

1125    Arai, Keiyû. "Jitsuzon to Komponchi - Yasupasu to Haideggâ" (Existence and Essential Knowledge - Jaspers and Heidegger). *Tetsugaku Zasshi* (Tôkyô) (Tôkyô Daigaku Tetsugakukai), vol. 754, 1967, 128-156.

1126    Arai, Sato-o. "Sonzai to Sonzai-Ryôkai" (Being and Understanding-Being). In *Tokyôdaigaku-Kyôyôgakubu-Jinmonkagakuka- Kijô.* Tôkyô, 1965.

1127    Aramoto, Toyozô. "Haideggâ ni okeru Jiyû no Monda" (Freedom in Heidegger). *Tetsugaku* (Hiroshima) (Hirochima Diagaku), vol. 12, 1960, 77-89.

1128    Aranguren, J. L. L. "Sobre 'Holzwege' de Martin Heidegger." *Arbor* (Madrid), vol. 16, 1950, 243-253.

1129 Arce Carrascoso, José Luis. "Lenguaje y pensamiento en Heidegger." *Annales del Seminario de Metafísica,* vol. 12, 1977, 11-73.

1130 Arcoleo, S. Rev. of *Heraklit. Seminar Winter semester 1966/1967,* by M. Heidegger and E. Fink. Frankfurt: Klostermann, 1970, 261 p. *Rivista di Filosofia Neo-Scolastica* (Milano), vol. 68, 1976, 535-537.

1131 Arcoleo, S. Rev. of *Séminaire du semestre dàiver 1966-1967,* by M. Heidegger and E. Fink. Trans. Jean Launay and Patrick Levy. (Classiques de la philosophie). Paris: Gallimard, 1973, 222 p. *Rivista di Filosofia Neo-Scholastica* (Milano), vol. 68, 1976, 535-537.

1132 Arendt, Hannah. "La philosophie de l'existence." *Deucalion* (Paris), vol. 1, 1946, 217-252.

1133 Arendt, Hannah. "La philosophie de l'existence." *Deucalion* (Paris), vol. 2, 1947, 215-245, (specifically pages 232-239).

1134 Arendt, Hannah. "Martin Heidegger ist achtzig Johre alt." *Merkur* (Stuttgart), vol. 10, 1969, 893-902.

1135 Arendt, Hannah. "Martin Heidegger, octogenario." *Revista de Occidente* (Madrid), vol. 84, 1970, 255-271.

1136 Arendt, Hannah. "Martin Heidegger a quatre-vingts ans." Trans. Patrick Lévy et Babara Cassin. Revue par l'antor. *Critique* (Paris), vol. 27, 1971, 918-928.

1137 Arendt, Hannah. "Osiemdziesiecioletni Heidegger" (The Eighty Year Old Heidegger). Trans. H. Krzeczkowski. *ZnaK,* vol. 6, 1974.

1138 Arendt, Hannah. "Martin Heidegger at Eighty." Trans. Albert Hofstadter. In *Heidegger and Modern Philosophy. Critical Essays.* Ed. Michael Murray. New Haven, Connecticut: Yale Univ. Press, 1978, 293-303.

1139 Argyros, Alexander. *The Question of Truth in Sartre, Heidegger, and Derrida.* Romance Lit. Diss. Cornell Univ. 1977. *Dissertation Abstracts International,* vol. 38/12-A, 7362.

1140 Arifuku, Kogaku. "Shinshin-Sôkantai to shite no Ningen-Sonzai no Shomondai; Kanto, Haideggâ, Zenbukkyô ni Kansetsu shite" (The Problems of Human Being as the Correlative of Body and Soul; on Kant, Heidegger and Zen-Buddhism). *Nara Kyôiku Daigaku Kiyô* (Nara), vol. 23, no. 1, 1974, 45-78.

1141 Arifuku, Kôgaku. "Kanto to Haideggâ: Kûkan to Jikan no Mondai ni kotoyosete" (Kant and Heidegger: On the Problem of Space and Time). *Riso* (Tôkyô), vol. 498, 1974, 47-62.

1142 Arikuku, Kôgaku. "Mono e no Toi o megute: Haideggâ no Kanto Kaishaku" (On the Kant-Interpretation of M. Heidegger in 'Die Frage nach dem Ding'). *Riso* (Tokyo), vol. 542, 1978, 230-254.

1143 Aron, R. *Marxism and the Existentialists.* New York, 1970, 182 p.

1144 Aronson, Ronald. "Interpreting Husserl and Heidegger: The Root of Sartre's Thought." *Telos* (Buffalo), vol. 5, 1972, 47-67.

1145 Aróstegui, A. "Sobre la ontologia." *Actes du XIe congrés international de philosophie, Bruxelles 20-26 August 1953* (Amsterdam/Louvain), vol. 3, 1953, 14-20.

1146 Arruda Campos, Francisco. "A Reelaboraçño Do Tomismo No Mundo De Hoje: A Pensamento De Joño Baptista Lotz." *Revista Portuguesa de Filosofia,* vol. 33, April-September 1977, 196-234.

1147 Artingstoll, T. M. "Existentialism: Is Existentialism Buddhism?" *Hibbert Journal,* vol. 63, 15-18.

1148 Artola Barrenecha, José María. "Kant en la interpretación de Martin Heidegger." *Annales de Seminario de Metafisica,* vol. 12, 1977, 37-57.

1149 Asai, Masao. "Haideggâ ni okeru 'Shisaku'" ('Poetizing' in Heidegger). *Riso* (Tôkyô), vol. 305, Oktober 1958.

1150 Asô, Ken. "Martin Heidegger: Nietzsches Wort 'Gott ist tot'--sono Kaishaku to Ichizuke" (Martin Heidegger: Nietzsche's dictum: 'Gott ist tot'--Explication and Discussion). *Doitsu Bunka* (Tôkyô) (Chuo Daigaku Doitsu Gakkai), vol. 7, 1968, 31-43.

1151 Assaad-Mikhail, Fawzia. "Heidegger interprète de Nietzsche." *Revue de Métaphysique et de Morale* (Paris), vol. 73, no. 1, 16-55.

1152 Assaad-Mikhail, Fawzia. "Bradley et Heidegger." *Revue de Metaphysique et de Morale* (Paris), vol. 75, no. 2, 1970, 151-188.

1153 Aster, E. von. *Geschichte der Philosophie.* Kröner, I. Bd. 1st ed. Leipzig, 1932. 13th ed. Stuttgart, 1956, 437-441. 14th ed. 1963.

1154 Aster, E. von. *Die Philosophie der Gegenwart.* Leiden, 1935, 135-167.

1155 Asti-Vera, A. "El lenguaje del existencialismo." In *Symposion sobre existencialismo 2.* Rosario, 1955, passim.

1156 Astrada, Carlos. *Idealismo fenomenologico y metafisica existencia.* Buenos Aires, 1936, (specifically page 49).

1157 Astrada, Carlos. *Temporalidad.* Buenos Aires, 1943, (specifically pages 153-157, passim).

1158 Astrada, Carlos. Rev. of *Platons Lehre von der Wahrheit,* by Martin Heidegger. Bern, 1947. *Cuadernos de filosofia,* vol. 1, 1948, 55-64.

1159 Astrada, Carlos et al. *Martin Heideggers Einfluss auf die Wissenschaften. Aus Anlass Seines 60. Geburtstages.* Bern, 1949, 174 p.

1160 Astrada, Carlos. "Uber die Möglichkeit einer existenzialgeschichtlichen Praxis". In *Martin Heideggers Einfluss auf die Wissenschaften.* Bern,, 1949, 165-171.

1161 Astrada, Carlos. "El existencialismo, filosofia de nuestra época." *Actas del primer Congreso nacional de Filosofia* (Mendoza), vol. 1, 1949, 349-358.

1162 Astrada, Carlos. "Relacion del ser con la ec-sistencia." *Actas del primer Congreso nacional de Filosofia* (Mendoza), vol. 2, 1949, 655-659.

1163 Astrada, Carlos. "Ser, Humanismo, 'Existencialismo'." In *Una aproximación a Heideger.* Buenos Aires, 1949.

1164 Astrada, Carlos. "La etapa actual del último Heidegger. Qué significa pensar?" *Cuadernos de Filosofia* (Buenos Aires), no. 7-9, 1952, 104-108.

1165 Astrada, Carlos. "La historia como categoria del ser social" (Heidegger y Marx). In *Ensayos filosóficos* (Bahia Blanca), Univ. Nacional del Sur, Departamento de Humanidades). Bahia Blanca, 1963, 237-245.

1166 Astrada, Carlos. "El humanismo del Hölderlin (un paralelo con Heidegger)." In *Ensayos filosóficos*. (Univ. Nacional del Sur, Departamento de Humanidades). Bahia Blanca, 1963, 293-302.

1167 Astrada, Carlos. "En torno al ultimo Heidegger. Sobre Holzwege." In *Ensayos filosoficos.* (Univ. Nacional del Sur, Departamento de Humanidades). Bahia Blanca, 1963, 253-263.

1168 Astrada, Carlos. "El tiempo en San Augustin con referencia a Plotino y Heidegger." In *Ensayos filosoficos.* (Univ. Nacional del Sur, Departamento de Humanidades). Bahia Blanca, 1963, 177-291.

1169 Astrada, Carlos. "Temporalidad e historicidad en Heidegger." *Dialogos* (Rio Piedras), (Puerto Rico), vol. 5, no. 11/12, 1968, 7-12.

1170 Astrada, Carlos. *Martin Heidegger. De la analitica ontológica a la dimensión dialectica.* Buenos Aires, 1970, 271 p.

1171 Aubenque, Pierre. Rev. of *Chemins qui ne mènent nulle part,* by Martin Heidegger. Paris, 1962. *Revue Philosophique de la France et de l'Étranger* (Paris), vol. 96, 1071, 470-471.

1172 Aubenque, Pierre. Rev. of *Le principe de raison,* by Martin Heidegger. Paris, 1962. *Revue Philosophique de la France et de l'Étranger* (Paris), vol. 96, 471-472.

1173 Aubenque, Pierre. "Presentation à E. Cassirer--M. Heidegger, Débat sur le Kantisme et la Philosophie." March, 1929. *Davos* (Paris), 1972, 7-16.

1174 Aubenques, Pierre. "Martin Heidegger (1889-1976). Im memoriam." *Les Études Philosophiques* (Paris), no. 3, 1976, 259-272.

1175 Aubenque, Pierre. "Travail et 'Gelassenheit' chez Heidegger." *Etudes Germaniques* (Paris), vol. 32, no. 3, 1977, 259-267.

1176 Avelino, A. "Il problema dell'esistenzialismo (Riassunto), Roma 15-20 Novembre 1946, II: L'esistenzialismo." *Atti del congresso internazionale di filosofia, promosso dall'Istituto di Studi Filosofici* (Milano), 1948, 45-49, passim.

1177 Avila Crespo, Remedios. "Heidegger y Hölderlin." *Annales del Semenario de Metafisica,* vol. 12, 1977, 95-101.

1178 Awerkamp, D. "Heidegger and the Problem of God." *Annual Report Duns Scotus Philosophical Association,* vol. 29, 1965, 75-97.

1179 Axelos, Kristos. *Einführung in ein künftiges Denken. Über Marx und Heidegger.* Tübingen, 1966, x and 104 p.

1180 Axelos, Kristos. "On Heidegger." (In Polish). *Studia Filozoficzne* (Warszawa), vol. 17, no. 11-12, 1973, 75-80.

1180a    Baba, Yoshiyuki. "Haideggâ-Ron." *Tokyo Kasei Daigaku Kiyo* (Tokyo), vol. 2, 1961, 121-126. (Treatise on Heidegger).

1181    Baboc, Al. "Heidegger et l[ntologie de làumain." (In Romanian). *Revista de Filozofia,* vol. 25, March-April 1978, 206-222.

1182    Babosov, E. M. "Irracionalizm, christianstvo i XX vek" (Irrationalism, Christianity and the 20th Century). *Nauka i religija* (Moskva), vol. 2, 1967, 66-73.

1183    Bachmann, I. "Die kritische Aufnahme der Existenzialphilosophie Martin Heideggers." Phil. Diss. Wien 1949 130 p.

1184    Baciero, C. Rev. of *Sobre Heidegger,* by G. de Fraga. Coimbra, 1965. *Pensamiento* (Madrid), vol. 24, 1968, 133-134.

1185    Baglietto, C. "La formazione del pensiero di M. Heidegger nei suoi scritti giovanili." *Annali dell Scuola normale superiore di Pisa. Lettere, Storia e Filosofia* (Paris), Ser. 2, vol. 26, 1957, 190-221.

1186    Bailiff, John D. *Coming to Be: An Interpretation of the Self in the Thought of Martin Heidegger.* Phil. Diss. Univ. Park Pennsylvania State Univ. 1966. *Dissertation Abstracts International,* vol. 27, 09-A. 3075.

1187    Bailiff, John Delaware. *Coming to Be. An Interpretation of the Self in the Thought of Martin Heidegger.* Phil. Diss. The Pennsylvania State Univ. 1966. Ann Arbor, Michigan: Univeristy Microfilms Inc., 1977, iv-118 p.

1188    Bakan, Mildred. "The Tradition Via Heidegger." *Philosophy of the Social Sciences. An International Journal* (Aberdeen), vol. 4, no. 2-3, 1974, 293-300.

1189    Bakker, R. "Heidegger en de technick." *Wijsgerig Perspectief op Maatschappij en Wetenschap* (Amsterdam), vol. 3, 1962-1963, 294-306.

1190    Bakker, R. *De Geschiedenis van het fenomenologische Denken.* Utrecht/Antwerpen, 1964, 504 p.

1191    Bakker, R. "De vraag naar het transcendentale, vooral in verband met Heidegger en Kant." *Tijdschrift voor Filosofie* (Leuven), vol. 30, 1968, 366-374.

     [Zu: O. D. Duintjer, De vraag naar het transcendentale. Vooral in verband met Heidegger en Kant. Leiden, 1966.]

1192    Bakker, R. "Heideggers interpretatie van de Logos bij Herakleitos." *Tijdschrift voor Filosofie* (Leuven), vol. 31, 1969, 290-324.

     [Dt. Zusammenfassung: Heideggers Interpretation vom Logos bei Herakleitos, 324-325.]

1193    Bakker, R. "Augustinus en het moderne Denken." *Tijdschrift voor Filosofie* (Leuven), vol. 36, 1974, 442-465.

1194    Bakker, R. "Kanttekeningen bij het 'Spiegel'-interview." *Wijsgerig Perspectief op Maatschappij en Wetenschap* (Amsterdam), vol. 17, 1976-1977, 338-347.

1195    Bakradze, K. S. "Ekzistencializm" (Existentialism). Tiblisi, 1962, 87 p.

1196 Bakradze, K. S. "Interesnaja rabota o Chajdeggere O knige Gajdenko 'Ekzistencializm i problema kul'tury', Kritika filosofii M. Chajdeggera" (An Interesting Publication on Heidegger: Review: Gajdenko's book. *Existentialism and the Problem of Culture. The Criticism of Philosophy by M. Heidegger.* Moscow, 1963. *Voprosy filosofii,* vol. 12, 1964, 162-167.

1197 Balca, N. "Interpretarea existentii omenesti in filosofia lûi M. Heidegger." *Revista de filosofia* (Bucuresti), vol. 24, 1939, 302-325.

1198 Ballard, Edward G. "A Brief Introduction to the Philosophy of Martin Heidegger." (Studies in Recent Philosophy). *Tulane Studies in Philosophy* (New Orleans), vol. 12, Tulane Univ., s'Gravenhage, 1963, 106-151.

1199 Ballard, Edward G. "Heidegger's View and Evaluation of Nature and Natural Science." In *Heidegger and the Path of Thinking.* Ed. J. Sallis. Pittsburgh, 1970, 37-64.

1200 Ballard, Edward G. "On the Pattern of Phenomenological Method." *The Southern Journal of Philosophy* (Memphis), vol. 8, 1970, 421-431.

1201 Ballard, Edward G. and Charles E. Scott, eds. *Martin Heidegger: In Europe and America,* with contributions by Robert Cooper, Otto Pöggeler, Karl Löwith, et al. The Hague: Martinus Nijhoff, 1973, 1974, xii-200 p.

1202 Ballard, Edward G. "On the Pattern of Phenomenological Method." In *Martin Heidegger: In Europe and America.* Eds. Edward G. Ballard and Charles E. Scott. The Hague, 1973, 183-193.

1203 Ballard, Edward G. "The Idea of Being: A Platonic Speculation." *Tulane Studies in Philosophy* (New Orleans), vol. 27, 1978, 13-25.

1204 Ballauf, Th. "Philosoph Martin Heidegger." *Hessenland* (Kassel), vol. 50, 1939, 86.

1205 Ballauf, Th. "Die Wendung der pädagogischen Fragestellung durch die Philosophie Martin Heideggers." In *Philosophische Begründungen der Pädagogik.* Berlin, 1966, (specifically pages 205-246, and passim).

1206 Ballmer, K. *Aber Herr Heidegger Zur Freiburger Rektoratsrede Martin Heideggers.* Basel, 1933.

1207 Balthasar, H. U. "Heideggers Philosophie vom Standpunkt des Katholizismus." *Stimmen der Zeit* (Freiburg), vol. 137, 1939, 1940, 1-8.

1208 Balthasar, H. U. "Die Vergöttlichung des Todes." In *Apokalypse der deutschen Seele,* by H. U von Balthasar, Bd. III. Salzburg, 1939, xix-459, (specifically pages 193-315).

1209 Balthasar, H. U. "La filosofia de Heidegger a la luz dél catolicismo." *Rev. Col. Mayor N.S. del Rosario* (Bogatá), vol. 426, 1950, 81-88.

1210 Balthasar, H. U. *Herrlichkeit.* Bd. 3, Teil 1. Einsiedeln, 1965, 769-787.

1211 Ban, Hiroshi. "Haideggâ no 'Sonzai no Yûgen-sei' ni tsuite" (On 'The Finitude of Being' in Heidegger). *Philosophia* (Tokyo), 1956, 150-169.

1213    Ban, Kazunori. "Shutaisei towa nanika - Haideggâ o Chûshin ni" (What is
        Subjectivity?). *Waseda Daigaku Daigakuin Bungaku Kenkyûka Kiyo*
        (Tôkyô), vol. 7, 1961, 203-206.

1214    Ban, Kazunori. "Haideggâ no Mono-ron" (On Heidegger's 'Thing').
        *Philosophia* (Tôkyô), vol. 53, 1968, 189-208.

1215    Banchetti, S. "Romanticismo e filosofia dell'esistenza." *Cenolio*, 1956,
        549-554.

1216    Banchetti, S. L'ermetismo estetistico nel pensiero di M. Heidegger." *Giornale
        di Metafisica* (Genova/Torino), vol. 14, 1959, 155-188.

1217    Banfi, A. "Il problema dell'esistenza." *Studi filosofici* (Milano), vol. 2, 1941,
        170-192, (specifically page 181, and passim).

1218    Barden, G. Rev. of *Hermeneutics: Interpretation Theory in Schleiermacher,
        Dilthey, Heidegger and Gadamer*," by R. E. Palmer. *Philosophical Studies*
        (Dublin), vol. 20, 1972, 243-246.

1219    Barents, J. Rev. of *Platons Lehre von der Wahrheit*, by Martin Heidegger. (Mit
        einem Brief über den 'Humanismus). *De Gids* (Utrecht), October 1948,
        77-79.

1220    Barion, J. Rev.of *Platons Lehre von der Wahrheit*, by Martin Heidegger. (Mit
        einem Brief uäer den Humanismus). Bern, 1947. *Philosophisches Jahrbuch*
        (Fulda), vol. 60, 1950, 97-98.

1221    Barjau Riu, E. "Sobre la finitud del 'Ser' en el pensamiento de Heidegger."
        *Convivium* (Barcelona), vol. 3, no. 5-6, 1958, 107-114.

1222    Barjau Riu, E. "Bosquejo de algunos conceptos de la filosofia de Heidegger."
        *Episteme* (Caracas), vol. 2, 1958, 277-302.

1223    Barjau, E. "Heidegger: Hölderlin y la esencia de la poesia. In memoriam Jaume
        Bofill i Bofill." *Convivium* (Barcelona), vol. 21, 1966, 53-62.

1224    Barnes, W. *The Philosophy and Literature of Existentialism*. New York:
        Woodbury, 1968, 245 p.

1225    Barrett, William. "What is Existentialism?" *The New York Partisan Review*,
        1947.

1226    Barrett, William. *Irrational Man: A Study in Existential Philosophy*.
        London/Melbourne/Toronto, 1958, 278 p., (specifically pages 184-212).

1227    Bartels, Martin. "Selbstbewusstsein und Unbewusstes. Studien zu Freud und
        Heidegger." *Quellen und Studien zur Philosophie*, vol. 10, Berlin, New
        York: de Gruyter, 1976, x-200 p. [Phil. Diss. Heidelberg, 1971.]

1228    Barth, Heinrich. "Die Philosophie und das Christentum." *Zwischen den
        Zeiten* (München), vol. 7, 1919, 142-156.

1229    Barth, Heinrich. "Kant und die moderne Metaphysik." (Vortrag vor der
        Ortsgruppe Stuttgart der Kantgesellschaft). *Zwischen den Zeiten*
        (München), vol. 6, 1928, 406-428.

1230    Barth, Heinrich. "Zur Philosophie unserer Zeit." *Neue Schweizer Rundschau*
        (Zürich), vol. 22, 1929, 912-917.

1231    Barth, H. Rev. of *Sein und Zeit,* by Martin Heidegger. Halle, 1927. *Annalen der Philosophie* (Leipzig), vol. 8, 1929, 162; *Neue Schweizer Rundschau,* vol. 22, 1929, 912.

1232    Barth, H. Rev. of *Was ist Metaphysik?,* by Martin Heidegger. Bonn, 1929. *Theologische Blätter,* vol. 39, 1929, 139-146.

1233    Barth, H. "Ontologie und Idealismus. Eine Auseinandersetzung mit M. Heidegger." *Zwischen den Zeiten* (München), 1929, 511-540.

2134    Barth, H. "Zu Martin Heideggers Buch über: Kant und das Problem der Metaphysik." Bonn, 1929. *Theologische Blätter* (Leipzig), (Kartellzeitung), vol. 40, N.F. 9, 1930, 139-146.

1235    Barth, H. "Philosophie, Theologie und Existenzproblem." *Zwischen den Zeiten* (München), vol. 10, 1932, 99-124, passim.

1236    Barth, Hans. "Vom Ursprung des Kunstwerks. Vortrag von Martin Heidegger." *Neue Zürcher Zeitung,* vol. 157, no. 105, 20 January 1936, 1.

1237    Barth, Karl. *Kirchliche Dogmatik I, 2, Die Lehre vom Worte Gottes, 1938.* Zollikon/Zürich, 1948, 50.

1238    Barth, Karl. *Kirchliche Dogmatik, III, 3: Die Lehre von der Schöpfung.* Zollikon/Zürich, 1950, 383-402.

1239    Barth, Karl. "Gott und das Nichtige (1950)." In *Heidegger und die Theologie, Beginn und Fortgang der Diskussion.* Ed. G. Noller. München, 1967, 197-225.

1240    Barth, T. "Heidegger - ein Durchbruch zur Transzendenz?" *Wissenschaft und Weisheit* (Düsseldorf), vol. 12, 1949, 27-44.

1241    Barth, T. "Identität und Differenz. Eine Begegnung mit M. Heidegger." *Wissenschaft und Weisheit* (Düsseldorf), vol. 22, 1959, 81-92.

1242    Bartky, Sandra L. "'Seinsverlassenheit' in the Later Philosophy of Heidegger." *Inquiry,* vol. 10, Spring 1967, 74-88.

1243    Bartky, Sandra L. "Originative Thinking in the Later Philosophy of Heidegger." *Philosophy and Phenomenological Research* (Buffalo), vol. 30, 1970, 368-381.

1244    Bartky, Sandra L. "Heidegger's Philosophy of Art." *British Journal of Aesthetics* (London), vol. 9, no. 4, 1969, 353-371.

1245    Bartky, Sandra L. *A Study of 'Being' in the Philosophy of Heidegger.* Phil. Diss. Urbana: Univ. of Illinois 1963 208 p. *Dissertation Abstracts International,* vol. 24, no. 12, 5462.

1246    Bartky, Sandra L. Rev. of *On Heidegger and Language.* Ed. Joseph Kockelmans, Evanston, Illinois, 1972/73. *Philosophy and Phenomenological Research* (Buffalo, New York), vol. 34, 1974, 442-444.

1246a   Bartky, Sandra L. "Heidegger and the Modes of World-Disclosure." *Philosophy and Phenomenological Research* (Buffalo), vol. 40, 1979/80, 212-236.

1247    Bartky, Sandra L. *A Study of 'Being' in the Philosophy of Heidegger.* Authorized facsimile of the dissertation of the Univ. of Illinois 1963. Ann Arbor, Michigan; London: Univ. Microfilms International, 1977, vii-200 p.

1248    Bartlett, Steven. "Phenomenology of the Implicit." *Dialectica,* vol. 29, 1975, 173-188.

1249    Bartolomei, M. C. Rev. of *Fenomenologie e teologia,* by Martin Heidegger. Florence: la Nuova Italia, 1974. *Bolletino Filosofico* (Padova), vol. 9, no. 8-9, 1975, 114-115.

1250    Barton, Jr., W.B. "An Introduction to Heidegger's 'What Is a Thing'." *The Southern Journal of Philosophy* (Memphis), vol. 11, 1973, 15-25.

1251    Baruzzi, Arno. "Untersuchungen zur Philosophie als Zeitkritik in Hinblick auf Martin Heidegger." Phil. Diss. München 1974.

1252    Basave Fernández del Valle, Agustín. *Tres filósofos alemanes de nuestro tiempo (Scheler, Heidegger y Wust).* Mexico: Univ. Autónoma de Nuevo León, 1977, 130 p.

1253    Bast, Rainer A. "Philologisches zur 15. Auflage von *Sein und Zeit* und zum "Humanismusbrief," I." *Man and World,* vol. 13, 1980, 241-250.

1254    Bast, Rainer A. and Heinrich P. Delfosse. "Report: Philological Remarks on the Two New Editions of *Sein und Zeit.*" *Man and World* (The Hague), vol. 12, no. 3, 1979, 387-401.

1255    Bast, Rainer A. and Heinrich P. Delfosse. Rev. of *Sein und Zeit.* Gesamtausgabe, Abt. 1, Bd II. Ed. Friedrich-Wilhelm von Hermann. *Philosophisches Jahrbuch* (München), vol. 86, 1971, 185-190.

1256    Bast, Rainer A. and Heinrich P. Delfosse. *Handbuch zum Textstudium von Heideggers 'Sein und Zeit'.* Bd 1: Stellenindices - Philologisch - kritischer Apparat. Bd 2: Wortindices - Verzeich nisse zu Wortgebrauch und Wortbildung - Literatur und Fundstellenliste announced to be published in 1981. Stuttgart: Holzboog, 1980, 500 p.

1257    Bastable, J. D. Rev. of *Heidegger, Essays in Metaphysics. Philosophical Studies* (Maynooth), vol. 11, 1961-62, 326.

1258    Battaglia, F. "Idealismo ed esistenzialismo." *Atti del congresso internazionale di filosofia, promosso dell'Istituto di Studi Filosofici* (Roma), 15-20 November 1946. II: "L'esistentialismo." Milano, 1948, 57-68.

1259    Battaglia, F. "Esistenza e coesistenza nel pensiero di Martino Heidegger." *Esistenzialismo. Quaderno dell'Archivio di filosofia* (Roma), vol. 15, 1946, 42-60.

1260    Battaglia, F. *Heidegger e la metafisica dell'essere finito.* 2nd ed. Bologna, 1949.

1261    Battaglia, F. *Heidegger e la filosofia dei valori,* Bologna, 1967, 111 p.

        [Rev. by J. Decerf in *Revue Philosophique de Louvain* (Louvain), vol. 69, 1971, 161.]

1262    Battaglia, F. "'La scienza non pensa' nota sull'ultimo Heidegger." *Ethica* (Forli), vol. 9, 1970, 81-104.

1263    Bauch, B. Rev. of *Heidegger, Hölderlin und das Wesen der Dichtung*. München, 1937. *Blätter für deutsche Philosophie* (Berlin), vol. 13, 1939/40, 217-218.

1264    Bauch, K. "Die Kunstgeschichte und die heutige Philosophie." In *Martin Heidegger Einfluss auf die Wissenschaften Aus Aulap Seines 60. Geburestges Berfasst,* Bern, 1949, 88-93.

1265    Baum, H. "Le 'cercle ontologique': Contre une ontologie de 'l'Etre et de l'étant'." *Laval Théologique et Philosophique* (Québec), vol. 34, no. 2, 1978, 115-128.

1266    Baumann, G. "Martin Heidegger. Unterwegs zur Dichtung." *Études Germainiques* (Paris), vol. 32, no. 3, 1977, 268-278.

1267    Baumgardt, D. "Rationalism and the Philosophy of Despair: Pre-Nazi Ethics." *Sewanee Review* (Sewanee, Tennessee), 1947, 223-237.

1268    Beau, A. E. "O Humanismo no pensamento de Heidegger." *Humanitas* (Coimbra), vol. 2, 1949, 195-210.

1270    Beaufret, Jean. "Heidegger et le problème de la vérité." *Fontaine* (Paris), vol. 63, 1947, 758-785.

1271    Beaufret, Jean. "A propos de l'existentialisme." *Confluences* (Lyon), vol. 2, 1945, 192-199. (196ff).

1272    Beaufret, Jean. "La Fable de Monde." In *Martin Heidegger zum 70. Geburtstag. Festschrift.* Pfullingen, 1959, 11-18.

1273    Beaufret, Jean. "La pensée du néant dans l'oeuvre de Heidegger." *La table ronde* (Paris), no. 182, 1963, 76-81.

1274    Beaufret, Jean. "Heidegger vu de France." In *Die Frage Martin Heideggers.* Ed. H. G. Gadamer. Berlin, 1969, 9-16.

1275    Beaufret, Jean. "Heidegger Seen From France." *The Southern Journal of Philosophy* (Memphis), vol. 8, 1970, 433-438. Rpt. in *Martin Heidegger in Europe and America.* The Hague, 1973, 195-200.

1276    Beaufret, Jean. *Introduction aux philosophies de l'existence. De Kierkegaard à Heidegger.* Paris, 1971, 213 p.

1277    Beaufret, Jean. *Dialogue avec Heidegger.* Tom I, Paris: Les éditions de Minuit, 1973.

1278    Beaufret, Jean. *Dialogue avec Heidegger. Vol. II: Philosophie moderne* (Arguments, 58). Paris: Éditions de Minuit, 1973, 224 p.

1279    Beaufret, Jean. *Dialogue avec Heidegger. Vol III: Approche de Heidegger* (Arguments). Paris: éditions de Minuit, 1974, 239 p.

1280    Beaufret, Jean. *Wege zu Heidegger.* Trans. from French by Christina Maihofer. Frankfurt: Klostermann, 1976, 175 p.

1281    Beaufret, Jean. "A propos de Questions IV de Heidegger." *Les Études Philosophiques* (Paris), no. 2, 1978, 235-245.

1282   Beaufret, Jean, Dominique Buhan, and Eryck de Rubercy. "Dwanaácie pytaá w sprawie Heideggera" (Twelve Questions Concerning Heidegger). Trans. M. Ochab. *Teksty,* March, 1977.

1283   Beaufret, Jean. "Le chemin de Heidegger." *Etudes Germaniques* (Paris), vol. 32, no. 3, 1977, 279-298.

1284   Beaufret, Jean. "En France." In *Erinnerung an Martin Heidegger.* Ed. Günther Neske. Pfullingen: Verlag Günther Neske, 1977, 9-13.

1285   Beaufret, Jean. "Martin Heidegger and the Problem of Truth." In *Heidegger's Existential Analytic.* Ed. and trans. Frederick Elliston. The Hague/New York: Mouton, 1978, 197-217.

1286   Beaufret, Jean. "A propos de *Questions IV* de Heidegger." *Les Etudes Philosophiques* (Paris), no. 2, 1978, 235-245.

1286a  Beaufret, Jean. "Heidegger et la Théologie." *Heidegger et la Question de Dieu.* Ed. R. Kearney and J. S. O'Leary. Paris: B. Grasset, 1980, 19-36.

1287   Beck, E. L. "Der ontologische Imperativ. Hoffentlich ein Beitrag zum Verständnis M. Heideggers." *Wissenschaft und Weltbild* (Wien), vol. 8, 1955, 206-212.

1288   Beck, Joel Isaac. "Plato and the Problem of Metaphysics: An Inquiry into the Meaning of Being in Plato and Heidegger." Phil. Diss. Univ. of Chicago 1978.

1289   Beck, Lewis White. "Review: *Heidegger, Kant and the Problem of Metaphysics.* " *The Philosophical Review* (Ithaca), vol. 72, 1963, 396-398.

1290   Beck, M. "Referat und Kritik von Martin Heideggers: *Sein und Zeit.*" *Philosophische Hefte* (Berlin), vol. 1, 1928, 5-44. (Sonderheft über Heidegger: Sein un

1291   Beck, M. "Die neue Problemlage der Erkenntnistheorie." *Zwischen den Zeiten* (München), 1928, 611-639.

1292   Beck, M. "Hermeneutik und philosophia perennis." *Philosophische Hefte* (Berlin), vol. 2, 1930, 13-46.

1293   Beck, M. "Der phänomenologische Idealismus, die phänomenologische Methode und die Hermeneutik." *Philosophische Hefte* (Berlin), vol. 2, 1930, 97-101.
       [Rev. by Th. Celms in *Der Phänomenologische Idealismus Husserls,* 1928.]

1294   Beck, M. "Kritik der Schelling-, Jaspers-, Heideggerschen Ontologie." *Philosophische Hefte* (Prag), vol. 4, 1934, 97-164.

1295   Beck, Karl. Rev. of *Das Göttliche und der Gott bei Heidegger,* by Helmut Danner. Meisenheim, 1971. *Zeitschrift für Philosophische Forschung* (Meisenheim), vol. 28, 1974, 315-317.

1296   Becker, Oskar. "Mathematische Existenz. Untersuchungen zur Logik und Ontologie mathematischer Phänomene." *Jahrbuch für Philosophie und phänomenologische Forschung* (Halle), vol. 8, 1927, 439-809.

1297   Becker, Oskar. "Para-Existenz. Menschliches Dasein und Dawesen." *Blätter für deutsche Philosophie* (Berlin), vol. 17, 1943/44, 62-95. Rpt. in *Heidegger.* Ed. O. Poeggeler. Koeln/Berlin, 1969, 261-285.

1298   Becker, Oskar. *Grösse und Grenze der mathematischen Denkweise.* Freiburg/München, 1959, v-174.

1299   Becker, Oskar. *Dasein und Dawesen. Gesammelte philosophische Aufsätze.* Pfullingen, 1963, 191 p.

1301   Beerling, Reinier F. *Antithesen. Mit een Voorwoord von J. Hiuzinga.* Haarlem, 1935, 310 p., (specifically pages 195-310: De existentie - philosophie van M. Heidegger).

1302   Beerling, Reinier F. *Moderne Dood's Problematiek.* Delft, 1945, viii-306.

1303   Beerling, Reinier F. "De existentiephilosophie van M. Heidegger." In *Antithesen. Vier Studies* (Haarlem), vol. 4, 1945.

1304   Beerling, Reinier F. *Moderne doodsproblematiek. Een vergelijkende studie over Simmel, Heidegger en Jaspers.* Delft, 1946, 306 p., (specifically pages 88-248).

1305   Beerling, Reinier F, C. Debrot and J. De Kadt. *Het Existentialisme.* 's-Gravenhage, 1947, 97 p.

1306   Beerling, Reinier F. "Waarheid." *Wijsgerig Perspectief op Maatschappij en Wetenschap* (Amsterdam), vol. 17, 1976-1977, 78-84.

1307   Beerling, Reinier F. *Van Nietzsche tot Heidegger. Drie Studies.* Deventer: Van Loghum Slaterus, 1977, 184 p.

1308   Behl, L. "Wittgenstein and Heidegger." *Duns Scotus Philosophical Association,* vol. 27, 1963, 70-115.

1309   Behler, E. Rev. of *Was heisst Denken?,* by Martin Heidegger. Tübingen, 1954; *Vom Wesen der Wahrheit.* Frankfurt, 1954. *Literarischer Ratgeber* (Köln), vol. 41, 1954/1955, 118.

1310   Behler, W. "Realität und Ek-sistenz. Auseinandersetzung mit der Konzeption Martin Heideggers in Konfrontation mit den ontologischen Schriften von Hedwig Conrad-Martius." Phil. Diss. München 7.8 1956 200 Bl.

1311   Beierwaltes, Werner. *Identität und Differenz: Zum Prinzip cusanischen Denkens.* Opladen, 1977.

1312   Benda, J. *Tradition de l'existentialisme ou les philosophies de la vie.* Paris, 1947. Passim.

1313   Benda, J. *Trois idoles romantiques. Le dynamisme - l'existentialisme - la dialectique matérialiste.* Genève, 1948, 97-144, passim.

1314   Benedikt, M. "Das Problem des Grundes bei Martin Heidegger als ein Problem der Grundlegung oder Überwindung von Metaphysik." Phil. Diss. Wien 1952 iii and 200 p.

1315   Beneyto, J. "La historia, carga y contorno del hombre." *Revista de estudios politicos* (Madrid), vol. 185, 1972, 5-16.

1316    Benincasa, Carmine. "Feldweg e Holzwege heideggeriani." *Sapienza* (Roma), vol. 24, 1971, 163-174.

1317    Benoist, Jean-Marie. "De Héraclite à la Forêt Noire. Heidegger redécouvre, tout au long de sa pensée, les présocratiques; mais n travestit-il pas Héraclite en Parménide? Et où mèment les chemins da sa pensée?" *Magazine Littéraire* (Paris), no. 117, 1976, 9-11.

1318    Bense, M. Rev. of *Heideggers Brief über den Humanismus. Merkur* (Stuttgart), vol. 3, 1949, 1021-1025.

1319    Bense, M. "Beständig im Gedärm der Wahrheit Wühlen. Bermerkungen zu Heideggers 'Holzwege." *Deutsche Zeitung und Wirtschaftszeitung* (Stuttgart), vol. 5, no. 54, 1950, 17.

1319a   Berciano Villalibre, Modesto. "Formas de Pensamiento y Modos de Producción: Su Relación en Martin Heidegger. Un Modelo no Marxista Entre Teoria y Praxis Económica." *Rev Agust Esp,* vol. 19, no. 58-59, 1978, 75-134.

1320    Berciano, Modesto. "Herbert Marcuse. El Primer marxista heideggeriano." *Pensamiento,* vol. 36, no. 142, 1980, 131-164.

1321    Berens, V. "In the Neighbourhood of Being." *Revue de l'Université Laurentienne* (Sudbury), vol. 9, no. 2, 1977, 7-14.

1322    Berg, Richard. "Heidegger on Language and Poetry." *Kinesis. Graduate Journal in Philosophy* (Carbondale, Illinois), vol. 7, no. 2, 1977, 75-89.

1323    Berghs, H. M. "Nederlandse Heidegger Bibliothek." *Duitse Kroniek,* vol. 21, 1969, 164-166.

1324    Berghs, H. M. "Het zakelijk krarkter van Heideggers vragg naar de techniek." *Tijdschrift voor Filosofie* (Leuven), vol. 33, 1971, 250-278.

1325    Berlinger, R. *Das Nichts und der Tod.* Frankfurt, 1972, 197 p.

1327    Bernard-Maitre, H. Rev. of these Martin Heidegger works in *Revue de Synthèse* (Paris), vol. 85, 1964, 153-155.

        [*Approche de Hölderlin.*]

        [*Chemins qui ne mènent nulle part.*]

        [*Le principe de raison.*]

1328    Bernet, A. "M. Heidegger, F. Himpele, L. Marcuse." *Leserbriefe zu: Mitternacht einer Weltnacht, Der Spiegel,* Jg. 20, no. 7, Hamburg, 7.2 1966, 110-113. Der Spiegel Jg. 20, no. 11, Hamburg, 7.3, 1966, 9-12.

1329    Bertholet, Edmond. "La question de L'Être chéz Heidegger et chez Gonseth." *Dialectica* (Lausanne), vol. 31, no. 1-2, 1977, 99-105.

1330    Bertman, M. A. "La vérité comme coulisse mythique chez Nietzsche." *Revue Philosophique de Louvain* (Leuven), vol. 71, 1973, 62-71.

1331    Bertman, Martin A. "Truth as Mythic Coulisse in Nietzsche." *Philosophy Today* (Celina, Ohio), vol. 18, 1974, 41-46.

1331a    Berezdivin, Ruben. "Fire and Logos: The Speech of Fire and Its Cotradictions." *Heraclitean Fragments*, Univ. of Alabama Press, 1980, 68-85.

1332    Bespaloff, R. "Lettre sur Heidegger à M. Daniel Halévy." *Revue Philosophique de la France et de l'Etranger* (Paris), vol. 58, no. 116, 1933, 321-339.

1333    Betancourt, E. "El problema de la existencia humana en Heidegger." *Montezuma* (Mexico), no. 108, 1950, 237-253.

1334    Betschart, I. Zu philosophischen und psychologischen Neuerscheinungen. Rev. of *Einführung in die Metaphysik*, by Martin Heidegger. Tübingen, 1953. *Civitas* (Immensee), vol. 9, 1953/54, 278-279.

1335    Beyer, W. R. "Herr Heidegger - und die Friedensfrage." *Deutsche Zeitschrift für Philosophie* (Berlin), vol. 10, 1962, 1533-1553.

1336    Beyer, W. R. "Heideggers Katholizität." *Deutsche Zeitschrift für Philosophie* (Berlin), vol. 12, 1964, 191-209, 310-324.

1337    Beyer, W. R. "Philosophische Perspektiven des Differenzbegriffs." (Hegel, Heidegger, Marx). *Filosoficky Casopis* (Prag), 1964, 208.

1338    Beyer, W. R. "Heidegger über sich selbst." *Die Tat* (Frankfurt), vol. 24.10, 1964, 9.

1339    Beyer, W. R. *Hegelbilder. Kritik der Hegeldeutungen.* Berlin, 1964, 2nd edition, Berlin, 1967. (especially: 180-192; 335)

1340    Beyer, W. R. "'Marxistische Ontologie' - Eine idealistische Modeforschung." *Deutsche Zeitschrift für Philosophie*, vol. 17, 1969, 1310-1331.

1341    Beyer, W. R. *Vier Kritiken: Heidegger, Sartre, Adorno, Lukács.* Köhn, 1970. 232 p.

    [Rev. by K.-D. Block and E. Galander in *Deutsche Zeitschrift für Philosophie* (Berlin), vol. 19, no. 2, 1971, 241-243.]

1342    Beydoun, Afaf. "Das vergessene Geheimnis des Daseins nach Heidegger." Phil. Diss. München 1974.

1343    Bhattacharya, Rajlukshmee Debee. "Personal Man and Personal God: The Tagorean Conception Revisited." *International Philosophical Quarterly*, vol. 15, December 1975, 425-437.

1344    Bianco, F. Rev. of *Die Frage nach dem Ding*, by Martin Heidegger. *Archivio de Filosofia* (Roma), no. 3, 1965, 151-153.

1345    Bianco, F. "Rassegna di studi heideggeriani." *Archivio di Filosofia* (Roma), vol. 1, 1967, 139-151.

1346    Biehl, P. "Welchen Sinn hat es, von 'theologischer Ontologie' zu reden." *Zeitschrift für Theologie und Kirche* (Tübingen), vol. 53, 1956, 349-372.

1347    Biemel, Walter. "Heideggers Begriff des Daseins." *Studia Catholica* (Nijmegen), vol. 24, 1949, 113-129.

1348    Biemel, Walter. *Le concept de monde chez Heidegger.* Paris: Louvain, 1950, 184 p.

[Rev. by H. Kuhn in *Archiv für Philosohie* (Stuttgart), vol. 4, 1952, 416-417; J. B. Lotz *Scholastik* (Freiburg), vol. 29, 1954, 131-132.]

1349    Biemel, Walter. "Husserls Encyclopaedia-Britiannica Artikel und Heideggers Anmerkungen dazu." *Tijdschrift voor Philosophie* (Leuven), vol. 12, 1950, 246-280. Mit Auszügen aus Brief Heideggers an Husserls, 274.

1350    Biemel, Walter. "El articulo de Husserl para le Encyclopaedia Britiannica y las observaciones de Heidegger al mismo." *Arkhé* (Cordoba), vol. 3, 1966, 3-37.

1351    Biemel, Walter. "Dichtung und Sprache bei Heidegger." *Man and World* (Pittsburgh), vol. 2, 1969, 487-514. Rpt. in *Filosoficky Casopis* (Tschechoslowakei), no. 5/6, 1969, 768-787.

1352    Biemel, Walter. "Poetry and Language in Heidegger." In *On Heidegger and Language*. Ed. J. J. Kockelmans, 65-105.

1353    Biemel, Walter. "Kunst und Situation. Bermerkugen zu einem Aspekt der aktuellen Kunst." *Philosophische Perspektiven* (Frankfurt), vol. 4, 1972, 27-44.

1354    Biemel, Walter et al. "Panel-discussion." Ed. J. J. Kockelmans. In *On Heidegger and Language*. Evanston, Illinois, 1972, 261-277.

1355    Biemel, Walter. *Martin Heidegger in Selbstzeugnissen und Bilddokumenten*. Reinbek, 1973, 173 p. (Trans. into English by Joneva L. Nehta, New York, 1976; London, 1977.)

1356    Biemel, Walter. "Husserls Encyclopaedia-Britiannica-Artikel und Heideggers Anmerkungen dazu." In *Husserl*. Ed. Hermann Noack. *Wege der Forschung* (Darmstadt), Wissenschaftliche Buchgesellschaft, vol. 40, 1973, 282-315. Rpt. in *Tijdschrift voor Philosophie*, vol. 12, 1950, 246-280.

1357    Biemel, Walter. "L'interprétation heideggérienne du sacré chez Hölderlin." In *Prospecttive sul sacro. Contributi al Convegno su Il sacro* indetto dal Centro Internazionale di Studi Umanistici e dall'Istituto di Studi Filosofici. Roma, 4-9 Gennaio 1974. Ed. Enrico Castelli. (Centro Internazionale di Studi Umanistici Roma). Roma: Istituto di Studi Filosifici, 1974, 185-198.

1358    Biemel, Walter. "Husserl's *Encyclopaedia Britannica* Article and Heidegger's Remarks Thereon." Eds. and trans. Peter McCormick and Frederick A. Elliston. In *Husserl. Expositions and Appraisals*. Notre Dame, Indiana; London: Univ. of Notre Dame Press, 1977, 286-303.

        [German version published in 1950 and 1973.]

1359    Biemel, Walter. "Erinnerungsfragmente." In *Erinnerung an Martin Heidegger*. Ed. Günther Neske. Pfullingen: Günther Neske, 1977, 15-24.

1360    Biemel, Walter. "Heidegger and Metaphysics." Trans. Thomas J. Sheehan. *Listening. Journal of Religon and Culture* (River Forest, Illinois), vol. 12, no. 3, 1977, 50-60.

1361    Biemel, Walter. "Reminiscing Heidegger." (In Serbocroat). *Delo* (Belgrad), vol. 23, no. 12, 1977, 52-74.

1362 Biemel, Walter. "Erinnerungen an Heidegger." *Allgemeine Zeitschrift für Philosophie* (Stuttgart), vol. 2, no. 1, 1977, 1-23.

1363 Biemel, Walter. "Heidegger's Concept of Dasein." In *Heidegger's Existential Analytic.* Ed. Frederick Elliston. The Hague/New York: Mouton, 1978, 111-131.

1364 Biemel, Walter. "Heideggers Stellung zur Phänomenologie in der Marburger Zeit." In *Husserl, Scheler, Heidegger in der Sicht neuer Quellen.* Contributions by Ernst Wolfgang Orth and others. *Phänomenologische Forschungen,* 6/7. Freiburg: Karl Alber, 1978, 141-223.

1364a Biemel, Walter. "Philosophy and Art." Trans. by Emad Parvis. *Man and World* (The Hague), vol. 12, 1979, 267-283.

1365 Bindeman, Steven Lee. "The Role of Silence in the Philosophies of Martin Heidegger and Ludwig Wittgenstein." Authorized facsimile of the dissertation of the Duquesne Univ. Phil. Diss. 1978. Ann Arbor, Michigan; London: University Microfilms International, 1979, 218 p. *Dissertation Abstracts International,* vol. 39, 103-A, 2343.

1366 Binswanger, Ludwig. *Grundformen und Erkenntnis menschlichen Daseins.* Zürich, 1942, 726 p., passim.

1367 Binswanger, Ludwig. "Über die daseinsanalytische Forschungsrichtung in der Psychiatrie." *Schweizer Archiv für Psychiatrie und Neurologie* (Zürich), vol. 57, 1946, 209-235, passim.

1368 Binswanger, Ludwig. "Die Bedeutung der Daseinsanalytik Martin Heideggers für das Selbstverständnis der Psychiatrie" (Martin Heideggers Einfluss auf die Wissenschaften). Bern, 1949, 58-72. Rpt. in *Ausgewählte Vorträge und Aufsätze,* by L. Binswanger. Bern, Bd. 2, 1955, 264-278.

1369 Binswanger, Ludwig. "Daseinsanalytik und Psychiatrie." *Der Nervenartz* (Berlin), vol. 22, Göttingen, Heidelberg, 1951, 1-10, passim. Rpt. in *Ausgewählte Vorträge und Aufsätze,* by L. Binswanger. Bern, Bd. 2, 1955, 279-302.

1370 Binswanger, Ludwig. "Daseinsanalytik und Psychotherapie." *Ausgewählte Vorträge und Aufsätze* (Bern), Bd. 2, 1955, 303-307.

1371 Binswanger, Ludwig. "Martin Heidegger und die Psychiatrie." *Neue Züricher Zeitung,* no. 2898/1 and 2 vol. 27.9.1959. (Fernausgabe no. 264, 26.9.1959)

1372 Birault, Henri. "Existence et vérité d'après Heidegger." *Revue de métaphysique et de morale* (Paris), vol. 56, 1951, 35-87.

1373 Birault, Henri. "Existence et vérité d'après Heidegger." *Phénoménomologie-Existence,* recueil d'études par H. Birault, H. L. van Breda, A. Gurvitch, E. Levinas, P. Ricoeur, J. Wahl. Paris, 1953, 139-191.

1374 Birault, Henri. "La foi et la pensée d'après Heidegger." *Richerches et débats,* vol. 10, 1955, 108-132.

1375 Birault, Henri. "L'onto-theo-logique hegelienne et la dialectique." *Tijdschrift voor Philosophie* (Leuven), vol. 20, 1958, 646-723.

1376 Birault, Henri. "Heidegger et la pensée de la finitude." *Revue inernationale de Philosophie* (Bruxelles), vol. 14, 1960, 135-162.

1377 Birault, Henri. "De l'être, du Divin et des Dieux chez Heidegger." (L'Existence de Dieu). *Coll. 'Cahiers de l'actualité religieuse'* (Paris), vol. 16, 1960, 1961, 49-76.

1378 Birault, Henri. "Thinking and Poetizing in Heidegger" in *On Heidegger and Language*. Ed. J. J. Kockelmans. Evanston, Illinois, 1972, 147-168.

1379 Birault, Henri. "Heidegger und Frankreich. Faszination vom Existentialismus zum Strukturalismus." *Frankfurter Allgemeine Zeitung* (Frankfurt), no. 122, May 27, 1977, 25.

1380 Birault, Henri. "Heidegger und Frankreich. Überlegungen zu einer alten Verbindung." In *Martin Heidegger. Fragen an sein Werk*. Ein Symposium (Universal-Bibliothek, 9873). Stuttgart: Reclam, 1977, 46-53.

1381 Birault, Henri. *Heidegger et l'expérience de la pensée*. In *Bibliothèque de la philosophie*. Paris: Gallimard, 1978, 628 p.

1382 Bixio, Andrea. "Esistenza, colpa e dike (M. Heidegger e la filosofia de diritto)." *Rivista internazionale di Filosofia del Diritto* (Milano), vol. 50, 1973, 379-424.

1383 Bixler, Julius Seelye. "The Contribution of Existenz-Philosophie." *Harvard Theological Review*, vol. 33, January 1940, 35-63.

1384 Bixler, Julius Seelye. "The Failure of Martin Heidegger." *The Harvard Theological Review* (Cambridge), vol. 56, 1963, 121-143.

1385 Blackham, H. J. *Six Existentialist Thinkers*. London, 1952, 86-109.

1386 Blackham, H. J. *Seis pensadores existencialistas Kierkegaard, Nietzsche, Jaspers, Marcel, Heidegger, Sartre,* Trans. R. Jordana. Barcelona, 1965, 196 p.

1387 Blaisdell, Chuck. "Heidegger's Structure of Time and Temporality. A New Repudiation of the Classical Conception." *Dialogue. Journal of Phi Sigma Tau* (Milwaukee, Wisconsin), vol. 18, no. 2-3, 1975-1976, 44-53.

1388 Blanchot, M. "L'Altenti." In *Martin Heidegger zum 70. Geburtstag. Festschrift.* Pfullingen, 1959, 217-224.

1389 Blanco, J. E. "Diàlogos de mitografia heideggeriana." *Universidad de Antioquia* (Medellin), no. 146, 1961, 589-616.

1390 Blanco, J. E. "Mitografia heideggeriana." *Universidad de Antioquia* (Medellin, Columbia), vol. 40, 1963, 493-520.

1391 Bloch, E. "Wissen und Hoffen," especially "Ontologien der Fülle und Vergänglichkeit." *Scheler and Heidegger* (Berlin), 1955, 24-31.

1392 Block, Klaus Dieter. Rev. of *Vier Kritiken: Heidegger, Sartre, Adorno, Lukacs,* by Wilhelm Raimund Beyer. Köln, 1970. *Deutsche Zeitschrift für Philosophie* (Berlin), vol. 19, 1971, 241-243.

1393 Blocker, Gene. *The Meaning of Meaningless*. The Hague: Nijhoff, 1974.

1394 Blondel, Eric. Rev. of *Dialogue avec Heidegger, Vol. 2: Philosophie Moderne,* by Jean Beaufret. (Arguments, 56). Paris, 1973. *Revue Philosophique de la France et de l'Etranger* (Paris), vol. 166, 1976, 338-339.

1395 Blorer, J. Rev. of *Das Schicksal der Metaphysik von Thomas zu Heidegger,* by Gustav Siewer. Einsiedeln, 1959. *Revista de Filosofia* (Madrid), vol. 20, 1961, 98-99.

1396 Bobbio, N. "Persona e società nella filosofia dell'esistenza." *Archivio di filosofia* (Roma), vol. 11, 320-336, (specifically pages 325-328).

1397 Bobbio, N. *La filosofia del decadentismo.* Torino, 1944.

1398 Bobbio, N. "Tre breve scritti di Heidegger." *Rivista di Filosofia Neo-Scolastica* (Milano), vol. 3, 1948, 1-39.

1399 Bochenski, I. M. *Europäische Philosophe der Gegenwart.* Bern, 1947, 164-174.

1400 Bock, I. *Heideggers Sprachdenken.* Phil.Diss. München 1965 184 p. Auch Meisenheim, 1966, 117.

1402 Bocorisvili, A. T. "O nacale chudozestvennogo proizvedenija v ontologii M. Chajdeggera" (On the Origin of the Work of Art in Martin Heidegger's Ontology). *Mecniereba* (Tbilisi), 1973.

1403 Bodewils, Sophie Dorothee. "Er hat Heidegger übersehen: Letter to the Editor." *Frankfurter Allgemeine Zeitung* (Frankfurt), May 17, 1979.

1404 Bodnár, J. "Fundamentálná ontologia M. Heidegger" (Fundamental Ontology - M. Heidegger). *Otázky marxistickej filosofii* (Bratislava) (Die Fragen der marxistischen Philosophie), 1965, 557-568.

1405 Bodnár, J. "Heideggerova nová initiativa vo filozofii." In *Existentializmus a fenomenológia,* by J. Bodnár et al. Bratislava, 1967, 213-241.

1406 Böckenhoff, J. *Die Begegnungsphilosophie. Ihre Geschichte - ihre Aspekte.* Freiburg/München, 1970, 464 p.

1407 Boeder, H. "Weshalb 'Sein des Seienden'?" *Philosophisches Jahrbuch* (München), vol. 78, 1971, 111-133.

1408 Böhm, F. *Ontologie der Geschichte.* Tübingen, 1933, 140 p.

1409 Boehm, R. "Une introduction à la philosophie phénoménologique." *Archivio di Filosofia* (Milano), 1954, 169-172.

1410 Boehm, R. "Pensée et technique. Notes préliminaires pour une question touchant la problématique heideggerienne." *Revue internationale de Philosophie* (Bruxelles), vol. 14, 1960, 194-220.

1411 Boehm, R. "De kritiek van Levinas op Heidegger." *Tijdschrift voor Filosofie* (Leuven), vol. 25, 1963, 585-604.

1412 Boehm, R. "Progrès, arrêt et recul dans l'histoire." *Archives de Philosophie* (Italy), 1963, 1-2; 55-67.

1413 Boehm, R. "Chiasma. Merleau-Ponty und Heidegger." In *Durchblicke.* Ed. V. Klostermann. Frankfurt, 1970, 369-393.

1414    Boekenkamp, Werner. "'Der grösste Philosoph unserer Zeit'. Pariser Zeitungen zum Tod Heideggers." *Frankfurter Allgemeine Zeitung* (Frankfurt), vol. 115, May 29, 1976, 23. (Vol. 3, no. 2, 1976).

1415    Boelen, B. J. "Martin Heidegger's Approach to Will, Decision, and Responsibility." *Review of Existential Psychology and Psychiatry* (Pittsburgh), vol. 1, 1961, 197-204.

1416    Boelen, B. J. *Existential Thinking. A Philosophical Orientation.* Pittsburgh, 1968, ix-288 p.

1417    Boelen, B. J. "The Question of Ethics in the Thought of Martin Heidegger" In *Heidegger and the Quest for Truth.* Ed. M. S. Frings. Chicago, 1968, 76-105.

1418    Boelen, Bernhard. "Martin Heidegger as a Phenomenologist." In *Phenomenological Perspectives. Historical and Systematic Essays in Honor of Herbert Spiegelberg.* Ed. Philip j. Bossert. The Hague: Martinus Nijhoff, 1975. *Phaenomenologica,* vol. 62, 93-114.

1419    Boer, W. de. "Positivismus und Existenzphilosophie." *Merkur* (Stuttgart), vol. 6, 1952, 12-35.

1420    Boer, W. de. "Heideggers Missverständnis der Metaphysik." *Zeitschrift für philosophische Forschung* (Meisenheim), 1955, 500-545.

1421    Bogdan, V. "Martin Heidegger." *Istoria filosofie moderne* (Bukarest), vol. 3, 1938, 447-464.

1422    Bogliolo, V. "Dall'X di Kant al Nichts di Heidegger." *Rivista di Filosofia* (Roma), vol. 14, 1971, 271-289; *Aquinas,* vol. 14, 1971, 271-289.

1423    Bogomolov, A. S. "Istorija burzuaznof filosofii épochi imperializma" (The History of Bourgeois Philosophy During the Period of Imperialism). Moskva, 1967, 71-83.

1424    Bogomolov, A. S. "Nemeckaja burzuaznaja filosofija posle 1865 g" (German Bourgeois Philosophy After 1865). *Izdatel'stvo MGU,* 1969, 310-332, 383-391.

1425    Bogomolov, A. S. "Osnovyne tecenija sovremennoj burzuaznoj filosofii" (Main Currents in Contemporary Bourgeois Philosophy). *Vypusk tretij.* Moskva, 1970.

1426    Bogomolov, A. S. "Sovremennyj ekzistencializm 'povorot' ili krizis?" (Contemporary Existentialism: "The Turning" or the Crisis). *Izdatel'stvo Moskovskogo Universiteta* (Moskva), 1971, 217-223.

1427    Bogomolov, A.S. "Filosofija, osnovannaja na naucnom znanii, ili lingvisticeskaja metafizika?" (Philosophy Based on Scientific Cognition or Linguistical Metaphysics?). *Filosofskie nauki,* 1973, 2.

1428    Bohe, L. "Le roi Oedipe a pent-être un oeil de trop. Heidegger, commentateur de Parménide et de Sophocle." *Revue de l'Université d'Ottawa* (Ottawa), vol. 38, no. 4, 1968, 599-627.

1429    Bokelmann, H. "Heidegger und die Erziehungswissenschaft." *Zeitschrift für Pädagogik* (Weinheim/Bergstr.), vol. 6, 1960, 261-264.

1430   Boku, Shoko. "Haideggâ ni okeru Chiheino Mondai" (The Problem of the Horizon in Heidegger). *Riso* (Tôkyô März), 1935.

1431   Boliek, Lynn. "The Integrity of Faith." *Philosophia Reformaia* (Kampen, Netherlands), vol. 39, 1974, 41-68.

1432   Bolkestein, M. H. *Het Ik-Gij schema in de nieuwere Philosophie en Theologie.* Wageningen, 1941, 173 p., (specifically pages 125-130).

1433   Bollack, Jean and Heinz Wismann. "Heidegger l'incontournable." *Actes de la Recherches en Sciences Sociales* (Paris), no. 5-6, 1975, 157-161.

1434   Bollack, Jean and Heinz Wismann. Appendix to "Die politische Ontologie Martin Heideggers," by Pierre Bourdieu. In *Heidegger der Unumgängliche.* Frankfurt: Syndikat, 1976.

1435   Bollnow, O. F. Rev. of *Vom Wesen des Grundes,* by Martin Heidegger. Halle, 1929. *Deutsche Literaturzeitung* (Berlin), vol. 3, Sp. 1879-1887.

1436   Bollnow, O. F. "Über Heideggers Verhältnis zu Kant." *Neue Jahrbücher für Wissenschaft und Jugendbildung* (Berlin), vol. 9, 1933, 222-231.

1437   Bollnow, Otto Friedrich. Rev. of *Hölderlin und das Wesen der Dichtung,* by Martin Heidegger. München, 1936/37. *Die Literatur* (Stuttgart/Berlin), 1937/38, 59.

1438   Bollnow, Otto Friedrich. *Das Wesen der Stimmungen.* Frankfurt, 1941, x-224.

1439   Bollnow, Otto Friedrich. *Existenzphilosophie.* Systematische Philosophie, Stuttgart/Berlin, 1942, 313-430, passim. 2nd ed. Auflage Stuttgart, 1947. 3rd ed. Auflage Stuttgart, 1949. Expanded 4th ed. Auflage Stuttgart, 1955.

1440   Bollnow, Otto Friedrich. "Deutsche Existenzphilosophie und französischer Existentialismus." *Zeitschrift für philosophische Forschung* (Reutlingen), vol. 2, 1947/48, 231-243.

1441   Bollnow, Otto Friedrich. "Zur Diskussion über die Existenzphilosophie auf dem Philosophischen Kongress in Garmisch-Partenkirchen." *Zeitschrift für Philosophische Forschung* (Reutlingen), vol. 2, 1947, 587-596.

1442   Bollnow, Otto Friedrich. *Das Wesen der Stimmungen.* 1st ed. 1941. Expanded 2nd ed. Frankfurt, 1943, x-255, passim.

1443   Bollnow, Otto Friedrich. "Existentialismus und Ethik." *Die Sammlung,* vol. 4, 1949, 321-335; *Actas del primer Congreso nacional de Filosofia* (Mendoza), vol. 2, 1949, 723-728.

1444   Bollnow, Otto Friedrich. "Heideggers neue Kehre." *Zeitschrift für Religions-und Geistesgeschichte* (Erlangen), vol. 2, 1949/50, 113-128.

1445   Bollnow, Otto Friedrich. "Der Begriff des Heilen." *Situation. Beiträge zur phänomenologischen Psychologie und Psychopathologie* (Utrecht-Antwerpen), 1954, 15-25, (specifically pages 20-21).

1446   Bollnow, Otto Friedrich. "Die Tugend der Hoffnung. Eine Auseinandersetzung mit dem Existenzialismus." *Universitas* (Stuttgart), vol. 10, 1955, 153-164.

1447    Bollnow, Otto Friedrich. *Philosophie der Erkenntnis.*
        (Stuttgart/Berlin/Köln/Mainz), 1970, 160 p., (specifically pages 44-51).

1448    Bollnow, Otto Friedrich. "The Objectivity of the Humanities and the Essence
        of Truth." *Philosophy Today* (Celina, Ohio), vol. 18, 1974, 3-18.

1449    Bollnow, Otto Friedrich. "Zur Gesamtausgabe der Werke Martin Heideggers.
        Anlässlich des ersten erschienenen Bandes." *Universitas* (Stuttgart), vol. 31,
        no. 8, 1976, 827-833.

1450    Bollnow, Otto Friedrich. "Gespräche in Davos." In *Erinnerung an Martin
        Heidegger.* Ed. Günther Neske. Pfullingen: Verlag Günther Neske, 1977,
        25-29.

1451    Bondy, François. "Zum Thema, Martin Heidegger und die Politik." *Merkur*
        (Stuttgart), vol. 22, Heft 1/2, no. 238, 1968, 189-192.

1452    Bondy, François, ed. "Une lettre de Heidegger à François Bondy." *Critique*
        (Paris), vol. 24, 1968, 433-435.
        [Remarks on "A propos de Heidegger," by F. Fédier. 1967.]

1453    Bondy, François. "Prophet in Frankreich." *Weltwoche* (Zürich) vol. 22, June
        2, 1976, 2, (3, no. 2, 1976).

1454    Bonetti, A. Rev. of *Dell'essenza della verità,* by Martin Heidegger. Milano,
        1952. *Rivista di Filosofia Neo-Scolastica* (Milano), vol. 44, 1952, 371-372.

1455    Bonilla, A. "El pensiamento estetico de Martin Heidegger." *Revista de la
        Universidad de Costa Rica* (San José, Costa Rica), vol. 16, 1958, 53-62.

1456    Bonomi, G. *I grandi sistemi filosofici nella storia del pensiero. Vol. III:
        Movimenti filosofici dei secoli XIX-XX.* Milano, 1953, 377-386.

1457    Bontadini, G. "L posizione dell'esistenzialismo nella filosofia
        contemporanea." *Atti del congresso internazionale di filosofia, promosso
        dell'Istituto di Studi Filosofici, Roma 15-20 novembre 1946. II:
        L'esistenzialismo.* (Milano), 1948, 113-128 uö.

1458    Bonvecchio, C. Rev. of *La dottrina delle categorie e del significato in Duns
        Scoto,* by Martin Heidegger. Ed. Albino Babolin. (Piccola biblioteca
        filosofica Laterza, 92). Roma-Bari: Laterza, 1974, xxvi-261 p. *Rivista
        internazionale di filosofia del Diritto* (Milano), vol. 53, 1976, 305-6.

1459    Borello, Oreste. "Aspetti del naturalismo antologico di Heidegger." *Teoresi,*
        vol. 31, January-June 1976, 67-95.

1460    Borgmann, Albert. "The Transformation of Heidegger's Thought." *The
        Personalist* (Los Angeles), vol. 47, 1966, 484-499.

1461    Borgmann, Albert. "Philosophy and the Concern for Man." *Philosophy Today*
        (Celina, Ohio), vol. 10, 1966, 236-246.

1462    Borgmann, Albert. "Language in Heidegger's Philosophy." *The Journal of
        Existentialism* (New York), vol. 7, 1966/67, 161-180.

1463    Borgmann, Albert. "Heidegger and Symbolic Logic." In *Heidegger and the
        Quest for Truth.* Ed. M. S. Frings. Chicago, 1968, 139-162.

1464    Borgmann, Albert. "Heidegger and Symbolic Logic." In *Heidegger and Modern Philosophy. Critical Essays.* Ed. Michael Murray. New Haven, Connecticut: Yale Univ. Press, 1978, 3-22.

1465    Bork, Egon. *Language and Heidegger.* Maschinenschrift. Edmonton, Alberta, 1967, 147 p.

1466    Bork, Egon. "Heidegger's 'Frage nach der Technik'." Phil. Diss. The Univ. of Alberta 1976.

1467    Bornheim, Gerd A. "Hegel e o problema da tese do processo dialético." *Revista Brasileira de Filosofia* (Sao Paulo), vol. 20, 1970, 401-419.

1468    Bornheim, Gerd A. *M. Heidegger. L'être et le temps.* Paris: Hatier, 1976, 95 p.

1469    Bornkamm, H. "Die Sendung der deutschen Universitäten in der Gegenwart." *Volk im Werden* (Leipzig), vol. 2, 1934, 25-35.

1470    Borrello, Oreste. *L'Estetica dell'esistenzialismo.* Messina/Firenze, 1956, 327 p.

1471    Borrello, Oreste. "Aspetti del naturalismo ontologico di Heidegger." *Teoresi* (Catania), vol. 31, 1976, 67-95.

1472    Borrello, Oreste. "Sull-ontologismo psicolinguistico di Heidegger." *Teoresi Catania), vol. 32, 1977, 293-312.*

1473    Borrello, Oreste. "Le variazioni linguistico sociologiche del permanente in Heidegger." *Rassegna di Scienze filosofiche* (Napoli), vol. 30, no. 2-3, 1977, 66-90.

1474    Borzaga, Reynold. *Contemporary Philosophy. Phenomenological and Existential Currents.* Milwaukee, 1966, XXV, 290 p.

1475    Bosch, R. "La estética de Heidegger." *Revista de filosofia* (Madrid), vol. 13, 1954, 271-289.

1476    Boss, Medard. "Die Bedeutung der Daseinsanalyse für die Psychologie und Psychiatrie." *Psyche* (Stuttgart), vol. 6, 1952/53, 178-186. (Vortrag innerhalb der RIAS-Funk-universität am 25.2.1952).

1477    Boss, Medard. *Psychoanalyse und Daseinsanalytik.* Bern, 1957, 155 p., passim.

1478    Boss, Medard. "Martin Heidegger und die Ärzte." In *Martin Heidegger zum 70. Geburtstag (26.IX.59) Festschrift.* Pfullingen, 1959, 276-290.

1479    Boss, Medard. "Ein Freundesbrief. An Martin Heidegger." *Neue Zürcher Zeitung.* No. 606, v.5.10.1969, 52.

1480    Boss, Medard. "Martin Heidegger." In *Martin Heidegger im Gespräch.* Ed. R. Wisser. Freiburg/München, 1970, 20-22.

1481    Boss, Medard. *Grundriss der Medizin.* Bern/Stuttgart/Wien, 1971, 599 p.

1482    Boss, Medard. "Zollikoner Seminare." In *Erinnerung an Martin Heidegger.* Ed. Günther Neske. Pfullingen: Verlag Günther Neske, 1977, 31-45.

1483    Boss, Medard. "Martin Heidegger's Zollikon Seminars." *Review of Existential Psychology & Psychiatry* (Northwestern Univ. Evanston), vol. 16, nos. 1, 2, and 3, 1978/9.

1484    Bossart, William H. "Heidegger's Theory of Art." *Journal of Aesthetics and Art Criticism* (Baltimore), vol. 27, 1968/69, 57-66.

1485    Bossert, Philip J. "The Explication of the World in Constructionalism and Phenomenology." *Man and World* (The Hague), vol. 6, 1973, 231-247.

1486    Bossert, Philip J. "A Note on Heidegger's 'Opus One'." *The Journal of the British Society for Phenomenology* (Manchester), vol. 4, 1973, 61-63.

1487    Botelho, Afonso. "Martin Heidegger. In Memoriam." *Revista Brasileira de Filosofia* (Sao Paulo), vol. 26, 1976, 364-66.

1488    Bouckaert, Luk. "Het zijnsdenken en de ethiek. Enkele beschouwingen over de kritiek van E. Levinas op M. Heidegger." *Bijdragen. Tijdschrift voor filosofie en theologie* (Nijmegen), vol. 32, 1970, 313-328.

1489    Bouckaert, Luk. "Ontology and Ethics: Reflections on Levinas' Critique of Heidegger." *International Philosophical Quarterly* (New York), vol. 10, no. 3, 1970, 402-419.

1490    Bouckaert, Luk. "De uitgangspunten van de filosofie van E. Levinas." *Tijdschrift voor Filosofie* (Leuven), vol. 34, 1972, 680-702.

1491    Bouffard, Albert. "Language and the Ontological Difference. Heidegger's Quest for an Experience With Authentic Language." Phil. Diss. Duquesne Univ. 1970. Ann Arbor, Michigan: University Microfilms, 1977, v-309 p. *Dissertation Abstracts International,* vol. 32/01-A, 482.

1492    Bourdieu, Pierre. "L'ontologie politique de Martin Heidegger." *Actes de la Recherche en Sciences Sociales* (Paris), no. 5-6, 1975, 109-56.

1493    Bourdieu, Pierre. *Die politische Ontologie Martin Heideggers.* Trans. from French by Bernd Schwibs. Appendix: "Heidegger der Unumgängliche," by Jean Bollack and Heinz Wismann. Frankfurt: Syndikat, 1976, 120 p.

1494    Bourel, Dominique. "La leçon de Martin Heidegger." *Documents. Revue des Questions Allemands* (Strasbourg-Neudorf), no. 4-5, 1976, 77-80.

1495    Borrel, J.-R. "Malraux et la pensée allemande de 1921 à 1949." *Revue des Lettres Modernes* (Paris), no. 425-431, 1975, 103-34.

1496    Bowman, Leonard J. "Bonaventure's Contuition and Heidegger's Thinking. Some Parallels." *Franciscan Studies* (St. Bonaventure), vol. 37, 1977, 18-31.

1497    Boxtel, J. J. P. van. *Waarde-Ethiek en Zijnsleer.* Nijmegen/Utrecht, 1948, 24 p.

1498    Braido, P. "L'umanesimo ontologico di M. Heidegger contro l'umanesimo esistenzialistico di J. P. Sartre." *Salesianum* (Torino), vol. 14, 1952, 1-25.

1499    Brajovic, S. M. "Ob odnoj popytke sblizenija marksizma i ekzistencializma." *Voprosy filosofii* (Moskau), vol. 7, 1971, 39-47.

        [An attempt of reconciliation between marxism and existentialism.]

1500    Brajovic, S. M. "Angesichts eines Versuchs, Marxismus und Existentialismus einander anzunähern." *Voprosy filosofii* (Moskau), vol. 7, 1971, 39-47.

        [English abstract, 185.]

1501     Brand, G. *Die Lebenswelt. Eine Philosophie des konkreten Apriori.* Berlin, 1971, XXXVI, 651 p.

         [Rev. by L. B. Geiger in *Freiburger Zeitschrift für Philosophie und Theologie* (Freiburg), vol. 86, 1972, 152-153.]

1502     Brandao, A. J. "A caminho de um novo direito natural?" *Revista Portuguesa de Filosofia* (Braga), vol. 4, 1945, 377-385.

1503     Brandao, A. J. "Martinho Heidegger." *Rumo* (Lissabon), vol. 2, 1946, 275-278.

1504     Braque, George. "Widmung." *Martin Heidegger zum 70. Geburtstag. Festschrift.* Pfullingen, 1959, 173.

1505     Braun, C. "Ritual des Denkens. Kritische Anmerkungen zu Martin Heideggers 80. Geburtstag." *Die Weltwoche,* no. 37, v.26.9.1969, 69.

1506     Brecht, F. J. Rev. of *Kant und das Problem der Metaphysik,* by Martin Heidegger. Bonn, 1929. *Literarischer Handweiser für das katholische Deutschland* (Freiburg), vol. 66, 1930, 30.

1507     Brecht, F. J. "Die Situatin der Gegenwärtigen Philosophie." *Neue Jahrbücher für Wissenschaft und Jugendbildung* (Berlin), vol. 6, 1930, 42-58, (specifically page 55 ff).

1508     Brecht, F. J. *Bewusstsein und Existenz. Wesen und Weg der Phänomenologie.* Bremen, 1948, 170 p., (specifically pages 114-160 u.ö.).

1509     Brecht, F. J. *Heidegger und Jaspers. Die beiden Grundformen der Existenzphilosophie.* Wuppertal, 1948, 34 p.

1510     Brecht, F. J. *Einführung in die Philosophie der Existenz.* Heidelberg, 1948, (specifically pages 105-174).

1511     Brecht, F. J. "Martin Heidegger un die Frage nach dem Sein." *Deutsche Zeitung und Wirtschaftszeitung* (Stuttgart), Jg. 4, no. 76, 1949, 11.

1512     Brecht, F. J. *Vom lebendigen Geist des Abendlandes. Aufsätze und Vorträge.* Wuppertal, 1949, (specifically pages 406-436: Heidegger und Jaspers. Zusammenhang und Differenz von Existenzialontologie und Existenzerhellung).

1513     Brechtken, J. "Geschichtliche Transzendenz bei Heidegger. Die Hoffnugsstruktur des Daseins und die gott-lose Gottesfrage." *Monographien zur philosophischen Forschung* (Meisenheim), vol. 99, 1972, 142 p.

1514     Brechtken, J. "Geschichte und Transzendenz oder die Gottesfrage am Ende der Metaphysik." *Tijdschrift voor Filosofie* (Leuven), vol. 39, no. 4, 1977, 587-609.

1515     Breek, B. *Critische existentiephilosophie en christelijk geloof.* Assen, 1953, 172 p.

1516     Breek, B. "Heidegger en de ethiek." *Nederlands theologisch Tijdschrift* (Wageningen), vol. 13, 1958-59, 190-205.

1517　　Breek, B. "Martin Heidegger en de ethiek." In *Handelingen van het vijfentwintigste nederlands filologencongres gehouden te Leiden op Donderdag 10 en vrijdag 11 April 1958.* Groningen, 1958, 89-90.

1518　　Bréhier, E. *Histoire de la philosophie allemande.* 3rd ed. Paris, 1954, 239-258, und passim.

1519　　Brelage, M. *Studien zur Transzendentalphilosophie.* Ed. Aenne Brelage. Berlin, 1965, XI, 256 p., (specifically pages 188-229).

1520　　Breton, Stonisau. "From Phenomenology to Ontology." *Philosophy Today* (Celina, Ohio), vol. 4, 1960, 227-237.

1521　　Bretschneider, W. "Sein und Wahrheit Über d. Zusammengehörigkeit von Sein und Wahrheit im Denken Martin Heideggers." *Monographien z. philosophischen Forschung* (Meisenheim/Glan), vol. 37, 1965, 201.

1522　　Bretschneider, W. "'Über-Seiendes' und 'Sein', Ein Vergleich zwischen Eugen Bisers und Martin Heideggers Nietzsche Interpretation." *Philosophisches Jahrbuch* (Freiburg), vol. 77, 1970, 147-156.

1523　　Bretschneider, W. Rev. of *Nietzsche. Bd I-II,* by Martin Heidegger. Pfullingen: Neske, 1961, 661 and 492 p. *Philosophisches Jahrbuch* (München), vol. 77, 1970, 147-56.

1524　　Bridges, Thomas William. "The Concept of Meaning in Heidegger's *Sein und Zeit.*" Authorized facsimile of the Columbia Univ. Phil. Diss. 1972. Ann Arbor, Michigan: University Microfilms International, 1977, iii-230 p. *Dissertation Abstracts International,* vol. 35/10-A, 6757.

1525　　Brinkmann, C. Rev. of *Sein and Zeit,* by Martin Heidegger. Halle, 1927. *Kant-Studien* (Berlin), vol. 34, 1929, 209.

1526　　Brinkmann, D. "Existentialismus und Tiefenpsychologie." *Actas del primer Congreso nacional de Filosofia* (Mendoza), vol. 2, 1949, 1346-1360, passim.

1527　　Briod, Marc E. "The Primacy of Discourse in Determining the Sense of Heidegger's Authenticity: Ground for a Sensitive Education." Phil. Diss. Evanston, Illinois. Chicago, 1968, 249 p. *Dissertation Abstracts International,* vol. 29/10-A, 3635.

1528　　Brissoni, A. "Piccola memoria sull'esistenzialismo." *Rivista di Studi Crociani* (Napoli), vol. 11, no. 2, 1974, 191-201.

1529　　Brito, E. "Hegel y las estéticas." *Revista Latino-Americano de Filosofia* (Buenos Aires), vol. 4, no. 3, 1978, 213-54.

　　　　 [Summary in English]

1530　　Brock, Werner. *An Introduction to Contemporary German Philosophy.* Cambridge, 1935, 109-117.

1531　　Brock, Werner. "Introduction." In *Existence and Being,* by Martin Heidegger. London, 1949. 2nd ed. 1956, 13-19.

1532　　Brock, Werner. "A Brief Outline of the Career of M. Heidegger." In *Existence and Being,* by M. Heidegger. London, 1949. 2nd ed. 1956, 20-24.

1533    Brock, Werner. "An Account of Being and Time; 1. The Three Main Problems: Dasein, Time and Being. The projekt and the Published Version; 2. Some Aspects of the Analysis of Dasein; 3. Dasein and Temporality; 4. Some Reflections on the Significance of the Work." In *Existence and Being,* by Martin Heidegger. London, 1949. 2nd ed. 1956, 25-131.

1534    Brock, Werner. "An Account of 'The Four Essays'; 1. A Brief General Characterisation of the Four Essays; 2. On the Essence of Truth; 3. The Essay on Friedrich Hölderlin; 4. What is Metaphysics?" In *Existence and Being,* by Martin Heidegger. London, 1949. 2nd ed. 1956, 132-248.

1535    Brockard, Hans. Rev. of *Durchblicke. Martin Heidegger Zum 80. Geburtstag.* Frankfurt: Vittorio Klostermann, 1970. *Philosophisches Jahrbuch* (München), vol. 18, 1971, 221-28.

1536    Bröcker, Walter. "Über die geschichtliche Notwendigkeit der Heideggerschen Philosophie." *Actas del primer Congreso nacional de Filosofia* (Mendoza), vol. 2, 1949, 998-1004.

1537    Bröcker, Walter. "Der Mythos vom Baum der Erkenntnis." *Anteile, Martin Heidegger zum 60. Geburtstag.* Frankfurt, 1950, 29-50.

1538    Bröcker, Walter. "Heidegger und die Logik." In *Einführung in die Metaphysik,* by Martin Heidegger. Tübingen, 1953. *Philosophische Rundschau* (Tübingen), vol. 1, 1953-54, 48-56. (Auch als Sonderdruck).

1539    Bröcker, Walter. *Dialektik, Positivismus, Mythologie.* Frankfurt, 1958, 113 p.

1540    Bröcker, Walter. "Zu Hölderlins ]dipus-Deutung." In *Martin Heidegger zum 70. Geburtstag. Festschrift.* Pfullingen, 1959, 19-23.

1541    Bröcker, Walter. *Auseinandersetzungen mit Hegel.* Frankfurt, 1965, 57 p., (specifically pages 7-32: Hegel zwischen Kant und Heidegger).

1542    Bröcker, Walter. "Heidegger und die Logik." In *Heidegger.* Ed. O. Pöggeler. Köln/Berlin, 1969, 298-304. Früher erschienen in: Philosophische Rundschau, 1953/54.

1543    Bröcker, Walter. "Heideggers Hören auf das Sprechen der Sprache." In *Materialien zur Geschichte der Philosophie.* Frankfurt, 1972, 38 p.

1544    Bröcker, Walter. "Rückblick auf die Existenzphilosophie." *Philosophische Perspektiven* (Frankfurt/Main), vol. 4, 1972, 191-197.

1545    Bröcker, Walter. "Rückblick auf Heidegger." *Allgemeine Zeitschrift für Philosophie* (Stuttgart), vol. 2, 1977, 24-28.

1546    Brod, M. "Kierkegaard - Heidegger - Kafka." *Prisma, 1, H.11* (München), 1947, 17-20.

1547    Brod, M. *Das Unzerstörbare.* Stuttgart, 1968, 240 p., (specifically pages 144-154).

1548    Brown, R. H. "Bibliographie on Martin Heidegger." In *Existentialism, a Bibliography. The Modern Schoolman,* XXXI, 1953/54, 19-33. (22-24).

1549    Brown, J. *Kierkegaard, Heidegger, Buber and Barth. Subject and Object in Modern Theology.* (Croall lectures, 1953) (New York, 1962, 192 p.).

1550    Brown Jr., Wilson George. "An Inquiry Into the Question About Truth and
        Sense in the Thinking of Heidegger and Aristotle." Phil. Diss. Pennsylvania
        State Univ. 1978. *Dissertation Abstracts International,* vol. 39/12-A, 7376,
        386 p.

1551    Brück, M. V. "Was sollen wir tun? Eine Betrachtung zu Heideggers
        'Holzwege'." *Die Gegenwart* (Freiburg), Jg. 5, no. 3, 1950, 19-20.

1552    Brüning, W. "La filosofia de la historia en Husserl y Heidegger." *Humanitas*
        (Tucumán), vol. 7, 1959, 65-78.

1553    Brüning, W. "Existencialismo e historia." *Arbor* (Madrid), vol. 49, 1961,
        23-22.

1554    Brunner, A. "Die Entwertung des Seins in der Existentialphilosophie."
        *Scholastik* (Eupen), vol. 12, 1937, 233-238.

1555    Brunner, A. "Ursprung und Grundzüge der Existentialphilosophie."
        *Scholastik* (Eupen), vol. 13, 1938, 173-205, passim.

1556    Brunner, A. "Filosofia existencialistica." *Revista Portuguesa de Filosofia*
        (Braga), vol. 8, 1952, 379-412, (specifically pages 385-391).

1557    Brunner, A. "Die Rückkehr ins Sein. Martin Heideggers Weg." *Stimmen der
        Zeit* (Freiburg), vol. 154, 1953-54, 401-414.

1558    Brunner, A. "'Das Ding dingt die Welt'. Zur Philosophie Martin Heideggers."
        *Stimmen der Zeit* (Freiburg), vol. 156, 1954/55, 59-72.

1559    Brunner, A. Rev. of *Der Satz vom Grund,* by Martin Heidegger. Pfullingen,
        1957. *Stimmen der Zeit* (Freiburg), vol. 163, 1958/59, 313.

1560    Brunner, E. "Theologie und Ontologie - oder die Theologie am Scheidewege."
        *Zeitschrift für Theologie und Kirche* (Tübingen), N.F. 12, 1931, 111-222,
        passim.

1561    Brunner, E. "Theologie und Ontologie oder die Theologie am Scheidewege."
        *Heidegger und die Theologie. Beginn und Fortgang der Diskussion.* Ed. G.
        Noller. München, 1967, 125-135.

1562    Brusco, P. "Inhospitalidad del ser-en-el-mundo y temporalidad del Dasein en
        Heidegger." *Revista de Humanidades* (Cordoba), vol. 6, 1963, 138-147.

1563    Bruyne, E. De. "De philosophie van Martin Heidegger." *Tijdschrift voor
        Philosophie* (Leuven), vol. 4, 1942, 581-586.

1564    Bruzina, Ronald. "Heidegger on the Metaphor and Philosophy." *Cultural
        Hermeneutics* (Dordrecht), vol. 1, 1974, 305-24.

1565    Bruzina, Ronald. "Heidegger on the Metaphor and Philosophy." In *Heidegger
        and Modern Philosophy. Critical Essays.* Ed. Michael Murray. New Haven,
        Connecticut: Yale Univ. Press, 1978, 184-200.

1566    Buber, Martin. "Die Verwirklichung des Menschen. Zur Anthropologie M.
        Heideggers." *Philosophia* (Belgrad), vol. 3, 1938, 289-308.

1567    Buber, Martin. "Religion und modernes Denken." *Merkur* (Stuttgart), vol. 6,
        1952, 101-120, passim.

1568    Buber, Martin. "Geltung und Grenzen des politischen Prinzips." *Hinweise* (Zürich), 1953, 330-346, (specifically pages 339-341).

1569    Buber, Martin. *Das Problem des Menschen.* 4th ed. Heidelberg, 1971, 172 p., (specifically pages 99 ff).

1570    Buber, Martin. "Ostvarenje coveka." Trans. Danilo Basta. In *Rani Hajdeger - Recepcija i Kritika.* Eds. Dragan Stojanovic and Danilo Basta. *Bivstva i vremena* (Biblioteka Zokijak) (Beograd), 1979, 7-25.

1571    Bubnoff, N. V. Rev. of *Holzwege,* by Martin Heidegger. Frankfurt, 1950. *Universitas* (Stuttgart), vol. 6, 1951, 905-906.

1572    Bucceri, A. "La metafisica di Heidegger." *Rivista di Filosofia Neo-Scolastica* (Milano), vol. 38, 1946, 38-51.

1573    Buchana, James Henry. "Heidegger and the Problem of Ground. An Evaluation." *Philosophy Today* (Celina, Ohio), vol. 17, 1973, 232-45.

1574    Buchanan, James Henry. "Ground as Unity and Primordial Ground in the Thought of Martin Heidegger." Phil. Diss. Pennsylvania State Univ. 1970. Ann Arbor, Michigan: University Microfilms, 1977, iv-127 p. *Dissertation Abstracts International,* vol. 32/02-A, 1009.

1575    Buchdahl, Gerd. Rev. of *Heidegger, Kant and Time,* by Charles M. Sherover. Introd. by William Barrett. Bloomington, London, 1971. *Isis* (Cambridge, Massachusetts), vol. 63, 1972, 369-70.

1576    Buchenau, A. Rev. of *Kant und das Problem der Metaphysik,* by Martin Heidegger. Bonn, 1929. *Die Deutsche Schule* (Leipzig), vol. 33, 1928, 178.

1577    Buchenau, A. Rev. of *Was ist Metaphysik?,* by Martin Heidegger. Bonn, 1929. *Geistes-Kultur* (Berlin), vol. 42, 1933, 29.

1578    Bucher, A. J. "Martin Heidegger. Metaphysikkritik als Begriffsproblematik." *Mainzer philosophische Forschungen* (Bonn), vol. 14, 1972, XII, 263 p.
        [Rev. by G. Haeffer in *Philosophisches Jahrbuch* (Freiburg/München), vol. 80, 1973, 433-435,]
        [Rev. by W. Simonis in *Theologie und Philosophie* (Freiburg/Basel/Wien), vol. 48, 1973, 419-423.]

1579    Buchner, Hartmut. "Heidegger and Christianity." *Risô* [Japanese] (Tôkyô), vol. 319, Dezember 1959.

1580    Buchner, Hartmut. "Kotoba ni tsuite no Haideggâ no Ron-Kyu" (Heidegger's Discussion of Language). *Kansaigakuin-Tetsugakukenkyûnenpô* (Nishinomiya), November 1961.

1581    Buchner, Hartmut. "Fragmentarisches." In *Erinnerung an Martin Heidegger.* Ed. Günther Neske. Pfullingen: Verlag Günther Neske, 1977, 47-51.

1582    Buchner, Hartmut. "Heidegger-Gesamtausgabe: Letter to the Editor." *Frankfurter Allgemeine Zeitung* (Frankfurt), 25 November 1978.

1583    Buckley, Frank M. "The Everyday Struggle for the Leisurely Attitude." *Humanitas* (Pittsburgh), vol. 8, 1972, 307-321.

1584    Buddeberg, E. *Heidegger und die Dichtung. Hölderlin, Rilke.* Stuttgart, 1953.

[Rev. by W. Stembeck in *Philosophischer Literaturanzeiger* (München), vol. 7, 1954/55, 166-170; Offprint of *Deutsche Vierteljahresschrift für Literaturwissenschaft und Geistesgeschichte* (Tübingen), vol. 26 and 27, 1952 and 1953, 68 p.]

1585   Buddeberg, E. "Heideggers Rilkedeutung." *Deutsche Vierteljahresschrift für Literaturwissenschaft und Geistesgeschichte* (Tübingen), vol. 27, 1953, 387-412.

1586   Buddeberg, E. *Denken und dichten des Seins. Heidegger, Rilke.* Stuttgart, 1956, 210 p.

[Rev. by J. Allemann in *Euphorion* (Heidelberg), vol. 51, 1957, 335-337.]

1587   Bürkle, H. "Dialektisches Zeitverständnis und existentialer Zeitbegriff. Eine Untersuchung über die Beziehung zwischen der frühen dialektischen Theologie Karl Barths und der Ontologie Martin Heideggers." Phil. Diss. Hamburg 1957 236 p.

1588   Buess, E. "Die Philosophie Martin Heideggers und ihre theologische Deutung." In *Denken und Sein,* by H. Ott. Zolikon, 1959. *Kirchenblatt für die reformierte Schweiz* (Basel), vol. 116, 1960, 340-345.

1589   Buggle, H. "Der Begrif der 'Zeit'," by Victor V. Weizsäcker und Martin Heidegger. "Eine vergleichende Untersuchuntung zur Grundlagenforschung der medizinischen Anthropologie." Phil. Diss. Heidelberg 1964 76 Bl.

1590   Buhr, Heinrich. "Der weltliche Theolog." In *Erinnerung an Martin Heidegger.* Ed. Günther Neske. Pfullingen: Verlag Günther Neske, 1977, 53-59.

1591   Buhr, Heinrich, and Erika Reichle. "Vor der Gemeinde als vor dem lieben Gott." In *Erinnerung an Martin Heidegger.* Ed. Günther Neske. Pfullingen: Verlag Günther Neske, 1977, 59-63.

1592   Buhr, M., and G. Klaus, eds. *Philosophisches Wörterbuch.* 6th ed. 2 vol. Leipzig, 1969, (specifically page 1198).

1593   Bultmann. *Die Religion in Geschichte und Gegenwart.* 2nd ed. Vol. 2. Tübingen, 1928. *Handwörterbuch für Theologie und Religionswissenschaft,* (specifically pages 1687-1688).

1594   Burgert, H. Rev. of *Kant und das Problem der Metaphysik,* by Martin Heidegger. Bonn, 1929. *Germania* (Berlin), vol. 17, no. 5, 1930.

1595   Burgert, H. Rev. of *Vorträge und Aufsätze,* by Martin Heidegger. Pfullingen, 1954. *Die Zeichen der Zeit, Evangelische Monatsschrift* (Berlin), vol. 9, 1955, 400.

1596   Burgert, H. "Heidegger und Russell. Gegensätzliche Aspekte westlicher Philosophie." *Zeichen der Zeit. Evangelische Monatsschrift für Mitarbeiter der Kirche* (Berlin), vol. 14, 1960, 270-276.

1597   Burska, F., and Irena Krónska. "Heidegger osiemdziesiecioletni" (The Eighty Year Old Heidegger). *Twórczoáá,* December 1969.

1598 Busche, Jürgen. "Der Denker des Jahrhunderts, Zum Tod des Philosophen Martin Heidegger." *Frankfurter Allgemeine Zeitung* (Frankfurt), vol. 114, 28 May 1976, 1 and 25.

1599 Busche, Jürgen. "Der Denker des Jahrhunderts. Zum Tod des Philosophen Martin Heidegger." In *Fragen an sein Werk. Ein Symposium,* by Martin Heidegger, (Universal-Bibliothek), 9873. Stuttgart: Reclam, 1977, 5-15.

1600 Busche, Jürgen. "Wie lesbar darf ein Philosoph sein? Zum Streit um die Heidegger-Gesamtausgabe." *Frankfurter Allgemeine Zeitung* (Frankfurt), 21 October 1978.

1601 Bushkovitch, Maureen Lorna. "The Historical Dimension in Heidegger's Thought." Authorized facsimile of the New School for Social Research. Phil. Diss. 1977. Ann Arbor, Michigan; London: University Microfilms International, 1979, iv-201 p. *Dissertation Abstracts International,* vol. 38/09-A, 5518. [HGK78-00609]

1602 Busse, Guenther. "War Heidegger regimetren? Bemerkungen zu dem Aufsatz 'Wege zu Aussprache' ous dem Jahre 1937." *Philosophisches Jahrbuch,* 1980, 117 ff.

1603 Bussmann, L. *Der Gewissensbegriff bei Martin Heidegger und Karl Jaspers.* Phil. Diss. Würzburg 1951 102 p.

1604 Butchvarov, Penayot. *Being Qua Being. A Theory of Identity, Existence, and Predication.* Bloomington: Indiana Univ. Press, 1979.

1605 Butkus, Robert George John. *Heidegger's Thought and Ethics.* Phil. Diss. Univ. of Waterloo (Canada) 1976. *Dissertation Abstracts International,* vol. 37/06-A, 3688.

1606 Bychovskij, B. *Main Currents of Modern Idealistic Philosophy* (In Russian). Moscow, 1957, (34 f. on Heidegger; Rpt. in *Nachlese zu Heidegger,* by G. Scheeberger. Bern 1962, 268-269).

1607 Byrum, Charles Stephen. "Philosophy as Play." *Man and World* (West Lafayette), vol. 8, no. 3, 1975, 315-326.

1608 C., A.P. de. Rev. of *Zur Seinsfrage,* by Martin Heidegger. *Kriterion* (Belo Horizonte), 11, 1958, no. 43-44, 314-315.

1609 Caba, P. "La nada y la angustia." *Cuadernos Hispano-americanos* (Madrid), vol. 27, 1952, 410-418.

1610 Cabado Castro, M. *Sein und Gott bei G. Siewerth.* Düsseldorf, 1971, 342 p.

1611 Cadin, F. "Imperturbabilita e turbamento in Martin Heidegger. Commento alla 'Gelassenheit' heideggeriana." *Rivista di Filosofia Neo-Scolastica* (Milano), vol. 54, 1962, 552-584.

1612 Cady, Frank Cullison. *The Unitary Phenomen: The Phenomenology of Martin Heidegger and the Poetry of Ezar Pound, William Carlos Williams and Charles Olson.* Modern Language and Literature. Phil. Diss. Stanford Univ. 1973. *Dissertation Abstracts International,* vol. 33/12-A, 6903.

1613 Cahú, M. *Filosofijá otcajanija i stracha. Ekzistencializm.* Tiblissi, 1962, 128 p.

1614    Caleo, M. Rev. of "La dottrina delle categorie e del significato in Duns Scoto," by Martin Heidegger. Ed. Albino Babolin. (Piccola biblioteca filosofica Laterza, 92). Roma-Bari: Laterza, 1974, xxyi-261 p. *Rassegna di Scienze filosofiche* (Napoli), vol. 28, 1975, 114-115.

1615    Calin, M. D. *Filosofija otcajanija i stracha?* (The Philosophy of Despair and Fear). Gospolitizdat, Moskva 1962, 128 p.

1616    Calin, M. L. "V plenu individualizma" (Captured by Individualism). In *Izdatel'stvo 'Mysl'.* Moskva, 1966.

1617    Calin, M. L. "Ekzistencializm kak sistema mirovozzrenija" (Existentialism as the System of Ideology). In *Avtoreferat dissertacii na soiskanie ucĕnoj stepeni doktora filosofskich nauk.* Moskva, 1969.

1618    Calogero, C. "L'intramontabile." *Cultura* (Rom), vol. 9, 1971, 543-545.

1619    Calogero, G. "Leggendo Heidegger." *Rivista di Filosofia Neo-Scolastica* (Milano), vol. 41, 1950, 136-149.

1620    Caltofen, R. "Martin Heidegger und die bretonische Bäuerin." *Die Anregung* (Köln), vol. 6, 1954, 257-258.

1621    Camele, A. "Martin Heidegger and Meaning for Man." *Listening* (Dubuque, Iowa), vol. 1, 1966, 140-149.

1622    Camele, Anthony M. "Time in Merleau-Ponty and Heidegger." *Philosophy Today,* vol. 19, Fall 1975, 256-268.

1623    Camele, Anthony M. "Heideggerian Ethics." *Philosophy Today* (Celina, Ohio), vol. 21, no. 3-4, 1977, 284-93.

1624    Camón-Aznar, J. "El tiempo en Heidegger y su versión artistica." *Cuadernos Hispanoamericanos* (Madrid), vol. 33, 1958, no. 97, 5-18.

1625    Campbell, R. "Sur une interprétation de Parménide par Heidegger." *Revue internationale de philosophie* (Bruxelles), vol. 5, 1951, 390-399.

1626    Campbell, R. *L'esistenzialismo. S. Kierkegaard, K. Jaspers, G. Marcel, M. Heidegger, J.P. Sartre.* Napoli, Ed. Rocco, 1955, 150 p.

1627    Campbell, R. "Sur 'L'introduction à la métaphysique' de Heidegger." *Etudes germaniques* (Paris), vol. 15, 1960, 29-43.

1628    Campbell, R. "Martin Heidegger, philosophie de la vérité." *La Revue de Paris* (Paris), vol. 67, no. 2, 1960, 95-106.

1629    Campo, M. "Psicologia, logica e ontologia nel primo Heidegger." *Rivista di filosofia neoscolastica* (Milano), vol. 31, 1939, 474-491.

1630    Campo, A. del. "El trabajo material en la filosofia de Martin Heidegger." *Laye* (Barcelona), vol. 21, 1952, 3-18.

1631    Campo, A. del. "El trabajo material en la filosofia de Martin Heidegger." *Revista dominicana de Filosofia,* 1959, 19-40.

1632    Cancelo, José Luis. "Filosofia y sacerdocio. Texto y contexto de un discurso familiar de Martin Heidegger." *Revista Augustiana de Espiritualidad* (Calahorra), vol. 11, 1970, 409-425.

1633 Cancelo, José Luis. "Reflexiones de Martin Heidegger sobre un agustino (Abraham a Santa Clara)." *Revista Agustiniana de Espiritualidad* (Calahorra), vol. 13, 1972, 33-61.

1634 Cancelo, José Luis. "El optimismo de M. Heidegger." *Revista Agustiniana de Espiritualidad* (Longrono), vol. 16, no. 49-50, 1975, 115-43.

1635 Cancelo, José Luis. "En recuerdo de Martin Heidegger. Un pensar en camino." *Arbor* (Madrid), vol. 96, no. 373, 1977, 21-47.

1636 Candau, J. M. R. *Ser y vida. Analisis fenomenologice de los problemas basicos de la filosofia.* Madrid, 1950, 398 p., (specifically pages 132 ff).

1637 Candáu, J. M. Rubert y. "La función de la filosofi ante el momento histórico actual. Un diálogo con M. Heidegger." *Verdad y Vida* (Madrid), vol. 20, 1962, 433-446.

1638 Capánaga, Victorino. "Martin Heidegger y el P. Abraham de Santa Clara." *Crisis* (Madrid), vol. 21, no. 81, 1974, 89-97.

1639 Caputo, John David. *The Way Back Into the Ground: An Interpretation of the Path of Heidegger's Thought.* Phil. Diss. Bryn Mauwr 1968 384 p. *Dissertation Abstracts International,* A, vol. 29/11-A, 1969, 3046A. *See also* 1654.

1640 Caputo, John David. "Being, Ground and Play in Heidegger." *Man and World* (Pittsburgh), vol. 3, 1970, 26-48.

1641 Caputo, John David. "Heidegger's Original Ethics." *The New Scholasticism* (Washington), vol. 45, 1971, 127-138.

[Rev. of *A Critique of Heidegger's Concept of 'Solicitude',* by R. Weber. Washington, 1968.]

1642 Caputo, John David. "The Rose is Without Why. An Interpretation of the Later Heidegger." *Philosophy Today* (Celina, Ohio), vol. 15, 1971, 3-16.

1643 Caputo, John David. Rev. of *Frühe Schriften,* by Martin Heidegger. Frankfurt: Vittorio Klostermann, 1972, xii-386 p. *Research in Phenomenology* (Pittsburgh), vol. 3, 1973, 147-55.

1644 Caputo, John David. "Time and Being in Heidegger." *The Modern Schoolman* (Saint Louis), vol. 50, 1973, 325-49.

1645 Caputo, John David. "The Problem of Being in Heidegger and the Scholastics." *The Thomist* (Washington), vol. 38, no. 3-4, 1974, 62-91.

1646 Caputo, John David. "Phenomenology, Mysticism and the Grammatica Speculativa. A Study of Heidegger's Habilitationsschrift." *The Journal of the British Society for Phenomenology* (Manchester), vol. 5, 1974, 101-17.

1647 Caputo, John David. "Meister Eckhart and the Later Heidegger: The Mystical Element in Heidegger's Thought, I." *Journal of the History of Philosophy* (Claremont), vol. 12, 1974, 479-494.

1648 Caputo, John David. "Meister Eckhart and the Later Heidegger: The Mystical Element in Heidegger's Thought, II." *Journal of the History of Philosophy* (Claremont), vol. 13, 1975, 61-80.

1649    Caputo, John David. "The Principle of Sufficient Reason. A Study of Heideggerian Self-Criticism." *The Southern Journal of Philosophy* (Memphis), vol. 13, no. 4, 1975, 419-426.

1650    Caputo, John David. Rev. of *M. Heidegger: In Europe and America.* Eds. E. G. Ballard and Charles E. Scott. With contributions by Robert Cooper, Otto Pöggeler, Karl Löwith, et al. The Hague, Martinus Nijhoff, 1973/74, xii-200 p. *Review of Metaphysics* (Washington), vol. 29, 1975/76, 335-336.

1651    Caputo, John David. "The Poverty of Thought. A Reflection on Heidegger and Eckhart." *Listening* (River Forest, Illinois), vol. 12, no. 3, 1977, 84-91.

1652    Caputo, John David. "The Problem of Being in Heidegger and Aquinas." *Thomist,* vol. 41, January 1977, 62-91.

1653    Caputo, John Dovid. "The Question of Being and Transcendental Phenomenology: Reflections on Heidegger's Relationship to Husserl." *Research in Phenomenology* (Pittsburgh), vol. 7, 1977, 84-105.

1654    Caputo, John David. "The Way Back Into the Ground. An Interpretation of the Path of Heidegger's Thought." Phil. Diss. Brynn Mawr College 1968. Ann Arbor, Michigan: University Microfilms Inc., 1977, viii-374 p. *Dissertation Abstracts International,* vol. 29/11-A, 1969, 3046 A.

1655    Caputo, John David. "Fundamental Ontology and the Ontological Difference." *Proceedings of the American Catholic Philosophical Association* (Washington), vol. 51, 1977, 28-35.

1656    Caputo, John David. *The Mystical Element in Heidegger's Thought.* Athens, Ohio: Ohio Univ. Press, 1978, 292 p.

1656a   Caputo, John D. Rev. of "Martin Heidegger. Early Greek Thinging." *Review of Metaphysics* (Washington), vol. 32, 1978/79, 759-760.

1657    Caputo, John David. "Transcendence and the Transcendental in Husserl's Phenomenology." *Philosophy Today,* vol. 23, Fall 1979, 205-16.

1657a   Caputo, John D. "Heidegger's 'Dif-ference' and the Distinction Between Esse and Ens." *International Philosophical Quarterly* (New York), vol. 20, 1980, 161-182.

1657b   Capuzzi, Frank A. "Heraclitus: Fire, Dream, and Oracle." *Heraclitean Fragments.* Ed. John Sallis and Kenneth Maly. Univ. of Alabama Press, 1980, 135-148.

1658    Caracciolo, A. *La struttura dell-essere nel mondo e il modo del Besorgen in Sein und Zeit di Heidegger.* Genova, 1960, 141 p.

1659    Caracciolo, A. "Evento e linguaggio in un recente scritto di Martin Heidegger." Review of *Unterwegs zur Sprache,* by Martin Heidegger. Pfullingen, 1959. *Giornale Critico della Filosofia Italiana* (Firenze), vol. 40, 1961, 222-246.

1660    Caracciolo, A. Rev. of *Essere e tempo. L'essenza del fondamento,* by Martin Heidegger. Torino, 1969. *Proteus* (Roma), vol. 1, 1970, 184-190.

1661    Carcano, P. Filiasi. *Problematica della Filosofia odierna.* Roma-Milano, 1953, 140-142, und passim.

1662 Cardoletti, P. Rev. of *Sentieri interrotti,* by Martin Heidegger. *La Scuola Cattolica* (Varese), vol. 97, 1969, suppl. bibl., 112-113.

1663 Cardoletti, P. Rev. of *Introduzione alla metafisica,* by Martin Heidegger. *La Scuola Cattolica* (Varese), vol. 97, 1969, suppl. bibl., 110-112.

1664 Cardoletti, P. Rev. of *Kant e il problema della metafisica,* by Martin Heidegger. *La Scuola Cattolica* (Varese), vol. 93, Venegono Infer., 1965, 95-97.

1665 Carifi, R. "Nietzsche e bataille." *Nuova Corrente* (Milano), no. 75, 1978, 88-93.

1666 Carlini, A. *Traduzione Commento di 'Dell'essenza della verita' di Heidegger.* Milano, 1952.

1667 Carlini, A. *Il problema del nella metafisica di Heidegger.* In appendice a *Principi metafisici del mondo storico.* Urbino, 1943.

1668 Carlini, A. *Avviamento alla filosofia.* Firenze, 1936, 278-279, passim.

1669 Carlini, A. *Il mito del realismo.* Firenze, 1936, (specifically pages 57 ff, 69 ff, and passim).

1670 Carlini, A. "Introduction." In *Martin Heidegger: Che cos'è la metafisica.* Firenze, 1953.

1671 Carmona, N. F. "La significación social del Ser y el tiempo de Heidegger." *Universitas* (Bogatá), 1955, 15-24.

1672 Carmona, F. "El punto de partida de 'El ser y tiempo' de Heidegger." *Ideas y Valores* (Bogotá), vol. 2, 1951, 159-164.

1673 Carmo Silva, C. H. do. "Nota bibliográfica: Martin Heidegger." *Revista Portuguesa de Filosofia* (Braga), vol. 33, no. 4, 350-373.

1674 Carmo Silva, C. H. do. "O mesmo e a sua indiferença temporal. O paramenidianismo de Heidegger perspectiv a do a partir de *Zeit und Sein.* " *Revista Portuguesa de Filosofia* (Braga), vol. 33, no. 4, 1977, 299-349.

1675 Carnap, Rudolf. "Überwindung der Metaphysik durch logische Analyse der Sprache." *Erkenntnis,* vol. 2, 1932, 219-241.
    [English translation *See* 01676.]

1676 Carnap, Rudolf. "The Overcoming of Metaphysics Through Logical Analysis of Language." Rpt. from *Logical Positivism,* by A. J. Ayer. London, 1959. In *Heidegger and Modern Philosophy. Critical Essays.* Ed. Michael Murray. New Haven, Connecticut: Yale Univ. Press, 1978, 23-34.

1677 Carpio, Adolfo P. "La pregunta por el ser." *Cuadernos de Filosofia* (Buenos Aires), vol. 11, no. 15-16, 1971, 65-104.

1678 Carpio, Adolfo P. "El sentido de la pregunta por el ser segun Heidegger." In *II. Congreso Nacional de Filosofia. Actas.* Vol. II: Simposios, Buenos Aires, 1973, 21-27.

1679 Carrolo, C. A. "Reflexao sobre a fenomenologia. A propósito do 7o do Sein und Zeit de Heidegger." *Revista Portuguesa de Filosofia* (Braga), vol. 24, 1968, 222-224.

1679a    Caracciolo, Alberto. "Heidegger e il problema del nihilismo." *Il pensiero di Martin Heidegger/L'Uomo, un segno* (Milano), vol. 3, no. 1-2, 1979, 19-42.

1680    Carrasco de la Vega, R. *Heidegger y la formulacion de la pregunta por el ser.* Cochabamba. Bolivia, 1964, 25 p.

1681    Cartechini, Sisto. "Pensiero di Heidegger e teologia." *Doctor Communis. Rivista Quadrimestrale della Pontificia Accademia di S. Tommaso* (Cittá del Vaticano), vol. 31, no. 3, 1978, 406-11.

1682    Carvallo, D. *Die ontische Stimme.* Freiburg, 1965, 195 p.

        [Translated from Spainish by M. Preusse.]

1683    Casalone, P. "La filosofia ultima di Heidegger." *Rivista di Filosofia neo-scolastica* (Milano), vol. 50, 1958, 117-137.

1684    Casas, M. G. "Un problema metafisico en Martin Heidegger." *Norte* (Tucumán), vol. 1, 1951, 13-31.

1685    Casañas, Mario. "Oficio de Tinieblas. A propósito de Martin Heidegger y de nuestra época." *Conflicto* (San Salvador), vol. 1, no. 1, 1978, 49-52.

1686    Casares, A. J. "Sobre una valoración del pensamiento de Heidegger." *Universidad* (Santa Fé), no. 33, 1956, 155-171.

1687    Casares, A. J. Rev. of *Introducción a la metafisica,* by Martin Heidegger. *Humanitas* (Tucumán), vol. 3, 1957, 244-252.

1688    Casares, A. J. "La autenticidad existencial." *Humanitas* (Bresica), vol. 9, 1961, 14, 97-104.

1689    Casares, A. J. "Notas sobre tres conceptos fundamentalels de 'Ser y tiempo'." *Diálogos* (Rio Piedras, Puerto Rico), vol. 5, no. 11-12, 1968, 109-129.

1690    Cassirer, A., and Martin Heidegger. *Débat sur le Kantisme et la philosophie* (und andere Texte). Ed. P. Aubenque. Trans. P. Aubenque, P. Quillet and J.M. Fataud. Appendix *Théologie et Philosophie,* by Martin Heidegger. 101-103. Paris, 1972, 134 p.

1691    Cassirer, E. "Remarques sur l'interpretation de Kant proposée par M. Heidegger dans 'Kant et le problème de la métaphysique' ders 'Kant und das Problem der Metaphysik'." *E. Cassirer u. M. Heidegger, Débats sur le Kantisme.* Paris, 1972, 53-84.

        [French trans. of *Kant und das Problem der Metaphysik,* 1931, 1-26.]

1692    Cassirer, E. "Kant und das Problem der Metaphysik." *Kant-Studien* (Berlin), vol. 36, 1931, 1-26.

        [Trans. into Spanish in *Idess y Volones* (Bogatá), no. 48-49, 1977, 105-129.]

1693    Cassirer, T. *Aus meinem Leben mit Ernst Cassirer.* New York, 1950, (specifically pages 165-167).

1694    Castaneda, Hector N. "El lenguaje como factor de integración dei hombre y el mundo." *Revista del Maestro,* 11-12, 1948/49, 130-138.

1695    Castanos de Médicis, St. *Réponse à Heidegger sur l'humanisme.* Paris, 1966, 92 p.

1696　Castellon, Enrique Lopez. "Dimensiones christianas de la etica de situacion." *Estud Filosof,* vol. 21, May-August 1972, 377-442.

1697　Caussimon, J. "L'intuition métaphysique de l'existence chez Saint Thomas et dans l'existentialisme contemporain." *Revue de Métaphysique et de Moral* (Paris), vol. 55, 1950, 392-407.

1698　Cavaliere, Renata Viti. Rev. of *In cammino verso il linguaggio,* by Martin Heidegger. Milano: Mursia, 1973. *Rivista di Studi Crociani* (Napoli), vol. 4, 1973, 478-480.

1699　Cayard, W. Wallace. "Bertrand Russell and Existential Phenomenologists on Foundations of Knowledge." *Journal of the West Virginia Philosophical Society,* Fall 1976, 17-22.

1700　Cedrins, J. *Gedanken über den Tod in der Existenzphilosophie.* Phil. Diss. Bonn 1948.

1701　Celan, Paul. *Todtnauberg am 12.* January, 1968.

　　　　[Privatdruck, wiederabgedruckt in Paul Celan: Lichtzwang, 2nd ed.]

1702　Célis, Raphaël. "La mondanité du jeu et de l'image selon Eugen Fink." *Revue Philosophique De Louvain,* vol. 76, Fall 1978, 54-66.

1703　Celms, Th. Rev. of *Kant und das Problem der Metaphysik,* by Martin Heidegger. Bonn, 1929. *Deutsche Literaturzeitung* (Berlin), vol. 51, 1930, 2311-2317.

1704　Cenacchi, Giúseppe. "Pensare heideggeriano e problematica teologica." *Aquinas, Rivista di Filosofia* (Roma), vol. 14, 1971, 645-653.

1705　Ceñal, R. "La filosofia de Martin Heidegger." *Revista de filosofia* (Madrid), vol. 4, 1945, 347-365.

1706　Ceñal, R. "El problema de la verdad en Heidegger." *Actas del primer Congreso nacional de Filosofia* (Mendoza), vol. 2, 1949, 1009-1014.

1707　Ceñal, R. Rev. of *De l'essence de la vérité,* by Martin Heidegger. Louvain, 1948. *Pensamiento) (Madrid), vol. 5, 1949, 214-216.*

1708　Ceñal, R. "Un nuevo escrito de Heidegger." *Pensamiento* (Madrid), vol. 5, 1949, 473-485. Rev. of these Martin Heidegger works:

　　　　[*Was ist Metaphysik?* 4th ed. Frankfurt, 1949.]

　　　　[*Vom Wesen der Wahrheit.* Frankfurt, 1943.]

　　　　[*Platons Lehre von der Wahrheit mit einem Brief über den Humanismus.* 1942.]

　　　　[*De l'essence de la vérité.* Louvain, 1948.]

1709　Ceñal, R. Rev. of *Holzwege,* by Martin Heidegger. Frankfurt, 1950. *Pensamiento* (Madrid), vol. 6, 1950, 534-537.

1710　Ceñal, R. Rev. of *Vom Wesen des Grundes,* by Martin Heidegger. 3rd ed. Frankfurt, 1949. *Pensamiento* (Madrid), vol. 6, 1950, 387-388.

1711　Ceñal, R. "El problema de la verdad en Heidegger." *Sapientia. Revista Tomista de Filosofia* (La Plata), vol. 5, 1950, 19-40.

1712    Ceñal, R. "Tiempo e historia en Heidegger." *Revista de filosofía* (Madrid), vol. 10, 1951, 354-358.

1713    Ceñal, R. Rev. of *Erläuterungen zu Hölderlins Dichtung,* by Martin Heidegger. 2nd ed. Frankfurt, 1951. *Pensamiento* (Madrid), vol. 8, 1952, 532-533.

1714    Ceñal, R. "Introduction." In *La filosofía de Martin Heidegger,* by A. de Waelhens. Trans. by R. Ceñal. 1952.

1715    Ceñal, R. "El problema de la ontologia fundamental." *Actes du XIe congrès international de philosophie,* Bruxelles, 20-26 Août 1953 (Amsterdam-Louvain), vol. 3, 1953, 21-25.

1716    Ceñal, R. "Los vericuetos de Martin Heidegger." *Universidad de Antioquia* (Medellin, Colombia), vol. 31, 1955, 298-306.

1717    Ceñal, R. "Ser y fundamento en Heidegger." *Finis Terrae,* vol. 6, 1959, 3-15.

1718    Ceñal, R. "Palabra, ser y fundamento. Tres lecciones sobre Heidegger." *Cuadernos hispanoamericanos* (Madrid), vol. 42, 1960, 19-53.

1719    Cerezo-Galán, P. *Arte, verdad y ser en Heidegger.* La estética en el sistema de Heidegger. Publicaciones de la Fundación Universitaria Española (Madrid), IX, 1963, 273 p.

1720    Cerf, Walter. "An Approach to Heidegger's Ontology." *Philosophy and Phenomenological Research* (Buffalo, New York), vol. 1, 1940/41, 177-190.

1721    Cerf, Walter. Rev. of *Vorträge und Aufsätze,* by Martin Heidegger. Pfullingen, 1954. *The Philosophical Review* (Ithaca), vol. 66, 1957, 417-420.

1722    Cerf, Walter. Rev. of *An Introduction to Metaphysics,* by Martin Heidegger. New Haven, 1959. *Philosophy and Phenomenological Research* (Buffalo, New York), vol. 22, 1961/62, 109-112.

1723    Ceriotto, C. L. "La pregunda por Dios en la pensar de Heidegger." *Philosophia* (Mendoza), vol. 37, 1971, 5-15.

1724    Ceriotto, C. L. "La pregunta por Dios en el pensar de Heidegger." Eds. E. Sosa Lopez and A. Caturelli. *Temas de Filosofía Contemporanea* (Buenos Aires), 1971, 13-25.

1725    Cerná, J. "Heideggerovo 'Zasláno'." *Literarni noviny* (Czechoslovakia), vol. 15, 1966, no. 14, 9.

1726    Cerná, J. "Jak to bylo s Heideggerem?" *Literarni noviny* (Czechoslovakia), vol. 15, no. 11, 1966, 8.

1727    Cerná, J. "Fink und Heidegger." *Filosofichá Casopis* (Czechoslovakia), no. 5-6, 1969, 751-759.

1728    Cerná, V. *Prvni sesit o existencialismu.* Praha, 1948, 90 p.

1729    Cervinka, J. "Pokus existenciálni filosofie." *Ohnice* (Praha), Sbornik soucasné literatury, II, 1947, 7-15.

1730    César, Constança Marcondes. "A crítica de Lukács a Heidegger." *Reflexao* (Campinas), vol. 1, no. 1, 1975/76, 53-57.

1731    Chacon, Vamireh. "Crise e esperança do ocidente em Heidegger." *Revista brasileira de Filosofia* (Sâo Paulo), vol. 28, no. 109, 1978, 12-27.

1732 Chaeil, Sô. *Haidegkae issôsôûi chonjae kaenyôm* (The Notion of Being in Heidegger). M. A. Thesis, Chonnam Univ., 1976.

1733 Chajdegger, V. "'filosofskoj enciklopekii' upominaetsja." *Philosophical Encyclopedia* (Moscow). Tom I - str. 78, 210, 213, Tom II - str. 147, 216, 261, 300, 325, 352, 386, 482, Tom III - str. 89, 91, 119, 159, 406, 464, Tom IV - str. 28, 29, 66, 78, 79, 142, 191, 314, 344, 362, 567, Tom V - str. 36, 108, 109, 139, 150, 154, 167, 168, 174, 203, 230, 315, 340, 341, 351, 405, 413, 426, 484, 538, 540, 542, 573, 600, 609, 620, 622, 624.

1734 Champagne, R. "Chemins qui mènent à la pensée chez Heidegger." *Revue de l'Université Laurentienne* (Sudbury), vol. 9, no. 2, 1977, 93-102.

1735 Champigny, R. "Sartre et Heidegger: deux sensibilités." *Modern Language Notes* (Baltimore), vol. 70, 1955, 426-428.

1736 Chandra, S. S. *Das Phänomen des Todes im Denken Heideggers und in der Lehre Buddhas.* Köln, 1966, 244, II p. (Phil. Diss. Köln v.31.3.1966)

1737 Chang, Chung-Y. "Commentary on J. Glenn Gray's 'Splendor of the Simple'." *Philosophy East and West* (Honolulu), vol. 20, 1970, 241-246.

1738 Chang, Chung-Y. "'The Essential Source of Identity' in Wang Lung-Chi'i's Philosophy." *Philosophy East and West* (Honolulu), vol. 23, 1973, 31-47.

1739 Chang, Chung-Yang. "Pre-rational Harmony in Heidegger's Essential Thinking and Ch'an Thought." *The Eastern Buddhist* (Kyoto), vol. 5, no. 2, 1972, 153-170.

1740 Chang, Chung-Yuan. "Tao: A New Way of Thinking." *Journal of Chinese Philosophy* (Dordrecht, Netherlands), vol. 1, 1974, 127-152.

1741 Chang, Chung-Yuan. "Kant's Aethetics and the East." *Journal of Chinese Philosophy,* vol. 3, 1976, 399-411.

1742 Chang, Chung-Yuan. "Tao and Heidegger." *Lier en Boog* (Purmerend), vol. 2, 1976/77, 66-74, 87.

1743 Chang, Chung-Yuan. "The Philosophy of Taoism According to Chuang Tzu." *Philosophy East and West,* vol. 27, 1977, 409-422.

1744 Chang, Chung-Yuan. "Taoist Philosophy and Heidegger's Poetic Thinking." *Indian Philosophical Quarterly* (Poona-7, India), vol. 4, 1977, 305-311.

1745 Chang, Chung-Yuan. "The Philosophy of Chuang Tzu." *Zeitschrift für Ästhetik und allgemeine Kunstwissenschaft* (Bonn), vol. 22, no. 2, 1977, 177-192.

1746 Chang, Chung-Yuan. "Reflections." In *Erinnerung an Martin Heidegger,* by Günther Neske. Pfullingen: Verlag Günther Neske, 1977, 65-70.

1747 Chapelle, A. *L'ontologie phénoménologique de Heidegger. Un Commentaire de Sein und Zeit.* Coll. Encyclopédie universitaire. Paris, 1962, XXIII, 267 p.

1748 Char, René. "Widmung." *Martin Heidegger zum 70. Geburtstag. Festschrift.* Pfullingen, 1959, 299.

1749    Char, René. "Eindrücke von früher." Trans. Clemens Graf Podewils. In
        *Erinnerung an Martin Heidegger.* Ed. Günther Neske. Pfullingen: Verlag
        Günther Neske, 1977, 75-78.

1750    Char, René. "Souvent Isabelle d'Egypte. A Martin Heidegger - Oftmals
        Isabella von Ägypten." Trans. Clemens Graf Podewils. In *Erinnerung an
        Martin Heidegger.* Ed. Günther Neske. Pfullingen: Verlag Günther Neske,
        1977, 72-74.

1751    Charles, D. "Dire, entendre, parler: l'herméneutique et le langage selon Paul
        Ricoeur." *Algemeen Nederlands Tijdschrift voor Wijsbegeerte* (Assen), vol.
        68, no. 2, 1976, 75-98.

1752    Châtelet, Frederick. Rev. of *Questions ... II,* by Martin Heidegger. Paris, 1968.
        *La Quinzaine littéraire,* no. 48, 1968, 21.

1753    Cheng, Chung-Ying. "Remarks on Ontological and Trans-Onto-Logical
        Foundations of Language." *Journal of Chinese Philosophy,* vol. 5, Summer
        1978, 335-340.

1754    Chikamatsu, Yoshiyuki. "Geijutsusakuhin ni okeru Sekai" (The World in the
        Work of Art). *Saikyôdaigadu-Gakujutsuhôkoku* (Kyôto), 1955.

1755    Chin, Chông. "Haidegkaûi samulûi munje" (The Problem of the Thing in
        Heidegger). *Ch'ôrhak Yôngu* (Sôul), vol. 5, 1976, 26-47.

1756    Chin, Chông. "K'antûe issôsôûi samulmunje" (The Problem of the
        Thing-In-Itself in Kant). *Ch'ôrhak Yôngu* (Sôul), vol. 6, 1978, 31-68.

1757    Chin, Chông. "K'antûi sunsuisôngbip'snûi chonjaeronjôk haesôk"
        (Ontological Interpretation of Kant's *Kritik der reinen Vernunft*). Phil.
        Diss. Sôul Univ. 1979.

1758    Chindae, Kim. "K'antûi siganrone taehan Haidegkaûi haesôke kwanhayô"
        (On Heidegger's Exegesis of Space and Time in Kant). M. A. Thesis,
        Kyôngbuk Univ., 1956.

1759    Chinen, Hideyuki. "Haidegga to 18 Seiki Doitsu Bunka" (Heidegger and
        German Culture in the 18th Century). *Ryûtsû Keizai Ronshû* (Tôkyô), vol.
        3, 1970, 51-66.

1760    Ching, Julia. "'Authentic Selfhood'. Wang Yang-ming and Heidegger." *The
        Monist* (La Salle), vol. 61, 1978, 3-27.

1761    Chinhûng, I. "Haidegka sironûi il koch'al" (Poetry in Heidegger). M. A.
        Thesis, Kyôngbuk Univ., 1975.

1762    Chestov, L. *Kierkegaard et la philosophie existentielle.* Traduction de Rageot
        et Boris de Schloezer. Paris, 1936.

1763    Chiodi, P. *L'esistenzialismo di Heidegger.* Torino, 1947, 207 p. 2nd ed. 1955.

1764    Chiodi, P. *L'ultimo Heidegger.* Torino, 1949. 2nd ed. 1960.

1765    Chiodi, P. *Heideggers Einfluss auf die Wissenschaften.* Bern, 1949.

1766    Chiodi, P. "Heidegger e Anassimandro: La metafisica come oblio dell'essere."
        *Rivista critica di storia della filosofia* (Milano), vol. 7, 1952, 161-172.

1767 Chiodi, P. Rev. of *Dell'essenza della verita*, by Martin Heidegger. Milano, 1952. *Rivista critica di storia della filosofia* (Milano), vol. 7, 1952, 236.

1768 Chiodi, P. Rev. of *Platons Lehre von der Wahrheit. Mit einem Brief über den 'Humanismus'*, by Martin Heidegger. Bern, 1947. *Rivista critica di storia della filosofia* (Milano), vol. 7, 1952, 325-327.

1769 Chiodi, P. "La *Einführung in die Metaphysik* di Heidegger." *Rivista di Filosofia* (Torino), vol. 44, 1953, 424-446.

1770 Chiodi, P. Rev. of *Heidegger, Denker in dürftiger Zeit*, by Karl Lôwithy. Frankfurt, 1953. *Rivista di Filosofia* (Torino), vol. 44, 1953, 464-467.

1771 Chiodi, P. "L'estetica di Martin Heidegger." *Il pensiero critico* (Milano), vol. 9-10, 1954, 1-12.

1772 Chiodi, P. "Essere e linguaggio in Heidegger e nel *Tractatus* di Wittgenstein." *Rivista di filosofia* (Torino), vol. 46, 1955, 170-191.

1773 Chiodi, P. *L'esistenzialismo di Heidegger. Con una appendice su la Einführung in die Metaphysik.* Prefazione di Nicola Abbagnano (Collezione de filosofia, 3). 2nd ed. Torino, 1955, 212 p. 3rd ed. 1965.

1774 Chiodi, P. "Il problema della tecnica in un incontro fra Heidegger e Heisenberg." *Aut Aut* (Milano), no. 32, 1956, 87-108.

1775 Chiodi, P. Rev. of *Was heisst Denken?*, by Martin Heidegger. Tübingen, 1954. *Rivista di Filosofia* (Torino), vol. 47, 1956, 85-88.

1776 Chiodi, P. "Tempo ed essere nell'ultimo Heidegger." *Archivo di Filosofia* (Roma), no. 1, 1958, (Il tempo), 175-189.

1777 Chiodi, P., ed. *Il pensiero esistenzialista. Kierkegaard, Jaspers, Heidegger, Marcel, Sartre, Merleau-Ponty, Abbagnano, Paci. Antologia a cura di P. Chiodi.* (Antologie del saper tutto, 136-138). Milano, 1959, 194 p.

1778 Chiodi, P. "Heidegger e la fine della ragione astuta." *Rivista di Filosofia* (Torino), vol. 51, 1960, 399-425.

1779 Chiodi, P. "Husserl e Heidegger." *Rivista di Filosofia* (Torino), vol. 52, 1961, 192-211.

1780 Chiodi, P. "Esistenzialismo e marxismo. Contributo a un dibattio sulla dialettica." *Rivista di Filosofia* (Torino), vol. 54, 1963, 164-190.

1781 Chiodi, P. "Husserl e Heidegger." *Revista di Filosofia* (Torino), vol. 52, 1965, 192-211.

1782 Chôlhwa, Hong. "Haidegkaûi ônôe kwanhayô" (On Language in Heidegger). M. A. Thesis, Chonnam Univ., 1975.

1783 Chôngbok, I. "The Problem of Philosophical Method Concerning the Dispute of the History of Occidental Philosophy." *Ch'ôrhak Yôngu* (Sôul), vol. 6, 1971, 87-114.

1784 Chôngbok, I. "The Basic Ontological Structure(s) of Old Chinese Thinking." *Ch'ungnam University Collection of Essays* (Ch'ungnam), vol. 11, 1972, 91-145.

1785 Chôngbok, I. "Hyondaee issôsôûi yôksasôngûi munje" (Historicity and Its Problems in Heidegger, M. Müller, W. Schulz, Pannenberg und Gadamer). *Collection of Essays.* Ed. *Institute of Humanities* (Ch'ungnam), vol. 1, part I, 1974, 297-311.

1786 Chônghong, Pak. "Haidegkae issôsôûi chip'ôngûi munje" (The Problem of the Horizon in Heidegger). *Risho* (Rishosha, Tôkyô), no. 4, 1935.

1787 Chônghong, Pak. "Ihaewa sayu - Haidegkawa Yasûp'ôsûûi pangbôpjôk ch'ai" (Understanding and Thinking - Methodological Difference Between Heidegger and Jaspers). *Munye* (Sôul), vol. I, no. 2, 1949,

1788 Chôngok, Pak. *Haidegka chonjaeronûi pangpôbronjôk Chôngwi* (Methodological Orientation of Ontology in Heidegger). M. A. Thesis, Kyongbuk Univ., 1975.

1789 Chonghu, I. "Haidegkajôk sayueûi immunûl wihan ch'obojôk siron" (Introduction to Heideggerian Thinking). *Yôngnam University Collection of Essays* (Taegu), vol. 6, 1972, 107-122.

1790 Choron, J. *Der Tod im abendländischen Denken.* Stuttgart, 1967, 335 p., (specifically pages 239-248).

1791 Christ. Rev. of *Einführung in die Metaphysik,* by Martin Heidegger. Tübingen, 1953. *Die Schulwarte* (Stuttgart), vol. 7, 1954, 368-369.

1792 Christoff, Daniel. "Raison suffisante et idoneisme, fermeture et ouverture." *Dialectica, Revue Internationale de Philosophie de la Connaissance* (Bienne, Switzerland), vol. 31, 1977, 165-176.

1793 Christopher, P. "Heidegger, Hegel, and the Problem of 'das Nichts'." *International Philosophical Quarterly* (New York), vol. 8, 1968, 379-405.

1794 Chryssides, George D. "Concepts of Freedom in Bultmann and Heidegger." *Sophia. A Journal for Discussion in Philosophical Theology* (Parkville, Australia), vol. 17, no. 1, 1978, 20-27.

1795 Chuhûi, Cho. "Haidegkawa Sartûtrûe issôsô chukûmûi siljonjôk haesôk" (Existential Interpretation of Death in Heidegger and Sartre). M. A. Thesis, Koryô Univ., 1978.

1796 Chuhwan, Cho. "Haidegkaûi K'antû yônyôk" (Heidegger on Kant). M. A. Thesis, Kyôngbuk Univ., 1978.

1797 Churchill, James Spencer, trans. *Kant and the Problem of Metaphysics,* by Martin Heidegger. Phil. Diss. Indiana Univ. 1960. *Dissertation Abstracts International,* vol. 21/05, 1217, 361 p.

1798 Chuun, I. "Haidegka ch'ôrhake issôsôûi chônhoe munje" (The Problem of the Turning in Heidegger's Philosophy). M. A. Thesis, Sônggyungwan Univ., 1976.

1799 Ciaravolo, P. "La ricerca dell'assoluto in 'Essere e tempo' di Heidegger." *Sapienza* (Rom), vol. 25, 1972, 227-234.

1800 Cichowicz, S. "Po ostatnim slowie" (After the Last Word). *Teksty,* vol. 3, 1977.

1801 Cichowicz, S. Rev. of *Heidegger i filozofia współczesna* (Heidegger and Contemporary Philosophy), by Krzysztof Michalski. Warszawa, 1978. *Nowe Ksiazki,* vol. 15, 1978.

1802 Ciloberto, Vicente O. "El Ser En Santo Tomás Y En La Fenomenologia." *Sapientia,* vol. 32, April-June 1977, 93-110.

1803 Clark, Orville. "Pain and Being: An Essay in Heideggerian Ontology." In: Heidegger issue *The Southwestern Journal of Philosophy* (Norman), vol. 4, no. 3, 1973, 179-90.

1804 Clark, Orville. "Heidegger and the Mystery of Pain." *Man and World* (The Hague), vol. 10, no. 3, 1977, 334-50.

1805 Cleveland, Harlan. "Welcome." *Philosophy East and West* (Honolulu), vol. 20, 1970, 223-225.

1806 Cobb, J. B. "Hat der spätere Heidegger Relevanz für die Theologie?" *Der spätere Heidegger und die Theologie* (Zürich, Stuttgart), 1964, 207-231.

1807 Cobo Suero, J. M. "La cuestión por el 'sentido del ser' en M. Heidegger." *Pensamiento* (Madrid), vol. 30, 1974, 131-48.

1808 Cochrane, Arthur C. *The Existentialists and God. Being and the Being of God in the Thought of Sören Kierkegaard, Karl Jaspers, Martin Heidegger, Jean-Paul Sartre, Paul Tillich, Etienne Gilson, Karl Barth.* Philadephia, Westminster Press, 1956, 174 p.

1809 Cohen, E. "The Ontological Position of God in Existentialist Philosophy." *Iyyun* (Jerusalem), vol. 16, 1965, 3-38.

1810 Cohn, Priscilla. "The Idea of the Nothing in the Philosophy of Martin Heidegger." Phil. Diss. Bryn Mawr College 1969.

1811 Cohn, Priscilla. *Heidegger. Su filosofia a través de la nada.* Madrid: Guadarrama, 1974, 208 p.

1812 Colette, J. "Kierkegaard, Bultmann et Heidegger." *Revue des Sciences Philosophiques et Théologiques* (Paris), vol. 49, 1965, 597-608.

1813 Colette, J. "Pourquoi la philosophie?" *Esprit. Changer la Culture et la Politique* (Paris), no. 6, 1977, 114-119.

1814 Colletti, L. Rev. of *Nietzsches Wort 'Gott ist tot',* by Heidegger. In *Holzwege.* 1950. *Giornale Critico della Filosofia italiana* (Firenze), vol. 30, 1951, 132-141.

1815 Collins, James. "The German Neoscholastic Approach to Heidegger." *Modern Scholastic,* vol. 21, 1944, 143-152.

1816 Collins, James. *The Existentialists. A Critical Study.* Chicago, 1952, 150-187, und passim.

1817 Collins, James. Rev. of *An Introduction to Metaphysics,* by Martin Heidegger. *Cross Currents,* vol. 10, 1960, 158-159.

1818 Collins, James. Rev. of *Discourse on Thinking,* by Martin Heidegger. *Cross Currents* (West Nyack), vol. 17, 1967, 207-208.

1819    Colnort-Bodet, S. Rev. of *Lettre sur l'humanisme,* by Martin Heidegger. *Revue de Synthèse* (Paris), vol. 79, 1958, 152-157.

1820    Colombi, G. "Spunti interpretativi sull'ultimo Heidegger." *Humanitas* (Brescia), vol. 17, 1962, 228-237.

1821    Colombo, A. "Martin Heidegger: Il ritorno dell'essere." *Saggi* (Bologna), vol. 47, 1964, 728.

1822    Colombres, Carlos A. I. "La ontologia modificada." *Revista Sapientia* (La Plata), vol. 26, 1971, 389-410.

1823    Colomer, E. "Martin Heidegger y las diversas interpretaciones de su filosofia." *Espiritu* (Barcelona), vol. 7, 1958, 158-168.

1824    Colomer, E. "Heidegger, pensament i poesia en l'absence de Deu," *Biblioteca Teologica del seglar,* 11. Barcelona, 1964, 104 p.

1825    Colonnello, Pio. "Kant nella interpretazione di Heidegger. Parte I: La tematica dell'immaginazione trascendentale. Parte II: L'immaginazione trascendentale e il problema della finitudine umana." *Università degli studi di Napoli. Facoltà di lettere e filosofia, Istituto di filosofia teoretica.* Quaderni, 2, 8. Napoli: Guannini, 1979, 2o, 14.

1826    Come, A. B. *Advocatus Dei - Advocatus hominis et mundi, Der spätere Heidegger und die Theologie.* Zürich/Stuttgart, 1964, 135-159.

1827    Condrau, G. "Martin Heidegger und die schweizerische Psychatrie." *Neue Zürcher Zeitung* (Fernausgabe), vol. 579, no. 260, vom 21.9.1969, 51.

1828    Conkling, Mark L. "Notes on Death." *Southwest Philosophical Studies,* vol. 1, April 1976, 21-7.

1829    Conrad-Martius, Hedwig. Rev. of *Sein und Zeit,* by Martin Heidegger. Halle, 1927. *Deutsche Kunstwissenschaft* (München), vol. 46, 1933, 246-251. Rpt. in *Schriften zur Philosophie* (München), 3 Bde., 1 Bd., 1963, 185-193, 461.

1830    Consentino, A. "Bagliori sperduti nel buio." *Filosofia dell' 'Unicita'* (Rom), 72 f., 1970, 47-81.

1831    Contri, S. "Heidegger in una luce rosminiana." *Rivista Rosminiana di Filosofia et di Cultura* (Comodossola-Milano), vol. 52, 1958, 161-176, 243-257.

1832    Contri, S. "Heidegger in una luce rosminiana." *Rivista Rosminiana di Filosofia et di Cultura* (Comodossola-Milano), vol. 54, 1960, 81-95.

1833    Conway, Jeremiah Patrick. *Why to Poetry? A Study of Martin Heidegger's Philosophy of Language.* Phil. Diss. Yale Univ. 1978. *Dissertation Abstracts International,* vol. 40/01-A, 305, 248 p.

1834    Copleston, Frederik C. "Pensadores influyentes de hoy: Russel, Heidegger, Jaspers." *Razon y Fe* (Madrid), vol. 143, 1951, 45-60.

1835    Copleston, Frederik C. Rev. of *Existence and Being,* by Martin Heidegger. 1949. *Philosophy) (London), vol. 26, 1951, 187-188.*

1836    Copleston, Frederik C. Rev. of *The Question of Being,* by Martin Heidegger. *The Month* (London), vol. 23, 1960, 353-354.

1837 Corbin, H. "Transcendental et existential." *Congres Descartes,* vol. VIII, 1937, 24-31.

1838 Corbin, H. Rev. of *Qu'est-ce que la Métaphysique,* by Martin Heidegger. Suivi d'extraits sur l'être et le temps et d'une conference sur Hölderlin. Traduit de l'allemand avec un avant-propos et des notes. Paris, 1938, 254 p.

1839 Corcoran, P. "The Influence of Existentialism on Contemporary Theology, III: Waiting for the Later Heidegger." *The Irish Ecclesiastical Record* (Dublin), vol. 108, 1967, no. 1, 1-18, 105-113.

1840 Cordua, Carla. "Heidegger o comenzar a pensar." *Diálogos* (Rio Piedras, Puerto Rico), vol. 13, no. 31, 1978, 7-37.

1841 Coreth, E. "Das fundamentalontologische Problem bei Heidegger und Hegel." *Scholastik* (Freiburg), vol. 29, 1954, 1-23.

1842 Coreth, E. "Auf der Spur der entflohenen Götter? M. Heidegger und die Gottesfrage." *Wort und Wahrheit* (Wien), vol. 9, 1954, 107-125.

1843 Coreth, E. "Zum Verhältnis Heideggers zu Hegel." *Analecta Gregoriana* (Romae), vol. 67, 1954; Studi intorno al' 'Esistenza', al Mondo, al Trascendente, 81-90.

1844 Coreth, E. "Heidegger in heutiger Sicht. Heideggers jüngste Schriften." *Orientierung, Katholische Blätter für weltanschauliche Information* (Zürich), vol. 19, 1955, 153-156, 157-170.

1845 Coreth, E. "Heidegger und Kant. Kant und die Scholastik heute." *Pullacher Philosophische Forschungen* (Pullach), Bd 1, 1955, 208-255.

1846 Coreth, E. *Grundfragen der Hermeneutik. Ein philosophischer Beitrag.* Freiburg, 1969, 230 p.

[Rev. by T. Kisiel in *Zeitschrift für Allgemeine Wissenschaftstheorie* (Wiesbaden), vol. 3, 1972, 156-158.]

1847 Coreth, E. "From Hermeneutics to Metaphysic." *International Philosophical Quarterly* (New York/Heverlee-Leuven), vol. 11, 1971, 249-259.

1847a Corngold, Stanley. " *Sein und Zeit.* Implications for Poetics." *Martin Heidegger and the Question of Literature.* Ed. by William V. Spanos. Bloomington, Indiana; London: Indiana Univ. Press, 1979, 99-114.

1848 Corts Grau, J. *Anotaciones previas al pensamiento ético-juridico de Martin Heidegger.* (Lección inaugural del curso 1970-71). Valencia, 1970, 88 p.

1849 Corvez, Maurice. "La place de Dieu dans l'ontologie de Martin Heidegger." *Revue Thomiste* (Paris), vol. 53, 1953, 287-320.

1850 Corvez, Maurice. "Chronique heideggérienne." *Revue Thomiste* (Paris), vol. 53, 1953, 591-619.

Rev. of Martin Heidegger's:

[*Vom Wesen der Wahrheit.* Frankfurt, 1943, 593-597.]

[*Qu'est-ce que la métaphysique?* Suivi d'extraits sur l'Etre et le Temps et d'une conférence sur Hölderlin. 2nd ed. Paris, 1951, 597-598.]

[*Was ist Metaphysik?* 5th ed. Frankfurt, 1949, 598-605.]

[*Vom Wesen des Grundes.* 3rd ed. Frankfurt, 1949, 605-608.]

[*Über den Humanismus.* Frankfurt, 1947, 609-619.]

1851 Corvez, Maurice. "La place de Dieu dans l'ontologie de Martin Heidegger." *Revue Thomiste* (Paris), vol. 54, 1954, 79-102, 559-583.

1852 Corvez, Maurice. "Chronique heideggérienne." *Revue Thomiste* (Paris), vol. 54, 1954, 414, 429.

[Rev. of *Kant et le problème de la métaphysique,* by Martin Heidegger. Paris, 1953, 414-417.]

[Rev. of *Einführung in die Metaphysik,* by Martin Heidegger. Tübingen, 1953, 418-420.]

1853 Corvez, Maurice. "La place de Dieu dans l'ontologie de Martin Heidegger." *Revue Thomiste* (Paris), Jg. 63, Bd 55, 1955, 377-390.

1854 Corvez, Maurice. "L'Etre de Heidegger est-il objectif?" *Revue Tomiste* (Paris), Jg. 63, Bd 55, 1955, 565-581.

1855 Corvez, Maurice. *La philosophie de Heidegger.* (Coll. 'Initiation philosophique', 51). Paris, 1961, 136 p. 2nd ed. 1966.

1856 Corvez, Maurice. Rev. of *L'être et le temps,* by Martin Heidegger. Paris, 1964. *Revue Thomiste* (Toulouse), vol. 64, 1964, 658.

1857 Corvez, Maurice. "La pensée de l'être chez Martin Heidegger." *Revue Thomiste* (Toulouse), vol. 65, 1965, 536-553.

1858 Corvez, Maurice, and M.-V. Leroy. "Etudes sur Heidegger." *Revue Thomiste* (Toulouse), vol. 65, 1965, 638-642.

1859 Corvez, Maurice. "L'Être et l'étant dans la philosophie de Martin Heidegger." *Revue Philosophique de Louvain* (Louvain), vol. 63, 1965, 257-279.

1860 Corvez, Maurice. "L'idée de vérité dans l'oeuvre de Martin Heidegger." *Revue Thomiste* (Toulouse), vol. 66, 1966, 48-61.

1861 Corvez, Maurice. Rev. of *Introducion à la métaphysique,* by Martin Heidegger. Paris, 1967, 231 p. (Übersetzt von G. Kahn) *Revue Thomiste* (Toulouse), vol. 67, 1967, 665.

1862 Corvez, Maurice. Rev. of *Questins III,* by Martin Heidegger. *Revue Thomiste* (Toulouse), vol. 67, 1967, 516-517.

1863 Corvez, Maurice. *La Filosofia de Heidegger.* Trans. Agustin Ezcurdia Hijar (Breviario, 211). Mexico: F.C.E., 1970, 136 p.

1864 Corvez, Maurice. Rev. of *Humanism and Ethics. An Introduction to Heidegger's Letter on Humanism With a Critical Bibliography,* by Robert H. Cousineau. Louvain, 1972. *Revue Thomiste* (Toulouse), vol. 75, 1975, 306-307.

1865 Corvez, Maurice. Rev. of *Heidegger du l'experience de la pensée,* by René Scherer and Arion Lothar Kelkel. Paris, 1973. *Revue Thomiste* (Toulouse), vol. 75, 1975, 505-508.

1866 Costa, Filippo. *Heidegger e la teologia.* (L'Agorà. Filosofia, Pedagogia, Sociologia, 3). Ravenna: A. Longo, 1974, 444 p.

1867 Cotten, Jean-Pierre. *Heidegger.* (Ecrivains de toujours, 95). Paris: Éditions du Seuil, 1974, 189 p.

1868 Cotten, Jean-Pierre. "Quelques remarques sur la notion de crise." *Revue de l'Enseignement Philosophique* (Gagny), vol. 25, no. 5, 1975, 11-19.

1868a Cotten, Jean-Pierre. "Où en est-on sur le thème 'Heidegger et la politique?'" *Pensée* (Paris), no. 200, 1978, 102-114.

1869 Courtine, J. F. "Du besoin de la philosophie." *Critique* (Paris), vol. 34, no. 369, 1978, 138-153.

1869a Courtine, Jean-Francois. "Anthropologie et Anthropomorphisme (Heidegger Lecteur de Schelling)." *Nachdenken über Heidegger.* Ed. by Ute Guzzoni. Hildesheim: Gerstenberg Verlag, 1980, 9-35.

1870 Cousineau, Robert H. Rev. of *On the Way to Language,* by Martin Heidegger. Trans. Peter D. Hertz. New York: Harper & Row, 1971, 200 p. *Theological Studies* (Baltimore), vol. 32, 1971, 677-680.

1871 Cousineau, Robert H. *Humanism and Ethics. An Introduction to Heidegger's Letter on Humanism With a Critical Bibliography.* Louvain, 1972.

1872 Cousineau, Robert H. Rev. of *Poetry, Language, Thought,* by Martin Heidegger. Trans. and intr. Albert Hofstadter. New York: Harper & Row, 1971, 229 p. *Theological Studies* (Baltimore), vol. 33, 1972, 561-564.

1873 Couturier, Fernand. *Monde et être chez Heidegger. Mit einem Vorwort von B. Welte.* Montréal, 1971, VIII, 584 p.

1874 Couturier, Fernand. *Monde et être chez Heidegger.* Département de philosophie de l'Université du Québec à Montréal, 1971, 586 p.

1875 Cowan, Joseph L. "Can and Can'ts." *Philosophy Research Archives* (Bowling Green), vol. 3, no. 1171, 1977.

1876 Cranaki, M. "De Husserl à Heidegger ou les voies du silence." *Critique* (Paris), vol. 10, no. 86-87, 1954, 676-688.

1877 Crandall, J. W. "Criteria of Authentic Family Relationships as Conceptualized Within an Ontological Framework." Phil. Diss. New York 1968 231 p.

1878 Cranston, Maurice. "The Light Within. The Encounter of Word and World in the 'Poem' of Martin Heidegger and René Char." *Rivista di Letterature Moderne e Comparate* (Firenze), vol. 29, no. 4, 1976, 298-308.

1879 Crescini, Angelo. "Tramonto del pensiero occidentale? Saggio su Heidegger." (Saggi classici e contemporanei, 2). Udine: La Nuova Base, 1977, 221 p.

1880 Cress, Donald W. "Heidegger's Criticism of 'Entitative Metaphysics' in His Later Works." *International Philosophical Quarterly* (New York), vol. 12, 1972, 69-86.

1881 Cristaldi, M. "Nota sulla ripresa del fondamento nella filosofia contemporanea." *Teoresi* (Catania), 1961.

1882 Cristaldi, M. "Nota sulla possibilità di un'ontologia del linguaggio in Wittgenstein e in Heidegger." *Teoresi* (Catania), vol. 22, 1967, 47-86.

1883    Croce, B. Rev. of *Die Selbstbehauptung der Deutschen Universität,* by Martin Heidegger. Breslau, 1933. *La Critica* (Napoli), vol. 32, 1934, 69-70.

1884    Croce, B. "Martin Heidegger et l'ontologie." *Recherches philosophiques* (Paris), CXIII, 1932.

1885    Croce, B. "Intorno allo Hölderlin e ai suoci critici." *La Critica* (Napoli), vol. 39, 1941, 201-214, (specifically pages 211-212).

1886    Cruz-Hernández, M. "La filosofia de Martin Heidegger en el horizonte de nuestro tiempo." *Boletin de la Universidad de Granada,* vol. 18, 1946, 79-96.

1887    Cruz-Hernández, M. "Filosofia y estética del lenguaje en Martin Heidegger." *Revista de filosofia* (Madrid), vol. 8, 1949, 253-277.

1888    Cruz Jaimes, L. "El existencialismo de Martin Heidegger." *Duc in Altum* (Tlalpan, Mexico), vol. 16, 1951, 280-289.

1889    Cruz Vélez, D. "El punto de partida del filosofar." *Cuadernos de Filosofia* (Rosario), 1961, 17-42.

1890    Cruz Vélez, D. *Filosofia sin supuestos, de Husserl a Heidegger.* Buenos Aires, 1969, 310 p.

1891    Cuesta, S. "El valor humano de la metafisica según los grandes filósofos." (Aristóteles, Descartes, Kant, Heidegger). *Pensamiento* (Madrid), vol. 10, 1954, 147-168.

1892    Cuisenier, J. "Heidegger et Sartre." *La Nef* (Paris), vol. 3, 1946, 133-137.

1893    Cullberg. *Das Du und die Wirklichkeit. Zum ontologischen Hintergrund der Gemeinschaftskategorie.* Uppsala, 1933, (specifically pages 101-111).

1894    Cullmann, O. *Heil als Geschichte. Heilsgeschichtliche Existenz im Neuen Testament.* Tübingen, 1965, XII, 328 p.

1895    Cumming, R. Rev. of *Existence and Being,* by Martin Heidegger. Chicago, 1949. *The Journal of Philosophy* (New York), vol. 48, 1951, 102-107.

1895a   Cumming, Robert Denoon. *Starting Point: An Introduction to the Dialectic of Existence.* Chicago: Univ. of Chicago Press, 1979.

1896    Currás Rábade, Angel. "Heidegger: el arduo sosiego del exilio." *Anales Del Seminario De Metafisica,* vol. 12, 1977, 59-94.

1897    Curtin, John Claude. "Waiting and Truth." *The New Scholasticism* (Baltimore), vol. 47, no. 4, 1973, 469-477.

1898    Curtin, John Claude. "Death and Presence: Martin Heidegger." *Philosophy Today* (Celina, Ohio), vol. 20, 1976, 262-266.

1899    Czaplinski, W. Rev. of *Der europäische Nihilismus,* by Martin Heidegger. Pfullingen, 1967. *Ruch Filozoficzny,* February 1971.

1900    Czerniak, S. Rev. of *Budowaá, mieszkaá, myále Eseje wybrane,* by Martin Heidegger. (Bauen Wohnen, Denken. Ausgewählte Essays). Ed. Krzysztof Michalski. Warszawa, 1977. *Literatura na swiecie,* January 1978.

1901    Da Cunha, C. E. J. "Qué es esto: i la Introducción a la metafisica?" Trans. Á. J. Casasares. *Diálogos* (Rio Piedras, Puerto Rico), vol. 5, 1968, no. 11/12, 141-157.

1902 Daech'un, I. "Haidegkaûi kich'ojonjaerone taehan koch'al - Segyeûi segesongûl chungsimûro" (A Contemplation on the Fundamental Ontology in Heidegger Especially in Regard to the Notion of Worldhood of World). M. A. Thesis, Koryô Univ., 1964.

1903 D'Agostino, F. Rev. of *Saggi e discorsi,* by Martin Heidegger. Trans. Gianni Vattimo. Milano: Mursia, 1976. *Rivista internazionale di Filosofia del Diritto* (Milano), vol. 54, 1977, 444-446.

1904 Daim, W. "Das Trauma der Geburt und Heideggers Existentialismus." *Wissenschaft und Weltbild* (Wien), vol. 4, 1951, 14-21.

1905 Dahlhaus, F. Rev. of *Einführung in die Metaphysik,* by Martin Heidegger. Tübingen, 1953. *Diskus* (Frankfurt), Jg. 3, no. 7, 1953, 8-9.

1906 Dalledone, A. "Dal nihilismo alla dignità dell'uomo in Heidegger." *Divus Thomas. Commentarium de philosophia et theologia* (Piacenza), no. 3-4, 1973, 396-404.

1907 Dallmayr, Winfried. "Expérience du sens et réflexion sur la validité: K O Apel et la transformation de la philosophie." *Archives De Philosophie,* vol. 39, July-September 1976, 367-406.

1908 D'Amore, Benedetto. "La metafisica del nulla e dell'essere à M. Heidegger." *Sapienta* (Roma), vol. 9, no. 4-5, 1956, 334-369.

1909 D'Amore, Benedetto. "Esistenzialismo tedesco ed esistenzialismo italiano." *Incontri Culturali* (Roma), vol. 1, 1968, 414-424.

1910 D'Amore, Benedetto. "La Filosofia Christiana, Oggi (Presupposti Necessari Per Un'adeguata Comprensione)." *Sapienzia,* vol. 31, July-September 1978, 275-295.

1911 Daniélou, M. "La philosophie de Heidegger." *Cahiers de Neuilly,* vol. 7, 1949, 57-59.

1912 Danner, H. *Das Göttliche und der Gott bei Heidegger.* Meisenheim/Glan, 1971, 187 p.

1913 Dantlo, R. *A la rencontre de Martin Heidegger.* Toulouse, 1969, 135 p.

1914 Dary, M.-M. "La notion de curiosité du point de vue de l'existencialisme." (Heidegger-Sartre). *Actas del primer Congreso nacional de Filosofia* (Mendoza), vol. 2, 1949, 1015-1019.

1915 Dastur, Françoise. "Poésje et pensée selon Heidegger." *Bulletin de la Faculté des Lettres de Strasbourg* (Strasbourg), vol. 48, no. 2, 1969, 161-165.

1916 Dastur, Françoise. "Heidegger." In *Histoire de la philosophie, III: Du xixe siècle à nos jours.* Ed. Yvon Belaval. *Encyclopédie de la Pléiade* (Paris), vol. 38, 1974, 608-630.

1917 Dauenhauer, Bernhard P. "An Approach to Heidegger's Way of Philosophizing." *The Southern Journal of Philosophy* (Memphis), vol. 9, 1971, 265-275.

1918 Dauenhauer, Bernhard P. "On Death and Birth." *Personalist,* vol. 57, Spring 1976, 162-170.

1919    Dauenhauer, Bernhard P. "Renovating the Problem of Politics." *Review of Metaphysics* (Washington), vol. 29, no. 4, 1976, 626-641.

1920    Dauenhauer, Bernhard P. "Heidegger, the Spokesman for the Dweller." *The Southwestern Journal of Philosophy* (Norman), vol. 15, no. 2, 1977, 189-199.

1921    Dauenhauer, Bernhard P. "Does Anarchy Make Political Sense: A Response to Schürmann's 'Questioning the Foundation of Practical Philosophy'." *Human Studies,* vol. 1, October 1978, 369-375.

1922    D'Avack, L. Rev. of *Essere e tempo. L'essenza del fondamento,* by Martin Heidegger. Ed. Pietro Chiodi. (Classici della filosofia, 5). Torino: U.T.E.T., 1969, 700 p. *Rivista internazionale di Filosofia del Diritto* (Milano), vol. 49, 1972, 659-661.

1923    Dean, Thomas J. *The Logic of Language and Persons: A Methodological Introduction to the Interpretative Metaphysics of Heidegger.* Phil. Diss. New York 1968 361 p. *Dissertation Abstracts International,* vol. 30/04-A, 1597.

1924    De Andia, Ysabel. "Réflexions sur les rapports de la philosophie et de la théologie à partir de deux textes de Martin Heidegger (à suivre)." *Mélanges de Science Religieuse* (Lille), vol. 32, 1975, 133-152.

1925    De Andia, Ysabel. *Présence et eschatologie dans la pensée de Martin Heidegger.* (Encyclopédie Univ.). Villeneuve d'Ascq, Univ. de Lille III; Paris: Editions Universitaires, 1975, 298 p.

1926    De Andia, Ysabel. "Réflexiones sur les rapports de la philosophie et de la théologie à partir de deux textes de Martin Heidegger." *Mélanges de Science Religieuse* (Lille), vol. 32, no. 3, 1975, 133-152.

1927    De Andia, Ysabel. "Réflexions sur les rapports de la philosophie et de la théologie à partir de deux textes de Martin Heidegger (suite)." *Mélanges de Science Religieuse* (Lille), vol. 33, 1976, 89-122.

1928    De Boer, Theo. "Heideggers Kritiek op Husserl, I-II." *Tijdschrift voor Filosofie* (Leuven), vol. 40, 1978, 202-249, 453-501.

        [Résumé: *La critique heideggerienne de Husserl, I-II,* 250, 501.]

1929    De Boer, Wolfgang. "Das Verhängnis des Idealismus." *Zeitschrift für Philosophische Forschung* (Meisenheim), vol. 29, no. 4, 1975, 521-543.

1930    De Brie, G. A. Rev. of *Logik. Die Frage nach der Wahrheit,* by Martin Heidegger. Gesamtausgabe, Abt. 2, Bd 21. Ed. Walter Biemel. Frankfurt: Klostermann, 1976. *Tijdschrift voor filosofie* (Leuven), vol. 38, 1976, 502-503.

1931    De Brie, G. A. Rev. of *Sein und Zeit,* by Martin Heidegger. Gesamtausgabe, Abt. 1: Veröffentlichte Schriften 1914-1970. Bd 2. Ed. Friedrich-Wilhelm von Herrmann. Frankfurt: Klostermann, 1976. *Tijdschrift voor Filosofie* (Leuven), vol. 39, 1977, 747.

1932    De Brie, G. A. Rev. of *Wegmarken,* by Martin Heidegger. Gesamtausgave, Abt. 1: Veröffentlichte Schriften 1914-1970. Bd 9. Ed. Friedrich-Wilhelm von Herrmann. Frankfurt: Klostermann, 1976. *Tijdschrift voor Filosofie* (Leuven), vol. 39, 1977, 747.

1933   De Brie, G. A. Rev. of *Phänomenologische Interpretation von Kants Kritik der reinen Vernunft,* by Martin Heidegger. Gesamtausgabe, Abt. 2, Bd 25. *Tijdschrift voor Filosofie* (Leuven), vol. 39, 1977, 748.

1934   De Carolis, Massimo P. "Metafisica e tecnica in Heidegger." *Sapienza* (Roma), vol. 31, no. 3, 1978, 330-346.

1935   De Carolis, Massimo P. "Differenza: analitica esistenziale e problema dell'essere." *Filosofia,* vol. 29, April 1978, 199-209.

1936   De Carolis, Massimo P. "Il 'linguaggio originario' in Heidegger." *Filosofia,* vol. 29, no. 2, 1978, 193-220, 477-498, 613-634.

1937   De Cecchi Duso, G. *L'interpretazione heideggeriana dei Presocratici.* (Pubblicazioni della Scuola de prefezionamento in filosofia dell'Università de Padova, 14). Padova, 1970, 148 p.

   [Rev. by L. Fontaine-de Vischer in *Revue Philosophique du Louvain* (Louvain), vol. 69, 1971, 587-589.]

1938   De Cecchi Duso, G. "Teologia e filosofia in due inediti di Martin Heidegger." *Bolletino filosofico* (Padova), vol. 4, 1970, 35-39.

1939   Deck, Barbara Ann. *The Healing Power of Poetry. From Heidegger's Poesis to Illustrations From Representative Nineteenth-Century Thinkers.* Authorized facsimile of the dissertation of the Brandeis University. Phil. Diss. 1977. Ann Arbor, Michigan; London: University Microfilms International, 1979, iii-204. [Hgk77-22808] *Dissertation Abstracts International,* vol. 38/05-A, 2843.

1940   Deckers, H. "L'Existence est-elle lumineuse et béatifique?" *Revue internationale de métaphysique, sociologie et économie,* vol. 6-7, 1950, 215-221.

1941   Declève, Henri. "Le second avant-propos de 'Kant et le problème de la métaphysique'." *Dialogue* (Montréal/Kingston), vol. 6, 1967/68, 555-566.

1942   Declève, Henri. "Heidegger et Cassirer interprètes de Kant. Traduction et commentaire d'un document." *Revue Philosophique de Louvain* (Leuven), vol. 67, 1969, 517-545.

1943   Declève, Henri. *Heidegger et Kant.* The Hague, 1970, 380 p. (Phänomenologica 40).

   [Rev. by von B. de Gelder in *Revue Philosophique de Louvain* (Louvain), vol. 70, 1972, 443-453.]

1944   Deely, John N. "The Situation of Heidegger in Tradition of Christian Philosophy." *The Thomist* (Washington), vol. 31, 1967, 159-244.

1945   Deely, John N. *The Tradition via Heidegger. An Essay on the Meaning of Being in the Philosophy of Martin Heidegger.* The Hague, 1971, XXVIII, 200 p.

1946   De Gelder, B. "Heidegger et Kant." *Revue philosophique de Louvain* (Leuven), vol. 70, 1972, 443-453.

1947   De George, Richard T. "Heidegger and the Marxists." *Studies in Soviet Thought,* vol. 5, 1965, 289-298.

1948    De Guzman Vicente, Lorenzo. "Sobre la semántica del ser en Martin Heidegger." *Estudios Filosóficos* (Valladolid), vol. 24, 1975, 35-54.

1949    De Jong, A. *Een wijsbegeerte van het woord. Een godsdienstwijsgerige studie over de taalbeschouwing van Martin Heidegger.* Amsterdam, 1966, 232 p.

1950    Delfgaauw, Bernhard. "De Existentie-Philosophie van Martin Heidegger." *Katholiek Cultureel Tijdschrift* (Amsterdam), vol. 76, 1947, 368-380.

1951    Delfgaauw, B. *Praedviezen over het Existentialisme. Het 'atheistische Existentialisme': Nietzsche, Heidegger, Sartre.* Den Haag, 1947.

1952    Delfgaauw, B. "Het Niets." *Tijdschrift voor Philosophie* (Leuven), vol. 9, 1947, 371-380.

        [German trans. "Das Nichts." *Zeitschrift für philosophische Forschung* (Meisenheim/Glan), vol. 4, 1949/50, 393-401.]

1953    Delfgaauw, B. "Heidegger en Sartre." *Tijdschrift voor Philosophie* (Leuven), vol. 10, 1948, 289-336, 403-446.

1954    Delfgaauw, B. "Notes sur Heidegger et Sartre." *Les Etudes Philosophiques* (Marseille), N.F. 4, 1949, 371-374.

1955    Delfgaauw, B. *Heidegger, het denken van het zijn.* (Hedendaagse op den mens, Gespreken of Drakenburgh, bijgebracht door J. Peters). C.S.S.R. Heerlen, 1950, 99-116.

1956    Delfgaauw, B. Rev. of *Erläuterungen zu Hölderlins Dichtung,* by Martin Heidegger. Frankfurt, 1944. *Kultuurleven) (Amsterdam), vol. 7, 1951, 566.*

1957    Delfgaauw, B. Rev. of *Kant und das Problem der Metaphysik,* by Martin Heidegger. Bonn, 1929. *Kultuurleven* (Antwerpen), vol. 7, 1951, 566.

1958    Delfgaauw, B. *Wat is Existentialisme?* 3rd ed. Amsterdam, 1952. 7th revised ed. 1969.

1959    Delfgaauw, B. "Heidegger et Hölderlin." *Actes du XIe congrès international de philosophie, Bruxelles 20-26 Août 1953* (Amsterdam/Louvain), vol. 14, 1953, 312-316.

1960    Delfgaauw, B. "De religieuze vraag als kernpunt van het denken van Martin Heidegger." *Tijdschrift voor Philosophie* (Leuven), vol. 16, 1954, 85-102.

1961    Delfgaauw, B. "La phenoménologie chez Martin Heidegger." *Les Etudes philosophiques* (Paris), vol. 9, 1954, 50-56.

1962    Delfosse, Heinrich P. *See* Bost, Reiner, and H. P. Delfosse.

1963    Dell, A. "Ontologische Daseinsanalyse und theologisches Daseinsverständnis." *Imago Die. Beitr. z. theologischen Anthropologie. Gustav Krüger zum 70. Geburtstag.* Ed. H. Bornkamm. Giessen, 1932, 215-232.

1964    Della Volpe, G. "Da un programma antiromantico." *Studi filosofici* (Milano), vol. 18, 1940, 337-352, (specifically pages 348-349).

1965    Della Volpe, G. *Crisi critica dell'estetica romantica.* Messina, 1941, 42-45.

1966    Della Vople, V. *Discorso sull'ineguaglianza, con due saggi sull'tica dell'esistenzialismo.* Roma, 1943, 9-12.

1967    Dello, Preite, M. "Karl Jaspers e Martin Heidegger. Appunti per un confronto." *Sapienza* (Roma), vol. 31, no. 1, 1978, 74-82.

1968    Del Negro, W. "Die Existenzphilosophie Heideggers." *Die Philosophie der Gegenwart* (Leipzig), 1942, 47-49.

1969    Del Negro, W. Rev. of *Martin Heidegger und die Existential-philosophie,* by R. Marcic. Bad Ischl, 1949. *Philosophischer Literaturanzeiger* (Schlehdorf, Obb), vol. 1, 1949, 153-154.

1970    Del Negro, W. "Von Brentano über Husserl zu Heidegger." *Zeitschrift für philosophische Forschung* (Meisenheim/Glan), vol. 7, 1953, 571-585.

1971    Delp, A. *Tragische Existenz. Zur Philosophie Martin Heidegger.* Freiburg, 1935.

1972    Delp, A. "Modern German Existential Philosophy." *The Modern Schoolman* (St. Louis, Missouri), vol. 14, 1936, 62-66.

1973    Delpech, L. J. Rev. of *Introductin à la métaphysique,* by Martin Heidegger. *Les Études Philosophiques* (Paris), vol. 22, 1967, 339-340.

1974    Delpech, L. J. Rev. of *Questions III,* by Martin Heidegger. *Les Études Philosophiques* (Paris), vol. 22, 1967, 553-554.

1975    *Dem Andenken Martin Heideggers. Zum 26. Mai 1976.* Frankfurt: Klostermann, 1977, 65 p.

1976    De Medicis, Stelios Castanos. "Actualité de la pensée d'Héraclite." *Philosophia* (Athens), vol. 4, 1974, 137-154.

1977    Dempf, Alois. *Kierkegaards Folgen.* Leipzig, 1935, (specifically pages 26-43).

1978    Demske, James M. "Heidegger's Quadrate and Revelation of Being." *Philosophy Today,* vol. 7, Winter 1963, 245-257.

1979    Demske, James M. "Heidegger's Quadrate and Revelation of Being." *Philosophy Today,* vol. 7, 1963, 245-257.

1980    Demske, James M. *Sein, Mensch und Tod. Das Todesproblem bei Martin Heidegger.* (Symposion, 12). Freiburg/München, 1963, 207 p.

        [Rev. by H. Hülsmann in *Salzburger Jahrbuch für Philosohie,* vol. 8, 1964, 274-276.]

1981    Demske, James M. "Sein, Mensch und Tod: Das Todesproblem bei Martin Heidegger." *International Philosophical Quarterly* (Heverlee/Louvain), vol. 4, 1964, 488-490.

1982    Demske, James N. *Being, Man and Death. A Key to Heidegger.* Lexington, Kentucky, 1970, VII, 234 p.

1892a   Demske, James M. *Sein. Mensch und Tod: Das Todesproblem bei Martin Heidegger.* (Symposion, 12). Xerox-Reprint. Freiburg: Alber, 1979, 207 p.

1983    De Raeymaker, L. *Philosophie de lêtre. Essai de synthèse métaphysique.* 3rd ed. Louvain, 1970, 432 p.

1984    Derbolav, J. Rev. of *Einführung in die Metaphysik,* by Martin Heidegger. Tübingen, 1953. *Wissenschaft und Weltbild* (Wien), vol. 7-8, 1954, 314-316.

1985    Derisi, Octavio Nicolas. "Método, sentido y alcance de la investigacion metafisica en Heidegger y Santo Tomás." *Sapientia* (La Plata), vol. 35, 1954/55, 159-180.

1986    Derisi, Octavio Nicolas. "El Método, sentido y alcance de la investigación metafisica em M. Heidegger y em Santo Tomás." *Angelicum* (Roma), vol. 32, 1955, 141-177; II: *Sapientia,* vol. 10, 1955, 91-108, 168-181.

1987    Derisi, Octavio Nicolas. "Ser y hombre en la Introdución a la metafisica de M. Heidegger." *Cuadernos Hispanoamericanos,* vol. 31, 1957, 321-332. *See Veritas* (Porto Allegre), vol. 2, 1957 and *Xenium* (Cordoba), vol. 1, 1957.

1988    Derisi, Octavio Nicolas. "En torno a la moral de Heidegger y Sartre." *Sapientia. Revista Tomista de Filosofia* (La Plata), vol. 12, 1957, 139-141.

1989    Derisi, Octavio Nicolas. "Ser y pensar en Martin Heidegger." Rev. of *Que significa pensar?,* by Martin Heidegger. *Sapientia. Revista Tomista de Filosofia* (La Plata), vol. 14, 1959, 38-45.

1990    Derisi, Octavio Nicolas. "Reflexiones acerca del sentido del 'esse' en santo Tóma frente a la concepción respectiva en Aristóteles, en la Escolástica y en Heidegger." *Sapientia. Revista Tomista de Filosofia* (La Plata), vol. 14, 1959, 289-292.

1991    Derisi, Octavio Nicolas. "Aproximaciones y diferencias entre la fenomenologia existencial de Martin Heidegger y la ontologia de Santo Tomás." *Sapientia* (La Plata), vol. 22, 1967, 185-192.

1992    Derisi, Octavio Nicolas. *El último Heidegger. Aproximaciones y diferencias entre la fenomenologia existencial de Martin Heidegger y la ontologia de Santo Tomás.* Buenos Aires, 1968, 112 p. 2nd ed. 1969.

1993    Derisi, Octavio Nicolas. "El ser en Martin Heidegger." In *II. Congresso Nacional de Filosofia. Actas. Tomo I: Sesiones Plenarias.* Buenos Aires, 1973, 551-557.

1994    Derisi, Octavio Nicolas. "La vía inaccesible al ser. A propósito de la filosofía existencial de M. Heidegger." *Sapientia* (La Plata), vol. 31, no. 121, 1976, 217-222.

1995    Derrida, Jaques. *L'écriture et la différence.* Paris, 1967.
        [Partly trans. into German: *Die Schrift und die Differenz.* Frankfurt/Main, 1972, 452 p., (specifically pages 203-234).]

1996    Derrida, Jaques. "The Ends of Man." *Philosophy and Phenomenological Research* (Buffalo), vol. 30, 1969, 31-57.

1997    Derrida, Jacques. "'Ousia and Gramme': A Note to a Footnote in Being and Time." Trans. E. S. Casey. *Phenomenology in Perspective.* Ed. F. J. Smith. The Hague, 1970, 231 p., (specifically pages 54-93). First publ. in *L'endurance de la pensée.* Paris, 1968, 219-266.
        [Trans. by Sreten Morie in *Rami Hajdeger - Recepcija i kritika Bivstva i Veremena.* Ed. D. Stojanovic and D. Basta. Beogrod, 1979, 175-224.]

1998    Derrida, Jacques. "Restitutions of Truth to Size." *Research and Phenomenology,* vol. 8, 1978, 1-44.

1999    Deschepper, J.-P. Rev. of *Zur Sache des Denkens,* by Martin Heidegger. *Revue Philosophique de Louvain* (Leuven), vol. 68, 1970, 547.

2000    De Soto, Anthony E. "Heidegger, Kneller, and Vandenberg." *Educational Theory,* vol. 16, July 1966, 239-241.

2001    Dessauer, F. *Streit um die Technik.* Frankfurt, 1956, 348-368.

2002    Deutsch, Eliot. "Commentary on J. L. Mehta's: Heidegger and the Comparison of Indian and Western Philosophy." *Philosophy East and West* (Honolulu), vol. 20, 1970, 319-321.

2003    De Vitiis, Pietro. Rev. of *La dottrina del giudizio nello psicologismo,* by Martin Heidegger. Ed. Albino Babolin. *Aquinas* (Roma), vol. 16, 1973, 142-146.

2004    De Vitiis, Pietro. *Heidegger e la fine della filosofia.* Firenze: La Nuova Italia, 1974, 256 p.

2005    De Vitiis, Pietro. Rev. of *Scritti filosofici (1912-1917),* by Martin Heidegger. Ed. Albino Babolin. (Univ. di Parma. Istituto di scienze religiose, Saggi, 2). Padova: La Garangola, 1972, 246 p. *Incontri Culturali* (Roma), vol. 7, 1974, 268-270.

2006    De Vitiis, Pietro. "Schelling secondo Heidegger." *Rivista di Filosofia Neo-Scolastica* (Milano), vol. 67, no. 3, 1975, 516-524.

2007    De Vitiis, Pietro. "Il problema di Dio in Martin Heidegger." *Rivista di Filosofia Neo-Scolastica* (Milano), vol. 67, 1975, 24-42.

2008    De Vitiis, Pietro. Rev. of *La dottrina delle categorie e del significato in Duns Scoto,* by Martin Heidegger. Ed. Albino Babolin. (Piccola biblioteca filosofica Laterza, 92). Roma-Bari: Laterza, 1974, xxvi-261. *Rivista di Filosofia Neo-Scolastica* (Milano), vol. 68, 1976, 158-162.

2008a   De Vitis, Pietro. "Heidegger e la fine della filosofia." *Aquinas* (Roma), vol. 22, no. 2-3, 1979, 259-264.

2009    Diaz de Tuesta, V. "Exploración del ser que concreta al ente material. Que es eso que Ilamanos materia?" *Estudio Agustiniano* (Valladolid), vol. 5, 1970, 297-372.

2010    Diaz Diaz, Gonzalo. "Martin Heidegger en las letras españolas. Nota bibliográfica." *Anales Del Seminario De Metafisica,* vol. 12, 1977, 133-156.

2011    Dech, G. "Altes Buch." *Martin Heidegger zum 70. Geburtstag. Festschrift.* Pfullingen, 1959, 301.

2012    Diéguez, Manuel de. "Chez Heidegger à Fribourg." *Les Nouvelles Littéraires artistiques et scientifiques* (Paris), vol. 31, no. 1295, 1952, 1, 5.

2013    Diéguez, Manuel de. "Heidegger et la postérité de Nietzsche." Rev. of *Heidegger, Nietzsche, Bd I-II. Critique* (Paris), Jg. 18, no. 183-184, 744-757.

2014    Diéguez, Manuel de. "Henry Corbin et Heidegger." *La nouvelle revue francaise* (Paris), vol. 230, 1972, 27-39.

2015    Diéguez, Manuel de. "Contestation philosophique I. A propos de Qu'est-ce qu'une chose?" *La nouvelle revue francaise* (Paris), vol. 237, 1972, 69-78.

2016　　Diemer, Alwin. "Grundzüge des Heideggerschen Philosophierens." *Zeitschrift für philosophische Forschung* (Meisenheim/Glan), vol. 5, 1950/51, 547-567.

2017　　Diemer, Alwin. "Vom Sinn ontologischen Fragens." *Sinn und Sein. Ein philosophisches Symposion.* Ed. R. Wisser. Tübingen, 1960, 231-244.

2018　　Diez Blanco, A. *Evolution del pensamiento filosofico. De Thales de Mileto a Martin Heidegger.* Valladolid, 1942.

2019　　Dilworth, David A. "Whitehead's Process Realism, the Abhidharma Dharma Theory and the Mahayana Critique." *International Philosophical Quarterly,* vol. 18, June 1978, 151-169.

2020　　Di Norcia, V. "Heidegger's Concept of Physis and Ecology." *Revue de l'Université Laurentienne* (Sudbury), vol. 9, no. 2, 1977, 25-38.

2021　　Dios Vial, Juan de. "Sobre el ser y la verdad en Heidegger." *Anales de la Universidad de Chile,* vol. 102, 1956, 63-70.

2022　　Dios Vial, Juan de. *Tres Ideas de la Filosofia y una Teoria.* Santiago, 1979.

2023　　Dittmann, L. "Die Kunsttheorie Kurt Badts." *Zeitschrift für Ästhetik und allgemeine Kunstwissenschaft,* vol. 16, 1971, 58-78.

2024　　Doering, Renate. "Ein König der Philosophie. Zum Tode des Existenzphilosophen Martin Heidegger." *Trierischer Volksfreund* (Trier), vol. 120, 27 May 1976, 14.

2025　　Doering, Renate. "Wie ein Rebell brach er ein in den akademischen Lehrbetrieb. Feldweg im Atomzeitalter. Zum Tod von Martin Heidegger." *Kölnische Rundschau* (Köln), vol. 31, no. 114, 27 May 1976, 15.

2026　　Doherty, J. E. *Sein, Mensch und Symbol. Heidegger und die Auseinandersetzung mit dem neukantianischen Symbolbegriff.* Bonn, 1972, 278

2027　　Dollé, Jean-Paul. "La mort de Heidegger. A-t-elle marqué, cette mort, la disparition du dernier philosophe, ou, au contraire, la reconnaissance et le déploiement, à niveau, de la Métaphysique?" *Magazine Littéraire* (Paris), no. 117, 1976, 8-9.

2028　　Dominguez Hernández, Javier. "El pensar moderno y las tareas del pensar según Martin Heidegger." *Escritos, Univ. Pont. Bolivariana* (Médellin, Columbia), no. 6-7, 1977, 91-112.

2029　　Dominguez Hernández, Javier. "El pensar moderno y las tareas del pensar según Martin Heidegger." *Escritos, Univ. Pont. Bolivariana* (Médellin, Colombia), vol. 3, no. 8, 1978, 3-17' vol. 3 no. 9, 1978, 70-82.

2029a　Dominguez Hernández, Javier. "El pensar moderno y las tareas del pensar según Martin Heidegger (conclusion)." *Escritos* (Medellín), vol. 3, no. 10, 1979, 123-138.

2030　　Dondeyne, A. "L'historicite dans la philosophie contemporaine." *Revue Philosophique de Louvain,* vol. 54, 1956, 5-25.

2031　　Dondeyne, A. "La difference ontologique chez M. Heidegger." *Revue Philosophique de Louvain* (Louvain), vol. 56, 1958, 35-62, 251-293.

2032    Donghûi, Ch'oe. "Haidegkae issôsôûi inganjonjewa sigong" (Being of Man and
        Space-Time in Heidegger). M. A. Thesis, Koryo Univ., 1954.

2033    Dooyeweerd, H. *De Wijsbegeerte der wetsidee. Bd II: De functioneele
        zinstructuur der tijdelijke werkelijkheid en het probleem der kennis.*
        Amsterdam, 1935, (specifically pages 19-22, 451-468).

2034    Dornseiff, F. "Wie wenn am Feiertage das Feld zu sehn ein Landmann geht..."
        Rev. of *Hölderlins Hymne 'Wie Wenn am Feiertage',* by Martin Heidegger.
        Halle, 1941. *Geistige Arbeit. Zeitung aus der wissenschaftlichen Welt*
        (Berlin), Jg. 9, no. 19, 1942, 5.

2034    aDottori, Ricardo. "Nota: La questione della dialettica in Hegel, Heidegger,
        Gadamer." In *Hans Georg Gadamer: La dialettica di Hegel.* (Classici del
        pensiero moderno e contemporaneo a cura di Umberto Margiotta, 7).
        Toriono: Marietti, 1973, 152-178.

2035    Dottori, Ricardo. "Kritisches Nachwort zu *Hegels Dialektik* von H. G.
        Gadamer und zum Verhältnis Hegel-Heidegger-Gadamer." *Bijdragen*
        (Nijmegen, Brugge), vol. 38, 1977, 176-192.

2036    Doty, Stephen Charles. "Heidegger's Kant-Interpretations. Through Retrieve
        to Dialogue." Authorized facsimile of the dissertation of the Paul Univ.
        Phil. Diss. 1973. Ann Arbor, Michigan; London: University Microfilms
        International, 1979, iv-172 p. *Dissertation Abstracts International,* vol.
        34/06-A, 3963.

2037    Douglas, George H. "Heidegger's Notion of Poetic Truth." *The Personalist*
        (Los Angeles), vol. 47, 1966, 500-508.

2038    Douglas, George H. "Heidegger on the Education of Poets and Philosophers."
        *Educational Theory* (Urbana), vol. 22, 1972, 443-449.

2039    Doyle, John P. "Heidegger and Scholastic Metaphysics." *The Modern
        Schoolman* (St. Louis), vol. 49, 1972, 201-220.

2040    Doz, André. "Remarques sur Heidegger et le problème de l'histoire."
        *Recherches et Débats* (Paris), vol. 17, 1956, 70-88.

2041    Doz, André. "L'ontologie fondamentale et le problème de la culpabilité."
        *Revue de Máaphysique et de Morale* (Paris), vol. 61, 1956, 166-194.

2042    Doz, André. "Martin Heidegger." *Revue de Métaphysique et de Morale* (Paris),
        vol. 81, no. 4, 1976, 433-437.

2043    Dreyfus, Hubert L. "Wild on Heidegger." *The Journal of Philosophy* (New
        York), vol. 60, 1963, 677-680.

2044    Dreyfus, Hubert L., and S. Todes. "The Existentialist Critique of Objectivity:
        Kierkegaard, Nietzsche and Heidegger." In *Patterns of the Life-World.* Ed.
        J. M. Edie. Evanston, Illinois, 1971, 346-381.

2045    Dreyfus, Hubert L. "What Computers Can't Do: A Critique of Artificial
        Reason." New York, 1972, 259 p., (specifically pages 173-188).

2046    Dreyfus, Hubert L. "The Priority of the World to my World: Heidegger's
        Answer to Husserl (and Sartre)." *Man and World* (The Hague), vol. 8, 1975,
        121-130.

2047    Dreyfus, Hubert, and John Haugeland. "Husserl and Heidegger: Philosophy's Last Stand." In *Heideger and Modern Philosophy. Critical Essays.* Ed. Michael Murray. New Haven, Connecticut: Yale Univ. Press, 1978, 222-238.

2048    Dubsky, Ivan. "Über Hegels und Heideggers Begriff der Zeit." In *Hegel-Jahrbuch.* 1 Halbband. München, 1961, 73-84.

2049    Dubsky, Ivan. "Heidegger o technice a byti" (Heidegger on Technology and on Being). *Dejiny a soucasnos* (Geschichte und Gegenwart), vol. 2, 1965, 10-12.

2050    Dubsky, Ivan. "Domov a bezdomovi" (Home and Unhomeliness). *Filosoficky casopis* (Prag), 1966, 64-72.

2051    Dubsky, Ivan. "Unterwegs." (Czechoslovakia). *Filosoficky Caspopis* (Praha), no. 5-6, 1969, 703-713.

2052    Dubská-Novozámská, J. "Existencionalismus v anglosaském svete." *Filosoficky Casopis* (Praha), vol. 16, 1968, 425-443.

2053    Ducoin, G. "A propos de la vérité αληδεια." *Analecta Gregoriana* (Romae), vol. 67, 1954, 31-34, passim.

2054    Ducot, C. *Présence et absence de l'être.* Paris, 1960, 192 p.

2055    Duda, S. *Selbstwerdung und Sprache bei M. Heidegger als Grundlage für pädagogische Anthropologie.* Phil. Diss. Wien 1966 II and 116 Bl.

2055a   Düsing, Klaus. "Objektive and subjektive Zeit." *Kant-Studien 71.* Berlin: Walter de Gruyter, 1979, 1-34.

2056    Dufrenne, Mikel, and Paul Ricoeur. *Karl Jaspers et la philosophie de l'existence.* Paris, 1947, (specifically pages 363-372).

2057    Dufrenne, Mikel. "Heidegger et Kant." *Revue de métaphysique et de morale* (Paris), vol. 54, 1949, 1-28. Rpt. in *Phaenomenologica.* Collection publée sous le patronage des centres d'Archives Husserl, 20. La Haye, 1966.

2058    Dufrenne, Mikel. "La mentalité primitive et Heidegger." *Les Etudes philosophiques* (Paris), vol. 9, 1954, 284-306. Rpt. in *Phaenomenologica* (La Haye), vol. 20, 1966, 127-149.

2059    Dufrenne, Mikel. *Pour l'homme.* Paris, 1968.

2060    Duintjer, O. D. Rev. of *Was ist Metaphysik?,* by Martin Heidegger. Bonn, 1929. *Wijsgerig Perspectief op Maatschappij en Wetenschap* (Amsterdam), vol. 3, 1962/63, 152-154.

2061    Duintjer, O. D. *De Vraag naar het transcendentale vooral in verband met Heidegger en Kant.* (Summary written in German). Leiden, 1966, VII, 417 p.

        [Rev. by K. Oedingen in *Kant-Studien* (Bonn), vol. 63, 1972, H. 3, 384-385.]

2062    Dultz, W. *Eine Untersuchung über die Philosophie Martin Heideggers.* Phil. Diss. Heidelberg 1940 62 p.

2062a  Dupuy, Bernard. "Heidegger et le Dieu inconnu." In *Heidegger et la question de Dieu.* Ed. by Richard Kearney and Joseph Stephen O'Leary. Paris: B. Grasset, 1980, 103-121.

2063  Duroché, Leonard L. "Aspects of Literary Criticism in Present Day Germany, With Special Reference to the Thought of Martin Heidegger." Phil. Diss. Stanford Univ. 1965 350 p. *Dissertation Abstracts International,* vol. 26/01, 353.

2064  Dussort, H. "L'artiste dépassé par l'art." (Note sur Mallarmé et Heidegger). *Revue Philosophique de la France et de l'étranger* (Paris), Jg. 82, Bd 147, 1957, 41-46.

2065  Dybel, P. "Martina Heideggera mysl o mowie" (Heidegger's Thinking Concerning Language). *Przeglad humanistyczny,* 8 July 1978.

2066  Dybel, P. Rev. of *Heidegger i filozofia wspóczesna* (Heidegger and Contemporary Philosophy), by Krzysztof Michalski. Warszawa, 1978. *Miesiecznik Literacki,* September 1978.

2067  Dybel, P. Rev. of *Budowac, mieszkac, myálec. Eseje wybrane* (Bauen, Wohnen, Denken. Ausgewählte Essays), by Martin Heidegger. Ed. Kryzysztof Michalski. Warszawa, 1977. *Nowy Wyraz,* April 1978.

2068  Dyroff, A. Rev. of *Die Kategorien und Bedeutungslehre des Duns Scotus,* by Martin Heidegger. Tübingen, 1916. *Historische Zeitschrift* (München/Berlin), vol. 119, 1919, 497-499.

2069  Dyroff, A. "Glossen zu Heideggers 'Sein und Zeit'." *Philosophia perennis* (Regensburg), vol. II, [Festgabe Josef Geyser], 1930, 772-796.

2070  Earle, William. "Wahl on Heidegger on Being." Rev. of *Einführung in die Metaphysik,* by Martin Heidegger. Tübingen, 1953. *Philosophical Review* (Ithaka/New York), vol. 67, 1958, 85-90.

2071  Earle, William. "Phenomenology and Existentialism." *The Journal of Philosophy,* vol. 57, 1960, 75-83.

2072  Ebeling, Georg. "Verantwortung des Glaubens in Begegnung mit dem Denken M. Heideggers." *Zeitschrift für Theologie und Kirche* (Tübingen), Beih. 2, 1961, 119-124.

2073  Echauri, Raúl. "El ser como luz y como acto." *Cuadernos de Filosofia* (Rosario), 1961, 43-52.

2074  Echauri, Raúl. *El ser en la filosofia de Heidegger.* Rosario, 1964, 175 p.

2075  Echauri, Raúl. "La diferencia ontológica en Heidegger y Santo Tomás." *Philosophia* (Argentinia), no. 28, 1964, 16-28.

2076  Echauri, Raúl. Rev. of *Kants These über das Sein,* by Martin Heidegger. *Documentación Critica Iberoamericana de Filosofia y Ciencias Afines* (Sevilla), vol. 3, 1966, 29-35.

2077  Echauri, Raúl. *Heidegger y la metafisica tomista.* (Introduction by E. Gilson). Buenos Aires, 1970, 189 p.

2078  Echauri, Raúl. *Heidegger y la metafisica tomista.* Buenos Aires, 1971, 189 p.

2079   Echauri, Raúl. "Ser y realidad en *El ser y el tiempo* de Heidegger." Eds. E. Sosa Lopez and A. Caturelli. *Temas de Filosofia Contemporanea* (Buenos Aires), 1971, 45-51.

2080   Echauri, Raúl. *Heidegger y la metafisica tomista.* Buenos Aires: Eudeba, 1971, 189 p.

2081   Echauri, Raúl. "Heidegger y el *esse* tomista." *Cuadernos de Filosofia* (Buenos Aires), vol. 11, no. 15-16, 207-214.

2082   Echauri, Raúl. "Desocultamiento y creación." *Sapientia* (La Plata), vol. 29, 1974, 35-42.

2083   Echizenyd, Etsuko. "Haideggâ no 'Tenkai' ni tsuite" (On Heidegger's Reversal). *Kokugakuin-Zasshi* (Tôkyô), vol. 77, no. 11, 1976, 115-128.

2084   Eckstein, W. Rev. of *Heidegger und die Tradition,* by W. Marx. Stuttgart, 1961. *Journal of Philosophy* (New York), vol. 60, 1963, 251-252.

2085   Ecole, J. Rev. of *Introduction à la métaphysique,* by Martin Heidegger. *Les Etudes Philosophiques* (Paris), vol. 13, 1958, 276-377.

2086   Ecole, J. Rev. of *Essais et conférences,* by Martin Heidegger. (Préface de J. Beaufret). Paris, 1958. *Les Etudes Philosophiques* (Paris), N.S. 14, 1959, 223-224.

2087   Ecole, J. Rev. of *Qu'appelle-t-on penser?,* by Martin Heidegger. Paris, 1959. *Les Etudes Philosophiques* (Paris), N.S. 15, 1960, 106-107.

2088   Ecole, J. Rev. of *Le principe de raison,* by Martin Heidegger. Paris, 1962. *Les Etudes Philsophiques* (Paris), vol. 17, 1962, 547-548.

2089   Ecole, J. Rev. of *Chemins qui ne ménent nulle part,* by Martin Heidegger. Paris, 1962. *Les Etudes Philosophiques* (Paris), N.S. 17, 1962, 546-547.

2090   Edwards, A. "Martin Heidegger y el pensar. Una semblanza." *Teologia y Vida* (Santiago de Chile), vol. 18, no. 1, 1977, 49-60.

2091   Edwards, A. "Persona Humana conquista, destruccion y nueva bûqueda." *Stromata* (San Miguel, Argentinia), no. 1-2, 1978, 3-25.

2092   Edwards, Paul. "Existentialism and Death: A Survey of Some Confusions and Absurdities." *Philosophy, Science and Method.* (Essays in honor of Ernest Nagel). Eds. S. Morgenbesser, P. Suppes and M. White. London, 1971, 473-505. [1st ed. New York, 1969]

2093   Edwards, Paul. "Heidegger and Death as 'Possibility'." *Mind* (Oxford), vol. 84, 1975, 548-566.

2094   Edwards, Paul. "Heidegger and Death. A Deflationary Critique." *Revue d'Histoire des Mines et de la Métallurgie* (Jarville, France), vol. 59, no. 2, 1976, 161-186. Rpt. in *The Monist* (La Salle), vol. 56, 1976, 161-186.

2094a  Edwards, Paul. *Heidegger and Death. A Critical Evaluation.* (Monistmonograph, 1). La Salle: Hegeler Inst., 1979, 71 p.

2095   Egidi, R. Rev. of *Die Frage nach dem Ding; Zu Kants Lehre von den transzendentalen Grundsätzen,* by Martin Heidegger. *Archivio di Filosofia* (Roma), no. 3, 1965.

2096    Ehman, Robert. "Temporal Self-Identity." *Southern Journal of Philosophy* (Memphis), vol. 12, 1974, 333-341.

2097    Ehrentreich, A. "Versuche mit Schriften Martin Heideggers in der philosophischen Arbeitsgemeinschaft." *Die Sammlung* (Zeitschrift für Kultur und Erziehung), (Göttingen), vol. 13, 1958, 274-278.

2098    Ehrentreich, A. "Schwyzer Fehde Gegen Heideggers Vergangenheit." *Neue Sammlung. Göttinger Blätter für Kultur und Erziehung* (Göttingen), vol. 2, 1962, 382-384.

2099    Eisenhuth, E. *Der Begriff des Irrationalen als philosophisches Problem. Ein Beitrag zur Religionsbegründung.* Göttingen, 1931, (specifically page 216 ff).

2100    Eisenhuth, H. E. Rev. of *Platons Lehre von der Wahrheit. Mit einem Brief über den 'Humanismus',* by Martin Heidegger. Bern, 1947. *Theologische Literaturzeitung* (Berlin), vol. 76, 1951, 494-495.

2101    Eisenhuth, H. E. Rev. of *Holzwege,* by Martin Heidegger. Frankfurt, 1950. *Theologische Literaturzeitung* (Berlin), vol. 78, 1953, 306-309.

2102    Eisenhuth, H. E. Rev. of *Vom Wesen des Grundes,* by Martin Heidegger. 3rd ed. Frankfurt, 1949. *Theologische Literaturzeitung* (Berlin), vol. 78, 1953, 362-364.

2103    Eisenhuth, H. E. Rev. of *Vorträge und Aufsätze,* by Martin Heidegger. Pfullingen, 1954. *Theologische Literaturzeitung* (Berlin), vol. 82, 1957, 458-461.

2104    Elliston, Frederick. "Phenomenology Reinterpreted. From Husserl to Heidegger." *Philosophy Today* (Celina, Ohio), vol. 21, no. 3, 1977, 273-283.

2105    Elliston, Frederick A., ed. *Heidegger's Existential Analytic.* The Hague/Paris/New York: Mouton Publishers, 1978, xiv-273.

2106    Elliston, Frederick A. "Heidegger's Phenomenology of Social Existence." In *Heidegger's Existential Analytic.* Ed. Frederick Elliston. The Hague/New York: Mouton Publishers, 1978, 61-77.

2107    Emad, Parvis. "'Sein und Zeit im Bereich' der englischen Sprache." *Wissenschaft und Weltbild* (Wien), vol. 3, 1969, 227-230.

2108    Emad, Parvis. Rev. of *Zur Sache des Denkens,* by Martin Heidegger. *Philosophy and Phenomenological Research* (Buffalo), vol. 31, 1970/71, 617-618.

2109    Emad, Parvis. Rev. of *Hegels Concept of Experience,* by Martin Heidegger. *Philosophischer Literaturanzeiger* (Meisenheim/Glan), vol. 25, 1972, H. 3, 181-183.

2110    Emad, Parvis. Rev. of *A Commentary of Heidegger's Being and Time,* by Martin Heidegger. *Philosophischer Literaturanzeiger* (Meisenheim/Galn), vol. 3, 1973, 169-171.

2111    Emad, Parvis. Rev. of *Poetry, Language, Thought,* by Martin Heidegger. *Philosophischer Literaturanzeiger* (Meisenheim/Glan), vol. 2, 1973, 117-119.

2112    Emad, Parvis. "Über den gegenwärtigen Stand der Interpretation des Denkens Heideggers in englische Sprache." *Zeitschrift für Philosophische Forschung* (Meisenheim), vol. 27, 1973, 289-301.

2113    Emad, Parvis. "C. M. Sherover's Heidegger, Kant and Time." *The Southern Journal of Philosophy* (Memphis), vol. 11, no. 4, 1973, 367-374.

2114    Emad, Parvis. Rev. of *Poetry, Language, Thought,* by Martin Heidegger. Trans. and intr. Albert Hofstadter. New York: Harper & Row, 1971, 229 p. *Philosophischer Literaturanzeiger* (Meisenheim/Glan), vol. 26, 1973, 117-120.

2115    Emad, Parvis. Rev. of *On Time and Being,* by Martin Heidegger. Trans. Joan Stambaugh. New York: Harper & Row, 1972, 84 p. *Philosophischer Literaturanzeiger* (Meisenheim/Glan), vol. 27, 223-125.

2116    Emad, Parvis. Rev. of *On the Way to Language,* by Martin Heidegger. Trans. Peter D. Hertz. New York: Harper & Row, 1971, 200 p. *Philosophischer Literaturanzeiger* (Meisenheim/Glan), vol. 27, 1974, 161-163.

2117    Emad, Parvis. Rev. of *M. Heidegger: In Europe and America.* Eds. E. G. Ballard and Charles E. Scott. With contributions by Robert Cooper, Otto Pöggeler, Karl Löwith et al. The Hague: Martinus Nijhoff, 1974, xii-200. *Philosophischer Literaturanzeiger* (Meisenheim/Galn), vol. 28, 1975, 297-298.

2118    Emad, Parvis. Rev. of *On Heidegger and Language,* by Joseph Kockelmans. Evanston, Illinois, 1972/73. *Philosophischer Literaturanzeiger* (Meisenheim/Mainz), vol. 28, 1975, 344-346.

2119    Emad, Parvis. Rev. of *The End of Philosophy,* by Martin Heidegger. Trans. Joan Stambauch. New York, 1973. *Philosophischer Literaturanzeiger* (Meisenheim/Mainz), vol. 28, 1975, 296.

2120    Emad, Parvis. "Heidegger on Schelling's Concept of Freedom." *Man and World* (The Hague), vol. 8, 1975, 157-74.

2121    Emad, Parvis. "Heidegger's Value-Criticism and Its Bearing on the Phenomenology of Values." *Research in Phenomenology* (Pittsburgh), vol. 7, 1977, 190-208.

2122    Emad, Parvis. "Das Ringen um die Sprache Heideggers. Wiederübersetzung seiner Werke." *Philosophischer Literaturanzeiger* (Meisenheim), vol. 31, 1978, 184-190.

2122a   Emad, Parvis. "Foucault and Biemel on Representation: A Beginning Inquiry." *Man and World* (The Hague), vol. 12, 1979, 284-297.

2123    Emad, Parvis. Rev. of *Early Greek Thinking,* by Martin Heidegger. Trans. David Farrell Krell and Frank A. Capuzzi. New York: Harper & Row, 1975. *Philosophischer Literaturanzeiger* (Meisenheim/Glan), vol. 32, 1979, 60-61.

2123a   Emad, Parvis. Rev. of "Martin Heidegger: Metaphysische Anfangründe der Logik." *Research in Phenomenology* (Pittsburgh), vol. 9, 1979, 233-246.

2124    Engelhardt, P. M. "Eine Begegnung zwischen Martin Heidegger und thomistischer Philosophie?" *Freiburger Zeitschrift für Philosophie und Theologie* (Freiburg, Schweiz), vol. 3, 1956, 187-196.

2125    Engler, Helmut. "Introduction." *Heidegger. Freiberger Universitätsvorträge zu seinem Gedenken.* (Alber-Broschur Philosophie). Freiburg: Alber, 1977.

2126    Englert, L. "Als Student bei den zweiten Davoser Hochschulkursen." *Die Zweiten Davoser Hochschulkurse 17. März bis 6. April 1929* (Davos), 64 p.

2127    Enoda, Tatsumi. "Haideggâ ni okeru Ningensonzai no Konponkozô" (The Fundamental Structure of the Human Being by Heidegger). *Kyôto Daigaku Kyoiku Gakubu Kiyô* (Kyôto), vol. 23, 1977, 74-84.

2128    Entralgo, P. L. "Quevedo und Heidegger." *Deutsche Vierteljahresschrift für Literaturwissenschaft und Geistesgeschichte* (Halle/Saale), vol. 17, 1939, 405-418.

2129    Erickson, Stephen Anthony. "The Metaphysician as Constructive Thinker: An Interpretation of Heidegger's Thought." Phil Diss. Yale Univ. 1964.

2130    Erickson, Stephen Anthony. "Martin Heidegger." *Review of Metaphysics* New Haven, Connecticut), vol. 19, 1965/66, 462-492.

2131    Erickson, Stephen Anthony. "Meaning and Language." (Heidegger and Wittgenstein). *Man and World* (Pittsburgh), vol. 1, 1968, 563-586.

2132    Erickson, Stephen Anthony. "Worlds and Worlds Views." *Man and World* (Pittsburgh), vol. 2, 1969, 228-247, (specifically pages 242-244).

2133    Erickson, Stephen Anthony. *Language and Being. An Analytic Phenomenology.* New Haven/London, 1970, 165 p.

2134    Erickson, Stephen Anthony. "Views and Perspectives." *Man and World* (West Lafayette), vol. 7, no. 2, 1974, 103-117.

2135    Erlach, E. Rev. of *Was heisst Denken,* by Martin Heidegger. Tübingen, 1954. *Oberösterreichische Nachrichten* (Linz), 4.1.1955.

2136    Erlach, E. "Heidegger fragt: 'Was heisst Denken'?" *Oberösterreichische Nachrichten* (Tages-Post), 4.6.1955.

2137    Ernst, W. "Moderne Versuche zur Gewinnung eines neuen Lebensverständnisses in Philosophie und Theologie (M. Heidegger und die dialektische Theologie)." *Zeitschrift für systematische Theologie* (Gütersloh), vol. 9, 1931, 25-46.

2138    Ernst, W. "Theologische Begriffe in der modernen Existentialphilosophie." *Zeitschrift für systematische Theologie* (Gütersloh), vol. 10, 1933, 589-612.

2139    Ernst, W. "Der moderne Existenzgedanke in seiner Auswirkung und Auswertung für das Handeln der Kirche." *Der Geisteskampf der Gegenwart* (Gütersloh), vol. 66, 1933, 97-110.

2140    Erro, C. *El diálogo existencial. Exposición y análisis de la filosofía de Heidegger.* Buenos Aires, 1938.

2141 Ersov, M. V. "Filosofija jazyka i religii M. Chajdeggera" (M. Heidegger's Philosophy of Language and Philosophy of Religion). *Problemy bor'by protiv burzuaznoj ideologii* (Leningrad), vol. 2, 1973, 54-65.

2142 Ertel, Chr. "Von der Phänomenologie und jüngeren Lebensphilosophie zur Existentialphilosophie M. Heidegger." *Philosophisches Jahrbuch* (Fulda), vol. 51, 1938, 1-28.

2143 Escamilla, M. L. *La metafisica de El ser y el tiempo de Heidegger.* Editorial Univ., San Salvador, 1961, 284 p.

2144 Esposito, Joseph L. "Play and Possibility." *Philosophy Today* (Celina, Ohio), vol. 18, 1974, 137-146.

2145 Estall, H. M. Rev. of *German Existentialism,* by Martin Heidegger. *Dialogue* (Montreal, Kingston), vol. 4, 1965/66, 415-416.

2146 Estiú, E. "El problema metafisico en las ultimas obras de Heidegger." Introduction to *Introduccion a la metafisica,* by Martin Heidegger. Trans. E. Estiú. Buenos Aire, 1956.

2147 Etô, Tarô. "Haideggâ ni okeru Kikyô no Mondai" (The Problem of Home-Coming in Heidegger). *Risô* (Tôkyô), vol. 223, Dezember 1951.

2148 Etô, Tarô. "Sonzai no Akarumi no Kôzô" (The Structure of the Clearing of Being). *Risô* (Tôkyô), vol. 444, 1970, 11-20.

2149 Etô, Tarô. "Dôgen-Tetsugaku to Heideggâ" (Dôgen's Philosophy and Heidegger). *Risô* (Tôkyô), vol. 349, Juni 1962.

2150 Evain, F. Rev. of *Was ist das - die Philosophie?,* by Martin Heidegger. Pfullingen, 1956; and *Qu'est-ce que la Philosophie?,* 2nd ed. Paris 1957. *Archives de Philosophie* (Paris), vol. 21, 1958, 146-147.

2151 Evain, F. "L'être en question dans la personne. Un affrontement entre Rosmini et Heidegger." *Rivista rosminiana di Filosofia e di Cultura* (Domodossola-Milano), vol. 58, 1964, 29-34.

2152 F.C.C. Rev. of *Being and Time,* by Martin Heidegger. *Heythrop Journal* (Oxford), vol. 4, 1963, 104.

2153 F., I. Rev. of *Essais et conferences,* by Martin Heidegger. Paris, 1958. *Revue Bénédictine* (Maredsous), vol. 69, 1959, 172.

2154 Fabro, Cornelio. *Introduzione all'esistenzialismo.* Milano, 1943, 73-88.

2155 Fabro, Cornelio. *Problemi dell'esistenzialismo.* Roma, 1945, 24-31.

2156 Fabro, Cornelio. "Arte e poesia nell'ultimo Heidegger." *Estetica, Atti del VII convegno di studi filosofici cristiani tra professori univ.,* Padova, 1951, 434-441.

2157 Fabro, Cornelio. "Ontologia dell'arte nell'ultimo Heidegger." *Giornale Critico dell Filosofia Italiana* (Firenze), Jg. 31, Ser. 3, vol. 6, 1952, 344-361.

2158 Fabro, Cornelio. "Ontologia esistenzialistica e metafisica tradizionale." *Rivista di Filosofia Neo-Scolastica* (Milano), vol. 45, 1953, 581-618, passim.

2159 Fabro, Cornelio. "Il problema di Dio nell'ultimo Heidegger." *Atti del Congresso per il IV Centenario della Pont. Univ. Gregoriana,* 14-17 ottobre 1953. Sezione Filosofica.

2160 Fabro, Cornelio. "Il problema di Dio nel pensiero di Heidegger." *Analecta Gregoriana* (Romae), vol. 67, 1954, (Studi filosofici intorno all 'Existenza' al Mondo, al Trascendente), 17-29.

2161 Fabro, Cornelio. *Dall'essere all'esistente.* Brescia, 1957, 521 p.

[Specifically pages 337-424: Ontologia metaphysica nell'ultimo Heidegger.]

2162 Fabro, Cornelio. "L'essere e l'esistente nell'ultimo Heidegger." *Giornale Critico della Filosofia Italiana* (Firenze), vol. 38, 1959, 240-258.

2163 Fabro, Cornelio. "Il ritorno al fondamento. Contributo per un confronto fra l'ontologia di Heidegger e la metafisica di S. Tommaso d'Aquino." *Sapienza* (Roma), vol. 26, 1973, 265-278.

2164 Fabro, Cornelio, Johannes B. Lotz, and G. Bontadini. "Dibattito Congressuale: Allocusioni Introduttive Al Dibattito." *Sapienza,* vol. 26, July-December 1973, 357-370.

2165 Fabro, Cornelio. "Il trascendentale esistenziale e la riduzione al fondamento." *Giornale Critico della Filosofia Italiana* (Firenze), vol. 52, no. 4, 1973, 469-516.

2166 Fabro, Cornelio. "Freedom and Existence in Contemporary Philosophy and in St. Thomas." *The Thomist* (Baltimore), vol. 38, no. 3, 1974, 524-556.

2167 Fabro, Cornelio. "Il ritorno al fondamento. Contributo per un confronto fra l'ontologia di Heidegger e la metafisica di S. Tommaso d'Aquino." *Scripta Theologica* (Pamplona), vol. 6, no. 1, 1974, 93-109.

2168 Fabro, Cornelio. "L'interpretazione dell'atto in S. Tommaso e Heidegger." *Tommaso d'Aquino nel suo VII Centenario.* Congresso Internazionale. Roma, Napoli, 17-24 aprile, 1974, Roma: Via Panisperna, 261, 505-517.

2169 Fabro, Cornelio. "L'interpretazione dell'atto in S. Tommaso e Heidegger." *Tommaso d'Aquino nella storia del pensiero.* Vol. I: Le fonti del pensiero di S. Tommaso (Atti del Congresso internazionale. Roma-Napoli, 17/24 aprile 1974. Tommaso d'Aquino nel suo settimo centenario), Napoli: Edizioni Domenicane Italiane, 1975, 119-128.

2170 Fabro, Cornelio. "Edith Stein, Husserl e Martin Heidegger." *Humanitas* (Brescia), vol. 33, no. 4, 485-517.

2171 Fackeldey, H. "Essentia und esse und die Seinsmomente des Soseins und Daseins. Eine begriffsvergleichende Studie." *Philosophia Naturalis* (Meisenheim/Glan), vol. 9, 1965, 114-137.

2172 Fagone, Virgilio. "Unita o frattura nel pensiero di M. Heidegger?" *Civiltà cattolica* (Roma), 107, vol. 2, 1956, 21-34.

2173 Fagone, Virgilio. "Unité ou discontinuité dans la pensée de M. Heidegger?" *Sciences ecclésiastiques* (Montréal), vol. 8, 1956, 317-333.

2174 Fagone, Virgilio. "Il problema della verità in Heidegger." *La Civiltà Cattolica* (Roma), 110, vol. III, 1959, 140-154.

2175 Fagone, Virgilio. "Verità e libertà in Heidegger." *La Civiltà Cattolica* (Roma), 110, vol. III, 1959, 487-502.

2176 Fagone, Virgilio. "Tempo e intenzionalità. Brentano-Husserl-Heidegger." *Archivio di Filosofia* (Roma), no. 1, 1960, 105-131.

2177 Fagone, Virgilio. "Demitizzazione ed ermeneutica esistenziale." *Civiltà cattolica* (Roma), 113, 1962, 2680, 325-337.

2178 Fagone, Virgilio. Rev. of *Introduzione alla metafisica,* by Martin Heidegger. *La Civiltà Cattolica* (Roma), vol. 120, no. 3, 1969, 200-201.

2179 Fagone, Virgilio. "M. Heidegger e il superamento della metafisica." *La Civiltà Cattolica* (Roma), vol. IV, 127, 1976, 126-141.

2180 Fagone, V. S. I. "Il fondamento ontologico della communicazione nell'analisi esistenziale di Martin Heidegger." *La Civiltà Cattolica* (Roma), 116, 1965, 414-427.

2181 Fahrenbach, Helmut. *Existenzphilosophie und Ethik.* Frankfurt, 1969, XII, 216 p., (specifically pages 99-131).

2182 Fahrenbach, Helmut. "Heidegger und das Problem einer 'philosophischen' Anthropologie." *Durchblicke.* Ed. V. Klostermann. Frankfurt, 1970, 97-131.

2183 Fales, W. Rev. of *Platons Lehre von der Wahrheit. Mit einem Brief über den 'Humanismus',* by Martin Heidegger. Bern, 1947. *Philosophy and Phenomenological Research* (Buffalo, New York), vol. 10, 1949/50, 605-606.

2184 Falk, W. "Heidegger und Trakl." *Literaturwissenschaftliches Jahrbuch* (Berlin), vol. 4, 1963, 191-204.

2185 Fandozzi, Phillip Robert. *The Heideggerian Perspective on Nihilism: A Critique of Modern Technology Through Its Manifestations in Literature, Philosophy and Social Thought.* Phil. Diss. Univ. of Hawaii 1974. *Dissertation Abstracts International,* vol. 36/02-A, 935.

2186 Farber, Marvin. "Experience and Transcendence: A Chapter in Recent Phenomenology and Existentialism." *Philosophy and Phenomenological Research,* vol. 12, 1951, 1-23.

2187 Farber, Marvin. Rev. of *Existence and Being,* by Martin Heidegger. Chicago, 1949. *Philosophy and Phenomenological Research* (Buffalo, New York), vol. 12, 1951/52, 580-581.

2188 Farber, Marvin. "Heidegger On the Essence of Truth." *Philosophy and Phenomenological Research* (Buffalo, New York), vol. 18, 1957/58, 523-532.

2189 Farber, Marvin. "What is Philosophy?" Rev. of *What is Philosophy?,* by Martin Heidegger. New York, 1958. *Philosophy and Phenomenological Research* (Buffalo, New York), vol. 21, 1960/61, 255-259.

2190    Farber, Marvin. *Phenomenology and Existence. Toward a Philosophy Within Nature.* New York, 1967, 244 p.

2191    Farber, Marvin. "Heidegger on the Essence of Truth." *Radiation Research* (New York/London), 1971, 79-89.

2192    Farrelly, John. "Religious Reflection and Man's Transcendence." *The Thomist* (Washington), vol. 37, 1973, 1-68.

2193    Fasquelle, Jean-Claude, ed. "Heidegger aujourd'hui. Dossier." *Magazine Littéraire* (Paris), no. 117, 1976, 6-27.

2194    Fatone, V. *La existencia human y sus filósofos. Heidegger. Jaspers. Barth. Chestov. Berdiaeff. Zubiri. Marcel. Lavelle. Sartre. Abagnano.* Buenos Aires, 1953, 193 p., (specifically pages 9-3 und passim).

2195    Favino, F. "L'umanità dell'uomo in Heidegger." *Aut Aut* (Milano), no. 40, 1957, 331-344.

2196    Favino, F. "La cosa come vicinanza pensata in Heidegger." *Aut Aut,* no. 41, 1957, 407-414.

2197    Favino, F. *Il pensoso abitare dei mortali in Heidegger.* Roma, 1959, 11 p.

2198    Fay, Thomas A. *Heidegger on Logic: An Encounter of His Thought With Wittgenstein.* Phil. Diss. New York 1971 350 p. *Dissertation Abstracts International,* vol. 32/02-A, 1012.

2199    Fay, Thomas A. "Early Heidegger and Wittgenstein on World." *Philosophical Studies* (Maynooth), vol. 21, 1971, 161-171.

2200    Fay, Thomas A. "Heidegger: Thinking as *Noein.* " *The Modern Schoolman* (Saint Louis), vol. 51, no. 1, 1973, 17-28.

2201    Fay, Thomas A. "Heidegger on Logic: A Genetic Study of His Thoughts on Logic." *Journal of the History of Philosophy* (Claremont), vol. 12, 1974, 77-94.

2202    Fay, Thomas A. "Heidegger on the History of Western Metaphysics as Forgetfulness of Being. A Thomistic Rejoinder." *Tommaso d'Aquino nella storia del pensiero. Vol. II: Dal medioevo ad oggi* (Atti del Congresso internazionale. Roma, Napoli, 17-24 aprile 1974. Tommaso d'Aquino del suo settimo centenario). Napoli: Edizioni Domenicane Italiane, 1976, 480-484.

2203    Fay, Thomas A. "Heidegger. The Role of Logic in His Thought." *The Journal of the British Society for Phenomenology* (Manchester), vol. 8, no. 2, 1977, 103-109.

2204    Fay, Thomas A. *Heidegger: The Critique of Logic.* The Hague: Martinus Nijhoff, 1977, x-136 p.

        [Rev. by Robert Brisart in *Revue Philosophique de Louvain,* 1979, 594-598.]

2205    Fay, Thomas A. "Heidegger. The Origin and Development of Symbolic Logic." *Kant-Studien,* vol. 69, no. 4, 1978, 444-460.

2206    Fay, Thomas A. "Heidegger and Wittgenstein on the Question of Ordinary Language." *Philosophy Today,* vol. 23, no. 2-4, 1979, 154-159.

2206a    Fay, Thomas A. "Two Approaches to the Philosophy of Ordinary Language: Heidegger and Wittgenstein." *Rivista critica di Storia della Filosofia* (Milano), vol. 35, 1980.

2207    Faye, J. P. "Heidegger et la 'révolution'." *Médiations* (Paris), no. 3, 1961, 151-159.

2208    Faye, J. P. "Attaques nazies contre Heidegger." *Médiations* (Paris), no. 5, 1962, 137-154.

2209    Faye, J. P. "La lecture et l'énoncé." Rev. of *Trois attaques contre Heidegger,* by Fr. Fédier. *Critique* (Paris), vol. 23, 1967, 288-295.

2210    Faye, J. P. "La chaine de la 'durete'." *Etudes Germaniques* (Lyon), vol. 23, 1968, 283-286.

2211    Fédier, François. "Trois attaques contre Heidegger." Rev. of *Nachlese zu Heidegger,* by Guido Schneeberger. Bern, 1962. *Jargon der Eigentlichkeit,* by Theodor W. Adorno. Frankfurt, 1964. *In Sachen Heidegger,* by Paul Hühnerfeld. München, 1961. *Critique* (Paris), vol. 234, 1966, 883-904.

2212    Fédier, François. "A propos de Heidegger. Une lecture dénoncée." Rev. of *La lecture et l'énonce,* by J. P. Faye. *Critique* (Paris), vol. 24, 1967, 672-686.

2213    Fédier, François. "Le point." *Critique* (Paris), vol. 24, 1968, 435-437.

         [Remarks to: A propos de Heidegger, 1967.]

2214    Fédier, François. "Andenken..." Trans. Eva-Maria Bergmann-Schmitt. Ed. Günther Neske. In *Erinnerung an Martin Heidegger.* Pfullingen: Verlag Günther Neske, 1977, 79-85.

2214a    Fédier, Francois. "Heidegger et Dieu." In *Heidegger et la question de Dieu.* Ed. by Richard Kearney and Joseph Stephen O'Leary. Paris: B. Grasset, 1980, 37-45.

2215    Fehrenbach, Dr. "Der unbequeme Philosoph." *Technische Rundschau,* 25.9.1954.

2216    Fehrenbach, O. Rev. of *Nietzsche, Bd I-II,* by Martin Heidegger. Pfullingen, 1961. *Philosophischer Literaturanzeiger* (Meisenheim/Glan), vol. 15, 1962, 3-11.

2217    Fehse, W. "Blick auf die Philosophie unserer Zeit: Hartmann und Heidegger." *Die Hilfe* (Berlin), vol. 42, 1936, 114-117.

2218    Feick, H. *Index zu Heideggers Sein und Zeit.* Tübingen, 1961, VI, 108 p. 2nd ed. Revised and enlarged, 1968, IX, 132 p.

2219    Feist Hirsch, Elisabeth. "The Problem of Speech in 'Being and Time'." Ed. Frederick Elliston. In *Heidegger's Existential Analytic.* The Hague/New York: Mouton Publishers, 1978, 159-178.

2220    Feldmann, J. Rev. of *Die Kategorien und Bedeutungslehre des Duns Scotus,* by Martin Heidegger. Tübingen, 1916. *Theologie und Glaube* (Paderborn), vol. 11, 1919, 454-455.

2221    Fellermeier, J. "Wahrheit und Existenz bei Heidegger und Thomas von
        Aquin." *Salzburger Jahrbuch für Philosophie* (Salzburg), vol. 15-16,
        1971/72, 39-70.

2222    Fellermeier, J. "Heidegger - der Begründer einer neuen Metaphysik?"
        *Münchener theologische Zeitschrift* (München), vol. 22, 1971, 234-251.

2223    Fellermeier, J. "Der Begriff der Existenz in der Scholastik und in der
        modernen Existenzphilosophie." In *Festschrift Kardinal Faulhaber zum 80.
        Geburtstag.* München, 1949, 191-205, (specifically page 198).

2224    Fell, Joseph. "Heidegger's Notion of Two Beginnings." *The Review of
        Metaphysics* (Washington), vol. 25, 1971, 213-237.

2225    Feo, N. M. de. "Il principio d'identità ed il tempo nell'ontologia di Heidegger."
        *Annali della Facoltà di Lettere e Filosofia* (Bari), vol. 7, 1961, 223-267.

2226    Feo, N. M. de. "Il principio d'identità ed il tempo nell'ontologia di Heidegger."
        *Annali dell Facoltà di Lettere e Filosofia* (Bari), vol. 8, 1962, 223-267.

2227    Feo, N. M. de. *Kierkegaard, Nietzsche, Heidegger.* ('Laocoonte'). Milano,
        1964, 279 p.

2228    Feo, N. M. de. "Ancora a proposito del *Was ist das - die Philosophie?* di
        Heidegger." *Teoresi* (Catania), vol. 21, 1966, 97-108.

2228a   Feo, N. M. de. "Heidegger e l'autonomia del negativo." *Aquinas* (Roma), vol.
        22, no. 2-3, 1979, 242-258.

2228b   Ferguson, Frances C. "Reading Heidegger. Paul de Man and Jacques
        Derrida." In *Martin Heidegger and the Question of Literature.* Ed. by
        William V. Spanos. Bloomington, Indiana; London: Indiana Univ. Press,
        1979, 253-270.

2229    Ferrara, Lawrence. *Referential Meaning in Music: A Conceptual Model Based
        on the Philosophy of Martin Heidegger.* Phil. Diss. New York Univ. 256 p.
        *Dissertation Abstracts International,* vol. 39/08-A, 4979.

2230    Ferrari, O. H. "Filosofia y metafisica de Heidegger." *Philosophia* (Argentinia),
        1964, no. 28, 41-47.

2231    Ferrari, O. H. "El ser en la fenomenologia de Husserl y de Heidegger."
        *Philosophia* (Mendoza, Argentinia), vol. 35, 1969, 65-110.

2232    Ferrari, O. H. "Heidegger y la filosofia." *Philosophia* (Mendoza), no. 27, 1963,
        43-49.

2233    Ferreira da Silva Filho, V. "A última fase do pensamento de Heidegger."
        *Revista Brasileire de Filosofia* (Sao Paulo), vol. 1, 1951, 278-289.

2234    Ferry, Luc, and Alain Renaut. "Heidegger en question. Essai de critique
        interne." *Archives de Philosophie* (Paris), vol. 41, 1978, 597-639.
        [Summary, 597.]

2235    Ferry, Luc, and Alain Renaut. "Universite et System." *Archives de Philosophie,*
        vol. 42, January-March 1979, 59-90.

2235a    Ferry, Luc and alain Renaut. "La dimension éthique dans la pensée de Heidegger. De Heidegger à Kant." In *Nachdenken über Heidegger.* Ed. by Ute Guszzoni. Hildesheim: Gerstenberg Verlag, 1980, 35-54.

2236     Fessard, G. Rev. of *Chemins qui ne ménent nulle part; Approche de Hölderlin. Le principe de raison,* by Martin Heidegger. *Etudes* (Paris), vol. 315, 1962, 290.

2237     Fetz, Reto Luzius. "La notion hégélienne de l'expérience et son interprétation par M. Heidegger et H. G. Gadamer." *Revue de Theologie et de Philosophie,* vol. 111, 1979, 1-12.

2238     Fetz, Reto Luzius. "Expérience et histoire." *Revue de Theologie et de Philosophie,* vol. 111, 1979, 1-12.

2239     Feuling, D. "Le mouvement phénoménologique: position historique, idées directes, types prinvipaux. Discussion." *La Phénoménologie* (Journées d'études de la Société Thomiste) (Juvisy), 12 septembre 1932, 17-55, (specifically pages 36-40).

2240     Fegurelli, Roberto. "A origem da obra de arte segundo M. Heidegger." *Revista brasileira de Filosofia* (Sao Paulo), vol. 28, no. 109, 1978, 28-44.

2241     Filipe, A. "Heidegger e a sua influência." *Brotéria* (Lisboa), vol. 90, 1970, 587-595.

2242     Filipiak, T. Rev. of *Lettre sur l'Humanisme,* by Martin Heidegger. Paris, 1964. *Ruch Filozoficzny,* 4 March 1967.

2243     Filippini, E. "Nota su Husserl e Heidegger." *Rivista di Filosofia* (Torino), vol. 52, 1961, 212-216.

2244     Finazzo, G. "L'uomo e il mondo nella filosofia di M. Heidegger." ('Cultura', 27). *Editrice Studium* (Roma), vol. 22, 1963, 164 p.

2245     Finazzo, G. "L'eristica nell'ontologia di Martin Heidegger." *Aquinas* (Ephemerédes Thomisticae) (Roma), vol. 6, 1963, 109-126.

2246     Fink, Eugen. "Philosophie als Überwindung der 'Naivität'." (Bruchstücke einer Vorlesung zum Begriff der ontologischen Differenz bei Heidegger). *Lexis* (Lahr), vol. 1, 1948, 107-127.

2247     Fink, Eugen. "Zum Problem der ontologischen Erfahrung." *Actas del primer Congreso nacional de Filosofia* (Mendoza), vol. 2, 1949, 733-747.

2248     Fink, Eugen. "L'analyse intentionelle et la pensée specultive." *Problèmes actuels de la Phénoménologie* (Paris), 1952, 53-87.

2249     Fink, Eugen. *Sein, Wahrheit, Welt. Vor-Fragen zum Problem des Phänomen-Begriffs.* La Haye, 1958, 156 p.

2250     Fink, Eugen. "Welt und Geschichte." In *Husserl et la pensée moderne. Husserl und das Denken der Neuzeit. Actes du deuxième Colloque International de Phénoménologie, Krefeld, 1-3 November 1956.* Eds. H. L. van Breda and J. Taminiaux. Den Haag, 1959, 143-159. [Phaenomenologica 2]

2251     Fink, Eugen, and Martin Heidegger. *Heraklit. Seminar Wintersemester 1966/67.* Frankfurt, 1970, 261 p.

2252 Fink, Eugen. "Filozofija kao prevladavanje 'Naivnosti'." Trans. Danilo Basta. In *Rani Hajdeger - Recepcija i kritika Bivstva i vremena.* (Biblioteka Zodijak). Eds. Dragan Stojanovic and Danilo Basta. Beograd, 1979, 68-89.

2253 Fink, Eugen, and R. Berlinger. "Anathesis für Martin Heidegger." *Philosophische Perspektiven. Ein Jahrbuch.* Eds. R. Berlinger and E. Fink. Bd 1, 317.

2254 Fiorito, M. A. "Heidegger en diálogo con la filosofia cristiana." *Ciencia y Fe* (San Miguel), vol. 13, 1957, no. 1, 41-53.

2255 Fischer, A. *Die Existenzphilosophie Martin Heideggers. Darlegung und Würdigung ihrer Grundgedanken.* Leipzig, 1935, XV, 134 p.

2256 Fischer-Barnicol, Hans A. "Spiegelungen - Vermittlungen." Ed. Günther Neske. *Erinnerung an Martin Heidegger.* Pfullingen: Verlag Günther Neske, 1977, 87-103.

2257 Flach, W. Rev. of *Der europäische Nihilismus,* by Martin Heidegger. Pfullingen, 1967. *Philosophy and History* (Tübingen), vol. 3, 1970, 9-10.

2258 Flam, L. "Geschiedenis en historiciteit bij Martin Heidegger." *Dialoog* (Brussel), vol. 2, 1961/62, 145-161.

2259 Flam, L. "De problematik van Heidegger." *Dialoog* (Brussel), vol. 2, 1961/62, 73-86.

2260 Flam, L. "Le devenir de la vérité de Hegel à Heidegger." *Actes du XIIe Congrès des Sociétés de Philosohie de Langue française Organisé à Bruxelles et à Louvain du. 22 au 24 août 1964 par la Société belge de Philosophie et la Société Philosophique de Louvain.* Thème principal: L Vérité (Vol. I: Communications). Louvain Nauwelaerts/Paris/Béatrice-Nauwelaerts, 1964, 286-292.

2261 Flam, L. "Les symboles, de Hegel à Heidegger." *Revue de Université de Bruxelles* (Bruxelles), vol. 19, 1966/67, 225-236.

2262 Flaumbaum, I. "Meister Eckhart y Martin Heidegger." *Minerva* (Buenos Aires), vol. 1, 1944.

2263 Flechsig, Hartmut. "Anstösse Heideggers zum Selbstverständnis in der Musikwissenschaft." *Musikforschung* (Kassel), vol. 30, no. 1, 1977, 26-30.

2264 Fleischmann, K. Rev. of *Einführung in die Metaphysik,* by Martin Heidegger. Tübingen, 1953. *Iyyun. Hebrew Philosophical Quarterly* (Jerusalem), vol. 5, 1954, 239-243.

2265 Floistad, Guttorm. "Tanker fra Martin Heideggers filosofi." *Frisprog* (Oslo), 17.6.1961.

[*See* "Norsk filosofi og prosessen i Jerusalem." Ed. J. Torgersen. *Verdens Gang* (Oslo), 16.5.1961.]

2266 Floistad, Guttorm. *Heidegger.* Oslo, 1968.

[Rev. by T. Sirnes in *Morgenbladet,* 19.7.1970.]

2267    Floistad, Guttorm. "On Understanding Heidegger: Some Difficulties."
        *Contemporary Philosophy in Scandinavia* (Baltimore/London), 1972,
        431-454.

2268    Flórez-Ochoa, R. "Una moral existencialista atea." *Franciscanum* (Bogotà),
        vol. 9, 1967, 179-230.

2269    Flückinger, F. *Existenz und Glaube. Kritische Betrachtungen zur existentialen
        Interpretation.* Wuppertal, 1966, 108 p.

2270    Flüe, B. Von. "Heideggers Erfahrung von Sein und die Frag-würdigkeit einer
        'bonum'. Dimension." *Freiburger Zeitschrift für Philosophie und Theologie*
        (Freiburg, Schweiz), vol. 19, 1972, 3-95.

2271    Flügel, G. Rev. of *Sein und Zeit,* by Martin Heidegger. Halle, 1927.
        *Philosophisches Jahrbuch* (Fulda), vol. 42, 1929, 104-109.

2272    Flügge, J. "Die Wissenschaft, die Technik und die Wahrheit des Seins.
        Bemerkungen zu Martin Heideggers Buch 'Holzwege'." *Die Kommenden*
        (Freiburg), Jg. 5, no. 1, 1951, 8.

2273    Fogeler, Ja G. *Dritika ontologii nemeckogo ekzistencializma* (The Criticism of
        Ontology in German Existentialism). In *Avtoreferat dissertacii na soiskanie
        ucěnoj stepeni kandidata filosofskich nauk.* Moskva, 1965.

2274    Fogeler, Ja. G. "Koncepija poznanija nemeckogo ekzistencializma" (The
        Concept of Cognition in German Existentialism). In *V sbornike
        'Sovremennaja idealisticeskaja gnoseologija'.* Moskva, 1968.

2275    Fogeler, Ja. G. "K kritike ekzistencialistskoj koncepcii suscestvovanija"
        (Criticism of the Existentialist Conception of Existence). *Vestnike
        Moskovskogo universiteta,* vol. VIII, no. 5, 1962, 53-63.

2276    Follesdal, Dagfinn. "Husserl and Heidegger on the Role of Actions in the
        Constitution of the World." In *Essays in Honour of Jaakko Hintikka.* Eds.
        Esa Saarinen, Risto Hilpinen, Ilkka Niiniluoto and Merrill Provence
        Hintikka. (Synthese Library, 124). Dordrecht, Boston: D. Reidel pub. Co.,
        1979, 365-378.

2277    Folwart, H. *Kant, Husserl, Heidegger. Kritizismus, Phänomenologie.
        Existentialontologie.* Ohlau, 1936.

2278    Fondane, B. "Sur la route de Dostoyewski." *Cahiers du Sud* (Marseille), vol.
        19, 1932, 378-392.

2279    Fondane, B. *La conscience malheureuse.* Paris, 1936, 309 p., (specifically pages
        169-198 u.ö.).

2280    Fontaine-de Visscher, Luce. "La pensée du langage chez Heidegger." *Revue
        philosophique de Louvain* (Louvain), vol. 64, 1966, 224-262.

2281    Fontaine-de Visscher, Luce. "La pensée du langage comme forme." *Revue
        Philosophique du Louvain* (Louvain), vol. 68, 1970, 449-472, (specifically
        pages 464-471).

2282    Fontaine-de Visscher, Luce. "En parlant du langage." *Revue Philosophique de
        Louvain* (Leuven), vol. 70, 1972, 453-465.

2283    Forest, Aime. "Pascal et Heidegger." *Giornale di Metafisica* (Genova/Torino), vol. 17, 1962, 590-610.

2284    Forest, Aime. "La sacré fondamental." *Teoresi* (Catania), vol. 27, 1972, 147-174.

2285    Fornari, Anibal. "Proyección el pensamiento de Heidegger como critica del positivismo cultural." *Revista Latinoamericana de Filosofia* (Argentinia), vol. 3, no. 5-16, 1977/78, 143-69.

2286    Forni, E. M. *L'impossibilità della storiografia. Significato e senso della storicità in Heidegger.* Genova/Milano: Silva ed., 1961, 172.

2287    Forni, E. M. "'Fundamentalontologie' e ontocoscienzialismo." *Giornale di Metafisica* (Genova/Torino), vol. 17, 1962, 416-453.

2288    Foulquié, P. *Existentialisme.* Paris, 1947, (specifically pages 50 ff, und passim).

2289    Fraga, Gustavo de. "De Husserl a Heidegger. Elementos para una problemáica de fenomenologia." *Biblos* (Coimbra), vol. 40, 1964, 1-260.

2290    Fraga, Gustavo de. *Sobre Heidegger.* Coimbre/Livr. Almedina, 1965, 60 p.

2291    Fraga, Gustavo de. *De Husserl a Heidegger. Elementos para una problematica de fenomenologia.* Coimbra, 1966, 260 p.

    [Rev. by E. Colomer in *Pensamiento* (Madrid), vol. 26, 1970, 312-313.]

2292    Fragata, J. Rev. of these Martin Heidegger works in *Revista Portuguesa de Filosofia* (Braga), vol. 8, 1952, 442-443:

    [*Erläuterungen zu Hölderlins Dichtung.* 2nd ed. Frankfurt, 1951.]

    [*Was ist Metaphysik?* 6th ed. Frankfurt, 1951.]

    [*Vom Wesen des Grundes.* 3rd ed. Frankfurt, 1949.]

    [*Kant und das Problem der Metaphysik.* 2nd ed. Frankfurt, 1951.]

    [*Über den Humanismus.* Frankfurt, 1947.]

    [*Vom Wesen der Wahrheit.* 3rd ed. Frankfurt, 1949.]

    [*Platons Lehre von der Wahrheit.* Bern, 1947.]

2293    Fragata, J. Rev. of *Einführung in die Metaphysik,* by Martin Heidegger. Tübingen, 1953. *Revista Portuguesa de Filosofia* (Braga), Supl. Bibl. 2, 1954, 252.

2294    Fragata, J. Rev. of *Was heisst Denken?,* by Martin Heidegger. Tübingen, 1953. *Revista Portuguesa de Filosofia* (Braga), 1955, 371-372.

2295    Fragata, J. Rev. of *Introduction à la métaphysique,* by Martin Heidegger. Paris, 1958. *Revista Portuguesa di Filosofia* (Braga), vol. 15, 1959, 207-208.

2296    Fragata, J. "Existencialismo e cristianismo." *Broteria. Revista contemporanea de cultura* (Lisboa), vol. 80, 1965, 273-283.

2297    Fragata, J. "O problema de Deus na fenomenologia." *Revista Portuguesa de Filosofia* (Braga), vol. 26, 1970, 225-236.

2298    Franchi, G. Rev. of *Was ist Metaphysik?,* by Martin Heidegger. Bonn, 1929. *Rivista di Filosofia-Neo-Scolastica* (Milano), vol. 25, 1933, 362-363.

2299　　Franchi, G. "A proposito del 'rapporto' Heidegger-Moretti Costanzi." *Ethica* (Forli), vol. 2, 1963, 129-140.

2300　　Franchini, A. *Metafisica e Storia.* Napoli, 1958.

2301　　Franchini, Raffaello. "Heidegger: la formazione e il tramonto." *Nuova Antologia* (Roma), vol. 530, no. 2118-2120, 1977, 114-133.

2302　　Franco, R. de. "La idea della morte e il suicidio." *Giornale Critico della Filosofia Italiana* (Firenze), vol. 1, 1970, 566-579.

2303　　Frank, E. *Wissen, Wollen, Glauben. Gesammelte Aufsätze zur Philosophiegeschichte und Existenzialphilosophie.* Ed. L. Edelstein. Stuttgart, 1955, 508 p.

2304　　Frank, Manfred. "Eine fundamental-semiologische Herausforderung der abendlaendischen Wissenschaft." *Philosophische Rundschau,* vol. 23, 1976, 1-16.

2305　　Franks, Dean. "An Interpretation of Technology Through the Assertorical-Problematic Distinction." *Kinesis* (Carbondale, Illinois), vol. 4, 1971, 22-29.

2306　　Franquiz, J. A. "Appraisal of Heidegger's Epistemology as a Foundation for a Metaphysics of Religion." *Wesleyan Studies in Religion,* vol. 57, 1964/65, 23-29.

2307　　Franz, H. "Das Denken Heideggers und die Theologie." *Zeitschrift für Theologie und Kirche* (Tübingen), Beiheft 2, 1961, 81-118. Rpt. in *Heidegger und die Theologie.* Ed. G. Noller. München, 1967, 249-289. Rpt. in *Heidegger.* Ed. O. Pöggeler. Köln/Berlin, 1969, 179-216.

2308　　Franzen, Winfried. Rev. of *Philosophie und Politik bei Heidegger,* by Otto Pöggeler. *Philosophisches Jahrbuch* (München), vol. 80, 1973, 1.Halbbd., 212-216.

2309　　Franzen, Winfried. *Von der Existenzialontologie zur Seinsgeschichte. Eine Untersuchung über die Entwicklung der Philosophie Martin Heideggers.* (Monographien zur philosophischen Forschung, 132). Meisenheim/Glan: Verlag Anton Hain, 1975, x-237.

2310　　Franzen, Winfried. *Martin Heidegger.* (Sammlung Metzler, 141: Abt. D, Literaturgeschichte). Stuttgart: J. B. Metzlersche Verlagsbuchhandlung, 1976, x-136.

2311　　Frenzel, Ivo. "Heideggers Absage an die Metaphysik." Rev. of *Einführung in die Metaphysik,* by Martin Heidegger. Tübingen, 1953. *Frankfurter Hefte* (Frankfurt), Hefte 8, 1953, 965-970.

2312　　Frenzel, Ivo. "'Sein und Zeit' in historischer Sicht. Als Auftakt der grossen Heidegger-Ausgabe: frühe Marburger Vorlesung." *Süddeutsche Zeitung* (München), no. 19, 24 January 1976, 110.

2313　　Frenzel, Ivo. "Abschied von einer Epoche. Zum Tode von Martin Heidegger." *Süddeutsche Zeitung* (München), vol. 122, 28 May 1976, 14, (3, no. 2, 1976).

2314 Frenzel, Ivo. Rev. of *Die Grundprobleme der Phänomenologie,* by Martin Heidegger. Gesamtausgabe, Abt. 2: Vorlesungen 1923-1944. Bd 24. Ed. Friedrich-Wilhelm von Herrmann. Frankfurt: Klostermann, 1975. *Süddeutsche Zeitung* (München), 24 January 1976.

2315 Fresco, M. F. "Literatuur ten dienste van de wijsbegeerte. Heidegger gebruikt Hölderlin." *Wijsg Persp Maatsch Wet,* vol. 19, 1978/79, 50-56.

2316 Freund, E. H. "Man's Fall in M. Heidegger's Philosophy." *The Journal of Religion* (Chicago), vol. 24, 1944, 180-187.

2317 Friedmann, G. "Heidegger et la crise contemporaine de l'idée de progrès." *Cahiers internationaux de sociologie* (Paris), vol. 16, 1954, 118-125.

2318 Friedman, M. "Phenomenology and Existential Analysis. Existential Phenomenology: Temporality, Distancing, and Immediacy." *Review of Existential Psychology and Psychiatry* (Pittsburgh), vol. 9, 1968/69, 151-168.

2319 Frings, Manfred S. Rev. of *Nietzsche,* by Martin Heidegger. Pfullingen, 1961. *The Journal of Philosophy* (New York), vol. 69, 1962, 830-835.

2320 Frings, Manfred S., ed. *Heidegger and the Quest for Truth.* (With a letter by Martin Heidegger). Ed. and intr. by Manfred S. Frings. Chicago: Quadrangle Books, 1968, 205 p.

[Rev. by P. Emad in *Philosophischer Literaturanzeiger* (Meisenheim/Glan), vol. 23, 97-99.]

2321 Frings, Manfred S. "Heidegger and Scheler." *Philosophy Today* (Celina, Ohio), vol. 12, 1968, 21-30.

2322 Frings, Manfred S. *Person und Dasein. Zur Frage der Ontologie des Wertseins.* (Phaenomenologica, vol. 32). The Hague, 1969, 118 p.

2323 Frings, Manfred S. "Insight - Logos - Love (Lonergan - Heidegger - Scheler)." *Philosophy Today* (Celina, Ohio), vol. 14, 1970, 106-115.

2324 Frings, Manfred S. "Max Scheler: Focusing on Rarely Seen Complexities of Phenomenology." *Phenomenology in Perspective.* Ed. F. J. Smith. The Hague, 1970, 54-93.

2325 Frings, Manfred S. "Demut und Existenz." *Die Anregung* (Wirtschaftsausgabe), vol. IV, 1971.

2326 Frings, Manfred S. "Protagoras Re-Discovered: Heidegger's Explication of Protagoras' Fragment." *The Journal of Value Inquiry* (Genesco/The Hague), vol. 8, 1974, 112-123.

2327 Frings, Manfred S. "Nothingness and Being: A Schelerian Comment." *Research in Phenomenology* (Pittsburgh), vol. 7, 1977, 182-189.

2328 Frutos Cortés, E. "La vinculación metafisica del problema estético en Heidegger." *Revista de ideas estéticas,* vol. 6, 1948, 335-342.

2329 Frutos Cortés, E. "Inmanencia y transcendencia del ser y del concocer en Heidegger." *Revista de Filosofia* (Madrid), vol. 9, 1950, 199-215.

2330    Fu, Charles Wei-Hsun. "Creative Hermeneutics. Taoist Metaphysics and
        Heidegger." *Journal of Chinese Philosophy* (Dordrecht), vol. 3, 1975/76,
        115-143.

2331    Fu, Charles Wei-Hsun. "The Trans-Onto-Theo-Logical Foundations of
        Language in Heidegger and Taoism." *Journal of Chinese Philosophy*, vol.
        5, 1978, 301-33.
        [Erratum: Page 316 of the above paper inadvertently mis-printed, *Journal
        of Chinese Philosophy*, vol. 6, 1979, 114.]

2332    Fuchs, Ernst. "Theologische Exegese und philosophisches Seinsverständnis.
        Zum 'Gespräch' zwischen Bultmann und Heidegger." *Zeitschrift für
        Theologie und Kirche* (Tübingen), vol. 13, 1932, 307-323.

2333    Fuchs, Ernst. "Theologie und Metaphysik. Zu der theologischen Bedeutung
        der Philosophie Heideggers und Grisebachs (1933)." In *Heidegger und die
        Theologie. Beginn und Fortgang der Diskussion*. Ed. G. Noller. München,
        1967, 136-146.

2334    Fuchs, Ernst. "Vom Sinn des menschlichen Daseins. Eine Auseinandersetzung
        mit M. Heidegger." *Deutsche Zeitschrift für Philosophie* (Berlin), vol. 10,
        1962, 982-994.

2335    Fuchs, Ernst. "Aus der Marburger Zeit." In *Erinnerung an Martin Heidegger*.
        Ed. Günther Neske. Pfullingen: Verlag Günther Neske, 1977, 105-108.

2336    Fürstenau, P. Rev. of *Vorträge und Aufsätze*, by Martin Heidegger. Pfullingen,
        1954. *Zeitschrift für philosophische Forschung* (Meisenheim/Glan), vol. 10,
        1956, 645-646.

2337    Fürstenau, P. *Heidegger. Das Gefüge seines Denkens*. (Philosophische
        Abhandlungen XVI). Frankfurt, 1958, 185 p.

2338    Fuertes Y Carreras, Juan Carlos de. "Heidegger, Existencial." (En sus
        coordenadas de trancedencia historicidad y moral). *Logos* (Mexico City),
        vol. 4, 1976, 111-120.

2339    Fujii, Satoshi. "Sonzaironteki Sabetsu ni yosete" (On the Ontological
        Difference. *Tetsugaku Ronshû* (Ôtani Daigaku) (Kyôto), no. 23, 1977,
        31-46.

2340    Fujimoto, Tadashi. "Sonzaironteki Jiyû, Haideggâ ni okeru Sonzai to Jiyu"
        (Ontological Freedom. On Being and Freedom in Heidegger). In
        *Kansaidaigaku Bungakuronshû*. Ôsaka, 1953.

2341    Fujimoto, Tadashi. "Shi no Kyokugensei to Chôetsusei, Haideggâ-Tetsugaku
        ni okeru Hititsu no Mondaiten" (The Boundary and Transcendence of
        Death. A Questionable Aspect in Heidegger's Philosophy). In
        *Kansaidaigaku-Bungakuronshu*. Ôsaka, 1960.

2342    Fujimoto, Tadashi. "Kanto no 'Junsui Risei Hihan' ni okeru Chôetsu no
        Mondai; Haideggâ no Kantokaishaku ni Kanren shite" (The Problem of
        Transcendence in Kant's Critique of Pure Reason: Concerning Heidegger's
        Interpretation of Kant). *Bungaku Ronshû* (Kansai Daigaku), vol. 25, no.
        1, 2, 3, 4, 1975, 155-198.

2343 Fujinaga, Yoshizumi. "Haideggâ ni okeru Keijijyôgaku no Kokufuku to Rinrigaku no Kanousei" (Overcoming of Metaphysics and Probability of Ethics in Heidegger). *Tetsugaku* (Hiroshima Tetsugakukai) (Hiroshima), vol. 28, 1976, 85-100.

2344 Fujita, Kenji. "Haideggâ no tetsugakuteki Kiyo" (Philosophical Contributions of Heidegger). *Jitsuzonshugi* (Tôkyô), vol. 69, 1974, 2-14.

2345 Fujita, Kenji. "Haideggâ to Yasupâsu" (Heidegger and Jaspers). *Jitsuzonshugi* (Tôkyô), vol. 77, 1976, 129-133.

2346 Fujita, Sekiji. "Haideggâ no 'Inakano Michi' ni tsuite" (On Heidegger's 'Feldweg'). *Risô* (Tôkyô), vol. 255, 1954, 54-59.

2347 Fujita, Sekiji. "Haideggâ ni okeru Shi e no Sonzai to Nôryoku to Ai no Mondai" (The Problems 'Being Towards Death, Faculty and Love' in Heidegger). *Philosophia* (Tôkyô), vol. 29, 1956.

2348 Fulton, James Street. "The Event of Being." (Symposium Honoring James Street Fulton). *The Southwestern Journal of Philosophy* (Norman), vol. 6, no. 1, 1975, 7-30.

2349 Fumet, S. "Heidegger et les mystiques." *La table ronde* (Paris), no. 182, 1963, 82-89.

2350 Funabashi, Hiroshi. "Haideggâ Tetsugaku no Ayumi I - Shinri-ron no Tenkai o tsûjite" (The Development of Heidegger's Philosophy on His Theory of Truth). *Miyagi Kyôiku Daigaku Kiyô* (Sendai), vol. 1, 1967, 87-104.

2351 Funabashi, Hiroshi. "Haideggâ Tetsugaku no Ayumi II - Shinri-ron no Tenkai o tôshite" (The Development of Heidegger's Philosophy). *Miyagi Kyôiku Daigaku Kiyô* (Sendai), vol. 3, 1969, 73-84.

2352 Funayama, Shin'ichi. "Haideggâ-Sekaijimbutsu Sunappu." *Kaizô* (Tôkyô), XXII-3, 1940, 339.

2353 Fushimi, Fumio. "Haideggâ no Gengoron ni tsuite" (Heidegger's Thought on Language). *Kenkyû Ronshû* (Kansai Gaikokugo Daigaku) (Ôsaka), no. 23, 1975, 327-353.

2354 Fushimi, Fumio. "Haideggâ Tetsugaku no Ichi-Kosatsu" (A Study of the Philosophy of Heidegger). *Kenkyû Ronshû* (Kansai Gaikokugo Daigaku) (Hirakata), no. 25, 1977, 585-603.

2355 Funke, Gerhard. "Crisis de la Hermenéutica?" *Cuadernos de Filosofia,* vol. 14, 1974, 7-29.

2356 Gabitova, R. M. "Martin Heidegger and Classical Philosophy." (In Russian). *Voprosy filosofii* (Moskau), vol. 11, 1972, 144-149.

2357 Gabitova, R. M. "Celovek i obcžestvo v nemeckom ekzistenci alizme" (Man and Society in German Existentialism). *Nauka* (Moskva), vol. 1, 1972, 5-138.

2358 Gabitova, R. M. "M. Chajdegger i anticnaja filosofija" (Heidegger and the Classical Antiquity). *Voprosy filosofii,* vol. 11, 1972, 144-149.

2359    Gabitova, R. M. "Antiistorizm pod maskoj 'istoricnosti'" (The Anti-Historicism in the Mask of 'Historicity'). *Filosofskie nauki,* vol. 1, 1966, 73-80.

2360    Gabitova, R. M. "Problema 'celostnosti' celoveka i ee ekzistencialistskaja interpretacija" (The Problem of the "Totality" of Man and Its Existentialist Interpretation). In *Celovek v socialisticeskom i burzuaznom obscestve, Simpozium* (doklady i soobscenija). Moskva, 1966.

2361    Gabitova, R. M. "Koncepcija licnosti i obscestvennoj zizni v nemeckom ekzistencializme" (The Concept of Personality and of Social Life in the German Existentialism). In *Sovremennhj ekzistencializm.* Moskva, 1966, 125-145.

2362    Gabitova, R. M. "Koncepcija celoveka i obscestvav nemeckom ekzistencializme" (The Concept of Man and of Society in the German Existentialism). In *Avtoreferat dissertacii na soiskanie ucënoj stepeni kandidata filosofskich nauk.* Moskva, 1966.

2363    Gabriel, Leo. *Existenzphilosophie. Von Kierkegaard bis Sartre.* Wien, 1951, 416 p., (specifically pages 113-166).

2364    Gabriel, Leo. "Erfahrung des Seins in der Zeit. Kritischer Bericht über drei Wiener Vorträge von Martin Heidegger, Arnold Gehlen, Johannes Lotz." *Wissenschaft und Weltbild* (Wien), vol. 11, 1958, 144-152, (specifically pages 144-146, Heideggers Vortrag am 11. Mai 1958 im Wiener Burgtheater über 'Denken und Dichten').

2365    Gabriel, Leo. "Wege zum Sein: Martin Heidegger und Gabriel Marcel zum 70. Geburtstag." *Wissenschaft und Weltbild* (Wien), vol. 12, 1959, 610-617.

2366    Gabriel, Leo. "Sinn und Wahrheit. Aus dem gegenwärtigen Stand der Wahrheitsfrage." *Sinn und Sein. Ein philosophisches Symposion.* Ed. R. Wisser. Tübingen, 1960, 135-153.

2367    Gabriel, Leo. "Lebensphilosophie, Existentialphilosophie und Fortschrittsglaube." *Der Fortschrittsglaube. Sinn und Gefahren. Festschrift für Franz König.* Ed. Ulrich Schöndorfer. (Studien der Wiener Katholischen Akademie, Bd 5). Graz 1965, 109-120, (specifically pages 116-120).

2368    Gabriel, Leo. "Martin Heidegger. Gedenken zum 80. Geburtstag." *Wissenschaft und Weltbild* (Wien), vol. 22, 1969, no. 3, 174-175.

2369    Gabriel, Leo. "Martin Heidegger." *Martin Heidegger im Gespräch.* Ed. R. Wisser. Freiburg/München, 1970, 35-37.

2370    Gabriel, Leo. *Filosofia de la existencia. Kierkegaard, Heidegger, Jaspers, Sartre. Dialogo de las posiciones.* Trans. from German by Pelayo Arribas. Madrid: La Editorial Católica, 1974, 352 p.

2371    Gaboriau, F. "Introduction." In *Traité des catégories et de la signification chez Duns Scotus,* by Martin Heidegger. Paris, 1970.

2372    Gadamer, Hans-Georg. "Zur Vorgeschichte der Metaphysik." In *Anteile, Martin Heidegger zum 60. Geburtstag.* Frankfurt, 1950, 51-79.

2373 Gadamer, Hans-Georg. "Vom Zirkel des Verstehens." In *Martin Heidegger zum 70. Geburtstag. Festschrift.* Pfullingen, 1959, 24-34.

2374 Gadamer, Hans-Georg. *Wahrheit und Methode.* Tübingen, 1960, (specifically pages 240-290).

2375 Gadamer, Hans-Georg. "Zur Einführung." *Martin Heidegger: Der Ursprung der Kunstwerkes. Mit einer Einführung von H.-G. Gadamer.* Stuttgart, 1960, 102-125.

2376 Gadamer, Hans-Georg. "Martin Heidegger et la signification de son 'herméneutique de la facilitá pour les sciences humaines." In *Le Problème de la conscience historique.* Préface de L. De Raeymaeker (Chaire Cardinal Mercier 1957). Paris: Louvain Pub. Univ. de Louvain, 1963, 39-48.

2377 Gadamer, Hans-Georg. "Martin Heidegger und die Marburger Theologie." In *Zeit und Geschichte.* Dankesgabe an Rudolf Bultmann zum 80. Geburtstag im Auftrage der Alten Marburger und in Zusammenarbeit mit Hartwig Thyen. Ed. Erich Dinkler. Tübingen, 1964, 479-490.

2378 Gadamer, Hans-Georg. "Die Universalität des hermeneutischen Problems." *Philosophisches Jahrbuch* (München), vol. 73, 1965/66, 215-225.

2379 Gadamer, Hans-Georg. "Anmerkungen zu dem Thema 'Hegel und Heidegger'." In *Natur und Geschichte.* Karl Löwith zum 70. Geburtstag. Stuttgart/BerlinKöln/Mainz, 1967, 123-131.

2380 Gadamer, Hans-Georg. *Kleine Schriften, I. Philosophie. Hermeneutik.* Tübingen, 1967, 230 p., (specifically page 82 ff).

2381 Gadamer, Hans-Georg, ed. *Die Frage Martin Heideggers.* Beiträge zu einem Kolloquium mit Heidegger aus Anlass seines 80. Geburtstages von J. Beaufret, H.-G. Gadamer, K. Löwith, K.-H. Volkmann-Schluck. Sitzungsberichte der Heidelberger Akademie der Wissenschaften. Philosophisch-historische Klasse, Abh. 4. Berlin, 1969, 68 p.

2382 Gadamer, Hans-Georg. "Der Denker Martin Heidegger." In *Die Frage Martin Heideggers.* Ed. H.-G. Gadamer. Berlin, 1969, 62-68.

2383 Gadamer, Hans-Georg. "Über leere und erfüllte Zeit." *Die Frage Martin Heideggers.* Ed. H.-G. Gadamer. Berlin, 1969, 17-35.

2384 Gadamer, Hans-Georg. "Martin Heidegger und die Marburger Theologie." In *Heidegger.* Ed. O. Pöggeler. Köln/Berlin, 1969, 169-178. From *Kleine Schriften, I. Philosophische Hermeneutik,* by H.-G. Gadamer. Tübingen, 1967, 82-92. 1st pub. 1964 in *Zeit und Geschichte.* Ed. E. Dinkler; vgl. no. XXXX.

2385 Gadamer, Hans-Georg. "Concerning Empty and Ful-Filled Time." *The Southern Journal of Philosophy* (Memphis), vol. 8, 1970, 341-353. Rpt. in *Martin Heidegger in Europe and America.* Eds. E. G. Ballard and C. E. Scott. The Hague, 1973, 77-89.

2386 Gadamer, Hans-Georg. *Hegels Dialektik.* Tübingen, 1971, 96 p.

[Chapter V: Hegel und Heidegger, 83-96.]

2387　　Gadamer, Hans-Georg. *Kleine Schriften, III. Idee und Sprache. Platon. Husserl. Heidegger.* Tübingen, 1972, 271 .

2388　　Gadamer, Hans-Georg. "Heidegger et le langage de la metaphysique." *Archives de Philosophie* (Chantilly/Paris), vol. 36, 1973, 3-13.

2389　　Gadamer, Hans-Georg. *La dialettica di Hegel. Con due lettere di M. Heidegger a H. G. Gadamer.* Trans. and annotations by Riccardo Dottori. (Classici del pensiero moderno e contemporaneo, 7). Torino: Marietti, 1973, 178 p.

2390　　Gadamer, Hans-Georg. "L'herméneutique philosophique." *Studies in Religion* (Toronto), vol. 5, no. 1, 1975, 3-13.

2391　　Gadamer, Hans-Georg. "The Problem of Historical Consciousness." *Graduate Faculty Philosophy Journal* (New York), vol. 5, 1975, 8-52.

2392　　Gadamer, Hans-Georg. "Kant und die philosophische Hermeneutik." *Kant-Studien* (Bonn), vol. 66, 1975, 395-403.

2393　　Gadamer, Hans-Georg. *Philosophical hermeneutics.* Trans. David E. Linge. Berkeley, 1976.

2394　　Gadamer, Hans-Georg. "Plato und Heidegger." Eds. Ute Guzzoni, Bernhard Rang and Ludwig Siep. In *Der Idealismus und seine Gegenwart.* Festschrift für Werner Marx zum 65. Geburtstag, Hamburg: Felix Meiner Verlag, 1976, 166-175.

2395　　Gadamer, Hans-Georg. "Ser, espíritu, Deus." Trans. Manuel Augusto Esteves. *Revista Portuguesa de Filosofia* (Braga), vol. 33, no. 4, 1977, 285-298.

2396　　Gadamer, Hans-Georg. "Einzug in Marburg." *Erinnerung an Martin Heidegger,* by Günther Neske. Pfullingen: Verlag Günther Neske, 1977, 109-113.

2397　　Gadamer, Hans-Georg. "The Historicity of Understanding as Hermeneutic Principle." Rpt. from *Truth and Method,* by H.-G. Gadamer. New York, 1975. In *Heidegger and Modern Philosophy. Critical Essays.* Ed. Michael Murray. New Haven, Connecticut: Yale Univ. Press, 1978, 161-83.

2397a　　Gadamer, Hans-Georg. "Plato and Heidegger." In *The Question of Being.* Ed. M. Sprung. Univ. Park, 1978, 45-54.

2398　　Gadamer, Hans-Georg. "Il pensatore Martin Heidegger." *Humanitas* (Brescia), vol. 33, no. 4, 1978, 416-422.

2399　　Gadamer, Hans-Georg, Werner Marx, and Carl Friedrich von Weizäcker. *Heidegger.* Freiburger Universitätsvorträge zu seinem Gedenken. Ed. Werner Marx. With intr. by Helmut Engler. (Alber- Broschur Philosophie). Freiburg: Alber, 1977, 88 p.

2400　　Gadamer, Hans-Georg. "Hajdeger i jezik metafizike." Trans. Danilo Basta. In *Rani Hajdeger - Recepcija i kritika Bivstva i vremena,* by Draga Stojanovic and Danilo Basta. (Biblioteka zodijak). Beograd, 1979, 57-68.

2401　　Gadamer, Hans-Georg. "Heidegger's Paths." Trans. C. Kayser and G. Stack. *Philosophic Exchange,* vol. 2, no. 5, Summer 1979, 80-91.

2401a    Gadamer, Hans-Georg. "Heidegger und die Griechen-Heidegger e i Greci." Trans. Fulvio Longato. *Verifiche* (Trento), vol. 8, no. 1, 1979, 4-33.

2402    Gajdenko, P. P. "Filosofija M. Chajdeggera kak vyrazenie krizisa sovremennoj burzuaznojkultury" (M. Heidegger's Philosophy as the Expression of the Crisis of Contemporary Bourgeois Culture). In *Avtoreferat dissertacii na soiskanie ucënoj stepeni kandidata filosofskich nauk.* Moskva, 1962.

2403    Gajdenko, P. P. "Filosofija istorii M. Chejdeggera i sud'by buzuaznogo romantizma" (M. Heidegger's History of Philosophy and the Paths of Bourgeois Romantism). *Voprosy Filosofii,* no. 4, 1962, 73-84.

2404    Gajdenko, P. P. "'Fundamental'naja ontologija' M. Chajdeggera kak forma obosnovanija filosofskogo irracionalizma" ('The Fundamental-Ontology' by Heidegger as the Way of Founding the Philosophical Irrationalism). *Voprosy filosofii,* vol. 2, 1963, 93-104.

2405    Gajdenko, P. P. *Ekzistencializm i problema kultury. Kritika filosofii M. Chajdeggera.* Moskva, 1963, 121 p.

2406    Gajdenko, P. P. "Ekzistencializm i problemy kul'tury (Kritika filosofii M. Chajdeggera)" (Existentialism and the Problem of Culture (Heidegger's Criticism of Philosophy)). In *Vyssaja skola.* Moskva, 1963.

2407    Gajdenko, P. P. "The 'Fundamental Ontology' of M. Heidegger as an Attempt of Founding the Philosophical Irrationalism." (In Russian). *Voprosy Filosofii* (Moskau), 1963, H. 2, 93-105.

2408    Gajdenko, P. P. "Problema vremeni v ontologii M. Chajdeggera" (The Problem of Time in M. Heidegger's Ontology). *Voprosy filosofii,* vol. 12, 1965, 109-120.

       [In Russian with a summary in English.]

2409    Gajdenko, P. P. "The 'Fundamental Ontology' of Heidegger as a Basis of Philosophical Irrationalism." *Soviet Studies in Philosophy* (New York), vol. 4, no. 3, 1965/66, 44-55.

2410    Gajdenko, P. P. "Problema intencional'nosti u Gusserlja i ekzistencialistskaja kategorija trncendental'nosti" (The Problem of Intentionality in Husserl and the Existentialist Category of Transcendentality). In *V sbornike 'Sovremennyj ekzistencializm. Kriticeskij ocerk' (Izdatel'stvo 'Mysl').* Moskva, 1966, 77-107.

2411    Gajdenko, P. P. "Suscestvovanie" (The Existence). *Filosofskoj enciklopedii* (Moskva), tom 4, 1970, 167-168.

2412    Gajdenko, P. P. "Filosofija iskusstva Martina Chajdeggera" (Heidegger's Philosophy of Art). *Voprosy literatury,* vol. 7, 1969, 94-115.

2413    Gajdenko, P. P. "Smert" (Death). *Filosofskoj enciklopedii* (Moskva), vol. 5, 1970, 36.

2414    Gajdenko, P. P. "Ekzistencializm" (Existentialism). *Filosofskoj enciklopedii* (Moskva), vol. 5, 1970, 538-542.

2415    Gajdenko, P. P. "Chajdegger" (Heidegger). *Filosofskoj enciklopedii* (Moskva), vol. 5, 1970, 426-428.

2416    Gajdenko, P. P. "Problema vremeni v ontologii M. Chajdeggera" (The Problem of Time in Heidegger's Ontology. *V sbornike 'Filosofija marksizma i ekzistencializma' (Izdatel'stvo Moskovskogo Universiteta),* 1971, 98-113.

2417    Gajdenko, P. P. "Problem czasu w ontologii M. Heideggera" (The Problem of Time in M. Heidegger's Ontology). Trans. from Russian. In *Czlowiek i swiatopoglad,* vol. 6, 1973.

2418    Gajdenko, P. P. "Problem czasu w ontologii M. Hideggera" (The Problem of Time in M. Heidegger's Ontology). In *Filozofia marksizmu a egzystencjalizm* (Marxist Philosophy and Existentialism). Warszawa, 1974, also 1973.

2419    Gajdenko, P. P. "Chajdegger i sovremennaja filosofskaja germenevtika" (Heidegger and the Contemporary Philosophical Hermeneutics). *Novejsie tecenija i problemy filosofii v FRG, Nauka* (Moskva), vol. I, paragraph 1, 1978, 27-80.

2420    Gajdenko, P. P. "Ekzistencializm M. Chajdeggera" (Heidegger's Existentialism). *Sovremennaja burzuaznaja filosofija, Mysl* (Moskva), Part IV, paragraph 2, 1978, 291-310.

2421    Galamini, L. "Persona e società in alcuni aspetti della filosofia dell'esistenza." *Rivista internazionale di filosofia del diritto* (Milano), vol. 29, 1952, 68-75, passim.

2421a   Galán, Francisco V. "La revelación del ser en el tiempo." *Revista de Filosofia* (UIA), vol. 12, no. 34, 1979, 7-105.

2422    Galeazzi, Umberto. "Kant, la metafisica e lo scientismo." *Revista di Filosofia Neo-Scolastica* (Milano), vol 65, 1973, 119-150.

2424    Galimberti, Umberto. "Introduction." In *Sull'essenza della verita,* by Martin Heidegger. Brescia: La Scuola, 1973.

2425    Galimberti, Umberto. *Heidegger, Jaspers e il tramonto dell'Occidente.* Torino: Marietti, 1975, 271 p.

2426    Galimberti, Umberto. *Linguaggio e civiltà. Analisi del linguaggio occidentale in Heidegger e Jaspers.* (Studi di filosofia, 15). Torino: Mursia, 1977, 252 p.

2427    Gallagher, Kenneth. "La pensée créatrice: Marcel et Heidegger." *Dialogue* (Montréal/Kingston), vol. 8, 1969, 22-43.

2428    Galli, D. Rev. of *La dottrina del giudizio nello psicologismo,* by Martin Heidegger. Ed. Albino Babolin. Padova: La Garangola, 1972, 167 p. *Revista Rosminiana di Filosofia e di Cultura* (Domodossola/Milano), vol. 68, 1974, 162-164.

2429    Galli, D. Rev. of *Scritti filosofici (1912-1917),* by Martin Heidegger. Ed. Albino Babolin. (Univ. de Parma. Istituto di scienze religiose. Saggi, 2). Padova: La Garangola, 1972, 246 p. *Rivista Rosminiana di Filosofia e di Cultura* (Domodossola/Milano), vol. 69, 1975, 146-147.

2430    Galli, D. "Nietzsche nell'interpretaziona heideggeriana." *Sacra Doctrina. Studio generale domenicano di Bologna* (Milano), vol. 82, 1976, 525-528.

2431    Gandillac, M. de. "Entretien avec Martin Heidegger." *Les temps modernes* (Paris), vol. 1, 1945/46, 713-716.

2432    Gandillac, M. de. "Martin Heidegger." In *Martin Heidegger im Gespräch.* Ed. R. Wisser. Freiburg/München, 1970, 16-19.

2433    Ganduglia Pirovano, Mirtha Evelia. "La nouvelle aurore de Heidegger." *Akten des Internationalen Kongresses für Philosophie. Wien, 2 - 9 September 1968* (Wien), 1968, 485-488.

2434    Gans, Stephen Lawrence. "Ethics or Ontology. Levinas and Heidegger." *Philosophy Today* (Celina, Ohio), vol. 16, 1972, 117-121.

2435    Gans, Steven Lawrence. "An Analysis of the Philosophical Methodology of Martin Heidegger." Phil. Diss. The Pennsylvania State Univ. 1967. Ann Arbor, Michigan: University Microfilms Inc., 1977, iv-164 p. *Dissertation Abstracts International,* vol. 29/03-A, 929.

2436    Gans, Steven Lawrence. Rev. of *Materialien zur Heidegger-Bibliographie 1917-1972,* by Hans-Martin Sass (ed.). Meisenheim, 1975. *The Journal of the British Society for Phenomenology* (Manscheseter), vol. 8, 1977, 64.

2437    Gaos, J. "El ser y el tiempo de Martin Heidegger." *Filosofía y Letras* (Mexico), vol. 16, 1948, 205-240.

2438    Gaos, J. *Introducción a 'El ser y el Tiempo' de Martin Heidegger.* Mexico, 1952, 5-27. 2nd ed. 1971.

2439    Garceau, Beudit. "Heidegger et le concept traditionnel de la vérité." *Revue de l'Université d'Ottawa* (Ottawa), vol. 37, 1967, 101-113.

2440    Garcia, Mário. "Cuidado e temporalidade em 'Ser e Tempo' de Heidegger." *Revista Portuguesa de Filosofia* (Braga), vol. 28, 1972, 206-211.

2441    Garcia, Mário. "Cuidado e temporalidade em 'Ser e tempo'." *Revista Portuguesa de Filosofia* (Braga), vol. 28, 1972, 206-211.

2442    Garcia Bacca, J. D. "El 'Dasein' en la filosofia de Heidegger." *Letras de México* (Mexico), vol. 3, no. 22, 1940.

2443    Garcia Bacca, J. D. "El sentido de la nada en la fundmentación de la 'metafisica' según Heidegger y el sentido de la nada como fundamentación de la Experiencia mistica, según San Juan de la Cruz." *Cuadernos Americanos* (Mexico), vol. 18, 1944, 87-100.

2444    Garcia Bacca, J. D. *Nueve grandes filósofos contemporáneos y sus temas.* Vol. 1. Caracas, 1947.

2445    Garcia Bacca, J. D. "Los conceptos de ontologia general y de ontologia fundamental en Heidegger." *Universidad Nacional de Colombia* (Bogotá), vol. 8, 1947, 57-96.

2446    Garcia Bacca, J. D. "La filosofia de Heidegger." *Universidad de Mexico,* vol. 2, 1947/48, 13-14.

2447    Garcia Bacca, J. D. *Siete modelos de filosofar.* Caracas, 1950. (Heidegger o el modelo existencial de filosofar, 139-168).

2448     Garcia Bacca, J. D. "Comentarios a 'La esencia de la poesia' de Heidegger."
         *Revista nacional de Cultura* (Caracas), vol. 18, 1955, 112-113; 220-234;
         1956: 18, 108-115; 117-118; 147-153.

2449     Garcia Bacca, J. D. Rev. of *Aus der Erfahrung des Denkens,* by Martin
         Heidegger. Pfullingen, 1954. *Revista nacional de Cultura* (Caracas), no. 18,
         no. 114, 1956, 207-209.

2450     Garcia Bacca, J. D. *Antropologia filosofica contemporanea.* Caracas, 1957, 193
         p.
         [El plan de la antropologia filosofica, en Heidegger, 161-175.]

2451     Garcia Bacca, J. D. *Existencialismo.* Xalapa, Mexico, 1962, 289 p.

2452     Garcia Bacca, J. D. "Existencialismo alemán y existencialismo francés."
         (Heidegger y Sartre). *Cuadernos Americanos* (Mexico), vol. 216, no. 1, 1978,
         69-96.

2453     Garcia-Navarro, S. Rev. of *L'être et le temps, I,* by Martin Heidegger.
         *Convivium* (Barcelona), no. 19-20, 164, 1965.

2454     Garcia San Miguel, L. "Moral y derecho en la filosofia existencialista. Un
         estudio sobre Heidegger y Sartre." *Revista general de legislación y
         jurisprudencia* (Madrid), vol. 113, 1965, 543-575.

2455     Gardet, L. "A propos Heidegger: valeur d'expérience de la 'Question du sens
         de l'être'." *Revue Thomiste* (Toulouse), vol. 68, 1968, 381-418.

2456     Garelli, J. "Le champ de présence." *Temps modernes* (Paris), vol. 27, 1970,
         538-556.

2457     Garin, Eugenio. "Kant, Cassirer e Heidegger." *Revista critica di Storia della
         Filosofia* (Milano), vol. 28, 1973, 203-206.

2458     Garulli, Enrico. "Problemi della filosofia giovanile heideggeriana." *Il Pensiero*
         (Roma/Urbino), vol. 11, 1966, 226-253.

2459     Garulli, Enrico. "L'unité idéale de la pensée heideggérienne d'après un essai
         de Gianni Vattimo, Essere storia e linguaggio in Heidegger." (Sguardi su
         la filosofia contemporanea, 50). *Revue de Métaphysique et de Morale* (Paris),
         vol. 72, 1967, 116-125.

2460     Garulli, Enrico. *Problemi dell'Ur-Heidegger.* Urbino, 1967, 185 p.

2461     Garulli, Enrico. Rev. of *Essere e tempo,* by Martin Heidegger. Trans. Pietro
         Chiodi. (Il labirinto, 24). 11th ed. Milano: Longanesi, 1970, xl-691. *Bolletino
         Filosofica* (Padova), vol. 5, 1971, 145-149.

2462     Garulli, Enrico. Rev. of "In cammino verso il linguaggio," by Martin
         Heidegger. Ed. Alberto Caracciolo. Trans. Alberto Caracciolo a. Maris
         Perotti Caracciolo. (Biblioteca di Filosofia, Testi, 5). Milano: U. Mursia,
         1973, 217 p. *Bollettino Filosofico* (Padova), vol. 7, 1973, 62-64.

2463     Garulli, Enrico. "Ontologia, linguaggio e salvezza in Martin Heidegger."
         *Bollettino Filosofica* (Padova), vol. 8, no. 4, 1974, 52-53.

2464     Garulli, Enrico. "Per una modalità ontologica del sacro e del divino in
         Heidegger." In *Prospettive sul sacro,* by Enrico Castelli (ed.). (Centro

Internazionale di Studi Umanistici Roma). Roma: Istituto di Studi Filosofici, 1974, 89-103.

2465    Garulli, Enrico. *Heidegger.* Assisi: Cittadella, 1974, 153 p.

2466    Garulli, Enrico. "Prospettive attuali della ontologia heideggeriana." *Bollettino filosofica* (Padova), vol. 11, 1977, 1-5.

2466a   Garulli, Enrico. "Aspetti e problemi della coscienza storica e della coscienza speculativa in Heidegger." *Verifiche* (Trento), vol. 8, no. 1, 1979, 81-105.

2467    Gashû, Hideo. "Haideggâ ni okeru 'Shi' o Mondai; Heruderurin no Shiku o Chûshin to shite" (The Problem of 'Poetry' in Heidegger). *Gendai Kagaku-Ronsô,* vol. 2, 1968, 36-48.

2468    Gashû, Hideo. "Haideggâ Tetsugaku no Shisaku-Katei ni tsuite; tokuni Tenkai no Mondai o Chûshin to shite" (Heidegger's World of Ideas and the Problem of "The Turning"). *Gendaikagaku-ronsô,* vol. 3, 1969, 14-28.

2469    Gauger, H.-M. *Wort und Sprache.* Tübingen, 1970, 137 p., (specifically page 76 ff).

2470    Gauthier, Yvon. "Ontologie et langage de l'être: à propos de l'ontologie du dernier Heidegger." *Proceedings of the Seventh Inter-American Congress of Philosophy Under the Auspices of the Canadian Philosophical Association* (Quebec), vol. I, 1967, 335-340.

2471    Gauthier, Yvon. "Cronologia y topologia en el pensamiento de Heidegger." Trans. Angel J. Casares. *Dialogos* (Rio Piedras, Puerto Rico), vol. 5, no. 11-12, 1968, 55-61.

2472    Gauthier, Yvon. "Heidegger, le langage et la psychanalyse." *Revue de l'Université Laurentienne* (Sudbury), vol. 9, no. 2, 1977, 67-77.

2473    Gawroáski, A. "O dialogu krytycznie. Publicystyka katolicka o M. Heideggerze" (Critical Evaluation of the Dialogue. The Catholic Journalism Concerning Heidegger). *Tyg. Powszechny,* vol. 22, 1973.

2474    Gay, W. "Kosik's Concept of Dialectics." *Philosophy and Social Criticism and Cultural Hermeneutics* (Chestnut Hill, Massachusetts), vol. 5, no. 3-4, 1978, 417-425.

2475    Gazitúa Navarrete, V. *Formulación ontológica-cientifica de El ser y el tiempo.* Buenos Aires, 1963, 101 p.

2476    Gebser, J. *Ursprung and Gegenwart.* Stuttgart, 1966.

2477    *Gedenkschrift der Stadt Messkirch an ihren Sohn und Ehrenbürger Professor Martin Heidegger.* Foreword and postscript by Siegfried Schühle. Messkirch: Stadt Messkirch, 1977, 46 p.

2478    Geiger, Louis-Bertrand. "Bulletin de Philosophie. Philosophie de l'existence. Heidegger." *Revue des science philosophiques et théologiques* (Paris), vol. 38, 1954, 66-72.

2479    Geiger, Louis-Bertrand. "Heideggers Denken. Eine Wegweisung." *Freiburger Zeitschrift für Philosophie und Theologie* (Freiburg, Schweiz), vol. 23, 1976, 233-352.

2480    Gelley, A. de. "Staiger, Heidegger and the Task of Criticism." *Modern Language Quarterly* (Washington), vol. 23, 1962, 195-216.

2481    Gelven, Charles M. *Martin Heidegger's Theory of Fundamental Ontology.* Phil. Diss. Washington Univ. 1966 252 p. *Dissertation Abstracts International,* vol. 27/06-A, 1866.

2482    Gelven, Michael. *A Commentary on Heidegger's 'Being and Time'. A Section-By-Section Interpretation.* New York, 1970, XIV, 234 p.

        [Rev. by E. Feist Hirsch in *Journal of the History of Philosophy* (Berkeley), vol. 9, no. 3, 1971, 400-403. *See* "Hegel, Heidegger, and 'Experience'," by H. W. Schneider. *Journal of the History of Philosophy,* 1972.]

2483    Gelven, Michael. "Guilt and Human Meaning." *Humanitas* (Pittsburgh), vol. 9, 1972, 69-81.

2484    Gelven, Michael. "Eros and Projection: Plato and Heidegger." Heidegger issue. *The Southwestern Journal of Philosophy* (Norman), vol. 4, no. 3, 1973, 125-136.

2485    Gelven, Michael. "Authenticity and Guilt." In *Heidegger's Existential Analytic,* by Frederick Elliston (ed.). The Hague/New York: Mouton Publishers, 1978, 233-246.

2485a   Gelven, Michael. "Heidegger and Tragedy." In *Martin Heidegger and the Question of Literature.* Ed. William V. Spanos. Bloomington, Indiana; London: Indiana Univ. Press, 1979, 215-228.

2485b   Gelven, Michael. "Heidegger's Understanding of the Ultimate Meaning and Reality." *Ultimate Reality and Meaning* (Assen), vol. 3, 1980, 114-134.

2486    Gendlin, Eugene T. "Befindlichkeit: Heidegger and the Philosophy of Psychology." *Review of Existential Psychology & Psychiatry* (Northwestern Univ., Evanston, Illinois), vol. 16, no. 1, 2 and 3, 1978/79.

2487    Gent, W. *Die Raum-Zeit-Philosophie des neunzehnten Jahrhunderts. Historische, kritische und analytische Untersuchungen. Die Geschichte der Begriffe des Raumes un der Zeit vom kritischen Kant bis zur Gegenwart.* Bonn, 1930, 351-358.

2488    Gent, W. "Existenzphilosophie und Ethik." *Philosophische Studien* (Berlin), vol. 2, 1950/51, 126-136 u.ö.

2489    Gentile, G. Rev. of *Platons Lehre von der Wahrheit. Mit einem Brief über den 'Humanismus',* by Martin Heidegger. Bern, 1947. *Giornale di Metafisica* (Torino), vol. 5, 1950, 520-521.

2490    Gérard, J. Rev. of *Kant und das Problem der Metaphysik,* by Martin Heidegger. Bonn, 1929. *Revue internationale de philosophie* (Bruxelles), vol. 7, 1953, 404-408.

2491    Gérard, J. "Heidegger et ses lieux." *Etudes* (Paris), vol. 2, 1954, 41-42.

2492    Gérard, J. Rev. of *Einführung in die Metaphysik,* by Martin Heidegger. Tübingen, 1953. *Revue Internationale de Philosophie* (Bruxelles), vol. 9, 1955, 158-160.

2493     Gerardo, J. Rev. of *Gelassenheit,* by Martin Heidegger. (Heideggeriana, I). Trans. E. Landolt. Milano, 1967. *Pensamiento* (Madrid), vol. 25, 1969, 303-304.

2494     Gerber, Rudolph J. "Heidegger: Thinking and Thanking Being." *The Modern Schoolman* (St. Louis, Missouri), vol. 44, 1966/67, 205-222.

2495     Gerber, Rudolph J. "Focal Points in Recent Heidegger Scholarship." *The New Scholasticism* (Washington), vol. 42, 1968, 561-577.

2496     Gerber, U. "Heideggers Denkweg und die Fragen der Theologie." *Deutsches Pfarrerblatt* (Essen), vol. 63, 1963, 454-455.

2497     Gerken, Alexander. Rev. of *Das Verhältnis von Philosophie und Theologie im Denken Martin Heideggers,* by Annemarie Gethmann-Siefert. Phil. Diss. Bochum 1974. *Theologische Revue* (Münster), vol. 72, 1976, 223-226.

2498     Gerken, Alexander. "Bonaventura und Heidegger. Ein Vergleich." *Franciscan Studies* (St. Bonaventure), vol. 37, 1977.

2499     Gerlach, Hans-Martin. "Spätbürgerliche Philosophie und Konservatismus." *Deutsche Zeitschrift für Philosophie* (Berlin), vol. 24, 1976, 603-617.

2500     Gerlach, Hans-Martin. "Der bürgerliche Mensch zwischen Existenz und Sein. Marxistische Bemerkungen zum philosophischen Entwicklungsgang Martin Heideggers." *Deutsche Zeitschrift für Philosohie* (Berlin), vol. 25, no. 6, 1977, 671-682.

2501     Gethmann, Carl Friedrich. "Die Möglichkeit der Seinsfrage in einer operativen Sprachtheorie." *Zeitschrift für Katholische Theologie* (Wien), vol. 91, 1969, 554-566.

2502     Gethmann, Carl Friedrich. "Heideggers These vom Sein des Daseins als Sorge und die Frage nach der Subjektivität des Subjekts." *Zeitschrift für Katholische Theologie* (Wien), vol. 32, 1970, 425-453.

2503     Gethmann, Carl Friedrich. *Untersuchungen zum Methodenproblem in der Philosophie Martin Heideggers.* Bonn, 1972, XVI, 375 p.

        [Phil. Diss. Bochum 1971.]

2504     Gethmann, Carl Friedrich. "Zu Heideggers Wahrheitsbegriff." *Kant-Studien* (Bonn), vol. 65, 1974, 186-200.

2505     Gethmann, Carl Friedrich. *Verstehen und Auslegung. Das Methodenproblem in der Philosophie Martin Heideggers.* (Abhandlungen zur Philosophie, Psychologie und Pädagogik, 81). Bonn: Bouvier Verlag Herbert Grundmann, 1974, 416 p.

        [Phil. Diss. 1971; 1st pub. 1972.]

2506     Gethmann-Siefert, Annemarie. *Das Verhältnis von Philosophie und Theologie im Denken Martin Heideggers.* (Symposion. Philosophische Schriftenreihe, 47). Freiburg/München: Verlag Karl Alber, 1975, 340 p.

        [Phil. Diss. Brochum 1972.]

2507    Gethmann-Siefert, Annemarie. "The Significance of *Time and Being* for the Foundation of Theology." (In Serbocroat). *Delo* (Beograd), vol. 23, no. 12, 1977, 177-194. Rpt. in *Rani Hajdeger - Recepcija i kritika Bivstva i vrenema.* Trans. Dragon Stojanovic and Danilo Basta. (Biblioteka Zodijak). Beograd, 1979, 290.

2508    Geurtsen, H. "M. Heidegger: De metaphysiek van de eindigheid." *Studia Catholica* (Nijmegen), vol. 12, 1936, 469-487.

2509    Geuss, Artuno. "Martin Heidegger a umelecké dilo." *Filosoficky Casopis* (Praha), vol. 15, no. 5, 1967, 676-685.

2510    Geyer, H. G. "Gespräch mit Heidegger. Verkündigung und Forschung." *Jahrbuch 1958/59* (München), 1960/62, 173-185.

2511    Ghanotakis, George. *The Notion of 'Essence' (Wesen) in Heidegger's Thought: Heidegger's Phenomenological Explication of the Ecstatico-Horizontal Dimension of Intelligibility.* Phil. Diss. Univ. of Toronto 1978. *Dissertation Abstracts International,* vol. 40/03-A, 1515.

2512    Giannarás, A. "Martin Heidegger und sein Verhältnis zur philosophischen Tradition." *Hellenika. Zeitschrift für deutsch-griechische kulturelle und wirtschaftliche Zusammenarbeit* (Bochum), no. 3, 1969, 8-10.

2513    Giannini, Giorgio. "Parmenide, Heidegger e S. Tommaso." *Sapientia Aquinatis, I; Communicationes IV Congressus Thomistici Internationalis, Romae 13-17 Septembris 1955.* (Bibliotheca Pontificiae Academiae Romanae S. Thomae Aquinatis, Vol. I). Romae, 1955, 482-488.

2514    Giannini, Giorgio. Rev. of *Kant e il problema della metafisica,* by Martin Heidegger. *Humanitas* (Brescia), vol. 19, 1964, 936-937.

2515    Giannini, Giorgio. "Postille Heideggeriane." *Aquinas* (Roma), vol. 20, no. 2, 1977, 163-179.

2516    Gibson, W. R. Boyce. "Excerpts From a 1928 Freiburg Diary." *The Journal of the British Society for Phenomenology* (Manchester), vol. 2, 1971, 63-76.

2517    Gibson, W. R. Boyce. "From Husserl to Heidegger. Excerpts From a 1928 Freiburg Diary." Ed. H. Spiegelberg. *The Journal of the British Society for Phenomenology* (Manchester), vol. 1, 1971, 58-83.

2518    Gier Jr., Nicholas Francis. *Heidegger and the Ontological 'Differenz': A Historical-Philosophical Analysis.* Phil. Diss. Claremont Graduate School 1972. *Dissertation Abstracts International,* vol. 33/09-A, 5233, 242 p.

2519    Giesecke, H. Rev. of *Einführung in die Metaphysik,* by Martin Heidegger. Tübingen, 1953. *Die Zeichen der Zeit. Evangelische Monatsschrift* (Berlin), vol. 9, 1955, 279.

2520    Gignoux, V. *La philosophie existentielle. Kierkegaard-Jaspers-Heidegger-Sartre-Marcel.* Paris, 1950, 19-25.

2521    Gilson, E. *Being and Some Philosophers.* Toronto, 1949, XI, 219 p.

2522    Gilson, E. "L'être et Dieu." *Revue Thomiste* (Toulouse), vol. 72, 1962, 398-416.

2523 Giordani, M. C. "Heidegger, o filosofo em busca do sentido do Ser." *Vozes* (Petópolis), vol. 56, 1962, 568-588.

2524 Giorgiantonio, M. Rev. of *Qu'appelle-t-on penser?*, by Martin Heidegger. *Sophia* (Padova), vol. 36, 1968, 122-123.

2525 Giovannangeli, Daniel. "Heidegger pris au mot." *Revue de l'Université de Bruxelles* (Bruxelles), no. 2, 1977, 459-471.

2526 Gipper, H. *Bausteine zur Sprachinhaltsforschung.* Düsseldorf, 1963, 174 ff.

2527 Gironella, J. R. "Metafisica de la forma." (Kant, Suaréz, Tomismo, Escotismo, Heidegger). *Pensamiento* (Madrid), vol. 14, 1958, 263-285.

2528 Giroux, Laurent. *Durée pure et temporalité: Bergson et Heidegger.* Tournai, 1971, 136 p.

2529 Giroux, Laurent. "Heidegger et la metaphysique: Vers un double dépassement." *Philosophiques,* vol. 20, 1975, 207-228.

2530 Giroux, Laurent. "L'historialité chez Heidegger et son rapport à la philosophie de la vie de W. Dilthey." *Dialogue* (Montreal/Kingston), vol. 15, no. 4, 1976, 583-594.

2531 Giroux, Laurent. "Heidegger et la migration des concepts. Les chances de la philosophie." *Revue de l'Université Laurentienne* (Sudbury), vol. 9, no. 2, 1977.

2432 Giulietti, G. *Alla ricerca dell'essere perduto. Una introduzione al pensiero di Heidegger.* Treviso, 1972, 294 p.

2533 Glazman, M. S. "Chajdeggerovskaja koncepcija vzaimootnosênija nauânogo i chudozestvennogo mâslenija" (Heidegger's Concept of the Relationships Between Scientific and Artistic Thinking). *Kritika nekotorych napravlenij sovremennoj burzuaznoj filosofii* (Moskva), 1973, 90-101.

2534 Gleason, Robert W. "Toward a Theology of Death." *Thought,* vol. 32, 1957, 39-68.

2535 Glicksman, M. "A Note on the Philosophy of Heidegger." *The Journal of Philosophy* (New York), vol. 35, 1938, 93-104.

2536 Glockner, H. *Die europäische Philosophie von den Anfängen bis zur Gegenwart.* 2nd ed. Stuttgart, 1958, 1127-1136.

2537 Gloege, G. "Existenzphilosophie und Seinsdenken. Eine Nachlese im Umkreis ihrer Literatur." *Theologische Literaturzeitung* (Berlin), vol. 91, 1966, 481-498.

2538 Gmeiner, Conceiçao Neves. "Martin Heidegger e o Nacional-Socialismo." *Leopoldianum. Revista de Estudos e Comunicaçoes* (Santos), vol. 2, no. 1, 1975, 26-33.

2539 Gneo, Corrado. "M. Heidegger 'educatore'." *Aquinas* (Roma), vol. 20, no. 2, 1977, 281-289.

2540 Goeze-Wegner, Ilse. *Paul Tillich - Martin Heidegger: Philsophische Theologie im Horizont neuzeitlicher Metaphysik. Ein kritischer Versuch über Tillichs*

*Theologie in ihrer Beziehung zu Heideggers Philosophie.* Phil. Diss. Tübingen 1973.

2541 Goff, Robert A. "Wittgenstein's Tools and Heidegger's Implements." *Man and World* (Pittsburgh), vol. 1, 1968, 447-462.

2542 Goff, Robert A. "Saying and Being With Heidegger and Parmenides." *Man and World* (The Hague), vol. 5, 1972, 62-78.

2543 Goldmann, Lucien. "Lukács et Heidegger." *Revue de l'Institut de Sociologie* (Bruxelles), no. 3-4, 1973, 503-523.

2544 Goldmann, Lucien. *Lukács et Heidegger.* Fragments posthumously published and annotated by Youssef Ishaghpour. (Bibliothèque Médiations, 112). Paris/Denoël: Gonthier, 1973, 182 p. English trans. by William Q. Zielhawer. New York, 1979, 136 p.

2545 Goldmann, Lucien. *Lukács und Heidegger.* Nachgelassene Fragmente. Ed. and intr. Youssef Ishagpour. Trans. Rainer Rochlitz. (Sammlung Luchterhand, 176). Darmstadt, Neuwied: Luchterhand, 1975, 194 p.

[German trans. of 2544.]

2546 Goldmann, Lucien. "Lukács et Heidegger." In *Lucien Goldmann et la sociologie de la littérature.* Hommage à Lucien Goldmann. (Etudes de Sociologie de la Littérature). Bruxelles: Editions de l'Univ. de Bruxelles, 1975, 11-31.

2547 Goldmann, Lucien. *Lukács y Heidegger. Hacia una filosofia nueva.* Trans. José Luis Etcheverry. (Col. Biblioteca de filosofia). Buenos Aires: Amorrortu Ed., 1975, 152 p.

[Spanish trans. of 2544.]

2548 Goldmann, Lucien. *Lukács e Heidegger.* Posthumous fragments published by Youssef Ishagpour. Trans and ed. Emanuela Dorigotti Volpi. (Il lavoro critico, 10). Verona: Bertani, 1976, 156 p.

[Italian trans. of 2544.]

2549 Goldmann, Lucien. *Lukács and Heidegger. Toward a New Philosophy.* Trans. William Q. Boelhower. London/Boston, Massachusetts: Routledge & Kegan Paul, 1977, xxii-112 p.

[English trans. of 2544.]

2550 Goldstein, Jeffrey. "Buber's Misunderstanding of Heidegger. Being and the Living God. *Philosophy Today* (Celina, OHio), vol. 22, no. 2-4, 1978, 156-167.

2551 Gomá-Fusté, F. "Conclusiones sobre 'El estudio tematico de la nada en Heidegger'." *Convivium* (Barcelona), vol. 4, 1959, 21-31.

2552 Gombrowicz, W. "Guide de la philosophie en six heures en quart. Schopenhauer-Hegel-Existentialisme - La liberté chez Sartre - Le regard d'autrui-Heidegger." *L'Herne* (Paris), vol. 14, 1971, 390-417, (specifically pages 413-417).

2553 Gómez-Lobo, Alfonso. "Martin Heidegger." *Mensase* (Santiago, Chile), no. 255, 1976, 623-629.

2554 González, Gonzalo. "R. Bultmann y M. Heidegger. Un ejemplo de relación filosofia-teologia." *La Ciencia Tomista* (Salamanca), vol. 104, 1977, 3-19.

2555 Gonzalez-Caminero, Nemesio. "Ortega y el primer Heidegger." *Gregorianum* (Roma), vol. 56, 1975, 89-138.

[Summary, 138-9.]

2556 Gonzalez-Caminero, Nemesio. "Ortega y el segundo Heidegger." *Gregorianum* (Roma), vol. 56, 1975, 733-162.

[Summary, 762-3.]

2557 González-Caminero, Nemesio. "Ortega y Heidegger: postrera valoración mutua." *Miscelanea Comillas* (Comillas, Santander), vol. 64, 1976, 5-38.

2558 Gonzalo Casas, M. "Un Problema metafisico en Martin Heidegger." *Norte* (Tucumán), vol. 1, 1951, 13-31.

2559 Gonzalo Casas, M. "Apuntes sobre el fundamento de la sociedad. En torno a Heidegger." *Norte* (Tucumán), vol. 3, 1953, 5-15.

2560 Gonzalo Casas, M. "Heidegger y la filosofia existencial." *Introduction a la filosofia* (Tucumán), 1954, 269-292.

2561 Gonzalo Casas, M. "El problema del fundamento en Heidegger. La búsqueda del ser." *Giornale di Metafisica* (Torino), vol. 9, 1954, 660-664.

2562 Gonzalo Casas, M. "Notas criticas de filosofia." *Sapientia* (Buenos Aires), vol. 12, 1957, 115-121.

2563 Goodman, Harvey Louis. *Heidegger's Aesthetic Theory: Truth and the Work of Art.* Phil. Diss. The Univ. of Tennessee 1974. *Dissertation Abstracts International,* vol. 35/11-A, 7350.

2564 Gordeziani, P. S. *Problema 'suââestvovanija' v ekzistencializme (Kritika fundamental'noj ontologii Chajdeggera)* (The Problem of 'Existence' in Existentialism (The Criticism of Heidegger's Fundamental-Ontology)). *Avtoreferat dissertacii na soiskanie uâënoj stepeni kandidata filosofskich nauk.* Tbilisi, 1969.

2565 Gotô, Taira. "Pasukaru to M. Haideggâ - Pasukaru to Gendai Jitsuzonshugi" (Pascal and Heidegger - Pascal and the Modern Existentialism). *Shizuoka Daigaku Jimbunronshû* (Shizuoka), vol. 12, 1961, 1-19.

2566 Gotô, Taira. "Pasukaru to M. Haideggâ" (Pascal and M. Heidegger). In *Jinmonronshu.* Shizuoka, 1962.

2567 Gottfredson, Ches. *Prophecy and Philosophy.* (Vol. I: Elijah, Isaiah, Heidegger). New York: Vantage Press, 1977, 213 p.

2568 Gould, Carol Cirelle. "Authenticity and Being - With Others. A Critique of Heidegger's 'Sein und Zeit'." Authorized facsimile of the dissertation of the Yale Univ. Phil. Diss. 1971. Ann Arbor, Michigan; London: University Microfilms International, 1977, iv-251 p. *Dissertation Abstracts International,* vol. 32/12-A, 7042.

2569    Graaf, F. de. *Het schuldprobleem in de existentiephilosophie van Martin Heidegger.* 's-Gravenhage, 1951, 161 p.

2570    Graaf, F. de. *Het Europese nihilisme.* Amsterdam, 1957.

2571    Graff, W. L. "Rilke in the Light of Heidegger." *Laval Théologique et Philosophique* (Quebec), vol. 17, 1961, 165-172.

2572    Grampon, R. "Heidegger." *Témoignages* (Saint Léger), vol. 46, 1954, 32-43.

2573    Granarolo, P. "Heidegger, penseur de l'époque planétaire." *Annales de la Faculté des Lettres et Sciences Humaines de Nice* (Nice), no. 20, 1973, 41-66.

2574    Granel, G. *Le sens du temps et de la percipation chez Husserl.* Paris, 1969, 281 p.

2575    Granel, G. *L'equivoque ontologique de la pensée kantienne.* Paris, 1970, 192 p.

2576    Granel, G. "Remarques sur le rapport de Sein und Zeit et de la phénoménologie Husserlienne." *Durchblicke.* Ed. V. Klostermann. Frankfurt, 1970, 350-368.

2577    Granier, J. Rev. of *Zur Sache des Denkens,* by Martin Heidegger. Tübingen: Max Niemeyer Verlag, 1969, 94 p. *Revue Philosophique de la France et de l'Etranger* (Paris), vol. 100, 1975, 376-378.

2578    Granier, J. "Réfexions sur l'essence de la métaphysique." *Revue de Métaphysique et de Morale* (Paris - CDSH), vol. 83, no. 4, 1978, 433-446.

2578a   Grant, Grellv. "Heidegger on Inauthenticity and Authenticity." *Gnosis,* vol. 1, 1979, 81-94.

2579    Grasselli, G. "La fenomenologia di Husserl e l'ontologia di M. Heidegger." *Rivista di filosofia neoscolastica* (Milano), vol. 19, 1928, 330-347.

2580    Grasselli, G. Rev. of *Kant und das Problem der Metaphysik,* by Martin Heidegger. Bonn, 1929. *Rivista di filosofia* (Bologna), vol. 21, 1930, 275-280.

2581    Grasselli, G. Rev. of *Vom Wesen des Grundes,* by Martin Heidegger. Halle, 1929. *Rivista di filosofia* (Bologna), vol. 23, 1932, 179.

2582    Grasselli, G. "La fenomenologia di Husserl e l'ontologia di M. Heidegger." *Rivista di filosofia* (Bologno), vol. 29, 1938, 330-347.

2583    Grassi, Ernesto. "Sviluppo e significato della scuola fenomenologica nella filosofia tedesca contemporanea." *Rivista di filosofia* (Milano), vol. 20, 1929, 129-151, (specifically pages 135, 147-151).

2584    Grassi, Ernesto. "Il problema della metafisica immanente di Heidegger." *Giornale critico della filosofia italiana* (Firenze), vol. 11, 1930, 288-314.

2585    Grassi, Ernesto. *Dell'appaire e dell'essere. Seguito da linee della filosofia tedesca contemporanea.* Firenze, 1933.

2586    Grassi, Ernesto. "Il probleme del logo." *Archivio di filosofia* (Roma), vol. 6, 1936, 151-183, passim.

2587    Grassi, Ernesto. "Il problema del nulla nella filosofia di M. Heidegger." *Giornale Critico della Filosofia Italiana* (Firenze), vol. 18, 1937, 319-334.

2588 Grassi, Ernesto. *Vom Vorrang des Logos.* (Das Problem der Antike in der Auseinandersetzung zwischen italienischer und deutscher Philosophie). München, 1939, 43-65, passim.

2589 Grassi, Ernesto. *Verteidigung des individuellen Lebens.* München, 1946, 176 p.

2590 Gravely, James William. *Heidegger and Metaphysics, an Attempt to Found a Dialogue.* Phil. Diss. Tulane Univ. 1974. *Dissertation Abstracts International,* vol. 35/03-A, 1699.

2591 Gray, Glenn J. "The Idea of Death in Existentialism." *The Journal of Philosophy* (Lancaster, Pennsylvania), vol. 48, 1951, 113-127, passim.

2592 Gray, Glenn J. "Heidegger's 'Being'." *The Journal of Philosophy* (Lancaster, Pennsylvania), vol. 49, 1952, 415-422.

2593 Gray, Glenn J. "Heidegger 'evaluates' Nietzsche." *Journal of the History of Ideas* (Lancaster, Pennsylvania/New York), vol. 14, 1953, 304-309.

2594 Gray, Glenn J. "Heidegger's Course: From Human Existence to Nature." *The Journal of Philosophy* (Lancaster, Pennsylvania/New York), vol. 54, 1957, 197-207.

2595 Gray, Glenn J. "Martin Heidegger: On Anticipating My Own Death." *The Personalist* (Los Angeles), vol. 46, 1965, 439-458.

2596 Gray, Glenn J. "Einleitung." Rev. of *What is Called Thinking?,* by Martin Heidegger. New York, 1968, XII-XXVII.

2597 Gray, Glenn J. "Splendor of the Simple." (M. Heidegger). *Philosophy East and West* (Honolulu), vol. 20, 1970, 227-240.

2598 Gray, Glenn J. "Heidegger on Remembering and Remembering Heidegger." *Man and World* (West Lafayette), vol. 10, no. 1, 1977, 62-78.

2599 Grebe, W. *Heideggers Existenzontologie.* (Der tätige Mensch. Untersuchungen zur Philosophie des Handelns). Berlin, 1937, 16-50.

2600 Greef, J. de. "Philosophy and It's 'Other'." *International Philosophical Quarterly* (New York/ Heverlee/Leuven), vol. 10, 1970, 252-275, (specifically pages 254-256, 262-263).

2601 Greenier, David Laurence. *Meaning and Being in Heidegger's 'Sein und Zeit'.* Phil. Diss. Heidelberg 1976.

2602 Greisch, J. "Identité et différence dans la pensée de Martin Heidegger. Le Chemin de *l'Ereignis.*" *Revue des Sciences Philosophiques et Théologiques* (Le Saulchoir), vol. 1, 1973, 71-112.

2603 Greisch, J. "Les mots et les roses. La métaphore chez Martin Heidegger." *Revue des Sciences Philosophiques et Théologiques* (Le Saulchoir), vol. 3, 1973, 433-456.

2603a Greisch, Jean. "La contrée de la sérénité et l'horizon de l'espérance." In *Heidegger et la question de Dieu.* Ed. Richard Kearney and Joseph Stephen O'Leary. Paris: B. Grasset, 1980, 168-193.

2604 Gremmels, H. Rev. of *Einführung in die Metaphysik,* by Martin Heidegger. Tübingen, 1953. *Schwäbische Landeszeitung* (Augsburg), 28/29.6.1953.

2605 Gremmels, H. "Martin Heideggers Landschaft." *Schwäbische Landeszeitung* (Augsburg), 28/29.6.1953.

2606 Grene, Marjorie. *Dreadful Freedom.* Chicago, 1948, (specifically pages 41-94). New title: *Introduction to Existentialism.* Chicago, 1959.

2607 Grene, Marjorie. *Martin Heidegger.* (Studies in modern european literature and thought). London, 1957, 128 p.

[Rev. by A. Shalom in *Les Etudes philosophiques* (Paris), no. 13, 1958, 215.]

2608 Grene, Marjorie. *Heidegger: Philosopher and Prophet.* (The Twentieth Century, 164 [N. 982]). London, 1958, 545-555.

2609 Grene, Marjorie. "Heidegger." *The Encyclopedia of Philosophy.* Ed. P. Edwards. New York/London, 1967, Bd III, 459-465.

2610 Grene, Majorie. "The Paradoxes of Historicity." *The Review of Metaphysics* (Washington), vol. 32, no. 1, 1978, 15-36.

2611 Grieshaber, H. "Martin Heidegger zum 70. Geburtstag." *Festschrift* (Pfullingen), 1959, 349.

2612 Grigorjan, B. T. "Na putjach filosofskogo poznanija celoveka" (On the Paths of Man's Philosophical Cognition). *V knige 'Problema celoveka v sovremennoj filosofii' Izdatel'stvo 'Nauka'* (Moskva), 1969, 405-408.

2613 Grimm, Ruediger Hermann. "Introduction: Being as Appropriation." *Philosophy Today* (Celina, Ohio), vol. 19, 1975, 146-151.

2614 Grimsley, R. *Existentialist Thought.* Cardiff, 1955, 39-89, passim.

2615 Grisebach, E. "Interpretation oder Destruktion? Zum kritischen Verständnis von Martin Heideggers 'Kant und das Problem der Metaphysik'." *Deutsche Vierteljahrsschrift für Literaturwissenschaft und Geistesgeschichte* (Halle), vol. 8, 1930, 199-232.

2616 Grolman, A. von. Rev. of *Hölderlin und das Wesen der Dichtung,* by Martin Heidegger. München, 1936/37. *Die Neue Literatur* (Leipzig), vol. 38, 1937, 468-469.

2617 Grooten, J. Rev. of *Einführung in die Metaphysik,* by Martin Heidegger. Tübingen, 1953. *Dietsche Warande en Belfort* (Antwerpen), 1955, 244-249.

2618 Groth, H. Miles. "Messkirch: Martin Heidegger. June 1976." *Philosophy Today* (Celina, Ohio), vol. 20, 1976, 259-261.

2619 Groves, John L. *The Influence of Heidegger in Latin-American Philosophy.* Phil. Diss. Boston Univ. 1960, 537 p. *Dissertation Abstracts International,* vol. 21/04, 926.

2620 Gruber, W. *Vom Wesen des Kunstwerkes nach Martin Heidegger. Eine Untersuchung über die Möglichkeit und Notwendigkeit d. Kunst.* (Schriften und Vorträge im Rahmen d. Grazer Theol. Fakultät, Reihe D, Heft 1/2). Graz, 1956, 90 p.

2621 Gründer, Karlfried. "Martin Heideggers Wissenschaftskritik in ihren geschichtlichen Zusammenhängen." *Archiv für Philosophie* (Stuttgart), vol. 11, 1961, 312-335.

2622 Gründer, Karlfried. "Heidegger's Critique of Science." *Philosophy Today,* vol. 7, Spring 1963, 15-32.

2623 Grugan, Arthur Anthony. "Thought and Poetry. Language as Man's Homecoming. A Study of Martin Heidegger's Question of Being and Its Ties to Friedrich Hölderlin's Experience of the Holy." Authorized facsimile of the dissertation Duquesne Univ. Phil. Diss. 1972. Ann Arbor, Michigan; London: University Microfilms International, 1977, vii-236 p. *Dissertation Abstracts International,* vol. 33/08-A, 4473.

2624 Grundmann, W. "Heideggers 'Sein und Zeit' und die christliche Verkündigung." *Die Furche* (Berlin), vol. 17, 1931, 163-179.

2625 Grunert, E. Rev. of *Was heisst Denken?*, by Martin Heidegger. Tübingen, 1954. *Freiburger Zeitschrift für Philosophie und Theologie* (Freiburg, Schweiz), vol. 6, 1959, 101-102.

2626 Grygiel, S. Rev. of *Budowaá, mieszkaá, myáleá. Eseje wybrane,* by Martin Heidegger. (Bauen, Wohnen, Denken. Ausgewählte Essays). Ed. Krzysztof Michalski. Warszawa, 1978. *Znak,* vol. 9, 1978.

2627 Grzesik, J. *Die Geschichtlichkeit als Wesensverfassung des Menschen - Eine Untersuchung zur Anthropologie Wilhelm Diltheys und Martin Heideggers.* Bonn 1.6.1960. Bonn, 1960, 325 p.

2628 Guardini, Romano. "Leib und Leiblichkeit in Dantes 'Göttlicher Komödie'." In *Anteile, Martin Heidegger zum 60. Geburtstag.* Frankfurt, 1950, 154-177.

2628a Günter, Peter. "Heideggers Vergessen und das Er-innern von Gesellschaft im Begriff logischer Zeit." In *Nachdenken über Heidegger.* Ed. Ute Guzzoni. Hildesheim: Gerstenberg Verlag, 1980, 55-79.

2628b Günther, Gotthard. "Martin Heidegger und die Weltgeschichte des Nichts." In *Nachdenken über Heidegger.* Ed. Ute Guzzoni. Hildesheim: Gerstenberg Verlag, 1980, 80-116.

2629 Guerriere, Daniel. "Ontology as the Symbolics of the Future." *Philosophy Today* (Celina, Ohio), vol. 17, 1973, 213-219.

2629a Guerriere, Daniel. "Physis, Sophia, Psyche." In *Heraclitean Fragments.* Ed. John Sallis and Kenneth Maly. Univ. of Alabama Press, 1980, 86-134.

2630 Guggenberger, A. "Orientations métaphysiques dans l'Allemagne d'aujourd'hui." *Revue Philosophique de Louvain* (Louvain), vol. 51, 1953, 541-554, (specifically pages 549-552).

2631 Guibal, Francis. "Martin Heidegger et l'attente du 'Dieu divin'." *Études* (Paris), no. 334, 1971, 595-624, 753-774.

2632 Guibal, Francis. ... *et combien de dieux mauveaux, approches contemporaines: Heidegger.* Paris: Aubier-Montaigne, 1980, 168 p.

2633 Guibal, Francis. "Martin Heidegger, penseur de notre modernité." *Projet,* no. 145, mai 1980, 595-608.

2634    Guignon, Charles Burke. *Heidegger and the Structure of Traditional Epistemological Arguments.* Phil. Diss. Univ. of California Berkeley 1979 384 p. *Dissertations Abstracts International,* vol. 40/07-A, 4083.

2635    Guilead, R. *Etre et liberté. Une étude sur le dernier Heidegger.* Intr. Paul Ricoeur. (Philosophies contemporains. Textes et études, 12). Louvain/Paris, 1965, 184 p.

        [Rev. by A. Erickson in *Journal of the History of Philosophy* (Berkeley), vol. 5, 1967, 307.]

2636    Guilead, R. "Heidegger et l'échec." In *Les hommes devant l'échec.* Ed. J. Lacroix. Paris, 1968, 165-175.

2637    Guise, Alice M. *What are Poets For? Coleridge and Heidegger.* Phil. Diss. The American Univ. 1976. Ann Arbor, Michigan: University Microfilms International, 44. [HGK76-19781]. *Dissertation Abstracts International,* vol. 37/03-A, 1608.

2638    Guitton, J. "Visite à Heidegger." *La Table ronde* (Paris), vol. 123, 1958, 143-155.

2639    Guitton, J. "Chemins de campagne. Méditation sur Heidegger." *La Table ronde* (Paris), no. 162, 1961, 9-15.

2640    Guitton, J. *Le clair et l'obscur. Théétète ou l'obscurité - Claudel et Heidegger - Mystère humain et mystère divin - Les disciples d'Emmaüs.* Paris, 1962, 128 p.

2641    Guitton, J. *Profils parallèles, Pascal, Leibniz, Newman, Teilhard, Bergson, Claudel, Heidegger.* Paris, 1970, 497 p.

        [Polish trans. by S. Cichowicz, a chapter on Claudel and Heidegger, Warszwawa, 1973.]

2642    Gullvag, I. *Referanse, Mening og Eksistens.* Philosophy Institute, Trondheim, 1965.

2643    Gupta, Rajender Kumar. "What Does Heidegger Understand by Being?" *Journal of the Philosophical Association,* vol. 7, 29-44.

2644    Gupta, Rajender Kumar. "Heidegger's Notion of Truth." *Journal of the Philosophical Association,* vol. 7, 145-152.

2645    Gupta, Rajender Kumar. "Ein Schwierigkeit in Kants 'Kritik der reinen Vernunft' und Heideggers Kant-Interpretation." *Zeitschrift für Philosophische Forschung* (Meisenheim/Glan), vol. 16, 1962, 429-450.

2646    Gupta, R. W. "What is Heidegger's Notion of Time?" *Revue internationale de Philosophie* (Bruxelles), vol. 14, 1960, 163-193.

2647    Gurvitch, G. *Les tendances actuelles de la philosophie allemande.* Paris, 1930, 235 p., (specifically pages 207-234). 2nd ed. 1949.

2648    Gutenbrunner, Siegfried. "Was bedeutet *Sein?* M. Heidegger zum 85. Geburtstag mit verehrungsvollem Dank gewidmet." *Zeitschrift für Philosophische Forschung* (Schlehdorf a. Kochelsee, Meisenheim/Glan), vol. 28, 1974, 434-442.

2649    Gutiérrez Alemán, C. B. "El neokantianismo como punto de partida de la filosofia de Heidegger." *Ideas y Valores* (Bogotá), no. 48-49, 1977, 47-65.

2650    Gutiérrez, Carlos Bernardo. *Die Kritik des Wertbegriffes in der Philosophie Heideggers.* Phil. Diss. Heidelberg 1976.

2651    Guy, A. Rev. of *Sendas perdidas,* by Martin Heidegger. Buenos Aires, 1960. *Les Etudes Philosophiques* (Paris), no. 16, 1961, 254-255.

2652    Guy, A. "Ortega y Gasset, critique de Heidegger." *Annales publiées trimestriellement par l'Université de Toulouse - Le Mirail* (Toulouse), vol. 8, no. 3, Philosophie 1, 1972, 123-141.

2653    Guzzo, Augusto. *Sguardi sulla filosofia contemporanea.* Roma, 1940, 53-58.

2654    Guzzo, Augusto. "In morte di Martin Heidegger." *Filosofia* (Torino), vol. 27, 1976, 453-456.

2655    Guzzoni, A. "Recenti sviluppi del pensiero di Heidegger." *Il Pensiero* (Milano), vol. 2, 1957, 74-91.

2656    Guzzoni, A. "Il 'Movimento' della differenza ontologica in Heidegger." *Il Pensiero* (Milano), vol. 3, 1958, 193-199.

2657    Guzzoni, A. Rev. of *Der Satz vom Grund,* by Martin Heidegger. *Il Pensiero* (Milano), vol. 3, 1958, 232.

2658    Guzzoni, A. "Ontologische Differenz und Nichts." *Martin Heidegger zum 70. Geburtstag, Festschrift* (Pfullingen), 1959, 35-48.

2659    Guzzoni, G. Rev. of *Lettre sur l'Humanisme* and *Essais et conférences,* by Martin Heidegger. Paris, 1958. *Il Pensiero* (Milano), vol. 5, 1960, 128-132.

2660    Guzzoni, G. Rev. of *Qu'appelle-t-on penser?,* by Martin Heidegger. *Il Pensiero* (Milano), vol. 6, 1961, 392-394.

2661    Guzzoni, G. Rev. of *Gelassenheit,* by Martin Heidegger. *Il Pensiero* (Milano), vol. 7, 1962, 403-405.

2662    Guzzoni, G. *Considerazioni intorno alla prima sezione di 'Sein und Zeit'.* (Studi filosofici). Urbino, 1969, 248 p.

2663    Guzzoni, G. Rev. of *Introduzione alla metafisica,* by Martin Heidegger. *Il Pensiero* (Roma/Urbino), vol. 14, 1969, 92-95.

2663a   Guzzoni, Ute. "'Anspruch' und 'Entsprechung' und die Frage der Intersubjektivität." In *Nachdenken über Heidegger.* Ed. Ute Guzzoni. Hildesheim: Gerstenberg Verlag, 1980, 117-135.

2663b   Guzzoni, Ute, ed. *Nachdenken über Heidegger. Eine Bestandsaufnahme.* Hildesheim: Gerstenberg Verlag, 1980, 306 p.

2664    Haag, K. H. *Kritik der neuren Ontologie.* Stuttgart, 1960, 95 p.

2665    Haar, Michel. "La pensée et la moi chez Heidegger: les dons et les épreuves de l'Etre." *Revue de Métaphysique et de Morale* (Paris), vol. 80, no. 4, 1975, 456-484.

2666    Haar, Michel. "Heidegger et l'essence de la technique." *Etudes Germaniques* (Paris), vol. 32, no. 3, 1977, 299-316.

2666a   Haar, Michel. "Structures hégéliennes dans la pensée heideggérienne de l'histoire." *Revue de Métaphysique et de Morale* (Paris), vol. 85, 1980, 48-59.

2667   Habermas, Jürgen. "Mit Heidegger gegen Heidegger denken - Zur Veröffentlichung von Vorlesungen aus dem Jahre 1935." *Frankfurter Allgemeine Zeitung* (Frankfurt), 1953, Nr. 170 v.25.7.1953.

2668   Habermas, Jürgen. "Ein anderer Mythos des zwanzigsten Jahrhunderts." *Frankfurter Hefte,* vol. 14, 1959, H.3.

2669   Habermas, Jürgen. "Die grosse Wirkung. Eine chronistische Anmerkung zu Martin Heideggers 70. Geburtstag." *Frankfurter Allgemeine Zeitung,* 26.9.1959.

2670   Habermas, Jürgen. *Philosophisch-politische Profile.* Frankfurt, 1971, 254 p. (Heidegger, 67-92).

2671   Habermas, Jürgen. "Martin Heidegger. On the Publication of Lectures From the Year 1935." Trans. Dale Ponikvar. *Graduate Faculty Philosophy Journal,* vol. 6, 1977, 155-80.

2671a   Habermas, Jürgen. "Urbanisierung der Heideggerschen Provinz." In *Das Erbe Hegels.* (Suhrkamp-Taschenbücher, 596). Frankfurt: Suhrkamp, 1979.

2672   Hachez. Rev. of *Einführung in die Metaphysik,* by Martin Heidegger. Tübingen, 1953. *Medizinische Monatsschrift* (Stuttgart), vol. 7, 1953, 745.

2673   Hachin, A. "Existentialisme et phénoménologie. Trois étapes: Husserl-Heidegger-Sartre." *Bull Cercle thomiste* (Caen), vol. 15, 1953, 25-32.

2674   Hacquarrie, John. *An Existentialist Theology. A Comparison of Heidegger and Bultmann.* Middlesex, England, 1973.

2675   Hadot, P. "Heidegger et Plotin." *Critique* (Paris), vol. 15, no. 145, 1959, 539-556.

2676   Haeffner, Gerd. Rev. of *Die Kunst und der Raum,* by Martin Heidegger. *Theologie und Philosophie* (Frankfurt/Pullach/Freiburg), vol. 45, 1970, 457-458.

2677   Haeffner, Gerd. Rev. of *Metaphysikkritik als Begriffsproblematik,* by Martin Heidegger. *Philosophisches Jahrbuch* (Freiburg/München), vol. 80, 1973, 433-435.

2678   Haeffner, Gerd. *Heideggers Begriff der Metaphysik.* (Pullacher philosophische Forschungen, 10). München: Berchmannskolleg-Verlag, 1974, 174 p.

2679   Haeffner, Gerd. "Denken im Ende der Metaphysik. Ein Rückblick auf das Werk Martin Heideggers." *Stimmen der Zeit* (Freiburg), vol. 194, 1976, 517-529.

2680   Haeffner, Gerd. "Heidegger: Busca do carácter filosófico da *Antropologia Filosófica.*" Trans. Manuel Losa. *Revista Portuguesa de Filosofia* (Braga), vol. 33, no. 4, 1977, 257-269.

2681    Haeffner, Gerd. "Neue Literatur zur Problematik von 'Sein und Zeit'." *Theologie und Philosophie* (Frankfurt/Pullach/Freiburg), vol. 52, no. 3, 1977, 408-428.

2682    Haeffner, Gerd. Rev. of *Materialien zur Heidegger-Bibliographie 1917-1972*, by Hans-Martin Sass (ed.). Meisenheim, 1975. *Theologie und Philosophie* (Freiburg), vol. 52, 1977, 156-177.

2682a    Haeffner, Gerd. Rev. of "Martin Heidegger: Sein und Zeit." *Theologie und Philosophie* (Frankfurt/Pullach/Freiburg), vol. 53, 1978, 457-458.

2683    Haegil, Sô. *Haidegkaûi ch'ôlhake issôsôûi Stimmunggwa Geschick* (Mood and Common Fortune in Heidegger). M. A. Thesis, Ch'ungnam Univ., 1966.

2684    Haegil, Sô. "Haidegkae issôsôûi sigansônge kwanhan yôngu" (On the Notion of Temporality in Heidegger). *Ch'ungnam University Collection of Essays* (Ch'ungnam), vol. 9, 1970, 211-228.

2685    Härting, T. "Tauton. Untersuchungen zum Wesen des Begriffes." *Philosophisches Jahrbuch* (Freiburg), vol. 77, 1970, 190-214.

2686    Härting, Th. "Ideologiekritik und Existenzphilosophie." *Zeitschrift für philosophische Forschung* (Meisenheim/Glan), vol. 21, 1967, 282.

2687    Haeussling, Ansgar. *Physik und Didaktik: Versuch der Standortbestimmung einer Didaktik der Physik durch die Seinsphilosophie.* Kastellaun, 1976.

2688    Haga, Mayumi. "Haideggâ no Shiron" (Heidegger's Discussion of Poetry). *Risô* (Tôkyô), vol. 319, December 1959.

2689    Haga, Mayumi. "Haideggâ no 'Kotoba' no mondai" (The Problem of 'Language' in Heidegger). *Risô* (Tôkyô), vol. 322, March 1960.

2690    Hagiwara, Hiroshi. "Haideggâ Shûnin-Enzetsu-Hihan" (Criticism on Heidegger's Inaugural Lecture). *Dôtoku-Kyôiku* (Tôkyô), Juni 1934, 18-29.

2691    Hagmann, M. *Descartes in der Auffassung durch die Historiker der Philosophie. Zur Geschichte der neuzeitlichen Philosophiegeschichte.* Winterthur, 1955, 157-164.

2691a    Hahn, Robert. "Truth (Aletheia) in the Context of Heidegger's Critique of Plato and in the Tradition." *Southwest Philosophical Studies,* vol. 4, 1979, 51-57.

2692    Halder, A. "Martin Heidegger." *Lexikon der Pädogogik* (Freiburg), vol. 2, 1970, 200.

2693    Halebitses, Chrestos Ch. *He Philosophia tou Chaintenker.* Athens, 1974.

2694    Hall, David L. "Whitehead's Speculative Method." *Philosophy Today* (Celina, Ohio), vol. 16, 1972, 193-209.

2695    Hall, R. L. "Heidegger and the Space of Art." *The Journal of Existentialism* (New York), vol. 8, 1967/68, 91-108.

2696    Hamada, Yosuke. "Haideggâ no Tetsugaku no ichi Kôsatsu; Sekai to Chôetsu no Gainen o Chûshin toshite" (A Contemplation on Heidegger's Philosophy the Notions World and Transcendence). *Tetsugaku-Nempô, Dôshisha Daigaku* (Kyôto), November 1942, 1-94.

2697    Hamada, Yosuke. "Haideggâ no Kanto Kaishaku ni tsuite - Kanto ni okeru Jissen Tetsugaku no Mondai 1, 2" (Heidegger's Explication of Kant - The Problem of the Practical Philosophy in Kant). *Bunkagaku-Nempô, 2, Jimbungaku* (Dôshisha Daigaku, Kyôto), vol. 5, 1951, 1952, 1-11, 1-18.

2698    Hamburg, Carl H. "A Cassirer-Heidegger Seminar." *Philosophy and Phenomenological Research* (Buffalo), vol. 25, 1964/65, 208-222.

2699    Hammett, Jenny Lee Yates. *Existential Conceptions of Death: Heidegger, Tillich, Rilke.* Phil. Diss. Syracuse Univ. 1973. *Dissertation Abstracts International,* vol. 34/10-A, 6699.

2700    Hamrick, William S. "Heidegger and the Objectivity of Aesthetic Truth." *The Journal of Value Inquiry* (Akron), vol. 5, 1970/71, 120-130.

2701    Hamrick, William S. "Fascination, Fear and Pornography: A Phenomenological Typology." *Man and World* (The Hague), vol. 7, 1974, 52-66.

2702    Hanak, T. Rev. of *Perspektiven zur Deutung seines Werkes,* by Martin Heidegger. Ed. O. Pöggeler. *Zeitschrift für Philosophische Forschung* (Meisenheim/Glan), vol. 25, 1971, 467-469.

2703    Hancke, K. "Die Philosophie Martin Heideggers." *Geistige Arbeit. Zeitung aus des wissenschaftlichen Welt* (Berlin), vol. 21, 1934, 5.

2704    Hancke, K. "Um Heidegger. Gefolgschaft und Kritik." *Geistige Arbeit. Zeitung aus der wissenschaftlichen Welt* (Berlin), vol. 6, 1935, 5-6.

2705    Hanselmann, Johannes F. S. *Martin Heidegger's Fundamental Ontology and Its Theological Implications.* Hartford, Connecticut, May 1952.

2706    Hanselmann, Johannes F. S. "Ist Gott tot? Ein Versuch über das Problem der Stellung Heideggers zur Theologie." *Evangelisch-lutherische Kirchenzeitung* (Berlin), vol. 7, 1953, 113-117.

2707    Hanselmann, Johannes F. S. "Fundamentalontologie oder Kryptotheologie? Ein Beitrag zum theologischen Verständnis Martin Heidegger." *Evangelisch-lutherische Kirchenzeitung* (Berlin), vol. 7, 1953, 183-186.

2708    Hansen-Löve, F. "Fundamentalontologie oder Seinsmystik? Zur jüngsten Schrift Martin Heideggers." Bern, 1947. *Wort und Wahrheit* (Wien), vol. 4, 1949, 219-223.

2709    Hansen-Löve, F. "Parusie des Seins? Zu Martin Heideggers neuer Schrift *Holzwege.*" *Wort und Wahrheit* (Wien), vol. 5, 1950, 60-68.

2710    Hansen-Löve, F. "Der Einfluss Heideggers auf das Denken der Gegenwart, Literaturbericht." *Wort und Wahrheit* (Wien), vol. 6, 1951, 386-387.

2711    Hara, Tasuku. "Haideggâ no Tenkai o megutte" (On Heidegger's "Turning"). *Tetsugkuzasshi* (Tôkyô), vol. 725-726, October-November 1954.

2712    Hara, Tasuku. "Haideggâ." *Gendai Tetsugaku Kôza* (Kawade-Shobô) (Tôkyô), vol. 3, 1955, 83-102.

2713    Hara, Tasuku. "Haideggâ no Sonzaironshiteki Jikaku" (Heidegger's ''Ontological'' Historical Identity). *Tôkyôdaigaku-Kyôyôgakubu-Jinmonkagakuka-Kiyô* (Tôkyô), March 1956.

2714    Hara, Tasuku. "Haideggâ-Kenkyû-Oboegaki" (Notes on the Heidegger-Studies). *Todai-Kyôyôsakubu-Jinmonkagakuka-Kiyô* (Tôkyô), March 1957.

2715    Hara, Tasuku. "Haideggâ ni okeru Shi to Tetsugaku" (Poetry and Philosophy in Heidegger). *Tôkyôkaigaku-Kyôyôgakubu-Jinmonkagakuka-Kiyô* (Tôkyô), March 1958.

2716    Hara, Tasuku. "Haideggâ no Saikin no Mondaiishiki" (Heidegger's Final Problems). *Risô* (Tôkyô), vol. 305, October 1958.

2717    Hara, Tasuku. *Haidegga* (Heidegger). Tokyo, 1958.

2718    Hara, Tasuku. "Haideggâ 'Shikô no Keiken kara'." Rev. of (Notes on Heidegger: *Aus der Erfahrung des Denkens*). *Tôkyô Daigaku Kyôyôgakubu Jinbunkagakuka Kiyô* (Tôkyô), vol. 18, 20, 1959, 1960, 119-151, 71-104.

2719    Hara, Tasuku. *Jitsuzonshugi no Shisôkatachi* (Existentialist Thinkers). Tôkyô, 1962, 245-282.

2720    Hara, Tasuku. "Haideggâ to Gendai" (Heidegger and the Present). *Tetsugaku to Jensei* (Tôkyô) (Tôkyô Daigaku Shuppankai), Mai 1962, 213-225.

2721    Hara, Tasuku. "Haideggâ no Sekai" (Heidegger's World). *Sôbun* (Tôkyô), vol. 5, 1962, 4-5.

2722    Hara, Tasuku. "Haideggâ to Kirukegôru" (Heidegger and Kierkegaard). *Linmon Kagaku Kiyô* (Tôkyô) (Tôkyô Daigaku Kyoyô Gakubu), vol. 57, 1974, 1-16.

2723    Harder, R. Rev. of *Die Selbstbehauptung der Deutschen Universität,* by Martin Heidegger. Breslau, 1933. *Gnomon* (Berlin), vol. 9, 1933, 440-442.

2724    Harding, C. "Der Seher ins dritte Jahrtausend. Zum Tode von Martin Heidegger." *Deutsche Annale* (Leoni), vol. 6, 1977, 193-204.

2725    Harding, R. "Hühnerfeld contra Heidegger." *Neue deutsche Hefte. Beiträge zur europäischen Gegenwart mit den kritischen Blättern* (Gätersloh), vol. 2, 1959, 254-256.

2726    Harms, J. "Vom Deutsch deutscher Philosophen." *Muttersprache. Zeitschrift des deutschen Sprachvereins* (Berlin), vol. 49, Heft 1, 1934, 1-4.

2727    Harper, Ralph. *Existentialism: A Theorie of Man.* Cambridge, Massachusetts, 1948, XII, 163 p. (specifically 67-93).

2728    Harries, Karsten. "A Note on John Wild's Review of 'Being and Time'." *The Review of Metaphysics* (New Haven, Connecticut), vol. 17, 1963/64, 296-300.

2729    Harries, Karsten. "Heidegger and Hölderlin: The Limits of Language." *The Personalist* (Los Angeles), vol. 44, 1963, 5-23.

2730    Harries, Karsten. "Heidegger's Conception of the Holy." *The Personalist* (Los Angeles), vol. 47, 1966, 169-184.

2731     Harries, Karsten. "Wittgenstein and Heidegger: The Relationship of the Philosopher to Language." *The Journal of Value Inquiry* (Akron), vol. 2, 1968, 281-291.

2732     Harries, Karsten. "Das befreite Nichts." *Durchblicke.* Ed. V. Klostermann. Frankfurt, 1970, 39-62.

2733     Harries, Karsten. Rev. of *On the Way to Language,* by Martin Heidegger. New York, 1971. *The Philosophical Review* (Ithaca, New York), vol. 81, no. 3, 1972, 387-389.

2734     Harries, Karsten. "Heidegger as a Political Thinker." *Review of Metaphysics* (Washington), vol. 29, no. 4, 1975/76, 642-669. Rpt. in *Heidegger and Modern Philosophy.* Ed. M. Murray. Yale Univ. Press, 1978, 304-328.

2735     Harries, Karsten. "Death and Utopia: Towards a Critique of the Ethics of Satisfaction." *Research in Phenomenology* (Pittsburgh), vol. 7, 1977, 138-152.

2736     Harries, Karsten. "Fundamental Ontology and the Search for Man's Place." In *Heidegger and Modern Philosophy. Critical Essays.* Ed. Michael Murray. New Haven, Connecticut: Yale Univ. Press, 1978, 65-79.

2736a    Harries, Karsten. "Language and Silence. Heidegger's Dialogue With Georg Trakl." In *Martin Heidegger and the Question of Literature.* Ed. William V. Spanos. Bloomington, Indiana; London: Indiana Univ. Press, 1979, 155-171.

2737     Hart, James G. Rev. of *Der hermeneutische Zirkel. Untersuchungen zu Schleiermacher, Dilthey und Heidegger,* by John C. Maraldo. Phil. Diss. München 1970. Freiburg/München 1974. (Symposion, 48). *International Philosophical Quarterly* (New York), vol. 16, 1976, 365-367.

2738     Hart, Samuel G. Rev. of *Logik. Die Frage nach der Wahrheit,* by Martin Heidegger. Gesamtausgabe, Abt. 2. Bd 21. Ed. Walter Biemel. Frankfurt: Klostermann, 1976. *Philosophy and Phenomenological Research* (Buffalo, New York), vol. 38, 1977, 142-144.

2739     Hart, S. L. Rev. of *Heidegger, das Gefüge seines Denkens,* by Fürstenau. Frankfurt, 1958. *Philosophy and Phenomenological Research* (Buffalo, New York), vol. 20, 1959/60, 133-134.

2740     Hart, S. L. Rev. of *In Sachen Heidegger,* by Hühnerfeld. München, 1961; and *Nachlese zu Heidegger,* by Schneeberger. Bern, 1962. *Philosophy and Phenomenological Research* (Philadelphia), vol. 24, 1963/64, 601-603.

2741     Hartmann, H. *Denkendes Europa. Ein Gang durch die Philosophie der Gegenwart.* Berlin, 1936, 385-390.

2742     Hartmann, Klaus. "The Logic of Deficient and Eminent Modes in Heidegger." *The Journal of the British Society for Phenomenology* (Manchester), vol. 5, 1974, 118-134.

2743     Hartmann, Nicolai. *Zur Grundlegung der Ontologie.* Berlin/Leipzig, 1935, 43-46.

2744    Hartmann, Otto Julius. *Der Mensch im Abgrund e seiner Freiheit, Prolegomena zu einer Philosophie der christlichen Existenz.* Frankfurt, 1932, 186 p.

2745    Hartmann, Otto Julius. "Begegnungen mit Martin Heidegger. Ein Nachtrag zu seinem 80. Geburtstag." *Die Kommenden. Eine unabhängige Zeitschrift für geistige und soziale Erneuerung* (Freiburg), no. 22, 1969, 21-23.

2746    Hartmann, Otto Julius. "Zum Tode Martin Heideggers. Ging mit ihm die Philosophie zu Ende?" *Die Kommenden. Eine unabhängige Zeitschrift für geistige und soziale Erneuerung* (Freiburg/Breisgau), vol. 30, no. 13, 1976, 13-14.

2747    Hasegawa, Akira. "Haideggâ; aru 'KKontonari' no Raai" (Heidegger; A Case of "Differecnce"). *Gendai-Shisô* (Tôkyô), vol. 2, no. 1, 1974, 151-156.

2748    Hasegawa, Akira. "Sonzai to Jikan ni okeru Kôzô" (The Concept of Strucutre in "Being and Time"). *Gendai-Shisô* (Tôkyô), vol. 2, no. 10, 1974, 188-193.

2749    Hasegawa, Hiroshi. "Haideggâ no Gengoshiso" (Heidegger's Thought of Language). *Gendai-Shisô* (Tôkyô), vol. 1, no. 10, 1973, 157-169.

2750    Hasegawa, Noboru. "Haideggâ Môsô" (Hallucinations on Heidegger). *Jitsuzonshugi* (Tôkyô), vol. 56, July 1971, 56-62.

2751    Hasenfuss, J. *Ersatzreligionen heute. Soziologismus und Existentialismus.* Aschaffenburg, 1965. (Der Christ in der Welt, Reihe 18, Bd 1).

2752    Hassett, Joseph D. "Heidegger, Being and a World in Turmoil." *Thought* (New York), vol. 36, 1961, 537-554.

2753    Hatta, Yoshiho. "Haideggâ no Kagaku Ron" (Heidegger's Conception of the Science). *Philosophia* (Tôkyô), vol. 60, 1972, 91-113.

2754    Haule, John Ryan. *'Imagination and Myth': A Heideggerian Interpretation of C. G. Jung.* Relig. Diss. Temple Univ. 1973. *Dissertation Abstracts International,* vol. 34/07-A, 4391.

2755    Hayashida, Shinji. "Haideggâ to Yasupâsu" (Heidegger and Jaspers). *Jitsuzonshugi* (Tôkyô), April 1966.

2756    Hayen, A. Rev. of *Lettre sur l'humanisme,* by Martin Heidegger. Paris, 1957. *Nouvelle Revue Théologique* (Tournai), vol. 81, 1959, 543-544.

2757    Hayes, D. G. "Nietzsche's Eternal Recurrence: A Prelude to Heidegger." *The Journal of Existentialism* (New York), vol. 6, 1965/66, 189-196.

2758    Hazelton, Roger, ed., and David E. Roberts. *Existentialism and Religious Belief.* New York: Oxford Univ. Press, 1957.

2759    Heaton, J. M., et al. "Symposium on Saying and Showing in Heidegger and Wittgenstein." *The Journal of the British Society for Phenomenology* (Manchester), vol. 3, 1972, 27-45.

2760    Hector, J. "Heidegger ou le prolongement de la question." ('Hommage à Gandhi 1869-1969'). *Synthèses* (Belgien), vol. 24, no. 282, 1969, 64-66.

2760a   Hederman, Mark Patrick. "De l'interdiction à l'écoute." In *Heidegger et la question de Dieu.* Ed. Richard Kearney and Joseph Stephen O'Leary. Paris: B. Grasset, 1980, 285-295.

2761 Heftrich, E. "Nietzsche im Denken Heideggers." *Durchblicke*. Ed. V. Klostermann. Frankfurt, 1970, 331-349.

2762 *Heidegger aujourd'hui*. Dossier. *Magazine Litteraire* (Paris), no. 117, 1976, 6-27.

2763 *Heidegger (1889-1976). Revista Portuguesa de Filosofia* (Braga), vol. 33, no. 4, 1977. Braga: Faculdade de Filosofia, 1977, 257-384.

2763a *Heidegger et la question de Dieu*, with contributions by J. Beaufret, F. Fédier, E. Levinas, J.-L. Marion, et al. Ed. by Richard Kearney and Joseph Stephen O'Leary. Paris: B. Grasset, 1980, 346 p.

2764 Heidegger, Fritz. "Ein Geburtstagsbrief an den Bruder." In *Martin Heidegger zum 80. Geburtstag von seiner Heimatstadt Messkirch*. Frankfurt, 1969, 58-63.

2765 Heidemann, I. *Der Begriff des Spieles und das ästhetische Weltbild in der Philosophie der Gegenwart*. Berlin, 1968, IX, 378 p. (Die Problematik des Spielbegriffs bei Heidegger, 278-372 und passim).

[Rev. by W. Ritzel in *Kant-Studien* (Köln), vol. 59, 1968, 487-494.]

2766 Heim, Karl. *Der evangelische Glaube und das Denken der Gegenwart. 1.* Band: Glaube und Denken. Berlin, 1931.

2767 Heim, Karl. "Ontologie und Theologie." *Zeitschrift für Theologie und Kirche* (Tübingen), N.F. 11, 1930, 325-338, passim. Rpt. in *Heidegger und die Theologie. Beginn und Fortgang der Diskussion*. Ed. G. Noller. München, 1967, 59-71.

2768 Heimpel, Hermann. "Der gute Zuhörer." In *Erinnerung an Martin Heidegger*, by Günther Neske (ed.). Pfullingen: Verlag Günther Neske, 1977, 115-117.

2769 Heinemann, Fritz. *Neue Wege der Philosohie*. Geist-Leben-Existenz. Eine Einführung in di Philosophie der Gegenwart. Leipzig, 1929, (besonders, 370-391).

2770 Heinemann, Fritz. "Was ist lebendig und was ist tot in der Existenzphilosophie?" *Zeitschrift für philosophische Forschung* (Meisenheim/Glan), vol. 5, 1950/51, 3-24, (specifically pages 7-21).

[English trans. "What is Alive and What is Dead in Existentialism?" *Revue internationale de Philosophie* (Bruxelles), vol. 3, 1949, 306-319, (specifically page 311ff).]

2771 Heinemann, Fritz. *Existenzphilosophie Lebendig oder tot?* Stuttgart, 1954. 2nd ed. 1956. 3rd ed. Stuttgart, 1963, 215 p. 4th ed. 1971.

2772 Heinemann, F. H. *Existentialism and the Modern Predicament*. London, 1953, 227 p., (specifically pages 84-103). 2nd ed. 1954.

2773 Heinemann, W. *Die Relevanz der Philosophie Martin Heideggers für das Rechtsdenken*. Freiburg, 1970, 425 p.

[Phil. Diss. 17.6.1970.]

2774 Heiniel, Erich. Rev. of *Das Göttliche und der Gott bei Heidegger,* by Helmut Danner. Meisenheim, 1971. *Wiener Jahrbuch für Philosophie* (Wien/Stuttgart), vol. 6, 1973, 242-250.

2775 Heinrichs, Hans Jürgen. "Was nützt uns heute die Philosophie. Zum Tode von Martin Heidegger." *Frankfurter Rundschau* (Frankfurt), vol. 115, 29 May 1976, 7.

2776 Heintel, Peter. *Gedanken zu einigen Aporien der Philosophie Heideggers.* Phil. Diss. Wien 1962 VII 185 p.

2777 Heise, Wolfgang. *Philosophie als Krisenbewusstsein und illusionäre Krisenüberwindung. Eine Untersuchung zu den Gesetzmässigkeiten der Entwicklungstendenzen in der modernen bürgerlichen Philosophie in Deutschland.* Berlin, 1963, 498 p. Habilitationsschrift v.17.Juli 1963. Also published under the title *Aufbruch in die Illusion. Zur Kritik der bürgerlichen Philosophie in Deutschland.* Berlin, 1964, 498 p., (specifically pages 458-491).

2778 Heisenberg, Werner. "Grundlegende Voraussetzungen in der Physik der Elementarteilchen." *Martin Heidegger zum 70. Geburtstag. Festschrift.* Pfullingen, 1959, 276-290.

2779 Heiss, Rudolph. "Psychologismus, Psychologie und Hermeneutik." In *Martin Heideggers Einfluss auf die Wissenschaften.* Bern, 1949, 22-36.

2780 Heissennbüttel, H. "Einsätze." In *Martin Heidegger zum 70. Geburtstag, Festschrift.* Pfullingen, 1959, 302-304.

2781 Held, Klaus. "Der Logos-Gedanke des Heraklit." *Durchblicke.* Ed. V. Klostermann. Frankfurt, 1970, 162-206.

2781a Held, Klaus. "Heideggers These vom Ende der Philosophie." Zeitschrift für Philosophische Forschung. Meisenheim: Glan, vol. 34, no. 2, 1980, 535-560.

2782 Hellebrand, W. "Hirt des Alls und Platzhalter des Nichts. Der Mensch in der Philosophie Martin Heideggers. Zum 60. Geburtstag des Philosophen." *Die Zeit* (Hamburg), Jg 4, no. 38, 1949, 5.

2783 Hempel, Hans-Peter. "Politische Philosophie im Denken Heideggers." *Zeitschrift für Philosophische Forschung* (Meisenheim/Glan), vol. 22, 1968, 432-440.

2784 Hempel, Hans-Peter. Rev. of *Wegmarken,* by Martin Heidegger. *Philosophischer Literaturanzeiger* (Meisenheim/Glan), vol. 21, 1968, 138-143.

2785 Hempel, Hans-Peter. Rev. of *Philosophie und Politik bei Heidegger,* by Otto Pöggler. Freiburg, 1972. *Philosophischer Literaturanzeiger* (Meisenheim/Mainz), vol. 26, 1973, 194-196.

2786 Hengstenberg, Haus Edward. "Die Kairos-Lehre bei Stefan George und M. Heidegger." *Die Kirche in der Welt* (Münster), vol. 6, 1953, 27-32.

2787 Hengstenberg, Hans Edward. "Was ist Existenzialontologie?" *Zeitschrift für Philosophische Forschung* (Meisenheim/Glan), vol. 26, no. 2, 1972, 171-195.

2788    Henrich, D. "Über die Einheit der Subjektivität." Rev. of *Kant und das Problem der Metaphysik,* by Martin Heidegger. 2nd ed. Frankfurt, 1951. *Philosophische Rundschau* (Tübingen), vol. 3, 1955, 28-69.

2789    Henry, Michael. "Le concept de l'être comme production." *Revue Philosophique De Louvain,* vol. 73, 1975, 79-107.

2790    Henry, Michael. "Qu'est-ce que cela que nous appelons la vie?" *Philosophiques,* vol. 5, 1978, 133-150.

2791    Hentrich, John James. *The Private Self in Heidegger and the Search for Genuine Community.* Phil. Diss. Yale Univ. 1975. *Dissertation Abstracts International,* vol. 36/05-A, 2897.

2792    Hepburn, R. W. Rev. of *Being and Time,* by Martin Heidegger. *The Philosophical Quarterly* (St. Andrews), vol. 14, 1964, 276-278.

2793    Herbert, G. S. "The Concept of Future in Bergson and Heidegger: A Comparative Study." *Indian Philosophical Quarterly* (Poona-7, India), vol. 4, 1977, 597-604.

2794    Herbertz, R. "Die Philosophie Martin Heideggers als 'schlechtes' Barock." *Der kleine Bund Literarische Beilage des 'Bund'* (Bern), vol. 23, no. 45, 8.11.1942, 354-356.

2795    Herman, Paul Edward. *The Contributions of Ramana Mahrachi and Heidegger to an East-West Integral Psychology.* Phil. Diss. California Institute of Asian Studies 1974 246 p. *Dissertation Abstracts International,* vol. 35/12-B, 6072.

2796    Hermann, R.-D. "Heidegger and Logic (Sophia)." *Rassegna critica di filosofia e storia della filosofia* (Padova), vol. 29, 1961, 353-357.

2797    Herrmann, R.-D. "M. Heidegger und die Idee der Kunst." *Filosofia* (Torino), vol. 13, Supplement to Fasc IV, 1961, 648-657.

2798    Herra, Rafael A. "Un Heidegger redivivo." *Revista de Filosofia de la Universidad de Costa Rica* (San José), vol. 14, no. 39, 1976, 199-200.

2798a   Herre, Rafael A. "Un Heidegger redivivo." *Revista de Filosofia de la Universidad de Costa Rica* (San José), vol. 14, 1976, 199-200.

2799    Herrigel, H. "Denken dieser Zeit. Fakultäten und Nationen treffen sich in Davos." *Frankfurter Zeitung* (Abendblatt), 22.4.1929.

2800    Herrigel, H. "Der Philosoph Heidegger nach Berlin berufen." *Frankfurter Zeitung,* 29.3.1930.

2801    Herrigel, H. "Die politische Universität." *Deutsche Zeitschrift. Unabhängige Monatshefte für die politische und geistige Gestaltung der Gegenwart* (München), vol. 46, 1932/33, 802-806.

2802    Herrigel, H. "Der Ansatz der Ontologie." *Zeitschrift für Philosophische Forschung,* vol. 8, 1954, 267-292.

2803    Herrmann, Friedrich-Wilhelm von. "Die Selbstinterpretation Martin Heideggers." *Monographien z. philosophischen Forschung* (Meisenheim/Glan), vol. 32, 1964, 278 p.

[Rev. by O. Lechner in *Salzburger Jahrbuch für Philosophie* (Salzburg/München), vol. 9, 1965, 321-322. Phil. Diss. Freiburg 1961, xi und 328 Bl.]

2804 Herrmann, Friedrich-Wilhelm von. "Sein und Cogitationes. Zu Heideggers Descartes-Kritik." *Durchblicke.* Ed. V. Klostermann. Frankfurt, 1970, 235-254.

2805 Herrmann, Friedrich-Wilhelm von. "Lebenswelt und In-der-Welt-sein. Zum Ansatz des Weltproblems bei Husserl und Heidegger." *Weltaspekte der Philosophie. Rudolph Berlinger zum 26.Okt.1972.* Eds. Werner Beierwaltes und Wiebke Schrader. Amsterdam, 1972, 123-141.

2806 Herrmann, Friedrich-Wilhelm von. "Zeitlichkeit des Daseins und Zeit des Seins. Grundsätzliches zur Interpretation von Heideggers Zeit-Analysen." *Philosophische Perspektiven* (München), vol. 4, 1972, 198-210.

2807 Herrmann, Friedrich-Wilhelm von. "Befindlichkeit und Verstehen in ihrer Stellung zur Seinsfrage. Eine Einleitung in das Denken von 'Sein und Zeit'." *Philosophische Perspektiven* (Frankfurt), vol. 5, 1973, 162-170.

2808 Herrmann, Friedrich-Wilhelm von. *Subjekt und Dasein. Interpretationen zu 'Sein und Zeit'.* Frankfurt: Vittorio Klostermann, 1974, 90 p.

2809 Herrmann, Friedrich-Wilhelm von. "Observations on the Definitive Collected Edition of the Works of Martin Heidegger." *Universitas. A German Review of Arts and Sciences* (Stuttgart), vol. 17, 1975, 29-37.

2810 Herrmann, Friedrich-Wilhelm von. "Fichte und Heidegger. Phänomenologische Anmerkungen zu ihren Grundstellungen." In *Der Idealismus und sein Gegenwart.* Eds. Ute Guzzoni, Bernhard Rang and Ludwig Siep. Festschrift für Werner Marx zum 65. Geburtstag. Hamburg: Felix Meiner Verlag, 1976, 231-256.

2811 Herrmann, Friedrich-Wilhelm von. *Heideggers Philosophie der Kunst.* Frankfurt: Vittorio Klostermann, 1979, 260 p.

2811a Herrmann, Friedrich-Wilhelm von. *Heideggers Philosophie der Kunst: Eine systematische Interpretation der Holzwege-Abhandlung 'Der Ursprung des Kunstwerks'.* Frankfurt: Klostermann, 1980, xxv-379 p.

2811b Herrmann, Friedrich-Wilhelm von. "Remarks on the Difference Between Fink's and Heidegger's Approaches to Heracleitus." In *Heraclitean Fragments.* Ed. John Sallis and Kenneth Maly. Univ. of Alabama Press, 1980, 19-21.

2812 Hersch, Jeanne. "Discontinuité des perspectives humains." *Le choix, le monde, l'existence.* (Cahiers du Collège philosophique). Grenoble, 1947, 199 p.

2813 Hertz, Peter Donald. "Martin Heidegger. Language and the Foundations of Interpretation." Authorized facsimile of the dissertation of the Stanford Univ. Phil. Diss. 1967. Ann Arbor, Michigan; London: University Microfilms International, 1976, 315 p.

2814 Herz, K. Rev. of *Sein und Zeit,* by Martin Heidegger. 2nd ed. Halle, 1929. *Monatsschrift für höhere Schulen,* vol. 29, 1930, 520.

2815    Hessen, Johannes. *Die Philosophischen Strömungen der Gegenwart.*
        Rottenburg, 1940, 133-137.

2816    Hessen, Johannes. *Existenzphilosophie.* (Grundlinien einer Philosohie des
        menschlichen Daseins). Essen, 1947, 32-38.

2817    Heyen, Erk Volkmar. "Zum Verhältnis von philosophischer und
        wissenschaftlicher Anthropologie." *Archiv Für Rechts-Und
        Sozialphilosophie,* vol. 64, 1978, 509-533.

2818    Higami, Hidehiro. "Shutaigâ to Haideggâ" (Staiger and Heidegger). *Doitsu
        Bungaku* (Tôkyô), vol. 15, 1955, 6-14.

2819    Higashi, Sen'ichirô. "Shûkyôteki-Shi to Shûkyôteki-Jikan; Haideggâ,
        Kirukegôru, Dôgen" (Religious Death and the Religious Period; Heidegger,
        Kierkegaard and Dôgen). *Risô* (Tôkyô), vol. 443, 1970, 17-28.

2820    Higashi, Sen'ichirô. "Shûkyôteki-Shi to Shûkyôteki-Jikan; Haideggâ,
        Kirukegôru, Dôgen (2)" (Religious Death and the Religious Period;
        Heidegger, Kierkegaard and Dôgen (2)). *Kansai Daigaku Bungaku Ronshû*
        (Ôsaka), XX - 3, Januar 1971, 48-68.

2821    Higashi, Sen'ichirô. "Haideggâ ni okeru Keijijôgaku no Mondai to Nippon
        no tetsugakuteki Dentô" (The Problem of Metaphysics by Heidegger and
        the Japanese Philosophical Tradition). *Tôzai Gakujutsu Kenkyûsho* (Kiyô),
        vol. 8, 1975.

2822    Higashi, Sen'ichirô. "Haideggâ ni okeru Toki no Mondai" (The Problem of
        Time by Heidegger). *Risô* (Tôkyô), vol. 500, 1975, 43-60.

2823    Higgins, David J. *Possibility in Peirce and Heidegger: A Propaedeutic for
        Synthesis.* Phil. Diss. Columbia 1968 196 p. *Dissertation Abstracts
        International,* vol. 29/03-A, 931.

2824    Hildebrandt, Dieter. "Heidegger und die Stehlampe." *Der Tagesspiege*
        (Berlin), Ausgabe A, 32, no. 9337, 13 June 1976, 4. (Jg. 3, 1976, Nr. 3).

2825    Hildebrandt, K. Rev. of *Hölderlins Hymne 'Wie wenn am Feiertge',* by Martin
        Heidegger. Halle, 1942. *Zeitschrift für philosophische Forschung*
        (Retlingen), vol. 1, 1946/47, 416-417.

2826    Hiller, K. "Dokument über Martin Heidegger." In *Köpfe und Tröpfe. Profile
        aus einem Vierteljahrhundert,* by K. Hiller. Hamburg, 1950, 70-73.

2827    Hindel, R. "Martin Heideggers 'System'." *Wissenschaft und Weltbild* (Wien),
        vol. 3, 1950, 79-83.

2828    Hines, Thomas J. *The Outline of Beings and Its Expressings: Husserl,
        Heidegger, and the Later Poetry of Wallace Stevens.* Phil. Diss. Univ. of
        Oregon Eugene 1969 408 p. *Dissertation Abstracts International,* vol.
        31/06-A, 2975.

2829    Hines, Thomas J. *The Later Poetry of Wallace Stevens. Phenomenological
        Parallels With Husserl and Heidegger.* Lewisburg, Pennsylvania: Bucknell
        Univ. Press, 1976, 298 p.; London: Associated Univ. Presses.

2830    Hinman, Lawrence H. "Heidegger, Edwards, and Being-Toward-Death." *The
        Southern Journal of Philosophy* (Memphis), vol. 16, no. 3, 1976, 193-212.

2831 Hinners, Richard C. "Martin Heidegger's Conception of the Question: 'What is the Meaning of to-be?' in 'Sein und Zeit'." Phil. Diss. Univ. of Toronto Canada 1955. *Dissertation Abstracts International,* vol. W, 1955, 3.

2832 Hinners, Richard C, and Q. Lauer. "Being and God in Heidegger's Philosophy." *Proceedings of the American Catholic Philosophical Association* (Washington), vol. 31, 1957, 157-165.

2833 Hinners, Richard C. "The Freedom and Finiteness of Existence in Heidegger." *The New Scholasticis:n* (Washington), vol. 33, 1959, 32-48.

2834 Hinzmann-Fürstenau, P. *Heidegger. Das Gefüge seines Denkens.* Phil. Diss. Berlin. Vom 10.12.1956, 202 Bl.

2835 Hirano, Tomomi. "Haideggâ no jiyû-Gainen no Kyôikugakuteki ichi Kôsatsu" (A Pedagogical Contemplation on Heidegger's Notion of Freedom). *Jôchi Daigaku Kyôikugaku, Shinrigaku Ronshû* (Tôkyô), vol. 4, 1970, 54-63.

2836 Hiromatsu, Wataru. "Sonzai no Tetsugaku to busshokateki Sakushi" (Heidegger's Philosophy and Reification). *Gendaishisô* (Tôkyô), vol. 1, no. 1, 1973, 119-134.

2837 Hiromatsu, Wataru. "Haideggâ to busshokateki Sakushi" (Heidegger and Reification) in "Kototeki Sekaikan e no Zenshô" (The Outpost Toward the View of the World as the Matter). *Keisô Shobô* (Tôkyô), 1975, 95-122.

2838 Hirose, Bungô. "Hosshin no Shisô to Haideggâ" (The Buddhist Notion 'Hosshin' and Heidegger). *Tetsugaku-Kaizô,* vol. 4, 1932, 3-5.

2839 Hirsch, Elisabeth F. "Heidegger und die Dichtung." *Journal of the History of Philosophy* (Berkeley), vol. 6, 1968, 271-283.

2840 Hirsch, Elisabeth F. "Martin Heidegger and the East." *Philosophy East and West* (Honolulu), vol. 20, 1970, 247-263.

2841 Hirsch, Elisabeth F. Rev. of *Poetry, Language, Thought,* by Martin Heidegger. Trans. and intr. Albert Hofstadter. New York: Harper & Row, 1975. *Journal of the History of Philosophy* (Claremont, California), vol. 16, 1978, 489-492.

2842 Hirsch, Elisabeth F. Rev. of *Early Greek Thinking,* by Martin Heidegger. Trans. David Farrell Krell and Frank A. Capuzzi. New York: Harper & Row, 1975. *Journal of the History of Philosophy,* vol. 16, 1978, 489-492.

2843 Hirsch, Elisabeth F. "Remembrances of Martin Heidegger in Marburg." *Philosophy Today,* vol. 23, no. 2-4, 1979, 160-169.

2844 Hirsch, Wilfried. "Die Zukunftsproblematik im Werk Martin Heidegger nach Erscheinen von 'Sein und Zeit'." *Freiburger Zeitschrift für Philosophie und Theologie* (Freiburg, Schweiz), vol. 21, 1974, 139-184.

2845 Hirsch, W. "Platon und das Problem der Wahrheit." In *Durchblicke.* Ed. V. Klostermann. Frankfurt, 1970, 207-234.

2846 Hirsch, Walter. "An Ethical Issue? Remarks Concerning the Analysis of Culpability in 'Being and Time'." (In Serbocroat). Trans. Danilo Basta. In *Rani Hajdeger - Recepcija i kritika Bivstvai vremena,* by Dragan Stojanovic and Danilo Basta (eds.). (Biblioteka Zodijak). Beograd, 1979, 265-76. Rpt. of *Delo* (Beograd), vol. 23, no. 12, 1977, 142-150.

2847 Hirschberger, J. *Geschichte der Philosophie*. 2. Teil: Neuzeit und Gegenwart, Freiburg 1952, 579-589. 2nd ed. 1955. 6th ed. 1963, (Martin Heidegger: Specifically pages 640-650).

2848 Hisamatsu, Hoseki Shinichi. "Begegnung in Wien." In *Erinnerung an Martin Heidegger*, by Gäther Neske (ed.). Pfullingen: Verlag Günther Neske, 1977, 216-217.

2849 Hislop, I. Rev. of *De l'essence de la vérité*, by Martin Heidegger. *Dominican Studies* (Oxford), vol. 2, 1949, 401-402.

2850 Hobe, Konrad. "Zwischen Rickert und Heidegger. Versuch über eine Perspektive des Denkens von Emil Lask." *Philosophisches Jahrbuch* (München), vol. 78, 1971, 360-376.

2851 Hobe, Konrad, and Orlando Puugliese. "La logica de E. Lask como transición entre la teoría del juicio en H. Rickert y el concepto de verdad en M. Heidegger." *Cuadernos de Filosofía*, vol. 11, no. 15-16, 1971, 105-136.

2852 Hoberg, A. *Das Dasein des Menschen. Die Grundfrage der Heideggerschen Philosophie*. Zeulenroda, 1937.

2853 Hochkeppel, Willy. "Martin Heideggers langer Marsch durch die 'verkehrte Welt'." *Merkur* (Stuttgart), vol. 30, no. 341, 1976, 911-921.

2854 Hochkeppel, Willy. "'Der erregendste Denker - durch nichts?' Heidegger - Erinnerungen zwischen Bewunderung und Ablehnung." *Merkur* (Stuttgart), vol. 32, no. 6, 1978, 615-619.

2855 Hodgson, P. C. "Heidegger, Revelation, and the Word of God." *The Journal of Religion* (Chicago), vol. 49, no. 3, 1969, 228-52.

2856 Högel, M. "Heidegger Martin, Holzwege der Philosophie. Vortrag Heideggers im Prinz-Carl-Palais zu München." *Neues Abendland* (Augsburg), vol. 5, 1950, 299-300.

2857 Hoegen, M. "Das Sein und der Mensch bei Martin Heidegger." *Salzburger Jahrbuch für Philosophie* (Salzburg), vol. 4, 1960, 29-112.

2858 Hoeller, Keith. "Heidegger Bibliography of English Translations." *The Journal of the British Society for Phenomenology* (Manchester), vol. 6, 1975, 206-208.

2859 Hoeller, Keith, ed. "Heidegger and Psychology." (Heidegger Issue). *Review of Existential Psychology & Psychiatry* (Northwestern Univ., Evanston, Illinois), vol. 16, no. 1, 2, and 3, 1978/79.

2860 Hoeller, Keith. "Phenomenology, Psychology, and Science." *Review of Existential Psychology & Psychiatry* (Northwestern Univ., Evanston, Illinois), vol. 16, no. 1, 2, and 3, 1978/79.

2861 Höllhuber, I. "Acotaciones al problema de un aquende y un allende el conocimiento racional." *Sapientia* (La Plata), vol. 30, no. 118, 1975, 283-292.

2862    Hoeven, J. van der. *Heidegger en de geschiedenis der wijsbegeerte.* (Openbare le, uitgesproken bij de aanvssrding van det ambt van lector in de Faculteit der Letteren aan de Vrije Univ. op 15 november 1963). Amsterdam, 1963, 19 p.

2863    Hoeven, J. van der. "Waarheid en methode (Inzake de slotfase van het fenomenologisch denken bij Heidegger en Sartre)." *Algemeen Nederlands Tijdschrift voor Wijsbebeerte en Psychologie* (Assen), vol. 56, 1963/64, 1-18.

2864    Hofer, H. "Existenz und Nihilismus bei Nietzsche und drei verwandten Denkern (Jacobi, Sartre, Heidegger)." In *Jahresverzeichnis schweiz. Geschichtsschr.* 1956-1060. Bern, 1960, 52-63.

2865    Hofmann, Paul. Rev. of *Sein und Zeit,* by Martin Heidegger. Halle, 1927. *Deutsche Literaturzeitung für Kritik der internationalen Wissenschaft* (Berlin), vol. 50, N.F. 6, 1929, 155-172.

2866    Hofmann, Paul. Rev. of *Was ist Metaphysik?,* by Martin Heidegger. Bonn, 1929. *Deutsche Literaturzeitung* (Berlin), vol. 51, 1930, 1063-1068.

2867    Hofmann, Paul. "Metaphysik oder verstehende Sinn-Wissenschaft? Gedanken zur Neugründung der Philosophie im Hinblick auf Heideggers 'Sein und Zeit'." Unaltered rpt. of the Berlin edition. *Kantstudien* (Berlin) (Ergänzungsheft 64), 1929, 65 p. Rpt. Vaduz/Liechtenstein: Topos-Verlag, 1978.

2868    Hofstadter, Albert. "Truth of Being." *Journal of Philosophy* (New York), April 1965.

2869    Hofstadter, Albert. "Introduction." In *Poetry, Language, Thought,* by Martin Heidegger. New York: Harper & Row, 1975.

2869a   Hofstadter, Albert. "Enownment." In *Martin Heidegger and the Question of Literature.* Ed. William V. Spanos. Bloomington, Indiana; London: Indiana Univ. Press, 1979, 17-37.

2870    Hogan, John. "Gadamer and the Hermeneutical Experience." *Philosophy Today* (Celina, Ohio), vol. 20, 1976, 3-12.

2871    Hohmann, F. *Bonaventura und das existenzielle Sein des Menschen.* Würzburg, 1935.

2872    Hohoff, C. "Martin Heidegger in München." *Die Zeit* (Hamburg), Jg. 5, no. 24, 1950, 3.

2873    Hohoff, C. "Denken, Sein und Sprache bei Heidegger." Rev. of *Was heisst Denken,* by Martin Heidegger. Tübingen, 1954. *Süddeutsche Zeitung* (München), no. 174, 31.7./1.8.1954.

2874    Hôjiro, Ki. "Jitsuzon Tetsugaku no Genkai" (The Limit of Existential Philosophy). *Tetsugaku-Zasshi* (Tôkyô), vol. 734, 735, 1957, 40-49.

2875    Holata, Ladislav. "Kritik der heideggerschen Konzeption des Menschen." *Filozofia* (Bratislava), vol. 27, 1972, 347-358.

2876    Holata, Ladislav. "Die Offenheit der marxistisch-leninistischen Philosophie und einige Probleme des philosophischen Revisionismus (Zur Kritik über

Heideggers Philosophie)." *Zbornik Ustavu Marxismu-Leninizmu Univerzity Komenského. Marxistická Filozofia* (Bratislava), vol. 4, 1973, 79-95. [German summary of a Czechoslovakian article.]

2877    Holenstein, Elmar. Rev. of "Martin Heidegger as a Phenomenologist," by Bernhard Boelen. In *Phenomenological Perspectives. Historical and Systematic Essays in Honor of Herbert Spiegelberg,* by Philip J. Bossert. (Phenomenologica, 62). The Hague, 1975, 93-114. *The Journal of the British Society for Phenomenology* (Manchester), vol. 8, 1977, 62-64.

2878    Holk, L. J. van. "Wat betekent Heideggers uitspraak: 'Das Fragen ist die Frömmigkeit des Denkens'?" *Nederlands theologisch Tijdschrift* (Wageningen), vol. 11, 1956/57, 119-129.

2879    Hollenbach, J. M. *'Sein und Gewissen'. Über den Möglichkeitsgrund der Gewissensregungen. Eine Auseinandersetzung zwischen Martin Heidegger und Thomas von Aquin.* Phil. Diss. Frankfurt, 1952, IV, 245 p.

2880    Hollenbach, J. M. *'Sein und Gewissen'. Über den Ursprung der Gewissensregung. Eine Begegnung zwischen Martin Heidegger und thomistischer Philosophie.* Baden-Baden, 1954, 373 p.

2881    Hollenbach, J. M. "Heidegger oder Thomas von Aquin?" *Stimmen der Zeit* (Freiburg), vol. 157, 1955/56, 70-72.

2882    Holz, Hans-Heinz. Rev. of *Was ist Metaphysik,* by Martin Heidegger. 5th ed. Frankfurt, 1949. *Philosophischer Literaturanzeiger* (Schlehdorf, Obb.), vol. 1, 1949/50, 13-16.

2883    Holz, Hans-Heinz. Rev. of *Einführung in die Metaphysik* and *Was heisst Denken,* by Martin Heidegger. Tübingen, 1953, 1954, respectively. *Deutsche Zeitschrift für Philosophie* (Berlin), vol. 2, 1954, 740-746.

2884    Holz, Hans-Heinz. "Martin Heideggers Rückweg zu Kant." Rev. of *Die Frage nach dem Ding,* by Martin Heidegger. *Allgemeine Zeitung Mainz,* 24./25.August 1963.

2885    Holz, Hans-Heinz. "Der vornehme Ton in der Philosophie (Neues von und über Heidegger)." *Die literarische Tat,* 28.Jg., Nr.81, 23.3.1963, 26.

2886    Holz, Hans-Heinz. "'Im Angesicht des abwesenden Gottes untergehen'. Die Identität von Heideggers Denken mit den geistigen Wurzeln des Faschismus. Zum Tode des Philosophen." *Deutsche Volkszeitung* (Düsseldorf), no. 25, 17 June 1976, 14. (Jg. 3, 1976, Nr. 2).

2887    Holzamer, Karl. "Zum Geleit." In *Martin Heidegger im Gespräch.* Ed. R. Wisser. Freiburg/München, 1970, 7-8.

2888    Holzhey, Helmut. "Martin Heidegger gestorben." *Neue Züricher Zeitung* (Zürich), no. 123, 29 May 1976, 33. (Jg. 3, 1976, Nr. 2).

2889    Holzhey, Helmut. "Ein literarisches Mausoleum? Die Gesamtausgabe als Ende der 'Wege' Martin Heidegger." *Neue Züricher Zeitung* (Zürich), no. 208, 8 September 1979, 65-66.

2890    Homann, K., and W. Weymann-Weyhe. "Martin Heidegger." *Frankfurter Hefte* (Frankfurt), vol. 5, 1950, 527-531.

2891    Hommes, J. "Das Anliegen der Existentialphilosophie." *Philosophisches Jahrbuch* (Fulda), vol. 60, 1950, 175-199 u.ö.

2892    Hommes, J. *Zwiespältiges Dasein. Die existenziale Ontologie von Hegel bis Heidegger.* Freiburg, 1953.
        [Rev. by W. Rüfner in *Scholastik* (Freiburg), vol. 29, 1954, 405-407.]

2893    Hommes, J. *Krise der Freiheit. Hegel - Marx - Heidegger.* Regensburg, 1958, 332 p.

2894    Hommes, U. *Die Existenzerhellung und das Recht.* Frankfurt, 1962, 224 p.

2895    Honda, Tetsuo. "Haideggâ ni okeru Herundârin no Shi no Kaishaku o megutte" (On the Interpretations of Hölderlin's Poetry by Heidegger). *Daigakuin Kiyô* (Tôkyô Daigaku) (Tôkyô), no. 13, 1977, 43-53.

2896    Honma, Hideyo. "Haideggâ no Gengokan" (Heidegger's Conception of the Language). *Jôchi Daigaku Doitsu Bungaku Ronsyû* (Tôkyô), no. 9, 1972, 79-94.

2897    Hood, Webster F. *A Heideggerian Aproach to the Problem of Technology.* Phil. Diss. Pennsylvania, 1968, 258 p. *Dissertation Abstracts International,* vol. 29/10-A, 3637.

2898    Hopkins, Jasper. "Are Moods Cognitive? A Critique of Schmitt on Heidegger." *The Journal of Value Inquiry* (Geneseo/Den Haag), vol. 6, 1972, 64-71.

2899    Hoppe, H. "Wandlungen in der Kant-Auffassung Heidegger." In *Durchblicke.* Ed. V. Klostermann. Frankfurt, 1970, 284-317.

2900    Hoppe, H. Rev. of *Heidegger, Kant and Time,* by Charles Sherover. *Kant-Studien* (Bonn), vol. 1, 1973, 131-37.

2901    Horgby, I. "The Double Awareness in Heidegger and Wittgenstein." *Inquiry,* vol. 2, 1959, 235-264.

2902    Hori, Mitsuo. "Haideggâ to Gendai Shingaku; Shoki Haideggâ no Burutoman Shingaku e no Eikyô" (Heidegger and Theology Today; Influence of the Early Heidegger on Bultmann's Theology). *Gendai-Shisô* (Tôkyô), vol. 2, no. 10, 1974, 168-174.

2903    Horiuchi, Misao. "Kindai Hihan no Keihu; Haideggno Hinirizumu Shiso" (The Genealogy of Critique to the Modern World; Heidegger's Thought on Nihilism). *Takachiho Ronsô* (Tôkyô), no. 1, 1971, 1972, 186-204; 1971, no. 2, 1972, 191-213.

2904    Horiuchi, Misao. "Gijutsu ni tsuite" (On Heidegger's Philosophy of Technique). *Tekachiho Ronsô* (Tôkhô), vol. 2, 1973, 69-85; *Takachiho Ronsô,* vol. 3, 1973, 67-79.

2905    Horiuchi, Misao. "Ningensonzai no Yûgensei ni tsuite" (On the Finiteness of Dasein). *Takachiho Ronshû,* 1974, (1), 1975, 477-502.

2906    Horiuchi, Misao. "Haideggâ no 'Gelassenheit' ni tsuite" (On Heidegger's Thought of Gelassenheit; A Comparative Study). *Takachiho Ronsô* (Tôkyô), no. 2, 1978; 1979, 39-52.

2907  Horn, Uwe. *Dialogische Bildung und pädgogische Dimension: Versuch einer Studie und Frage nach dem Verhältnis von Sein und Nichtsein im Hinblick auf die ontologische Dimension des Pädagogischen unter besonderer Berücksichtigung von Aristoteles, Hegel und Heidegger.* Phil. Diss. Freiburg, 1975.

2908  Hornedo, Florentino H. "Truth, Man, and Martin Heidegger." *Saint Louis University Research Journal* (Baguio City), vol. 2, 1971, 1-18.

2909  Hornstein, H. *Probleme der Metaphysik und das Denken Martin Heideggers.* Phil. Diss. Wien, 1950, 73 p.

2910  Hornstein, H. "Das Haus des Seins. Zu Martin Heideggers Sprachphilosophie." *Neues Abendland* (München), vol. 10, 1955, 433-438.

2911  Horosz, William. *The Promise and Peril of Human Purpose.* St. Louis, 1970, 332 p.

2912  Horvath, Nicholas. *Essentials of Philosophy: Hellenes to Heidegger.* Woodbury, New York: Barron's Educ. Ser., 1974, 353.

2913  Hosoi, Yusuke. "The Tragic Atmosphere." (In Japanese). *Bigaku,* vol. 27, December 1976, 38.

2914  Hosokawa, Ryôichi. "Sonzai to Jikan no Kisokôzô" (The Basic Structure of 'Being and Time')." *Tetsugaku (Nihon Tetsugakukai)* (Tôkyô), vol. 24, 1974, 160-172.

2915  Hosoya, Sadao. "Sonzai to Jikan no Honyaku ni tsuite" (The Problem of the Translation of 'Sein und Zeit'). *Bunka,* XXVII-4, Tôhoku Daigaku Bungakubu. Sendai, 1963, 112-125.

2916  Hosoya, Sadao. "Haideggâ no Gyôseki" (Heidegger's Works). *Risô* (Tôkyô), vol. 444, 1970, 2-10.

2917  Hosoya, Sadao. "Haideggâ no Shisaku to Nihirizumu no Tenkai" (Heidegger's Thought and the Reversal of Nihilism). In *Tetsugaku no Sakubun* (The Composition of Philosophy). Miraisha, Tôkyô, 1975, 171-239.

2918  Hosoya, Sadao. "Haideggâ o shinobu" (The Reminiscence of Prof. Heidegger). *Jitsuzonshugi* (Tôkyô), vol. 77, 1976, 134-137.

2919  Hosoya, Sadao. "Heideggâ no Shi ni tsuite omoukoto" (Mouring for Heidegger's Death). *Rinsha-Seikei Kenkyû,* vol. 5, 1977.

2920  Hosoya, Tadao. "Gendai Sonzai-ron no Mondai" (Problems of the Newer Ontology). *Risô* (Tôkyô), vol. 305, 1958, 40-51.

2921  Hosoya, Tsuneo. "Genshôgaku ni okeru Nichijôsei no Mondai tokuni Fusseru to Haideggeru o Chûshin toshite" (The Problem of Everydayness in Phenomenology, Particularly in Husserl and Heidegger). *Risô* (Tôkyô), vol. 41, Juli 1933.

2922  Hosoya, Tsuneo. "Genshogaku no Genmitsusei to Kongensei. Fussaru to Haidegga" (Severity and Originality in Phenomenology. Husserl and Heidegger). *Risô* (Tôkyô), March 1935.

2923    Hosoya, Yoshio. "Haideggâ Sonzai to Jikan" (On Heidegger's 'Sein und Zeit'). *Risô* (Tôkyô), vol. 422, 1968, 47-54.

2924    Hossfeld, P. "Das Sein in Heideggers späteren Schriften und Gott." *Theologie und Glaube. Zeitschrift für den Katholischen Klerus* (Paderborn), vol. 54, 1964, 332-344.

2925    Hottois, Gilbert. "Aspects du rapprochement par K. O. Apel de la philosophie de M. Heidegger et de la philosophie de L. Wittgenstein." *Revue Internationale de Philosophie* (Bruxelles), vol. 30, no. 117-118, 1976, 450-485.

2926    Hottois, Gilbert. "L'insistance du langage dans la phénoménologie post-husserlienne." *Revue Philosophique de Louvain,* Louvain, vol. 77, 1979, 51-70.

2927    Howey, Richard L. *Heidegger and Jaspers on Nietzsche.* The Hague, 1973, XI, 218 p. *Dissertation Abstracts International,* vol. 30/05-A, 2076.

2928    Hoy, David Couzens. "History, Historicity and Historiography in 'Being and Time'." In *Heidegger and Modern Philosophy. Critical Essays.* Ed. Michael Murray. New Haven, Connecticut: Yale Univ. Press, 1978, 329-353.

2928a   Hoy, David Couzens. "The Owl and the Poet. Heidegger's Critique of Hegel." In *Martin Heidegger and the Question of Literature.* Ed. William V. Spanos. Bloomington, Indiana; London: Indiana Univ. Press, 1979, 53-70.

2929    Hoyos Vásquez, J. "Un neuvo punto de partida del filosofar. Anotaciones sobre la manera como filosofia Heidegger." *Ecclesiastica Xaveriana* (Bogotá), vol. 15, 1965, 29-36.

2930    Hoyos Vásquez, J. "Presentación." *Ideas y Valores* (Bogotá), no. 48-49, 1977, 67-77.

2931    Hrachovec, Herbert. "Welt und Sein beim frühen Heidegger." *Salzburger Jahrbuch für Philosophie* (Salzburg/München), vol. 14, 1970, 127-151.

2932    Hrachovec, Herbert. Rev. of *Das Göttliche und der Gott bei Heidegger,* by Helmut Danner. Meisenheim, 1971. *Wort und Wahrheit. Zeitschrift für Religion und Kultur* (Freiburg), vol. 28, 1973, 270-271.

2933    Hrachovec, Herbert. Rev. of *Geschichtliche Transzendenz bei Heidegger. Die Hoffnungsstruktur des Daseins und die Gott-lose Gottesfrage,* by M. Brechtken. Meisenheim, 1972. *Wort und Wahrheit* (Freiburg), vol. 28, 1973, 70-71.

2934    Hsiao, Paul Shih-Yi. "Wir trafen uns am Holzmarktplatz." In *Erinnerung an Martin Heidegger.* Ed. Günther Neske. Pfullingen: Verlag Günther Neske, 1977, 119-129.

2935    Huch, K. J. *Philosophiegeschichtliche Voraussetzungen der Heideggerschen Ontologie.* Frankfurt, 1967, 72 p. Kritische Studien zur Philosophie. Eds. K. H. Haag, Herb Marcuse, O. Negt, Alfred Schmidt.

2936    Hübener, W. "Untersuchungen zur Denkart Martin Heideggers." Phil. Diss. F.U. Berlin 1960. Berlin, 1960, 127 p.

2937    Hübscher, A. "Martin Heidegger." In *Philosophen der Gegenwart,* by Arthur Hübscher. München, 1949, 73-76.

2938    Hübscher, A. Rev. of *Einführung in die Metaphysik,* by Martin Heidegger. Tübingen, 1953. *Der Allgäuer* (Kempten), 15.10.1954.

2939    Hübscher, A. "Martin Heidegger." *Westermanns Monatshefte* (Braunschweig), Jg. 100, 1959, 61.

2940    Hübscher, A. *Von Hegel zu Heidegger. Gestalten und Probleme.* Stuttgart, 1961, 243-265; 278.

2941    Huegli, Anton. "Zur Geschichte der Todesbedeutung: Besuch einer Typologie." *Studia Philosophica,* vol. 32, 1972, 1028.

2942    Hühnerfeld, P. "Ursprung, Existenz und Romantik. Zu neuen Büchern von Heidegger, Jaspers und Rehm." *Die Zeit* (Hamburg), Jg. 4, no. 27, 1949, 5.

2943    Hühnerfeld, P. "Glauben mit und ohne Christus. Neue Schriften von Gabriel Marcel und Martin Heidegger." *Die Zeit* (Hamburg), Jg. 5, no. 12, 1950, 11.

2944    Hühnerfeld, P. *Die Kategorie der Befindlichkeit in der Philosophie Martin Heideggers.* Phil. Diss. Hamburg 1951 125 p.

2945    Hühnerfeld, P. *In Sachen Heidegger. Versuch über ein deutsches Genie.* Hamburg, 1959, 118 p. New edition, München, List-Buecher, 1961, 132.

2946    Hühnerfeld, P. "Die deutsche Philosohie und das Vaterland. In Sachen Heidegger." *Die Zeit* (Hamburg), vol. 14, no. 11, 1959, 7.

2947    Hueni, Heinrich. *Rekonstruktion des Fragens: Ein systematischer Versuch zum Ansatz von M. Heideggers Frage nach dem Sinn von Sein.* Phil. Diss. Bonn 1973.

2948    Hülsmann, H. "Epoché und Existenz." *Salzburger Jahrbuch für Philosophie* (München), vol. 9, 1965, 7-40, (specifically pages 23-40).

2949    Hülsmann, H. "Hermeneutik und Reflexion." *Salzburger Jahrbuch für Philosophie* (Salzburg/München), vol. 14, 1970, 153-163.

2950    Hufnagel, A. Rev. of *Die Frage dem Ding. Zu Kants Lehre von den transzendentalen Grundsätzen,* by Martin Heidegger. Tübingen, 1962. *Freiburger Zeitschrift für Philosophie und Theologie* (Freiburg, Schweiz), vol. 11, 1964, 447-448.

2951    Hûisông, Kil. "Haidegkae issôsôûi muwa chonjaee taehan koch'al" (Non-Being and Being in Heidegger). M. A. Thesis, Sôul Univ., 1967.

2952    Humann, Ursula. Rev. of *Lukac und Heidegger: Nachgelassene Fragmente,* by Lucien Goldmann. Darmstadt, Neuwied, 1975. *Philosophischer Literaturanzeiger* (Meisenheim), vol. 30, 1977, 141-144.

2953    Hunnex, M. D. *Existentialism and Christian Belief.* Chicago, 1969, 126 p.

2954    Husserl, E. *Vorlesungen zur Phänomenologie des inneren Zeitbewusstseins.* Ed. Martin Heidegger. (Handbuch für Philosophie und phänomenologische Forschung). Halle, vol. 9, 1928, 132.

2955    Husserl, E. "Zu einer reinen Phänomenologie und phänomenologischen Philosophie. Nachwort zu meinen Ideen." *Jahrbuch für Philosophie und phänomenologische Forschung* (Halle), vol. 11, 1930, 549-570.

2956    Husserl, E. *Briefe an Roman Ingarden. Mit Erläuterungen und Erinnerungen an E. H.* Ed. von R. J. Den Haag, 1968, IX, 186 p.

2957    *Husserl, Scheler, Heidegger in der Sicht Neuer Quellen.* (Contributions by Ernst Wolfgang ORTH a.o.). Freiburg, 1978, 223 p.

2958    Hvidtfelt Nielsen, K. "De la production du sens: Heidegger et la sémiotique." *Semiotica* (The Hague), vol. 17, no. 3, 1976, 191-210.

2959    Hyland, Drew A. "Art and the Happening of Truth. Reflexions on the End of Philosophy." *The Journal of Aesthetics and Art Criticism* (Cleveland), vol. 30, 1971, 177-187.

2960    Hyônggon, Ko. "Sônûi chonjaeronjôk kumyông" (Ontological Analysis of Zen). Phil. Diss. Sôul Univ. 1970.

2961    Hyônggon, Ko. "Chonjae hyônjônûrosôûi chayôn" (Nature as Being-Present-At-Hand). *Ch'ôrhak Yôngu* (Sôul), vol. 4, 1969, 79-94.

2962    Hyônggon, Ko. *Sônûi segye* (The World of Zen). Sôul, 1977.

2963    Hyôngwôn, Min. "Haidegka ch'ôrhake issôsô yesulûi ch'egyejôk ûimie Kwanhan yôngu" (The Significance of Poetry in Heidegger). M. A. Thesis, Sôul Univ., 1977.

2964    Hyppolite, Jean. "Du bergsonisme à l'existentialisme." *Actas del primer Congreso nacional de Filosofia* (Mendoza), vol. 1, 1949, 442-445, passim.

2965    Hyppolite, Jean. "Un texte de Heidegger. Note en manière d'introduction." *Mercure de France* (Paris), vol. 317, 1953, 385-391.

2966    Hyppolite, Jean. *Ontologie et phénoménologie chez Martin Heidegger.* Paris, 1954, 75-143; 307-314.

2967    Hyppolite, Jean. *Figures de la pensée philosophique.* (Ecrits 1931-1968, vol. 1 and II). Paris, 1971, 512 p.

2968    Ibanez, M. "Heidegger y una nueva interpretación de lo poetico." *Cuadernos de Filosofia* (Buenos Aires), VIII, 13, 14, 15, 1953/54, 41-43.

2969    Ibuki, Yû. "Haideggâ no Shii ni okeru Shintekinamono to Shingaku" (The Godly in Heidegger's Thinking and Theology). *Jitsuzonshugi* (Tôkyô), vol. 69, 1974, 102-111.

2970    Ichikura, Hirosuke. "Haideggâ to Sarutoru" (Heidegger and Sartre). *Shisô* (Tôkyô), vol. 366, 1954.

2971    Ichikura, Hirosuke. "Haideggâ no Sonzai ni tsuite" (On Being in Heidegger). *Jitsuzon* (Tôkyô), Mai 1955.

2972    Ichikura, Hirosuke. "Haideggâ; Sonzai to Jikan" (Heidegger's 'Being and Time'). In *Tetsugaku no Mêcho* (Library of the Philosophical Classics). Ed. H. Huruta. Gakuyôshobô, Tôkyô, 1972, 251-274.

2973    Ignatov, Assen. "Das Problem der Beziehung zwischen Existenz und Mensch in der Philosophie Heideggers." *Filosofska Misal* (Sofia), vol. 9, 1971, 65-74.

2974    Ignatow, Assen. Rev. of *Martin Heidegger und Ludwig Klages: Daseinsanalytik und Metaphysik,* by Hans Kunz. *Philosophischer Literaturanzeiger* (Meisenheim), vol. 30, 1974, 195-197.

2975    Ignatow, Assen. "Das Existenzialismus-Bild der Filosofskaja Enciklopedija." *Studies in Soviet Thought* (Dordrecht, Netherlands), vol. 15, 1975, 225-251.

2976    Ignatow, Assen. Rev. of *Von der Existenzialontologie zur Seinsgeschichte: Eine Untersuchung über die Philosophie Martin Heideggers,* by Winfried Franzen. Phil. Diss. Giessen 1972. *Philosophischer Literaturanzeiger* (Meisenheim/Mainz), vol. 30, 1977, 92-94.

2977    Ignatow, Assen. "Das schwierige Gespräch oder: Heideggers Entfremdungsauffassung und der Marxismus." *Studies in Soviet Thought* (Friebourg/Dordrecht), vol. 19, 1979, 1-36.

2978    Ignatow, Assen. *Heidegger und die philosophische Anthropologie. Eine Untersuchung über die anthropologische Dimension des Heideggerschen Denkens.* Königstein, 1979, ii-325 p.

2979    Ihde, Don. *Hermeneutic phenomenology.* Evanston, Illinois, 1971.

2980    Ihde, Don. "Language and Two Phenomenologies." In *Martin Heidegger: In Europe and America.* Eds. Edward Goodwin Ballard and Charles E. Scott. The Hague, 1973, 147-156.

2981    Ihde, Don. "Phenomenology and the Later Heidegger." *Philosophy Today* (Celina, Ohio), vol. 18, 1974, 19-31.

2982    Ihde, Don. *Technics and Praxis.* (Boston Studies in the Philosophy of Science, vol. xxiv. Synthese Library 130). Dordrecht: D. Reidel Pub. Co., 1978, xxviii-151.

2983    IJsseling, Samuel. *Denken en danken, geven en zijn.* Antwerpen, 1964.

2984    IJsseling, Samuel. *De filosofie en het technische Denken. Een studie over Martin Heidegger.* (Uitzicht van onze wereld. Wijsgerige essays door B.J. De Clercq, S. IJsseling, J. Mertens, H. Parret, H. Roelants, Cl. Van Reeth, N. Versluis). Brugg/Utrecht, 1964, 31-48.

2985    IJsseling, Samuel. "Van en over Heidegger. Kroniek van de Heidegger-literatuur 1955-1965." *Tijdschrift voor Filosofie* (Leuven), vol. 27, 1965, 587-609.

2986    IJsseling, Samuel. "Het zijn en de zijnden. Een studie over de ontologische differenz bij Martin Heidegger." *Tijdschrift voor Filosofie* (Leuven), vol. 28, 1966, 3-51.

        [Summary: Being and Beings, 51-52]

2987    IJsseling, Samuel. "Martin Heidegger over Abraham a Santa Clara. Een voordracht van Heidegger, ingeleid en vertaald door Samuel IJsseling." *Streven* (Amsterdam), vol. 20, 1966/67, 743-753.

2988    IJsseling, Samuel. "Heidegger en Marx." *Tijdschrift voor Filosofie* (Leuven), vol. 28, 1966, 264-274.

        [Résumé: Heidegger et Marx, 274-275]

2989    IJsseling, Samuel. "Heidegger als interpretator. Bouwstenen voor een filosofische hermeneutiek." *Tijdschrift voor Filosofie* (Leuven), vol. 29, 1967, 65-97.

2990    IJsseling, Samuel. "De waarheid bij Husserl en Heidegger." *Tijdschrift voor Filosofie* (Leuven), vol. 31, 1969, 771-785.

2991    IJsseling, Samuel. "Filosofie en psychoanalyse. Enige opmerkingen over het denken van Martin Heidegger en J. Lacan." *Tijdschrift voor Filosofie* (Leuven), vol. 31, 1969, 261-289.

2992    IJsseling, Samuel. "Van en over Heidegger, II. Kroniek van de Heidegger-literatuur 1965-1970." *Tijdschrift voor Filosofie* (Leuven), vol. 32, 1970, 721-739.

2993    IJsseling, Samuel. "Novalis: Een fragment over de taal." *Tijdschrift voor Filosofie* (Leuven), vol. 33, 1971, 636-658.

2994    IJsseling, Samuel. "Martin Heidegger." In *Filosofen van de 20e, Eeuw.* Eds. C. P. Bertels, E. Petersman. Assen/Amsterdam/Brüssel, 1972, 101-111.

2995    IJsseling, Samuel. "Heidegger en de fenomenologie." *Tijdschrift voor Filosofie* (Leuven), vol. 38, no. 4, 1976, 511-534.

        [Summary: Heidegger und die Phänomeologie, 534.]

2996    IJsseling, Samuel. Rev. of *Die Grundprobleme der Phänomenologie.* Ed. Friedrich-Wilhelm von Herrmann. Gesamtausgabe, Abt. 2: Vorlesungen 1923-1944. Bd XXIV. Frankfurt: Vittorio Klostermann, 1975, x-473 p. *Tijdschrift voor Filosofie* (Leuven), vol. 38, 1976, 264-276.

2997    IJsseling, Samuel. Rev. of *Logik. Die Frage nach der Wahrheit,* by Martin Heidegger. Ed. Walter Biemel. Gesamtausgabe, Abt. 2, Bd 21. Frankfurt: Klostermann, 1976. *Tijdschrift voor Filosofie* (Leuven), vol. 38, 1976, 276.

2998    IJsseling, Samuel. "Heidegger: Tijd en zijn." *Wijsgerig Perspectief op Maatschappij en Wetenschap* (Amsterdam), vol. 17, 1976/77, 340-349.

2998a   Ijssling, Samuel. "Macht, taal en begeerte." *Tijdschrift voor Filosofie* (Leuven/Belgium, vol. 41, 1979, 375-404.

2999    Ijun, Kim. "Haidegkae issôsôûi hyôngisanghakûi kûgbok" (On the Over-Coming of Metaphysics in Heidegger). M. A. Thesis, Sôul Univ., 1965.

3000    Ikegami, Jun'ichi. "Haideggâ 'Sonzai to Jikan' ni mirareru Gensonzai Gainen no Nijusei ni tsuite" (On Ambiguity of the Concept 'There-Being' in Heidegger's 'Being and Time'). *Kyôyôgakka Kiyô* (Tôkyô Daigaku) (Tôkyô), vol. 8, 1975, 91-128.

3001    Ikegami, Jun'ichi. "Haideggâ Sonzairon no Kôzô Kaimei e no Kokoromi, 2; Haideggâ no 'Chôetsu' Gainen ni tsuite" (Essay on the Structure of Heidegger's Ontology). *Gaikokugoka Kenyû Kiyô* (Tôkyô Daigaku Kyôyôgakubu) (Tôkyô), 1976, 91-128.

3002    Ikegami, Kenzô. "Heidegga no Kanto-Kaishaku" (Heidegger's Kant-Interpretation). *Risô* (Tôkyô), March 1935.

3003　Ikeo, Kenichi. "Kindai-Hihan no Keifu, Haidegga" (The Genealogy of the Criticism of Modern Times. Heidegger). *Jitsuzn* (Tôkyô), April 1945.

3004　Ikeo, Ken'ichi. "Haideggâ" (Heidegger). *Jitsuzon* (Tôkyô), vol. 5, 1954, 18-26, 46.

3005　Ikeo, Ken'ichi. "Haideggâ no Anakushimandorousu-Ron" (Heidegger's Essay on Anaximander). *Risô* (Tôkyô), vol. 367, August 1955.

3006　Ikeo, Ken'ichi. "Haideggâ no Anakushimandorosu-Ron; Shiteki Kaishaku no ichi-Rei" (Heidegger's Explication on Anaximandros - An Example of Poetic Interpretation). *Risô* (Tôkyô), vol. 267, 1955, 66-80.

3007　Ikimatsu, Keizo. "Shisaku to Shikô' (Poem-Writing and Thinking). *Bungei* (Tôkyô), vol. 15, no. 8, 1976, 216-219.

3008　Ikimatsu, Keizo. "Shisaku to Shikô; Haideggâ no Sokuseki" (Poem-Writing and Thinking; Footsteps of M. Heidegger). In *Gendai-Shisô no Genryû.* Kawade-Shobô-Shinsha, Tôkyô, 1977, 171-180.

3009　Iljo, Chang. "Haidegkaûi ihaeûi kaenyôm" (The Notion of Understanding in Heidegger). M. A. Thesis, Yônse Univ, 1967.

3009a　*Il pensiero di Martin Heidegger.* Atti del Convegno Internazionale di Monteripido. (*L'Uomo, un segno* (Milano), vol. 3, no. 1-2). Milano: Ed. Dov'e la tigre/Via Melzo 34, 1979, 131 p.

3010　Ilting, K.-H. "Sein als Bewegtheit. Zu Heidegger, Vom Wesen und Begriff der Physis; Aristoteles Physik B 1." *Philosophische Rundschau* (Tübingen), vol. 10, 1962, 31-49.

3011　Imamichi, T. A. "Die gegenwärtige Lage der japanischen Philosophie." *Philosophische Perspektiven* (Frankfurt), vol. 1, 1969, 318-330.

3012　Inaba, Minoru. "Haideggâ no Shii no Shûkyôsei" (Religious Aspects in Heidegger's Thinking). *Risô* (Tôkyô), vol. 444, 1970, 40-54.

3013　Inatomi, Eijirô. "Haideggâ no Hyûmanizumu-Ron" (Heidegger's Discussion on Humanism). *Risô* (Tôkyô), vol. 223, December 1951.

3014　Irfan, Niaz. "Nothingness in the Existentialistic Philosophy." *Pakistan Philosophical Congress,* vol. 5, 1958, 193-200.

3015　Iriarte, J. "La poesia no quiere ser filosofia. Un parangon entre el 'Hölderlin' de Heidegger y el 'Platon' de Laercio." *Revista de la Facultad de Filosofia y Humanidades* (Córdoba), vol. 4, 1952, 44-60.

3016　Iriarte, J. Rev. of *Martin Heidegger zum 70. Geburtstag, Festschrift.* Pfullingen, 1959. *Razón y Fe* (Madrid), vol. 163, 1961, 423-426.

3017　Iriarte, J. "La angustia existencial nos abandona." *Razon y Fe* (Madrid), vol. 161, 1960, 257-270.

3018　Iriarte, J. "Heidegger en la miscelánea jubilar (26-IX-59)." *Razon y Fe* (Madrid), vol. 163, 1961, 423-426.

3019　Isaga, A. "Es posible hablar de una ética en Martin Heidegger?" *Franciscanum* (Bogota), vol. 6, 1964, 48-56.

3020 Ishaghpour, Youssef. "Le monologue de Heidegger à propos du marxisme." *Magazine Littéraire* (Paris), no. 117, 1976, 15-16.

3021 Ishida, Akira. "Zwischen der Kunst und dem Kunstwerk - Über die ontologische Differenz der Kunst." (In Japanese). *Bigaku,* vol. 26, December 1975, 27-39.

3022 Ishida, Tadashi. "Gêjutsu no Imi; Haideggâ no Baai" (The Meaning of the Art; The Case of Heidegger). In *Gêjutsuteki Sekai no Ronri* (The Logics of the World of the Art). Ed. Kyôto Daigaku Bigaku-Bizitsushi Kenkyûkai. Sôbunsha, Tôkyô, 1972, 49-57.

3023 Ishihara, Shizuo. "'Actus essendi' to shiteno Sonzai Gainen - Makkusu Myura no Haideggâ Rikai" (The Notion of Time as Actus Essendi - Max Müller's Exegesis of Heidegger). *Yamanashi Daigaku Gakugei Gakubu Kenkyû-Hôkoku* (Kôfu), vol. 3, 1953, 33-37.

3024 Ishihara, Shizuo. "Sonzairon-teki-Ninshiki ni kansuru Oboegaki" (Notes on Existential Cognition). *Yamanashi Daigaku Gakugei Gakubu Kenkyû-Hôkoku* (Kôfu), vol. 5, 1954, 31-39.

3025 Ishihara, Shizuo. "Sonzai-rn to Rinrigaku; Haideggâ no Hyûmanizumu Shokan kar (Ontology and Ethics; From Heidegger's Letter on Humanism). *Yamanashi Daigaku Gakugeibu Kenkyû Hôkoku* (Kôfu), vol. 10, 1959, 47-52.

3026 Ishihara, Tatsuzô. "Haideggâ no Geijutsu Tetsugaku" (Heidegger's Philosophy of the Fine Arts). *Kôza Bigaku Shinshichô* (Geijutsu Shuppansha) (Tôkyô), vol. 1, 1965, 37-108.

3027 Ishizu, Shôji. "Shûkyô no Konkyo ni kansuru Kenkyû; Kirukegôru to Haideggâ no Ginmi ni sotte" (A Study in the Origin of Religion; According to Kierkegaard and Heidegger). *Tôhoku Daigaku Bungaku-bu Kenkyû Nempô* (Sendai), vol. 8, 1957, 171-221.

3028 Ishizu, Shôji. *Shûhyô no Konkyo ni kansuru Kenkyû, Kierukegôru to Haideggâ no Shoron no Ginmi ni sotte* (Searching for the Origin of Religion, by Means of the Respective Discussin in Kierkegaard and Heidegger). In *Tôhokudaigaku-Bungkubu-Kenkyûnenpô.* Sendai, 1958.

3029 Ishizuka, Tameo. *Kyomu to Mu, Jitsuzon no Kiwamini Hairu* (The Nugatory Non-Being and Non-Being. On the Entering into the Most Remote Existence). In *Shinshûdaigaku-kenkyûronshu.* Nagano, 1960.

3030 Itô, Kanichi. "Sonzai to Kotoba, Haideggâ no Gengoron" (Being and Language. On Heidegger's Discussion of Language). *Jinmonronkyû* (Hakodate), vol. 9, 1953.

3031 Itô, Yukio. "Kirisuto-kyô Rikai o hiraku Mushin-ron; Haideggâ to Sarutoru" ("Irreligion" as a Possibility of the Understanding of Christianity; Heidegger and Sartre). *Risô* (Tôkyô), vol. 408, 1967, 33-42.

3032 Ittel, G. W. "Der Einfluss der Philosophie M. Heideggers auf die Theologie R. Bultmanns." *Kerygma und Dogma* (Göttingen), vol. 2, 1956, 90-108.

3033 Itturralde Columbres, C. A. "La ontologia modifacada." *Sapientia* (La Plata), 100-200, 1971, 389-410.

3034 Iturrioz, J. "Abstracciones en Heidegger." *Pensamiento* (Madrid), vol. 1, 1945, 353-357.

3035 Iturrioz, J. "Heidegger, octogenario." *Ráon y Fe* (Madrid), vol. 180, 1969, 431-436.

3036 Itzkowitz, Kenneth. "Difference and Identity." *Research and Phenomenology,* vol. 8, 1978, 127-143.

3037 Ivánka, E. von. "Was bleibt von der Existenzphilosohie?" Rev. of *Existenzphilosophie von Kierkegaard bis Sartre,* by L. Gabriel. Wien, 1951. *Scholastik* (Freiburg), vol. 27, 1952, 400-408, passim.

3038 Iwakiri, Masakazu. "Haideggâ ni okeru Genshoteki-Shii ni tsuite" ("Initial Thinking" in Heidegger). *Tetsugaku Ronbunshû* (Kyûshâ Daigaku Tetsugakukai) (Fukuoka), vol. 4, 1968, 39-55.

3039 Iwanami, Tetsuo. "Haideggâ no Tenkai ni tsuite" (On Heidegger's Reversal). *Jitsuzonshugi* (Tôkyô), vol. 77, 1976, 100-103.

3040 Iwasaki, Tsutomu. "Yasupâsu to Haideggâ" (Jaspers and Heidegger). *Risô* (Tôkyô), vol. 203, 1950, 66-70.

3041 Iwata, Yasuo. "Sonzai e no Sekkin - Haideggâ no Konkyo o megutt (The Aproach to Being - Concerniing Heidegger's Ground). In *Kôza "Tetsugagu"* 1. Tokyodaigaku-Shuppankai, 1973, 27-66.

3042 Iwayama, Saburô. "Haideggâ ni okeru Nihirizumu" (Nihilism in Heidegger). *Bunka* (Sendai), Juni 1949.

3043 Iwayama, Saburô. "'Martin Heidegger; Holzwege' Kenkyû (Heideggers 'Holzwege')." *Lôbe Daigaku Bungakukai* (Kôbe), vol. 1, 1951, 110-113.

3044 J.B.B. Rev. of *German Existentialism,* by Martin Heidegger. *Review of Metaphysics* (New Haven, Connecticut), vol. 19, 1965/66, 162.

3045 Jacob, A. Rev. of *L'être et le temps,* by Martin Heidegger. Paris, 1964. *Les Etudes Philosophiques* (Paris), N.S. 19, 1964, 610-611.

3046 Jacobelli-Isoldi, A. M. *Il tempo in Kant e suoi sviluppi in Husserl e Heidegger. Anno accademico 1962-63.* (Univ. degli studi di Roma). Facoltà di magistero Roma, 1963, 168 p.

3047 Jadacki, J. J. "Próba odczarowani Heideggera" (Attempt of Taking the 'Entzauberung' Away From Heidegger). *Odra,* vol. 3, 1977.

3048 Jäger, Alfred. *Gott: nochmals Martin Heidegger.* Tübingen: Mohr, 1978, x-514 p.

3049 Jaeger, Hans. *Heidegger's Existentialphilosophy and Modern German Literature.* (Publications of the Modern Language Association of America, 67). Menasha, Wisconsin, 1952, 655-683. Rpt. in *Essays on German Literautre 1935-1962,* by H. Jaeger. Bloomington, Indiana, 1968, 103-136.

3050 Jaeger, Hans. "Heidegger and the Work of Arts." *Journal of Aesthetics and Art Criticism* (Baltimore), vol. 17, 1958/59, 58-71. Rpt. in *Essays on German Literature 1935-1962,* by H. Jaeger. Bloomington, Indiana, 1968, 137-158.

3051 Jaeger, Hans. *Heidegger und die Sprache.* Bern/München, 1971, 138 p.

3052 Jaeger, Petra. *Heideggers Ansatz zur Verwindung der Metaphysik in der Epoche von 'Sein und Zeit'.* (Europäische Hochschulschriften; Reihe 20: Philosophie, 20). Frankfurt: Peter Lang; Bern: Herbert Lang, 1976, 319 p.

3053 Jäggli, A. Rev. of *Einführung in die Metaphysik,* by Martin Heidegger. Tübingen, 1953. *Das Bücherblatt* (Zürich), 24.9.1954.

3054 Jähnig, Dieter. "Die Kunst und der Raum." In *Erinnerung an Martin Heidegger,* by Günther Neske (ed.). Pfullingen: Verlag Günther Neske, 1977, 131-148.

3055 Jafella, S. A. Rev. of *Que es eso de filosofia?,* by Martin Heidegger. Buenos Aires, 1960. *Revista de Filosofia* (La Plata), no. 10, 1961, 99-101.

3056 Jancke, R. "Die Kant-Interpretation Heideggers." *Archiv für systematische Philosophie,* N.F. 34, 1931, 267-286.

3057 Jancsary, Peter. *Die Bedeutung der Stimmung im Werk Martin Heideggers. Versuch einer topologischen Pathologie.* Phil. Diss. Innsbruck 1976.

3058 Janicaud, Dominique. "Dépasser la métaphysique?" *Annales de la Faculté des Lettres et Sciences Humaines de Nice* (Nice), no. 20, 1973, 67-76.

3059 Janicaud, Dominique. "L'apprentissage de la contiguité." *Critique* (Paris), vol. 31, no. 349-350, 1976, 664-676.

3060 Janicaud, Dominique. "Heidegger and Method." *Man and World* (The Hague), vol. 9, no. 2, 1976, 140-152.

3061 Janicaud, Dominique. Rev. of *Questions. Vol. IV: Temps et être. La fin de la philosophie et la tâche de la pensée. Le tournant. La phénoménologie et la pensée de l'être. Les séminaires de Thor. Le séminaire de Zähringen,* by Martin Heidegger. Trans. Jean Beaufret, François Fédier, Jean Lauxerois and Claude Roels. (Classiques de la philosophie). Paris: Gallimard, 1976, 339 p. *Critique* (Paris), vol. 31, 1976, 664-676.

3062 Janicaud, Dominique. "Savoir philosophique et pensée méditante. Penser à partir de Hegel et de Heidegger aujourd'hui." *Revue de l'Enseignement Philosophique* (Paris), vol. 27, no. 3, 1977, 1-14.

3063 Janicaud, Dominique. "Le penseur en son atelier." *Etudes Germaniques* (Paris), vol. 32, no. 3, 1977, 317-325.

3064 Janicaud, Dominique. "Presence and Appropriation." *Research and Phenomenlogy,* vol. 8, 67-75.

3065 Janke, Wolfgang. "Die Zeitlichkeit der Repräsentation. Zur Seinsfrage bei Leibniz." *Durchblicke.* Ed. V. Klostermann. Frankfurt, 1970, 255-283.

3066 Janke, Wolfgang. "The Unvailing of the Being-There Through the Mirror of Art. A Contribution to the Fundamental-Ontological Solution of the Poetic Antinomies." (In Sebocroat). *Delo* (Beograd), vol. 23, no. 12, 1977, 127-141.

3067    Janke, Wolfgang. "The Unvailing of the Being-There Through the Mirror of
        Art. A Contribution to the Fundamental-Ontological Solution of the Poetic
        Antinomies." (In Serbocroat). Trans. Danilo Basta. In *Rani Hajdeger -
        Recepcija i kritika Bivstva i vremena.* Eds. Dragan Stojanovic and Danilo
        Basta. (Biblioteka Zodijak). Beograd, 1979, 247-265. Rpt. in *Delo*
        (Beograd), vol. 23, no. 12, 1977, 127-141.

3068    Jansen, B. *Aufstiege zur Metaphysik heute und ehedem.* Freiburg, 1933,
        441-484.

3069    Janssen, O. *Das erlebende Ich und sein Dasein.* Berlin/Leipzig, 1932.

        [Specifically pages 199-218: Die Verirrungen des Seinsproblems in der
        'Hermeneutik' des 'Daseins'.]

3070    Janssen, O. "Von dem 'Felde des Daseienden' und seiner Übersteigerung. Eine
        ontologische Untersuchung." *Zeitschrift für Philosophische Forschung*
        (Meisenheim/Galn), vol. 18, 1964, 627-655.

3071    Jaroszewski, T. M. "Antynomie egzystenojalnej wolnosci: Heidegger i
        pochwala "zycia autentycznego" - J.P. Sartre i absolutyzacja ludzkiej
        subiektywnosci" (Antinomies of Existential Freedom: 'Heidegger and the
        Praise' of True Life - J. P. Sartre and the Absolutisierung of Human
        Subjectivity). *Argumenty,* vol. 29, 1965.

3072    Jaroszewski, T. M. "Koncepcja zycia autentycznego Martina Heideggera"
        (Heidegger's Concept of True Life). In *Etyka.* 1969.

3073    Jaroszewski, T. M. "Koncepcija 'podlinnoj zizni' Martina Chajdeggera" (The
        Concept of "The Essence of Life" in Heidegger). *Filosofskie nauki,* vol. 5,
        1970, 117-126.

3074    Jaroszewski, T. M. "Im gepriesenen Bezirk des 'Cogito'. Tendenzen und
        Antinomien des bürgerlichen Humanismus." *Filozofia* (Bratislava), vol. 1,
        1972, 51-65.

3075    Jaspers, Karl. *Philosophische Autobiographie.* New enlarged edition. München,
        1977.

        [Heidegger: 92-111.]

3076    Jaspers, Karl. "Acerca de Martin Heidegger." *Folia Humanistica* (Barcelona),
        vol. 15, no. 174, 1977, 401-416.

3077    Jaspers, Karl. *Notizen zu Martin Heidegger.* Ed. Hans Saner.
        München/Zürich: R. Piper & Co. Verlag, 1978, 342 p.

3078    Jaspers, Karl. "On Heidegger." *Graduate Faculty Philosophy Journal,* vol. 7,
        1978, 107-128.

3079    Jaspers, Karl. "Heidegger and the Practical Implications of Philosophy."
        *Graduate Faculty Philosophy Journal. New School for Social Research,* vol.
        7, 1978.

3080    Jaworski, W. "Zaklety spokoj Heideggera" (M. Heidegger's 'verzauberte
        Stille'). *Odra,* vol. 10, 1977.

3081    Jeannière, A. "L'itinéraire de Martin Heidegger." *Etudes* (Paris), vol. 280, 1954, 64-74.

3082    Jelke. Rev. of *Sein und Zeit,* by Martin Heidegger. Halle, 1927. *Theologisches Literaturblatt* (Leipzig), vol. 51, 1930, 314.

3083    Jens, Walter. "Marginalien zur modernen Literatur." *Martin Heidegger zum 70. Geburtstag, Festschrift.* Pfulligen, 1959, 225-236.

3084    Jens, Walter. "Nachruf der Akademie der Künste Berlin." In *Erinnerung an Martin Heidegger,* by Günther Neske (ed.). Pfullingen: Verlag Günther Neske, 1977, 149-153.

3085    Jetmarová, M. "Existenciálni filosofie." Ed. E. Tondl. *Soucasná západni filosofie* (Praha), 1958, 86-122.

3086    Jiménez, J. F. "La verdad come problema ontológico." *Revista nacional de Cultura* (Caracas), vol. 24, 1962, 151-152, 158-172.

3087    Jiménez Moreno, L. Rev. of *Nietzsche,* by Martin Heidegger. *Aporia* (Madrid), vol. 1, 1964/65, 99-101.

3088    Jobin, Jean-Francois. "Heidegger et la technique." *Studia Philosophica* (Basel), vol. 35, 1975, 81-127. Also separately Basel: Verlag für Recht und Gesellschaft, 1975, 19 p.

3089    Jörgensen, P. H. "Martin Heidegger, en ny filosofisk religionsstifter." *Dansk teologisk Tidsskrift* (Kopenhagen), vol. 21, 1958, 65-94, 159-177.

3090    Jörgensen, P. H. *Die Bedeutung des Subjekt-Objektverhältnisses für die Theologie. Der theo-onto-logische Konflikt mit der Existenzphilosophie.* (Aus dem Dänischen übersetzt von Susanne Diderichsen). Hamburg-Bergstedt, 1967, 461 p.

3091    Jolivet, R. *Les doctrines existentialistes de Kierkegaard à J.-P. Sartre.* Abbaye S. Wandrille, 1948, 75-143.

3092    Jolivet, R. *Le problème de la mort chez M. Heidegger et J.-P. Sartre.* Abbaye S. Wandrille, 1950, 111 p.

3093    Jolivet, R. "Le problème métaphysique dans 1 philosophie de Heidegger." *Actes du XIe congrès international de philosophie, Bruxelles 20 - 26 Août 1953* (Amsterdam/Louvain), vol. 3, 1953, 44-46.

3094    Jonas, Hans. "Gnosticism and Modern Nihilism." *Social Research,* vol. 19, 1952, 430-552. Rpt. in *Gnosis, Existentialismus und Nihilismus. Zwischen Nichts und Ewigkeit,* by H. Jonas. Göttingen, 1963, 77 p.
        [Rev. by W. J. Richardson in *Thought,* vol. 40, 1965, 13-40; and Ch. E. Scott in *The Harvard Theological Review,* vol. 59, 1966, 175-185.]

3095    Jonas, Hans. "Heidegger and Theology." *Review of Metaphysics* (New Haven, Connecticut), vol. 18, 1964/65, 207-233. *See* "Heidegger und die Theologie," by H. Jonas. *Evangelische Theologie,* vol. 24, 1964, 621-642. Rpt. in *Heidegger und die Theologie. Beginn und Fortgang der Diskussion.* Ed. G. Noller. München, 1967, 316-340.

3096    Jonas, Hans. *The Phenomenon of Life.* New York, 1966, 303 p.

[Specifically pages 211 ff: Gnosticism, Existentialism an Nihilism; 235 ff: Heidegger and Theology.]

3097 Jonas, Hans. "Wandlung und Bestand. Vom Grunde der Verstehbarkeit des Geschichtlichen." In *Durchblicke*. Ed. V. Klostermann. Frankfurt, 1970, 1-26.

3097a Jones, B. J. Rev. of "Frederick Elliston (ed). Heidegger's Existential Analytic." *The Journal of the British Society for Phenomenology* (Manchester), vol. 11, 1980, 99-100.

3098 Joos, Ernest. "Langage et mythe ou temps à trois dimensions chez Heidegger." *Dialogue* (Montréal/Kingston), vol. 10, 1971, 47-59.

3099 Jordan, B. Rev. of *Die Kategorien und Bedeutungslehre des Duns Scotus,* by Martin Heidegger. Tübingen, 1916. *Literarisches Zentralblatt für Deutschland* (Leipzig), vol. 68, 1917, 847-848.

3100 Jordan, B. "Angst und Sorge. Was leistet die Ontologie Heideggers für die Neubegründung der Anthropologie?" *Die Tatwelt* (Jena), vol. 8, 1931, 81-89.

3101 Jung, Hwa Yol, and Petee Jung. "To Save the Earth." *Philosophy Today* (Celina, Ohio), vol. 19, 1975, 108-117.

3101a Jung, Hwa Yol. "Confucianism and Existentialism: Intersubjectivity as the Way of Man." *Philosophy and Phenomenological Research* (Buffalo, New York), vol. 30, 1969/70, 186-202.

3101b Jung, Hwa Yol. "The Life-World, Historicity, and Truth. Reflections on Leo Strauss's Encounter With Heidegger and Husserl." *The Journal of the British Society for Phenomenology* (Manchester), vol. 9, no. 1, 1978, 11-25.

3102 Jüngel, Eberhard. "Der Schritt zurück. Eine Auseinandersetzung mit der Heidegger-Deutung Heinrich Otts." *Zeitschrift für Theologie und Kirche* (Tübingen), vol. 58, 1961, 104-122.

3103 Jüngel, Eberhard. "Vor Gott schweigen? Theologie in der Nachbarschaft des Denkens von Martin Heidegger." *Frankfurter Allgemeine Zeitung* (Frankfurt), no. 120, 25 May 1977, 25.

3104 Jüngel, Eberhard. "Gott entsprechendes Schweigen? Theologie in der Nachbarschaft des Denkens von Martin Heidegger." In *Martin Heidegger. Fragen an sein Werk. Ein Symposium.* (Universal-Bibliothek, 9873). Stuttgart: Reclam, 1977, 37-45.

3105 Jünger, Ernst. "Über die Linie." In *Anteile, Martin Heidegger zum 60. Geburtstag.* Frankfurt, 1950, 245-284.

3106 Jünger, Ernst. "Vom Ende des geschichtlichen Zeitalters." In *Martin Heidegger zum 70. Geburtstag, Festschrift.* Pfullingen, 1959, 309-341.

3107 Jünger, Ernst. "Federbälle." In *Martin Heidegger zum 80. Geburtstag. Ansprache und Notizen.* Ad Hoc, Stuttgart, 1970, 31 ff.

3108 Jünger, Ernst. "Martin Heidegger." In *Martin Heidegger im Gespräch.* Ed. R. Wisser. Freiburg/München, 1970, 23-26.

3109    Jünger, Friedrich-Georg. "Die Wildnis." In *Anteile, Martin Heidegger zum 60. Geburtstag.* Frankfurt, 1950, 235-244.

3110    Jünger, Friedrich-Georg. "Abendgang." In *Martin Heidegger zum 70. Geburtstag, Festschrift.* Pfullingen, 1959, 343 ff.

3111    Juenger, Friedrich-Georg. "'Der europäische Nihilismus'. Gedanken zu Martin Heideggers Buch, *Scheidewege Vierteljahresschrift für skeptisches Denken*" (Stuttgart), vol. 3, 1973, 184-211.

3112    Junyi, Tang. "Shu Hai Dege zhi conzaizhexue" (On Heidegger's Existential Philosophy). Appendix to Tang Junyi. *Zhexue Gailun* (Fundamental Aspects of Philosophy). Hong Kong: Mengshi jiaoyu jijin hui, 1961. (In Chinese).

3113    Jurkschat, E.-M. *Martin Heidegger. Eine Bibliographie der ausländischen Literatur über ihn und seine Werke.* (Unpublished Diplom-Prüfungsarbeit des Bibliothekar-Lehrinstituts des Landes Nordrh-Westfalen). Köln, 1956.

3114    K. K. Rev. of *Platons Lehre von der Wahrheit,* by Martin Heidegger. Berlin, 1942. *Algemeen Nederlands Tijdschrift voor Wijsbegeerte en Psychologie* (Assen), vol. 42, 1950, 105-106.

3115    K. K. Rev.of *Was ist Metaphysik?,* by Martin Heidegger. Bonn, 1929. *Algemeen Nederlands Tijdschrift voor Wijsbegeerte en Psychologie* (Assen), vol. 42, 1950, 104-105.

3116    Kaam, A. van. "Clinical Implications of Heidegger's Concepts of Will, Decision and Responsibility." *Review of Existential Psychology and Psychiatry* (Pittsburgh), vol. 1, 1961, 205-216.

3117    Kaelin, E. F. *Art and Existence: A Phenomenological Aesthetics.* Lewisburg, 1970, 357 p.

3118    Kästner, E. *Martin Heidegger - Eduardo Chillida: Die Kunst und der Raum.* (Rede v.12.10.1969 bei Ausgabe des Buches 'Die Kunst und der Raum' in der Galerie 'im Erker' in St. Gallen). St. Gallen, 1970, 5 p.

        [Numerierte Aufl. von 500 Exemplaren]

3119    Kahl-Furthmann, Gertrud. *Das Problem des Nicht. Kritisch-historische und systematische Untersuchungen.* Berlin, 1934. 2nd ed. 1968, 592 p., (specifically page 307ff).

3120    Kahl-Furthmann, Gertrud. Rev. of *Kants These über das Sein,* by Martin Heidegger. Frankfurt, 1963. *Philosophischer Literaturanzeiger* (Meisenheim/Glan), vol. 16, 1963, 193-194.

3121    Kahl-Furthmann, Gertrud. Rev. of *Zur Sache des Denkens,* by Martin Heidegger. Tübingen, 1969. *Philosophischer Literaturanzeiger* (Meisenheim/Glan), vol. 24, 1971, 141-143.

3122    Kahl-Furthmann, Gertrud. Rev. of *Le destin de la pensée et la mort de dieu selon Heidegger,* by Odette Laffoucriere. La Haye, 1968. *Zeitschrift für Philosophische Forschung* (Meisenheim/Glan), vol. 25, 1971, 621-626.

3123 Kahl-Furthmann, Gertrud. Rev. of *Zur Sache des Denkens,* by Martin Heidegger. Tübingen: Max Niemeyer Verlag, 1969, 94 p. *Philosophischer Literaturanzeiger* (Meisenheim/Glan), vol. 24, 1971, 141-143.

3124 Kai, Hiromi. "U no Shinsei to Haideggâ no Shii" (The Truth of Being and Heidegger's Thinking; A Preparatory Consideration in Order to Read "Being and Time"). *Tetsugaku Ronbunshû* (Fukuoka), vol. 10, 1974, 53-72.

3125 Kainz, F. *Über die Sprachverführung des Denkens.* Berlin/München, 1972, 518 p.

3126 Kainz, Howard. Rev. of *Hegel's Concept of Experience,* by Martin Heidegger. New York: Harper & Row, 1970, 155 p. *The New Scholasticism* (Washington), vol. 47, 1973, 418-420.

3127 Kakihara, Tokuya. "Haideggâ no Kotoba ni tsuite" (On the 'Language' of Heidegger). *Doitsu Bunka* (Chûô Daigaku Doitsu Gakki) (Tôkyô), vol. 1, 1962, 1-11.

3128 Kakihara, Tokuya. "Haideggâ to Niche - Seiyô no Shikô no Unmei" (Heidegger and Nietzsche - Destiny of European Thinking). *Doitsu Bunka* (Chûô Daigaku Doitsu Gakkai) (Tôkyô), vol. 4, 1965, 182-248.

3129 Kakihara, Tokuya. "'U' no Toi o megutte; Haideggâ no 'U to Toki' ni sokushite" (On Heidegger's "Being-Question"; a Discussion of "In His Being" in "Sein und Zeit"). *Seikei Daigaku Bungakubu Kiyô* (Tôkyô), vol. 2, 1966, 125-155.

3130 Kakihara, Tokuya. "Haideggâ Sensei o meguru Omoide" (Remembering Prof. Heidegger). *Jitsuzonshugi* (Tôkyô), vol. 35, 1966, 117-126.

3131 Kakihara, Tokuya. Minutes to a report on Hegel's logics. The session on January 11th, 1957 of Professor Heidegger's seminar. *Seikei Daigaku Bungakubu Kiyô* (Tôkyô), vol. 3, 1967, 1-5.

3132 Kakihara, Tokuya. "Intâpuretachion-Shôron" ("Interpretation" - Heidegger and Staiger). *Jitsuzonshugi* (Tôkyô), vol. 50, 1969, 83-93.

3133 Kakihara, Tokuya. "Haideggâ no Konkyo-Settei 'Aida'" (Heidegger's Initial Position 'Between'). *Seikei Daigaku Bungakubu Kiyô* (Tôkyô), vol. 6, 1970, 33-45.

3134 Kakihara, Tokuya. "Shii no Jishô - Hêgeru to Haideggâ o meguri" (On Thinking - Hegel and Heidegger). *Jitsuzonshugi* (Tôkyô), vol. 52, 1970, 19-30.

3135 Kakihara, Tokuya. "Jûjifu o kaserareta U no Shosô" (Different Aspects of 'Being Bearing its Cross'). *Risô* (Tôkyô), vol. 44, 1970, 21-30.

3136 Kakihara, Tokuya. "Haideggâ no Gengo-kan" (Heidegger's 'Language'). *Germanist* (Daigakushorin-Verlag) (Tôkyô), 87, 88, 89, 90, 92, 93, 96, 97, 1970/71. (insgesamt 37 p.)

3137 Kakihara, Tokuya. "Kenen-Kôzô ni tsuite" ('Structure of Care' in 'Sein und Zeit'). *Seikei Daigaku Bungakubu Kiyô* (Tôkyô), vol. 7, February 1972, 32-64.

3138    Kakihara, Tokuya. "Haideggâ no 'Mono' kan" (On Heidegger's Conception of "Thing"). *Jitsuzonshugi* (Tôkyô), vol. 61, 1972, 73-89.

3139    Kakihara, Tokuya. "Kenen Kôzô (Sorge-Struktur) ni tsuite" (On the Structure of "Concern" in Heidegger's "Being and Time"). *Seikei Daigaku Bungakubu Kiyô* (Tôkyô), vol. 7, 1972, 34-64.

3140    Kakihara, Tokuya. "Haideggâ no Toki" (Heidegger's Concept of Time). *Jitsuzonshugi* (Tôkyô), vol. 66, 1973, 74-82.

3141    Kakihara, Tokuya. "Konkyo Settei 'Itsuno Hi ni ka', Haideggâ Rikai no Tojô de" (Setting the Ground 'Some Day' - On the Way to Understanding of Heidegger). *Jitsuzonshugi* (Tôkyô), vol. 69, 1974, 72-84.

3142    Kakihara, Tokuya. "Haideggâ no 'Kotoba no Honshitsu' ni tsuite" (On Heidegger's 'The Essence of Language'). *Risô* (Tôkyô), vol. 500, 1975, 30-42.

3143    Kakihara, Tokuya. "'U to Toki' no 'Rekishisei' ni tsuite" (On Historicity in "Being and Time"). *Bungakubu Kiyô* (Seikei Daigaku) (Tôkyô), vol. 11, 1976, 25-40.

3144    Kakihara, Tokuya. "Tomurai" (The Condolence). *Risô* (Tôkyô), vol. 517, 1976, 137-138.

3145    Kakihara, Tokuya. "Haideggâ no Herudârin Kaishaku" (Heidegger's Interpretation of Hölderlin). *Seikei Daigaku Bungakubu Kiyô* (Tôkyô), vol. 13, 1977, 32-64.

3146    Kakihara, Tokuya. "Shisô to Shii; Herudârin to Haideggâ" (Poetizing and Thinking; Hölderlin and Heidegger). *Risô* (Tâyô), vol. 542, 1978, 191-210.

3147    Kalinowski, Georges. "La philosophie de S. Thomas d'Aquin face à la critique de la métaphysique par Kant, Nietzsche et Heidegger." In *San Tommaso e il Pensiero Moderno*. Roma: Accademia di S. Tommaso d'Aquino, Città Nuova Editrice, 1974, 257-83.

3148    Kallimach. "Nie mnózmy mitów" (No More Myths). *Literatura,* vol. 42, 1974.

3149    Kallimach. "Heidegger i odpowiedzialnoáá filozofa" (Heidegger and the Philosopher's Responsibility). *Literatura,* vol. 42, 1974.

3150    Kallimach. "Smierá filozofa" (Death of a Philosopher). *Literatura,* vol. 25, 1976.

3151    Kallimach. "Skryty fundament/teoria bytu Heideggera/" (The Hidden Fundament/ Heidegger's Theory of Being). *Literatura,* vol. 21, 1978.

3152    Kallimach. "Za i przeciw" (Pro and Contra). *Literatura,* vol. 33, 1978.

3153    Kallimach. "Trop Heideggera" (Heidegger's Path). *Literatura,* vol. 22, 1978.

3154    Kallimach. Rev. of *Heidegger i filozofia wspóczesna* (Heidegger and Contemporary Philosophy), by Krzysztof Michalski. Warszawa, 1978. *Literatura,* vol. 40, 1978.

3155    Kallimach. "Pomiedzy" (In Between). *Literatura,* vol. 3, 1979.

3156    Kaltenbrunner, Gerd-Klaus. "Die Holzwege und die Feldwege. Ein Zeitalter verliert seinen Denker. Zum Tode Martin Heideggers." *Deutsche Zeitung - Christ und Welt* (Stuttgart), vol. 23, 6 April 1976, 3. (Jg. 3, 1976, Nr. 2).

3157    Kmeyama, Kenkichi. *Haideggâ no Shisôshiteki Ichi ni tsuite* (Heidegger's Place in the History of Ideas). Nipponjoshidai-Kiyô, Tôkyô, 1961.

3158    Kameyama, Kenkichi. "Haideggâ to Herudarin" (Heidegger and Hölderlin). *Jitsuzonshugi* (Tôkyô), April 1966.

3159    Kameyama, Kenkichi. "Haideggâ to W. v. Funboruto" (Heidegger and W. v. Humboldt). *Jitsuzonshugi* (Tôkyô), vol. 77, 1976, 108-114.

3160    Kamlah, Wilhelm. *Christentum und Geschichtlichkeit.* 2nd ed. Stuttgart/Köln, 1951, 348 p.

3161    Kamlah, Wilhelm. "Martin Heidegger und die Technik. Ein offener Brief." *Deutsche Universitätszeitung* (Göttingen), Jg. 9, Heft 11, 1954, 10-13.

3162    Kamo, Hideomi. "'Sonzai to Jikan' no Genshôgaku" (Phenomenology in "Being and Time"). *Jitsuzonshugi* (Tôkyô), vol. 69, 1974, 49-61.

3163    Kan, Moritsune. "Haidaggâ ni okeru keijijôgaku to Kisoteki-Sonzairon 1-5" (Heidegger's Metaphysics and the Fundamental-Ontology). *Kansai Daigaku Gakuho* (Ôsaka), 77-81, 1930, insgesamt 30 p.

3164    Kan, Moritsune. "Haideggâ no Kanto Kaishaku 1-6" (Heidegger's Interpretation of Kant). *Kansai Daigaku Gakuhô* (Ôsaka), 83, 85, 90, 93, 94, 97, 1930/32. (insgesamt 29 p.)

3165    Kan, Moritsune. "Jissen-Risei to chôetsuronteki Kôsôryoku, Haideggâ Kenkyû no Issetsu." (Die praktische Vernunft und die transzendentale Einbildungskraft). *Kansai Daigaku Gakuhô* (Ôsaka), vol. 103, 1932, 26-29.

3166    Kan, Moritsune. "Kongen-Kaiji no Shikata narabini 'Sonzai' oyobi 'Chôetsu' ni tsuite; Haideggâ no Kanto Kaishaku" (The Mode of the Genuine Disclosedness - Being and Transcendence). *Kansai-Daigaku Gakuhô* (Ôsaka), vol. 105, 1933, 13-17.

3167    Kane, Francis Ignatius. *Heidegger's 'Sein' and Linguistic Analytic Objections to Metaphysics.* Authorized facsimile of the dissertation of the Georgetown Univ. Phil. Diss. 1976. Ann Arbor, Michigan; London: University Microfilms International, 1979, iv-412 p. [HGJ77-06182] *Dissertation Abstracts International,* vol. 37/09-A, 5884.

3168    Kaneko, Takezô. *Haideggâ no Shiso* (The Thought of Heidegger). Tôkyô, 1958.

3169    Kaneko, Takezô. "Yasupâsu to Haideggâ - Yôroppa no Tabi kara kaette" (Jaspers and Heidegger). *Jitsuzonshugi* (Tôkyô), vol. 31, 1965, 65-85.

3170    Kaneko, Takezô. *Haideggâ no Shisô* (Heidegger's Thinking). Shimizukôbundô-Verlag, Tôkyô, 1969, 264 p.

3171    Kaneko, Takezô. "Haideggâ ni tauite; Mittsu no Gimonten" (On Heidegger; Three Questions). *Jitsuzonshugi* (Tôkyô), vol. 69, 1974, 85-91.

3172 Kaneko, Takezô. "Haideggâ to Yasupâsu" (Heidegger and Jaspers). In *Jitsuzonshisô no Seiriitsu to Keifu.* Ibunsha, Tôkyô, 1977, 172-179.

3173 Kaniowski, W. "The Ideal of the Future: Superman." (In Polish). *Studia Filozoficzne* (Warszawa), vol. 18, no. 1, 1974, 93-108.

3174 Kanthack, K. *Vom Sinn der Selbsterkenntnis.* Berlin, 1958, VIII, 211 p.
[Rev. in *The New Scholasticism* (Washington), vol. 35, 1961, 243-248.]

3175 Kanthack, K. *Das Denken Martin Heideggers. Die Grosse Wende der Philosophie.* Berlin, 1959, VIII, 80 p. 2nd ed. 1964.

3176 Kanthack, K. "Das Wesen der Dialektik im Lichte Martin Heideggers." *Studium Generale* (Berlin), vol. 21, 1968, 538-554.

3177 Kariatsumari, Hideo. "Haideggâ no genshôgakuteki Hakai no Hôho; Kanto to Keijijôgaku no Mondai o chûshin to shite" (The Method of Heidegger's Phenomenological Destruction; in Connection with "Kant and the Problem of Metaphysics"). *Gendaikagaku Ronsô* (Chiba), vol. 7, 1973, 12-21.

3178 Kariatsumari, Hideo. "Haideggâ Tetsugaku no Hôho; Kaizon ni yoru Kangen ni tsuite" (On the Methodology of Heidegger's Philosophy; in Centering Around His 'Restoration of EK-Sistenz'). *Gendai Kagaku Ronsô* (Chiba), vol. 8, 1974, 33-40.

3179 Kariatsumari, Hideo. "Haideggâ Bunken 1" (Heidegger's Bibliography 1). *Gendaikagaku Ronsô* (Chiba), vol. 9, 1975, 89-120.

3180 Kariatsumari, Hideo. "Haideggâ Tetsugaku no Kiso; kaishakugakuteki-genshogakuteki Hôhô" (The Foundation of Heidegger's Philosophy; Hermeneutical Phenomenological Method). *Gendaikagaku Ronso* (Chiba), vol. 6, 1972, 28-37.

3181 Kariatsumari, Hideo. "Haideggâ to Nîche; Nihirizumu to no Kanren ni oite" (Heidegger and Nietzsche; in Connection With Nihilism). *Gendaikagaku Ronsô* (Chiba), vol. 9, 1975, 14-24.

3182 Kariatsumari, Hideo. "Haideggâ to Watsuji Tetsurô; 'Gensonzai' to 'Ningen' to no Kanren ni oite" (Heidegger and Tetsurô Watsuji; in Connection With 'Dasein' and 'Human Being'). *Gendai Kagaku Ronsô* (Chiba), vol. 10, 1976, 68-80.

3183 Kariatsumari, Hideo. "Haideggâ Bunken, 2" (Heidegger's Bibliography, 2). *Gendai Kagaku Ronsô* (Chiba), vol. 10, 1976, 90-93.

3184 Kariatsumari, Hideo. "Haideggâ Bunken, 3" (Heidegger's Bibliography, 3). *Gendai Kagaku Ronsô* (Chiba), vol. 11, 1977, 87-89.

3185 Kariatsumari, Hideo. "Shoki Haideggâ Tetsugaku ni tsuite; Shûgaku Jidai kara 'Sonzai to Jikan' no Seiritsu made" (On Heidegger's Philosophy in His Early Period; From His School Days to Completion of "Being and Time"). *Gendai Kagaku Ronsô* (Chiba), vol. 11, 1977, 55-66.

3186 Kariatsumari, Hideo. "Nihon ni okeru Haideggâ Kenkyû; Shôwa 10 Nen made o Chûchin ni" (A Study for Heidegger's Philosophy in Japan; in Centering Around Till Ten Years of Shôwa). *Kenkyû-Kiyô* (Chibakeiai Gakuen) (Chiba), vol. 1, 1977, 6-17.

3187    Kariatsumari, Hidea. "Haideggâ Bunken, 4" (Heidegger's Bibliography, 4). *Gendai Kagaku Ronsô* (Chiba), vol. 12, 1978, 47-52.

3188    Kariatsumari, Hideo. "Haideggâ no Jikan Gainen; 'Sonzai to Jikan' o Chûshin ni" (The Concept of Time by Heidegger; in Connection With 'Sein und Zeit'). *Gendai Kagaku Ronsô* (Chiba), vol. 12, 1978, 1-11.

3189    Karimskij, A. M. "K probleme funkcii vremeni v ékzistencializme" (On the Problem of the Role of Time in Existentialism. *Voprosy filosofii,* 1978, 9.

3190    Karsz, S. "La filosofia, según Martin Heidegger." *Revista de Humanidades* (Buenos Aires), vol. 2, 1962, 287-294.

3191    Kashiwabara, Keiichi. "Kirukegôru ni okeru Kanôsei no Mondai; Heideggâ o tegakari ni shite" (On "Potentiality" in Kierkegaard - Seen From Heidegger's Viewpoint). *Tetsugaku Zasshi* (Tôkyô), vol. 753, 1966, 178-197.

3192    Kashiyama, Kinshiro. "Heidegga no Kisotekisonzairon" (Heidegger's Foundamental Ontology). *Risô* (Tôkyô März), 1935.

3193    Katayama, Masanao. "Shi ni tsuite - Haideggâ to Kirukegôru" (On Death - Heidegger and Kierkegaard). *Kirukegôru Kenkyû* (Kirukegôru Kyôkai) (Ôsaka), vol. 5, 1968, 85-105.

3194    Katayama, Masanao. "Haideggâ no Tetsugaku to Shûkyô" (Heidegger's Philosophy and Religion). *Risô* (Tôkyô März), 1935.

3195    Kates, Carol. "Heidegger and the Myth of the Cave." *The Personalist* (Los Angeles), vol. 50, 1969, 532-548.

3196    Katô, Kiyoshi. "Haideggâ ni okeru Gijutsuteki-Sakusei to Kyôikugaku" (Technics in Heidegger, and Educational Science). *Ôsaka Sangyô Daigaku Ronshû* (Ôsaka), vol. 27, 1969, 14-25.

3197    Katô, Kiyoshi. "Haideggâ no Jitsuzon ni tsuite" (On the Existence in Heidegger). *Ôsaka Sangyô Daigaku Ronshû* (Ôsaka), vol. 29, 1970, 9-37.

3198    Katô, Kiyoshi. "Haideggâ - Shisô ni okeru Tenkai ni tsuite" (On the "Turning" in Heidegger's Way of Thinking). *Ôsaka Sangyô Daigaku Ronshû - Jimbun Kagaku Hen 33* (Ôsaka), October 1971, 19-41.

3199    Katô, Takamasa. "Fuan, Zetsubô to Mu - Haideggâ o Chûshin to Shite" (Anxiety, Despair, Non-Being With Regard to Heidegger). *Ôtani Gakuhô* (Kyôto), XL-3, 1960, 27-42.

3200    Katô, Takao. "'Sonzai to Jikan' o Chûshin to suru Haideggâ no Konkyo ni tsuite" ('Ground' in "Sein und Zeit"). *Ôtani Gakuhô* (Kyôto), XXXIV-3, 1954, 37-58.

3201    Katô, Takao. "Fuan, Zetsubô to Mu, Haideggâ o Chushin toshite" ("Fear and Despair" and Non-Being, in Regard to Heidegger). *Ôtanigakuhô* (Kyôto), 1961.

3202    Katô, Yasuyoshi. "Genshogakuteki-Hoho no Tenkai" (The Development of the Phenomenological Method). *Riso* (Tôkyô), vol. 319, December 1959.

3203    Katô, Yasuyoshi. "Riruke to Haideggâ tachi" (Rilke and the Heideggerian School). *Jitsuzonshugi* (Tôkyô), vol. 33, 1965, 51-64.

3204 Katô, Yasuyoshi. "Sumu-Ba o Hirakumono - Haideggâ no Geijutsu-ron" (The Opening in the Place of Dwelling - Heidegger's Theory of the Fine Arts). *Risô* (Tôkyô), vol. 44, 1970, 31-39.

3205 Katô, Yoshijirô. *Haideggâ ni okeru Ningen to Sonzai no Mondai* (The Problem of Man and Being in Heidegger). Kansaidaigaku-Bungakuronshû, Ôsake, 1960.

3206 Katô, Yasuyoshi. "Toki to Eien; Bashô to Haideggâ no Baai" (Time and Eternity; in Cases of Basho and Heidegger). *Risô* (Tôkyô), vol. 489, 1974, 74-86.

3207 Katô, Takao. "Jitsuzonronteki na Rekishigainen ni tsuite; Haideggâ, Kirukegôru" (The Existential Concept of History; Heidegger, Kierkegaard). *Dohô Daigaku Ronsô* (Nagoya), vol. 31, 1974.

3208 Katô, Kiyoshi. "Gijutsu to Ningen (sono 1, 2); Haideggâ Tetsugaku no Kenkyû" (Technic and Man; Studies in Heidegger's Philosophy). *Ôsaka Sangyô Daigaku Ronshû* (Ôsaka), no. 40, 1975.

3209 Katô, Kiyoshi. *Haideggâ ni okeru Gijutsu no Mondai* (The Problem of Technic in Heidegger). Hôritsu Bunkasha, Tokyo, 1975, 208 p.

3210 Kaufmann, F. "Geschichtsphilosophie der Gegenwart." *Philosophische Forschungsberichte* (Berlin), Heft 10, 1931, 118-129.

3211 Kaufmann, F. W. "The Value of Heidegger's Analysis of Existence for Literary Criticism." *Modern Language Notes* (Baltimore), vol. 48, 1933, 487-491.

3212 Kaufmann, Fritz. "Discussion. Concerning Kraft's 'Philosophy of Existence'." *Philosophy and Phenomenological Research* (Buffalo, New York), vol. I, 1940/41, 359-364.

3213 Kaufmann, Fritz. "Ethik und Metaphysik. Betrachtungen zu Helmut Kuhns *Begegnung mit dem Nichts* (Tûbingen 1950) und *Begegnung mit dem Sein* (Tûbingen 1954)." *Zeitschrift für philosophische Forschung* (Meisenheim/Glan), vol. 10, 1956, 279-286.

3214 Kaufmann, Walter Arnold. "Le château de Heidegger." *Iyyun* (Jerusalem), vol. 9, 1958, 76 ff.

3215 Kaufmann, Walter Arnold. *The Owl and the Nightingale: From Shakespeare to Existentialism.* London: Faber, 1960.

3216 Kaufmann, Walter Arnold. *The Faith of a Heretic.* New York: Doubleday, 1961.

3217 Kaufmann, Walter Arnold. *Without Guilt and Justice, From Decidophobia to Autonomy.* New York: Wyden, 1973.

3218 Kaufmann, Walter Arnold. "Nietzsche and Existentialism." *Symposium* (Syracuse, New York), vol. 28, no. 1, 1974, 7-16.

3219 Kaufmann, Walter Arnold. *Existentialism, Religion, and Death.* New York: New American Library, 1976.

3220    Kaufmann, Walter Arnold. "Nietzsche als der erste grosse Psychologe."
        *Nietzsche-Studien* (Berlin), vol. 7, 1978, 261-275.

3221    Kaufmann, Walter Arnold. *From Shakespeare to Existentialism.* Boston:
        Beacon Press, 1980.

3222    Kaufmann, Walter Arnold. *Discovering the Mind.* Vol. II, 4. [Heidegger's
        Dogmatic Anthropology] New York: McGraw Hill, 1980.

3223    Kaulbach, Friedrich. "Die kantische Lehre von Dingund Sein in der
        Interpretation Heideggers." Rev. of *Die Frage nach dem Ding* and *Kants
        These über das Sein,* by Martin Heidegger. *Kantstudien* (Köln), vol. 55,
        1964, 194-220.

3224    Kaurin, W. "En S. A. Filosofi." *Vinduet* (Oslo), vol. 3, 1948, 219-224.

3225    Kawada, Kumataro. "Haideggeru no Choetsu" (Transcendence in
        Heidegger). *Rinrikenkyu* (Tôkyô), vol. 11, Mai 1930.

3226    Kawado, Yoshitake. "Kanto to Haideggâ" (Kant and Heidegger).
        *Jinmonshakai* (Hirosaki), December 1954.

3227    Kawado, Yoshitake. "Haideggâ no Kanto Kaishaku" (Heidegger's
        Explication of Kant). *Kirisuto Kyôgaku* (Rikkyô Daigaku Kirisutokyô
        Gakkai) (Tôkyô), vol. 8, 1966, 1-23.

3228    Kawado, Yoshgitake. "Sonzai no Shinri e no Tojô - Haideggâ Kenkyû"
        (Towards the Truth of Being - A Study in Heidegger). *Kirisuto Kyôgaku*
        (Rikkyô Daigaku Kirisuto-kyô Gakkai) (Tôkyô), vol. 9, 1967, 61-102.

3229    Kawado, Yoshitake. "Kami no Shi; Haideggâ no Nîche Kôgi" (The Death
        of God; Heidegger's Lecture on Nietzsche). *Kirisuto Kyôgaku* (Rikkyô
        Daigaku Kirisutokyô Gakkai) (Tôkyô), vol. 10, 1968, 95-119.

3230    Kawado, Yoshitake. "Tetsugaku-teki Ningengaku ni tsuite; Kanto to
        Haideggâ" (On Philosophical Anthropology: Kant and Heidegger).
        *Kirisuto-Kyôgaku* (Rikkyô Daigaku Kirisutokyô Gakkai) (Tôkyô), vol. 11,
        1970, 14-36.

3231    Kawado, Yoshitake. "Haideggâ ni okeru Kami no Mondai" (Heidegger's
        Inquiry on God). *Kirisutokyôgaku, Rikkyô Daigaku Kirisuto kyôgakkai*
        (Tôkyô), vol. 13, December 1971, 17-37.

3232    Kawahara, Eihô. "Haideggâ ni okeru Gensonzai no Jitsuzonronteki Kôzô no
        Henka" (The Metamorphosis of the Existential Structure of There-Being
        in Heidegger). *Tetsugakunenpô* (Tôkyô), vol. 19, 1956.

3233    Kawahara, Eihô. "Haideggâ no Shinri-Ron" (Heidegger's Discussion of
        Truth). *Philosophia* (Tôkyô), vol. 30, Juni 1956.

3234    Kawahara, Eihô. "Sonzai no Rekishi" (The History of Being). *Philosophia*
        (Tôkyô), vol. 33, December 1957.

3235    Kawahara, Eihô. "Kibô to Yûryo - Borunô no Kôen 'Kibô no Ningenteki Imi'
        to Haideggâ no Kôen 'Genshi-Jidai ni yosete' to o kiite" (Two Reports;
        Bollnow's "Menschliche Bedeutung der Hoffnung" and Heidegger's "Zum
        Atomzeitalter"). *Risô* (Tôkyô), vol. 318, 1959, 20-31.

3236    Kawahara, Eihô. "Haideggâ ni okeru Mu" (The Non-Being in Heidegger). *Philosophia* (Tôkyô), vol. 41, 1961.

3237    Kawahara, Eihô. "Haideggâ no 'Kotoba' Ron" (Heidegger's Discussion of "Language"). In *Wasedahôgakkaishi*. Tôkyô, 1962.

3238    Kawahara, Eihô. "Haideggâ no 'Gen-sonzai'" ("There-Being" in Heidegger). *Mikkyôbunka* (Wakayama), vol. 59, no. 60, 1962.

3239    Kawahara, Eihô. "Haideggâ ni okeru Philosophieren" (Heidegger and Philosophizing). *Tetsugaku* (Nippon Tetsugakukai) (Tôkyô), vol. 18, 1968, 57-86.

3240    Kawahara, Eihô. "'Transzendental' ni tsuite - Haideggâ no Kanto Kaishaku no Ittan" (On "Transcendental" - Kant Exegesis in Heidegger). *Waseda Daigaku Daigakuin Bungaku Kenkyûka Kiyô* (Tôkyô), vol. 15, 1969, 1-21.

3241    Kawahara, Eihô. "Haideggâ no Topologi" (Heidegger's Topology). *Jitsuzonshugi* (Tôkyô), vol. 69, 1974, 15-25.

3242    Kawahara, Eihô. "Shijinteki ni sumu; Herudârin to Haideggâ" (Poetically Doth Man Dwell; Hölderlin and Heidegger). *Risô* (Tôkyô), vol. 500, 1975, 86-102.

3243    Kawahara, Eihô. "Gerassenhait Shoken" (On Heidegger's "Release"). *Jitsuzonshugi* (Tôkyô), vol. 77, 1976, 93-99.

3244    Kawahara, Eihô. "Tsutsushinde Aitô" (A Message of Condolence). *Risô* (Tôkyô), vol. 517, 1976, 131-137.

3245    Kawahara, Eihô. "Haideggâ." In *Gendai Jûdai Tetsugaku* (10 Modern Great Philosophies). Fujishoten, Tôkyô, 1977, 249-280.

3246    Kawahara, Eihô. "Haideggâ wa Nihilisto de wa nai" (Heidegger is not a Nihilist). In *Nihilism.* Kôdansha, Tôkyô, 1977, 145-231.

3247    Kawahara, Eihô. "Haideggâ ni okeru Kêre" (Heidegger's "Reversal"). *Risô* (Tôkyô), vol. 542, 1978, 211-229.

3248    Kawamura, Kakusho. "Haideggâ no Konpon Keiken suru Jitsuzon ni tsuite" (On the Existence Experienced Originally by Heidegger). *Kyoto Daigaku Kyoiku Gakubu Kiyô* (Kyoto), vol. 23, 1977, 85-95.

3249    Kayano, Yoshio. "Sonzai to Jitsuzon; Kiso-teki-Sonzairon no sonogoni tsuite" (Being and Existence - The Further Development of the Fundamental-Ontology). *Tetsugakuzasshi* (Tôkyô), vol. 717, 1952, 46-65.

3250    Kayano, Yoshio. "Haideggâ no Nîche-Kan" (Heidegger's Opinion of Nietzsche). *Tetsugakuzasshi* (Tôkyô), vol. 721, 1954.

3251    Kayano, Yoshio. "Yûgensei no Mondai; Haideggâ Zenki ni okeru Shisaku no Rikai e no Shian, I" (The Problem of Finitude; an Attempt to Comprehend Heidegger's Earlier Stage of Thinking, Part I). *Hokkai-Gakuen Ronshû* (Sapporo), no. 1, 1956, 1-30.

3252    Kayano, Yoshio. "Yûgensei to Jikansei; Haideggâ Zenki ni okeru Shisaku no Rikai e no Shian, II" (Finitude and Temporality; an Attempt to

Comprehend Heidegger's Earlier Stage of Thinking, Part II). *Hokkai-Gakuen Ronshû* (Sapporo), no. 2, 1957, 20-54.

3253 Kayano, Yoshio. "Haideggâ kara mita Sarutoru; Jitsuzonshugi, Hyûmanizumu, Genshôgaku" (Heidegger Versus Sartre; Existentialism, Humanism, Phenomenology). *Jitsuzonshugi* (Tôkyô), vol. 39, 1967, 47-59.

3254 Kayano, Yoshio. "Haideggâ to Dentô" (Heidegger and Tradition). Ed. T. Kaneko. In *Dentô* (Tradition). Risôsha, Tôkyô, 1967, 59-91.

3255 Kayano, Yoshio. "Haideggâ no Daigaku-ron" (Heidegger's Notion of University). *Jitsuzonshugi* (Tôkyô), vol. 47, 1969, 34-46.

3256 Kayano, Yoshio. *Shoki Haideggâ-Tetsugaku no Keisei* (The Shaping of Heidegger's Philosophy in his Early Period). Tôkai Shuppankai, Tôkyô März, 1972, 494 p.

3257 Kayano, Yoshio. "Jôtaisei to shie no Kibun" (Mood as Ontological Disposition). *Jitsuzonshugi Kôza* (Risôsha, Tôkyô), vol. 4, 1972, 35-80.

3258 Kayano, Yoshio. "Haideggâ to Rekishisei no Mondai" (Heidegger and the Problem of Historicity). *Risô* (Tôkyô), vol. 488, 1974, 66-80.

3259 Kayano, Yoshio. "Nîshe to Haideggâ" (Nietzsche and Heidegger). *Gendai Shisô* (Tôkyô), vol. II, no. 6, 1974, 102-117.

3260 Kayano, Yoshio. "Haideggâ to Jikan no Mondai" (Heidegger and the Problem of Time). *Episutêmê* (Tôkyô), no. 12, 1975, 86-103.

3261 Kayano, Yoshio. "'Der Shupîgeru' Shi Kisha, Aogusutain oyobi Boruhu tono Taiwa; 1977 Nen 9 Gatsu 23 Nichi" (Heidegger's Dialogue With Augstein and Wolff on 23 September 1966). *Jitsuzon Shugi* (Tôkyô), no. 77, 1976, 57-69.

3262 Kayano, Yoshio. "Haideggâ to Nîche; "Nîche" dai Ikkan ni sokushite" (Heidegger and Nietzsche; Some Reflections on Heidegger's "Nietzsche," Vol. 1). *Gendai-Shisô* (Tôkyô), vol. 4, no. 12, 1976, 223-247.

3263 Kayano, Yoshio. "Haideggâ to 'Sonzai no Imi e no Toi' no Hottan; Haideggâ Kenkyû, 1" (Heidegger and the Origin of 'The Question of the Sense of Being'; Studies on Heidegger, 1). *Episutêmê* (Tôkyô), no. 8 and 9, 1976, 288-308.

3264 Kayano, Yoshio. "'Sonzai no Imi' to 'Jikan'; Haideggâ Kenkyû, 2" ('The Sense of Being' and 'Time'; Studies on Heidegger, 2). *Episutêmê* (Tôkyô), no. 10, 1976, 257-276.

3265 Kayano, Yoshio. "'Sekai ni aru Koto' no jikanteki Imi; Haideggâ Kankyû, 3" (The Temporal Sense of 'To-be-in-the-World'; Studies on Heidegger, 3). *Episutêmê* (Tôkyô), no. 11, 1976, 223-243.

3266 Kayano, Yoshio. "Haideggâ o itamu" (I Grieved Over the Death of Martin Heidegger). *Gendai-Shisô* (Tôkyô), vol. 4, no. 7, 1976, 42-44.

3267 Kayano, Yoshio. "1930 Nendai ni okeru Haideggâ no Imi" (The Sense of Heidegger's Thinking in the 1930's). *Tetsugaku* (Tôkyô), no. 27, 1977, 35-54.

3268    Kayano, Yoshio. "'Sekai ni aru Koto' to 'Sonzai no Imi'; Haideggâ Kenkyû, IV" ('To-be-in-the World' and 'The Sense of Being'; Studies on Heidegger, IV). *Episutêmê* (Tôkyô), vol. 3, no. 1, 1977, 268-289.

3269    Kayano, Yoshio. "Haideggâ to Gendai no Tetsugaku" (Heidegger and Contemporary Philosophy). *Britanica Kokusai Nenkan* (Tôkyô), 1977, 302-303.

3270    Kayano, Yoshio. "Jinmeru to Haideggâ" (Simmel and Heidegger). *Gendai-Shisô* (Tôkyô), vol. 5, no. 11, 1977, 230.

3271    Kazarjan, A. T. "Problema bytija v filosofii rannego Chajdeggera" (The Problem of Being in Heidegger's Early Philosophy). *Istorija filosofii i sovremennost* (Moskva), vol. 1, 1976, 59-70.

3272    Kazarjan, A. T. "Ponimanie i samoosmyslenie filosofii v nemeckom ekzistencializme" (The Understanding and Identity in the Philosophy of German Existentialism). *Istorija filosofii i sovremennost* (Moskva), vol. 2, 1977.

3272a   Kearney, Richard and Joseph Stephen O'Leary. "Avant-propos." In *Heidegger et la question de Dieu.* Ed. Richard Kearney and Joseph Stephen O'Leary. Paris: B. Grasset, 1980, 9-14.

3272b   Kearney, Richard. "Heidegger, le possible de Dieu." In *Heidegger et la question de Dieu.* Ed. Richard Kearney and Joseph Stephen O'Leary. Paris: B. Grasset, 1980, 125-167.

3273    Kelkel, Arion L. "History as Teleology and Eschatology: Husserl and Heidegger." *Analecta Husserliana,* vol. 9, 1979, 381-411.

3274    Kelkel, Arion L. *La légende de l'être. Language et poésie chez Heidegger.* Paris: J. Vrin, 1980, 639.

3275    Keller, W. *Vom Wesen des Menschen.* Basel, 1943, VIII-142.

3276    Kelley, D. A. "The Earth as Home." *Religious Humanism* (Yellow Springs), vol. 6, 1972, 178 f.

3277    Kellner, Douglas Mackay. "Heidegger's Concept of Authenticity." Phil. Diss. Columbia Univ. 1973. *Dissertation Abstracts International,* vol. 34/07-A, 4327.

3278    Kelly, Arthur J. "The Gifts of the Spirit: Aquinas and the Modern Context." *The Thomist* (Baltimore), vol. 38, 1974, 193-231.

3278a   Kempf, Hans-Diedrich. *Martin Heideggers Sorge. Warum hat der Denker den 2. Teil von 'Sein und Zeit' nicht geschrieben?* Bonn, Brüssel: Kempf-Onoma, 1979, xxiii-399 p.

3279    Kempter, L. Rev. of *Allemann, B., Hölderlin und Heidegger.* Zürich/Freiburg, 1954. *Euphorion* (Heidelberg), vol. 51, 1957, 330-335.

3280    Kerényi, K. *Geistiger Weg Europas.* (Fünf Vorträge über Freud, Jung, Heidegger, Thomas Mann, Hofmannsthal, Rilke, Homer und Hölderlin). Zürich, 1955, 106 p., passim.

3281    Keogh, Andrew. *Authenticity and Self-Actualization: A Rapprochement Between the Philosophy of Heidegger and the Psychology of Maslow.* Phil. Diss. Univ. Toronto Canada 1978. *Dissertation Abstracts International,* vol. 39/07-A, 4323.

3282    Kerferd, G. B. Rev. of "Early Greek Thinking," by Martin Heidegger. Trans. David Farrell Krell and Frank A. Capuzzi. New York: Harper & Row, 1975, 129 p. *The Journal of the British Society for Phenomenology* (Manchester), vol. 8, 59-60.

3283    Kerkhoff, Manfred. "Hoelderlin y la filosofia." *Dialogos* (Rio Piedras, Puerto Rico), vol. 6, 1969, 17-34.

3284    Kerkhoff, Manfred. Rev. of *Die Grundprobleme der Phänomenologie,* by Martin Heidegger. *Diálogos* (Rio Piedras, Puerto Rico), vol. 13, 1978, 191-202.

3285    Kerr, F. "Heidegger Among the Theologians." *New Black Friars* (Cambridge), vol. 46, no. 538, 1965, 396-403. A monthly rev. ed. by the English Dominicans.

3286    Kersten, Fred. "Heidegger and Transcendental Phenomenology." *The Southern Journal of Philosophy* (Memphis), vol. 11, 1973, 202-215.

3287    Kersten, Fred. "Heidegger and the History of *Platonism.*" In *Der Idealismus und Sein Gegenwart,* by Ute Guzzoni, Bernhard Rang, and Ludwig Siep (eds.). Festschrift für Werner Marx zum 65. Geburtstag. Hamburg: Felix Meiner Verlag, 1976, 272-296.

3288    Kestenbaum, Victor. "Phenomenology and Dewey's Empiricism: A Response to Leroy Troutner." *Educational Theory* (Urbana), vol. 22, 1972, 99-108.

3289    Kettner, Otmar. *Die Gestalt der existenziellen Unsicherheit (Insecuritas Humana) bei Peter Wust und Martin Heidegger.* Phil. Diss. Wien 1974.

3290    Keyes, C. D. *Time, Ambiguity, Miracle; a Theological Investigation Based, in Part, on the Methods of M. Heidegger's 'Being and Time'.* Th. D. Trinity College Canada 1967.

3291    Keyes, C. D. "Trust as Art. An Interpretation of Heidegger's 'Sein und Zeit' (Sec. 44) and 'Der Ursprung des Kunstwerkes'." In *Heidegger and the Path of Thinking.* Ed. J. Sallis. Pittsburgh, 1970, 65-84.

3292    Keyes, C. D. "An Evaluation of Levinas' Critique of Heidegger." *Research in Phenomenology* (Pittsburgh), vol. 2, 1972, 121-142.

3293    Khan, Mohammad Ahmad. "Daseinanalyse or Existential Analysis." *The Pakistan Philosophical Journal* (Lahore, Pakistan), vol. 12, no. 3, 1973, 60-68.

3294    Khoobyar, Helen. *On Thinking: A Heidegger-Dewey Comparison for Philosophy of Education.* Phil. Diss. Univ. of California Berkeley 1973.

3295    Khoobyar, Helen. "Educational Import of Heidegger's Notion of Truth as Letting-Be." *Philosophy of Education* (Edwardsville, Illinois), 1974, 47-58.

3296    Kiba, Shinjô. *Shinri to Jitsuzon* (Truth and Existence). Tôkyô: Fukumurashoten, 1948, 201 p.

3297 Kiba, Shinjô. "Shinrigenshô no Sonzaironteki Imi" (The Ontological Meaning of the Phenomenon of Truth). *Risô* (Tôkyô), vol. 223, Dezember 1951.

3298 Kiba, Shinjô. "Haideggâ ni okeru 'Seinarumono'" (The Notion of the "Divine" in Heidegger). *Risô* (Tôkyô), vol. 305, October 1958.

3299 Kiba, Shinjô. "Haideggâ ni okeru 'Sei narumono' ni tsuite" (On the Holy in Heidegger). *Ôtani Gakuhô* (Kyôto), vol. 51, no. 4, 1972, 87-89.

3300 Kida, Hajime. "Kôzôshugi to Ningenshugi" (Structuralism and Humanism). *Sekai* (Tôkyô), vol. 363, 1976, 260-280.

3301 Kidûk, Song. *Haidegkaûi chilliûi ponjiljôk ûimi* (Essential Meaning of Truth in Heidegger). M. A. Thesis, Yônse Univ., 1964.

3302 Kiernan, Doris Josephine. *Existenziale Themen bei Max Frisch. Die Existenzialphilosophie Martin Heideggers in den Romanen 'Stiller', 'Homo Faber' und 'Mein Name sei Gantenbein'.* Germanic Lit. Phil. Diss. Univ. of California Berkely 1976. *Dissertation Abstracts International,* vol. 38/02-A, 817. Rpt. in *Quellen und Forschungen zur Sprach- und Kulturgeschichte der germanischen Völker. N. F. 73.* Berlin/New York: de Gruyter, 1978, 224 p.

3303 Kimmel, H. W. "Heidegger im Fernsehen." *Hochland* (München), vol. 62, 1970, 368-370.

[zu: Martin Heidegger im Gespräch. Ed. R. Wisser. Freiburg, 1970.]

3304 Kimmel, H. W. "Martin Heidegger im Gespräch. Ein geistesgeschichtliches Dokument." *Zeitschrift für Religions-und Geistesgeschichte* (Köln), vol. 24, 1972, 74-77.

3305 Kimmel, H. W. and J. T. Wilde. *The Search of Being.* New York, 1962, 507-520.

3306 Kimura, Chiharu. "Maruchin Haideggâ - 'Konkyo no Honshitsu' o Chûshin to shite" (Martin Heidegger - His Work "Vom Wesen Des Grundes"). *Aichi Gakugei Daigaku Tetsugaku Kaishi* (Nagoya), vol. 1, 1953, 35-38.

3307 Kimura, Satoshi. "Haideggâ Sensei o Shinobu" (The Reminiscence of Prof. Heidegger). *Gendai-Shiso* (Tôkyô), vol. 4, no. 7, 1976, 45-47.

3308 Kimura, Satoshi. "Sonzairontekisai to Seishinbyô" (The Ontological Difference and Psychosis). *Risô* (Tôkyô), vol. 542, 1978, 112-127.

3309 Kimura, Shôgo. "Haideggâ ni okeru Kotoba no Mondai" (The Problem of Language in Heidegger). *Gaikoku Bungaku Kenkyû* (Ritsumeikan Daigaku) (Kyôto), vol. 13, 1966, 25-8.

3310 Kimura, Shôgo. "Haideggâ" (Heidegger). In *Gendai no Tetsugakusha* (The Modern Philosophers). Ed. Shimizu and Inoue. Fukumura-Shuppan, Tôkyô, 1974, 237-256.

3311 King, Magda Y. *Heidegger's Philosophy.* A guide to his basic thought. New York, 1964, XX-193; Oxford, 1965, XX-193.

3312    King, Magda Y. "Heidegger Reinterpreted: On L. Versenyi's, Heidegger, Being and Truth." *International Philosophical Quarterly* (New York/Heverlee/Louvain), vol. 6, 1966, 483-491.

3313    King, Magda Y. "Truth and Technology." *The Human Context* (London), vol. 5, 1973, 1-34.

3314    Kirita, Kiyohide. "Haideggâ no Niche Ron; Nihirizumu no Mondai o megutte, 1" (Heidegger's Essay on Nietzsche; in Connection With the Question of Nihilism, 1). *Hanazono Daigaku Kenkyû Kiyô* (Kyôto), vol. 4, 1973, 1-18.

3315    Kisiel, Theodore. "The Happening of Tradition: The Hermeneutics of Gadamer and Heidegger." *Man and World* (Pittsburgh), vol. 2, 1969, 358-385.

3316    Kisiel, Theodore. "Phenomenology as the Science of Science." In *Phenomenology and the Natural Sciences.* Ed. J. J. Kockelmans and T. J. Kisiel. Evanston, Illinois, 1970, 5-44.

3317    Kisiel, Theodore. "Science, Phenomenology, and the Thinking of Being." In *Phenomenology and the Natural Sciences.* Ed. J. J. Kockelmans and T. J. Kisiel. Evanston, Illinois, 1970, 167-183.

3318    Kisiel, Theodore. "T he Language of the Event: The Event of Language." In *Heidegger and the Path of Thinking.* Ed. J. Sallis. Pittsburgh, 1970, 85-104.

3319    Kisiel, Theodore. "Zu einer Hermeneutik naturwissenschaftlicher Entdeckung." *Zeitschrift für Allgemeine Wissenschaftstheorie* (Düsseldorf), vol. 2, 1971, 195-221.

3320    Kisiel, Theodore. Rev. of *Hermeneutics: Interpretation Theory in Schleiermacher, Dilthey, Heidegger and Gadamer,* by Richard E. Palmer. Evanston, Illinois: Northwestern Univ. Press, 1969. *Zeitschrift für Allgemeine Wissenschaftstheorie* (Düsseldorf), vol. 2, 1971, 130-132.

3321    Kisiel, Theodore. "On the Dimensions of a Phenomenology of Science in Husserl and the Young Dr. Heidegger." *Journal of the British Society for Phenomenology,* October 1973, 217-234.

3322    Kisiel, Theodore. "The Mathematical and the Hermeneutical on Heidegger's Notion of the Apriori." In *Martin Heidegger: In Europe and America,* by Goodwin Ballard and Charles E. Scott. The Hague, 1973, 109-120.

3323    Kisiel, Theodore. Rev. of *Heidegger et Kant,* by Henri Decleve. Den Haag, 1970. *Philosophy and Phenomenological Research* (Buffalo, New York), vol. 4, 1973, 601-603.

3324    Kisiel, Theodore. Rev. of *Heidegger, Kant and Time,* by Charles M. Sherover. Bloomington/London, 1971. *Philosophy and Phenomenological* (Buffalo, New York), vol. 33, 1973, 601-603.

3325    Kisiel, Theodore. "Heidegger and the New Images of Science." *Research in Phenomenology* (Pittsburgh), vol. 7, 1977, 162-181.

3326    Kisiel, Theodore. "Towards the Topology of Dasein." *Listening. Journal of Religion and Culture* (River Forest, Illinois), vol. 12, no. 3, 1977, 38-49.

3327 Kisiel, Theodore. "Habermas Purge of Pure Theory: Critical Theory Without Ontology?" *Human Studies,* vol. 1, 1978, 167-183.

3328 Kisiel, Theodore. "A Prefatory Guide to Readers of 'Being and Time'." In *Heidegger's Existential Analytic,* by Frederick Elliston (ed.). The Hague, New York: Mouton Pub., 1978, 13-20.

3329 Kit'ae, Kim. *Haidegkae issôsôûi ch'owôlûi munje* (The Problem of Transcendence in Heidegger). M. A. Thesis, Kyôngbuk Univ., 1956.

3330 Kit'ae, Kim. *Haidegkae issôsôûi sagowa chaksiûi munje* (The Problem of Thinking and Poetizing in Heidegger). Kyôngbuk Univ. In *Collection of Essays.* Kyôngbuk, vol. 7, 1963, 241-256.

3331 Kit'ae, Kim. *Haidegkae issôsôûi yôksaûi yôngu* (Analysis of the History in Heidegger). Phil. Diss. Kyôngbuk Univ. 1975.

3332 Kit'ae, Kim. "Haidegkae issôsôûi kidokgyo sinanggwa chonjaeeûi murûm" (Christian Religion and the Ontological Question in Heidegger). *Ch'ôrhak Yôngu* (Taegu), vol. 20, 1977, 55-63.

3333 Kitô, Eiichi. "Kisotekisonzairon to Ningengaku" (Fundamental Ontology and Anthropology). *Risô* (Tôkyô), Januar 1932.

3334 Kitô, Eiichi. "Haideggâ no Ningengaku" (Heidegger's Anthropology). *Risô* (Tôkyô März), 1935.

3335 Kitô, Eiichi. *Haideggâ no Sonzaigaku* (Heidegger's Ontology). Tôkyô, 1935.

3336 Kitô, Eiichi. "Haideggâ to Yasupâsu" (Heidegger and Jaspers). *Bungei* (Tôkyô), vol. IV, no. 4, 1936, 133-137.

3337 Kitô, Eiichi. "Haideggâ no Tetsugaku to Rekishiteki Shakaiteki Genjitsu no Mondai" (The Philosophy of Heidegger and the Problem of the Historical-Social Reality). *Tetsugaku-ka Nempô* (Rikkyô-Daigaku) (Tôkyô), vol. 1, 1937, 41-57.

3338 Kitô, Eiichi. "Haideggâ (Heidegger). *Gakusei-Kyôyô* (Mikasa Shobô, Tôkyô), vol. 4, 1941.

3339 Kitô, Eiichi. *Jitsuzn no Kanôsei* (The Possibility of Existence). Kanazawa, 1957.

3340 Kitô, Eiichi. "Haideggâ ni okeru Fuan" ('Anxiety' in Heidegger). *Jitsuzonshugi* (Tôkyô), vol. 17, 1959, 13-17.

3341 Kitô, Eiichi. "Haideggâ" (Heidegger). *Jitsuzonshugi* (Tôkyô), vol. 26, 1962, 52-58.

3342 Kitô, Eiichi. "'Sonzai to Jikan' ni tsuite" (On "Being and Time"). *Jitsuzonshugi* (Tôkyô), April 1966.

3343 Klein, I. *Das Sein und das Seiende. Das Grundproblem der Ontologie N. Hartmanns und M. Heideggers.* Phil. Diss. Köln 1949 240 p.

3344 Klein, J. Rev. of *Die Kategorien und Bedeutungslehre des Duns Scotus,* by Martin Heidegger. Tübingen, 1916. *Theologische Revue* (Münster), vol. 17, 1918, 215-219.

3345 Klein, Ted. "Being as Ontological Predicate: Heidegger's Interpretation of 'Kant's Thesis About Being'." *The Southwestern Journal of Philosophy* (Norman), vol. 4, no. 3, 1973, 35-51, 88-100. [Heidegger issue]

3346 Klein, Ted. "A Shared Paradox." *The Southwestern Journal of Philosophy* (Memphis), vol. 6, 1975, 21-25.

3347 Klenk, G. F. "Das Sein und die Dichter. Zu Heideggers Hölderlin-Auslegung." *Stimmen der Zeit* (Freiburg), vol. 148, 1950/51, 419-428.

3348 Klenk, G. F. "Das doppelte Gesicht Heideggers im Spiegel der jüngsten Kritik." *Gregorianum* (Rom), vol. 32, 1951, 290-306.

3349 Klenk, G. F. "Heidegger und Kant." *Gregorianum* (Rom), vol. 34, 1953, 56-71.

3350 Klenk, G. F. "Rev. of *Einführung in die Metaphysik,* by Martin Heidegger. Tübingen, 1953. *Gregorianum* (Roma), vol. 36, 1955, 138-141.

3351 Klonoski, Richard. "A Journey Through the Middle of 'Being and Time' By Way of Section 42." *Dialogos* (Rio Piedras, Puerto Rico), vol. 14, 1979, 71-79.

3352 Klostermann, V., ed. *Durchblicke.* Festschrift für Martin Heidegger zum 80. Geburtstag. Mit Beiträgen von H. Jonas, H. Ott, H. Fahrenbach, E. Tugendhat, K. Harries, Kl. Held, W. Hirsch, Fr.-W. von Herrmann, W. Janke, H. Hoppe, R.-E. Schulz-Seitz, J. Taminiaux, E. Heftrich, G. Granel, R. Boehm, J. Patocka, G. Petrovic. Frankfurt, 1970, VIII, 436 p.

3353 Kluback, W. Rev. of *Heidegger. Das Gefüge seines Denkens,* by P. Fürstenau. Frankfurt, 1958. *The Journal of Philosophy* (Lancaster, Pennsylvania), vol. 55, 1958, 1114-1116.

3354 Klug, H. Rev. of *Die Kategorien und Bedeutungslehre des Duns Scotus,* by Martin Heidegger. Tübingen, 1916. *Franziskanische Studien* (Münster), vol. 5, 1918, 143-144.

3355 Kneller, George F. *Existential and Education.* New York Philosophical Lib., 1958. *See also* "Kneller, Heidegger, and Death," by Donald Vandenberg. *Educational Theory,* vol. 17, April 1967, 176-177; and "Heidegger, Kneller, and Vandenberg," by Anthony De Soto. *Educational Theory,* vol. 16, July 1966, 239-241.

3356 Knittermeyer, H. "Philosophie als Ontologie. Zu Martin Heideggers 'Sein und Zeit'." *Christliche Welt* (Gotha), vol. 44, 1930, 669-675, 720-725.

3357 Knittermeyer, H. Rev. of *Sein und Zeit,* by Martin Heidegger. Halle, 1927. *Theologische Literaturzeitung* (Leipzig), vol. 53, 1928, 481-493.

3358 Knittermeyer, H. Rev. of *Vom Wesen des Grundes,* by Martin Heidegger. Halle, 1929. *Theologische Literaturzeitung* (Leipzig), vol. 56, 1931, 279-284.

3359 Knittermeyer, H. "Der 'Übergang' zur Philosophie der Gegenwart." *Zeitschrift für Philosophische Forschung,* vol. 1, 1946, 266-540.

3360 Kobayashi, Eizaburô. R. M. Riruke to M. Haideggâ no Hikaku Kenkyû no tameno Kiso-Hôhôron" (An Elementary Method for Comparative Research on R. M. Rilke and Martin Heidegger). *Doitsu Bungaku* (Tôkyô), vol. 47, October 1971, 74-86.

3361 Kobayashi, Genkyô. "Haideggâ no Geijutsu-Ron" (Heidegger's Discussion of Art). *Jitsuzon* (Tôkyô), Mai 1955.

3362 Kobayashi, Toshihiro. "Haideggâ no 'Sonzai'" (Heidegger's 'Being'). *Tetsugaku* (Tôkyô), vol. 3, no. 4, 1954, 53-54.

3363 Kobayashi, Yasumasa. "Watsuji Tetsurô no Ningen no Gainen to M. Haideggâ no Gensonzai (Dasein) no Bunseki tono Hikakuteki-Kôsatsu" (A Comparative Contemplation of Watsujis Notion of "Man" and Heidegger's "There-Being"). *Daitô Bunka Daigaku Kiyô* (Tôkyô), vol. 2, 1967, 71-94.

3364 Kobayashi, Yasumasa. "Gengo to Kyôkô-Sonai - Haideggâ ni sokushite" (Language and With-Being - According to Heidegger). *Jitsuzonshugi* (Tôkyô), vol. 50, 1969, 22-30.

3365 Kockelmans, A. *Martin Heidegger. Een inleiding in zijn denken.* (Denkers over God en wereld, 4). 's-Gravenhage, 1962, 158 p.

3366 Kockelmans, Joseph J. *Martin Heidegger. A First Introduction to His Philosophy.* Pittsburgh, Pennsylvania, Duquesne Univ. Press/Louvain, 1965, VIII-182.

3367 Kockelmans, Joseph J. "Thanks-Giving: The Completion of Thought." *Heidegger and the Quest for Truth.* Ed. M. S. Frings. Chicago, 1968, 163-183.

3368 Kockelmans, Joseph J. "Einleitung und Kommentar." In *Wat is dat - Filosofie?* by Martin Heidegger. Tielt/Utrecht, 1970.

3369 Kockelmans, Joseph J. "Heidegger on the Essential Difference and Necessary Relationship Between Philosophy and Science." *Phenomenology and the Natural Sciences.* Ed. T. Kisiel and J. J. Kockelmans. Evanston, Illinois, 1970, 147-166.

3370 Kockelmans, Joseph J. Heidegger on Time and Being." *The Southern Journal of Philosophy* (Memphis), vol. 8, 1970, 319-340.

3371 Kockelmans, Joseph J. "Language, Meaning and Ek-Sistence." In *Phenomenology in Perspective,* by F. J. Smith (ed.). The Hague: Nijhoff, 1970. Rpt. in *On Heidegger and Language.* Ed. J. Kockelmans. Evanston, Illinois, 1972, 3-32.

3372 Kockelmans, Joseph J. "Ontological Difference, Hermeneutics, and Language." *On Heidegger and Language.* Ed. J. J. Kockelmans. Evanston, Illinois, 1972, 195-234.

3373 Kockelmans, Joseph J. "Heidegger on Time and Being." In *Martin Heidegger: In Europe and America,* by Edward Goodwin Ballard and Charles E. Scott. The Hague, 1973, 55-76.

3374 Kockelmans, Joseph J. "Heidegger on Theology." *The Southwestern Journal of Philosophy* (Norman), vol. 4, no. 3, 1973, 85-108. [Heidegger issue]

3375 Kockelmans, Joseph J. "Toward an Interpretative or Hermeneutic Social Science." *Graduate Faculty Philosophy Journal* (New York), vol. 5, 1975, 73-96.

3376 Kockelmans, Joseph J. "Destructive Retrieve and Hermeneutic Phenomenology in 'Being and Time'." *Research in Phenomenology* (Pittsburgh), vol. 7, 1977, 106-137.

3377 Kockelmans, Joseph J. "Daseinsanalysis and Freud's Unconscious." *Review of Existential Psychology & Psychiatry* (Northwestern Univ., Evanston, Illinois), vol. 16, no. 1, 2, and 3, 1978/79.

3378 Kockelmans, Joseph J. "Heidegger on the Self and on Kant's Conception of the Ego." In *Heidegger's Existential Analytic,* by Frederick Elliston (ed.). The Hague, New York: Mouton Pub., 1978, 133-156.

3379 Kockelmans, Joseph J. "Alcune riflessioni sulla concezione della terra in Heidegger." *Humanitas* (Brescia), vol. 33, no. 4, 1978, 445-468.

3380 Köchler, Hans. "Das Gottesproblem im Denken Heideggers." *Zeitschrift für katholische Theologie* (Wien), vol. 95, no. 1, 1973, 61-90.

3381 Köchler, Hans. *Der innere Bezug von Anthropologie und Ontologie: das Problem der Anthropologie im Denken Martin Heidegger.* Meisenheim/Glan: Hain, 1974, 83 p.

3382 Köchler, Hans. *Skepsis und Gesellschaftskritik im Denken Martin Heideggers.* Meisenheim/Glan: Verlag Anton Hain, 1978, viii-158.

3383 Koenker, Ernest B. "The Being of the Material and the Immaterial in Heidegger's Thought." *Philosophy Today* (Celina, Ohio), vol. 24, 1980, 54-61.

3384 Koenne, W. *Das Phänomen der Technik bei Dessauer, Jaspers und Heidegger. Ein Beitrag zum gegenwärtigen Verständnis der Technik.* Phil. Diss. Wien 1965 131 p.

3385 Koepp. "Merimna und Agape. Zur Analytik des Daseins in Heideggers 'Sein und Zeit'." *Reinhold-Seeberg-Festschrift* (Leipzig), 1929, 99-139.

3386 Köster, Peter. "Das Fest des Denkens. Ein polemisches Motto Heideggers und seine ursprüngliche Bedeutung in Nietzsches Philosophie." *Nietzsche - Studien* (Berlin/New York), vol. 4, 1975, 227-262.

3387 Köster, W. Rev. of *Einführung in die Metaphysik,* by Martin Heidegger. Tübingen, 1953. *Documents* (Strassburg) (Revue mensuelle des questions allemandes), vol. 9, 1954, 589-590.

3387a Köstler, Hermann, ed. "Heidegger schreibt an Grabmann." *Philosophisches Jahrbuch* (München), vol. 87, 1980, 96-109.

3388 Kodama, Tatsudo. "Haideggâ ni okeru niko no 'Sonzaimondai' no Kankei ni tsuite" (On the Relation of the Two "Problems of Being" in Heidegger). *Tetsugakuzasshi* (Tôkyô März), vol. 505, 1929.

3389 Kogan, J. "Filosofia y poesia en Heidegger y Hegel." *Cuadernos americanos* (Mexico), vol. 26, 1967, 106-132.

3390 Kogan, J. *Arte y metafísica.* Buenos Aires, 1971, 237 p.

3391 Kogawa, Tetsuo. "Shinjôteki Haideggârian no Otoshiana" (The Trap of the Sentimental Heideggerians; Heidegger's Participation in Nazism and the Problematical Points of its Apology). *Kokkaron Kenkyû* (Tôkyâ, vol. 10, 1976, 8-24.

3392 Koike, Minoru. *Haideggâ ni okeru Sonzai no Shii ni tsuite* (On the Thinking of Being in Heidegger). Bunka, Sendai, 1960.

3393 Kojima, Hiroshi. "Bûbâ to Haideggâ; Karera no Ningenkan e no Tebiki" (Buber and Heidegger - Their Conception of "Mankind"). *Iryô to Fukushi* (Tôkyô), vol. 15, 1965, 40-45.

3394 Kojima, Takehiko. "Orutega Maruseru Haideggâ" (Ortega Marcel Heidegger). *Risô* (Tôkyô), vol. 273, 1956, 58-65.

3395 Komija, Takehiko and M. Heidegger. "Briefwechsel mit einem japanischen Kollegen [Brief von T. Kojima an M. Heidegger, Tokio 5. Juli 1963]." *Begegnung.* Zeitschrift für Literatur, bildende Kunst, Musik und Wissenschaft, Nr. 4, Amriswil o.J. 1963, 2-7.

3396 Kolakowski, L. "Filozofia egzystencji i porazka egzystencji" (Existential Philosophy and the Defeat of Existence). *Filozofia egzystencjalna.* Ed. L. Kolakowski and K. Pomian. Warszawa, 1965.

3397 Kolleritsch, A. *Eigentlichkeit und Uneigentlichkeit in der Philosophie Martin Heideggers.* Phil. Diss. Graz 1965.

3398 Kolumban, O. M. *The Ontological Basis of Realism and Symbolism in Art.* Phil. Diss. The Pennsylvania State Univ. Univ. Park 1965 185 p.

3399 Komatsu, Setsurô. "Haideggâ no Rekishikan" (Heidegger's Conception of History). *Risô* (Tôkyô März), 1935.

3400 Komatsu, Setsurô. "Haideggâ Zakkô" (Something on Heidegger). *Tetsugaku-Zasshi* (Tôkyô), vol. 607, 1937, 48-55.

3401 Komatsu, Setsurô. "Haideggâ Hihan" (Critical Remarks on Heidegger). *Riron* (Tôkyô), vol. I, no. 6, 1947, 48-58.

3402 Kommerell, M. *Briefe und Aufzeichnungen 1919-1944.* Aus dem Nachlass herausgegeben von I. Jens. Olten/Freiburg, 1967. [Max Kommerell an Martin Heidegger am 29.1941 und 29.7.1942, 384-385, 396-402.]

3403 Kondô, Isao. *Haideggâ no Kanto-Kaishaku to sono Mondaiten* (A Questionable Aspect in Heidegger's Kant-Interpretation). Aichigakugeidaigaku-Kenkyûhôkoku, Nagoya, 1962.

3404 Kondô, Isao. "Kanto to Haideggâ" (Kant and Heidegger). *Rinrigaku Nenpô* (Tôkyô), vol. 25, 1976, 73-86.

3405 Kondô, Shigeaki. "Ryôkai ni tsuite" (On Understanding). *Tetsugakuronsô* (Tôkyô), Januar 1964.

3406 Kondô, Shigeaki. "Kôsôryoku ni tsuite - Koringuuddo to Haideggâ no Baai" (On Imagination - Collingwood and Heidegger). *Ehime Daigaku Kyôiku Gakubu Kiyô* (Matsuyama), vol. 1, 1968, 29-41.

3407    Kôno, Yoichi. "Haideggâ, Saikin no Geijutsuron" (Heidegger: His Recent Discussion of Art). *Sekai* (Tôkyô), vol. 55, Juli 1950.

3408    Koort, A. *Kaasaegset filosoofiat I.* (Tartu 1938). (Estinic).

[Nietzsche, Bergson, Dilthey, Scheler, Jaspers, Heidegger, Brunschvicq, Meyerson, Alexander, Whitehead.]

3409    Korn, Ernst R. "La question de l'être chez Martin Heidegger, I (Réflexions sur la pensée heideggérienne à partir de 'Qu'est-ce que la métaphysique')." *Revue Thomiste* (Toulouse), vol. 70, 1970, 227-263.

3410    Korn, Ernest R. "La question de l'être chez Martin Heidegger, II." *Revue Thomiste* (Toulouse), vol. 70, 1970, 560-603.

3411    Korn, Ernest R. "La question de l'être chez Martin Heidegger, III. Observations critiques concernant l'entreprise de Heidegger." *Revue Thomiste* (Toulouse), vol. 71, 1971, 33-58.

3412    Korn, Ernest R. "Le sacré dans l'oeuvre de Martin Heidegger." *Nova et Vetera* (Fribourg/Schweiz), vol. 1, 1970, 36-57.

3413    Korn, K. "Warum schweigt Heidegger? Antwort auf den Versuch einer Polemik." *Frankfurter Allgemeine Zeitung,* v.14.8.1953.

3414    Kortmulder, R. J. Rev. of *Kant und das Problem der Metaphysik,* by Martin Heidegger. Bonn, 1927. *Algemeen Nederlands Tijdschrift voor Wijsbegeerte en Psychologie* (Amsterdam/Assen), 1930, 149-157.

3415    Kos, J. "Heidegger in Slovenci." *Sodobnost* (Ljubljana), vol. 16, 1968, 1082-1103.

3416    Kôsaka, Masaaki. *Jitsuzontetsugaku* (Existential Philosophy). Tôkyô, 1948, 36-59.

3417    Kôsaka, Masaaki. *Kierukegooru kata Sarutoru e* (From Kierkegaard to Sartre). Tôkyô, 1949, 152-208.

3418    Kôsaka, Masaaki. "Haideggâ to Herudârin" (Heidegger and Hölderlin). *Shi to Tetsugaku* (Tôkyô), Februar 1952, 1-49.

3419    Kôsaka, Masaaki. *Haideggâ wa Nihirisuto ka* (Is Heidegger a Nihilist?) Tôkyô, 1953.

3420    Kôsaka, Masaaki. "Haideggâ no 'Kikyô', Saikin no Haideggâ no Keikô to Nishida-Tetsugaku" (Heidegger's "Home-Coming." Heidegger's Final Tendency and the Philosophy of Nishidea). *Kokoro* (Tôkyô), April 1953.

3421    Kôsaka, Masaaki. "Haideggâ no 'No no Michi'" (Heideggers 'Feldweg'). *Kokoro* (Tôkyô), VIII-1, 1955, 19-26.

3422    Kosik, K. *Dialektika konkrétniho.* Studie o problematice cloveka a sveta. Praha, 1963, 191 p. 3rd ed. 1966.

3423    Kottji, F. *Illusionen der Wissenschaft.* Eine notwendige Selbstbesinnung zur heutigen Kulturkrisis. Stuttgart/Berlin, 1931, 83-92.

3424    Kouropoulos, P. "Remarques sur le temps de l'homme selon Heidegger et Husserl." *Centre d'Etudes et de Recherches marxistes* (Paris), 1967, 1-33.

3425 Koutra, D. "Proeleusis kai ousia tou kollitechnématos kata Martin Heidegger." *Platon. Hetaireia Hellenon Philoloyon* (Athenai), vol. 21, no. 41-42, 1969, 93-102.

3426 Kouzuma, Tadashi. "Haideggâ Sensei no Gosêkyo o itamu" (The Condolence to Prof. Heidegger). *Jitsuzon Shugi* (Tôkyô), vol. 76, 1976, 106-109.

3427 Kouzuma, Tadashi. "Mu, Sonzai no Hirake, Shiichinarumono; Heideggâ no Sekaigainen" (Non-Being, the Open of Being, and Quadrate; Heidegger's Concept of the World). *Gendai-Shisô* (Tôkyô), vol. III, no. 10, 1974, 148-165.

3428 Kouzuma, Tadashi. "Haideggâ to doitsu Shinpishugi" (Heidegger and German Mysticism). *Jitsuzonshugi* (Tôkyô), vol. 69, 1974, 112-129.

3429 Kouzuma, Tadashi. "Haideggâ Tetsugaku to Ningengaku" (Heidegger's Philosophy and Anthropology). *Jitsuzonshugi* (Tôkyô), vol. 77, 1976, 9-30.

3430 Kozuma, Tadashi. "Haideggâ - Konkyo no Meidai" (Heidegger 'Der Satz vom Grund'). *Jitsuzon* (Tôkyô), vol. 11, 1957, 40-49.

3431 Kozuma, Tadashi. "Haideggâ Tetsugaku no Eikyô ni tsuite" (On the Position of Heidegger's Philosophy). *Jitsuzonshugi* (Tôkyô), vol. 35, 1966, 94-111.

3432 Kozuma, Tadashi. "Keijijôgaku to Kindai no Unmei - Heideggâ no Kindai Keijijôgaku Hihan o megutte" (Metaphysics and the Destiny of Modern Times - Heidegger's Criticism of Modern Metaphysics). *Seikei Daigaku Bungakubu Kiyô* (Tôkyô), vol. 1, 1966, 64-84.

3433 Kozuma, Tadashi. "Haideggâ" (Heidegger). *Jitsuzonshugi-Kôza* (Risôsha-Verlag, Tôkyô), 1968, 188-209.

3434 Kozuma, Tadashi. "Haideggâ Bunden" (Heidegger Bibliography). *Risô* (Tôkyô), vol. 444, 1970, 119-128.

3435 Kozuma, Tadashi. "Haideggâ to Hêgeru; Jikanron o Chûshin nishite" (Heidegger and Hegel; on the Problem of Time). *Risô* (Tôkyô), vol. 542, 1978, 172-190.

3436 Kozuma, Tadashi. "Haideggâ Bunken Moduroku" (Heidegger Bibliography). *Risô* (Tôkyô), vol. 542, 1978, 255-316.

3437 Kozuma, Tadashi. "Haideggâ Nenpu" (Heidegger's Chronological Record). *Risô* (Tôkyô), vol. 542, 1978, 317-329.

3438 Koyré, A. Rev. of *Was ist Metaphysik?*, by Martin Heidegger. Boon, 1929. *La Nouvelle Revue Française* (Paris), vol. 19, 1931, 750-753.

3439 Koyré, A. "L'évolution philosophique de Heidegger." *Critique* (Paris), vol. 1, 1946, 73-82, 161-183.

3440 Koyré, A. "'Vom Wesen der Wahrheit' par Martin Heidegger (1943)." *Fontaine* (Paris), vol. 52, 1946, 842-844.

3441 Koza, I. *Das Problem des Grundes in Heideggers Auseinandersetzung mit Kant.* Ratingen b. Düsseldorf, 1967, 147 p.

3442 Kozlowski, M. "Szkic pytania o Heideggera" (The Question Concerning Heidegger. An Outline). *Czlowiek i swiatopoglad,* 3 February 1979.

3443     Kraenzlin, G. *Max Schelers Phänomenologische Systematik.* Leipzig, 1934, 75-80.

3444     Kraenzlin, G. *Existenzphilosophie und Panhumanismus.* Schlehdorf am Kochelsee, 1950, 78-111.

3445     Kraft, Julius. *Von Husserl zu Heidegger. Kritik der phänomenologischen Philosophie.* Leipzig, 1932, 124 p. 2nd ed. Frankfurt, 1957, 148 p., (specifically pages 83-104).

3446     Kraft, Julius. "Philosophy of Existence." *Philosophy and Phenomenological Research* (Buffalo, New York), vol. I, 1940/41, 339-358.

3447     Kraft, Julius. "In Reply to Kaufmann's Critical Remarks About My 'Philosophy of Existence'." *Philosophy and Phenomenological Research* (Buffalo, New York), vol. 1, 1940/41, 364-365.

3448     Kraft, Julius. *Von Husserl zu Heidegger. Kritik der phänomenologischen Philosohie.* 2nd ed. Frankfurt, 1957, 148 p. 1st ed. 1932. 3rd ed. 1977, 151 p.

3449     Krajewski, V. *Heidegger und Portmann, Denker in 'dürftiger' Zeit.* Phil. Diss. Wien 1969 108 p.

3450     *Kratkij ocerk istorii filosofii* (The Outlines of the History of Philosophy). (Vtoroe perepecatannoe izdanie, Izdatel'stvo 'Mysl'). Moskva, 1967, 731-739.

3451     Kraus, F. "Denken und Dichten. Heidegger und seine Kritiker." *Neue literarische Welt* (Darmstadt), Jg. 4, Nr. 18, 25.9.1953, 3-4.

3452     Kraus, F. "Das Rätsel des Seins." Rev. of *Einführung in die Metaphysik,* by Martin Heidegger. *Badische Zeitung* (Freiburg), 21.9.1954.

3453     Kraus, F. "Die Wacht am Sein. Zu neuen Veröffentlichungen Martin Heideggers." Rev. of these Martin Heidegger works in *Badische Zeitung,* no. 133, 13.6.1955:

         ["Was heisst Denken?" 1954.]

         ["Aus der Erfahrung des Denkens." 1954.]

         ["Vorträge und Aufsätze." 1954.]

3454     Krebs, K. H. *Der strittige Rang des Seins: Eine Untersuchung des Heiligen in der Spätphilosophie Martin Heideggers.* Phil. Diss. Mainz 1970 161 p. [1971 erschienen]

3455     Krebs, K. H. Rev. of "Heraklit. Seminar Wintersemester 1966/1967," by Martin Heidegger and E. Fink. *Philosophy and History* (Tübingen), vol. 6, 1973, 23-25.

3456     Kreeft, Peter. "Zen in Heidegger's Gelassenheit." *International Philosophical Quarterly* (New York/Heverlee-Louvain), vol. 11, 1971, 521-545.

3457     Krell, David Farrell. *Nietzsche and the Task of Thinking: Martin Heidegger's Reading of Nietzsche.* Phil. Diss. Duquesne Univ. Pittsburgh 1971 390 p. *Dissertation Abstracts International,* vol. 32/09-A, 5288.

3458 Krell, David Farrell. Rev. of "Heraklit," by Martin Heidegger and E. Fink. *Research in Phenomenology* (Pittsburgh), vol. 1, 1971, 137-146.

3459 Krell, David Farrell. "The Heraclitus Seminar." *Research in Phenomenology* (Pittsburgh), vol. 1, 1971, 137-146.

3460 Krell, David Farrell. "Towards and Ontology of the Play." *Research in Phenomenology* (Pittsburgh), vol. 2, 1972, 63-93.

3461 Krell, David Farrell. "Heidegger and Zarathustra." *Philosophy Today* (Celina, Ohio), vol. 18, no. 4, 1974, 306-311.

3462 Krell, David Farrell. "Toward 'Sein und Zeit'. Heidegger's Early Review (1919-1921) of Jasper's 'Psychologie der Weltanschauungen'." *The Journal of the British Society for Phenomenology* (Manchester), vol. 6, no. 3, 1975, 147-156.

3463 Krell, David Farrell. "On the Manifold Meaning of 'Aletheia': Brentano, Aristotle, Heidegger." *Research in Phenomenology* (Pittsburgh), vol. 5, 1975, 77-94.

3464 Krell, David Farrell. "Nietzsche in Heidegger's 'Kehre'." *The Southern Journal of Philosophy* (Memphis), vol. 13, no. 2, 1975, 197-204.

3465 Krell, David Farrell. "Heidegger, Nietzsche, Hegel." *Nietzsche-Studien* (Berlin/New York), vol. 5, 1976, 255-262.

3466 Krell, David Farrell. "Being and Truth, Being and Time." *Research in Phenomenology* (Pittsburgh), vol. 6, 1976, 151-166.

3467 Krell, David Farrell. Rev. of "Logik. Die Frage nach der Wahrheit," by Martin Heidegger. Frankfurt: V. Klostermann, 1976, vii-418. *Research in Phenomenology* (Pittsburgh), vol. 6, 1976, 151-166.

3468 Krell, David Farrell. "Art and Truth in Raging Discord: Heidegger and Nietzsche on Will to Power as Art." *Boundary 2: A Journal of Postmodern Literature,* Winter, vol. IV, no. 2, 1976, 378-392.

3468a Krell, David Farrell. "The Question of Being." In *Martin Heidegger: Basic Writings.* Ed. D. F. Krell. New York: Harper & Row, 1976, 1-35.

3469 Krell, David Farrell. "Schlag der Liebe, Schlag des Todes: On a Theme in Heidegger and Trakl." *Research in Pehnomenology* (Pittsburgh), vol. 7, 1977, 238-258. Rpt. in *Radical Phenomenology.* Ed. J. Sallis. Atlantic Highlands, New Jersey: Humanities Press, 1978, 238-258.

3470 Krell, David Farrell. "Martin Heidegger, 1889-1976." *Journal of the British Society for Phenomenology* (Manchester), vol. 8, no. 1, 1977.

3471 Krell, David Farrell, ed. *Heidegger, Martin, Basic Writings.* From "Being and Time" (1927) to "The Task of Thinking" (1964). Ed. with general intr., and intr. to each sel. by David Farrell Krell. New York: Harper & Row, 1977, 397 p.

3472 Krell, David Farrell. "The Heidegger-Jaspers Relationship." *The Journal of the British Society for Phenomenology* (Manchester), vol. 9, no. 2, 1978, 126-129.

3473 Krell, David Farrell. "Death and Interpretation." In *Heidegger's Existential Analytic*, by Frederick Elliston (ed.). The Hague, New York: Mouton Pub., 1978, 247-255.

3474 Krell, David Farrell. Rev. of "Heidegger: An Illustrated Study," by Walter Biemel. *Journal of the British Society for Phenomenology* (Manchester), vol. 9, no. 3, 1978.

3475 Krell, David Farrell. "*Die Lichtung* in Transition." A lecture presented to the *Collegium Phaenomenologicum* at Perugia, Italy, 16 August 1978, (to be published in the *Proceedings*).

3476 Krell, David Farrell. "Hegel Heidegger Heraclitus." In *Heraclitean Fragments*, by John Sallis and Kenneth Maly (eds.). Univ. of Alabama Press, 1980, 22-42.

3477 Krell, David Farrell. "Art and Truth in Raging Discord. Heidegger and Nietzsche on the Will to Power." In *Martin Heidegger and the Question of Literature*. Ed. by William V. Spanos. Bloomington, Indiana/London: Indiana Univ. Press, 1979, 39-52.

3478 Krieck, E. "Germanischer Mythos und Heideggersche Philosophie." *Volk im Werden*. Ed. Ernst Krieck. Leipzig, vol. 2, 1934, 247-249. Rpt. in *Nachlese zu Heidegger*, by G. Schneeberger. Bern, 1962, 225-228.

3479 Krings, H. "Ursprung und Ziel der Philosophie der Existenz." *Philosophisches Jahrbuch* (Fulda), vol. 61, 1951, 433-445.

3480 *Krizis burzuaznoj filosofii v sovremennuju epochu* (The Present Crisis of Bourgeois Philosophy). *Istorija filosofii*, tom V, kniga 2, glava sed'maja. Moskva, 1965, II-14, 14-18, 21-25.

3481 *Krizis sovremennoj burzuaznoj sociologii estetiki, etiki, idealisticeskich koncepcij filosofii istorii i istorii filosofii* (The Crisis of Contemporary Bourgeois Sociology, Esthetics, Ethics, Idealistic Conceptions of the Philosophy of History and of the History of Philosophy). *Istorija filosofii*, tom V, kniga 2, glava vos'maja. Moskva, 1965, sec 1, 126, 127; sec 3, str. 176, 177; sec 4, str. 194-197; sec 5, str. 207-211.

3482 Krockow, Ch. Graf von. *Der Dezisionismus bei Ernst Jünger, Carl Schmitt und Martin Heidegger, seine soziale Funktion und seine sozialteoretische Bedeutung.* Göttingen, 1954, XIX, 233 p.

3483 Krockow, Ch. Graf von. *Die Entscheidung. Eine Untersuchung über Ernst Jünger, Carl Schmitt, Martin Heidegger.* Stuttgart, 1958, IV, 164 p., (specifically pages 68-81, 116-128).

3484 Kroner, R. "Heideggers Privatreligion." *Eckart* (Witten/Berlin), vol. 25, 1955, 30-41.

3485 Kroug, W. "Das Sein zum jode bei Heidegger und die Probleme des Könnens und der Liebe." *Zeitschrift für philosophische Forschung* (Meisenheim/Glan), vol. 7, 1953, 392-415.

3486 Krüger, G. "Sein und Zeit, zu Martin Heideggers gleichnamigem Buch." *Theologische Blätter* (Kartellzeitung) (Leipzig), vol. 39, no. 8, 1929, 57-64.

3487    Krüger, G. "Christlicher Glaube und Existentielles Denken." In *Festschrift Rudolf Bultmann.* Stuttgart, 1949. Rpt. in *Freiheit und Weltverwaltung,* by G. Krüger. München, 1958, 183-212.

3488    Krüber, G. "M. Heidegger und der Humanismus. Zur Auseinandersetzung mit den Schriften 'Platons Lehre von der Wahrheit' und 'Brief über den Humanismus'." *Studia philosophica* (Basel), vol. 9, 1949, 93-129. Rpt. in *Theologische Rundschau* (Tübingen), vol. 18, 1950, 148-178.

3489    Krüber, G. "Über Kants Lehre von der Zeit." In *Anteile, Martin Heidegger zum 60. Geburtstag.* Frankfurt, 1950, 178-211.

3490    Krüger, G. *Grundfragen der Philosophie.* Frankfurt, 1958, XII, 288 p., (specifically page 209 ff). 2nd ed. 1965.

3491    Krüger, G. "Heideggers Denken." *Frankfurter Rundschau* 11.10.1969. Leserzuschrift.

3492    Krzeczkowski, H. "Wina, kara, skrucha. Werner Heisenberg i Martin Heidegger w hitlerowskiej Rzeszy" (Guilt, Punishment, Repentance. Werner Heisenberg and Martin Heidegger During the Third Reich). *Tygodnik Powszechny,* vol. 40, 1974.

3493    Krzem. "Sad ostateczny" (The Final Judgement). *Polityka,* vol. 25, 1976.

3494    Kudrna, J. "K nekterám otázkam pojeti znaku u Diltheye, Freyera a Heideggera" (On Some Questions Concerning the Concept of the Symbol in Dilthey, Freyer and Heidegger). *Filosoficky casopis* (Prag), vol. 12, 1964, 640-656.

3495    Kudszus, H. Rev. of *Einführung in die Metaphysik,* by Martin Heidegger. Tübingen, 1953. *Die Neue Zeitung* (Berlin/Dahlem), 11.10.1953.

3496    Kudszus, H. "Spricht das 'Sein' wirklich deutsch? Martin Heidegger und Romano Guardini vor der Akademie der Künste." *Der Tagesspiegel,* 31.1.1959.

3497    Kuehn, Reinhold. *Hinweise auf die ontologische Differenz bei Martin Heidegger.* Phil. Diss. Tübingen 1974.

3498    Küng, H. *Menschwerdung Gottes. Eine Einführung in Hegels theologisches Denken als Prolegomena zu einer künftigen Christologie.* Freiburg/Basel/Wien, 1970, 704 p.

3499    Kuhlmann, G. *Die Theologie am Scheidewege.* Tübingen, 1935, passim.

3500    Kuhlmann, J. "Zum theologischen Problem der Existenz. Fragen an R. Bultmann." *Zeitschrift für Theologie und Kirche* (Tübingen), vol. 10, 1929, 27-57. Rpt. in *Heidegger und die Theologie. Beginn und Fortgang der Diskussion.* Ed. G. Noller. München, 1967.

3501    Kuhn, A. *Das Wertproblem in den Frühwerken Martin Heideggers und 'Sein und Zeit'.* München, 1968, II, 139 p. [Phil. Diss. 22.10.1968.]

3502    Kuhn, Helmut. *Encounter With Nothingness.* An essay on existentialism. Chicago, Illinois, 1949, passim.

3503 Kuhn, Helmut. *Begegnung mit dem Nichts.* Ein Versuch über die Existenzphilosophie. Tübingen, 1950, 173 p.

3504 Kuhn, Helmut. "Heideggers 'Holzwege'." *Archiv für Philosophie* (Stuttgart), vol. 4, 1952, 253-269.

3505 Kuhn, Helmut. "Philosophie in Sprachnot." Rev. of *Einführung in die Metaphysik,* by Martin Heidegger. Tübingen, 1953. *Merkur* (Stuttgart), vol. 7, 1953, 935-949.

3506 Kuhn, Helmut. *Begegnung mit dem Sein. Meditationen zur Metaphysik des Gewissens.* Tübingen, 1954, 225 p.

3507 Kuhn, Helmut. *Das Sein und das Gute.* München, 1962, 438 p., passim.

3508 Kuhr, A. "Neurotische Aspekte bei Heidegger und Kafka." *Zeitschrift für psychosomatische Medizin* (Göttingen), vol. 1, 1954/55, 217-227.

3509 Kuiper, M. V. "Aspetti dell'esistenzialismo." *Acta Pont. Academiae Romanae S. Thomae Aq. et Religionis Catholica* (Romae), vol. 9, 1944, 99-123, (specifically pages 103-116).

3510 Kuki, Shûzô. "Haideggâ no Tetsugaku" (Heidegger's Philosophy). *Iwanami-Kôza 'Tetsugaku'.* Tôkyô, 1933.

3511 Kuki, Shûzô. *Ningen to Jitsuzon* (Man and Existence). Tôkyô, 1939, 217-299.

3512 Kundaseva, D. "Kritika osnovnych polozenii teorii novogo gumanizma" (The Criticism of the Principles of the Theory of the "New Humanism"). *Avtoreferat dissertacii na soiskanie ucënoj stepeni kandidata filosofskich nauk.* Frunze, 1969.

3513 Kûnjun, Yu. *Haidegkawa yesuljakp'umûi kiwôn* (Heidegger and the Origin of the Work of Art). M. A. Thesis, Sôul Univ., 1960.

3514 Kuno, Akira. "Kaminakijidai no Shinpi Shisô" (The Mysticism in the Time Without God). *Risô* (Tôkyô), vol. 466, 1972, 60-69.

3515 Kuno, Akira. "Haideggâ ni totte Shisaku towa nan de attaka?" (What was the Thinking for Heidegger?) *Jitsuzonshugi* (Tôkyô), vol. 77, 1976, 90-92.

3516 Kuno, Akira. "Kami naki Jidai no Shinpi-Shisô" (Mysticism in the Age Without God). In *Nansôsha.* Tôkyô, 1976, 170 p.

3517 Kunz, Hans. "Die Bedeutung der Daseinsanalytik Martin Heideggers für die Psychologie und die philosophische Anthropologie." In *Martin Heideggers Einfluss auf die Wissenschaften.* Bern, 1949, 37-57.

3518 Kunz, Hans. Rev. of *Die Frage nach dem Ding. Zu Kants Lehre von den transzendentalen Grundsätzen,* by Martin Heidegger. Tübingen, 1962. *Studia Philosophica* (Basel), vol. 23, 1963, 236-237.

3519 Kunz, Hans. *Martin Heidegger und Ludwig Klages. Daseinsanalytik und Metaphysik.* München: Kindler, 1976, 96 p.

3520 Kunze, Robert W. *The Origin of the Self: A Presentation of the Philosophy of Levinas From the Standpoint of His Criticism of Heidegger.* Phil. Diss. Pennsylvania State Univ. 1974. *Dissertation Abstracts International,* vol. 35/11-A, 7350.

3521    Kurisu, Teruo. "Haideggâ no "Kotaba" ni tsuite" (On Heidegger's Conception of the Language; From Sign to Language). *Tetsugaku* (Hiroshima Daigaku Tetsugakukai) (Hiroshima), vol. 24, 1972, 57-70.

3522    Kûrisûdogyo ch'ôrhak yônguso, ed. *Haidegkaûi ch'ôrhak sasang* (Philosophical Thinking in Heidegger). (5 treatises). Sôul, 1978.

3523    Kurita, Kenzui. "Haideggâ no Kyôcô-Gensonzai 'Mitdasein' ni tsuite" (On the Meaning of the 'There-Being-With-Others' in Heidegger). *Mie Daigaku Gakugeibu Kenkyû Kiyô* (Tsu), vol. 19, 1958, 1-10.

3524    Kuschbert-Tölle, Helga. *Das Verhältnis von Denken und Sein bei Heidegger.* Phil. Diss. Tübingen 1961 IV und 163 p.

3525    Kuschbert-Tölle, Helga. "Heideggers Ansatz beim griechischen Seinsverständnis als Grundstruktur seines Denkens." *Philosophisches Jahrbuch* (München), vol. 70, 1962/63, 138-146.

3526    Kuschbert-Tölle, Helga. *Heidegger - der letzte Metaphysiker?* (Monographien zur philosophischen Forschung Band 180). Königstein: Hain, 1979, 150 p.

3527    Kuwaki, Tsutomu. "Haideggâ" (Heidegger). *Risô* (Tôkyô), vol. 200, Januar 1950.

3528    Kuwaki, Tsutomu. "Sein und Zeit o kiru" (Cutting the Leaves of "Being and Time"). *Shomotsu* (Tôkyô), vol. 2, Juni 1950.

3529    Kuwaki, Tsutomu. "Haideggâ Kenkyû no tameni" (On the Understanding of Heidegger). *Risô* (Tôkyô), vol. 223, 1951, 62-67.

3530    Kuwaki, Tsutomu. "'Sonzai to Jikan' ni tsuite" (On "Being and Time"). *Risô* (Tôkyô), vol. 223, Dezember 1951.

3531    Kuwaki, Tsutomu. "Sekai-zô yori Ningen-zô e" (From the World-As-Picture to the Picture of Mankind). *Risô* (Tôkyô), vol. 305, 1958, 63-66.

3532    Kuwaki, Tsutomu. "Chosaku Bunken Kaisetsu" (Introduction to the Writings of Heidegger). *Risô* (Tôkyô), vol. 305, 1958, 99-116.

3533    Kuwaki, Tsutomu. "Syuwarutsuwarudo no Sankakuten" (Triangular Points in Schwalzwald). *Jitsuzonshugi* (Tôkyô), vol. 77, 1976, 138-141.

3534    Kuwaki, Tsutomu. "Haideggâ Tetsugaku no Isan" (The Legacy From Heidegger's Philosophy). *Chûô-Hyôron* (Tôkyô), vol. 137, 1976, 111-118.

3535    Kuypers, K. "Heidegger en het griekse denken." *Algemeen Nederlands Tijdschrift voor Wijsbegeerte en Psychologie* (Assen), vol. 47, 1954/55, 34-44.

3536    Kuypers, K. "Fenomenologie en Kantianisme." *Algemeen Nederlands Tijdschrift voor Wijsbegeerte en Psychologie* (Assen), vol. 55, 1963, 225-239.

3537    Kuypers, K. "Heidegger en het Griekse denken." *K. Kuypers, Verspreide geschriften, Teil II: Wetenschap en kunde* (Assen), 1968, 289-301.

3538    Kuznecov, V. N. *Francuzskaja burzuaznaja filosofija XX veka* (French Bourgeois Philosophy of the 20th Century). (Izdatel'stvo *Mysl*). Moskva, 1970. (On Heidegger, pages: 184, 210, 228, 230, 246, 248, 255, 290, 297).

3539    Kwanghûi, So. *Haidegkai issôsôûi chonjaewa sayu* (Being and Thinking in Heidegger). M. A. Thesis, Sôul Univ., 1961.

3540    Kwanghûi, So. "Haidegkaui segye kaenyom" (The Notion of World in Heidegger). *Collection of Essays for Humanities and Social Sciences by Seoul Uni.* (Sôul), vol. 15, 1969, 83-112.

3541    Kwanghûi, So. "Haidegka ch'ôrhakûi hyôngsônggwajông I" (The Development of Heidegger's Philosophy). *Ch'ôrhak Yôngu* (Sôul), vol. 4, 1969, 79-94.

3542    Kyôngok, Ch'oe. "Muû munje - Haidegkae issôsôûi" (The Problem of Non-Being in Heidegger). M. A. Thesis, Sôul Univ., 1975.

3543    Kyôngyun, Kim. "Haidegkaûi siljongwa chonjae" (Existence and Being in Heidegger). M. A. Thesis, Yônse Univ., 1963.

3544    Kyuch'ôl, Cho. *Haidegkae issôsôûi chilliûi chonjaeronjôk ûimi* (Ontological Meaning of Truth in Heidegger). M. A. Thesis, Yônse Univ., 1970.

3545    L. S. Rev. of *Nietzsche, Bd I-II,* by Martin Heidegger. *Studi Urbinati di Storia, Filosofia e Letteratura* (Urbino), vol. 37, 1963, 146-148.

3546    Ladmiral, Jean-René. "Adorno contra Heidegger." *Revue d'Esthétique* (Paris), no. 1, 1975, 207-233.

3547    Ladmiral, Jean-René. "Lecture de Heidegger." *Allemagne d'Aujourd'hui* (Herblay), no. 49, 1975, 98-111.

3548    Ladmiral, Jean-René. "Après Heidegger, avec Heidegger." *Allemagne d'Aujourd'hui* (Herblay), no. 54, 1976, 101-108.

3549    Ladrière, J. "La philosophie de Martin Heidegger." *Essais et études universitaires,* vol. 1, 1945, 134-135.

3550    Ladrille, G. Rev. of "Phénoménologie et vérité. Essai sur l'évolution de l'idée de vérité chez Husserl et Heidegger," by A. De Waelhens. Paris, 1953. *Salesianum* (Torino), vol. 17, 179-182.

3551    Läpple, A. *Der Weg des Denkens.* Donauwörth, 1965, (specifically pages 257-268).

3552    Láubin, H. "Heidegger, Hebel und die Anthroposophie." *Das Goetheanum* (Basel), vol. 35, 1956, 205-207.

3553    Laffoucrière, O. "A propos de la crise de la métaphysique." *Dieu vivant* (Paris), vol. 27, 1953, 143-147.

3554    Laffoucrière, O. *Le destin de la pensée et 'La mort de Dieu' selon Heidegger.* (Phaenomenologica, 24). Den Haag, 1968, XI und 267 p.

        [Rev. by G. Kahl-Furthmann in *Zeitschrift für Philosophische Forschung* (Schlehdorf/Kochelsee/Meisenheim/Glan), vol. 25, no. 4, 1971, 621-626.]

3554a   Laffoucrière, Odette. "Etre autrement." In *Heidegger et la question de Dieu.* Ed. R. Kearney and J. S. O'Leary. Paris: B. Grasset, 1980, 296-303.

3555    La France, Yvon. "Platonisme et pensée contemporaine." *Dialogue* (Canada), vol. 14, March 1975, 147-158.

3556    Lain Entralgo, P. "Quevedo y Heidegger." *Jerarquia* (Pamplona), vol. 3, 1938, 97-215.

3557 Lakebrink, B. *Das Wesen der theoretischen Notwendigkeit unter besonderer Berücksichtigung der kantischen und ihrer modernen Interpretation. (Natorp, Heidegger).* Phil. Diss. Bonn 1931. [Teildruck]

3558 Lakebrink, B. *Klassische Metaphysik. Eine Auseinandersetzung mit der existentialen Anthropozentrik.* Freiburg, 1967, 288 p.

3559 Lampert, Laurence. *The Views of History in Nietzsche and Heidegger.* Phil. Diss. Evanston/Chicago 1971 304 p. *Dissertation Abstracts International,* vol. 32/06-A, 3370.

3560 Lampert, Laurence. "Heidegger's Nietzsche Interpretation." *Man and World* (The Hague), vol. 7, 1974, 353-378.

3561 Lampert, Laurence. "On Heidegger and Historicism." *Philosophy and Phenomenological Research* (Buffalo, New York), vol. 34, no. 4, 586-590.

3562 Lancellotti, Marco. "Il primo Heidegger in italiano." *Il veltro. Società Dante Alghieri* (Roma), vol. 19, no. 1-2, 1975, 92-99.

3563 Landgrebe, L. *Der Weg der Phänomenologie. Das Problem einer ursprünglichen Erfahrung.* Gütersloh, 1963, 208 p. 3rd ed. 1969.

3564 Landgrebe, L. "Husserl, Heidegger, Sartre. Trois aspects de la phénomènologie." *Revue de Métaphysique et de Morale* (Paris), vol. 69, 1964, 365-380.

3565 Landgrebe, L. *Phänomenologie und Geschichte.* Darmstadt, 1968, 206 p.

3566 Landgrebe, Ludwig. "Facticity and Individuation." (In Serbocroat). Trans. Danilo Basta. In *Rani Hajdeger - Recepcija i kritika Bivstva i vremena,* by Dragan Stojanovic and Danilo Basta (eds.). (Biblioteka Zodijak). Beograd, 1979, 132-148. Rpt. of *Delo* (Beograd), vol. 23, no. 12, 1977, 8-20.

3567 Landmann, M. *Philosophische Anthropologie. Menschliche Selbstdeutung in Geschichte und Gegenwart.* Berlin, 1955, 59-62, 232-235, und passim.

3568 Landmann, M. "Heidegger und Hitler." In *Das Ende des Individuums,* by M. Landmann. Anthropologische Skizzen. Stuttgart, 1971, 66-67.

3569 Landolt, Eduard. Rev. of *Aus der Erfahrung des Denkens,* by Martin Heidegger. Pfullingen, 1954. *Teoresi* (Messina), vol. 15, 1960, 261-263.

3570 Landolt, Eduard. "L'essere e il pensare in 'Kant e il problema della metafisica' di M. Heidegger." *Teoresi, Rivista di Cultura Filosofica* (Messina), vol. 10, 1955, 71-97.

3571 Landolt, Eduard. Rev. of *Unterwegs zur Sprache,* by Martin Heidegger. *Teoresi* (Catania), vol. 16, 1961, 181-209.

3572 Landolt, Eduard. Rev. of *Gelassenheit,* by Martin Heidegger. *Teorsi* (Messina), vol. 16, 1961, 66-77.

3573 Landolt, Eduard. Rev. of *Denken und Sein. Der Weg Martin Heideggers und der Weg der Theologie,* by H. Ott. 1959. *Teoresi* (Catania), vol. 16, 1961, 284-290.

3574 Landolt, Eduard. Rev. of *Zum 70. Geburtstag. Festschrift,* by Martin Heidegger. Pfullingen, 1959. *Teoresi* (Catania), vol. 16, 1961, 282-284.

3575     Landolt, Eduard. Rev. of *Die Frage nach dem Ding,* by Martin Heidegger. *Teoresi* (Catania), vol. 19, 1964, 281-282.

3576     Landolt, Eduard. Rev. of *Die Technik und die Kehre,* by Martin Heidegger. *Teorsi* (Catania), vol. 19, 1964, 114-124.

3577     Landolt, Eduard. "A proposito del 'Was ist das - die Philosophie?' di Heidegger." *Teoresi* (Catania), vol. 20, 1965, 66-86.

3578     Landolt, Eduard. "L'essere come ritmo o poiesia nell'interpretazione heideggeriana di Hölderlin." *Siculorum Gymnasi* (Catania), vol. 20, 1967, 36-82.

3579     Landolt, Eduard. "L'80. compleanno di Martin Heidegger." *Teoresi* (Catania), vol. 25, 1970, 301-322.

3580     Landolt, Eduard. "Rassegna Heideggerianna." *Teoresi* (Catania), vol. 27, 1972, 261-280.

3581     Landolt, Eduard. "*Opus postumum,* curato dallo stesso Heidegger? Un terzo Heidegger?" *Teoresi* (Catania), vol. 30, 1975, 131-134.

3582     Landsberger, F. "Mensch, Leben, Existenz." *Die Neue Rundschau* (Berlin/Leipzig), vol. 2, 1928, 310-319.

3583     Lang, H. "Zum Verhältnis von Strukturalismus, Philosophie und Psychoanalyse, konkretisiert am Phänomen der Subjektivität." *Tijdschrift voor Filosofie* (Leuven), vol. 38, 1976, 559-573.

3584     Lang, Zane A. "Preontological Mistakes." *Kinesis. Graduate School in Philosophy* (Carbondale, Illinois), vol. 5, no. 2, 1973, 76-86.

3585     Langan, Thomas D. "Heidegger in France." *The Modern Schoolman* (St. Louis, Missouri), vol. 33, 1955/56, 114-118.

3586     Langan, Thomas D. "Is Heidegger a Nihilist?" *The Thomist* (Washington), vol. 21, 1958, 302-319.

3587     Langan, Thomas D. "Transcendence in the Philosophy of Heidegger." *New Scholasticism* (Washington), vol. 32, 1958, 45-60.

3588     Langan, Thomas D. *The Meaning of Heidegger. A Critical Study of an Existentialist Phenomenology.* New York, Columbia Univ. Press, 1959; London, 1959, 247 p.

         [Rev. by W. Cerf in *Philosophy and Phenomenological Research* (Buffalo, New York), vol. 22, 1961/62, 112-113.]

         [Rev. by Quentin Lauer in *International Philosophical Quarterly,* vol. 1, 1961, 178-182.]

3589     Langan, Thomas D. "A Note in Response to Rukavina's Comment." *New Scholasticism* (Washington), vol. 33, 1959, 358-359.

3590     Langan, Thomas D. Rev. of *Essays in Metaphysics,* by Martin Heidegger. *The New Scholasticism* (Washington), vol. 35, 1961, 537-541.

3591     Langan, Thomas D. Rev. of *Heidegger: Through Phenomenology to Thought,* by W. J. Richardson. The Hague, 1963. *Theological Studies* (Woodstock/Baltimore), vol. 25, 1964, 679-682.

3592    Langan, Thomas D. "Heidegger Beyond Hegel: A Reflexion on 'The Onto-Theo-Logical Constitution of Metaphysics'." *Filosofia* (Torino), vol. 19, 1968, 735-746.

3593    Langan, Thomas D. "The Future of Phenomenology." In *Phenomenology in Perspective.* Ed. F. J. Smith. The Hague, 1970, 1-15.

3594    Langan, Thomas D. "The Problem of the Thing." In *Heidegger and the Path of Thinking.* Ed. J. Sallis. Pittsburgh, 1970, 105-115.

3595    Langan, Thomas D. *Heidegger Beyond Hegel.* (Sguardi su la filosofia contemporanea, 106). Torino: Edizioni di Filosofia, 1970, 12 p.

3596    Langan, Thomas D. "Heidegger and the Possibility of Authentic Christianity." *Proceedings of the American Catholic Philosophical Association* (Washington), vol. 46, 1972, 101-112.

3597    Langfelder, O. E. "La idea y el topos de la analitica existencial de Martin Heidegger." *Humanitas* (Tucumán), vol. 7, 1959, 13-34.

3598    Langfur, Stephen Joseph. *Death's Second Self. A Response to Heidegger's Question of Being Through the Insights of Buber and the Findings of Freud.* Authorized facsimile of the dissertation of the Syracuse Univ. Phil. Diss. 1977. Ann Arbor, Michigan; London: University Microfilms International, 1979, iv-558 p. [HGK77-30788] *Dissertation Abstracts International,* vol. 38/08-A, 4883.

3599    Langlois, J. "Heidegger, Max Müller et le thomisme." *Sciences ecclésiastiques* (Montreal), vol. 9, 1957, 27-48.

3600    Lanteri-Laura, G. Rev. of *De l'essence de la vérité,* by Martin Heidegger. *Les Etudes Philosophiques.* Marseille, 1950, 266-267.

3601    Lapointe, François H. "A Bibliography on Martin Heidegger for the Behavioral Scientists." *Review of Existential Psychology & Psychiatry* (Northwestern Univ., Evanston, Illinois), vol. 16, no. 1, 2, and 3, 1978/79.

3601a   Lapointe, Francois H. "The Italian Response to Martin Heidegger: A Bibliographic Essay." *Sapienza* (Roma), vol. 32, 1979, 314-343.

3601b   Lapointe, Francois H. "Martin Heidegger. A Bibliographical Essay." *Zeitschrift für Philosophische Forschung* (Meisenheim, Glan), vol. 34, 1980, 624-655.

3602    Lapointe, R. Rev. of *Questions, II,* by Martin Heidegger. *Dialogue* (Montreal/Kingston), vol. 8, 1969/70, 740-744.

3603    Laporte, R. Rev. of *Approche de Hölderlin,* by Martin Heidegger. Paris, 1962. *Critique* (Paris), vol. 24, 1968, 1019-1040.

3604    Lara, Luis. "Heidegger: un ayer para la historia." *Revista de Filosofía de la Universidad de Costa Rica* (San José), vol. 14, no. 39, 1976, 195-197.

3605    Larese, Dino. *Mit Heidegger in Hauptwil.* Amriswil, 1960, 20 p.

3606    Laruelle, François. "Heidegger et Nietzsche." *Magazine Littéraire* (Paris), no. 117, 1976, 12-14.

3607 Laruelle, François. *Nietzsche contre Heidegger. Thèses pour une politique nietzschéenne.* Paris: Payot, 1977, 252 p.

3608 Latzel, E. "Bemerkungen zum Umgang mit Existenzphilosophie." *Zeitschrift für philosophische Forschung* (Meisenheim/Glan), vol. 6, 1951/52, 399-410.

3609 Lauer, Quentin. Rev. of *Wat ist Metaphysik?* by Martin Heidegger. Bonn, 1929. *Goetheaneum* (Dornach), vol. 11, 1932, 238.

3610 Lauer, Quentin. Rev. of *An Introduction to Metaphysics,* by Martin Heidegger. *Thought* (New York), vol. 35, 1960, 301-302.

3611 Lauer, Quentin. "The Meaning of Heidegger, by T. Langan." *International Philosophical Quarterly,* vol. 1, 1960, 178-182.

3612 Lauer, Quentin. Rev. of *Being and Time,* by Martin Heidegger. *Theological Studies* (Baltimore), vol. 24, 1963, 350-351.

3613 Launay, M. B. de. Rev. of *Questions, IV,* by Martin Heidegger. Paris: Gallimard, 1976. *Allemagne d'Aujourd'hui* (Herblay), no. 56, 1976, 105-109.

3614 Lavelle, L. *L'angoscia e il nulla.* (Studi sul pensiero contemporaneo). Milano, 1943.

3615 Lavelle, L. *Le moi et son destin.* Paris, 1936, 93-103.

3616 Lawler, James. "Heidegger's Theory of Metaphysics and Dialectics." *Philosophy and Phenomenological Research* (Buffalo, New York), vol. 35, 1974/75, 363-375.

3617 Lawry, Edward G. "The Work-Being of the Work of Art in Heidegger." *Man and World* (The Hague), vol. 11, 1978, 186-198.

3618 Le Buhan, D., and De Rubercy, E. "Douze questions posées à Jean Beaufret à propos de Martin Heidegger." *Les Lettres Nouvelles* (Paris), no. 5, 1974/75, 11-39.

3619 Lechat, P. H. "'L'expérience sonde et fonde'. Hommage à Martin Heidegger." (L'Experience, XXIVe Semaine de Synthèse, 28 mai - 1er juin 1962. Centre international de Synthèse). *Revue de Synthèse* (Paris), vol. 84, no. 29-31, 1963; Paris, 1964, 442-444.

3620 Lechner, Robert. "Martin Heidegger." *Philosophy Today* (Celina, Ohio), vol. 19, 1975, 78.

3621 Lechner, Robert, H. Miles Groth, and Jean Claude Curtin. "For Martin Heidegger (1889-1976) Remembering and Thinking in Remembrance." *Philosophy Today* (Celina, Ohio), vol. 20, no. 4, 1976, 258-291.

3622 Le Cocq, Rhoda P. *The Radical Thinkers: Martin Heidegger and Sri Aurobindo.* Phil. Diss. California Institute of Asian Studies 1969.

3623 Lederer, L. "Existencionalismus, Heidegger a politika" (Existentialism, Heidegger and Politics). *Dejiny a soucastnost,* vol. 10, 1965, 9-11.

3624 Ledure, Yves. "Nietzsche et le polythéisme: une approche plurielle du divin." *Revue des Sciences Philosophiques et Theologiques,* vol. 61, 1977, 533-548.

3625 Lefebvre, H. *L'existentialisme.* Paris, 1946, (specifically pages 184-229).

3626 Legrand, Gérard. "Heidegger - Sartre, réflexions sur un malentendu." *Magazine Littéraire* (Paris), no. 117, 1976, 17-19.

3627 Lehmann, Gerhard. Rev. of *Kant und das Problem der Metaphysik,* by Martin Heidegger. Bonn, 1929. *Japanisch-deutsche Zeitschrift,* no. 2, 1930, 123-124.

3628 Lehmann, Gerhard. "Das Subjekt der Alltäglichkeit. Soziologisches in Heideggers Fundamentalontologie." *Archiv für angewandte Soziologie* (Berlin), vol. 5, 1932/33, 15-39.

3629 Lehmann, Gerhard. *Die Ontologie der Gegenwart in ihren Grundgestalten.* Halle, 1933, (specifically pages 15-21).

3630 Lehmann, Gerhard. *Die deutsche Philosophie der Gegenwart.* Stuttgart, 1943, XII, 575 p., (specifically pages 397-409).

3631 Lehmann, Gerhard. "Voraussetzungen und Grenzen systematischer Kantinterpretation." *Kant-Studien,* vol. 49, 1957, 364-388.

3632 Lehmann, K. *Der Tod bei Heidegger und Jaspers. Ein Beitrag zur Frage: Existenzialphilosophie - Existenzphilosophie und protestantische Theologie.* Heidelberg, 1938, 94 p.

3633 Lehmann, K. *Vom Ursprung und Sinn der Seinsfrage im Denken Martin Heideggers. Versuch einer Ortsbestimmung.* Phil. Diss. Gregoriana Roma 1962.

3634 Lehmann, K. "Metaphysik, Transzendentalphilosophie und Phänomenologie in den ersten Schriften Martin Heideggers (1912-1916)." *Philosophisches Jahrbuch* (München), vol. 71, 1963/64, 331-357.

3635 Lehmann, K. "Christliche Geschichtserfahrung und ontologische Frage beim jungen Heidegger." *Philosophisches Jahrbuch* (München), vol. 74, 1966/67, 126-153.

3636 Lehmann, K. "Christliche Geschichtserfahrung und ontologische Frage beim jungen Heidegger." In *Heidegger.* Ed. O. Pöggeler. Köln/Berlin, 1969, 140-168.

3637 Leick, Romain. "Der Hüter des Seins. Zum Tode von Martin Heidegger." *Vorwärts* (Bonn), no. 23, 3 June 1976, 14. (Jg. 3, 1976, Nr. 2).

3638 Leisegang, Hans. Rev. of *Vom Wesen des Grundes,* by Martin Heidegger. Halle, 1929. *Blätter für deutsche Philosophie* (Berlin), vol. 3, 1930, 433-445.

3639 Leist, Fritz. "Der Feldweg. Eine Einführung in die Philosophie Martin Heideggers." *Erziehung und Beruf* (Darmstadt), vol. 5, 1954, 277-282.

3640 Leist, Fritz. Rev. of *Nietzsches, Bd I-II,* by Martin Heidegger. Pfullingen, 1961. *Universitas* (Stuttgart), vol. 17, 1962, 1349-1351.

3641 Leist, Fritz. "Heidegger und Nietzsche." *Philosophisches Jahrbuch* (München), vol. 70, 1962/63, 363-394.

3642 Leland, Dorothy. "Edmund Husserl: Phenomenology and the Crisis of Language." *Philosophy Today,* vol. 23, Fall 1979, 226-237.

3643 Lemaigre, B. Rev. of *Questions III,* by Martin Heidegger. *Revue des Sciences Philosophiques et Théologiques* (Le Saulchoir), vol. 50, 1966, 577.

3644    Lenz, J. "Der moderne deutsche und französische Existentialismus." *Tierer theologische zeitschrift* (Trier), vol. 58, 1949/50, 99-108, 204-211.

3645    Leonard, Linda. "Towards and Ontological Analysis of Detachment." *Philosophy Today* (Celina, Ohio), vol. 16, 1972, 268-280.

3646    Leonard, Linda. "The Belonging-Together of Poetry and Death." *Philosophy Today* (Celina, Ohio), vol. 19, 1975, 137-145.

3647    Lepp, I. *Existence et existentialisme.* Paris, 1947, 35-36.

3648    *L'eredità filosofica di M. Heidegger.* [Relazioni e interventi del convegno, Padova, 9-10 gennaio 1979.] *Verifiche,* vol. 8, no. 1, 1979. Trento: Rivista Verifiche, (Casella Postale 269), 1979, 125 p.

3649    Lessing, Arthur. *'Man is Freedom': A Critical Study of the Conception of Human Freedom in the Philosophies of Martin Heidegger and Jean-Paul Sartre.* Phil. Diss. Tulane Univ. 1966 252 p. *Dissertation Abstracts International,* vol. 28/04-A, 1470.

3650    Levin, David Michael. "The Opening of Vision: Seeing Through the Veil of Tears." *Review of Existential Psychology & Psychiatry* (Northwestern Univ., Evanston, Illinois), vol. 16, no. 1, 2, and 3, 1978/79.

3651    Levinas, Emanuel. "Martin Heidegger et l'ontologie." *Revue philosophique de la France et de l'Etranger* (Paris), Jg. 57, Nr. 113, 1932, 395-431.

3652    Levinas, Emanuel. *En découvrant l'existence avec Husserl et Heidegger.* Paris, 1939.

3653    Levinas, Emanuel. "Il y a." *Deucalion* (Paris), vol. 1, 1946, 143-154.

3654    Levinas, Emanuel. *De l'existence à l'existant.* Paris, 1947.

3655    Levinas, Emanuel. *En découvrant l'existence avec Husserl et Heidegger.* Paris, 1949, 107 p.

3656    Levinas, Emanuel. *L'ontologie est-elle fondamentale?* (Phénoménologie-Existence. Recueil d'études par H. Birault, H. L. van Breda, A. Gurvitch, E. Levinas, P. Ricoeur, J. Wahl). Paris, 1953, 193-203, passim.

3657    Levinas, Emanuel. Rev. of *De l'essence de la Vérité,* by Martin Heidegger. *Revue Philosophique de la France et de l'Etranger* (Paris), vol. 84, 1959, 561-563.

3658    Levinas, Emanuel. "Sans identité." *L'Ephémère,* no. 13, 1970, 27-44.

3659    Lévinas, Emmanuel. *En découvrant l'existence avec Husserl et Heidegger.* (Bibliothèque d'histoire de la philosophie). 1st ed. 1967. 3rd ed, enlarged by recent essays. Paris: J. Vrin, 1974, 236 p.

3659a   Levinas, Emmanuel. *La traccia dell'altro (Scorciatoie).* [En découvrant l'existence avec Husserl et Heidegger.] Ed. Horst Künkler, with a preface by Emmanuel Levinas. Trans. Fabio Ciaramelli. (Il planetario, 3). Napoli: Libreria Tullio Pironti, 1979, 117 p.

3660 Levine, Stephen King. *Art and Being in the Philosophy of Martin Heidegger: An Interpretation and Critique of 'Der Ursprung des Kunstwerks'.* Phil. Diss. New York 1968 259 p. *Dissertation Abstracts International,* vol. 29/05-A, 1569.

3661 Levine, Stephen King. *Art and Being in the Philosophy of Martin Heidegger. An Interpretation and Critique of 'Der Ursprung des Kunstwerkes'.* New School for Social Research. Phil. Diss. 1968. Ann Arbor, Michigan: University Microfilms, 1977, v-253 p.

3662 Levy, H. "Heideggers Kantinterpretationen; zu Heideggers Buch: Kant und das Problem der Metaphysik." *Logos* (Tübingen), vol. 21, 1932, 1-43.

3663 Lewalter, Chr. E. "Heidegger und die 'Mystik'." *Die Zeit* (Hamburg), Jg. 5, Nr. 21, 1950, 5.

3664 Lewalter, D. E. "Wie liest man 1953 Sätze von 1935? Zu einem politischen Streit um Heideggers Metaphysik." *Die Zeit* (Hamburg), Jg. 8, Nr. 33, 13.8.1953, 6.

3665 Lewis, Donald. "Aristotle's Theory of Time: Destructive Ontology From Heideggerian Principles." *Kinesis,* vol. 2, 1970, 81-92.

3666 Lewkowitz, A. "Vom Sinn des Seins. Zur Existenzphilosophie Heideggers." *Monatsschrift für Geschichte und Wissenschaft des Judentums* (Breslau), vol. 80, N.F. 44, 1936, 184-195.

3667 Leyvraz, J.-P. "Heidegger et l'interrogation scientifique." *Studia philosophica* (Basel), vol. 27, 1957, 80-96.

3668 Leyvraz, J.-P. "Le moment du choix chez Heidegger." *Studia philosophica Gandensia* (Gent), vol. 26, 1966, 139-158.

3670 Lichtigfeld, A. "Imagination in Kant and Heidegger. A Survey." *Filosofia* (Torino), vol. 18, 1967, 807-836.

3671 Liebenthal, Walter. "Existentialism and Buddhism." *Visvabharati* (Quart), vol. 22, 293-313.

3672 Lieber, Hans-Joachim. "Die deutsche Lebensphilosophie und ihre Folgen." *Nationalsozialismus und die deutsche Universität, Universitätstage* (Berlin), 1966, 92 ff.

3673 Liebert, Arthur. Rev. of *Kant und das Problem der Metaphysik,* by Martin Heidegger. Bonn, 1929. *Berliner Tageblatt,* 12.11.1929.

3674 Liebert, Arthur. Rev. of *Was ist Metaphysik?* by Martin Heidegger. Bonn, 1929. *Kant-Studien* (Berlin), vol. 38, 1933, 243-244.

3675 Liebrucks, Bruno. *Probleme der Subjekt-Objektrelation.* Phil. Diss. v.7.7.1933. Königsberg 1934 109 p., (specifically pages 82-95 and passim).

3676 Liebrucks, Bruno. "Idee und ontologische Differenz." *Kant-Studien* (Köln), vol. 48, 1956, 268-301.

3677 Liebrucks, Bruno. *Erkenntnis und Dialektik.* Den Haag, 1972, 381 p.

3678 Liegler, L. Rev. of *Hölderlin und das Wesen der Dichtung,* by Martin Heidegger. München, 1937. *Monatsschrift für Kultur und Politik* (Wien), vol. 2, 1937, 849-852.

3679 Lindemann, H. A. "Critica del existencialismo y de la filosofia de Heidegger y Jaspers." *Anales de la Sociedad cientifica Argentina* (Buenos Aires), vol. 148, 1949, 77-92.

3680 Lingis, A. F. "On the Essence of Technique." *Heidegger and the Quest for Truth.* Ed. M. S. Frings. Chicago, 1968, 126-138.

3681 Lingis, Alphonso. "Truth and Art. Heidegger and the Temples of Constantinople." *Philosophy Today* (Celina, Ohio), vol. 16, 1972, 122-134.

3682 Lingis, Alphonso. "The Origin of Infinity." *Research and Phenomenology,* vol. 6, 1976, 27-45.

3683 Lingis, Alphonso. "Time to Exist in One's Own." *Analecta Husserliana* (Dordrecht), vol. 6, 1977, 31-40.

3684 Lingis, Alphonso. "Time of One's Own." *Diálogos* (Rio Piedras), vol. 11, no. 29-30, 1977, 113-122.

3685 Lingis, Alphonso. "Authentic Time." In *Crosscurrents in Phenomenology,* by Ronald Bruzina and Bruce Wilshire (eds.). (Selected studies in phenomenology and existential philosophy, 7). The Hague, Boston: Martinus Nijhoff, 1978, 276-296.

3686 Lingis, Alphonso. "Difference in the Eternal Recurrence of the Same." *Research and Phenomenology,* vol. 8, 1978, 77-91.

3687 Link, Wilhelm. "'Anknüpfung' 'Vorverständnis' und die Frage der 'Theologischen Anthropologie'." *Theologische Rundschau* (Tübingen) (Neue Folge), vol. 7, 1935, 205-254. Rpt. in *Heidegger und die Theologie. Beginn und Fortgang der Diskussion.* Ed. G. Noller. München, 1967, 147-193.

3688 Lio Brizzion, R. de. "Una conferenza di Heidegger su 'La cosa'." *Filosofia* (Torino), vol. 2, 1951, 430-431.

3689 Lipps, Hans. "Pragmatisme et philosophie de l'existence." *Recherches philosophiques* (Paris), vol. 6, 1936/37, 333-345.

3690 Liverziani, F. Rev. of "Scritti filosofici (1912-1917)," by Martin Heidegger. *Aquinas* (Roma), vol. 16, 1973, 28-30. Rpt. in *Rivista di Filosofia Neo-Scolastica* (Milano), vol. 66, 1974, 1050-1052.

3691 Livorsi, B. "'Il visible e l'invisible': Merleau-Ponty tra Marx e Heidegger." *Atti della Academie delle scienze di Torino. Classe di science morali, storiche e filologiche* (Turin), vol. 105, 1971, 475-497.

3692 Llambias de Azevedo, J. "Logos, dia-logos y filosofia." *Actas del primer Congreso nacional de Filosofia* (Mendoza), vol. 2, 1949, 1164-1171, passim.

3693 Llambias de Azevedo, J. "Der alte und der neue Heidegger." *Philosophisches Jahrbuch* (Fulda), vol. 60, 1950, 161-174. Rpt. in "El torno al último Heidegger." *Ciencia y Fe* (Buenos Aires), vol. 6, 1950, 7-30. Separate ed.: *El antiguo y el nuevo Heidegger y un diálogo con él.* (Instituto de filosofia, facultad de humanidades y ciencias). Montevideo, Univ. de la Republica, 1958, 30 p.

3694    Llera, Humberto Piñera. "Posibilidades epistemológicas de la filosofía existencial." *Philosophy and Phenomenological Research*, vol. 9, 1949, 400-415.

3695    Llewelyn, J. E. "Origins, Being and Nothingness." *The Journal of the British Society for Phenomenology* (Manchester), 1978. [Heidegger: 36, 42.]

3696    Lögstrup, K. E. "Le néant et l'action." *Danish Yearbook of Philosophy* (Kopenhagen), vol. 8, 1971, 159-167.

3697    Lögstrup, K. E. *Kierkegaards und Heideggers Existenzanalyse und ihr Verhältnis zur Verkündigung.* Berlin, 1951.

3698    Loen, A. E. *De Vaste Grond.* Amsterdam, 1946, VII, 332 p. (165 ff).

3699    Löwith, Karl. *Das Individuum in der Rolle des Mitmenschen.* München, 1928, (specifically page 79 ff).

3700    Löwith, Karl. "Grundzüge der Entwicklung der Phänomenologie zur Philosophie und ihr Verhältnis zur protestantischen Theologie." *Theologische Rundschau* (Tübingen), vol. 2, 1930, 26-64, 333-361.

3701    Löwith, Karl. "Phänomenologische Ontologie und protestantische Theologie." *Zeitschrift für Theologie und Kirche* (Tübingen), no. 11, 1930, 365-399.

3702    Löwith, Karl. "Existenz-Philosophie." *Zeitschrift für Deutsche Bildung* (Frankfurt/Main), vol. 8, 1932, 602-613, passim.

3703    Löwith, Karl. "M. Heidegger and F. Rosenzweig or Temporality and Eternity." *Philosophy and Phenomenological Research* (Buffalo, New York), vol. 3, 1942/43, 53-77.

3704    Löwith, Karl. "Les implications politiques de la philosophie de l'existence chez Heidegger." *Les temps modernes* (Paris), vol. 2, 1946/47, 343-360.

3705    Löwith, Karl. "Heidegger: Problem und Background of Existentialism." *Social Research* (New York), vol. 15, 1948, 345-369.

3706    Löwith, Karl. "Réponse à M. De Waelhens." *Les temps modernes* (Paris), vol. 4, 1948, 370-373.

3707    Löwith, Karl. "Background and Problem of Existentialism." *Actas del primer Congreso nacional de Filosofia* (Mendoza), vol. 1, 1949, 390-407, passim.

3708    Löwith, Karl. "Weltgeschichte und Heilsgeschehen." *Anteile, Martin Heidegger zum 60. Geburtstag* (Frankfurt), 1950, 106-153.

3709    Löwith, Karl. "Heideggers 'Kehre'." *Die neue Rundschau*, vol. 62, Heft 4, 1951, 48-79.

3709A   Löwith, Karl. "Martin Heidegger. Denker in dürftiger Zeit." *Die Neue Rundschau* (Frankfurt/Main), vol. 63, 1952, 1-27.

3710    Löwith, Karl. *Heidegger, Denker in dürftiger Zeit.* Frankfurt, 1953, 110 p. [Rev. by G. F. Klenk in *Gregorinum (Roma), vol. 36, 1955, 141-142. 2nd ed. 1960.]*

3711    Löwith, Karl. "Heideggers Auslegung des Ungesagten in Nietzsches Wort 'Gott ist tot'." *Die Neue Rundschau* (Frankfurt), vol. 64, 1953, 105-137.

3712    Löwith, Karl. *Heidegger, pensador de un tiempo indigente.* Estudio preliminar y trad. de Fernando Montero. (Biblioteca del pensamiento actual, 60). Madrid, Rialp, 1956, 253 p. (1st German ed. 1953).

3713    Löwith, Karl. "Martin Heidegger und Franz Rosenzweig. Ein Nachtrag zu 'Sein und Zeit'." *Zeitschrift für philosophische Forschung* (Meisenheim/Glan), vol. 12, 1958, 161-187.

3714    Löwith, Karl. "Heideggers Vorlesungen über Nietzsche." *Merkur* (Stuttgart) (Deutsche Zeitschrift für europäisches Denken), vol. 16, 1962, 72-83.

3715    Löwith, Karl. "La fine e il superamento della metafisica in Dilthey e in Heidegger." *Filosofi tedeschi d'oggi.* Ed. A. Babolin. Bologna, 1967, 279-302.

3716    Löwith, Karl. "Phänomenologische Ontologie und protestantische Theologie." *Heidegger.* Ed. O. Pöggeler. Köln/Berlin, 1969, 54-77.
        [Zuerst: Zeitschrift für Theologie und Kirche, 1930. Rpt. in *Heidegger und die Theologie.* 1967. Ed. G. Noller. *See* 3701.]

3717    Löwith, Karl. *Zu Heideggers Seinsfrage.* Sitzungsberichte der Heidelberger Akademie der Wissenschaften. Heidelberg, 1969.

3718    Löwith, Karl. "Martin Heidegger." *Martin Heidegger im Gespräch.* Ed. v. R. Wisser. Freiburg/München, 1970, 38-41.

3719    Löwith, Karl. "Martin Heidegger und F. Rosenzweig. Ein Nachtrag zu 'Sein und Zeit'." K. Löwith, *Gesammelte Abhandlungen. Zur Kritik der geschichtlichen Existenz.* 2nd ed. Stuttgart/Berlin/Köln/Mainz, 1969, 68-92. *See* 3703 and 3713.

3720    Löwith, Karl. "The Nature of Man and the World of Nature. For Heidegger's 80th Birthday." *The Southern Journal of Philosophy* (Memphis), vol. 8, 1970, 309-318.

3721    Löwith, Karl. "Philosophische Weltgeschichte?" *Merkur,* vol. 24, no. 269, 1970, 820-836.

3722    Löwith, Karl. "Die Frage Martin Heideggers." *Universitas* (Stuttgart), vol. 25, 1970, 603-616.

3723    Löwith, Karl. "Wahrheit und Geschichtlichkeit." *Universitas,* vol. 25, 1970, 1077-1089.

3724    Löwith, Karl. *Saggi su Heidegger.* Trans. by Cesare Cases and Alessandro Mazzone. Facsimile of the ed. di Torino, 1966. (Einaudi rpt., 21). Torino: G. Einaudi, 1974, xvi, 142 p.

3725    Lohmann, J. "M. Heideggers 'Ontologische Differenz' und die Sprache." *Lexis* (Lahr), vol. 1, 1948, 49-106.

3726    Lohmann, J. "Martin Heidegger's 'Ontological Difference' and Language." *On Heidegger and Language.* Ed. J. J. Kockelmans. Evanston, Illinois, 1972, 303-363.

3727 Lohmann, J. *Philosophie und Sprachwissenschaft.* Berlin, 1965, 297 p., (specifically pages 144, 157 ff and passim).

3728 Loi, A. M. "The Problem of Space in Heidegger's Ontology." (In Ukrain.). *Filosofs'ka Dumka* (Kiev), no. 6, 1974, 94-101.

3729 Lombardi, Franco. *L'esperienza e l'uomo.* Firenze, 1935, 276-278; 285.

3730 Lombardi, Franco. "Zeit als Existenz oder die Suche nach dem Sein. Martin Heidegger zum 80. Geburtstag." *Frankfurter Allgemeine Zeitung,* Nr. 224 v. 27.9.1969. [Aus dem Italienischen übersetzt von A. Giachi.]

3731 Long, Eugene T. "Being and Thinking." *The Southern Journal of Philosophy* (Memphis), vol. 9, 1971, 131-140.

3732 Long, W. "Existentialism, Christianity and Logos." *The Personalist* (Los Angeles), vol. 47, 1966, 149-168.

3733 Lopez Castallon, E. "Dimensiones cristianas de la ética de situación." *Estudios filosóficos* (Valladolid), vol. 21, 1972, 377-442.

3734 López, Jaime Sologuren. "Fin de la filosofia - comienzo del pensar." *Revista Venezolana de Filosof,* vol. 8, 1978, 97-133.

3735 López Quintás, Alfonso. "Filosofia y lenguaje." *Pensamiento,* vol. 29, 105-115.

3736 López Quintás, Alfonso. "El estilo de pensar del 'segundo Heidegger'." *Estudios* (Merced), vol. 33, no. 116, 1977, 21-34.

3737 López Quintás, Alfonso. "El sentido de la muerte en la filosofia de M. Heidegger." *Arbor* (Madrid), vol. 97, no. 377, 1977, 8-12.

3738 Loreau, M. "Heidegger et la technique moderne." *Morale et Enseignement* (Bruxelles), vol. 14, 1965, 3-4, 42-53.

3739 Lorenz, K. "Die Hintergehbarkeit der Sprache." *Kant-Studien,* vol. 58, 1967, 187-208.

3740 Loscerbo, J. "Martin Heidegger. Remarks Concerning Some Earlier Texts on Modern Technology." *Tijdschrift voor Filosofie* (Leuven), vol. 39, no. 1, 1977, 104-129.

3741 Lotz, Johannes Baptist. Rev. of *Hölderlins Hymne 'Wie wenn am Feiertage',* by Martin Heidegger. Halle, 1941. *Scholastik* (Ewen), vol. 18, 1943, 116-117.

3742 Lotz, Johannes Baptist. *Das christliche Menschenbild im Ringen der Zeit.* Heidelberg, 1947.

3743 Lotz, Johannes Baptist. "Existenzphilosophie, Nihilismus und Christentum." *Stimmen der Zeit* (Freiburg), vol. 142, 1948, 332-345.

3744 Lotz, Johannes Baptist. Rev. of these Heidegger's works in *Scholastik* (Freiburg), vol. 19-24, 1944-1949, 92-96:

[*Vom Wesen der Wahrheit.* 1943.]

[*Was ist Metaphysik?* 1943.]

[*Erläuterungen zu Hölderlins Dichtung.* 1944.]

[*Platons Lehre von der Wahrhet. Mit einem Brief über den 'Humanismus'.* 1947.]

3745    Lotz, Johannes Baptist. "Zum Wesen der Existenzphilosophie." *Scholastik* (Freiburg), vol. 25, 1950, 161-183, passim.

3746    Lotz, Johannes Baptist. "Zur Geschichtlichkeit des Menschen." *Scholastik* (Freiburg), vol. 26, 1951, 321-341.

3747    Lotz, Johannes Baptist. "Heidegger und das Sein." *Universitas* (Stuttgart), vol. 6, Bd 1, Heft 7, 1951, 727-734; Bd 1, Heft 8, 839-845.

3748    Lotz, Johannes Baptist. "Heidegger und das Christentum." *Doctor Communis* (Roma), vol. 4, 1951, no. 1, 63-73.

3749    Lotz, Johannes Baptist. Rev. of *Holzwege,* by Martin Heidegger. Frankfurt, 1952. *Scholastik* (Frieburg), vol. 27, 1952, 248-251.

3750    Lotz, Johannes Baptist. *Das Urteil und das Sein. Eine Grundlegung der Metaphysik.* [2., neubearbeitete und vermehrte Auflage von 'Sein und Wert 1' (1938).] Pullach/München, 1957, XXII, 218 p.

3751    Lotz, Johannes Baptist. "Denken und Sein nach den jüngsten Veröffentlichungen von M. Heidegger." *Scholastik* (Freiburg), vol. 33, 1958, 81-97.

3752    Lotz, Johannes Baptist. "Das Sein selbst und das subsistierende Sein nach Thomas von Aquin." In *Martin Heidegger zum 70. Geburtstag, Festschrift.* Pfullingen, 1959, 180-194.

3753    Lotz, Johannes Baptist. "El ser en el filosofar de Heidegger, Grandeza y limites." *Espiritu* (Barcelona), vol. 10, 1961, 93-101.

3754    Lotz, Johannes Baptist. "Being and Existence in Scholasticism and in Existence-Philosophy." *Philosophy Today,* vol. 8, 1964, 3-45.

3755    Lotz, Johannes Baptist. *Sein und Existenz. Kritische Studien in systematischer Absicht.* Freiburt/Basel/Wien, 1965, 420 p.

3756    Lotz, Johannes Baptist. *Der Mensch im Sein. Versuche zur Geschichte und Sache der Philosophie.* Freiburg/Basel/Wien, 1967, 672 p.

3757    Lotz, Johannes Baptist. *Neue Erkenntnisprobleme in Philosophie und Theologie.* Freiburg/Basel/Wien, 1968, 264 p.

3758    Lotz, Johannes Baptist. "Die Frage nach dem Fundament bei Heidegger und in der Scholastik - Il problema del fondamento in Heidegger e nella Scolastica." *Sapienza* (Roma), vol. 26, 1973, 280-331.

3759    Lotz, Johannes Baptist. "A atualidade do pensamento de S. Tomás. Um confronto entre o seu pensamento e o de Heidegger quanto ao problema do ser." *Presenca Filosófica* (Sao Paulo), no. 1, 2, and 3, 1974, 81-90.

3760    Lotz, Johannes Baptist. "Mensch - Zeit - Sein. Nachvollziehen einer Thematik von Heidegger bei Thomas von Aquin, I-II." *Gregorianum* (Roma), vol. 55, 1974, 238-271. [Summary, 272], 495-539 [Summary, 539-540].

3761 Lotz, Johannes Baptist. "Das Dasein nach Heidegger und Thomas von Aquin." In *Tommaso d'Aquino nel suo VII Centenario. Congresso Internazionale.* Roma, Napoli, 17-24 April 1974. Roma: Via Panisperna, vol. 261, 1974, 303-312.

3762 Lotz, Johannes Baptist. *Martin Heidegger und Thomas von Aquin. Mensch-Zeit-Sein.* Pfullingen: Verlag Günther Neske, 1975, 276 p.

3763 Lotz, Johannes Baptist. "Vom Sein durch die Zeit zum Menschen." *Gregorianum* (Roma), vol. 56, no. 1, 1975, 47-48.

3764 Lotz, Johannes Baptist. "Was von Heideggers Denken ins künftige Philosophieren einzubringen ist." In *Martin Heidegger. Fragen an sein Werk. Ein Symposium.* (Universal-Bibliothek, 9873). Stuttgart: Reclam, 1977, 28-32.

3765 Lotz, Johannes Baptist. "A diferença ontológica em Kant, Hegel, Heidegger e Tomás de Aquino." *Revista Portuguesa de Filosofia* (Braga), vol. 33, no. 4, 1977, 270-284.

3766 Lotz, Johannes Baptist. "Mi Pensamiemto Filosófico." *Revista de Filosofia (Mexico),* vol. 11, January-April 1978, 45-72.

3767 Lotz, Johannes Baptist. "Il valore religioso nella filosofia dell'essere di M. Heidegger." *Sapienza* (Roma), vol. 31, no. 3, 1978, 257-264.

3768 Lotz, Johannes Baptist. "Die ontologische Differenz in Kant, Hegel, Heidegger und Thomas von Aquin." *Theologie und Philosophie* (Frankfurt/Pullach/Freiburg), vol. 53, 1978, 1-26.

3769 Lotz, Johannes Baptist. "Mensch-Sein-Zeit-Gott. Zum Gespräch zwischen Heidegger und Thomas von Aquin." *Theologie und Philosophie* (Frankfurt/Pullach/Freiburg), vol. 54, 1979, 1-19.

3770 Lovitt, William. "A *Gespräch* With Heidegger on Technology." *Man and World* (Pittsburgh), vol. 1, 1973, 44-62.

3770a Lovitt, William. "Techne and Technology: Heidegger's Perspective on What is Happening Today." *Philosophy Today* (Celina), vol. 24, 1980, 62-72.

3771 Lowell Howey, R. *Heidegger and Jaspers on Nietzsche.* The Hague, 1973, xi and 218 p.

3772 Lowry, Atherton C. "Merleau-Ponty and Fundamental Ontology." *International Philosophical Quarterly,* vol. 15, 1975, 397-409.

3773 Luck, U. "Heideggers Ausarbeitung der Frage nach dem Sein und die existentialanalytische Begrifflichkeit in der evangelischen Theologie." *Zeitschrift für Theologie und Kirche* (Tübingen), vol. 53, 1956, 230-251. Rpt. in *Heidegger und die Theologie. Beginn und Fortgang der Diskussion.* Ed. G. Noller. München, 1967, 226-248. [Vgl. Nr. 1.2191]

3774 Lübbe, H. "Bibliographie der Heidegger-Literatur 1917-1955." *Zeitschrift für philosophische Forschung* (Meisenheim/Glan), vol. 11, 1957, 401-452.

3775 Lübbe, H. "M. Heidegger." In *Lexikon für Theologie und Kirche.* Bd 5. 2nd ed. 1960, 63-65.

3776 Lübbe, H. *Bewusstsein in Geschichten. Studien zur Phänomenologie. Mach Husserl Schapp. Wittgenstein.* Freiburg, 1972, 174 p.

3777 Luegenbiehl, Heinz Carl. *The Essence of Man. An Approach to the Philosophy of Martin Heidegger.* Authorized facsimile of the dissertation of the Purdue Univ. Phil. Diss. 1976. Ann Arbor, Michigan; London: University Microfilms International, 1979, vii-325 p. [HGK77-15438] *Dissertaton Abstracts International,* vol. 38/02-A, 847.

3778 Lützeler, Heinrich. "Die Frage nach dem Grund der Dinge. Mark Rothko (1903-1970)." *Zeitschrift für Ästhetik und allgemeine Kunstwissenschaft* (Bonn), vol. 21, no. 2, 1976, 187-197.

3779 Lugarini, Leo. "Sulla questione heideggeriana del superamento della metafisica." *Il Pensiero* (Milano), vol. 3, 1958, 157-192.

3780 Lugarini, Leo. "Die kantische transzendentale Idee in der Philosophie von Pantaleo Carabellese." *Kant-Studien* (Bonn), vol. 53, 1961, 225-234.

3781 Lugarini, Leo. *Heidegger e il problema della metafisica.* L'Aquila: Centro tecnico culturale ed assistenziale, 1971, 96 p.

3782 Luijpen, William A. M. *Existentiele fenomenologie.* Utrecht/Antwerpen, 1959, 322 p. ['Sein zum Tode': 312-328.] Rpt. in *Existential Phenomenology.* Pittsburgh, Duquesne Univ. Press, 1960.

3783 Luijpen, William, A. M. "Heidegger and 'Affirmation' of God, in: De Deo in philosophia S.Thomae et in hodierna philosophia." *Doctor Communis* (Roma) (Officium Libri Catholici), vol. XVIII, 1965, 303-310.

3784 Luijpen, William A. M. *Phenomenology and Humanism. A Primer in Existential Phenomenology.* Pittsburgh, 1966, 155 p.

3785 Lukács, G. *Existentialisme ou Marxisme?* Paris, 1948, passim.

3786 Lukács, G. "Heidegger redivivus." *Sinn und Form* (Potsdam), Jg. 1, H. 3, 1949, 37-62.

3787 Lukács, G. "Wozu braucht die Bourgeoisie die Verzweiflung?" *Sinn und Form* (Berlin), Jg. 3, Heft 4, 1951, 66-69, passim.

3788 Lukács, G. *Existentialismus oder Marxismus?* Berlin, 1951, 183 p.

3789 Lukács, G. *Die Zerstörung der Vernunft.* Berlin, 1954, 389-412.

3790 Luypen, W. "Heidegger and the 'Affirmation' of God." *Doctor Communis* (Roma), vol. 18, 1965, 303-310.

3791 Lynch, L. "Martin Heidegger: Language and Being." *Etienne Gilson Tribute Presented by his North American Students With a Response by Etienne Glison.* Ed. Charles J. O'Neil. Milwaukee, The Marquette Univ. Press, 1959, 135-147.

3792 Macann, C. Rev. of "Kant and the Problem of Metaphysics," by Martin Heidegger. 1962. *Man and World* (The Hague), vol. 9, 1976, 91-101.

3792a Macann, C. Rev. of "Martin Heidegger. Phänomenologische Interpretation von Kants Kritik der reinen Vernunft, ed. Ingtraud Görland." *Man and World* (The Hague), vol. 12, 1979, 515-521.

3793    Macdowell, J. A. A. *A gênese da ontologia fundamental de Martin Heidegger.*
        Sao Paulo, 1970, 240 p.

3794    Macedo, S. De. *Filosofia de Heidegger.* Maceio, Brazil, 1953.

3795    MacGregor, G. Rev. of *German Existentialism,* by Martin Heidegger. *The
        Personalist* (Los Angeles), vol. 46, 1965, 394-395.

3796    Mach. Rev. of *Hölderlin und das Wesen der Dichtung,* by Martin Heidegger.
        München, 1937. *Freie Welt* (Reichenberg), vol. 405, 1937, 59.

3797    Machácek, J. "Martin Heidegger." *Strucná filosofická slovnik* (Concise
        Philosophical Dictionary). Praha, 1966.

3798    Machella, V. "Il problema del comiciamento e la diagnosi nichilistica." *Rivista
        Rosminiana di filosofia e di Cultura* (Stresa), vol. 4, 1970, 176-186.

3799    MacIntyre, Alister. "Existentialism." *A Critical History of Western Philosophy.*
        Ed. D. J. O'Connor. New York/London, 1964, 509-529.

3800    Macomber, William Burns. *The Phenomenological Notion of Truth in Hegel
        and Heidegger.* Phil. Diss. Univ. of Toronto 1963.

3801    Macomber, William Burns. *The Anatomy of Disillusion. Martin Heidegger's
        Notion of Truth.* Northwestern Univ. Study in Phenomenology and
        Existential Philosophy. Evanston, Illinois, 1967, 227 p.

3802    Macquarrie, John. *Martin Heidegger.* London, 1968, 62 p.

3803    Macquarrie, John. *An Existentialist Theology. A Comparison of Heidegger and
        Bultmann.* [Previous ed. London: SCM Press, 1955.] (Pelican Books). W.
        Drayton. Middlesex, England: Penguin Books, 1973, 239 p.

3803    aMacquarrie, John. Rev. of "Martin Heidegger. The Piety of Thinking. Essays.
        Trans., Notes and Commentary by James G. Hart and John C. Maraldo."
        *Studi Internazionali di Filosofia* (Torino), vol. 9, 1977, 233-234.

3804    Madson, Peter. Rev. of "Logik. Die Frage nach der Wahrheit," by Martin
        Heidegger. 1976. *International Philsophical Quarterly* (New York), vol. 17,
        no. 4, 1977, 477-486.                                          ‹

3805    Maeda, Tadeshi. "Wakaki Haideggâ ni okeru Ningenteki Genjitsu - Rekishi
        e no Toi" (The Concept of the Actuality of Man in Heidegger's Early
        Writings - The Inquiry for History). *Kagoshima Daigaku Bunka Hôkoku
        7* (Kagoshima), September 1971, 1-42.

3806    Maeda, Tsuyoshi. "Wakaki Haideggâ ni okeru Shingaku teki Yurai" (The
        Theological Source in Young Heidegger). *Kagoshima Daigaku Bunka
        Hôkoku* (Kagoshima), vol. 9, 1974, 157-179.

3807    Maeda, Tsuyoshi. "Haideggâ ni okeru Shingaku no Mondai" (Theological
        Problems in Heidegger). *Shûkyô Kenkyû* (Tôkyô), vol. 214, 1973, 66-67.

3808    Maeda, Tsuyoshi. "Haideggâ to Shingaku" (Heidegger and Theology).
        *Jitsuzonshugi* (Tôkyô), vol. 69, 1974, 92-101.

3809    Maeda, Tsuyoshi. "Haideggâ ni okeru Shinkô to Shinkô no Gaku" (Faith and
        Study of Faith in Heidegger). *Shûkyô Kenkyû* (Tôkyô), vol. 230, 1976,
        65-66.

3810    Magerauer, Robert. "Toward Reading Heidegger's *Discourse on Thinking*." *Southwestern Journal of Philosophy*, vol. 8, Winter 1977, 143-156.

3811    Magnus, B. "Heidegger and the Truth of Being." *International Philosophical Quarterly* (New York/Louvain), vol. 4, 1964, 245-264.

3812    Magnus, Bernd. *Heidegger and Nietzsche's Doctrine of Eternal Recurrence*. Phil. Diss. Columbia Univ. New York 1967 257 p. *Dissertation Abstracts International*, vol. 31/06, 2975.

3813    Magnus, Bernd. *Heidegger's Metahistory of Philosophy: Amor fati, Being and Truth*. The Hague, 1970, XIV, 146 p.

3814    Magnus, Bernd. "Nihilism, Reason, and 'the Good'." *The Review of Metaphysics* (Washington), vol. 25, 1971, 292-310.

3815    Magurshak, Daniel John. *Death and Freedom. A Critical Analysis of Heidegger's Notion of Sein-zum-Tode*. Authorized facsimile of the dissertaton of the Northwestern Univ. Phil. Diss. 1976. Ann Arbor, Michigan; London: University Microfilms International, 1979, iii-174 p. *Dissertation Abstracts International*, vol. 37/07-A, 4419.

3815a   Magurshak, Dan. "Heidegger and Edwards on Sein-zum Tode." *The Monist* (La Salle), vol. 62, 1979, 107-118.

3816    Maheu, René, ed. *Kierkegaard vivant*. Colloque organisé par l'Unesco à Paris du 21 au 23 avril 1964. Allocution de R. Maheu. Textes de J.-P. Sartre, J. Beaufret, G. Marcel, L. Goldmann, M. Heidegger, Enzo Paci, K. Jaspers, J. Wahl, J. Hersch, N. Thulstrup. Paris, 1966, 320 p.

3817    Maihofer, Werner. *Recht und Sein. Prolegomena zu einer Rechtsontologie*. Frankfurt, 1954, 125 p.

3818    Majeres, J. "Jenseits von Subjekt und Objekt. Die philosophische Wende zum Sein im Denkweg Martin Heideggers." *Wort und Wahrheit* (Freiburg) (Monatsschrift für Religion und Kultur), vol. 15, 1960, 617-619.

3819    Major, L. "Heidegger a Hegel." *Filosoficky Casopis* (Tschechoslowakei), vol. 12, no. 4, 1964, 539-546.

3820    Major, L. "Svet jako 'ctverina'. O. Bröcknerove chápáni Heideggera." (Acta Univ. Carolinai, Philosophica et historica 1/1968). *Studia philosophica* (Praha), vol. I, 1968, 104-108.

3821    Maki, Yôzô. "Dirutai kara Haideggâ e; Futatsu no Bungei Kaishakugaku - Junkan-Shômeihô no Mondai o Chûshin ni shite" (From Dilthey to Heidegger - Two Ways of Approaching Hermeneutics - The Problem of the Circle Argument). *Ritsumeikan Bungaku* (Kyôto), vol. 250, 1966, 1-26.

3822    Makkreel, Rudolf. Rev. of *Discourse on Thinking*, by Martin Heidegger. New York, 1966. *Journal of the History of Philosophy* (Berkeley), vol. 6, 1968, 196-197.

3823    Maliandi, R. Rev. of *Sôbre a essência da verdade. - A tese de Kant sôbre o ser*, by Martin Heidegger. *Kant-Studien* (Bonn), vol. 63, H. 3, 1972, 389.

3824    Malik, Charles H. *The Metaphysics of Time in the Philosophies of A. N. Whitehead and M. Heidegger*. Phil. Diss. Harvard 1937.

3825   Malik, Charles Habib. "A Christian Reflection on Martin Heidegger." *The Thomist* (Washington), vol. 41, no. 1, 1977, 1-61.

3826   Mall, Ram Adhar. "On Heidegger's Concepts of 'Existenz' (Existence) 'Ek-sistenz' (Ek-or-ex-sistence) and 'Nichts' (Nothing)." *Journal of the Indian Academy of Philosophy,* vol. 4, 61-70.

3827   Maly, Kenneth. "Toward *Ereignis.* An Initiatory Thinking Through of the Granting in Heidegger's Essay *Zeit und Sein.*" *Research in Phenomenology* (Pittsburgh), vol. 3, 1973, 63-93.

3828   Maly, Kenneth. "Subject, Dasein, and Disclosure." *Research in Phenomenology* (Pittsburgh), vol. 5, 1975, 183-193. *See also* "Man and Disclosure." *Heroclitean Fragments.* Ed. J. Sallis and K. Ursly. Univ. of Alabma Press, 1980, 43-60.

3829   Maly, Kenneth. "To Reawaken the Matter of Being: The New Edition of *Sein und Zeit.*" *Research in Phenomenology* (Pittsburgh), vol. 7, 1977, 282-298.

3830   Man, P. de. "Les exégèses de Hölderlin par Martin Heidegger." [Rev. of *Heidegger und die Dichtung,* by Else Buddeberg. Stuttgart, 1952; *Hölderlin und Heidegger,* by Beda Allemann. Zürich/Freiburg, 1954.] *Critique.* Revue Générale des publications françaises et étrangères. Paris, 9. Jg., Bd 11, 1955, 800-819.

3831   Manasse, E. M. Rev. of *Platons Lehre von der Wahrheit, mit einem Brief über den Humanismus,* by Martin Heidegger. Bern, 1947. *Philosophische Rundschau* (Tübingen), vol. 5, Beiheft 1, 1957, 20-27.

3832   Manchester, Peter B. "Time in Whitehead and Heidegger: A Response." *Process Studies* (Claremont), vol. 5, 1975, 106-113.

3833   Mancini, I. Rev. of *Essere e tempo,* by Martin Heidegger. Milano, 1953. *Rivista di Filosofia Neo-Scolastica* (Milano), vol. 46, 1954, 497-498.

3834   Mancini, I. "Soteriologia e nazismo [saggio inedito]." *Filosofi esistenzialisti* (Urbino), 1964, 83-112.

3835   Mancini, I. "Heidegger. Il Nichten [saggio pubbl. in Drammaturgia, 1957, 369-424 col titolo Il Nichten heideggeriano e l'umanesimo ontologico.]" *Filosofi esistenzialisti* (Urbino), 1964, 9-82.

3836   Mandel, Ross. "Heidegger and Wittgenstein. A Second Kantian Revolution." In *Heidegger and Modern Philosophy. Critical Essays,* by Michael Murray (ed.). New Haven, Connecticut: Yale Univ. Press, 1978, 259-270.

3837   Manikath, Joseph. *From Anxiety to Releasement in Martin Heidegger's Thought.* Foreword by J. Van der Veken. Kottayam (address of the author), 1978, viii-58 p., paperback, (distributed by Bangalore, Asian Trading Corporation).

3838   Manno, A. Giacomo. *Esistenza ed essere in Heidegger.* Napoli, 1967, 524 p.

[*See Rossegna de Scienze filosofiche* (Napoli), vol. 23, 1970, 64-83, and *Teoresi* (Catania), vol. 25, 1970, 109-128. 2nd ed. 1977.]

3839    Manno, A. Giacomo. "Orizzonti antropologici in Hartmann, Heidegger e Jaspers." In *L'anima*. Contributions by F. Battaglia, F. Bellino, et al. (Problemi di attualità, 2). Napoli: Edizioni Dehoniane, 1979, 357-440.

3840    Manno, M. *Heidegger e la filosofia. A proposito del Was ist das - die Philosophie?* Roma, 1962, 244 p.

3841    Mansfeld, J. "Hermeneutische Techniek. Heideggers methodiek bij de Interpretatie van enige vroeggriekse denkers." *Algemeen Nederlands Tijdschrift voor Wijsbegeerte en Psychologie* (Assen), vol. 68, 1966, 19-34.

3842    Manzano, I. "La 'Habilitationsschrift' de M. Heidegger sobre Escoto." *Verdad y Vida* (Madrid), vol. 24, 1966, 305-325.

3843    Manzano, I. "Introducción a 'Sobre la esencia de la verdad' de Heidegger." *Verdad y Vida* (Madrid), vol. 26, 1968, 507-529.

3844    Manzapo, L. M. de. "Heidegger y la nada." *Logos* (Mexico), vol. 1, 1951, 60-72.

3845    Maraldo, John C. *Der hermeneutische Zirkel. Untersuchungen zu Schleiermacher, Dilthey und Heidegger.* (Symposion. Philosophische Schriftenreihe, 48). Freiburg: Verlag Karl Alber, 1974, 142 p.

3846    Marcel, Gabriel. "Autour de Heidegger." *Dieu vivant* (Paris), vol. 1, 1945, 89-100.

3847    Marcel, Gabriel. *L'Homme problématique.* Paris, 1955, 135-151.

3848    Marcel, Gabriel. "Der Mensch vor dem totgesagten Gott. Nihilismus oder 'Vieillissement'?" *Sinn und Sein.* Ein philosophisches Symposion. Ed. R. Wisser. Tübingen, 1960, 433-448.

3848a   Marcel, Gabriel. "Ma relation avec Heidegger." In *Gabriel Marcel et la pensée allemande. Nietzsche, Heidegger, Ernst Bloch.* Paris: Présence de Gabriel Marcel, 1979, 25-38.

3849    Marcic, R. *Martin Heidegger und die Existentialphilosophie.* Bad Ischl, 1949, 48 p.

3850    Marcic, R. *Vom Gesetzesstaat zum Richterstaat.* Wien, 1957, 548 p.

3851    Marck, S. *Die Dialektik in der Philosophie der Gegenwart.* I. Halbband. Tübingen, 1929, 144-166.

3852    Marck, S. *Die Dialektik in der Philosophie der Gegenwart.* II. Halbband. Tübingen, 1931, 149-160.

3853    Marck, S. "La philosophie de l'existence dans l'oeuvre de K. Jaspers et de M. Heidegger." *Revue philosophique de la France et de l'Etranger* (Paris), Jg. 61, Nr. 121, 1936, 197-219.

3954    Marcuse, Herbert. "Beiträge zu einer Phänomenologie des Historischen Materialismus." *Philosophische Hefte* (Berlin), vol. 1, 1928, 45-68.

3855    Marcuse, Herbert. "Über konkrete Philosophie." *Archiv für Sozialwissenschaft und Sozialpolitik* (Tübingen), vol. 62, 1929, 111-128.

3856    Marcuse, Herbert. "Enttäuschung." In *Erinnerung an Martin Heidegger,* by Günther Neske (ed.). Pfullingen: Verlag Günther Neske, 1977, 162-163.

3857     Marcuse, Herbert, et al. "Theory and Politics: A Discussion." *Telos,* vol. 38, 1978/79, 124-153.

3858     Marcuse, Herbert, and Frederick Olafson. "Heidegger's Politics." (An interview). *Graduate Faculty Philosophy Journal* (New York), vol. 6, 1977, 28-40.

3859     Marcuse, Ludwig. Rev. of *Existence and Being,* by Martin Heidegger. *The Personalist* (Los Angeles), vol. 32, 1951, 202-203.

3860     Marcuse, Ludwig. "Wer ist das - der Heidegger? Zu Heideggers Schrift: 'Was ist das - die Philosophie?'" *Rhein Neckar Zeitung,* 26.10.1956.

3861     Marcuse, Ludwig. "Das heikelste Thema der Gegenwärtigen Philosophie. Versuch einer Entmythologisierung Martin Heideggers." *Die Zeit* (Hamburg), vol. 14, no. 18, 1959, 9.

3862     Margvelasvili, G. T. "Rol'jazyka v filosofii M. Chajdeggera" (The Role of Language in M. Heidegger's Philosophy). *Vestnik Otdelenija obscestvennych nauk AN SSSR* (Tbilisi), vol. 1, 1969, 35-54.

3863     Margvelasvili, G. T. "Psichologizny v chajdeggerovskoj ekzistencial'noj analitike" (The Psychologism in Heidegger's "Existential-Analytic"). *Voprosy filosofii,* vol. 5, 1971, 124-128.

3864     Margvelzsvili, G. T. "Voprosy etiki v ekzistencial'no-ontologiceskom ucenii M. Chajdeggera" (The Problems of Ethics in M. Heidegger's Existential-Ontological Theory). *Vestnik Otdelenija obczestvennych nauk AN SSSR. Serija filosofii, psichologii, ekonomiki i prava* (Moskva), vol. 4, 1974, 53-65.

3865     Margvelasvili, G. T. "Sjuzetnoe vremja i vremja ekzistencii" (The Narrative Time and the Time of Existence). *Mecniereba* (Tbilisi), 1976.

3866     Marias, J. "Die literarische Ausdrucksform in der Philosophie und die Frage nach dem möglichen Sinn der Philosophie heute." *Sinn und Sein.* Ein philosophisches Symposion. Ed. R. Wisser. Tübingen, 1960, 31-45.

3867     Marino, L. "Husserl e Heidegger. Dialogo fecondo fra prospettive irriducibili." *Atti della Academia delle Scienze di Torino. Classe di Scienze morali, storiche e filologiche* (Torino), vol. 89, 1964/65, 777-810.

3867a    Marion, Jean-Luc. "L'angoisse et l'ennui. Pour interpréter 'Was ist Metaphysik?'." *Archives de Philosophie* (Paris), vol. 43, 1980, 121-146. [Summary, 121.]

3867b    Marion, Jean-Luc. "La double idolâtrie. Remarques sur la différence ontologique et la pensée de Dieu." In *Heidegger et la question de Dieu.* Ed. R. Kearney and J. S. O'Leary. Paris: B. Grasset, 1980, 46-74.

3867c    Marion, Jean-Luc. "Quelques objections à quelques réponses." In *Heidegger et la question de Dieu.* Ed. R. Kearney and J. S. O'Leary. Paris: B. Grasset, 1980, 304-309.

3868     Marquet, J.-F. Rev. of *Le principe de raison,* by Martin Heidegger. *Critique* (Paris), vol. 19, 1963, 239-247.

3869   Marray, M. *Modern Philosophy of History, Its Origin and Destination.* Den Haag, 1970, viii-137 p.

3870   Marrero, V. "Guardini, Picasso, Heidegger. Tres vistas." *Ensayos* (Madrid), vol. 3, 1959, 45 p.

3870a  Marshall, Donald G. "The Ontology of the Literary Sign. Notes Toward a Heideggerian Revision of Semiology." In *Martin Heidegger and the Question of Literature.* Ed. William V. Spanos. Bloomington, Indiana; London: Indiana Univ. Press, 1979, 271-294.

3871   Marshall, John M. *Martin Heidegger and Medard Boss: Dialogue Between Philosophy and Psycotherapy.* Phil. Diss. Univ. of Oklahoma 1974. *Dissertation Abstracts International,* vol. 36/01-A, 349. Rpt. in London: University Microfilms International, 1979, xvi-332 p.

3872   Marshall, Margaret Wiley. "Existentialism: Suspension Bridge to Indian Thought." *Visvabharati Quarterly,* vol. 28, 116-138.

3873   Marsik, M. "The Problem of the Essence and the Sources in Contemporary Philosophical Subjectivism." (In Czechoslovakian). *Filosoficky Casopis* (Praha), vol. 22, no. 2, 1974, 200-214.

3874   Martel, J. *Essai sur le concept d'existence.* Lyon, 1970, 155 p.

3875   Marten, R. *Existieren, Wahrsein und Verstehen. Untersuchungen zur ontologischen Basis sprachlicher Verständigung.* Berlin, 1972, 376 p.

3875a  Marten, Rainer. "Heideggers Heimat. Eine philosophische Herausforderung." In *Nachdenken über Heidegger.* Ed. Ute Guzzoni. Hildesheim: Gerstenberg Verlag, 1980, 160-175.

3876   Martin, F. David. "Heidegger's Being of Things and Aesthetic Education." *The Journal of Aesthetic Education* (Urbana), vol. 8, 1974, 87-105.

3877   Martin, V. R. "Martin Heidegger. Elementos de bibliographia." *Philosophia* (Mendoza), vol. 37, 1971, 125-171.

3877a  Martineau, Emmanuel. "La modernité de 'Sein und Zeit'. Réflexions au lendemain d'un cinquantenaire manqué." *Revue Philosophique de Louvain* (Louvain), no. 78, 1980, 160-175.

3878   Martinent, J. "Apercus sur la problématique de l'etre et du sens." *Revue de l'Enseignement Philosophique* (Gagny), vol. 26, no. 1, 1975, 5-9.

3879   *Martin Heidegger. Fragen an sein Werk.* Ein Symposium. (Universalbibliothek, 9873). Stuttgart: Reclam, 1977, 70 p.

3880   "Martin Heidegger 1889-1976." *Aquinas* (Roma), vol. 20, no. 2, 1977. Roma: Pontificia Univ. Lateranense, 1977, 161-315.

3881   Martinez-Gómez, L. "De nuevo Tomá-Heidegger." *Arbor* (Madrid), vol. 54, 1963, 92-93.

3882   Martins, D. "Una conferência de Heidegger." *Revista Portuguesa de Filosofia* (Braga), vol. 8, 1952, 424-427.

3883   Martins, D. "S. Tomás e Heidegger." *Revista Portuguesa di Filosofia* (Braga), vol. 9, 1953, 21-44.

3884    Maruyama, Ryôji. "Kisotekisonzairon no Mondai" (The Problem of Fundamental Ontology). *Tenridaigakugakuhô* (Tenri), Oktober 1951, Januar 1952.

3885    Maruyama, Ryôji. *HaideggÂ no Tenkai* (Heidegger's Notion of the Turning). *Tenridaigaku-Gakuhô* (Terni), 1960.

3886    Maruyama, Ryôji. *Haideggâ to Herudarin* (Heidegger and Hölderlin). *Tenridaigaku-Gakuhô* (Tenri), 1960.

3887    Maruyama, Ryôji. *Haideggâ to Kami no Mondai* (Heidegger and the Problem of God). *Tenridaigaku-Nenpô* (Tenri), 1961.

3888    Marx, Werner. "Heidegger's New Conception of Philosophy. The Second Phase of 'Existentialism'." *Social Research* (Albany, New York), vol. 22, 1955, 451-474.

3889    Marx, Werner. "Heidegger und die Metaphysik." *Beiträge zu Philosophie und Wissenschaft. Wilhelm Szilasi zum 70. Geburtstag.* München, 1960, 185-200.

3890    Marx, Werner. *Heidegger und die Tradition. Eine problemgeschichtliche Einführung in die Grundbestimmungen des Seins.* Stuttgart, 1961, 268 p.

3891    Marx, Werner. *Vernunft und Welt. Zwischen Tradition und anderem Anfang.* Den Haag, 1970.

3892    Marx, Werner. *Heidegger and the Tradition.* Evanston, Illinois, 1, XXXIII, 275 p.

3893    Marx, Werner. "The World in Another Beginning: Poetic Dwelling and the Role of the Poet." In *On Heidegger and Language.* Ed. J. J. Kockelmans. Evanston, Illinois, 1972, 235-259.

3894    Marx, Werner. "Thought and Issue in Heidegger." *Research in Phenomenology* (Pittsburgh), vol. 7, 1977, 12-30.

3895    Marx, Werner, ed. *Heidegger. Freiburger Universitätsvorträge zu seinem Gedenken.* Freiburg/München, 1977.

3896    Marx, Werner. "In Remembrance of Martin Heidegger." Trans. Richard S. Grabau. *Man and World* (The Hague), vol. 10, no. 1, 3-5.

3897    Marx, Werner. "Thought and Its Object." (In Serbocroat). *Delo* (Beograd), vol. 23, no. 12, 1977, 33-51.

3897a   Marx, Werner. "Il compito del pensiero. Discorso inaugurale al Convegno Internazionale dedicato a M. Heidegger dal Collegium Phaenomenologicum di Monteripido (Perugia, luglio 1978)." Trans. Anna Cazzullo. *L'Uomo, un segno* (Milano), vol. 3, no. 1-2, 7-18.

3897b   Marx, Werner. "Die Sterblichen." In *Nachdenken über Heidegger.* Ed. Ute Guzzoni. Hildesheim: Gerstenberg Verlag, 1980, 160-175.

3897    cMarx, Wolfgang. "Die ontologische Differenz in der Perspektive der regionalen Ontologie des Daseins. Ein Beitrag zur 'Unüberwindbarkeit' der Metaphysik." In *Nachdenken über Heidegger.* Ed. Ute Guzzoni. Hildesheim: Gerstenberg Verlag, 1980, 176-197.

3898    Marzano, S. Rev. of *Introduzione alla metafisica*, by Martin Heidegger. Milano, 1968. *Filosofia* (Torino), vol. 20, 1969, 517-522.

3899    Mascall, E. L. *Existence and Analogy*. Hamden, 1967, 188 p.

3900    Masi, G. "Ontologia e fenomenologia in Heidegger." *La Fenomenologia. Atti dell'XI Convegno del Centro di Studi Filosofici tra Professori Universitari-Gallarate 1955* (Brescia Morcelliana), 1956, 273-283.

3901    Masi, G. *La libertà in Heidegger*. (Ricerche sulla sua filosofia). Bologna, 1961, 196 p.

3902    Maslanka, John Stanley. *The Interrelationship of Being and Language in Heidegger's Thought*. Phil. Diss. Boston College 1974. *Dissertation Abstracts International*, vol. 36/04-A, 2260. Rpt. in London: University Microfilms International, 1979, vi-308 p.

3903    Mason, David R. *A Study of Time in the Philosophies of Alfred North Whitehead and Martin Heidegger With Implications for a Doctrine of Providence*. Phil. Diss. Univ. of Chicago 1973 431 p.

3904    Mason, David R. "Time in Whitehead and Heidegger: Some Comparisons." *Process Studies* (Claremont), vol. 5, 1975, 83-105.

3905    Massaia, Livia. "Note in margine a M. Heidegger. Saggi e discorsi." *Verifiche* (Trento), vol. 6, 1977, 644-653.

3905a   Massaia, Livia. "Recenti pubblicazioni heideggeriane Humanitas, Rassegna di Teologia." *Verifiche* (Trento), vol. 8, 1979, 438-441.

3906    Massolo, Arturo. "Heidegger e la fondazione Kantaina." *Giornale critico della filosofia italiana* (Firenze), vol. 22, 1941, 336-353.

3907    Massolo, Arturo. "Lezione su Heidegger." *Studi Urbinati di Storia, Filosofia e Letteratura* (Urbino), vol. 51, n.s. B, 1977, 477-486.

3908    Masson, Robert. "Rahner and Heidegger: Being, Hearing, and God." *The Thomist* (Washington), vol. 37, 1973, 455-488.

3909    Matoba, Tetsurô. "Haideggâ Ryakunenfu" (Heidegger's Chronological Records). *Jitsuzonshugi* (Tôkyô), vol. 77, 1976, 148-157.

3910    Matsui, Kyû. "Jituzonshugi no Kenkyû - Yasupâsu to Haideggâ no Mondaiten" (Existentialism - Jaspers and Heidegger). *Ryûkoku Daigaku Bukkyô Bunka Kenkyûsho kiyô* (Kyôto), vol. 8, 1969, 85-88.

3911    Matsumoto, Hikoyoshi. "Haideggâ no Sarutoru Hihan" (Heidegger's Criticism of Sartre). *Tembô* (Tôkyô), vol. 40, 1949, 23-24.

3912    Matusnami, Shinzaburo. "Herudârin no Kikyo" (Hölderlin's Homecoming). In *Varia Poetica*. Kawade Shobô Shinsha, Tôkyô, 1974, 265-288.

3913    Matsuno, Tatsuo. "'Tairaku' no Shakaigakuteki Arikata" (The Sociological Existence of "Decay"). *Gifudaigaku-Gakugeigakubu-Kenkyûhôkoku*. Gifu, 1961.

3914    Matsuzuka, Toyoshige. "Keijijôgaku to Nihirizumu" (Metaphysics and Nihilism; Studies on Heidegger's Nietzsche). *Shimane Daigaku Bunrigakubu Kiyô* (Matsue), vol. 10, 1976.

3915    Marz, R. "Gespräch mit M. Heidegger." *Horizont* (Vasa), vol. 20, 1973, 26-30.

3916    Matzat, H.-L. "Rev. of *Platons Lehre von der Wahrheit. Mit einem Brief über den 'Humanismus',* by Martin Heidegger. *Zeitschrift für philosophische Forschung* (Reutlingen), vol. 2, 1947/48, 646-648.

3917    Maurer, Reinhart. "Der angewandte Heidegger. Herbert Marcuse und das akademische Proletariat." *Philosophisches Jahrbuch* (München), vol. 77, 1970, 238-259.

3918    Maurer, Reinhart. "Von Martin Heidegger zur praktischen Philosophie." *Rehabilitierung der praktischen Philosophie.* Bd. I: Geschichte - Probleme - Aufgaben. Ed. M. Riedel. Freiburg, 1971, 415-454. Rpt. in English "From Heidegger to Practical Philosophy." *Idealistic Studies* (Worcester), vol. 3, 1973, 133-162.

3919    Maurer, Reinhart. *Revolution und Kehre. Studien zum Problem gesellschaftlicher Naturbeherrschung.* Frankfurt, 1975.

3920    Mauthner, J. "Dem Sein im Denken auf der Spur. Philosoph im Zeitalter der Angst: Martin Heidegger." *Westdeutsche Allgemeine Zeitung,* Nr. 229 v. 27.9.1969.

3921    May, William Francis. *Dread Before Death and Revolt Against Death: A Study of Heidegger and Camus.* Phil. Diss. Yale Univ. 1962.

3922    Mayer, A. "Martin Heideggers Beitrag zur Pädagogik." *Zeitschrift für Pädagogik* (Weinheim/Düsseldorf), 1960, 138-148.

3923    Mayorga, R. *Sein und Geschichte: Zur Kritik der negativen Ontologie und Geschichtsphilosophie Martin Heideggers.* Phil. Diss. Berlin- W 1971 411 p.

3924    Mayr, Franz K. "Heidegger und die neuscholastische Metaphysik." *Orientierung* (Katholische Blätter für weltanschauliche Information) (Zürich), vol. 28, 1964, 155-159.

3925    Mazzantini, C. "Martino Heidegger. Linee fondamentali della sua filosofia." *Rivista di filosofia neoscolastica* (Milano), vol. 27, 1935, 14-30.

3926    Mazzantini, C. "Il significato della realta nella filosofia di Martino Heidegger." *Rivista di filosofia neoscolastica* (Milano), vol. 27, 1935, 41-49.

3927    Mazzantini, C. "Martino Heidegger. Osservazioni critiche sulla sua dottrina dal punto di vista della filosofia neoscolastica." *Rivista di filosofia neoscolastica* (Milano), vol. 27, 1935, 268-282.

3928    Mazzantini, C. *Filosofia perenne e personalità filosofiche.* Padova, 1942. [M. Heidegger e la filos. neoscolastica: 261-305.]

3929    Mazzantini, C. *Il tempo.* Como, 1942, 55-91.

3930    Mazzantini, C. "Heidegger, Martin." *Enciclopedia filosofica* (Venezia/Roma), Bd II, 1957, 1032-1041.

3931    Mazzantini, C. *Il tempo e quattro saggi su Heidegger.* Parma, 1969, 231 p.

3932    McCormick, Peter J. "Heidegger's Meditation on the Word." *Philosophical Studies* (Maynooth), vol. 18, 1969, 76-99.

3933 McCormick, Peter J. "Interpreting the Later Heidegger." *Philosophical Studies* [Ireland] (Dublin), vol. 19, 1970, 83-101.

3934 McCormick, Peter J. "Saying and Showing in Heidegger and Wittgenstein." *The Journal of the British Society for Phenomenology* (New York), vol. 3, 1972, 27-35.

3935 McCormick, Peter J. Rev. of *Hermeneutics: Interpretation Theory in Schleiermacher, Dilthey, Heidegger and Gadamer,* by R. D. Palmer. *Philosophical Studies* (Dublin), vol. 20, 1972, 240-243.

3936 McCormick, Peter J. Rev. of "What is Called Thinking?" by Martin Heidegger. *The Journal of the British Society for Phenomenology* (Manchester), vol. 3, no. 1, 1972, 71-74.

3937 McCormick, Peter J. Rev. of "Identity and Difference?" by Martin Heidegger. *The Journal of the British Society for Phenomenology* (Manchester), vol. 3, no. 1, 1972, 71-74.

3938 McCormick, Peter J. Rev. of *Schellings Abhandlung über das Wesen der menschlichen Freiheit,* by Martin Heidegger. *Dialogue* (Montreal), vol. 12, 1973, 129-133.

3939 McCormick, Peter J. Rev. of "On Time and Being," by Martin Heidegger. *Dialogue* (Montréal/Kingston), vol. 13, 1974, 803-806.

3940 McCormick, Peter J. Rev. of "Identity and Difference," by Martin Heidegger. *Dialogue* (Montréal/Kingston), vol. 13, 1974, 217-220.

3941 McCormick, Peter J. "Heidegger sur le chemin du langage." *Philosophiques* (Montréal), vol. 1, no. 2, 1974, 15-36. [Summary, 80.]

3942 McCormick, Peter J. "A Note on *Time and Being.*" *Philosophy Today* (Celina, Ohio), vol. 19, 1975, 95-99.

3943 McCormick, Peter J. "Heidegger on Hölderlin." *Philosophical Studies* (Ireland), vol. 22, 1974, 7-16.

3944 McCormick, Peter J., ed. *Heidegger and the Language of the World. An Argumentative Reading of the Later Heidegger's Meditations on Language.* (Collection Philosophica). Ottawa: Univ. of Ottawa Press, 1976, xvi, 208 p.

3945 McCormick, Peter. "Phenomenology and Metaphilosophy." In *Husserl. Expositions and Appraisals,* by Frederick A. Elliston and Peter McCormick (eds.). Notre Dame, Indiana/London: Univ. of Notre Dame Press, 1977, 350-364.

3946 McCormick, Peter J. "Heidegger and the Philosophy of Mind." *Philosophy Today,* vol. 24, 1980, 153-160.

3947 McCown, Joe. "Phenomenology and Symbolics of Guilt." *Southern Journal of Philosophy,* vol. 14, 1976, 293-302.

3948 McCumber, John Albert. *The Communication of Philosophical Truth in Hegel and Heidegger.* Phil. Diss. Univ. of Toronto 1978. *Dissertation Abstracts International,* vol. 39/07-A, 4325.

3949 McCumber, John Albert. "Language and Appropriation: The Nature of Heideggerian Dialogue." *Personalist,* vol. 60, October 1979, 384-396.

3950 McEvilly, Wayne. "Kant, Heidegger, and the Upanisads." *Philosophy East and West* (Honolulu, Hawaii), vol. 12, 1963, 311-317.

3951 McGaughey, Douglas R. "Husserl and Heidegger on Plato's Cave Allegory: A Study of Philosophical Influence." *International Philosophical Quarterly* (New York), vol. 16, no. 3, 1976, 331-348.

3952 McGinley, John Willard. "The Essential Thrust of Heidegger's Thought." *Philosophy Today* (Celina, Ohio), vol. 15, 1971, 242-249.

3953 McGinley, John Willard. "Heidegger's Concern for the Lived-World in His Dasein-Analysis." *Philosophy Today* (Celina, Ohio), vol. 16, 1972, 92-116.

3954 McGinley, John Willard. "The Essential Thrust of Heidegger's Thought." *Philosophy Today* (Celina, Ohio), vol. 16, 1972, 242-249.

3955 McGinley, John Willard. "The Question of Life in Heidegger's *Being and Time.*" Authorized facsimile of the dissertation of the Boston College. Phil. Diss. 1971. Ann Arbor, Michigan; London: University Microfilms International, 1977, xi-167 p. *Dissertation Abstracts International,* vol. 32/01-A, 490.

3956 McGinley, John Willard. "Does God Exist?" *Philosophy Today* (Celina, Ohio), vol. 22, no. 2-4, 1978, 168-171.

3957 McNicholl, Ambrose. "Heidegger. Problem and Pregasp." *Irish Theological Quarterly* (Maynooth), vol. 44, no. 3, 1977, 208-231.

3958 McNicholl, Ambrose. "Heidegger: problema e precomprensione." *Aquinas. Rivista de Filosofia* (Roma), vol. 20, no. 2, 1977, 180-206.

3959 Mehta, Jarava Lal. *The Philosophy of Martin Heidegger.* Varanasi, Banares Hindu Univ. Press, 1967, XXII, 566 p. Rpt. in *Harper Torchbook,* 1971, 279.

3960 Mehta, Jarava Lal. "Heidegger and the Comparision of Indian and Western Philosophy." *Philosophy East and West* (Honolulu), vol. 20, 1970, 303-317.

3961 Mehta, Jarava Lal. *Martin Heidegger: The Way and the Vision.* Rev. ed. [Previous eds. pub. under title: *The Philosophy of Martin Heidegger.*] Honolulu: Univ. Press of Hawaii, 1976, 510 p.

3962 Mehta, Jarava Lal. "Finding Heidegger." *Research in Phenomenology* (Pittsburgh), vol. 7, 1977, 5-11.

3963 Mehta, Jarava Lal. "A Western Kind of Rishi." In *Erinnerung an Martin Heidegger.* Ed. Günther Neske. Pfullingen: Verlag Günther Neske, 1977, 165-171.

3964 Mehta, Jarava Lal. "Heidegger and Vedanta. Reflections on a Questionable Theme." *International Philosophical Quarterly* (New York), vol. 18, no. 2, 1978, 121-149.

3965 Meile, R. "Martin Heideggers Existentialphilosophie im Aufriss." *Annalen der Philosophischen Gesellschaft Innerschweiz* (Schwyz), vol. 2, 1945, 4-16.

3966    Meili, Cai. "Cunzaizhuyi dashi - Hai Dege" (Heidegger - Master of Existentialism). Taibei: *Daxue congkan*, vol. 15, 1970.

3966    Meile, R. "Martin Heideggers Existentialphilosophie im Aufriss." *Annalen der Philosophischen Gesellschaft Innerschweiz* (Schwyz), vol. 2, 1945, 4-16.

3967    Meinertz, J. *Moderne Seinsphilosophie in ihrer Bedeutung für die Psychologie.* Heidelberg, 1948.

3968    Meinertz, J. *Existenz, Psychologie, Ontologie. Versuch einer Ordnung existenzphilosophischer Probleme.* Meisenheim/Glan, 1952.

3969    Meinertz, J. "Das Sein und das Nichts, die Angst, der Tod und die Zeit." *Zeitschrfit für philosophische Forschung* (Meisenheim/Glan), vol. 9, 1955, 32-55, 461-489, 34-37, 50-52, 461-469.

3970    Meinertz, J. *Philosophie, Tiefenpsychologie, Existenz. Tiefenpsychologische Keime und Probleme in der Philosophie des Idealismus und in der Existenzphilosophie.* München/Basel, 1958, 131 p.

3971    Melander, Don Walter. *Wallace Stevens Meditations on Being: A Heideggerian Study.* Phil. Diss. Syracuse Univ. 1976.

3972    Melchinger, S. "In der Sackgasse des Denkens (Martin Heideggers neue Schrift/Zu seinem 65. Geburtstag)." *Stuttgarter Zeitung*, 25.9.1954.

3973    Mende, Georg. "Das Weltbild Martin Heideggers. Seine Wurzeln und seine Auswirkungen." *Wissenschaftliche Zeitschrift der Friedrich-Schiller-Universität.* (Gesellschafts und sprachwissenschaftliche Reihe). Jena, vol. 3, 1953/54, 201-251.

3974    Mende, Georg. *Studien über die Existenzphilosophie.* Berlin, 1956, 232 p.

3975    Mende, Goerg. "Holzwege der Philosophie (Heidegger)." *Wissenschaftliche Zeitschrift der Friedrich-Schiller-Universität Jena.* (Gesellschafts und Sprachwissenschaftl. Reihe). Jena, vol. 7, 1957/58, 93-96.

3976    Mende, Georg. Rev. of *Die Frage nach dem Ding,* by Martin Heidegger. Tübingen, 1962. *Deutsche Literaturzeitung für Kritik der internationalen Wissenschaft* (Berlin), vol. 85, 1964, 391-396.

3977    Menezes, Djacir. "Glosas Anti-Heideggerianas." *Revista Brasileira de Filosofia,* 1979, 29 or 30, 207-212.

3978    Menji, Shin'ichiro. "Parumenidesu to Haideggâ" (Parmenides and Heidegger). *Jitsuzonshugi* (Tôkyô), vol. 54, 1970, 52-68.

3979    Meny, James Frederick. *On Finitude and Truth: The Livability of the Philosophy of Martin Heidegger.* Phil. Diss. Univ. of Toronto 1975. *Dissertation Abstracts International,* vol. 38/09-A, 5528.

3980    Merlan, Philiph. "Time Consciousness in Husserl and Heidegger." *Philosophy and Phenomenological Research* (Buffalo, New York), vol. 8, 1947/48, 23-54.

3981    Merian, P. *Über 'Dichtung und Wahrheit' oder Forschung.* (Aus Anlass eines Werkes von Heidegger). Basel, 1945.

3982 Messer, A. "Über das Nichts." *Philosophie und Leben* (Leipzig), vol. 7, 1931, 47-50, 105-110.

3983 Metz, Johana Baptist. "Heidegger und das Problem der Metaphysik." *Scholastik* (Freiburg), vol. 28, 1953, 1-22.

3984 Metzger, Arnold. *Phänomenologie und Metaphysik.* Halle, 1933, 225-230, 270.

3985 Metzger, Arnold. *Freiheit und Tod.* Tübingen, 1955, XII, 290 p.

3986 Metzger, Arnold. *Existentialismus und Sozialismus. Der Dialog des Zeitalters.* Pfullingen, 1968, 281 p., (specifically pages 83-102).

3987 Metzger, Arnold. "Die Frage nach dem Menschen in der Philosophie unserer Zeit von Husserl bis Heidegger und Sartre." *Universitas* (Stuttgart), vol. 27, 1972, 65-77.

3988 Metzke, E. "Anweisung zum Denken." Rev. of *Was heisst Denken?* by Martin Heidegger. Tübingen, 1954. *Zeitwende* (Hamburg) (Die neue Furche), vol. 26, 1955, 566-567.

3989 Meulen, J. van der. *Heidegger und Hegel oder Widerstreit und Widerspruch.* Meisenheim/Glan, 1953, 216 p.

[Rev. by P. Chiodi in *Rivista di Filosofia* (Torino), vol. 47, 1956, 83-85.]

3990 Meurers, J. "Fortschrittsglaube und exakte Naturwissenschaft." *Der Fortschrittsglaube.* Festschrift f. Franz König, Graz, 1965, 68-83, (specifically pages 81-82).

3991 Meurers, J. "Der Satz des Anaximander und das Ding An Sich." *Kant-Studien,* vol. 70, 425-450.

3992 Meyer, G. Rev. of *Kant und das Problem der Metaphysik,* by Martin Heidegger. Bonn, 1929. *Hamburger Fremdenblatt,* 28.6.1930.

3993 Meyer, H. *Geschichte der abendländischen Weltanschauung.* V. Band: Die Weltanschauung der Gegenwart, Würzburg, 1949, 430-450.

3994 Meyer, H. Rev. of *Nietzsche, Bd I-II,* by Martin Heidegger. *Salzburger Jahrbuch für Philosophie* (Salzburg), vol. 7, 1963, 247-248.

3995 Meyer, H. *Martin Heidegger und Thomas von Aquin.* München/Paderborn/Wien, 1964, VIII, 154 p.

3996 "Mezdunarodnoe kommunisticeskoe dvizenie v borbe pravogo i 'levogo' opportunizma, ego filosofskich i sociologiceskich koncepcij" (The International Communist Movement Fighting Against Right and "Left" Opportunism, Its Philosophical and Sociological Conceptions). *Istorija filosofii,* tom V, kniga pervaja. Moskva, 1965, 386, 434.

3997 Michailov, A. A. *Filosofija obrecennych. Ekzistencializm rekcionnoe tecenie v sovo burzajaznoj filosofii.* Minsk, 1962, 32 p.

3998 Michailow, A. A. *Martin Heidegger und seine 'Kehre'.* Jena, 1966, IX, 114 p. Phil. Diss. Jena v.6.Juli 1966.

3999 Michajlov, A. A. "Martin Heidegger und der Humanismus." *Wissenschaftliche Zeitschrift der Friedrich-Schiller-Universität Jena*

(Berlin), vol. 20, 1971, 93-102. Rpt. in "Martin Chajdegger i gumanizm" (Martin Heidegger and Humanism). *Protiv burzuaznoj i reformistskoj ideologii.* Minsk, 1972, 129-137.

4000 Michalski, Krzysztof. "Martin Heidegger, Fenomenologia i Teologie." *Studia Filosoficzne* (Warszawa), vol. 10, 1972, 204-207.

4001 Michalski, Krzysztof. Rev. of "Schellings Abhandlung über das Wesen der menschlichen Freiheit," by Martin Heidegger. Tübingen, 1971. *Studia Filozoficzne,* vol. 12, 1972.

4002 Michalski, Krzysztof. Rev. of "Phänomenologie und Theologie," by Martin Heidegger. *Studia Filozoficzne,* vol. 10, 1972.

4003 Michalski, Krzysztof. "Milczenie Filosofia" (The Silence of the Philosopher). *Studia Filosoficzne* (Warszawa), vol. 11 and 12, 1972, 211-225.

4004 Michalski, Krzysztof. "Ku samej rzeczy" (To the Subject Itself). *Studia Filozoficzne,* vol. 10, 1973.

4005 Michalski, Krzysztof. "O odpowiedzialnosci filozofa" (On the Philosopher's Responsibility/a Discussion). *Znak,* vol. 6, 1974.

4006 Michalski, Krzysztof. "Heidegger i poltka" (Heidegger and Gossip). *Literatura,* vol. 42, 1974.

4007 Michalski, Krzysztof. "Uczucie i fenomenologie" (Feeling and Phenomenology). *Teksty,* vol. 2, 1974.

4008 Michalski, Krzysztof. "Heidegger i problem prawdy" (Heidegger and the Problem of Truth). *Studia Filozoficzne,* vol. 12, 1974.

4009 Michalski, Krzysztof. Rev. of "Frühe Schriften," by Martin Heidegger. Frankfurt, 1972. *Studia Filozoficzne,* vol. 1, 1974.

4010 Michalski, Krzysztof. "Filozof i czas" (Philosopher and Time). *Teksty,* vol. 6, 1974.

4011 Michalski, Krzysztof. "Heidegger." *Twórczósá* (Warszawa), vol. 31, no. 8, 1975, 87-100.

4012 Michalski, Krzysztof. "Granice filozofii transcendentalnej" (The Limits of Transcendental Philosophy). In *Dziedzictwo Kanta* (Kants Erfe). Warszawa, 1975.

4013 Michalski, Krzysztof. Rev. of "Heidegger in Selbstzeugnissen und Bilddokumenten," by W. Biemel. 1973. *Studia Filozoficzne,* vol. 7, 1975.

4014 Michalski, Krzysztof. Rev. of "Verstehen und Auslegung. Das Methodenproblem in der Philosophie M. Heidegger," by C. F. Gethmann. *Studia Filozoficzne,* 11 October 1975.

4015 Michalski, Krzysztof. "Heidegger." *Kultura,* vol. 29, 1976.

4016 Michalski, Krzysztof. Rev. of "Materialen zur Heidegger - Bibliographie 1917-1972," by Hans-Martin Sass. *Teksty,* vol. 2, 1976.

4017 Michalski, Krzysztof. "O áródlach filozofii" (On the Origins of Philosophy). *Teksty,* vol. 3, 1977.

4018　Michalski, Krzysztof. Rev. of "Logik," by Martin Heidegger. Frankfurt/Main, 1976. *Studia Filozoficzne,* vol. 7, 1977.

4019　Michalski, Krzysztof. *Heidegger i filozofia wspolczesna.* Warschau: Panstwowy Inst. Wydawniczy, 1978.

4020　Michalson, A. B. "Theologie als Ontologie und als Geschichte." *Der spätere Heidegger und die Theologie.* Zürich/Stuttgart, 1964, 161-186.

4021　Michalson, Carl. *Hinge of History: An Existential Approach to the Christian Faith.* Toronto: Saunders, 1959.

4022　Micheletti, M. Rev. of *La dottri na del giudizzio nello psicologismo,* by Martin Heidegger. *Revista di Filosofia Neo-Scolastica* (Mailand), vol. 64, 1972, 560-561.

4023　Micheletti, M. Rev. of *Scritti filosofici e La dottrina del giudizio nello psicologismo,* by Martin Heidegger. *Filosofia* (Torino), vol. 3, 1973, 350 ff.

4024　Micheletti, M. Rev. of "Scritti filosofici (1912-1917)," by Martin Heidegger. *Filosofia* (Torino), vol. 24, 1973, 350-353.

4025　Micheletti, M. Rev. of "La dottrina delle categorie e del significato in Duns Scoto," by Martin Heidegger. *Filosofia* (Torino), vol. 28, 1975, 319-320.

4026　Michnak, K. "Heidegger und das Schicksal des 'Gottes der Metaphysik'." *Filosoficky casopis* (Prag), no. 5, 1967, 686-703. (In Czechoslovakian).

4027　Mihalich, Joseph C. *Existentialism and Thomism.* New York Philosophical Lib., 1960.

4028　Mikhail, F. "'Qu'est-ce que la philosophie?' Heidegger en France (Décade de Cerisyla-Salle, 27 août - 4 septembre 1955)." *Aspects de la dialectique, Recherches de Philosophie* (Paris), Tome II, 1956, 353-359.

4029　Miki, Kiyoshi. "Haideggâ no Sonzairon" (Heidegger's Ontology). *Chûôkôron.* Tôkyô, [Supplement], 1930, 18-21.

4030　Miki, Masayuki. *Haideggâ no Herudârin-Kaishaku ni tsuite* (On Heidegger's Hölderlin-Interpretation). Kagoshima-daigakubunkahôkoku, Kagoshima, 1955.

4031　Miki, Masayuki. "Haideggâ no Riruke Kaishaku Oboegaki" (Remarks on Heidegger's Explications Concerning Rilke). (Bermerkungen zu Heideggers Erläuterung über Rilke). *Kindai* (Kôbe), vol. 31, 1961, 27-45.

4032　Millikan, James Dean. "Wild's Review of 'Being and Time'." *Review of Metaphysics* (New Haven, Connecticut), vol. 16, 1962/63, 780-785.

4033　Millikan, James Dean. "Heidegger, Time, and Self-Transcendence." Phil. Diss. Yale Univ. 1966. Ann Arbor, Michigan: University Microfilms Inc., 1977, v, 229 p. *Dissertation Abstracts International,* vol. 27/08-A, 2567.

4034　Mima, Chigusa. "Haideggâ no Geijutsuron" (Heidegger's Theory of Art). *Bigku* (Tôkyô), vol. XIII, no. 3, 1962, 11-13.

4035　Mindán, M. "Verdad y libertad." *Estudios Filosóficos* (Valladolid), vol. 28, no. 108-111, 1969, 5-25.

4036 Minder, R. "Hebel und die Sprache von Messkirch," by Martin Heidegger. *Der Monat,* Heft 214, (18.Jg.), Juli, 1966, 13-32.

4037 Minder, R. "Langage et nazisme." *Critique* (Paris), vol. 23, 1967, 284-287.

4038 Minejima, Akio. "Haideggâ no Geijutsuron ni yosete - Biteki Saisôzô ni okeru 'Jikan' no Igi" (Heidegger's Theory of Art - the Significance of 'Time' in Esthetic Representation). *Tetsugaku Ninshi* (Tôkyô) (Taishô Daigaku Tetsugakukai), vol. 1, 1963, 31-49.

4039 Minejima, Akio. "Nikorai Harutoman ni okeru Seishin-Kagaku no Kisozuke; Haideggâ Yasupâsu tono Taihi o tsûjite" (The Foundation of the Humanities Through Nikolai Hartmann; Compared With Heidegger and Jaspers). *Waseda Shôgaku* (Tôkyô), vol. 188, 1966, 57-90.

4040 Minges, P. "Die skotistische Literatur des 20. Jahrhunderts." Rev. of *Die Kategorien und Bedeutungslehre des Duns Scotus,* by Martin Heidegger. Tübingen, 1916. *Franziskanische Studien* (Münster), vol. 4, 1917, 177-178.

4041 Tavares de Miranda, M. C. "O pensar e o ser entre." *Revista filosofica do Nordeste* (Fortaleza, Brasil), vol. 2, 1961, 33-38.

4042 Tavares de Miranda, Maria C. "Martin Heidegger, filósofo do ser." *Revista brasileira de Filosofia* (Sao Paulo), vol. 26, 1976, 267-274.

4043 Mirri, E. "Il pensare del 'Medesimo'. Heidegger ed Hegel." *Aquinas* (Italy), vol. 21, no. 2-3, 1978, 212-239.

4044 Misaki, Gisen. "Haidegga no Kanto-Kaishaku ni okeru Choetsu" (Transcendence in Heidegger's Interpretation of Kant). *Philosophia* (Tôkyô), vol. 35, Dezember 1958.

4045 Misch, Georg. "Lebensphilosophie und Phänomenologie. Eine Auseinandersetzung mit Heidegger und Husserl." *Philosophischer Anzeiger* (Bonn), vol. 3, 1928/29, 267-368, 405-475; (Bonn), vol. 4, 1929/30, 181-330.

4046 Misch, Georg. *Lebensphilosophie und Phänomenologie.* Bonn, 1930. 2nd ed. Leipzig/Berlin, 1931, X, 324 p. Rpt. in 1967, X, 328 p.

4047 Misgeld, Dieter. "From the Existential Analytic to Social Inquiry. Heidegger and Contemporary Developments Toward a Hermeneutical Conception of Inquiry." *Revue de l'Université Laurentienne* (Sudbury), vol. 9, no. 2, 1977, 39-54.

4048 Mitchell, Donald W. Rev. of *Martin Heidegger and the East,* by E. F. Hirsch. *Philosophy East and West* (Honolulu), vol. 20, 1970, 265-279.

4049 Mitsusawa, Aritune. "Haideggâ no Geijutsutetsugaku" (Heidegger's Philosophy of Art). *Bigaku,* vol. 26, no. 3, 1975, 16-26.

4050 Miura, Hideharu. "Haideggâ no Tetsugaku to Nichijôsei no Mondai Josetsu - Nichijôsei to sono Hen'yô ni tsuite no ichi Shiron" (Heidegger's Philosophy and "Everydayness"). *Tôkyô Daigaku Daigakuin Kiyô* (Tôkyô), vol. 5, 1968, 23-37.

4051 Miura, Hideharu. "Haideggâ to Marukûze ni okeru Ketsuisei no Mondai" (Problems of Re-Solue in Heidegger's and Marcuse's Thought). *Tôyô Daigaku* (Bungakubu Hen) (Kiyô, Tôkyô), vol. 25, 1972, 15-32.

4052    Miura, Hideharu. "Jitsuzon to Sôzôryoku; Haideggâ o chûshin ni (Existence and Imagination; With Heidegger as the Central Figure). *Hakusan Tetsugaku* (Tôkyô), vol. 9, 1973, 92-123.

4053    Miura, Hideharu. "Haideggâ ni okeru Geijutsu to Jitsuzon Sekai; Gohho 'Nômin-Gutsu' no Aregorî-kô" (Art and Existence-World in Heidegger's Thought; Research for Allegory of 'Bauernschuhe' van Goghs). *Tôyô Daigaku Kiyô*; *Bungakubu Hen* (Tôkyô), vol. 28, 1974, 1-20.

4054    Miura, Hideharu. "Nichijôsei to Fuan" (Everydayness and Anxiety). *Hirosaki Daigaku Iryogijutsu Tanki-Daigkubu Kiyô* (Hirosaki), vol. 1, 1977, 1-17.

4055    Miura, Hideharu. "HOMO CURANS; Haideggâ no Ningenzô to Shêrâ" (HOMO CURANS; Presentment of 'An Image of Human Being' Heidegger's and Scheler). *Hirosaki Daigaku Iryogijutsu Tanki Daigakubu Kiyô* (Hirosaki), vol. 3, 1978, 1-19.

4056    Miyajima, Hajime. "Haideggâ no Daigaku-Honshitsuron" (The Nature of University in Heidegger). *Nippon Seishin Bunka* (Tôkyô), Februar 1934, 141-148.

4057    Miyake, Gôichi. "Haideggâ-Tetsugaku no Tachiba" (The Position of Heidegger's Philosophy). *Bunka* (Sendai), no. 1-3, 1934, 65-109.

4058    Miyake, Gôichi. *Haideggâ no Tetsugaku* (Heidegger's Philosophy). Tôkyô, 1950.

4059    Miyatsu, Eitarô. "Haideggâ no Tetsugaku" (Heidegger's Philosophy). *Bungakubu Kenkyû Nempô* (Tôkyô), vol. 1, 1935, 3-8.

4060    Miyauchi, Sanjirô. "Fidorâ to Haideggâ" (Fiedler und Heidegger). *Bigaku* (Tôkyô), XIX-3, 1968, 22-31.

4061    Mizoguchi, Kyôichi. "Haideggâ ni okeru U no Toi to Ningen-Sonzai, 1" (The Question of Being and Human Existence in Heidegger, 1). *Hyôgô Joshi Tanki Daigaku Ronshû* (Kakogawa), vol. 3, 1969, 26-36.

4062    Mizoguchi, Kyôichi. "Haideggâ ni okeru U no Toi to Ningen-Sonzai, 2" (The Question of Being and Human Existence in Heidegger, 2). *Hyôgô Joshi Tanki Daigaku Ronshû* (Kakogawa), vol. 4, 1970, 61-70.

4063    Mizoguchi, Kyôichi. "Haideggâ ni okeru U no Toi to Ningen-Sonzai, 3" (The Question of Being and Human Existence in Heidegger, 3). *Hyôgô Joshi Tanki Daigaku Ronchû* (Kakogawa), vol. 5, 1972, 96-104.

4064    Mizoguchi, Kyôichi. "Haideggâ ni okeru U no Toi to Ningen-Sonzai, 4" (The Question of Being and Human Existence in Heidegger, 4). *Hyôgô Joshi Tanki Daigaku Ronshû* (Kakogawa), vol. 9, 1975, 68-80.

4065    Mizoguchi, Kôhei. "Haideggâ ni okeru Gijutsu e no Toi" (The Question Concerning Technology in Heidegger). *Risô* (Tôkyô), vol. 500, 1975, 61-71.

4066    Mizoguchi, Kôhei. "Haideggâ to Toki no Mondai" (Heidegger and the Problem of Time). *Ôsaka Kyôiku Daigaku Kiyô* (Ôsaka), vol. 26, no. 3, 1978, 117-131.

4067    Mizoguchi, Kôhei. "Kaishakuteki Tetsugaku no Konpon Mondai; Sono Rironteki Kisozuke no Mondai to Tetsugaku no Kanôsei e no Toi"

(Fundamental Problem of Hermeneutical Philosophy; the Problem of Its Theoretical Foundation and the Question Concerning the Possibility of the Philosophy). *Shisô* (Tôkyô), vol. 659, 1979, 38-59.

4068   Mizuno, Osamu. "Haideggâ ni okeru Kindai ni tsuite" (On Heidegger's View of the Modern World; Through the Essential Determination of the Natural Science). *Shisaku* (Tôkyô), vol. 9, 1976, 20-39.

4069   Mnuskina, L. L. "Illjuzornyj mir ekzistencializma i problemy nravstvennoj orientacii individa" (The Illusionary World of Existentialism and Problems of the Moral Guidance of the Individual). 'Ucënye zapiski'. Moskovskij oblastnoj pedagogiceskij institut, t. 276. *Filosofija, vypusk,* 17, c. 2, 1970, 58-72.

4070   Moehling, Karl A. *Martin Heidegger and the Nazi Party: An Examination.* Phil. Diss. Northern Illinois Univ. DeKalb 1972 298 p. *Dissertation Abstracts International,* vol. 33/04-A, 1788.

4071   Moehling, Karl A. "Heidegger and the Nazis." *Listening. Journal of Religion and Culture* (River Forest, Illinois), vol. 12, no. 3, 1977, 92-105.

4072   Möller, Joseph P. *Existenzialphilosophie und katholische Theologie.* Baden-Baden, 1952, passim.

4073   Möller, Joseph P. "Nietzsche und die Metaphysik. Zu Heideggers Nietzscheinterpretation." *Theologische Quartalschrift* (Stuttgart), vol. 142, 1962, 283-309. Rpt. in "'Nietzsche and Metaphysics': Heidegger's Interpretation of Nietzsche." *Philosophy Today* (Celina, Ohio), vol. 8, 1964, 118-132.

4075   Möller, Joseph P. "Zum Thema: Der spätere Heidegger und die Theologie." *Theologische Quartalschrift* (Stuttgart), vol. 147, 1967, 386-431.

4076   Möller, Joseph P. *Wahrheit als Problem. Traditionen - Theorien - Aporien.* München/Freiburg, 1971, 302 p.

4077   Mörchen, H. "Die Einbildungskraft bei Kant." *Jahrbuch für Philosophie und phänomenologische Forschung* (Halle), vol. 11, 1930, 311 u.ö.

4078   Mörchen, H. "Heidegger in der Schule." *Pädagogische Provinz* (Frankfurt), vol. 12, 1958, 452-463.

4079   Mörchen, H. "Nachwort als Einleitung." *Heidegger, die Weltlichkeit der Welt.* [Ein Kapitel aus 'Sein und Zeit,' Texte für den Philosophieunterricht.] Frankfurt, 1959. 2nd ed. 1964.

4080   Mörchen, H. "Eine Möglichkeit, mit Heidegger anzufangen." *Pädagogische Provinz* (Frankfurt), vol. 14, 1960, 109.

4081   Moga, Michael David. *Intersubjectivity. A Heideggerian Reflection.* Phil. Diss. Tulane Univ. 1970. Ann Arbor, Michigan: University Microfilms, 1977, ii-285 p. *Dissertation Abstracts International,* vol. 31/06-A, 2977.

4082   Mohanty, J. N. "Consciousness and Existence: Remarks on the Relation Between Husserl and Heidegger." *Man and World* (West Lafayette), vol. 11, no. 3-4, 1978, 324-335.

4083    Moisio, F. Rev. of *Introduzione alla metafisica,* by Martin Heidegger. Milano, 1968. *Archivio di Filosofia* (Roma), no. 1, 1970, 171-177.

4084    Molina, Fernando R. *Existentialism as Philosophy.* Englewood Cliff, New Jersey: Prentice-Hall, 1962.

4085    Molina, Fernando R., ed. *The Sources of Existentialism as Philosophy.* Englewood Cliffs, New Jersey, 1969, 230 p.

4086    Molinaro, Aniceto. "Heidegger e l'etica." *Aquinas* (Roma), vol. 20, no. 2, 1977, 238-254.

4087    Molinuevo Martínez de Bujo, José Luis. *Kant en la superación heideggeriana de la metafísica, Excerpt From a Thesis.* Madrid: Facultad de filosofía y Letras, Univ. Complutense, 1974, 32 p.

4088    Molinuevo Martínez de Bujo, José Luis. "El diálogo de Heidegger con Kant en *Ser y Tiempo.*" *Anales del Seminario de Metafísica* (Madrid), vol. 9, 1974, 177-194.

4089    Molinuevo, José Luis. "El tema de la Trascendencia en *Kant y el problema de la metafísica.*" *Pensamiento* (Madrid), vol. 32, no. 128, 1976, 433-463.

4090    Molinuevo, José Luis. "La fundamentación kantiana de la metafisica según Heidegger. In memoriam." *Pensamiento* (Madrid), vol. 32, no. 127, 1976, 259-279.

4090a   Moneta, Giuseppina C. "Esperienza precategoriale Husserliana e *Gelassenheit* Heideggeriana." *L'Uomo, un segno* (Milano), vol. 3, no. 1-2, 1979, 101-110.

4091    Mongis, Henri. *Heidegger et la critique de la notion de valeur. La destruction de la fondation métaphysique.* [With a letter-preface by Martin Heidegger.] (Phaenomenologica, 74). La Haye: Nijhoff, 1976, xii-221 p.

4092    Montero-Moliner, F. "Heidegger y la reducción fenomenologica transcendental." *Revista de Filosofia* (Madrid), vol. 11, 1952, 443-465.

4093    Montero-Moliner, F. "La teoria de la significación en Husserl y Heidegger." *Revista de Filosofia* (Madrid), vol. 12, 1953, 393-426.

4094    Montero-Moliner, F. "El relativismo trascendental de Heidegger." *Revista de Filosofia* (Madrid), vol. 15, 1956, 43-53.

4095    Montull, T. "Boletin bibliografico existencialista." *Estudios Filosoficos* (Las Caldas de Besaya) (Santander), vol. 9, 1960, 135-178, 305-350.

4096    Mood, John J. "Poetic Languaging and Primal Thinking: A Study of Barfield, Wittgenstein, and Heidegger." *Encounter,* vol. 26, 1965, 417-433.

4097    Mood, John J. "Leadbelly on Angst. Heidegger on the Blues." *Philosophy Today* (Celina, Ohio), vol. 14, 1970, 161-167.

4098    Moore, A. "Existential Phenomenology." *Philosophy and Phenomenological Research* (Buffalo, New York), vol. 27, 1966/67, 408-414.

4099    Moore, J. T. Rev. of *Hegel's Concept of Experience,* by Martin Heidegger. *The Modern Schoolman* (St. Louis), vol. 49, 1971/72, 267-270.

4100    Moreau, Ch. "Veritas intellectus et veritas rei selon Saint Thomas et Heidegger." *Sapientia Aquinatis, I:* Communicationes IV Congressus

Thomistici Internationalis, Romae 13-17 Septembris 1955. (Bibliotheca Pontificiae Academiae Romanae S. Thomae Aquinatis, Vol. I). Romae, Officium Libri Catholici, 1955, 528-536.

4101   Moreau, Joseph. "Heidegger et la philosophie des valeurs." *Etudes Philosophiques* (Paris), vol. 2, 1968, 213-215.

4102   Moreau, Michel. Rev. of *Heidegger's Metahistory of Philosophy: amor fati, Being and Truth,* by Bernd Magnus. The Hague, 1970. *Revue Philosophique de Louvain* (Louvain), vol. 74, 1976, 307-308.

4103   Moreno, J. D. "El ser y el tiempo. La Libertad en Heidegger." *Universidad de Antioquia* (Medellin), vol. 30, no. 116, 1954, 57-66.

4104   Moreno, J. D. "Scholasticism Without God: Martin Heidegger (1889-1976)." *Group Psychotherapy, Psychodrama and Sociometry* (Beacon, New York), vol. 30, 1977, 135-137.

4105   Moretti-Costanzi, T. *L'ascetica di Heidegger.* Roma, 1949.

4106   Moretti-Costanzi, T. "Circa un giudizio dello Heidegger sulla mia Ascetica di Heidegger." *Teoresi* (Messina), vol. 6, 1951, 11-17.

4107   Moretti, Giampiero. "Metafisica e nihilismo in Heidegger." *Sapienza,* vol. 32, 1979, 478-492.

4108   Moretto, Giovanni. *L'esperienza religiosa del linguaggio in Martin Heidegger.* Firenze: Felice Le Monnier, 1973, 265 p.

4109   Mori, Kôichi. "Haideggâ no Hihan; 'Keijijôgaku towa nanzo' o Chûshin ni shite" (Criticism on Heidegger Concerning "Was ist Metaphysik"). *Yuibutsuron Kenkyû* (Tôkyô), vol. 16, 1934, 114-118.

4110   Mori, Kôichi. *Zen to Seiyôshiso* (Zen and Occidental Thought). Tôkyô, 1966.

4111   Morón, G. Rev. of *Was heisst Denken?* by Martin Heidegger. Tübingen, 1954. *Revista nacional de Cultura* (Caracas), vol. 18, no. 117-118, 1956, 198-199.

4112   Morpurgo-Tagliabue, G. *Le strutture del transcendentale. Piccola inchiesta sul pensiero critico, dialettico, esistenziale.* Milano, 1951.

4113   Morpurgo-Tagliabue, G. "M. Heidegger el il problema dell'arte." *El Pensiero* (Milano), vol. 4, 1959, 151-169.

4114   Morra, G. F. "Essenzialismo di Martin Heidegger." *Giornale Critico della Filosofia Italiana* (Firenze), Jg. 32, Ser. 3, Bd 7, 1953, 363-370.

4115   Morra, G. F. *Carabellese e Heidegger interpreti di Parmenide. Relazione presentata al Congresso di studi carabellesiani in Bolobna, 7-9 ottobre 1960.* Milano, Silva ed. 1962, 12.

4116   Morra, G. F. "Alienazione ontologica e nostalgia del rimpatrio nel 'Nietzsche' di Heidegger." *Giornale Critico della Filosofia Italiana* (Firenze), vol. 42, 1963, 515-521.

4117   Morra, G. "Martino Heidegger: la morale come abitazione nell'essere." *Ethica* (Forli), vol. 3, 1964, 205-220.

4118   Morra, G. "L'essere del dover-essere." *Proteus. Rivista di Filosofia* (Roma), vol. 5, no. 13, 1974, 47-72.

4119 Morrison, James C. "Heidegger's Criticism of Wittgenstein's Conception of Truth." *Man and World* (Pittsburgh), vol. 2, 1969, 551-573.

4120 Morrison, James C. "Husserl and Heidegger. The Parting of the Ways." In *Heidegger's Existential Analytic,* by Frederick Elliston. The Hague, New York: Mouton Pub., 1978, 47-59.

4121 Morrison, Ronald Philip. "Kant, Husserl, and Heidegger on Time and the Unity of 'Consciousness'." *Philosophy and Phenomenological Research* (Buffalo, New York), vol. 39, no. 2, 1978/79, 182-198.

4122 Morrison, Ronald Philip. "Man and the World. Heidegger and His Interpretation of Kant." Authorized facsimile of the dissertation of the Emory Univ. Phil. Diss. 1975. Ann Arbor, Michigan; London: University Microfilms International, 1979, vi-259 p.

4123 Morriston, W. "Heidegger on the World." *Man and World* (Pittsburgh), vol. 5, 1972, 452-466.

4124 Morscher, E. "Von der Frage nach dem Sein von Sinn zur Frage nach dem Sinn von Sein - der Denkweg des frühen Heidegger." *Philosophisches Jahrbuch* (München), vol. 80, 1973, 379-385.

4125 Morton, M. Rev. of *Poetry, Language, Thought,* by Martin Heidegger. *Dialogue* (Montreal), vol. 12, 1973, 372-373.

4126 Moser, Simon. Rev. of *Platons Lehre von der Wahrheit. Mit einem Brief über den 'Humanismus',* by Martin Heidegger. *Anzeiger für die Altertumswissenschaft* (Wien), vol. 3, 1950, 111-117.

4127 Moser, Simon. "Die Philosophie und ihre Geschichte." *Zeitschrift für philosophische Forschung* (Meisenheim/Glan), vol. 11, 1957, 255-261.

4128 Moser, Simon. *Metaphysik einst und jetzt. Kritische Untersuchungen zu Begriff und Ansatz der Ontologie.* Berlin, 1958, 294 p.

4129 Moser, Simon. "Toward a Metaphysics of Technology." *Philosophy Today* (Celina, Ohio), vol. 15, 1971, 129-156.

4130 Mougin, H. "Comme Dieu en France: Heidegger parmi nous." *Europe* (Paris), vol. 24, 1946, 132-138.

4131 Mougin, H. *Sa sainte famille existantialist.* Paris, 1947, passim.

4132 Mounier, E. *Introduction aux existentialismes.* Paris, 1947.

4133 Mounier, E. "Existenzphilosophie und Aktivismus." *Merkur* (Stuttgart), vol. 1, 1947, 679-699. Rpt. in *Introduction aux existentialismes,* by E. Mounier. Paris, 1947.

4134 Mraz, E. *Sprache und Sein bei Martin Heidegger.* Phil. Diss. Wien 13.12.68.

4135 Mühle, H. "Heidegger und das Wesen der Technik." *Handelsblatt* (Beilage, Düsseldorf), Jg. 8, no. 57, 1953.

4136 Müller, E. "Existentielle Sachlichkeit. Kritische Bemerkungen zu Heideggers Philosophie." *Stuttgarter Neues Tageblatt,* 21.8.1930.

4137 Müller, G. Rev. of *Kant und das Problem der Metaphysik,* by Martin Heidegger. Bonn, 1929. *Bund* (Bern), 24.1.1932.

4138    Müller, G. "Martin Heidegger und die Geschichte." *Evangelische Theologie* (München), vol. 13, N.F. 8, 1953, 319-339.

4139    Müller, G. "Martin Heideggers Philosophie als Frage an die Theologie." *Theologische Zeitschrift* (Basel), vol. 15, 1959, 357-375.

4140    Müller, G. "Vom nichtenden Nichts zur Lichtung des Seins. Zu Martin Heideggers 70. Geburtstag am 26.9.1959." *Deutsches Pfarrerblatt* (Essen), vol. 59, 1959, 414-415.

4141    Müller, H. E. *Der Zeitbegriff Deutingers und Heideggers.* Phil. Diss. Würzburg 1934.

4142    Müller, J. *Der Sprung. Untersuchung zur Logik bei Martin Heidegger.* Phil. Diss. München 26.3.1969 206 p.

4143    Müller, Max. "Zusammenfassung und Bericht über Martin Heidegger: Der Ursprung des Kunstwerks. Vortrag vom 11.11.1935 in der Kunstwissenschaftlichen Gesellschaft zu Freiburg." *Dichtung und Volkstum* (Stuttgart), vol. 38, 1937, 125-128.

4144    Müller, Max. *Existenzphilosophie im geistigen Leben der Gegenwart.* Heidelberg, 1949, 113 p. 2nd ed. 1958. 3rd revised ed. 1964.

4145    Müller, Max. "Phänomenologie, Ontologie und Scholastik." *Tijdschrift voor Philosophie* (Leuven), vol. 14, 1952, 63-86, passim.

4146    Müller, Max. Rev. of *Einführung in die Metaphysik,* by Martin Heidegger. Tübingen, 1953. *Universitas* (Stuttgart), vol. 9, 1954, 301-304, 409-413.

4147    Müller, Max. "Die Philosophie Martin Heideggers im Horizont der Gegenwart." *Badische Zeitung* (Freiburg), 26/27 September 1959.

4148    Müller, Max. "Klassische und moderne Metaphysik oder Sein als Sinn." *Sinn und Sein.* Ein philosophisches Symposion. Ed. R. Wisser. Tübingen, 1960, 311-332.

4149    Müller, Max. "Ende der Metaphysik? Für Martin Heidegger zum 75. Geburtstag am 26.9.1964." *Philosophisches Jahrbuch* (München), vol. 72, 1964/65, 1-48.

4150    Müller, Max. "Phänomenologie, Ontologie und Scholastik." *Heidegger.* Ed. O. Pöggeler. Köln/Berlin, 1969, 78-94.

4151    Müller, Max. *Erfahrung und Geschichte.* (Grundzüge einer Philosophie der Freiheit als transzendentale Erfahrung). Freiburg/München, 1971, 616 p., (specifically pages 521-531, und passim).

4152    Müller, Max. "Evolution und Geschichte." *Philosophisches Jahrbuch* (München), vol. 78, 1971, 17-23.

4153    Müller, Max. "Die Aktualität des Thomas von Aquin." *Philosophisches Jahrbuch* (München), vol. 82, no. 1, 1975, 1-9.

4154    Müller-Gangloff, E. "Gespräch mit Martin Heidegger." *Quatember, Evangelische Jahresbriefe* (Kassel), vol. 18, 1953/54, 99-100.

4155 Müller-Lauter, W. *Der Vorrang der Möglichkeit vor der Wirklichkeit im Denken Martin Heideggers.* Phil. Diss. F.U. Berlin 1959. Berlin, 1960, VII, 107 p.

4156 Müller-Schwefe, H.-R. "Die Angst." *Pastoralblätter* (Stuttgart), vol. 89, 1949, 847-857, (specifically pages 848-849).

4157 Müller-Schwefe, H.-R. *Existenzphilosophie.* Göttingen, 1961, 238 p., (specifically pages 51-74).

4158 Müller-Schwefe, H.-R. "Aufstand gegen das Sein. Der Nihilismus bei Heidegger, Sartre, Jaspers und Marcel." *Zeitwende. Die neue Furche* (Hamburg), vol. 32, 1961, 308-318.

4159 Münzberg, Olav. *Rezeptivität und Spontaneität. Die Frage nach d. ästhet. Subjekt oder soziolog. u. polit. Implikationen d. Verhältnisses Kunstwerk, Rezipient in d. ästhet. Theorien Kants, Schillers, Hegels, Benjamins, Brechts, Heideggers, Sartres u. Adornos.* (Studien zur Germanistik, Studienreihe Humanitas). Frankfurt: Akademische Verlagsgesellschaft, 1974, 219 p.

4160 Mugerauer, Robert. "Reading and Thinking With Heidegger." *Michigan Academian. Michigan Academy of Science, Art and Letters* (Ann Arbor, Michigan), vol. 9, no. 1, 1976, 83-96.

4161 Mugerauer, Robert. "Toward Reading Heidegger's *Discourse on Thinking.*" *The Southwestern Journal of Philosophy* (Norman), vol. 8, no. 1, 1977, 143-156.

4162 Munier, R. "Visite à Heidegger." *Cahiers du Sud* (Marseille), no. 312, 1952, 292-296.

4163 Munier, R. Rev. of *Einfuhrung in die Metaphysik,* by Martin Heidegger. Tübingen, 1953. *Cahiers du Sud* (Marseille), Jg. 41, Bd 40, 1954, 141-147.

4164 Munier, R. "La philosophie selon Heidegger." *Cahiers du Sud* (Marseille), vol. 43, 1956, 191-196.

4165 Munoz-Alonso, A. Rev. of *Da esencia da verdade,* by Martin Heidegger. *Crisis* (Madrid), vol. 3, 1956, 607.

4166 Munson, Thomas N. "Heidegger's Recent Thought on Language." *Philosophy and Phenomenological Research* (Buffalo, New York), vol. 21, 1960/61, 361-372.

4167 Murguia, A. Rev. of "Vier Seminare. Le Thor 1966, 1968, 1969; Zähringen 1973," by Martin Heidegger. 1977. *Pensamiento* (Madrid), vol. 34, 1978, 220-222.

4168 Murray, Michael. Rev. of *Heidegger and the Tradition,* by Werner Marx. *The Philosophical Review* (Ithaca), vol. 4, 1973, 252 ff.

4169 Murray, Michael. "Heidegger and Ryle: Two Versions of Phenomenology." *Review of Metaphysics* (Washington), vol. 27, 1973, 88-111.

4170 Murray, Michael. "A Note on Wittgenstein and Heidegger." *The Philosophical Review* (Ithaca), vol. 83, 1974, 501-503.

4171   Murray, Michael, ed. *Heidegger and Modern Philosophy. Critical Essays.* New Haven, Connecticut: Yale Univ. Press, 1978, xxiii-374 p.

4172   Murray, Michael. "Bibliographical Guide." [The Works of Heidegger in good English translations and a selection of additional secondary literature.] In *Heidegger and Modern Philosophy. Critical Essays,* by Michael Murray. New Haven, Connecticut: Yale Univ. Press, 1978, 355-365.

4173   Muschg, W. *Die Zerstörung der deutschen Literatur.* Bern, 1956, 93-109. 3rd ed. Bern, 1958, 214-230.

4174   Muskala, P. "Martin Heidegger czyli powrót do myálenia" (M. Heidegger: Return to 'Thinking'). *Politechnik,* 11.02.1979.

4175   Muth, F. *Edmund Husserl und Martin Heidegger in ihrer Phänomenologie und Weltanschauung.* Phil. Diss. München 1932 83 p.

4176   Myôngguk, Nam. *Sayuûi ponjil - Haidegkaûi hugisasanhesô* (The Nature of Thinking in the Late Heidegger). M. A. Thesis, Sôul Univ., 1975.

4177   Myôngo, Chông. *Haidegkae issôâo ponjiljôk sayuwa ônôûi munje* (The Problem of Essence Thinking and Language in Heidegger). M. A. Thesis, Sôul Univ., 1961.

4178   Myôngo, Chông. "Chilliûi ponjile taehan chonjaeronjôk kumyông" (Ontological Analysis of the Nature of Truth). *Ch'ôrhak Yôngu* (Sôul), vol. 7, 1972, 89-104.

4179   Myôngo, Chông. "Haidegka sironûi yôngu - siûi ponjile taehan chonjaeron-jôk-Siljonronjôk kumyông" (On Poetry in Heidegger - Ontological-Existential Explanation of the Nature of Poetry). *Ch'ôrhak Yôngu* (Sôul), vol. 8, 1973, 67-88.

4180   Myôngsu, Han. "Haidegkae issôsôûi yôksasônggwa chonjaeyôksaûi munje" (Historicity and the History of Being in Heidegger). *Ch'ôrhak Yôngu* (Taegu) (Ed. by the Kant-Society), vol. 2, 1965, 21-38.

4181   Myslivcenko, A. G. "Zapadnogermanskij ekzistencializm i ego klassovaja suscnost" (Existentialism in West Germany and Its Classical Nature). *Ucenye zapiski MOPI im N.K. Krupskoj,* vol. I, vypusk 4-j. Moskva, 1957, 20-248.

4182   Myslivcenko, A. G. "Kritika ekzistencialistskogo ponimanija svobody" (The Criticism of the Existentialist Conception of Freedom). *Voprosy filosofii* (Moskva), vol. 10, 1963, 91-101.

4183   Myslivcenko, A. G. "Ekzistencija i bytie - central'nye kategorii nemeckogo ekzistencializma" (The Existence and Being - The Central Categories of German Existentialism. *V sbornike 'Sovremennyj ekzistencializm. Kriticeskie ocerki' Izdatel'stvo 'Mysl'.* Moskva, 1966, 47-76.

4184   Myslivcenko, A. G. "Problema svobody v ekszistencializme" (The Problem of Freedom in Existentialism). *V sbornike ' Filosofija marksizma i ekzistencializm' Izdatel'stvo Moskovskogo Universiteta.* Moskva, 1971, 45-56.

4185 Mysliwczenko, D. "Problem wolnoáci w egzystencjalizmie" (The Problem of Freedom in Existentialism). Trans. from Russian. In *Filozofia marksizmu a Egzystencjalizm.* Warszawa, 1974.

4186 Mystrowytch, K. "La philosophie de l'existence et la finitude de la philosophie." *Revue Philosphique de Louvain* (Louvain), vol. 55, 1957, 470-486.

4187 Naber, A. "De existentialismo M. Heidegger, eiusque nota 'transcendentali'. Observationes quaedam." *Gregorianum* (Romae), vol. 25, 1944, 335-356.

4188 Naber, A. "Von der Philosophie des 'Nichts' zur Philosophie des 'Seins-selbst'. Zur grossen 'Wende' im Philosophieren M. Heideggers." *Gregorianum* (Roma), vol. 28, 1947, 357-378.

4189 Naber, A. "Wahrheit und Seinsdenken bei Martin Heidegger." *Analecta Gregoriana* (Romae), vol. 67, 1954, 45-58.

4190 Nachvatal, Paul. *Das Problem der Metaphysik bei Heidegger und Wittgenstein.* Phil. Diss. Wien 1973.

4191 Nadeau, Robert. "Cassirer et Heidegger: Histoire d'un affrontement." *Dialogue* (Montreal/Kingston), vol. 12, no. 4, 1973, 660-669.

4192 Nadler, K. "Die systematische Entwicklung des 'Grundes' in Hegels und Heideggers Philosophie." *De Idee* (Amsterdam), vol. 11, 1933, 3-37.

4193 Naess, Arne. "Modern filosofi i svensk press." *Dagens Nyheter,* 6.12.1961.

[Response by H. Ofstads in *Dagens Nyheter,* 4.1.1962.]

4194 Naess, Arne. *Moderne filosofer.* Stockholm, 1965. Rpt. in *Four Modern Philosophers: Carnap, Wittgenstein, Heidegger, Sartre,* by A. Hannay. Chicago/London, 1968, 367 p.

4195 Nagami, Isamu. "Human Existence and the Cartesian Ego in the Work of Heidegger and Watsuji: An Inquiry on Ethics and Technological Rationality." Phil. Diss. Univ. of Chicago 1977.

4196 Nagano, Mototsuna. "Haideggâ Sonzai to Jikan ni okeru Zentaisei no Gainen" (The Notion of "Totality" in Heidegger's "Sein und Zeit"). *Rinrigaku Kenkyû* (Tôkyô) (Tôkyô Kyôiku Daigaku Rinrigakukai), vol. 14, 1966, 80-95.

4197 Nagai, Shigeo. "Jitsuzonshugi to Ronrijisshôshugi no aida" (Existentialism and Logical Positivism). *Risô* (Tôkyô), vol. 473, 1972, 22-40.

4198 Nagai, Shigeo. "Haideggâ no Sonzairon to Gengobunseki no Hôô" (Heidegger's Ontology and the Method of Linguistic Analysis). In *Bunseki Tetsugaku towa nanika?* Kinokuniya Shoten, Tôkyô, 1973, 49-76.

4199 Nagai, Shigeo. "Haideggâ Sonzairon ni taisuru gegobunsekiteki Apurôchi no Kanôsei ni tsuite" (Heidegger's Ontology and Linguistic Analysis). *Tôyô Daigaku Tanki Daigaku Kiyô* (Tôkyô), vol. 4, 1973, 139-159.

4200 Nagata, Shin. "Haideggâ no Daigakuron ni tsuite" (On the Idea of the University in Heidegger). *Risô* (Tôkyô), vol. 54, 1935, 105-112.

4201 Nagley, W. E. "Introduction to the Symposion and Reading of a Letter From Martin Heidegger." *Philosophy East and West* (Honolulu), vol. 20, 1970, 221.

4202 Nakagawa, Eishô. "Haideggâ tetsugku ni okeru Hikari to Shinpisei" (The Lighting and Mysticism in Heidegger's Philosophy). *Taishô Daigaku Kenkyû Kiyô* (Tôkyô), vol. 57, 1972, 425-435.

4203 Nakagawa, Eishô. "Haideggâ no Tetsugaku to Bukkyo; shutoshite Haideggâ ni okeru 'Lichtung' to Jôdo Shisô no 'Prabhâ' ni tsuite" (Heidegger's Philosophy and Buddhism; Especially on 'Lichtung' in Heidegger and 'Prabhâ' in Jôdo Thought). In *Buddhism and Philosophy* (Chizan Gakuhô) (Tôkyô), vol. 24, 1974, 315-331.

4204 Nakagawa, Eishô. "Haideggâ no Tetsugaku ni okeru Hikari to Jikan ni tsuite" (On Lighting and Time in Heidegger's Philosophy). *Kenkyû Kiyô* (Taishô Daigaku) (Tôkyô), vol. 61, 1975, 211-221.

4205 Nakagawa, Hideyasu. "Haideggâ ni okeru Mu no Mondai" (The Non-Being in Heidegger). *Bunka* (Sendai), vol. VII, no. 11-12; vol. VIII, no. 8; vol. IX, no. 5, 1940/42.

4206 Nakagawa, Hideyasu. *Haideggâ Kenkyû* (Studies in Heidegger). Shunkôsha, 1949, 220 p.

4207 Nakagawa, Hideyasu. "Haideggâ" (Heidegger). *Tetsugaku-Kôza* (Chikuma-Shobô-Verlag, Tôkyô), vol. 1, 1959, 227-232.

4208 Nakagawa, N. "On 'Analogical Characteristics' in Heidegger's Philosophy." *Journal of Religious Studies* (Japan), vol. 33, no. 162, 1960, 55-56.

4209 Nakagawa, Shûkyô. "Jitsuzontetsugaku to sono Kadai Haideggâ o Chushin toshite" (The Task of Existential Philosophy, Particularly in Heidegger). *Risô* (Tôkyô), vol. 173, August 1947.

4210 Nakajima, Yoshio. "Haideggâ to Riruke" (Heidegger and Rilke). *Rinrigakunenpo* (Tôkyô), August 1955.

4211 Nakanishi, Masahiko. "Shizen, kono 'Tanjunnamono'" (Nature, the "Frugal"). *Risô* (Tôkyô), vol. 279, Juli 1956.

4212 Nakao, Kenji. "Haideggâ e no mittsu no Danpen" (Three Fragments About Heidegger). In *Shizuoka Daigaku Kyôyôgakubu Kenkyû Hôkoku*. Shizuoka, 1975, 69-80.

4213 Nakao, Takashi. "Haideggâ Sonzai to Jikan ni okeru Shinri-Gainen ni tsuite" (On the Notion of Truth in "Sein und Zeit"). *Kôbe Yamate Joshi Tanki Daigaku Kiyô* (Kôbe), vol. 12, 1969, 49-55.

4214 Nakayama, Kazunori. "Haideggâ ni okeru Gensonzai to Mu" (There Being and Nothing in Heidegger). *Kyôtosangyô Daigaku Ronshû*, vol. 2, no. 2, 1973, 144-165.

4215 Manjivako, Bmikkhu. "Karma - the Ripening Fruit." *Main Currents in Modern Thought* (New York), vol. 29, 1972, 28-36.

4216 Napoli, G. Di. "Essere e verità in S. Agostino e le grandi correnti della filosofia contemporanea." *Atti del Congresso italiano di filosofia agostiniana, Roma 20-23 ottobre 1954.* Edizioni Agostiniane, Deposito di Tolentino (Mercerata) 1956, 287-296.

4217 Napoli, G. Di. "Identità e differenza nell'ultimo Heidegger." *Rassegna di Scienze filosofiche* (Napoli), vol. 12, 1959, 119-143.

4218 Narbonne, J. "Peut-on parler de l'être?" On *Vers la Fin de l'ontologie,* by Jean Wahl. *Critique* (Paris), Jg. 10, vol. 12, no. 113, 1956, 863-875.

4219 Narski, Jgor S. "Ponjatija 'nigilizma' i 'nicto' v ekzistencializme M. Chejdeggera i antikommunizm" (The Termini 'Nihilism' and 'No-Thing' in M. Heidegger's Existentialism and the Anti-Communism). *Filosofskie Nauki,* Heft 3, 1964, 67-76.

4220 Narskij, I. S. "O ponjatijach 'nicto' i 'nigilism' v filosofii ekzistencializma" (On the Notions "the Nothing" and "Nihilism" in the Philosophy of Existentialism). *V sbornike 'Sovremennyj ekzistencializm. Kriticeskie ocerki' Izdatel'stvo 'Mysl'.* Moskva, 1966, 108-124.

4221 Narskij, I. S. "Problema otcuzdenija v ekzistencializme i religija" (The Problem of Alienation in Existentialism, and the Religion). *Filosofskie nauki,* vol. 1, 1966, 62-72.

4222 Narskij, I. S. "Marksistskaja koncepcija otcuzdenija i ekzistencializm" (The Marxist Conception of Alienation, and Existentialism). *V sbornike 'Filosofija marksizma i ekzistencializm' Izdatel'stvo Moskovskogo Universiteta.* Moskva, 1971, 24-27.

4223 Natanson, Maurice A. *Literature, Philosophy, and the Social Sciences. Essays in Existentialism and Phenomenology.* 3rd ed. The Hague, 1968, [1969], XII, 220 p.

4224 Natanson, Maurice A. "The Problem of Anonymity in Gurwitsch and Schutz." *Research in Phenomenology,* vol. 5, 1975, 51-56.

4225 Naumann, H. *Germanischer Schicksalsglaube.* Jena, 1934, (specifically pages 68-88: Sorge und Bereitschaft. Der Mythos und die Lehre Heideggers).

4226 Naumann, H. "Heideggers hermeneutisches Denken." Rev. of *Was heisst Denken?* by Martin Heidegger. Tübingen, 1954. *Frankfurter Allgemeine Zeitung,* 24.7.1954.

4227 Nauta, L. W. "Heideggers Latere commentaar op zijn in 1929 gehonden rede 'Was ist Metaphysik?'" *Vox Theologica* (Amsterdam), vol. 25, 1955, 80-97.

4228 Navarro Cordón, J. M. "Sentido de la ontologia fundamental en Heidegger." *Anales del Seminario de Metafisica* (Madrid), 1966, 29-52.

4229 Nayfal, Layla Pierre. "Method, Reversal and Way in Heidegger." Phil. Diss. Boston College 1977.

4230 Nebel, Georg. "Marburger Erinnerungen." *Neue Deutsche Hefte* (Berlin), vol. 22, no. 2, 1975, 270-286.

4231 Nelsen, K. H. "De la production du sens: Heidegger et la sémiotique." *Semiotica* (La Haye), vol. 17, no. 3, 1976, 191-209.

4232    Neske, Günther, ed. *Erinnerung an Martin Heidegger.* Ed. with a postscript by Günther Neske. Pfullingen: Verlag Günther Neske, 1977, 316 p.

4233    Neske, Günther. "Postscript." *Erinnerung an Martin Heidegger,* by Günther Neske. Pfullingen: Verlag Günther Neske, 1977.

4234    Neuber, Karl. Rev. of *Philosophie und Politik bei Heidegger,* by Otto Pöggeler. 1972. *Wissenschaft und Weltbild* (Wien/Zürich/München), vol. 26, 1973, 238-239.

4234a    Neuenschwander, Ulrich. *Gott im neuzeitlichen Denken, II.* Gütersloh: Gütersloher Verlagshaus Mohn, 1977, 244 p.

4235    Neufeld, Karl-Heinz. Rev. of *La theologie face au defi Hermeneutique. M. Heidegger, R. Bultmann, K. Rahner,* by Jean-Paul Reswever. 1975. *Theologie und Philosophie* (Freiburg), vol. 51, 1976, 413-417.

4236    Neuhäuser, Sylvia. Rev. of *Vier Seminare,* by Martin Heidegger. *Philosophischer Literaturanzeiger* (Meisenheim/Mainz), vol. 30, 1974, 340-341.

4236a    Neuhäuser, Silvia. Rev. of "Martin Heidegger. Vier Seminare. Le Thor 1966, 1968, 1969; Zähringen 1973. Postsript by Curd Ochwadt." *Philosophy and History* (Tübingen), vol. 11, 1978, 18-19.

4237    Neuhäusler, Anton. "Erinnerungen an das Sein. Zum Tode von Martin Heidegger." *Münchner Merkur* (München), no. 122, 28 May 1976, 19.

4238    Neulichedl, K. *Der Weltbegriff bei Martin Heidegger.* Phil. Diss. Wien 1967.

4239    Neumann, Harry. "Socrates and History: A Nietzschean Interpretation of Philosophy. To the Memory of Nietzsche's Only Student, Heidegger (1889-1976)." *Nietzsche-Studien* (Berlin/New York), vol. 6, 1977, 64-74.

4240    Neumann, Harry. "The Man on the Moon? The Question of Heidegger's 'Selfassertion of the German University'." *Journal of Value Inquiry,* vol. 13, 1979, 274-282.

4241    Neunheuser, K. "Heidegger und die Sprache." *Wirkendes Wort. Deutsches Sprachschaffen in Lehre und Leben* (Düsseldorf), vol. 8, 1957/58, 1-7.

4242    Nicholson, Graeme. *The Ontological Difference: A Study in Heidegger.* Phil. Diss. Toronto 1968 219 p. *Dissertation Abstracts International,* vol. 30/02-A, 767.

4243    Nicholson, Graeme. "The Commune of Being and Time." *Dialogue* (Montreal/Kingston), vol. 10, 1971, 708-726.

4244    Nicholson, Graeme. "Camus and Heidegger." *Anarchists* (Toronto) (Univ. of Toronto Quarterly), vol. 41, 1971, 14-23.

4245    Nicholson, Graeme. "Disclosure in Heidegger." *Studi Internazionali di Filosofia* (Torino), vol. 6, 1974, 139-154.

4246    Nicholson, Graeme. "Heidegger on Thinking." *Journal of the History of Philosophy* (Claremont, California), vol. 13, 1975, 491-503.

4247    Nicholson, Graeme. "Heidegger's Comments on Subjectivity." *Revue de l'Université Laurentienne* (Sudbury), vol. 9, no. 2, 1977, 15-24.

4248    Nicholson, Graeme. "The Meaning of the Word 'Being': Presence and Absence." In *Heidegger's Existential Analytic*, by Frederick Elliston (ed.). The Hague, New York: Mouton Pub., 1978, 179-194.

4249    Nielsen, Niel C. "Zen Buddhism and the Philosophy of Martin Heidegger." *Atti del XII Congresso internazionale di Filosofia (Venezia, 12-18 settembre 1958)*. Vol. X: Filosofie orientali e pensiero occidentale, Firenze, Sansoni, 1960, 131-137.

4250    Nielsen, Niels C. "Demythologizing and the Philosophia perennis: Bultmann, Jaspers and Heidegger." *Rice University Studies*, vol. 50, no. 1, 1964, 55-67.

4251    Nieto, Alfredo Zamarono. "El Concepto De Verdad En 'Ser Y Tiempo' De Martin Heidegger." *Revista de Filosofia (Mexico)* (Mexico), vol. 12, 1979, 363-372.

4252    Nieto Arteta, L. E. "Husserl y Heidegger (La fenomenologia y la analitica de la existencia." *Ciencia y Fe* (Buenos Aires), vol. 8, 1952, 29-39.

4253    Nieto Arteta, L. E. "Husserl y Heidegger: La fenomenologia y la analitica de la existencia." *Universidad de Antioquia* (Medellin), 1953, 243-262.

4254    Nink, Caspar. "Grundbegriffe der Philosophie Martin Heideggers." *Philosophisches Jahrbuch* (Fulda), vol. 45, 1932, 129-158.

4255    Nink, Caspar. *Ontologie. Versuch einer Grundlegung.* Freiburg, 1952, 494 p.

4256    Nink, Caspar. "Tí to ón: Zur Diskussion um den Seinsbegriff." *Philosophisches Jahrbuch* (München), vol. 63, 1954/55, 1-14.

4257    Nink, Caspar. "Zum Problem der Seinsdialektik." *Scholastik* (Freiburg), vol. 33, 1958, 506-528.

4258    Nishida, Hideki. "Haideggâ to Kotoba no Sekai" (Heidegger and the World of Language). *Kônan Daigaku Bungakukai Ronshû* (Kôbe), vol. 22, 1964, 153-190.

4259    Nishida, Kitaro. "Ippansha no Jikakuteki Taikei" (The System of the General, Growing Aware of Itself). *Sämtliche Werke* (Tôkyô), Bd. V, 1929, 289, 349, 351, 463, 477.

4260    Nishida, Kutaro. "Mu no Jikakuteki Gentei" (The Determination of the Non-Being, Growing Aware of Itself). *Sämtliche Werke* (Tôkyô), Bd. VI, 1932, 165, 168, 170, 171, 172, 175, 179.

4261    Nishida, Kitaro. "Tetsugaku no Konponmondai" (Elementary Problems of Philosophy). *Sämtliche Werke* (Tôkyô), Bd. VII, 1933/34, 79, 118, 179, 180, 330.

4262    Nishida, Kitaro. "Tetsugaku Ronbunshu, I" (Philosophical Treatises, I). *Sämtliche Werke* (Tôkyô), Bd. VIII, 1935, 20, 213.

4263    Nishida, Kitaro. "Tetsugaku Ronbunshu, 6" (Philosophical Treatises, 6). *Sämtliche Werke* (Tôkyô), Bd. XI, 1944, 178, 186.

4264    Nishii, Motoaki. "Jikan ni tsuite no sonzaironteki Kôsatsu" (The Ontological Investigation of Time: From Husserl, Heidegger to Sartre). *Ôtani Daigaku Kenkyû Nenpô* (Kyôto), vol. 24, 1972, 161-255.

4265   Nishimura, Keishin. "Haideggâ no Shêringuron" (On Schelling in Heidegger). *Shûkyô Kenkyû* (Tôkyô), vol. 214, 1973, 65-66.

4266   Nishitani, Keiji. "Haideggâ no Kôen 'Geijutsu-Sakuhin no Kigen'" (Heidegger's Lecture 'Der Ursprung des Kunstwerks'). *Tetsugakukikan* (Jsaka), no. 7, 1948.

4267   Nishitani, Keiji. *Nihirizumu* (Nihilism). Tôkyô, 1949, 181-223.

4268   Nishitani, Keiji. "Preliminary Remarks to Heideggers zwei Ansprachen in Messkirch." *The Eastern Buddhist* (Kyôtô), New Series, vol. 1, no. 2, 1966.

4269   Nishitani, Keiji. "Zatsukan" (Random Thoughts). *Risô* (Tôkyô), vol. 500, 1975, 160-165.

4270   Nishitani, Keisei Keiji. "Gedenken." In *Erinnerung an Martin Heidegger,* by Günther Neske. Pfullingen: Verlag Günther Neske, 1977, 232 ff.

4271   Nitta, Yoshihiro. *Haideggâ no Shinriron* (Heidegger's Discussion of Truth). Kenkyûnenpô, Sendai, 1958.

4272   Nitta, Yoshihiro. "Haideggâ ni okeru Shii to Shisaku - Kotoba no Mondai o megutte" ('Thinking' and 'Poetizing' in Heidegger; on the Question Concerning Language). *Tôkyô Daigaku Kyôyôgakubu Kiyô* (Tôkyô), vol. 2, 1961, 33-43.

4273   Nitta, Yoshihiro. *Haideggâ ni okeru Shii to Shisaku* (Thinking and Poetizing in Heidegger). Tôyôdaigaku-Kyôyôbu Kiyô, Tôkyô, 1963.

4274   Nitta, Yoshihiro. "Haideggâ" (Heidegger). *Jitsuzonshugi-Kôza* (Risôsha, Tôkyô), vol. 2, 1968, 187-201.

4275   Nitta, Yoshihiro. "Haideggâ to Fuihite" (Heidegger and Fichte). *Jitsuzonshugi* (Tôkyô), vol. 77, 1976, 115-121.

4276   Noack, H. "Gespräch mit Martin Heidegger." *Anstösse* (Berichte aus der Arbeit der Ev. Akademie Hofgeismar), vol. 1, 1954, 30-37.

4277   Noack, H. *Die Philosophie Westeuropas im zwanzigsten Jahrhundert.* Basel/Stuttgart, 1962, 315-333.

4278   Nóbrega Rodrigues, A. "Verdade e liberdade. Um tema de Martin Heidegger em Vom Wesen der Wahrheit." *Revista Portuguesa de Filosofia* (Braga), vol. 24, 1968, 215-221.

4279   Noël, L., M. De Wulf, and J. Haesaert. "Rapports concours annuel de 1942, 4e quesion: On demande une étude sur la philosophie de Martin Heidegger." *Bulletin de l'Académie Royale de Belgique. Lettres* (Bruxelles), vol. 28, 1942, 23-30.

4280   Nogales, S. G. "La abstraction del ser y el existencialismo." *Analecta Gregoriana* (Romae), vol. 67, 1954, 91-122, (specifically pages 101-108).

4281   Noguchi, Eiko. "Haideggâ ni okeru 'Genjitsusei' to 'Gengo' no Kankei ni tsuite" (On the Relationship Between 'Actuality' and 'Language' in Heidegger). (Seikyô Daigaku Gakujutsu-Hôkoku). *Jimbun* (Kyôto), vol. 5, 1954.

4282 Noguchi, Tsuneki. "Ningen no Mattanshiyô to Chûsûkonpon; Haideggâ to Asami Keisai" (Periphery and Kernel of Man; Heidegger and Keisai Asami). *Kôgakukan Daigaku Kiyô* (Ise), vol. 14, 1976, 242-260.

4283 Noguchi, Tsuneki. "Haideggâ no Gengoron kara Ware-Nanji Tetsugaku e" (From Heidegger's Theory of Language to the I-Thou Philosophy). *Kôgakkan Daigaku Kiyô* (Ise), vol. 15, 1977, 362-378.

4284 Noguchi, Tsuneki. "Von der Seinslehre Heideggers zur Ich-Du-Philosophie" (From Heidegger's Theory of Being to the I-Thou-Philosophy). *Kôgakkan Daigaku Kiyô* (Ise), vol. 17, 1979, 61-69.

4285 Noguchi, Tsuneki. "Haideggâ no Sonzairon kara Ware-Nanji Tetsugaku e" (From Heidegger's Theory of Being to the I-Thou Philosophy). *Kokoro* (Tôkyô), October 1976, 43-55.

4286 Nogueira, Joño Carlos. "Heidegger ou os novos caminhos da filosofia." *Reflexño* (Campinas), vol. 1, no. 3, 1975/76, 25-39.

4287 Nokes, D. "Pope and Heidegger: A Forgotten Fragment." *The Review of English Studies* (London), vol. 23, 1972, 308-313.

4288 Nolet, C. Rev. of *Vorträge und Aufsätze,* by Martin Heidegger. Pfullingen, 1954. *Rivista di Estetica* (Torino-Padova), vol. 1, 1956, 150-154.

4289 Noller, G. *Die Überwindung des Subjekt-Objekt-Schemas als philosophisches und theologisches Problem. Dargestellt an der Philosophie Heideggers und an der Theologie der Entmythologisierung.* Ev.-theol. Phil. Diss. Tübingen 1960 220 p. Rpt. in *Sein und Existenz. Die Überwindung des Subjekt-Objektschemas in der Philosophie Heideggers und in der Theologie der Entmythologisierung.* München, 1962, 166 p.

4290 Noller, G., ed. *Heidegger und die Theologie. Beginn und Fortgang der Diskussion.* München, 1967, 343 p.

 [Rev. by C. Pires in *Revista Portuguesa de Filosofia* (Braga), vol. 27, 1977, 328-329.]

4291 Noller, G. "Ontologische und theologische Versuche zur Überwindung des anthropologischen Denkens." *Heidegger und die Theologie. Beginn und Fortgang der Diskussion.* Ed. G. Noller. München, 1967, 290-315.

4292 Nomura, Shigeki. "Haideggâ no Jikansei ni tsuite" (On Heidegger's Temporality). *Kôka Joshi Tanki Daigaku Kenkyû Kiyô,* vol. 77, 1969, 18-29.

4293 Nomura, Shigeki. "Haideggâ no Shii no Tenkai ni tsuite" (On the Turning in Heidegger's Thinking). *Kôka Joshi Daigaku Kenkyû Kiyô,* vol. 9, Dezember 1971, 110-132.

4294 Nomura, Shigeki. "Haideggâ no Shii no Tenkai ni tsuite, Jo 2; Mu no Muka o megutte" (On Reversal of Heidegger's Thought, Introduction, 2; About Non-Being in Its Very Essence). *Kôka Joshi Daigaku Joshi Tanki Daigaku Kenkyû Kiyô* (Kyôto), vol. 10, 1972, 104-128.

4295 Nomura, Shigeki. "Haideggâ no Shii no Tenkai ni tsuite - Jo, 3 - Genzonsei no Kaijisei o megutte" (On Reversal of Heidegger's Thought - Introduction,

3 - About Disclosedness of There-Being). *Kôka Joshidaigaku Joshi-Tankidaigaku Kenkyû Kiyô* (Kyôto), vol. 12, 1974, 83-96.

4296 Nomura, Shigeki. "Haideggâ no Shii no Tenkai ni tsuite, Jo 4; Shinri no Honshitsu to shiteno Jiyû o megutte" (On Reversal of Heidegger's Thought, Introduction 4; About Freedom as Essence of Truth). *Kôka Joshi Daigaku Joshi-Tanki-Daigaku Kenkyû Kiyô* (Kyôto), vol. 13, 1975, 104-119.

4297 Nomura, Shigeki. "Haideggâ no Shii no Tenkai ni tsuite, Jo 5; Shinri no Honshitsu toshiteno Jiyû o megutte" (On Reversal of Heidegger's Thought, Introduciton 5; About Freedom as Essence of Truth). *Kôka Joshi Daigaku Joshi-Tanki-Daigaku Kenkyû Kiyô* (Kyôto), vol. 14, 1976, 106-120.

4298 Nomura, Shigeki. "Haideggâ niokeru Gensonzai no Akarumi toshiteno 'Da' kara Sonzai no Akarumi toshiteno 'Da' e no Shii no Tenkai ni tsuite" (On Change of Heidegger's Thought From 'Da' as Lighting-Process of There-Being to 'Da' as Lighting-Process of Being). *Kokâ Joshidaigaku Joshitanki-Daigaku Kenkyû Kiyô* (Kyôto), vol. 15, 1977, 156-171.

4299 Nordentoft, S. *Heideggers opgor med den filosofiske tradition, kritisk belyst.* Copenhagen, 1961, 186 p.

[Rev. by K. Tranoy in *Dagbladet,* 4.9.1962.]

4300 Nota, J. "Phaenomenologie als methode." *Tijdschrift voor Philosophie* (Leuven), vol. 3, 1941, 203-240, (specifically pages 237-240).

4301 "Notwendige Diskussion über Heidegger." [Leserzuschriften zu dem Artikel 'Mit Heidegger gegen Heidegger denken'. FAZ vom 25.7.1953 von Jürgen Habermas.] 'Freiheit, Anruf und Gewissen' (Jürgen Habermas, Bonn); 'Vor oben herab' (Peter Mehlhorn, Viersen); 'Wir wollen Klärung' (Gertrude Berthold, Überlingen); 'Im Stil der Proskynesis' (Prof. Dr. Heinrich Scholz, Münster); 'Was heisst Technik-Mensch?' (E. Schwarz, Neustadt a.d.W.); 'Eingefahrene ideologische Bahnen' (Wilfried Berghahn, Detmold); 'Noch ein Tadel' (Wilhelm Sander, Goslar). *Frankfurter Allgemeine Zeitung* (Frankfurt), 1953, no. 200 v.29.8.1953, Feuilleton.

4302 Nuno, J. A. "La revisión heideggeriana de la historia de la filosofia." *Episteme* (Caracas), vol. 3, 1959/60, 189-280.

4303 Nuno, J. A. *La revision Heideggeriana de la historia de la filosofia.* Caracas, Univ. Central, 1962, 94 p. [Separate from: *Episteme* (Caracas), vol. 3, 1959/60.]

4304 Nuno Montes, J. A. "En torno a una interpretación de Heidegger. Ser y devenir en la filosofia presocráica." *Revista nacional de Cultura,* vol. 26, no. 162-163, 1964, 97-104.

4305 Nwodo, Christopher S. "The Work of Art in Heidegger: A World Disclosure." *Cultural Hermeneutics* (Dordrecht/Boston), vol. 4, no. 1, 1976/77, 61-73.

4306 Nwodo, Christopher S. "The Role of Art in Heidegger's Philosophy." *Philosophy Today* (Celina, Ohio), vol. 21, no. 3-4, 1977, 294-304.

4307   Nwodo, Christopher S. "Friedländer Versus Heidegger: *A-lethei* Controversy." *The Journal of the British Society for Phenomenology,* vol. 10, May 1979, 84-93.

4308   N. N. Rev. of *Die Kategorien und Bedeutungslehre des Duns Scotus,* by Martin Heidegger. Tübingen, 1916. *Germania* (Berlin), 23.8.1917.

4309   N. N. Rev. of *Die Kategorien und Bedeutungslehre des Duns Scotus,* by Martin Heidegger. Tübingen, 1916. *Schwäbischer Merkur* (Stuttgart), 11.6.1919.

4310   N. N. Rev. of *Die Kategorien und Bedeutungslehre des Duns Scotus,* by Martin Heidegger. Tübingen, 1916. *Archivum Franciscanum historicum* (Firenze), vol. 14, 1925, 371.

4311   N. N. [gez. Snz.] Rev. of *Kant und das Problem der Metaphysik,* by Martin Heidegger. Bonn, 1929. *Annalen der Philosophie* (Leipzig) (Literaturberichte), vol. 8, 1929, 101.

4312   N. N. [gez. Snz.] Rev. of *Vom Wesen des Grundes,* by Martin Heidegger. Halle, 1929. *Annalen der Philosophie* (Leipzig) (Literaturberichte), vol. 8, 1929, 110.

4313   N. N. Rev. of *Kant und das Problem der Metaphysik,* by Martin Heidegger. Bonn, 1929. *Das Neue Reich* (Wien), vol. 12, 1930, 546.

4314   N. N. Rev. of *Was ist Metaphysik?* by Martin Heidegger. Bonn, 1929. *Das Neue Reich* (Wien), vol. 12, 1930, 502.

4315   N. N. "Martin Heidegger. Die Nachfolge von Troeltsch." *Berliner Tageblatt,* 28.3.1930.

4316   N. N. [gez. C.] "Martin Heidegger. Ein sozialistischer Minister beruft einen Kultur-Reaktionar nach Berlin." *Monistische Monatshefte* (Hamburg), vol. 15, 1930, 109-111.

4317   N. N. [gez. C.] "Heidegger-Philosophie." *Monistische Monatshefte* (Hamburg), vol. 15, 1930, 153-154.

4318   N. N. Rev. of *Die Selbstbehauptung der Deutschen Universität,* by Martin Heidegger. Breslau, 1933. *Die Hilfe* (Berlin), vol. 39, 1933, 504.

4319   N. N. [gez.-le] "Universität Freiburg. Feierliche Immatrikulation, verbunden mit Langemarckgedächtnis." *Freiburger Zeitung* (Morgenausgabe), 150 Jg., Nr. 323, 27.11.1933. Rpt. in *Nachlese zu Heidegger,* by G. Schneeberger. Bern, 1962, 156-158. [ein weiterer Bericht über diese Feier in *Breisgauer Zeitung,* 85. Jg., Nr. 297, 27.11.1933, 3.]

4320   N. N. [gez. H.E.] "Der Philosoph Heidegger in die NSDAP eingetreten." *Der Alemanne. Kampfblatt der Nationalsozialisten Oberbadens,* 3.Jg., Folge 121, 3.Mai 1933, 2.

4321   N. N. [gez. E.A.S.] "Rektoratsübergabe an der Universität Freiburg." *Freiburger Zeitung* (Abendausgabe), 150 Jg., Nr. 145, 29.5.1933. Rpt. in *Nachlese zu Heidegger,* by G. Schneeberger. Bern, 1962, 51-55; dort weitere Berichte über die Rektoratsübergabe, 49-58.

4322    N. N. [gez.-r-] "Verbandstag des Landesverbandes Badischer Schreinermeister." *Freiburger Zeitung* (Abendausgabe), 150 Jg., Nr. 240, 4.9.1933, 4, 7. Rpt. in *Nachlese zu Heidegger,* by G. Schneeberger. Bern, 1962, 120-122.

4323    N. N. [gez. S.] "Universität Freiburg. 3. Immatrikulation." *Freiburger Zeitung* (Morgenausgabe), 150 Jg., Nr. 139, 22.Mai 1933.

4324    N. N. [gez. A. von Sch.] "Arbeitsdienst, Wehrdienst, Wissensdienst. Das neue Gesicht der neuen Universität." *Freiburger Studenten-Zeitung,* 7. Semester, (14), Nr. 5, 14.Juni 1933, 2.

4325    N. N. "Schlageterfeier der Freiburger Universität." *Der Alemanne* (Kampfblatt der Nationalsozialisten Oberbadens), 3. Jg., Folge 145, 27.Mai 1933, 6.

4326    N. N. "Die Sonnenwendfeier der Freiburger Studenten." *Freiburger Zeitung* (Abendausgabe), 150 Jg., Nr. 170, 26.6.1933, 7. Rpt. in *Nachlese zu Heidegger,* by G. Schneeberger. Bern, 1962, 69-71.

4327    N. N. "Die Universität im neuen Reich. Ein Vortrag von Prof. Martin Heidegger." *Heidelberger neueste Nachrichten,* Nr. 150, 1.7.1933, 4.

4328    N. N. [gez. F.] "Philosophische Diskussion?" *Argis* (Krefeld) (Blätter zur Förderung der Humanität), vol. 1, 1935, 41 f.

4329    N. N. "Tragische Existenz. Auseinandersetzung mit der Philosophie Martin Heidegger." *Germania* (Berlin), 29.12.1935.

4330    N. N. [gez. H. P.] "Tragische Existenz." *Filosofická Revue* (Tschechoslowakei), vol. 8, no. 4, 1936, 165-167.

4331    N. N. Rev. of *Heidegger, Die Selbstbehauptung der deutschen Universität.* Breslau, 1933. *Zeitspiege* (Berlin), vol. II, 1936, 306.

4332    N. N. "Martinho Heidegger e 'Rumo'." *Rumo* (Lissabon), vol. 314, 1946, 475-480.

4333    N. N. "La postura politica de Martin Heidegger." *Arbor* (Madrid), vol. 7, 1947, 205-213.

4334    N. N. Rev. of *Platons Lehre von der Wahrheit. Mit einem Brief über den 'Humanismus',* by Martin Heidegger. Bern, 1947. *Die Weltwoche* (Zürich), 14.9.1948.

4335    N. N. [gez.a.bo.] "Heraklit - Hegel - Heidegger." *Christ und Welt* (Stuttgart), Jg. 2, no. 40, 1949, 9-10.

4336    N. N. [Lohmann, I.?] "Widmung." *Lexis* (Lahr), vol. 2, 1949, 1.

4337    N. N. [gez. R.] "Martin Heidegger über die Technik als das Wesen unserer Zeit. Bericht über einen Vortrag." *Die Kommenden* (Freiburg), Jg. 4, no. 9, 1950, 8.

4338    N. N. Rev. of *Platons Lehre von der Wahrheit. Mit einem Brief über den 'Humanismus',* by Martin Heidegger. Bern, 1947. *Algemeen Nederlands Tijdschrift voor Wijsbegeerte en Psychologie* (Assen), 1950, 105-106.

4339    N. N. Rev. of these works in *The Times Literary Supplement* (London), Jg. 49, no. 2522, 2.6.1950, 344:

[*Platons Lehre von der Wahrheit. Mit einem Brief über den 'Humanismus',* by Martin Heidegger. 1947.]

[*Heideggers Einfluss auf die Wissenschaften.* 1949.]

[*M. Heidegger und die Existentialphilosophie,* by Marcic. 1949.]

4340    N. N. [gez A.F.] "Bühler Höhen-Luft." *Deutsche Zeitung und Wirtschaftszeitung* (Stuttgart), Jg. 5, no. 82, 1950, 15.

4341    N. N. "Gespräch mit Heidegger." *Geistiges Frankreich* (Wien), vol. 4, 1950, 161-174.

4342    N. N. [gez. D.Sch.] "So wie bei Sarte geht es Nicht. Ein Mittwochabend bei Heidegger." *Sonntagsblatt* (Hamburg), Jg. 3, no. 17, 1950, 9.

4343    N. N. "Martin Heidegger fühlt sich missverstanden." *Deutsche Zeitung und wirtschaftszeitung* (Stuttgart), Jg. 6, no. 14, 1951, 2.

4344    N. N. "Gott braucht auch die 'Zerdenker'. Heidegger und Ortega y Gasset beim Darmstädter Gespräch." *Evangelische Welt* (Bethel/Bielefeld), vol. 5, 1951, 526-527.

4345    N. N. "Varia philosophica." *De Tyd,* 18.7.1953. Rev. of these works:

[*Denker in dürftiger Zeit,* by Martin Heidegger.]

[*Einführung in die Metaphysik,* by Martin Heidegger.]

[*Kant und die Probleme der Metaphysik,* by Walter Biemel.]

4346    N. N. "Der Magus von Freiburg." Rev. of *Einführung in die Metaphysik,* by Martin Heidegger. Tübingen, 1953. *Düsseldorfer Nachrichten* (Düsseldorf), 1.8.1953.

4347    N. N. Rev. of *Einführung in die Metaphysik,* by Martin Heidegger. *Neue Literarische Welt,* S. 2 vom 10.8.1953.

4348    N. N. Rev. of *Was heisst Denken?* by Martin Heidegger. Tübingen, 1954. *Europäischer Kulturdienst,* 3.Jg., A/5 u.A/6 vom 30.6.1954, 12.

4349    N. N. Rev. of *Was heisst Denken?* by Martin Heidegger. Tübingen, 1954. *Das neue Forum* (Darmstadt), vol. 4, 1954.

4350    N. N. "Frage und Einführung." Rev. of *Einführungin die Metaphysik,* by Martin Heidegger. Tübingen, 1953. *Schwäbisches Tageblatt,* 26.11.1954.

4351    N. N. Rev. of *Einführung in die Metaphysik,* by Martin Heidegger. Tübingen, 1953. *Das notwendige buch,* vol. III, 1954.

4352    N. N. "Heideggers Studie über das Denken." Rev. of *Was heisst Denken?* by Martin Heidegger. Tübingen, 1954. *Yedioth Hagom,* 19.4.1954.

4353    N. N. Rev. of *Was heisst Denken?* by Martin Heidegger. Tübingen, 1954. *Westdeutsche Zeitung,* 18.9.1954.

4354    N. N. Rückkehr zum Mysterium des Seins." Rev. of *Einführung in die Metaphysik,* by Martin Heidegger. Tübingen, 1953. *Salzburger Nachrichten,* 8.10.1954.

4355      N. N. Rev. of *Was heisst Denken?* by Martin Heidegger. Tübingen, 1954. *Das Antiquariat,* 1954.

4356      N. N. "Martin Heidegger bleibt unverständlich." *Die Gegenwart* (Frankfurt), vol. 8, 1953, 639-641.

4357      N. N. "Heideggers Vorlesung von 1953." *Forum Academicum* (Heidelberg), Buchbeilage, Jg. 5, no. 1, 1954.

4358      N. N. "Europa in der Zange." Rev. of *Einführung in die Metaphysik,* by Martin Heidegger. *Rhein-Neckar-Zeitung* (Heidelberg), 23./24.10.1954.

4359      N. N. Rev. of *Einführung in die Metaphysik,* by Martin Heidegger. Tübingen, 1953. *Katholika,* vol. 4, 1954, 184-185.

4360      N. N. Rev. of *Einführung in die Metaphysik,* by Martin Heidegger. Tübingen, 1953. *Deutsches Pfarrerblatt* (Essen), vol. 55, 1955, 93-94.

4361      N. N. Rev. of *Einführung in die Metaphysik,* by Martin Heidegger. Tübingen, 1953. *Rheinische Post* (Düsseldorf), 22.8.1955.

4362      N. N. Rev. of *Platons Lehre von der Wahrheit. Mit einem Brief über den 'Humanismus',* by Martin Heidegger. Bern, 1947. *International P.E.N. Bulletin of Selected Books* (London), September 1955, 97-98.

4363      N. N. "Martin Heidegger." *Der grosse Herder.* 5th ed. Freiburg, Bd 4, 1957, 739-740.

4364      N. N. "Ekzistencializm." *Bolsajasoretskaja enciklopedija* (Moskau), Bd 48, 1957, 358-359.

4365      N. N. "Meister und Schüler. Der fünfte deutsche Kongress für Philosophie in Deutschland." *Tübinger Chronik,* Jg. 13, no. 256, vom 5.11.1957.

4366      N. N. "Heidegger em diálogo com a filosofia crista." *Filosofia* (Lisboa), vol. 4, 1958, 290-291.

4367      N. N. "Ein deutscher Philosoph. Zu Martin Heideggers 70. Geburtstag." *Bücherschiff,* vol. 9, no. 9, September 1959.

4368      N. N. Rev. of *Hebel der Hausfrend,* by Martin Heidegger. Pfullingen, 1957. *Revue de Métaphysique et de Morale* (Paris), vol. 64, 1959, 238.

4369      N. N. *Martin Heidegger. 26. Sept. 1959.* [Reden anläss d. Verleihung d. Ehrenbürgerrechts d. Stadt Messkirch.] Messkirch, Brügerneisteramt, 1959, 36 p.

4370      N. N. Rev. of *Qu'appelle-t-on penser?* by Martin Heidegger. Paris, 1959. *Revue de Métaphysique et de Morale* (Paris), vol. 66, 1961, 483-484.

4371      N. N. Rev. of *Vom Wesen und Begriff,* by Martin Heidegger. *Ciencia y Fe* (San Miguel, FCSM Argentina), vol. 17, 1961, 99.

4372      N. N. "Philosophie - Heidegger: Die Wacht am Sein." *Der Spiegel* (Hamburg), vol. 16, no. 14, 1962, 72-74.

4373      N. N. "Heidegger." In *Trirucni Slovaik Nauong.* Praha, 1963, vol. II, 90.

4374      N. N. "Heidegger et les mystiques." *La Table Ronde* (Paris), vol. 182, 1963, 82-89.

4375 N. N. "Symposium: Martin Heidegger." *The Journal of Philosophy* (New York), vol. 60, 1963, 651-684.

4376 N. N. Rev. of *Die Frage nach dem Ding,* by Martin Heidegger. *Deutsche Kultur-Nachrichten* (Bonn), [inter nationes], Januar 1963, 22.

4377 N. N. Rev. of *Die Frage nach dem Ding,* by Martin Heidegger. *Ramat-Gan* (Israel), 20.2.1963.

4378 N. N. Rev. of *Die Frage nach dem Ding,* by Martin Heidegger. *IYYUN,* Bd 15, no. 3, Juli 1964.

4379 N. N. Rev. of *Die Frage nach dem Ding,* by Martin Heidegger. *Das Antiquariat,* Jg. 17, Nr. 5/8, 1964.

4380 N. N. "Martin Heidegger." *Welka Encyklopedia Powszechna pWN* (Warszawa), Bd 4, 1964, 592-593.

4381 N. N. [C.V.M.] Rev. of *German Existentialism,* by Martin Heidegger. *Espiritu* (Barcelona), vol. 14, 1965, 177-178.

4382 N. N. "Heidegger, Martin." *Encyclopaedia Britannica* (London), vol. 11, 1965, 305.

4383 N. N. "Mitternacht einer Weltnacht." *Der Spiegel* (Hamburg), Jg. 20, no. 7, 7.2.1966, 110-113.

4384 N. N. *Universitätstage 1966. Nationalsozialismus und die deutsche Universität.* Berlin, 1966, 223 p.

4385 N. N. Rev. of *What is a Thing?* by Martin Heidegger. Chicago, Illinois, 1968. *Review of Metaphysics* (Haverford), vol. 22, 1968, 379.

4386 N. N. Rev. of *What is Called Thinking?* by Martin Heidegger. New York, 1968. *Review of Metaphysics* (Haverford), vol. 22, 1969, 570.

4387 N. N. Rev. of *Introduzione alla metafisica,* by Martin Heidegger. *Sistematica* (Milano), vol. 2, 1969, 205-207.

4388 Oberti, E. "Lineamenti di un'estetica di Heidegger in un saggio su Rilke." *Rivista di filosofia neoscolastica* (Milano), vol. 46, 1954, 556-569.

4389 Oberti, E. "La teoria del pensiero nel piu recente Heidegger." *Rivista di filosofia neoscolastica* (Milano), vol. 47, 1955, 30-40.

4390 Oberti, E. *L'estetica nel pensiero di Heidegger.* Milano, 1955, 177 p.

4391 O'Brien, D. "Aristote et l'aiôn: Enqueête sur une Critique Recente." *Revue de Metaphysique et de Morales* (Paris), vol. 85, 1980, 94-108.

4392 O'Connor, David. "On the Viability of Macquarrie's God-Talk." *Philosophical Studies* (Ireland), vol. 23, 1975, 107-116.

4392a O'Connor, Tony. "L'appropriation et la trahison de l'autre absolu." In *Heidegger et la question de Dieu.* Ed. R. Kearney and J. S. O'Leary. Paris: B. Grasset, 1980, 271-284.

4393 Odebrecht, R. Rev. of *Kant und das Problem der Metaphysik,* by Martin Heidegger. Bonn, 1929. *Blätter für deutsche Philosophie* (Berlin), vol. 5, 1931/32, 132-135.

4394    Ôe, Seiichi. "Haideggâ 'Keijijôgaku towa nanika' no Kaisetse" (Comment on
        'Was ist Metaphysik'). *Risô* (Tôkyô), vol. 15, 1930, 148-190.

4395    Ôe, Seishirô. "Haideggâ no Kaishakuteki Sonzairon no Kiso" (The
        Foundation of Heidegger's Hermeneutic Ontology on "Vom Wesen des
        Grundes"). *Risô* (Tôkyô), vol. 23, no. 25, 1931, 37-71, 135-152.

4395A   Ôe, Seishirô. "Haideggâ no Ningengaku ni okeru Konponmondai" (The Basic
        Problem of Heidegger's Anthropology). *Risô* (Tôkyô), September 1931.

4396    Ôe, Seishirô. "Hegeru to Haideggâ" (Hegel and Heidegger). *Risô* (Tôkyô), vol.
        22, April 1931.

4397    Ôe, Seishirô. "Haideggâtetsugaku Gendai" (Heidegger's Philosophy and the
        Present). *Risô* (Tôkyô), März 1935.

4398    Ôe, Seishirô. "Haideggâ no Tetsugaku" (Heidegger's Philosophy). In *Gendai
        Tetsugaku*. Ed. by Kaneko Umaji. Risôsha-Verlag, Tôkyô, 1937.

4399    Ôe, Seishirô. "Kankyakusareteiru Kachi-Mondai, Haideggâ no
        Sonzai-Mondai o Chushin toshite" (Neglected Problem of Value. On
        Heidegger's Question of Being). *Risô* (Tôkyô), vol. 220, September 1951.

4400    Ôe, Seishirô. "Ningen-Sonzai no Konkyo eno Tankyû - Haideggâ 'Niche no
        Kotoba, Kami wa shindeiru' ni tsuite" (Searching for the Principles of the
        Human There-Being on Heidegger's "Nietzsches Wort Gott ist tot"). *Risô*
        (Tôkyô), vol. 234, 1952, 42-54.

4401    Ôe, Seishirô. "Ningen-Sonzai no Honshitsu, Haideggâ no Ningenron o
        Chushin toshite" (The Nature of Human Existence. Particularly in Respect
        to Heidegger's Discussion of Human Nature). *Philosophia* (Tôkyô), vol. 25,
        1953.

4402    Ôe, Seishirô. "Haideggâ" (Heidegger). *Risô* (Tôkyô), vol. 253, 1954, 68-71.

4403    Ôe, Seishirô. "Haideggâ to Bukkyô no Shinri (Shinnyo)" (Heidegger and the
        Truth of Buddhism). *Jitsuzon* (Tôkyô), November 1955.

4404    Ôe, Seishirô. "Haideggâ ni okeru 'Shinri' no Imi" (The Meaning of 'Truth'
        in Heidegger). *Risô* (Tôkyô), vol. 305, Oktober 1958.

4405    ôe, Seishirô. "Nishida Tetsugaku to Haideggâ Shisô tono Shinkinsei ni tsuite"
        (On the Relationship Between Nishida and Heidegger). *Risô* (Tôkyô), vol.
        326, 1960, 35-47.

4406    Ôe, Seishirô. "Haideggâ Tetsugku no Shôrai" (The Future of Heidegger's
        Philosophy). *Risô* (Tôkyô), vol. 444, 1970, 69-79.

4407    Oedingen, Karlo. "Die Erfahrung der 'Nichtung' und ihre Deutung bei Camus
        und Heidegger." *Tijdschrift voor Filosofie* (Leuven), vol. 27, 1965, 68-83.

4408    Oedingen, Karlo. "Das Problem der Gegensätze und die Traszendenz."
        *Kant-Studien* (Köln), vol. 61, 1970, 200-208.

4409    Oehme, C. Rev. of *Platons Lehre von der Wahrheit. Mit einem Brief über den
        'Humanismus'*, by Martin Heidegger. Bern, 1947. *Psyche* (Heidelberg), vol.
        1, 1947/48, 593-598.

4410 Oeing-Hanhoff, L. "Le problème de l'être à l'ère atomique. A propos d'un récent ouvrage de M. Heidegger: Du principe de raison." *Archives de Philosophie* (Paris), vol. 21, 1958, 5-25.

4411 Offerhaus, W. A. *De mens en zijn lot, een vonfrontatie tussen geloof en fatalisme in een mensbeschouwing.* Assen, 1970, XVII, 146 p.

4412 Ogawa, Hiroshi. *Sekai to Yûgenteki Chôetsu* (The World and the Finite Transcendence). Tôkyô: Tôkyôkyôikudaigaku-Bungakubu-Kiyô, 1956.

4413 Ogawa, Orii. "Jitsuzon Tetsugaku ni okeru Mu no Mondai" (The Problem of No-Thing in Existence-Philosophy; About Sartre, Heidegger and Marcel). *Bunkyô Joshi Tanki Daigaku Kiyô* (Tôkyô), vol. 9, 1976, 131-159.

4414 Ogden, Schubert M. "Dèr Begriff der Theologie bei Ott und Bultmann." In *Der spätere Heidegger und die Theologie.* Zürich/Stuttgart, 1964, 187-205.

4415 Ogiermann, Helmut. Rev. of *Kants These über das Sein,* by Martin Heidegger. Frankfurt, 1963. *Scholastik* (Freiburg), vol. 40, 1965, 144-145.

4416 Ogiermann, Helmut. "Anthropologie und Gottesaufweis." *Theologie und Philosophie,* vol. 44, 1969, 506-530.

4417 Ogiermann, Helmut. Rev. of *Zur Sache des Denkens,* by Martin Heidegger. *Theologie und Philosophie* (Frankfurt/Pullach/Freiburg), vol. 46, no. 1, 1971, 111-113.

4418 Ogiermann, Helmut. Rev. of "Heraklit," by Martin Heidegger and Fink. Seminar Wintersemester 1966/67. Frankfurt, 1970. *Theologie und Philosophie* (Frankfurt/Pullach/Freiburg), vol. 46, 1971, 464-465.

4419 Oguchi, Tadao. "Haideggâ ni okerû Jikan" (The Notion of Time in Heidegger). *Nihon Daigaku Bungakubu Kenkyû Nempô, Fûkkan* (Tôkyô), vol. 1, 1951, 27-42.

4420 Oguma, Jirô. "Haideggâ ni okeru 'Seiki' no Kyûmei o megutte" (On the Investigation of 'Event' in Heidegger). *Sôka Daigaku Bungakubu Ronshû* (Tôkyô), vol. 501, 1976, 127-132.

4421 Ogura, Sadahide. "Haideggâ ni okeru Shinsei no Mondai" (The Problem of Deity in Heidegger). *Rinrigakunenpô,* Tôkyô, 1953.

4422 Ogura, Shishô. "Haideggâ no 'Rekishisei no Hôsoku'" (Heidegger's 'Law of Historicity'). *Jitsuzon* (Tôkyô), Mai 1955.

4423 Ogura, Shishô. "Gendai no Nihirisumu, Haideggâ" (The Present Nihilism. Heidegger). *Jitsuzonshugi* (Tôkyô), vol. 15, September 1958.

4424 Ogura, Shishô. "Haideggâ to Girisha-Shisô" (Heidegger and the Greek Thinking). *Jitsuzonshugi* (Tôkyô), April 1966.

4425 Ogura, Yukiyoshi. "Haideggâ; Nihirizumu no Danmen" (Heidegger; an Aspect of Nihilism). *Jitsuzonshugi* (Tôkyô), vol. 15, 1958, 2-5.

4426 Ogura, Yoshiyuki. "Haideggâ no Shieringuron" (On Schelling in Heidegger). *Jitsuzonshugi* (Tôkyô), vol. 71, 1975, 125-136.

4427    Ogura, Yoshiyuki. "Haideggâ Tetsugaku no Kihon Seikaku" (Fundamental Character of Heidegger's Philosophy). *Jitsuzonshugi* (Tôkyô), vol. 77, 1976, 2-8.

4428    Ogurcov, A. P. "Ekzistencialistskaja mifologija jazyka (M. Chajdegger)" (The Existentialist Mythology of Language (M. Heidegger)). *V sbornike 'Filosofija marksizma i ekzistencialzm'*. Izdatel'stvo Moskovskogo Univ. Moskva, 1971, 24-27.

4429    Ogurcow, A. "Egzystencjalistyczna mitologia jezyka. Martin Heidegger" (Existential Mythology of Language). Trans. from Russian. In *Filozofia marksizmu a egzystencjalizm* (Marxist Philosophy and Existentialism). Warszawa, 1974.

4430    Ôhashi, Ryôsuke. "Haideggâ no Keiken to Kami no Mondai; Kindai no Tetsugaku to kanrenshite" (Heidegger's Experience and Problem of God; in Connection With Modern Philosophy). *Risô* (Tôkyô), vol. 500, 1975, 72-85.

4431    Ôhashi, Ryôsuke. *Ekstase und Gelassenheit. Zu Schelling und Heidegger.* (Münchener Univ., Reihe der Philosophischen Fakultät, 16). München: Wilhelm Fink Verlag, 1975, 184 p.

4432    Ohms, J. F. *Der Begriff der ontologischen Wahrheit bei Martin Heidegger. Seine Voraussetzungen und Konsequenzen.* Phil. Diss. Graz 1951 126 p.

4433    Ohyôn, Sin. "Ch'ojaegujôûi chonjaeronjôk haemyông" (Ontological Explanation of the Transcendental Structure in Heidegger). M. A. Thesis, Sôul Univ., 1966.

4434    Ohyôn, Sin. "Haidegkae issôsô haengûi kaenyôm" (The Notion of Dynamic Accomplishment in Heidegger). *Ch'ôrhad Yôngu* (Sôul), vol. 3, 1968, 73-98.

4435    Oizerman, Todor I. "Reakcionnaja suscnost' nemeckogo ekzistencializma" (The Reactionary Nature of German Existentialism). *V sbornike 'Sovremennyj sub-ektivnyj idealizm'.* Izdatel'stvo 'Gospolitizdat'. Moskva, 1957, 242-471.

4436    Oizerman, Todor I. "Ekzistencializm - filosofija krizisa" (Existentialism - the Philosophy of Crisis). *V sbornike 'Kritika sovremennoj burzuaznoj ideologii'.* Izdatel'stvo Vyssaja skola. Moskva, 1963, 60-88.

4437    Oizerman, Todor I. "Cennoe issledovanie svejcarskogo marksista" (A Valuable Research of the Swiss Marxists). *Posleslovie k knige T. Svarca 'Ot Sopengauera k Chajdeggeru'.* Moskva, 1964.

4438    Oizerman, Todor I., ed., L. N. Mitrochin, and A. G. Mislivcenko. *Sovremennyj ekzistencializm* (Kriticeskie ocerki). Moskva, 1966. [Heidegger, specifically pages 38-42, 52-56, 65-71, 90-104, 106-120, 132-137, 542-555.]

4439    Oizerman, Todor I. "Problemy istoriko-filosofskoj nauki" (The Problem of Historical-Philosophical Science). *Glava 2,* section 6. Izdatel'stvo 'Mysl'. Moskva, 1969.

4440    Oizerman, Todor I. "Filosofija krizisa i krizis filosofiii" (The Philosophy of Crisis and the Crisis of Philosophy). *V sbornike Svoremennyj ekzistencializm* (Kriticeskie ocerki). Izdatel'stvo 'Mysl'. Moskva, 1966.

4441    Oizerman, Todor I. "K kritike chajdeggerovskoj koncepcii filosofii" (The Criticism of Heidegger's Conception of Philosophy). *Naucnye doklady vyssej skoly, Filosofskie nauki,* vol. 4, 1969, 115-123.

4442    Oizerman, Todor I. "Glavnye filosofskie napravlenija" (Main Currents in Philosophy). *Glava 2,* section 5. Izdatel'stvo 'Mysl'. Moskva, 1971.

4443    Oizerman, Todor I. "Ekzistencializm - otrazenie krizisa burzuaznogo obscestva" (Existentialism as the Reflection of the Crisis of Bourgeois Society). *Problemy mira i socializma,* vol. 2, 1971.

4444    Oizerman, Todor I. "Osnovnye tecenija sovremennoj zapadnoevropejskoj filosofii" (The Main Currents of Contemporary Occidental Philosophy). *Politiceskoe samoobrazovanie,* vol. 11, 1971.

4445    Oizerman, Todor I. "Martin Heideggers Philosophie der Philosophie." In *Nachdenken über Heidegger.* Ed. Ute Guzzoni. Hildesheim: Gerstenberg Verlag, 1980, 198-212.

4446    Okabayashi, Katsumi. *Haideggâ no Tôki to Senku no Ichi-Kôsatu* (A Contemplation of the Projection and the Advancing in Heidegger). Shimanedai-Ronshû, Matsue, 1960.

4447    Okada, Noriko. "Haideggâ to Shijin no Mondai" (On Heidegger and the Poets). *Jimbun Gakuhô* (Tôkyô Toritsu Daigaku, Tôkyô), vol. 48, 1965, 83-103.

4448    Okada, Noriko. "Haideggâ no Ryôshin-ron to Furomu ni okeru Aku" (Heidegger's "Conscience" and E. Gromm's "Evil"). *Jitsuzonshugi* (Tôkyô), vol. 43, 1968, 28-35.

4449    Okada, Noriko. "'Jikan to Sonzai' o megutte" (On "Sein und Zeit"). *Tetsugakushi, Toritsu Daigaku Tetsugakukai* (Tôkyô), vol. 14, Dezember 1971, 1-24.

4450    Okada, Noriko. *Haideggâ Kenkyû* (Studies on Heidegger). Ibunsha, Tôkyô, 1976, 254 p.

4451    Okada, Noriko. "Haideggâ no Geijutsuron" (Heidegger's Theory of Art). *Jitsuzonshugi* (Tôkyô), vol. 77, 31-42.

4452    Okada, Noriko. "Haideggâ no Shinriron" (Heidegger's Theory of Truth). *Jinbun Gakuhô* (Tôkyô), no. 134, 1979, 1-70.

4453    Okada, Ryûhei. "Haideggâ Tetsugaku to sono Seikaku" (Heidegger's Philosophy and Its Particularity). *Risshô Daigaku Bungakubu Ronsô* (Tôkyô), vol. 4, 1955, 36-54.

4454    Okamoto, Hiromasa. "Haideggâ no Shinrikan" (Heidegger's Theory of Truth). *Tetsugaku Zasshi* (Tôkyô), vol. 87, no. 759, 1972, 207-226.

4455    Okano, Tomejirô. *Sonzaironteki Ryôiki toshite no Chôets ni tsuite* (On the Transcendence as an Ontological Region). Tomonagahakase-Kanrekikinen-Ronbunshu, Tôkyô, 1931.

4456   Okino, Masahiro. "Kôki Haideggâ to Hainrihi Otto" (The Later Heidegger and Heinrich Ott). *Ôsaka Denki Tsûshin Daigaku Kenkyû Ronshû* (Osaka), vol. 4, 1968, 67-91.

4457   Okino, Masahiro. "Haideggâ ni okeru Kaishaku-gaku to Kotoba no Mondai" (Hermeneutics and Language in Heidegger). *Ôsaka Denki Tsûshin Daigaku Kenkyû Ronshû* (Ôsaka), vol. 6, 1970, 16-31.

4458   Okojima, Shinji. "Haideggâ ni okeru 'Mu' ni tsuite" (On Heidegger's 'Non-Being'). *Kansai Dagaku Bungaku-Ronshû* (Ôsaka), November 1955, 46-60.

4459   Okojima, Shinji. "Haideggâ ni okeru Mu ni tsuite" (On the Notion of Non-Being in Heidegger). *Kansaidagaku-Bungakuronshu* (Ôsaka), Juni 1956.

4460   Oku, Masahiro. "Bittogenshutain to Haideggâ" (Wittgenstein and Heidegger). *Risô* (Tôkyô), vol. 444, 1970, 92-104.

4461   Okrent, Mark B. "The Becoming of Being." *Man and World,* vol. 11, 1978, 281-298.

4462   Olafson, Frederick A. *Principles and Persons. An Ethical Interpretation of Existentialism.* Baltimore, 1967, 258 p.

       [Rev. by B. Sitter in *Philosophische Rundschau* (Heidelberg/Tübingen), vol. 16, 1969, 273-282.]

4463   Olafson, Frederick A. "Interpretation and the Dialectic of Action." *The Journal of Philosophy* (New York), vol. 69, 1972, 718-734.

4464   Olafson, Frederick A. "Consciousness and Intentionality in Heidegger's Thought." *American Philosophical Quarterly* (Pittsburgh), vol. 12, 1975, 91-103.

4465   Olafson, Frederick A. "Heidegger's Politics. An Interview With Herbert Marcuse." *Graduate Faculty Philosophical Journal* (New York), vol. 6, 1977, 28-40.

4466   Olarte, T. "Sein und Zeit." *Revista de la Universidad de Costa Rica,* vol. 1, no. 1, 1957, 76-77.

4467   Olasagasti, M. *Introducción a Heidegger.* Madrid, 1967, 346 p.

4467   aO'Leary, Joseph Stephen. "Topologie de l'être et topographie de la révélation." In *Heidegger et la question de Dieu.* Ed. R. Kearney and J. S. O'Leary. Paris: B. Grasset, 1980, 194-237.

4468   Olivieri, Francisco José. "Nota sobre Heidegger y los griegos." *Cuadernos de filosofía* (Buenos Aires), vol. 11, no. 15-16, 1971, 181-194.

4469   Oltra, M. Rev. of *German Existentialism,* by Martin Heidegger. Trans. D. D. Runes. *Verdad y Vida* (Madrid), vol. 24, 1966, 616.

4470   O'Mahony, B. E. "Martin Heidegger's Existential Analysis of Death." *Philosophical Studies* (Maynooth), vol. 18, 1969, 58-75.

4471   O'Meara, Th. F. "Tillich and Heidegger: A Structural Relationship." *The Harvard Theological Review* (Cambridge), vol. 61, 1968, 249-261.

4472 Ômine, Ken. "Shinri towa ninika" (What is the Truth?) *Risô* (Tôkyô), vol. 534, 1977, 49-64.

4473 Onishi, Tomota. *Sheringu no Rekishiteki Shizen to Haidegga Yasupasu no Rekishiteki Ningen* (The Historical Nature in Schelling and the Historical Man in Heidegger and Jaspers). Tetsugakukenkyu, Kyoto, Dezember 1940.

4474 Ono, Ryôsei. "Haideggâ ni okeru U no Toi no Kôzô" (The Structure of Inquiry to Being in Heidegger). *Tetsugaku Ronshû,* vol. 21, 1975, 61-82.

4475 ônogi, Satoshi. "Haideggâ-Tetsugaku to Nihirizumu no Kokufuku" (Heidegger and an Overcoming of Nihilism). *Tetsugaku-Zasshi* (Journal of Philosophy) (Tôkyô), vol. 748, 1961, 38-52.

4476 Ônogi, Satoshi. "Haideggâ ni okeru Jiyû to Hitsuzen" (Heidegger's Conceptions of Freedom and Necessity). *Tetsugaku Zasshi* (Tôkyô), vol. 760, 1973, 44-61.

4477 Ônogi, Satoshi. "Haideggâ ni okeru Konkyoritsu no Mondai" (Heidegger's Thought on the Principle of Reason). *Jimbunkagaku Kenkyû* (Niigata), vol. 47, 1975, 75-108.

4478 Orendi Hinze, Diana. "Heidegger und Trakl: aus dem unveröffentlichten Briefwechsel Martin Heidegger - Ludwig von Ficker." *Orbis litterarum. Revue internationale d'études littéraires* (Kobenhavn), vol. 32, 1977, 247-253.

4479 Orr, Robert. *The Meaning of Transcendence: A Heideggerian Reflection.* Phil. Diss. Vanderbilt Univ. 1979 247 p. *Dissertation Abstracts International,* vol. 40/06-A, 3368.

4480 Osada, Arata. "Haideggâ no Daigakuron ni tsuite" (On Heidegger's 'Die Selbstbehauptung der deutschen Universität'). *Risô* (Tôkyô), März 1935.

4481 Ortega y Gasset, J. "Martin Heidegger und die Sprache der Philosophen." *Universitas* (Stuttgart), vol. 7, 1952, 897-903.

4482 Ortega y Gasset, J. "Martin Heidegger y el lenguaje de los filósofos." *Anales de la Universidad de Chile,* 1959, 7-10.

4483 Ortega Muñoz, J. F. "Lenguaje, estilo y método de la filosofía de Heidegger." *Analecta Malacitana* (Málaga), vol. 2, 1979, 137-164.

4484 Orth, Ernst Wolfgang. "Husserl, Scheler, Heidegger. Eine Einführung in das Problem der Philosophischen Komparatistik." In *Husserl, Scheler, Heidegger in der Sicht neuer Quellen.* Contributions by Ernst Wolfgang Orth, et al. (Phänomenologische Forschungen, 6/7). Freiburg: Verlag Karl Alber, 1978, 7-27.

4485 Ortiz Osés, Andrés. "Filosofia espannla y filosofia europea. Para una confrontación de Amor Ruibal con la filosofia de Heidegger." *Giornale di Metafisica* (Genova/Torino), vol. 26, 1971, 171-184.

4486 Ortiz-Osés, Andrés. "El Realismo Filosófico Españl: Amor Ruibal Y Zubiri." *Pensamiento,* vol. 33, 1977, 77-85.

4487 Ortner, E. "Das Nicht-Sein und das Nichts." *Zeitschrift für philosophische Forschung* (Meisenheim/Glan), vol. 5, 1950/51, 82-86, (specifically page 86).

4488 Ortúzar, M. "En torno al 'Sein und Zeit'." *Estudios, Revista Mensual* (Buenos Aires), vol. 3, 1947, 164-187.

4489 Oshima, Sueo. "Theology and History in Karl Barth: A Study of the Theology of Karl Barth in Reference to the Philosophy of Martin Heidegger." Phil. Diss. Univ. of Chicago 1970.

4490 Oshima, Sueo. "Barth's Analogia relationis and Heidegger's Ontological Difference." *The Journal of Religion* (Chicago), vol. 53, 1973, 176-194.

4491 Oshima, Sueo. "The Ontological Structures of Human Existence in Barth and Heidegger. Toward a Theology of Fellowship." *Rice University Studies* (Houston, Texas), vol. 60, no. 1, 1974, 103-129.

4492 Ôta, Akio. "Haideggâ Tetsugaku no ichi Kôsatsu" (On Heidegger's Philosophy). *Kyoto Gakuen Daigaku Ronsô* (Kyôto), vol. 1, no. 1, 1972, 198-207.

4493 Ôta, Akio. "Haideggâ to Mushinron no Mondai" (Heidegger and the Problem of Atheism). *Kyôto Gakuen Daigaku Ronsyû* (Kyôto), vol. 6, no. 1, 1977, 1-18.

4494 Ott, Heinrich. "Objektivierendes und existentielles Denken. Zur Diskussion um die theologie R. Bultmanns." *Kerygma und Mythos.* Ed. H. W. Bartsch. Hamburg, vol. IV, 1955, 107-131.

4495 Ott, Heinrich. *Denken und Sein. Der Weg Martin Heideggers und der Weg der Theologie.* Zollikon, 1959, 226 p.

4496 Ott, Heinrich. "Was ist systematische Theologie?" *Der spätere Heidegger und die Theologie* (Zürich/Stuttgart), vol. 1964, 95-133.

4497 Ott, Heinrich. "Antwort auf die amerikanischen Beiträge." *Der spätere Heidegger und die Theologie* (Zürich/Stuttgart), 1964, 233-248.

4498 Ott, Heinrich. *Wirklichkeit und Glaube, II: Der persônliche Gott.* Göttingen, 1969, 94-121: Das Gebet als Sprache des Glaubens und passim.

4499 Ott, Heinrich. "Die Bedeutung von Martin Heideggers Denken für die Methode der Theologie." In *Durchblicke.* Ed. V. Klostermann. Frankfurt, 1970, 27-38.

4500 Ott, Heinrich. "Martin Heidegger." In *Martin Heidegger im Gespräch.* Ed. R. Wisser. Freiburg/München, 1970, 45-47.

4501 Ott, Heinrich. "Hermeneutic and Personal Structure of Language." *On Heidegger and Language.* Ed. J. J. Kockelmans. Evanston, 1972, 169-193.

4502 Otto, W. F. "Die Zeit und das Sein." *Anteile.* Martin Heidegger zum 60. Geburtstag. Frankfurt, 1950, 7-28.

4503 Ottonelle, P. P. *Heidegger e il significate della decadenza. Dalle lezioni di Storia della filosofia tenute nell'anno accademico 1970-71 presso la Facoltà di magistero die Genova.* Genova, 1971, 162 p.

4504    Ôuchi, Susumu. "Gendai-Kagaku no Keijijôgaku" (Metaphysics of the Newer Sciences). *Aichi Gakugei Daigaku Kenkyû-Hôkoku* (Nagoya), vol. 4, 1954, 27-31.

4505    Ôushi, Susumu. *The Place-Keeper of Non-Being and the Shepherd of Being.* Aichigakugeidaigaku-Kenkyûhôkoku, Nagoya, 1957.

4506    Ôuchi, Susumu. "Haideggâ no Konkyo-ron" (Heidegger's "Satz vom Grund"). *Aichi Gakugei Daigaku Kenkyû Hôkoku* (Nagoya), vol. 8, 1959, 63-74.

4507    Ôuchi, Susumu. "Haideggâ Kenkyû I" (Heidegger Studies 1). *Aichi Gakugei Daigaku Kenkyû Hôkoku* (Nagoya), vol. 9, 1960, 721-771.

4508    Ôuchi, Susumu. *Haideggâ Kenkyû* (Studies on Heidegger). Tôkyô, 1962.

4509    Oyen, H. "Fundamentalontologie und Ethik." *Library of the Xth International Congress of Philosophy* (Amsterdam), vol. II, 1948, 107-121.

4510    Ozarowski, J. "Wokó siedemdziesieciolecia urodzin Martina" (On the Occasion of Martin Heidegger's Eightieth Birthday). *Argumenty,* vol. 4, 1959.

4511    Ozarowski, J. "Ujawnianie bytu w paustwi. Ontologia i polityka Martina Heideggera." *Studia filozoficzne* (Warschau), vol. 4, 1971, 87-100.

4512    Ozarowski, J. "Ujawnienie bytu w panstwie. Ontologia i polityka M. Heideggera" (The Revelation of Being in the State. M. Heidegger's Ontology and Politics). *Studia Filozoficzne,* vol. 4, 1971.

4513    Ozarowski, J. "Nieokreálonáá tragiczna Heideggera" (The Tragic Uncertainty M. Heidegger's). *Argumenty,* vol. 38, 1971.

4514    Ozarowski, J. "Kontynuacja "strony czynnej" w idealizmie niemieckim/Kant, Hegel, Husserl, Heidegger, Gadamer" (The Continuation of the 'Aktive Seite' of the German Idealism/Kant, Hegel, Husserl, Heidegger, Gadamer). Wydawnictwa Uniwersytetu Warszawskiego 1978.

4515    Paci, E. *Principi di una filosofia dell'essere.* Modena, 1939, 31-35, 159-161, 168-170, 185.

4516    Paci, E. "Il problema dell'esistenza." *Studi filosofici* (Milano), vol. 18, 1940, 93-105.

4517    Paci, E. "Introduzione alla traduzione di." In *Che cosa è la metafisica?* Milano, 1942.

4518    Paci, E. *L'esistenzialismo.* Padova, 1943, (specifically pages 28-29).

4519    Paci, E. *Esistenzialismo e storicismo.* Verona, 1950, (specifically pages 115-146: L'esistenzialismo di Heidegger e lo storicismo).

4520    Padeletti, H. "Arte y poesia en Heidegger." *Universidad,* Januar-März 1963, 55, 153-188.

4521    Padellaro, R. "A proposito di 'Un incontro tra Heidegger e la filosofia tomista'." *Giornale di Metafisica* (Genova/Torino), vol. 15, 1960, 16-41.

4522    Padellaro, R. *Heidegger e il problema kantiano.* Torino, 1960.

4523    Pageler, John C. *The Soul and Time: First Principles of Modern Metaphysical Speculation as Represented in the Thought of Martin Heidegger.* Phil. Diss. Claremont Graduate School and Univ. Center 1967 214 p. *Dissertation Abstracts International,* vol. 29/01-A, 292.

4524    Palmaers, M. "Het heilige en het onheilige. Commentaar op Heidegger." *Algemeen Nederlands Tijdschrift voor Wijsbegeerte en Psychologie* (Assen), vol. 63, 1971, 1-27.

4525    Palmer, Richard E. "'Phenomenology', Edmund Husserl's Article for the Encyclopaedia Britannica: A New Complete Translation." *The Journal of the British Society for Phenomenology,* vol. 2, May 1971, 77-90.

4526    Palmer, Richard E. *Hermeneutics. Interpretation Theory in Schleiermacher, Dilthey, Heidegger, and Gadamer.* (Northwestern Univ. studies in phenomenology and existential philosophy). Evanston, Illinois, 1969, XVIII, 283 p.

        [Rev. by P. Emad in *Philosophischer Literaturanzeiger* (Meisenheim/Glan), vol. 24, 1971, H. 5, 292 ff.]

        [Rev. by R. A. Makkreel in *Journal of the History of Philosophy* (Berkeley), vol. 9, no. 1, 1971, 114 ff.]

        [Rev. by Th. Kisiel in *Zeitschrift für allgemeine Wissenschaftstheorie,* vol. 2, no. 1, 1971, 130.]

4527    Palmer, Richard E. "The Postmodernity of Heidegger." *Boundary,* vol. 2, no. 4, 411-432. Rpt. in *Martin Heidegger and the Question of Literature.* Ed. William V. Spanos. Bloomington, Indiana/London: Indiana Univ. Press, 1979, 71-92.

4528    Palmier, J.-M. *Les écrits politiques de Heidegger.* Paris, 1968, 348 p. [Bibliographie, 335-341.]

4529    Palmier, J.-M., and F. de Towarnicki. "Conversación con Heidegger." *Ideas y valores* (Bogota), 35-37, 1970, 87-96.

4530    Palousová, A. "Martin Heidegger: bibliographie." *Filosoficky Casopis,* no. 5/6, 1969, 813-824. [Czechoslovakian and German sources.]

4531    Paluch, Stanley J. "Heidegger's 'What is Metaphysics?'" *Philosophy and Phenomenological Research* (Buffalo, New York), vol. 30, 1970, 603-609.

4532    Paluch, Stanley J. "Sociological Aspects of Heidegger's 'Being and Time'." *Inquiry,* vol. 6, 1963, 300-307.

4533    Paluch, Stanley J. "Heidegger and the *Scandal of Philosophy.*" *The Journal of the British Society for Phenomenology* (Manchester), vol. 6, 1975, 168-172.

4534    Paluch, Stanley J. "The Fall of the House of Being." *The Journal of the British Society for Phenomenology,* vol. 10, no. 2, 73-77.

4535    Panikkar, Raimundo. "Eine unvollendete Symphonie." In *Erinnerung an Martin Heidegger,* by Günther Neske. Pfullingen: Verlag Günther Neske, 1977, 173-178.

4536 Panis, D. Rev. of *Schelling: le traité de 1809 sur l'essence de la liberté humaine,* by Martin Heidegger. *Revue Internationale de Philosophie* (Bruxelles), vol. 31, 1977, 65-66.

4537 Panou, Stavros. "Logik des Nichts (in Greek)." *Philosophia* (Athens), vol. 4, 1974, 59-67.

4538 Pantazi, R. "Kritische Überlegungen zum Problem der Philosophie des Existentialismus im Lichte der leninistischen Wiederspiegelungstheorie." *Revue Roumaine des Sciences Sociales* (Bukarest) (Série de Philosophie et Logique), vol. 1, 1970, 15-20.

4539 Pardo, R. "La metaphysique existentialiste (Heidegger et Marcel) du point de vue d'une épistémologie radicalement évolutive de la raison." *Akten des XIV. Internationalen Kongresses für Philosophie* (Wien), vol. VI, 1968. Wien, 1971, 459-469.

4540 Pareyson, L. "Note sulla filosofia dell'esistenza." *Giornale critico della filosofia italiana* (Firenze), vol. 6, 1938, 407-438.

4541 Pareyson, L. "Panorama dell'esistenzialismo." *Studi filosofici* (Milano), vol. 2, 1941, 193-204, (specifically pages 196 ff, und passim).

4542 Pareyson, L. *Studi sull'esistenzialismo.* Firenze, 1943. 2nd ed. 1950, 207-258.

4543 Pareyson, L. "El existentialismo-Espejo de la conciencia contemporanea." *Universidad de Buenos Aires, Facultad de Filosofia y Letras* (Buenos Aires) (Instituto de Filosofia, Serie Ensayos), no. 2, 1949, 33 p.

4544 Pareyson, L. *Esistenza e persona.* 2nd ed. Torino, 1960.

4545 Parkes, Graham Ross. *Time and the Soul: Heidegger's Ontology as the Ground for an Archetypal Psychology.* Phil. Diss. Univ. of California Berkeley 1978 229 p. *Dissertation Abstracts International,* vol. 39/09-A, 5555.

4546 Paskow, Alan. "The Meaning of My Own Death." *International Philosophical Quarterly* (Bronx, New York), vol. 14, no. 1, 1974, 51-69.

4547 Paskow, Alan. "What do I Fear in Facing My Death?" *Man World,* vol. 8, May 1975, 146-156.

4548 Passweg, S. *Phänomenologie und Ontologie. Husserl-Scheler-Heidegger.* Zürich, 1939.

4549 Pastore, A. "Husserl, Heidegger, Chestov." *Archivio di storia della filosofia italiana* (Roma), vol. 2, 1933, 107-131.

4550 Pastore, A. "La comprensione emotiva del tempo. Considerazioni sopra l'analitica esistenziale di Heidegger." *Atti delle scienze de Torino. Classe di scienze morali storiche e filosofiche,* vol. 80, 1944/45, 3-25, 26-52.

4551 Pastore, A. "Whitehead e Heidegger contro Kant." *Rivista di filosofia* (Torino), vol. 38, 1947, 181-190.

4552 Pastore, A. *La volontà dell'assurdo. Storia e crisi dell'esistenzialismo.* Milano, 1948, 59-114.

4553    Pastore, A. "L'espressionismo metafisico di Heidegger." *Rendiconti della Classe di Scienze Morali dell'Accademia Naz. dei Lincei* (Roma), Serie 8, no. 9, 1954, 436-453.

4554    Pastuszka, J. "Proces myslenia u sw. Tomasze z Akwmu a v egzystencjalizme M. Heideggera" (The Procedure of Thinking in St. Thomas Aquinas and in the Existentialism of Martin Heidegger). *Roczniky filozoficzne.* Ed. Towarystwo Naukow Katolickiego Universitetu Lubelskiego (Scientific Society at the Catholic University of Lublin). Vol. XIII, no. 4, 1965, 33-48.

4555    Pastuszka, J. "Koncepcja czlowieka-blizniego w egzystencjalizmie" (The Concept of the 'Menschen-Nächsten' in Existentialism). In *Roczniki Filozoficzne,* KUL XIV, 1966.

4556    Pastuszka, J. "Koncepcja czlowieka - blizniego v egzystencjalizme" (The Concept of Fellow-Man in Existentialism). *Roczniky filozoficzne.* Ed. Towarystwo Naukowe Katolickiego Univ. Lubelskiego (Scientific Society at the Catholic Univ. of Lublin). Vol. XIV, 1966, 5-17.

4557    Patent, G. I. "K kritike ontologii Martina Chajdeggera" (Criticism of Heidegger's Ontology). *Ucënye zapiski Kurganskogo gosudarstvennogo pedagogiceskogo instituta,* vol. V, 1963, 36-61.

4558    Patent, G. I. "Praktika i poznanie v ekzistencializme i marksizme (K kritike 'Fundamental'noj ontologii' M. Chajdeggera)" (Practice and Cognition in Existentialism and Marxism (Criticism of Martin Heidegger's "Fundamental-Ontology")). V knige 'Leninskaja teorija otrazenija i sovremennost materialy jubilejnoj naucnoj sessii vuzov Ural'skoj zony'. *Filosofskie nauki* (Sverdlovsk), vol. I, 1967, 245-254.

4559    Patent, G. I. "Problema obscestvennogo soznanija v 'Fundamental'noj ontologii' M. Chajdeggera" (The Problem of Social Consciousness in M. Heidegger's "Fundamental-Ontology"). V knige 'Nekotorye voprosy marksistskoleninskoj filosofii'. *Sbornik statej* (Celjabinsk), vol. 2, 1969, 149-170.

4560    Patent, G. I. *Marksizm i apriorizm. Kritika irracionalisticeskogo apriorizma M. Chajdeggera* (Marxism and Apriorism. Criticism of the Irrationalistic Apriorism of M. Heidegger). Avtoreferat Phil. Diss. Sverdlovsk 1972.

4561    Patent, G. I. *Marsizm i ekzistencializm. K kritike irracionalisticeskoj 'Fundamental'noj Ontologii' M. Chajdeggera* (Marxism and Existentialism. On the Criticism of M. Heidegger's Irrationalistic 'Fundamental-Ontology'). Posobie dlja studentov, Celjabinsk, 1973.

4562    Pathak, Chintamani. *The Problem of Being in Heidegger.* (Bharata Manisha Research Series, 2). Varanasi, 1974.

4563    Patka, Frederik E. *Existentialist Thinkers and Thought.* New York, 1962, 170 p.

4564    Patocka, Jan. "Metafyzika ve XX, stoleti." *Dvacáté stoleti* (Praha), Teil 7, 1934, 608 p., (specifically pages 7-24).

4565 Patocka, Jan. "Heidegger vom anderen Ufer." In *Durchblicke*. Ed. R. Wisser. Frankfurt, 1970, 394-411.

4566 Patocka, Jan. "Hajdeger s druge obale." Trans. Dragan Stojanovic. In *Rani Hajdeger - Recepcija i kritika Bivstva i vremena*, by Dragan Stojanovic and Danilo Basta. (Biblioteka Zodijak). Beograd, 1979, 113-132.

4567 Patri, A. "Kant et le problème de la métaphysique selon Heidegger." *Le monde nouveau* (Paris), vol. 9, no. 73, 1953, 24-29.

4568 Patri, A. "Un exemple d'engagement (Heidegger)." *Le Contrat Social*, janvier-février 1962.

4569 Patri, A. "Serait-ce une querelle d'allemand?" *Critique* (Paris), vol. 23, 1967, 296-297.
[Rev. of *Trois attaques contre Heidegger*, by Fr. Fédier. 1966.]

4570 Patriccia, Nicholas A. "God and the Questioning of Being: An Analytical Comparison of the Thinking of Martin Heidegger and Paul Tillich." Phil. Diss. Univ. of Chicago 1972 223 p.

4571 Patriccia, Nicholas A. "Martin Heidegger's Understanding of Theology." *Listening*, vol. 10, Winter 1975, 59-72.

4572 Paumen, J. "La sagesse romantique de Martin Heidegger." *Revue international de philosophie* (Bruxelles), vol. 3, 1949, 281-289.

4573 Paumen, J. "Heidegger et le thème nietzschéen de la mort de Dieu." *Revue Internationale de Philosophie* (Bruxelles), vol. 14, no. 52, 1960, [Heidegger], 238-262.

4574 Paumen, J. "Eléments de bibliographie heideggérienne." *Revue Internationale de Philosophie* (Bruxelles), vol. 14, no. 52, 1960, 263-268.

4575 Paumen, J. "Heidegger et le sens du chemin." *Revue de l'Université de Bruxelles* (Bruxelles), vol. 17, 1964/65, 384-425.

4576 Paumen, J. *Temps et choix*. Brüssel, 1972, 238 p.

4577 Pavia, U. Rev. of *Che cos'è la metafisica?* by Martin Heidegger. Firenze, 1953. *Giornale Critica della Filosofia Italiana* (Firenze), Jg. 33, Serie 3, Heft 8, 1954, 279-282.

4578 Peatzeck, E. W. "La sentencia de Anaximandro a la luz del dilema heideggeriano." *Verdad y Vida* (Madrid), vol. 8, 1950, 299-324.

4579 Peccorini, Francisco L. "El 'ser' heideggeriano, como fundameto último del 'nous' aristotélico." *Revista de Filosofia de la Universidad de Costa Rica* (San José), vol. 15, no. 41, 1977, 255-260.

4580 Peccorini, Francisco L. "Sciacca's Case Against Heidegger's 'Oudenology'." *Filosofia Oggi* (Bologna/Italia), vol. 1, no. 1-4, 1978, 55-66.

4581 Peccorini, Francisco L. "Sciacca's Case Against Heidegger's 'Ondenology', II. Updating and Reevaluation." *Giornale di Metafisica* (Torino), vol. 1, no. 3, 1978, 225-250.

4582 Peccorini, Francisco L. "Sciacca's Case Against Heidegger's 'Oudenology'." (Continua). *Filosofia oggi*, vol. 1, no. 1, 1978, 55-66. [Summary, 98.]

4583   Pecka, D. "Zahada lidské existence." *Na hlubinu* (Czechoslovakian), vol. 11, no. 9, 1936, 618-624.

4584   Peery, Rebekah Smith. *An Interpretation of Personal Love Founded on the Phenomenological Ontology of Martin Heidegger.* Authorized facsimile of the dissertation of the Vanderbilt Univ. Phil. Diss. 1974. Ann Arbor, Michigan; London: University Microfilms International, 1979, ii-188 p.

4585   Pegorara, Olinto. "'Être et Temps' et 'Temps et Être'." *Revue Philosophique de Louvain* (Leuven), Mai 1973, (Quatrième série no. 10, 247-270).

4586   Pegoraro, Olinto. "Note sur la vérité chez saint Thomas et M. Heidegger." *Revue Philosophique de Louvain* (Louvain), vol. 74, 1976, 45-54. [Résumé, 54-55.]

4587   Pegoraro, Olinto. "La verità in S.Tommaso e M. Heidegger." In *Tommaso nel suo settimo centenario.* Atti del Congresso internazionale (Roma-Napoli, 17-24 aprile 1974). Vol. VI: L'essere. Napoli: Edizioni Domenicane Italiane, 1977, 311-319.

4588   Peiser, W. "M. Heidegger e il carattere ontologico della filosofia contemporanea tedesca." *Archivio di filosofia* (Lanciano), vol. II, no. 4, 1932, 75-79.

4589   Pelegri, Joan. "Martin Heidegger. Interpretaciones de su filosofar y su bibliographia puesta al dia." *Analecta Sacra Tarraconensia* (Barcelona), vol. 41, 1968, 87-142.

4590   Pelegri, Joan. "Ruptura o continuitat? A prop[sit d'una obra de Marti Heidegger." *Revista Catalana de Teologia* (Barcelona), vol. 1, 1976, 453-485. [Summary, 486-487.]

4591   Pellegrini, A. *Novecento tedesco.* Milano, 1942, 289-294.

4592   Pellegrini, A. *Hölderlin - Storia della critica.* Firenze, 1956, (German trans. Berlin, 1965, 594 p.)

4593   Pellegrino, A. "Massolo e Heidegger in 'Storicità della Metafisica'." *Studi in onore di Arturo Massolo.* Ed. L. Sichirollo. Urbino, 2. Teil, 1967, 521-537.

4594   Pelegri Valles, J. *El problema de Dios en el filosofar de Martin Heidegger.* (Lección inaugural del curso académico 1969/70). Barcelona, 1969, 86 p.

4595   Pelloux, L. "Heidegger - Register in Bibliografia italiana sull'esistenzialismo." *Esistenzialismo.* Saggi di vari autori a cura di L. Pelloux. Roma, 1943.

4596   Penati, G. *Alienazione e verità, Heidegger e l'ontologia come liberazione.* Brescia, 1972, 206 p.

4597   Penati, G. "Ricerca del fondamento e del significato: l'esperienza religiosa del linguaggio in Heidegger." *Humanitas* (Brescia), vol. 29, no. 7, 1974, 553-561.

4598   Renati, G. "Recenti interpretazioni heideggeriane in Italia." *Studium* (Roma), vol. 74, no. 5, 1978, 645-663.

4599 Penedos, A. dos. "A interpetacño heideggeriana da alegoria da caverna de Platño." *Revista da Faculdade de Letras* (Porto) (Série de Filosofia), vol. 1, 1971, 169-178.

4600 Penzo, Giorgio. "La teoria della conoscenza in Heidegger (una ontologia estetica)." *Studia Patavina* (Padova), vol. 11, 1964, 21-66.

4601 Penzo, Giorgio. "La Vor-Stellung (presentazione) in Heidegger e l'assimilatio in S. Tommaso (Riflessioni metafisiche sulla mistica heideggeriana)." *Studia Patavina* (Padova), vol. 11, 1964, 375-414.

4602 Penzo, Giorgio. "La Vor-Stellung (presentazione) in Heidegger e l'assimilatio' in S.Tommaso (Riflessioni metafisiche sulla mistica heideggeriana)." II. *Studia Patavina* (Padova), vol. 12, 1965, 65-107.

4603 Penzo, Giorgio. "Fondamenti ontologici del linguaggio in Heidegger." *Il problema filosofico del linguaggio*. A cura del Centro di Studi Filosofici di Gallarate. Padova, Gregoriana, 1965, 175-206.

4604 Penzo, Giorgio. "La dimensione ontologica heideggeriana dell 'und' di 'Sein und Zeit' e la metafisica." *Collana di Studi Filosofoci* (Padova), vol. 12, Editrice Gregoriana, 1966, 88-104.

4605 Penzo, Giorgio. "L'unità del pensiero in Martin Heidegger (Una ontologia estetica)." *Collana di Studi Filosofici* (Padova), vol. 11, 1965, 485 p.

4606 Penzo, Giorgio. "Riflessioni sulla intuitio tomista e sulla intuitio heideggeriana." *Aquinas* (Roma), vol. 9, 1966, 87-102.

4607 Penzo, Giorgio. "Essere 'e' tempo e tempo 'e' essere, I-II." *Studia Patavina* (Padova), vol. 13, 1966, 151-198, 359-426.

4608 Penzo, Giorgio. "La morte nel mistero pasquale e la morte nel mistro dell'essere di Heidegger." *Studia Patavina* (Padova), vol. 13, 1966, 211-225.

4609 Penzo, Giorgio. "L'intuito 'Pura' in Heidegger, l'intuitio 'Scintilla rationis' in S. Tommaso e il problema di Dio." *Doctor Communis* (Roma), vol. XIX, 1966, XX; Roma, 1967, 275-280.

4610 Penzo, Giorgio. "Fondamenti ontologici del linguaggio in Heidegger (Il loges heideggeriano ed il logos giovanneo)." *Studia Patavina* (Padova), vol. 14, 1967, 383-426.

4611 Penzo, Giorgio. "La Vor-Stellung in Kant e la Vor-Stellung in Heidegger." *Studia Patavina* (Padova), vol. 14, 1967, 77-120, 236-288.

4612 Penzo, Giorgio. *Pensare heideggeriano e problematica teologica*. Sviluppi della teologia radicale in Germania. Brescia, 1970, 229 p. 2nd ed. 1973.

4613 Penzo, Giorgio. "Riflessioni sulla dimensione dell'essere di Heidegger." *Aquinas. Rivista di Filosofia* (Roma), vol. 14, 1971, 49-62.

4614 Penzo, Giorgio. *Max Stirner. La rivalto eistenziale*. Torino, 1971, 384 p., passim.

4615 Penzo, Giorgio. *Essere e Dio in Karl Jaspers*. Firenze, 1972, 381 p.

4616 Penzo, Giorgio. *Friedrich Nietzsche nell'interpretazione heideggeriana*. Bologna: Pàtron Editore, 1976, 333 p.

4617    Penzo, Giorgio. "La tematica del linguaggion in Heidegger." *Aquinas* (Roma), vol. 20, no. 2, 1977, 207-237.

4618    Penzo, Giorgio. "Martin Heidegger: un filosofare a-teologico?" *Humanitas* (Brescia), vol. 33, no. 4, 1978, 389-415.

4618a   Penzo, Maurizio. *Tra Heidegger e Deleuze. Saggio sulla singolarità.* Venezia: Cluec, 1978, 33 p.

4619    Peperzak, A. "Denken in Parijs." *Algemeen Nederlands Tijdschrift voor Wijsbegeerte* (Assen), vol. 62, 1970, 175-210.

4620    Pereboom, Dirk. "Heidegger-Bibliographie 1917-1966." *Freiburger Zeitschrfit für Philosophie und Theologie* (Freiburg, Schweiz), vol. 16, 1969, 100-161.

4621    Pereboom, Dirk. "Heidegger: Etre, amour et art." *Cahiers de Faculté libre de philosophie comparée* (Paris), no. 4, 1971, 21-36.

4622    Pereboom, Dirk. *The Soterial Implications of Martin Heidegger's Concept of Being.* Thesis submitted to the Faculty of Letters of the Univ. of Fribourg, Switzerland for the Degree of Doctor of Philosophy. Fribourg: Imprimerie Renggli, 1972, v-178 p.

4623    Perini, C. M. G. "Rapporti tra pensiero heideggeriano e metafisica Tomistaca." *Divus Thomas P.* (Piacenza), vol. 76, 1973, 139-174. [Summary, 139.]

4624    Perkins, R. L. Rev. of "Heidegger and the Path of Thinking." Ed. John Sallis. *Journal of the British Society for Phenomenology* (Manchester), vol. 4, 1973, 80-81.

4625    Perotti, James L. *Heidegger on the Divine. The Thinker, the Poet, and God.* Athens, Ohio: Ohio Univ. Press, 1974, 134 p.

4626    Perotti, James L. Rev. of *The Piety of Thinking,* by Martin Heidegger. Trans. J. G. Hart and J. C. Maraldo. 1976. *Thomist,* vol. 43, 1979, 488-496.

4627    Perpeet, W. "Heideggers Kunstlehre." *Jahrbuch für Ästhetik und Allgemeine Kunstwissenschaft* (Köln), vol. 8, 1963, 158-189. Rpt. in *Heidegger.* Ed. O. Pöggeler. Köln/Berlin, 1969, 217-241.

4628    Petrick, Eileen Bagus. *Heidegger on Nihilism and the Finitude of Philosophy.* Phil. Diss. Pennsylvania State Univ. 1973 199 p. *Dissertation Abstracts International,* vol. 35/01-A, 520.

4629    Pesek, J. "Die Geschichtlichkeit und die 'Kehre' in der Philosophie von Martin Heidegger." (In Czechoslovakian). *Fiiosoficky Casopis,* no. 5/6, 1969, 759-767.

4630    Peter, A. Rev. of *Sein und Zeit,* by Martin Heidegger. Halle, 1927. *Die Eiche.* Vierteljahresschrift zur Pflege der fortschr. Beziehungen zwischen Grossbritannien und Deutschland, vol. 20, 1932, 387.

4631    Petersen, E. "Existentialismus und protestantische Theologie." *Wort und Wahrheit* (Wien), vol. 2, 1947, 409-412.

4632    Petroviá, Gajo. "Praxis und Sein." *Praxis.* Revue philosophique. Ed. Univ. Zagreb. Zagreb, 1965, 26-40.

4633    Petroviá, Gajo. "Der Spruch des Heidegger." In *Durchblicke*. Ed. V. Klostermann. Frankfurt, 1970, 412-436.

4634    Petroviá, Gajo. "Extra-Temporal Problems and Methodological Conscience of Philosophy. On the Case-History of *Sein und Zeit*." (In Serbocroat). *Delo* (Beograd), vol. 23, no. 12, 1977, 75-84.

4635    Petroviá, Gajo. "Heidegger und Marx." In *Nachdenken über Heidegger*. Ed. Ute Guzzoni. Hildesheim: Gerstenberg Verlag, 1980, 213-231.

4636    Petruzellis, N. *Filosofia dell'arte*. Roma, 1944, (specifically pages 71-86).

4637    Petruzellis, N. "Arte e veritá nell'ultimo libro di Heidegger." Rev. of *Holzwege,* by Martin Heidegger. 1950. *Rassegna di science filosofiche* (Roma), vol. 3, 1950, 92-106.

4638    Petzel, Heinrich Wiegand. "Reif ist die Traube und festlich die Luft." In *Martin Heidegger zum 70. Geburtstag*. Festschrift/Pfullingen, 1959, 239-248.

4639    Petzet, Heinrich Wiegand. "Emil Preetorius und Martin Heidegger über abstrakte Kunst." *Universitas* (Stuttgart), vol. 8, 1. Bd, 1953, 444-445.

4640    Petzet, Heinrich Wiegand. "Die Bremer Freunde. Den Bremer Hörerinnen der Freiburger Semester 1929/30 gewidmet." In *Erinnerung an Martin Heidegger,* by Günther Neske (ed.). Pfullingen: Verlag Günther Neske, 1977, 179-190.

4641    Peursen, C. A. van. *Riskante Philosophie*. Een karakteristiek van het dedendaagse existentielle denken. Amsterdam, 1948, VIII, 138 p.

4642    Peursen, C. A. van. "De Philosophie van Martin Heidegger als Wending tot het Zijn." *Tijdschrift voor Philosophie* (Leuven), vol. 13, 1951, 209-225.

4643    Peursen, C. A. van. "Ethik und Ontologie in der heutigen Existenzphilosophie." *Zeitschrift für evangelische Ethik* (Gütersloh), vol. 2, 1958, 98-112.

4644    Peursen, C. A. van. "Die Kommunikationshaftigkeit der Welt." In *Martin Heidegger zum 70. Geburtstag*. Festschrift/Pfullingen, 1959, 49-66.

4645    Pfeffer, Rose. *Nietzsche: Disciple of Dionysis*. Lewisburg, 1972, 297 p.

4646    Pfeiffer, J. *Existenzphilosophie*. Eine Einführung in Heidegger und Jaspers. Leipzig, 1934, 64 p. 3rd ed. 1952.

4647    Pfeiffer, J. Rev. of *Hölderlins Hymne 'Wie wenn am Feiertage',* by Martin Heidegger. Halle, 1941. *Der Bücherwurm* (Dessau), vol. 27, 1942, 214.

4648    Pfeiffer, J. "Zu Heideggers Deutung der Dichtung." *Der Deutschunterricht* (Stuttgart), vol. 2, 1952, 57-68.

4649    Pfeiffer, J. Rev. of *Einführung in die Metaphysik,* by Martin Heidegger. Tübingen, 1953. *Bücherei und Bildung,* vol. 5, 1953, 1153-1155.

4650    Pfeiffer, J. Rev. of *Einführung in die Metaphysik,* by Martin Heidegger. Tübingen, 1953. *Evangelischer Literaturbeobachter* (Müchen), vol. 13, 1954, 238.

4651 Pfeiffer, J. Rev. of *Was heisst Denken?* by Martin Heidegger. Tübingen, 1954; and *Vorträge und Aufsätze.* Pfullingen, 1954. *Bücherei und Bildung* (Reutlingen), vol. 7, 1955, 755-756.

4652 Pfeiffer, J. *Was haben wir an einem Gedicht?* [3 Kapitel über Sinn und Grenze der Dichtung. Anhang: Zu Heideggers Deutung der Dichtung.] Hamburg, 1955, 108 p.

4653 Pfeiffer, J. *Existenz und Offenbarung.* Die Existenzphilosophie von Heidegger und Jaspers als Weg zur Selbstprüfung des Glaubens. 5th ed. Berlin, 1966, 144 p.

4654 Pfeiffle, Horst. "Was sagt Heideggers Denken der Pädagogik?" *Wiener Jahrbuch für Philosophie* (Wien), vol. 9, 1976, 250-260.

4655 Pfeil, H. *Der Mensch im Denken der Zeit.* Paderborn, 1938, 199 p.

4656 Pfeil, H. *Existenzialistische Philosophie.* Paderborn, 1950, 94 p.

4657 Pfizer, Theodor. "Die Ausnahme." In *Erinnerung an Martin Heidegger,* by Günther Neske (ed.). Pfullingen: Verlag Günther Neske, 1977, 191-196.

4658 Pflaumer, R. "Sein und Mensch im Denken Heideggers." *Philosophische Rundschau* (Tübingen), vol. 13, 1966, 161-234. Rev. of these Heidegger works:

[ *Einführung in die Metaphysik.* 1953.]

[*Aus der Erfahrung des Denkens.* 1954.]

[*Was heisst Denken?* 1954.]

[*Vorträge und Aufsätze.* 1954.]

[*Was ist das - die Philosophie?* 1956.]

[*Zur Seinsfrage.* 1956.]

4659 Pfliegler, M. "Macht Martin Heidegger kehrt?" *Michael Pfliegler, Theologie auf Anruf.* Salzburg, 1963, 168-174, 315.

4660 Philippoussis, John. "Heidegger and Plato's Notion of Truth." *Dialogue* (Montreal/Kingston), vol. 15, 1976, 502-504.

4661 Picard, N. "Nuovi orizzonti dell'ontologia di M. Heidegger." *Esistenzialismo.* Acta Academiae Romanae S. Thomae Aq. et Religionis Catholicae. Torino, 1947, 65-84.

4662 Picard, N. "Essere e pensare. Intorno ad un recente scritto di M. Heidegger." *Teoresi* (Messina), vol. 8, 1953, 7-21.

4663 Picard, N. "La posizione della filosofia di M. Heidegger di fronte al problema metafisico." *Analecta Gregorina* (Romae), vol. 67, 1954. Studi filosofici intorno all 'Esistenza', al Mondo, al Trascendente, 3-15.

4664 Picard, Y. "Le temps chez Husserl et chez Heidegger." *Deucalion* (Paris), vol. 1, 1946, 95-124.

[Trans. *El tempo en Husserl y en Heidegger.* Trans. E. Tabering. Buenos Aires, 1959.]

4665 Piccione, Bruno L. G. "Heidegger y el hombre." *Cuadernos de Filosofía* (Buenos Aires), vol. 11, no. 15-16, 1971, 155-179.

4666 Picotti, De C., D. V. *Die Überwindung der Metaphysik als geschichtliche Aufgabe bei Martin Heidegger.* Phil. Diss. München 27.11.1969. 106 p.

4667 Picotti De C., D. V. "El concepto hegeliano de verdad y su discusión en M. Heidegger." *Stromata, Ciencia y Fe* (San Miguel), vol. 27, 1971, 403-416.

4668 Picht, Georg. "Die Macht des Denkens." In *Erinnerung an Martin Heidegger,* by Günther Neske (ed.). Pfullingen: Verlag Günther Neske, 1977, 197-205.

4669 Picht, Goerg. "Gewitterlandschaft. Erinnerung an Martin Heidegger." *Merkur* (Stuttgart), vol. 31, no. 10, 1977, 960-965.

4670 Piertersma, Henry. "Heidegger's Theory of Truth." In *Heidegger's Existential Analytic,* by Frederick Elliston (ed.). The Hague, New York: Mouton Pub., 1978, 219-229.

4671 Pietersma, H. "Husserl and Heidegger." *Philosophy and Phenomenological Research* (Buffalo, New York), vol. 40, 1979, 194-211.

4672 Pignato, L. "La filosofia del XX secolo." [In appendice alla 2a edizione della trad. italiana della.] *Storia della filosofia di G. Windelband.* Palermo, Milano, 1937, (specifically pages 451-466).

4673 Piguet, J.-C. "Les oeuvres récentes de Martin Heidegger." *Revue de Théologie et de Philosophie* (Lausanne), Ser. 2, Bd 8, 1958, 283-290.

4674 Piguet, J.-C. Rev. of *Introduction à la métaphysique,* by Martin Heidegger. Paris, 1958. *Revue de Théologie et de Philosophie* (Lausanne), Ser. 3, Bd 9, 1959, 102.

4675 Piguet, J.-C. Rev. of *Die Frage Nach dem Ding,* by Martin Heidegger. *Revue de Théologie et de Philosophie* (Lausanne), vol. 97, 1964, 62-63.

4676 Pindle, Arthur Jackson, Jr. *A Critical Study of Heidegger's Interpretation of Death.* Authorized facsimile of the dissertation of the Yale Univ. Phil. Diss. 1978 v-209. Ann Arbor, Michigan; London: University Microfilms International, 1979. [HGK78-19480] *Dissertation Abstracts International,* vol. 39/04-A, 2343.

4677 Pinera Llera, H. "Heidegger y Sartre o dos modos de la filosofia existencial." *Revista Cubana,* vol. 23, 1948, 22-54.

4678 Pinkard, Terry. "Social Philosophy and Social Categories." *Man and World,* vol. 11, 1978, 19-31.

4679 Pinto de Carvalho, A. "O humanismo de Heidegger." *Kriterion,* Belo Horizonte, (M. G., Brasil), vol. 13, 1960, 292-305.

4680 Piorkowski, H. "The Path of Phenomenology: Husserl, Heidegger, Sartre, Merleau-Ponty." *Duns Scotus Philosophical Association,* vol. 30, 1966, 177-221.

4681 Pires, Celestino. "Heidegger e o ser como história." *Revista Portuguesa de Filosofia* (Braga), vol. 19, 1963, 225-242.

4682    Pires, Celestino. Rev. of *Nietzsche,* by Martin Heidegger. Pfullingen, 1961. *Revista Portuguesa de Filosofia* (Braga), vol. 19, 1963, 94-96.

4683    Pires, Celestino. Rev. of *Qu'appelle-t-on penser?* by Martin Heidegger. Paris, 1959. *Revista Portuguesa de Filosofia* (Braga), vol. 19, 1963, 98.

4684    Pires, Celestino. Rev. of *Index zu Heideggers 'Sein und Zeit'* by Hildegard Feick. Tübingen, 1961. *Revista Portuguesa de Filosofia* (Braga), vol. 19, 1963, 96.

4685    Pires, Celestino. Rev. of *Qu'appelle-t-on penser?* by Martin Heidegger. Paris, 1959. *Revista Portuguesa de Filosofia* (Braga), vol. 20, 1964, 257-258.

4686    Pires, Celestino. "Ontologia e metafisica." *Revista Portuguesa de Filosofia* (Braga), vol. 20, 1964, 31-61.

4687    Pires, Celestino. Rev. of *Lettre sur l'Humanisme,* by Martin Heidegger. Paris, 1957. *Revista Portuguesa de Filosofia* (Braga), vol. 20, 1964, 258.

4688    Pires, Celestino. "Da fenomenologia a verdada. Un caminho de Martin Heidegger." *Revista Portuguesa de Filosofia* (Braga), vol. 22, 1966, 113-131.

4689    Pires, Celestino. "Deus e a teologia em Martin Heidegger." *Revista Portuguesa de Filosofia* (Braga), vol. 26, 1970, 237-284.

4690    Pires, Celestino. "Crise de metafisica, crise do homen." *Revista Portuguesa de Filosofia* (Braga), vol. 29, 1973, 3-20.

4691    Pitte, Frederik P. van de. "The Role of Hölderlin in the Philosophy of Heidegger." *The Personalist* (Los Angeles), vol. 43, 1962, 168-179.

4692    Piwko, S. Rev. of these A. de Waelhens's works in *Studia Filozoficzne,* vol. 2, 1962:

        ["Chemins et impasses de l'ontologie Heideggerienne." 1953.]

        ["La Philosophie De Martin Heidegger." 1955.]

4693    Plachte, K. "Das Seinsdenken und die Gottsfrage: Heidegger und Tillich." *Evangelisch-lutherische Kirchenzeitung* (Berlin), vol. 15, 1961, 41-43.

4694    Plachte, K. "Seinsdenken und Gottesfrage (Heidegger und Tillich)." *Pastoralblätter* (Stuttgart), Monatsschrift für den Gesamtbereich des evanglischen Pfarramtes, vol. 104, 1964, 269-277.

4695    Plate, B. *Die Erfahrung, die Zeit und das Mit-Dasein.* München, 1966, 224 p. [Phil. Diss. München v.6. Okt.1966.]

4696    Platen, A. *Das Nichts in der Ontologie der Existenz.* Phil. Diss. Bonn 1950 136 p.

4697    Platzeck, E. W. "La filosofia de Martin Heidegger." *Revista espaniola teologica,* vol. 6, 1946, 451-457.

4698    Platzeck, E. W. "La sentencia de Anaximandro a la luz del dilema heideggeriano." *Verdad y Vida* (Madrid), vol. 8, 1950, 299-324.

4699    Plebe, A. "Heidegger e il problema kantiano." *Studi e ricerche di storia della filosofia* (Torino: Ediz. di 'Filosofia'), vol. 41, 1960, 2.

4700    Pleydell-Pearce, S. "Philosophy, Poetry and Mysticism." *The Journal of the British Society for Phenomenology,* vol. 10, no. 2, 1979, 122-129.

4700a    Pleydell-Pearce, A. G. Rev. of "Martin Heidegger. Basic Writings From *Being and Time* (1927) to *The Task of Thinking* (1964)." Ed. with general intr. and intr. to each sel. by David Farrell Krell. *The Journal of the British Society for Phenomenology* (Manchester), vol. 10, 1979, 198-199.

4701    Podak, Klaus. "Philosoph gegen die Philosophie. Zum Tode von Martin Heidegger." *Stuttgarter Zeitung* (Ausgabe), vol. 32, no. 122, 28 May 1976, 37. (Jg. 3, 1976, no. 2).

4702    Podewils, Clemens. "Der Steig." In *Martin Heidegger zum 70. Geburtstag.* Festschrift/Pfullingen, 1959, 347-348.

4703    Podewils, Clemens. "Die nachbarlichen Stämme." In *Erinnerung an Martin Heidegger,* by Günther Neske (ed.). Pfullingen: Verlag Günther Neske, 1977, 207-213.

4704    Podewils, S. D. "Chrysaora." In *Martin Heidegger zum 70. Geburtstag.* Festschrift/Pfullingen, 1959, 345-346.

4705    Podlech, A. *Der Leib als Weise des In-der-Welt-Seins. Eine systematische Untersuchung innerhalb der phänomenologischen Existenzphilosophie.* Bonn, 1956, IV, 250 p. [Phil. Diss. Bonn 26.1.1955.]

4706    Pöggeler, Otto. Rev. of "Identität und Differenz," by Martin Heidegger. Pfullingen, 1957. *Philosophischer Literaturanzeiger* (Stuttgart/Bad Cannstatt), vol. 11, 1958, 294-298.

4707    Pöggeler, Otto. "Jean Wahls Heidegger-Deutung." *Zeitschrift für Philosophische Forschung* (Meisenheim/Glan), vol. 12, 1958, 437-458.

4708    Pöggeler, Otto. Rev. of *Der Satz vom Grund,* by Martin Heidegger. *Philosophischer Literaturanzeiger* (Stuttgart/Bad Cannstatt), vol. 11, 1958, 241-251.

4709    Pöggeler, Otto. "Sein als Ereignis. Martin Heidegger zum 26.9.1959." *Zeitschrift für philosophische Forschung* (Meisenheim/Glan), vol. 13, 1959, 597-632.

4710    Pöggeler, Otto. Rev. of *Was ist das - die Philosophie?* by Martin Heidegger. Pfullingen, 1956. *Philosophischer Literaturanzeiger* (Stuttgart/Bad Cannstatt), vol. 12, 1959, 194-198.

4711    Pöggeler, Otto. "Das Wesen der Stimmungen." *Zeitschrift für philosophische Forschung* (Meisenheim/Glan), vol. 14, 1960, 272-284.

4712    Pöggeler, Otto. "Metaphysik und Seinstopik bei Heidegger." *Philosophisches Jahrbuch* (München), vol. 70, 1962/63, 118-137.

4713    Pöggeler, Otto. *Der Denkweg Martin Heideggers.* Pfullingen, 1963, 318 p.

[Trans. *La pensée de Martin Heidegger.* Un cheminement vers l'être. Trans. M. Simon. Paris, 1967, 407 p. Netherlands trans. by M. Mok. Antwerpen, 1969, 335 p.]

4714    Pöggeler, Otto, ed. *Heidegger. Perspektiven zur Deutung seines Werks.* Köln/Berlin, 1969, 416 p.

4715    Pöggeler, Otto. "Hermeneutische und mantische Phänomenologie."
        *Heidegger.* Ed. O. Pöggeler. Köln/Berlin, 1969, 321-357. Rpt. from
        *Philosophische Rundschau* (Heidelberg/Tübingen), vol. 13, 1965, 1-39.

4716    Pöggeler, Otto. "Heideggers Topologie des Seins." *Man and World*
        (Pittsburgh), vol. 2, 1969, 331-357.

4717    Pöggeler, Otto. "Martin Heidegger." *Duitse Kroniek* (Den Haag), vol. 21, no.
        3, 1969, 100-120.

4718    Pöggeler, Otto. "Heidegger-Kolloquium der Pennsylvania State University
        (USA)." *Duitse Kroniek* (Den Haag), vol. 21, no. 3, 1969,

4719    Pöggeler, Otto. "Heidegger Today." *The Southern Journal of Philosophy*
        (Memphis), vol. 8, 1970, 273-308.

4720    Pöggeler, Otto. "Heidegger Hoy." Trans. from German by Elsa Taberning.
        Rev. by Ansgar Klein. *Cuadernos de Filosofia* (Buenos Aires), vol. 11, no.
        15-16, 1971, 11-64.

4721    Pöggeler, Otto. *Philosophie und Politik bei Heidegger.* Freiburg/München,
        1972, 152 p. Rev. under the title "Gegen Rasse und Masse" in *Der Spiegel,*
        vol. 26, no. 46, v.6.11.1972, 174-176. Revised version 1974, 159 p.

4722    Pöggeler, Otto. "Heidegger's Topology of Being." In *On Heidegger and
        Language.* Ed. J. J. Kockelmans. Evanston, 1972, 107-146.

        [Rev. by W. Franzen in *Philosophisches Jahrbuch* (Freiburg/München), vol.
        80, 1973, 212-215.]

        [Rev. by H. P. Hempel in *Philosophischer Literaturanzeiger*
        (Meisenheim/Glan), vol. 26, 1973, 194-196.]

4723    Pöggeler, Otto. "Die ethisch-politische Dimension der hermeneutischen
        Philosophie." Ed. G.-G. Grau. In *Probleme der Ethik.* Zur Diskussion
        gestellt auf der Wissenschaftlichen Tagung 1972 der Allgemeinen
        Gesellschaft für Philosophie in Deutschland. Freiburg/München, 1972,
        45-81.

4724    Pöggeler, Otto. "Heidegger Today." In *Martin Heidegger: In Europe and
        America,* by Edward Goodwin Ballard and Charles E. Scott (eds.). The
        Hague, 1973, 1-36.

4725    Pöggeler, Otto. "'Historicity' in Heidegger's Late Work." In *The Southwestern
        Journal of Philosophy* (Norman, Oklahoma), vol. 4, no. 3, 1973, 53-73.

4726    Pöggeler, Otto. "Hermeneutische Philosophie und Theologie." *Man and
        World* (West Lafayette), vol. 7, no. 1, 1974, 3-19.

4727    Pöggeler, Otto. "Philosophy in the Wake of Hölderlin." *Man and World,* vol.
        7, May 1974, 158-176.

4728    Pöggeler, Otto. "Being as Appropriation." Trans. by Ruediger Hermann
        Grimm. *Philosophy Today* (Celina, Ohio), vol. 19, 1975, 152-178.

4729    Pöggeler, Otto. "Metaphysics and Topology of Being in Heidegger." Trans.
        P. Emad. *Man and World* (The Hague), vol. 8, 1975, 3-27.

4730 Pöggeler, Otto. "Der Nachbar des Todes. Martin Heideggers Revision des philosophischen Ansatzes." *Rheinischer Merkur* (Koblenz), no. 23, 4 June 1976, 25-26. (Jg. 3, 1976, Nr. 2).

4731 Pöggeler, Otto. Rev. of *Logik. Die Frage nach der Wahrheit,* by Martin Heidegger. 1976. *Rheineischer Merkur* (Koblenz), 23 January 1976.

4732 Pöggeler, Otto. "The Interpretation of Time and Hermeneutical Philosophy." (In Serbocroat). *Delo* (Beograd), vol. 23, no. 12, 1977, 85-109.

4733 Pöggeler, Otto. "Zum Tode Martin Heideggers." *Research in Phenomenology* (Pittsburgh), vol. 7, 1977, 31-42.

4734 Pöggeler, Otto. "Heideggers Begegnung mit Hölderlin." *Man and World* (The Hague), vol. 10, no. 1, 1977, 13-61.

4735 Pöggeler, Otto. "Being as Appropriation." In *Heidegger and Modern Philosophy,* by Michael Murray. New Haven, Connecticut: Yale Univ. Press, 1978, 84-115.

4736 Pöggeler, Otto. "Filosofia ermeneutica e teologia." *Humanitas* (Brescia), vol. 33, no. 4, 1978, 427-444.

4736a Pöggeler, Otto. "Heideggers Neubestimmung des Phänomenbegriffs." In *Neuere Entwicklingen des Phänomenbegriffs,* with contributions by Heinrich Rombach, et al. (Phänomenologische Forschung, 9). Freiburg: Alber, 1980, 124-162.

4737 Poggi, Stefano. "Filosofia della vita, fenomenologia ed esistenzialismo in Ludwig Landgrebe." *Rivista de Filosofia* (Torino), vol. 64, 1973, 232-259.

4738 Pogorely, A. I. "Heidegger und die 'Selbstkritik' der modernen bürgerlichen Philosophie." [ukrainisch] *Filosofska Dumka,* no. 3, 1969, 128-136. [Zusammenfassung in Russisch]

4739 Pogorely, A. I. *Evoljucija ekzistencializma M. Chajdeggera i krizis sovremennoj burzuaznoj filosofii* (The Evolution of Existentialism of M. Heidegger and the Crisis of Contemporary Bourgeois Philosophy). Avtoreferat Phil. Diss. Kiev 1975.

4740 Pohl, B. "Heideggers und Gehlens Kulturkritik." *Eckart* (Witten), vol. 27, 1958, 75-78.

4741 Polak, C. *Studien zu einer existenzialen Rechtslehre.* Phil. Diss. Freiburg 1933 V 63 p.

4742 Poliakov, L., and J. Wulf. *Das dritte Reich und sein Denker.* Dokuments, Berlin, 1959.

4743 Pomedli, M. M. *Heidegger and Freud: The Power of Death.* Phil. Diss. Duquesne Univ. Pittsburgh 1972 299 p. *Dissertation Abstracts International,* vol. 33/05-A, 2430.

4744 Pomian, K. "Heidegger i antynomie idealu dzialznia" (Heidegger and the Antinomies of an Ideal of Dynamic Accomplishment). *Argumenty,* 41, 1960, and vol. 5, 1965.

4745 Pomian, K. "Egzystencjalizm i filozofia wspolczesna" (Existentialism and Contemporary Philosophy). In *Filozofia egzystencjalna.* Ed. L. Kolakowski and K. Pomian. Warszawa, 1965.

4746 Pongch'ôl, Hwang. "Haidegkaûi kibon chanjaeron koch'al" (A Contemplation on Fundamental Ontology in Heidegger). M. A. Thesis, Yônse Univ., 1977.

4747 Pongsu, Kim. "Haidegkae issôsôûi chonjaee kwanhayô" (Being in Heidegger). M. A. Thesis, Chungang Univ., 1965.

4748 Ponte, M. Da. "Essere e comprensione problematica dell'essere in Heidegger." *Studia Patavina* (Padova), vol. 5, 1958, 73-108.

4749 Pop, T. "The Main Theoretical Principles in Heidegger's Ontology." (In Roumane). *Studia Universitatis Babes-Bolyai. Series Philosophia* (Cluj), vol. 23, no. 1, 1978, 26-31.

4750 Popelová, J. *Tri studie z filosofie dejin.* Praha, 1947, 298 p.

4751 Porrino, S. "Dibattito su 'aspetti positivi e negativi del conformismo'." *Giornale di Metafisica* (Genova/Torino), vol. 19, 1964, 563-568.

4752 Posescu, A. "Der existentialistische Pluralismus." *Studii de Istorie a Filozofiei universale* (Rom), vol. 1, 1969, 177-235.

4753 Pouget, Pierre-Maire. *L'inevitable absolu a travers la difference ontico-ontologique.* Thèse lettres. Fribourg, Schweiz, 1975.

4754 Pouget, Pierre-Marie. *Heidegger ou le retour à la voix silencieuse.* Lausanne: Editions L'Age d'homme, 1975, 127 p.

4755 Powell, R. A. *Heidegger's Retreat From a Transcultural Structure of Dasein.* Chicago, St. Xavier College, 1966.

4756 Powell, R. A. "Has Heidegger Destroyed Metaphysics?" *Listening* (Dubuque, Iowa), vol. 2, 1967, 52-59.

4757 Powell, R. A. "A Late Heidegger's Omission of the Ontic-Ontologica Structure of Dasein." In *Heidegger and the Path of Thinking.* Ed. J. Sallis. Pittsburgh, 1970, 116-137.

4758 Prange, Kl. "Heidegger und die sprachanalytische Philosophie." *Philosophisches Jahrbuch* (München), vol. 79, 1972, 39-56.

4759 Prasad, Sanjiwan. "Religion and Atheistic Existentialism." *Indian Philosophical Quarterly,* vol. 4, July 1977, 619-626.

4760 Prauss, Gerold. *Erkennen und Handeln in Heideggers 'Sein und Zeit'.* (Reihe fermenta philosophica). Freiburg: Alber, 1977, 128 p.

4761 Préau, A. "Lâge technique d'après Martin Heidegger et Léopold Ziegler." *Cahiers du Sud* (Paris), vol. 40, no. 317, 1953, 93-102.

4762 Preetorius, E. "Vom Geheimnis des Sichtbaren." In *Martin Heidegger zum 70. Geburtstag.* Festschrift/Pfullingen, 1959, 249-251.

4763 Preite, Maria dello. "La fenomenologia de G. Funke tra metafisica e Metodo." *Giornale di Metafisica* (Genua/Turin), vol. 27, 1972, 543-550.

4764 Prenter, R. "Heideggers Filosofi og Teologien." *Teologisk Tidskrift* (Kopenhagen), vol. 5, 1933, 161-213.

4765 Presas, Mario A. Rev. of *Qué es eso de filosofia?* by Martin Heidegger. Buenos Aires, 1960. *Humanitas* (Brescia), vol. 9, no. 14, 1961, 226-228.

4766 Presas, Mario A. Rev. of *Sendas perdidas,* by Martin Heidegger. Buenos Aires, 1960. *Revista de Filosofia* (La Plata), no. 10, 1961, 89-99.

4767 Presas, Mario A. "Sobre la interpretación heideggeriana de la poesia." *Revista de Filosofia* (La Plata), vol. 11, 1962, 66-87.

4768 Presas, Mario A. "Un diálogo con Heidegger." *Folia Humanistica* (Barcelona), vol. 8, 1970, 367-371.

4769 Presas, Mario A. "Un encuentro con Heidegger." *Revista de Filosofia* (La Plata), vol. 22, 1970, 90-95.

4770 Presas, Mario A. "Filosofia e historia de la filosofia en Heidegger." *Man and World* (Pittsburgh), vol. 4, 1971, 294-312.

4771 Presas, Mario A. "Von der Phänomenologie zum Denken des Seins." *Zeitschrift für Philosophische Forschung* (Meisenheim), vol. 28, no. 2, 1974, 180-200.

4772 Presas, Mario A. "Heidegger y la fenomenologia." *Revista Latino-Americano de Filosofia* (Buenos Aires), vol. 3, no. 1, 1977, 23-39.

4773 Presas, Mario A. Rev. of *Die Grundprobleme der Phänomenologie,* by Martin Heidegger. 1976. *Revista Latino-Americano de Filosofia* (Buenos Aires), vol. 3, 1977, 93-97.

4774 Presas, Mario A. Rev. of *Wegmarken,* by Martin Heidegger. *Revista Latino-Americano de Filosofia* (Buenos Aires), vol. 3, 1977, 199-200.

4775 Presas, Mario A. Rev. of *Logik,* by Martin Heidegger. *Revista Lationo-Americano di Filosofia* (Buenos Aires), vol. 3, 1977, 200-201.

4776 Presas, Mario A. "En Torno a las Meditaciones Cartesianas de Husserl." *Revista Latino-Americano de Filosofia,* vol. 4, November 1978, 269-280.

4777 Prezioso, Faustino Antonio. "La riscoperta semantica di M. Heidegger nel pensiero di Duns Scoto." *Rassegna di Science filosofiche* (Napoli), vol. 25, 1972, 159-178, 287-302, 407-418.

4778 Prezioso, Faustino Antonio. "La riscoperta semantica di M. Heidegger nel pensiero di Duns Scoto." *Rassegna di Scienze filosofiche* (Napoli), vol. 26, 1973, 53-64.

4779 Prezioso, Faustino Antonio. "L'interpretazione Heideggeriana Della *Critica Della Ragion Pura Di Kant.*" *Sapienza,* vol. 32, 1979, 129-167.

4780 Prieur, M. Rev. of *Questions III,* by Martin Heidegger. *Revue Universitaire de Science Morale* (Genève), 6/7, 1966/67, 66-67.

4781 Prini, P. *Esistenzialismo.* Roma, 1950, 57-64.

4782 Prini, P. *Storia dell'esistenzialismo.* Roma, 1971, 209 p.

4783 Prucha, M. "Filosofické problémy existence cloveka." In *Sedmkrat o smyslu filosofie.* Ed. J. Coekl. Praha, 1964, 39-69.

4784 Prucha, M. "Existencialismus." In *J. Filopec, Clovek a moderni dova.* Praha, 1966, 8-67.

4785    Przywara, E. "Drei Richtungen in der Phänomenologie." *Stimmen der Zeit* (Freiburg), vol. 115, 1928, 252-264, (specifically page 258 ff).

4786    Przywara, E. "Wende zum Menschen." Rev. of *Kant und das Problem der Metaphysik,* by Martin Heidegger. Bonn, 1929. *Stimmen der Zeit* (Freiburg), vol. 119, 1930, 1-10.

4787    Przywara, E. *Kant heute. Eine Sichtung.* München/Berlin, 1930.

4788    Przywara, E. *Analogia entis, Metaphysik.* München, 1932, 154 p.

4789    Przywara, E. *Christliche Existenz.* Leipzig, 1934.

4790    Przywara, E. "Theologische Motive im philosophischen Werk Martin Heideggers." In *In und gegen. Stellungnahmen zur Zeit,* by E. Przywara. Nürnberg, 1955, 55-60.

4791    Przywara, E. Rev. of *Der Satz vom Grund,* by Martin Heidegger. Pfullingen, 1957. *Les Etudes Philosophiques* (Paris), N.S. 12, no. 4, 1957, 408.

4792    Przywara, E. "Husserl et Heidegger." *Les Etudes Philosophiques* (Paris), N.S. 16, 1961, 55-62.

4793    Psigotizev, I. S. "M. Chajdegger i neogumbol'dtianstvo" (M. Heidegger and the Neo-Humboldt Movement). *Vestnik Moskovskogo Universiteta, Filosofija,* vol. 3, 1970, 53-60.

4794    Psigotizev, I. S. "K probleme sootnosehija jazyka i istiny v filosofii M. Chajdeggera" (On the Problem of the Relation Between Language and Truth in M. Heidegger's Philosophy). *Vestnik Kabardino-Balkarskogo Naucnoissledovatel'skogo instituta pri Sovete Ministrov K. B. ASSR,* vol. 5, 1972, 140-143.

4795    Psigotizev, I. S. *Kritika ucenija M. Chajdeggera o jazyke* (The Criticism of Heidegger's Theory of Language). Avtoreferat Phil. Diss. Tbilisi 1975.

4796    Pucciarelli, Eugenio. "Hegel y el enigma del tiempo." *Cuadernos de Filosofia* (Buenos Aires), vol. 10, 1970, 257-290.

4797    Pucciarelli, Eugenio. "El origen de la noción vulgar de tiempo." *Cuadernos de Filosofia* (Buenos Aires), vol. 11, no. 15-16, 1971, 215-247.

4798    Pugliese, A. O. "Para una interpretación unitaria de la filosofia de Martin Heidegger." *Philosophia Argentinia,* no. 28, 1964, 29-40.

4799    Pugliese, A. O. "Vermittlung und Kehre. Grundzüge des Geschichtsdenkens bei Martin Heidegger." *Symposion* (Freiburg/München), vol. 18, 1965, 226 p. [Phil. Diss. Freiburg 1963.]

4800    Pugliese, A. O. "Zur Aufhebung der Methode bei Heidegger." *Akten des XIV. Internationalen Kongresses für Philosophie, Wien 2.-9.September 1968, III* (Wien), 1968, XVI, 694 p., (specifically pages 618-621).

4801    Pugliese, A. O. "Auseinandersetzung mit der Vermittlungsproblematik in einer 'nichtwissenschaftlichen' Philosophie. Anmerkungen zu Heideggers späterem Denken." *Philosophisches Jahrbuch der Görresgesellschaft* (Freiburg), vol. 77, Bd 1, 1970, 214 ff.

4802 Pyôngu, Kim. *Haidegkaûi chonjaee kwanhayô* (Being in Heidegger). M. A. Thesis, Sôul Univ., 1961.

4803 Pyôngu, Kim. "Haidegkaûi chonjae munje" (The Problem of Being in Heidegger). *Ch'ôrhak Yôngu* (Taegu) (Ed. by the Philosophers' Society), vol. 6, 1968, 32-40.

4804 Pyôngu, Kim. "Haidegkaûi sironjôk segye" (The World of Poetry in Heidegger). *Ch'ungnam Univ. Collection of Essays* (Ch'ungnam), vol. 2, part III, 1975, 263-279.

4805 Quattrocchi, L. Rev. of *Nietzsche Bd I-II,* by Martin Heidegger. *De Homine* (Roma), vol. 1, 1962, 103-114.

4806 Quelquejeu, B. "Herméneutique bultmannienne et analytique existentiale heideggérienne." *Revue des Sciences Philosophiques et Théologiques* (Paris), vol. 49, 1965, 577-596.

4807 Quenzer, W. "Herbstlicher Nebel - herbstliche Klarheit. Zum 75. Geburtstag Martin Heideggers." *Christ und Welt* (Stuttgart), Jg. 17, no. 39, 1964, 24.

4808 Quiles, I. *Heidegger: El existencialismo de la angustia.* Buenos Aires, 1948.

4809 Quiles, I. "La proyessión final del existencialismo." *Actas del primer Congreso nacional de Filosofia* (Mendoza), vol. 2, 1949, 1084-1089, passim.

4810 Quiles, I. Rev. of *Aus der Erfahrung des Denkens,* by Martin Heidegger. Pfullingen, 1954. *Ciencia y Fe* (Buenos Aires), vol. 13, 1957, 377-379.

4811 Quinterno, C. A. "Sobre el 'Logos' en el metodo de M. Heidegger." *Diálogo* (Buenos Aires), vol. 1, 1954, 132-135.

4812 Quinterno, C. A. "Repetición del pensamiento e historicidad." [Heidegger] *Diálogo* (Buenos Aires), vol. 1, 1954, 124-127.

4813 Raedemaeker, F. De. "Identität und Existenz." *Bijdragen, Tijdschrift voor Filosofie en Theologie* (Antwerpen), vol. 20, 1959, 157-174.

4814 Raggiunti, R. Rev. of "Heidegger e la teologia," by F. Costa. 1974. *Giornale Critico della Filosofia Italiana* (Firenze), vol. 6, no. 1, 1975, 147-152.

4815 Rahner, H. "Interoduction au concept de philosophie existentielle." *Recherches de science religieuse* (Paris), vol. 30, 1940. [L'increatum et le creatum, le finitum et l'infinitum chez Heidegger, 152-171.]

4816 Rahner, Karl. *Geist in Welt. Zur Metaphysik der endlichen Erkenntnis bei Thomas v. Aquin.* Innsbruck, 1939, XV, 296 p.

4817 Rahner, Karl. "The Concept of Existential Philosophy in Heidegger." *Philosophy Today* (Celina, Ohio), vol. 13, 1969, 127-137.

4818 Rahner, Karl. "Martin Heidegger." In *Martin Heidegger im Gespräch.* Ed. R. Wisser. Freiburg/München, 1970, 48-50.

4819 Rajl, Gilbert. "Martin Heidegger: Sein und Zeit." Trans. Ivan Jankovic. In *Rani Hajdeger - Recepcija i kritika Bivstva i vremena,* by Dragan Stojanovic and Danilo Basta (eds.). (Biblioteka Zodijak). Beograd, 1979, 89-113.

4820 Ralfs, G. "Kritische Bemerkungen zu Heideggers Lehre von der Wahrheit." *Kant-Studien* (Köln), vol. 48, 1956/57, 525-549.

4821    Ralfs, G. "Kritische Bemerkungen zu Heideggers Lehre von der Wahrheit."
        In *Lebensformen des Geistes. Vorträge und Abhandlungen.* Ed. Hermann
        Glockner. [Kant-studien. Ergänzungsheft, 86.] Köln, 1964, 291-320.

4822    Ramnoux, Clemence. "Sur quelques interpretations modernes de la pensée
        d'Anaximandre." *Revue de Métaphysique et de Morale* (Paris), vol. 59, 1954,
        233-252.

4823    Ramos, S. "Concepto y método de la metafisica de Heidegger." *Revista
        mexicana de Filosofia,* no. 1, 51-60.

4824    Ramos Gangoso, E. *La filosofia existencial de Martin Heidegger al alcance
        de todos.* Vigo, 1948.

4825    Rasmussen, Dennis. *Poetry and Truth.* The Hauge: Mouton Pub., 1974.

4826    Rather, L. J. "Existential Experience in Whitehead and Heidegger." *Review
        of Existential Psychology and Psychiatry* (Pittsburgh), vol. 1, 1961, 113-119.

4827    Rattner, J. *Das Menschenbild in der Philosophie Martin Heideggers.* Phil. Diss.
        Zürich 1952 108 p.

4828    Rauch, Leo. "What Philosophy is." *Independent Journal of Philosophy,* vol.
        1, Summer 1977, 29-30.

4829    Rauhala, L. "The Regulative Situational Circuit in Psychic Disturbance and
        Psychotherapy." (Studia philosophica in honorem Sven Krohn). In *Annales
        Universitatis Turkuensis Sarja-Ser: B. Humaniora* (Turku), vol. 126, 1973,
        157-176.

4830    Ravera, R. M. "En torno a 1 estética de Heidegger." *Cuadernos Filosoficos*
        (Rosario), vol. 2, 1961, 59-67.

4831    Reale, M. "Filosofia Alema no Brasil." *Revista Brasileira de Filosofia* (Sño
        Paulo), vol. 24, no. 93, 1974, 3-18.

4832    Rechsteiner, Alois. *Wesen und Sinn von Sein und Sprache bei Martin
        Heidegger.* Phil. Diss. Fribourg Switzerland 1969. Bern, 1977.

4833    Redan[, U. "L'ultimo Heidegger." *L'Italia che scrive. Rassegna per coloro che
        leggono* (Roma), vol. 37, 1954, 151-152.

4834    Redan[, U. "El problema de la libertad: de San Agustin a Heidegger." Trans.
        Luis Garayoa. *Augustinus* (Madrid), vol. 5, 1960, 175-190.

4835    Redeker, H. "Een psycholoog in Heideggers voetsporen." *Tijdschrift voor
        Philosophie* (Leuven), vol. 9, 1947, 465-472.

4836    Redeker, H. *Existentialisme, Een doortocht door philosophisch Frontgebied.*
        Amsterdam, 1949, 347 p. [Het existentialisme in Duitsland. M. Heidegger,
        65-130.]

4837    Reding, M. "Heidegger und Sartre." In *Der Mensch vor Gott.* Festschrift für
        Theodor Steinbüchel zum 60. Geburtstag. Düsseldorf, 1948, 333-348.

4838    Reding, M. *Die Existenzphilosophie. Heidegger, Sartre, Gabriel Marcel und
        Jaspers in kritisch-systematischer Sicht.* Düsserldorf, 1949, 236 p.

4839    Regina, Umberto. "Ontologia e trascendenza in Heidegger." *Rivista di
        Filosofia Neo-Scolastica* (Milano), vol. 58, 1966, 584-628.

4840 Regina, Umberto. *Il cammino speculativo di Heidegger in alcuni recenti studi.* (Contributi dell'Istituto di Filosofia, I). [Pubblicazioni dell'Università cattolica del Sacro Cuore. Contribuit. Serie terza. Scienze filosofiche, 14.] Milano, 1969, VIII, 320 p.

4841 Regina, Umberto. *Heidegger. Dal nichilismo alla dignità dell'uomo.* Milano, 1970, XV, 416 p.

4842 Regina, Umberto. "Il senso dell'Occidente in Heidegger e la salvezza della verità." *Rivista di Filosofia Neo-Scolastica* (Milano), vol. 63, 1971, 605-622.

4843 Regina, Umberto. *Heidegger. Esistenza e sacro.* Brescia: Morcelliana, 1974, 354 p.

4844 Regina, Umberto. Rev. of "La dottrina delle categorie e del significato in Duns Scoto," by Martin Heidegger. 1974. *Aquinas* (Roma), vol. 18, 1975, 417-427.

4845 Regina, Umberto. "In memoria di Martin Heidegger." *Humanitas* (Brescia), vol. 31, no. 7, 1976, 499-507.

4846 Regina, Umberto. "Tommaso d'Aquino e Heidegger. Le ragioni di un raffronto." In *Tommaso nel suo settimo centenario.* Atti del Congresso internazionale. (Roma-Napoli, 17-24 aprile 1974). Vol. VI: L'essere. Napoli: Edizioni Domenicane Italiane, 1977, 365-373.

4847 Regnier, Marcel. Rev. of *Zur Seinsfrage,* by Martin Heidegger. Frankfurt, 1956. *Archives de Philosophie* (Paris), vol. 20, 1957, 152-153.

4848 Regnier, Marcel. Rev. of *Vers la fin de l'ontologie. Etude sur l'introduction dans la Métaphysique par Heidegger,* by J. Wahl. 1956. *Archives de Philosphie* (Paris), vol. 20, 1957, 151-152.

4849 Regnier, Marcel. Rev. of these Heidegger works in *Archives de Philosophie* (Paris), vol. 22, 1959, 463-467:

[*Identität und Differenz.* 1957.]

[*Aus der Erfahrung der Denkens.* 1954.]

[*Introduction à la métaphysique.* 1958.]

[*Lettre sur l'humanisme.* 1957.]

[*Hebel der Hausfreund.* 1957.]

[*Qu'appelle-t-on penser?* 1959.]

4850 Reidemeister, K. *Die Unsachlichkeit der Existenzphilosophie. Vier kritische Aufsätze.* Berlin/Göttingen/Heidelberg, 1954, (specifically pages 18-21, und passim).

4851 Reidemeister, K. *Die Unsachlichkeit der Existenzphilosophie.* 2nd ed. Berlin, 1970, 95 p. 1st ed. Nr.1.1083.

4852 Reiner, H. *Phänomenologie und menschliche Existenz.* Halle, 1931, 26 p.

4853 Reiner, H. *Die Existenz der Wissenschaft und ihre Objektivität.* Halle, 1934, 48 p.

4854 Reiner, H. *Das Phänomen des Glaubens.* Halle, 1934, (specifically pages 86-94).

4855   Reinhardt, Kurt Frank. Rev. of *Existence and Being,* by Martin Heidegger. *The New Scholasticism* (Washington), vol. 25, 1951, 351-357.

4856   Reinhardt, Kurt Frank. *The Existentialist Revolt. The Main Themes and Phases of Existentialism. Kierkegaard, Nietzsche, Heidegger, Jaspers, Sartre, Marcel.* Milwaukee, 1952, VII, 242 p. 2nd ed. 1960, 281 p.

4857   Reiser, William Edward. "An Essay on the Development of Dogma in a Heideggerian Context: A Non-Theological Explanation of Theological Heresy." *The Thomist* (Washington), vol. 39, no. 3, 1975, 471-495.

4858   Reiser, William Edward. *What Calls Forth Heresy?: An Essay on the Development of Dogma Within a Heideggerian Context.* Theol. Diss. Vanderbilt Univ. 1977. *Dissertation Abstracts International,* vol. 38/03-A, 1479.

4859   Reisner, William Edward. "Was ist Existenz?" *Deutsches Volkstum* (Hamburg), vol. 14, 1932, 645-650, (specifically page 648 ff).

4860   Reisner, William Edward. "Existenzphilosophie und existentielle Philosophie." *Zwischen den Zeiten* (München), vol. 11, 1933, 57-78.

4861   Reiter, Josef. Rev. of *Heidegger e Brentano. L'aristotelismo e il problema dell'univocità dell'essere nella formazione filosofica del giovane Martin Heidegger,* by Franco Volpi. 1976. *Philosophischer Literaturanzeiger* (Meisenheim/Mainz), vol. 30, 1974, 290-293.

4862   Renaudière de Paulis, D. "Nota crítica sobre el sentido de la naturaleza en Martin Heidegger." *Sapientia, Revista Tomista de Filosofía* (La Plata), vol. 12, 1957, 129-132.

4863   Renaut, Alain. "Heidegger: 1927-1929." *Les Etudes Philosophiques* (Paris), no. 3, 1973, 355-370.

4864   Renaut, Alain. "Système et histoire de l'être." *Les Etudes Philosophiques* (Paris), no. 2, 1974, 245-264.

4865   Renaut, Alain. "Vers la pensée du déclin." *Les Etudes Philosophiques* (Paris), no. 2, 1975, 197-206.

4866   Renaut, Alain. "Qu-est-ce que l'homme?" *Man and World,* vol. 9, 1976, 3-44.

4867   Renaut, Alain. "La nature aime se cacher." *Revue de Metaphysique et de Morale,* vol. 81, January-March 1976, 62-111.

4868   Renaut, Alain. "'Qu'est-ce que l'homme?' Essai sur le chemin de pensée de Martin Heidegger." *Man and World* (The Hague), vol. 9, no. 1, 1976, 3-44.

4869   Renaut, Alain. "La fin de Heidegger et la tâche de la philosophie: de Heidegger à Hegel." *Les Etudes Philosophiques* (Paris), no. 4, 1977, 485-492.

4870   Rendtorff, Trutz. "Fragen ist die Frömmigkeit des Denkens. Am 26. Mai starb der Philosoph Martin Heidegger." *Deutsches Allgemeines Sonntagsblatt* (Hamburg), no. 23, 6 June 1976, 3. (Jg. 3, 1976, Nr. 2).

4871   Reniers, A. "Dichten en denken bij M. Heidegger." *Dialoog* (Brussel), vol. 3, 1962/63, 33-45.

4872    Reniers, A. "Het dichtende denken (Martin Heidegger)." *Dialoog* (Brussel), vol. 3, 1962/63, 169-176.

4873    Reniers, A. "Heidegger in Italie." *Dialoog* (Brussel), vol. 5, 1964/65, 219-223.

4874    Reniers, A. "De dialektiek bij M. Heidegger." *Dialoog* (Brussel), vol. 5, 1964/65, 138-144.

4875    Repsys, J. "The Humanisation of the Traditional Ontology in M. Heidegger's Philosophy." (In Lituanien). *Problemos* (Vilnius), no. 2, 1977, 60-72.

4876    Requet, A. "Survie, impensé et finitude." *Esprit* (Paris), N.S. 37, no. 9, 1969, 269-282.

4877    Rest, W. "Platons Lehre von der Paideia. Ein pädagogischer Essay zu Martin Heideggers Platon-Deutung. Robert Grosche zugeeignet." *Vierteljahrsschrift für wissenschaftliche Pädgogik* (Bochum), vol. 36, 1960, 249-261.

4878    Restrepo G., P. "La metafisica de Heidegger." *Franciscanum* (Bogotá), vol. 6, 1964, 87-129.

4879    Restrepo G., P. "Filosofia y teologia en Martin Heidegger." *Franciscanum* (Bogotá), vol. 9, 1967, 38-51.

4880    Resweber, Jean-Paul. *La pensée de Martin Heidegger.* Toulouse, 1971, 192 p.

4881    Resweber, Jean-Paul. *Essai sur le discours théologique à la lumière de la critique heideggérienne de la métaphysique.* Univ. de Lille III: Service de reproduction de thèses, 1974, 791 p.

4882    Resweber, Jean-Paul. *La théologie face au défi herméneutique. M. Heidegger, R. Bultmann, K. Rahner.* Louvain: Vander-Nauwelaerts, 1975, viii-376 p.; Bruxelles, 1975.

4883    Reutterer, A. "Kindliches und primitives Denken in der traditionellen Metaphysik." *Conceptus,* vol. 5, 1971, 67-78.

4884    Rey, W. H. "Heidegger-Trakl. Einstimmiges Zwiegespräch." *Deutsche Vierteljahresschrift für Literaturwissenschaft und Geistesgeschichte* (Stuttgart), vol. 30, 1956, 89-136.

4885    Rezzori, V. "Herr Nogoschiner empfiehlt Heidegger." *Die österreichische Furche* (Wien), Jg. 11, no. 22, 1955, Beilage Pfingsten, 5-6.

4886    Ricci Garotti, L. "Parmenide B 3 e 6 (D.-K) in alcune interpretazioni hiedeggeriane." *Studi Urbinati di Storia, Filosofia e Letteratura* (Urbino), vol. 35, n.s.B., 1961, 160-172.

4887    Ricci Garotti, L. "Leggendo Heidegger che legge Hegel." *Studi Urbinati* (Urbino), vol. 36, 1962, 258-281.

4888    Ricci Garotti, L. "Heidegger contra Hegel." *Il Pensiero* (Milano), vol. 8, 1963, 303-326.

4889    Ricci Garotti, L. *Heidegger contra Hegel e altri saggi di storiografia filosofica.* Urbino, 1965, V, 333 p.

       [Rev. by Livio Sichirollo in *Hegelstudien* (Bonn), vol. IV, 1967, 315-317.]

4890   Rice, Irvin K. "Pedagogic Theory and the Search for Being: Denton's Direction in the Epistemology of Education." *Educational Theory*, vol. 25, Fall 1975, 389-396.

4891   Richard, Lionel. "Langage et paroles de Heidegger." *Magazine Littéraire* (Paris), no. 117, 1976, 20.

4892   Richard, Lionel, and Robert Minder. "Le langage des origines." [Interview with R. Minder by L. Richard.] *Magazine Littéraire* (Paris), no. 117, 1976, 21-22.

4893   Richardson, William J. "Heidegger and the Origin of Language." *International Philosophical Quarterly* (Heverlee-Louvain), vol. 2, 1962, 404-416.

4894   Richardson, William J. "Heidegger and the Problem of Thought." *Revue Philosophique de Louvain* (Louvain), vol. 60, 1962, 58-78.

4895   Richardson, William J. "Heidegger and Plato." *The Heythrop Journal* (Oxford), vol. 4, 1963, 273-279.

4896   Richardson, William J. *Heidegger. Through Phenomenology to Thought.* Preface by Martin Heidegger. [Appendix: Courses, Seminars and Lectures of Martin Heidegger; Bibliography; Glossary; Indexes.] (Phaenomenologica. Collection publiée sous patronage des Centres d'Archives Husserl, 13). The Hague, 1963, XXXII, 764 p.

4897   Richardson, William J. "Heidegger and Aristotle." *The Heythrop Journal* (Oxford), vol. 5, 1964, 58-64.

4898   Richardson, William J. "Heideggers Weg durch die Phänomenologie zum Seinsdenken." *Philosophisches Jahrbuch* (München), vol. 72, 1964/65, 385-396.

4899   Richardson, William J. "Heidegger and God - and Prof. Jonas." *Thought*, vol. 40, 1965, 13-40.

4900   Richardson, William J. "Heidegger and Theology." *Theological Studies*, vol. 26, 1965, 86-100.

4901   Richardson, William J. "The Place of the Unconscious in Heidegger." *Review of Existential Psychology and Psychiatry* (Pittsburgh), vol. 5, 1965, 265-290.

4902   Richardson, William J. "Heidegger and the Quest of Freedom." *Theological Studies*, vol. 28, 1967, 286-307.

4903   Richardson, William J. "Kant and the Late Heidegger." *Phenomenology in America*. Chicago, 1967, 125-147.

4904   Richardson, William J. "Heidegger's Critique of Science." *The New Scholasticism* (Washington), vol. 42, 1968, 511-536.

4905   Richardson, William J. "Martin Heidegger: In Memoriam." *Man and World* (The Hague), vol. 10, no. 1, 1977, 6-12.

4906   Richardson, William J. "Heidegger's Way Through Phenomenology to the Thinking of Being." *Listening. Journal of Religion and Culture* (River Forest, Illinois), vol. 12, no. 3, 1977, 21-37.

4907    Richardson, William J. "The Mirror Inside: The Problem of the Self." *Review of Existential Psychology & Psychiatry* (Northwestern Univ., Evanston, Illinois), vol. 16, no. 1, 2, and 3, 1978/79.

4908    Richardson, William J. "Phenomenology and Psychoanalysis." In *Nachdenken über Heidegger.* Ed. Ute Guzzoni. Hildesheim: Gerstenberg Verlag, 1980, 232-252.

4909    Richey, Clarence W. "On the Intentional Ambiguity of Heidegger's Metaphysics." *The Journal of Philosophy* (Lancaster, Pennsylvania), vol. 55, 1958, 1144-1148.

4910    Rickert, H. *Die Logik des Prädikats und das Problem der Ontologie.* Heidelberg, 1930. [Auseinandersetzung mit Heideggers 'Was ist Metaphysik?'. Bonn, 1929, (specifically pages 227-236).]

4911    Ricoeur, Paul. "The Critique of Subjectivity and Cogito in the Philosophy of Heidegger." In *Heidegger and the Quest for Truth.* Ed. M. S. Frings. Chicago, 1968, 62-75.

4912    Ricoeur, Paul. "Heidegger i problem podmiotu" (Heidegger and the Problem of Subject). Trans. E. Bienkowskka. *Znak,* vol. 6, 1974.

4913    Ricoeur, Paul. "The Task of Hermeneutics." In *Heidegger and Modern Philosophy,* by Michael Murray (ed.). New Haven, Connecticut: Yale Univ. Press, 1978, 141-160.

4914    Ricoeur, Paul. "Hajdeger i pitanje o subjektu." Trans. Slavka Cavarkapa. In *Rani Hajdeger - Recepcija i kritika Bivstva i vremena,* by Dragan Stojanovic and Danilo Basta (eds.). (Biblioteka Zodijak). Beograd, 1979, 148-161.

4914a    Ricoeur, Paul. "Note Introductive [à Penser Dieu]." In In *Heidegger et la question de Dieu.* Ed. R. Kearney and J. S. O'Leary. Paris: B. Grasset, 1980, 17.

4915    Riddel, Joseph N. "From Heidegger to Derrida to Chance. Doubling and (Poetic) Language." In *Martin Heidegger and the Question of Literature.* Ed. William V. Spanos. Bloomington, Indiana/London: Indiana Univ. Press, 1979, 231-252.

4916    Riecke, H. Rev. of *Die Selbstbehauptung der Deutschen Universität,* by Martin Heidegger. 1933. *Berliner Börsenzeitung,* 13.8.1933.

4917    Riedel, Manfred. "Intervento." Trans. by Maria Giacin. *Verifiche,* vol. 8, no. 1, 1979, 107-112.

4918    Riega, Augustin de la. *Conocimiento, violencia y culpa: la fenomenologia frente al haber vital en la diferencia.* (Biblioteca del hombre contemporaneo, 249). Buenos Aires, 1973.

4919    Rieger, L. "Prispevek k problematice ontologie." *Ceská mysl* (In Czechoslovakian), vol. 37, no. 1-2, 1943, 1-2, 1-19.

4920    Rieger, L. "O váznamu filosofie existenciálni." *Listy* (In Czechoslovakian), vol. 1, no. 3, 1946/47, 327-336.

4921    Rifka, F. *Studien zur Ästhetik Martin Heideggers und Oskar Beckers.* Tübingen, 1965, III, 159 p. [Phil. Diss. Tübingen v.29.Okt.1965.]

4922    Rigobello, Armando. *Legge morale e mondo della vita.* Roma, 1958, 370 p.

4923    Rigobello, Armando. "Introduction and Commentary." In *Pensiero e poesia,* by Martin Heidegger. Rom: Armando Armando Ed., 1977.

4924    Rinieri, J.-J., and J. Beaufret. *Le poème de Parménide.* Paris, 1955.

4925    Rintelen, M., M. Söhngen, and E. Stein. "Interventions faites en langue allemande." *La Phénoménologie.* Journées d'études de la Société Thomiste. Juvisty 12 septembre 1932, 101-113.

4926    Rintelen, Fritz Joachim von. "Comprensión trágica del mundo en Rilke y Heidegger." *Revista de la Faculdad de Filosofia y Humanidades* (Córdoba), vol. 5, 1953, 9-18.

4927    Rintelen, Fritz Joachim von. "The Existentialism of Martin Heidegger." *The Personalist* (Los Angeles), vol. 38, 1957, 238-247, 376-382.

4928    Rintelen, Fritz Joachim von. *Philosophie der Endlichkeit als Spiegel der Gegenwart.* Meisenheim/Glan, 1951. 2nd ed. Meisenheim/Glan, XVIII, 490 p.

4929    Rintelen, Fritz Joachim von. "Martin Heidegger." In *Les grands courants de la pensée mondiale contemporaine.* Ouvrage publié sous la direction de N.F. Sciacca. IIIe Partie: Paris 1964, 697-737.

4930    Rintelen, Fritz Joachim von. "Humanismus und Existenzialismus Heideggers." *Staat und Gesellschaft.* Festabgabe für Günther Küchenhoff zum 60. Geburtstag am 21.8.1967, 173-183.

4931    Rintelen, Fritz Joachim von. *Contemporary German Philosophy and Its Background.* Bonn, 1970, X, 177 p.

4932    Rioux, B. *L'être et la vérité chez Heidegger et Saint Thomas d'Aquin.* Preface par Paul Ricoeur. Montreal/Paris, 1963, IX, 270 p.

4933    Rioux, B. "La notion de vérité chez Heidegger et Saint Thomas d'Aquin." In *S. Thomas d'Aquin aujourd'hui.* (Coll. 'Recherches de Philosophie', 6). Bruges, 1963, 197-217.

4934    Rioux, B. "Ontologie du signifier." *Man and World* (Pittsburgh), vol. 4, 1971, 243-258.

4935    Ritter, J, and F. Bollnow. "Arbeitsgemeinschaft Cassirer-Heidegger." In *Guido Schneeberger: Ergänzungen zu einer Heidegger-Bibliographie.* Bern, 1960, 17-27.

4936    Riu, Federico. "Sartre, Heidegger y el tema de la conciencia." *Cultura universitaria* (Caracas), no. 66-67, 1959, 42-46.

4937    Riu, Federico. "Existencialismo." *Revista nacional de Cultura* (Caracas), vol. 25, 81-90.

4938    Riu, Federico. "Reflexiones sobre el opusculo de Heidegger." *Dianoia* (Mesiko), vol. 18, 1972, 153-181.

4939    Riverso, E. "Fenomenologia e ontologia in Martino Heidegger." *Rassegna di Scienze filosofiche* (Napoli), vol. 15, 1962, 286-318.

4940 Riverso, E. Rev. of *Der Satz vom Grund,* by Martin Heidegger. *Rassegna di Scienze filosofiche* (Napoli), vol. 15, 1962, 100.

4941 Robbins, Harold J. *'Duns Scotus Theory of the Categories and of Meaning' by Martin Heidegger; Translated From the German and With Introduction.* Phil. Diss. De Paul Univ. 1978 291 p. *Dissertation Abstracts International,* vol. 39/04-A, 2343.

4942 Robert, Jean Dominique. "La vie de l'existentialisme en France." *Tijdschrift voor Philosophie* (Leuven), vol. 9, 1947, 711-754, (specifically page 730 ff).

4943 Robinet, André. "Leibniz und Heidegger: Atomzeitalter oder Informatikzeitalter?" Trans. Theodor A. Knust. *Studia Leitnitiana* (Wiesbaden), vol. 8, 1976, 241-256.

4944 Robinet, André. "Langage philosophique et informatique." *Revue de l'Université de Bruxelles* (Bruxelles), no. 1-2, 1976, 72-88.

4945 Robinson, Charles Kivet. "A Critical Analysis of Heidegger's Ontology in 'Sein und Zeit'." Phil. Diss. Duke Univ. 1958 172 p.

4946 Robinson, James M. "Heilsgeschichte und Lichtungsgeschichte." *Evangelische Theologie* (München), vol. 22, 1962, 113-141, (specifically pages 134-141).

4947 Robinson, James M., and John B. Cobb, Jr. *The Later Heidegger and Theology.* New York, 1963. Contributions by J. M. Robinson, H. Ott, A. B. Michalson, S. M. Ogden, J. B. Cobb, Jr. [German trans. *See* 4948.]

4948 Robinson, James M., and John B. Cobb, Jr., eds. *Der spätere Heidegger und die Theologie.* (Neuland in der Theologie. Ein Gespräch zwischen amerikanischen und europäischen Theologen, Bd 1). Contributions by J. M. Robinson, H. Ott, A. B. Michalson, S. M. Ogden, J. B.Cobb, Jr. Trans. E. Fincke. Zürich/Stuttgart, 1964, 248 p.

4949 Robinson, James M. "Die deutsche Auseinandersetzung mit dem späteren Heidegger." In *Der spätere Heidegger und die Theologie.* Zürich/Stuttgart, 1964, 15-93.

4950 Robinson, James M., and John B. Cobb, Jr. *Die neue Hermeneutik.* Zürich, 1965.

4951 Robinson, James M., and John B. Cobb, Jr. *New Frontiers in Theology: Discussions Among German and American Theologians. Vol. I, The Later Heidegger and Theology.* New York: Harper & Row, 1963.

4952 Rochlitz, R. "Lukács et Heidegger (suite d'un débat)." *L'Homme de la Société* (Paris), vol. 37-38, 1975, 87-94.

4953 Rodriguez, Martinez J. Rev. of *Kants These über das Sein,* by Martin Heidegger. *Ideas y Valores* (Bogotá), no. 17, 1963, 105-107.

4954 Rodriguez Martinez, J. "El concepto de la metafisica en Martin Heidegger." *Revista de Filosofia* (Madrid), vol. 20, 1960, 365-393.

4955 Rodriguex Martinez, J. "El concepto de la metafisica en Martin Heidegger." *Revista de Filosofia* (Madrid), vol. 20, 1961, 365-393.

4956    Rodriguez Paniagua, J. M. "De la propriedad derecho natural individual a la propiedad derecho humano y social." *Anales de la Catedra Francisco Suarez* (Granada), vol. 12, 1972, 325-328.

4957    Roesle, M. "Was ist Metaphysik? Ein Vergleich zwischen Heidegger und Thomas von Aquin." *Schweizer Kirchenzeitung,* vol. 111, 1943, 41-45, 54-57.

4958    Roessingh, K. H. *Der Godsdienstwijsgerige Problematiek in het denken van Martin Heidegger.* Assen, 1956, 240 p. Rpt. in *Martin Heidegger als Godsdienstwijsbegeer. Philosophia religionis, Bibliotheek van geschriften over de Godsdienstwijsbegeerte,* by K. H. Roessingh. Assen, vol. 8, 1957, 240 p.

4959    Rogalski, A. "Martin Heidegger." *Nurt,* 2, 1971.

4960    Rogalski, A. "Heidegger und Hölderlin." *Poezja,* 8 July 1975.

4961    Rogalski, A. "Dwa spojrzenia na Heideggera" (Heidegger Seen From Two Different Perspectives). *Zycie i myál,* 10, 1978.

4962    Rogel-H., Héctor. "Existencialismo y valores. La carta sobre el humanismo de Heidegger." *Logos* (Mexico), vol. 6, no. 17, 1978, 37-53.

4963    Rohatyn, Dennis. "A Note on Heidegger and Wittgenstein." *Philosophy Today* (Celina, Ohio), vol. 15, 1971, 69.

4964    Rohatyn, Dennis A. "An Introduction to Heidegger: Truth and Being." *Sapienza* (Roma), vol. 28, 1975, 211-218.

4965    Rohrmoser, G. "Anlässlich Heideggers Nietzsche." *Neue Zeitschrift für systematische Theologie und Religionsphilosophie* (Berlin), vol. 6, 1964, 35-50.

4966    Rohrmoser, G. "Platons politische Philosophie." *Studium Generale,* vol. 22, 1969, 1094-1134.

4967    Roig Girondella, J. "La filosofia de Martin Heidegger." *Razon y Fe* (Madrid), vol. 135, 1947, 270-271.

4968    Rolan-Gosselin, M.-D. Rev. of *Sein und Zeit,* by Martin Heidegger. Halle, 1927. *Revue des sciences philosophiques et théologiques* (Paris), vol. 21, 1932, 248-257.

4969    Rollin, Bernhard E. "Heidegger's Philosophy of History in 'Being and Time'." *The Modern Schoolman* (St. Louis), vol. 49, 1971/72, 97-112.

4970    Rollin, F. *La phénoménologie au départ. Husserl, Heidegger, Gaboriau.* Paris, 1967, 194 p.

        [Rev. by J. Echarri in *Pensamiento* (Madrid), vol. 26, 1970, 343-344.]

4971    Romano, Br. "Continuità e unità del pensiero di Martin Heidegger." *Rivista internazionale di Filosofia del Diritto* (Milano), vol. 44, 1967, 261-277.

4972    Romano, Br. Rev. of *Der europäische Nihilismus,* by Martin Heidegger. Pfullingen, 1967. *Rivista internazionale di Filosofia del Diritto* (Milano), vol. 45, 1968, 668-669.

4973	Romano, Br. *Tecnica e giustizia. Nel pensiero di Martin Heidegger.* (Pubblicazioni dell'Istituto di filosofia del diritto dell'Università di Roma. S. III, 7). Milano, 1969, XIV, 233 p. Rev. in *Gregorianum,* by J. De Finance. Roma, vol. 53, 1972, 181-182.

4974	Rombach, Heinrich. "Reflections on Heidegger's Lecture 'Time and Being'." *Philosophy Today* (Celina, Ohio), vol. 10, 1966, 19-29.

4975	Rombach, Heinrich. *Die Gegenwart der Philosophie. Eine geschichtsphilosophische und philosophiegeschichtliche Studie über den Stand des philosophischen Fragens.* Freiburg/München, 1962. 2nd ed. 1967, (specifically pages 71-116).

4976	Rorty, Richard. "Overcoming to Tradition: Heidegger and Dewey." *Review of Metaphysics* (Washington), vol. 30, 1976/77, 280-305. Rpt. in *Heidegger and Modern Philosophy. Critical Essays,* by Michael Murray (ed.). New Haven, Connecticut: Yale Univ. Press, 1978, 239-258.

4977	Rorty, Richard. "Derrida on Language, Being and Abnormal." *The Journal of Philosophy* (New York), vol. 74, no. 11, 1977, 673-681.

4978	Rorty, Richard. "Overcoming the Tradition. Heidegger and Dewey." In *Nachdenken über Heidegger.* Ed. Ute Guzzoni. Hildesheim: Gerstenberg Verlag, 1980, 253-274.

4979	Rosales, Alberto. "Observaciones criticas a la idea de tempralidad propia en 'Ser y tiempo' de Heidegger." *Revista Venezolana de Filosofia,* no. 8, 1978, 83-96.

4980	Rosales, Alberto. *Transzendenz und Differenz. Ein Beitrag zum Problem der ontologischen Differenz beim frühen Heidegger.* Den Haag, 1970, XVI, 320 p.

4981	Rosales, Alberto. "El problema de la diferencia ontológica en las obras tempranas de Heidegger." *Cuadernos de Filosofia* (Buenos Aires), vol. 11, no. 15-16, 1971, 195-205.

4982	Rosales, Alberto. "El giro del pensamiento de Heidegger." *Estudios Filosóficos* (Caracas), no. 1, 1974, 147-165.

4983	Rosales, Alberto. "Martin Heidegger y la crisis da la filosofia transcendental." *Estudios Filosóficos* (Caracas), no. 1, 1974, 113-128.

4984	Rosales, Alberto. "La critica de Heidegger al idealismo moderno." *Estudios Filosóficos* (Caracas), no. 1, 1974, 129-146.

4985	Rosales, Alberto. "El problema de la negatividad." *Revista Venezolana de Filosofia* (Caracas), no. 4, 1976, 123-174.

4986	Rosales, Alberto. "Una aprocimación a 'Tiempo y ser'." *Revista Venezolana de Filosofia* (Caracas), no. 4, 1976, 119-144.

4987	Rosales, Alberto. Rev. of *Die Grundprobleme der Phänomenologie,* by Martin Heidegger. 1975. *Revista Venezolana de Filosofia* (Caracas), 5/6, 1976/77, 119-144.

4988     Rosales, Alberto. "Observaciones criticas a la idea de temporalidad propia en 'Ser y Tiempo' de Heidegger." *Revista Venezolana de Filosofia* (Caracas), no. 8, 1978, 83-96.

4989     Rosales, Alberto. Rev. of *Qué es eso de filosofia?* by Martin Heidegger. *Cuadernos filosóficos* (Rosario), no. 3, 1962, 77-82.

4990     Rosen, Stanley H. "Curiosity, Anxiety, Wonder." *Giornale di Metafisica* (Genova/Torino), vol. 14, 1959, 465-474.

4991     Rosen, Stanley. "Heidegger's Interpretation of Plato." *The Journal of Existentialism* (New York), vol. 7, 1966/67, 477-504. Rpt. in *Essays in Metaphysics,* by C. G. Vaught (ed.). Park/London, 1970, 51-77.

4992     Rosen, Stanley. "Philosophy and Idealogy: Reflections on Heidegger." *Social Research* (Albany), vol. 35, no. 2, 1968, 260-285.

4993     Rosen, Stanley. *Nihilism: A Philosophical Essay.* New Haven, 1969, 241 p.

4994     Rosen, Stanley. "Return to the Origin: Reflections on Plato and Contemporary Philosophy." *International Philosophical Quarterly* (New York), vol. 16, no. 2, 1976, 151-177.

4995     Rosen, Stanley. "Thinking About Nothing." In *Heidegger and Modern Philosophy. Critical Essays.* Ed. Michael Murray. New Haven, Connecticut: Yale Univ. Press, 1978, 116-137.

4996     Rosenfeld, Alvin H. "'The Being of Language and the Language of Being'. Heidegger and Modern Poetics." In *Martin Heidegger and the Question of Literature.* Ed. William V. Spanos. Bloomington, Indiana/London: Indiana Univ. Press, 1979, 195-213.

4997     Rosenmayr, L. "Gesellschaftsbild und Kulturkritik Martin Heideggers." *Archiv für Rechts und Sozialphilosophie* (Bern), vol. 46, 1960, 1-38.

4998     Rosenstein, Leon. "The Ontological Integrity of the Art Object From the Ludic Viewpoint." *The Journal of Aesthetics and Art Criticism,* vol. 34, Spring 1976, 323-336.

4999     Rosenstein, Leon. "Heidegger and Plato and the Good." *Philosophy Today* (Celina, Ohio), vol. 22, no. 4, 1978, 332-354.

5000     Rosenstein, Leon. "Mysticism ad Preontology: A Note on the Heideggerian Connection." *Philosophy and Phenomenological Research* (Buffalo), vol. xxxix, no. 1, 1978, 57-73.

5001     Rosenthal, K. "Das Wesen der Sprache im Denken des späteren Heidegger." *Kerygma und Dogma. Zeitschrift für theologische Forschung und kirchliche lehre* (Göttingen), vol. 10, 1964, 284-290.

5002     Rosenthal, K. "Martin Heideggers Auffassung von Gott." *Kerygma und Dogma. Zeitschrift ür theologische Forschung und kirchliche Lehre* (Göttingen), vol. 13, no. 3, 1967, 212-229.

5003     Rosenthal, Sandra B., and Patrick I. Bourgeois. "Lewis, Heidegger, and Kant. Schemata and the Structure of Perceptual Experience." *Southern Journal of Philosophy,* vol. 17, 1979, 239-248.

5004     Rosenzweig, F. "Vertauschte Fronten, (Zur Hochschultagung in Davos 1929, Begegnung Cassirer-Heidegger)." *Morgen* (Berlin), vol. 6, 1930, 85-88.

5005     Rossi, F. Rev. of *La dottrina del giudizio nello psicologismo,* by Martin Heidegger. *Rassegna di Scienze filosofiche* (Napoli), vol. 26, 1973, 180-181.

5006     Rossi, F. Rev. of *Scritti filosofici (1912-1917),* by Martin Heidegger. 1972. *Sapienza* (Roma), vol. 29, 1976, 99-101.

5007     Rossi, P. "Martin Heidegger e Panalisi esistenziale della storicità." *Rivista di Filosofia* (Bologna/Torino), vol. 50, 1959, 15-37.

5008     Rossi, Sirpa. "Über das Problem der Verdinglichung bei Lukàcs und Heidegger." *Ajatus* (Helsinki), vol. 34, 1972, 155-161.

5009     Rossmann, K. "Martin Heideggers Holzwege." *Der Monat* (Berlin), Jg. 2, no. 21, 1949/50, 236-245.

5010     Rostenne, P. "L'ontologie entravée de Heidegger." *Revue de Métaphysique et de Morale* (Paris), vol. 71, 1966, 74-99.

5011     Rostenne, P. "L'exigence humaine du sacrifice." *Revue de Métaphysique et de Morale* (Paris), vol. 75, 1970, 218-252.

5012     Rota, Gian Carlo. "A Heidegger prospectus." *Phenomenology Information Bulletin* (Belmont), no. 1, 1977, 21-26.

5013     Rotenstreich, Nathan. "The Ontological Status of History." *American Philosophical Quarterly* (Pittsburgh), vol. 9, 1972, 49-58.

5014     Rotenstreich, Nathan. "Schematism and Freedom." *Revue Internationale de Philosophie,* vol. 28, 1974, 464-474.

5015     Rothacker, E. Rev. of *Die Selbstbehauptung der Deutschen Universität,* by Martin Heidegger. Breslau, 1933. *Kölnische Zeitung,* 30.7.1933.

5016     Rothacker, E. *Gedanken über Martin Heidegger.* Bonn, 1973, 38 p.

5017     Roubiczek, P. Rev. of *Der Satz vom Grund,* by Martin Heidegger. Pfullingen, 1957. *Erasmus* (Darmstadt), vol. 13, 1960, 266-268.

5018     Rotter, F. O. *Die Gabe unseres Daseins. Das Problem der Existenzphilosophie im Blickfeld der immerwährenden Philosophie.* Mainz, 1962, 144 p.

5019     Roustang, F. Rev. of *Lettre sur l'humanisme,* by Martin Heidegger. *Etudes* (Paris), vol. 294, 1957, 297.

5020     Routila, Lauri. "Wahrnehmung und Interpretation." *Ajatus,* vol. 36, 1974, 125-141.

5021     Roy, D. J. "Is *Philosophy* Really Possible? A Meditation on Heidegger and Wittgenstein with Karl-Otto Apel." *Revue de l'Université Laurentienne* (Sudbury), vol. 9, no. 2, 1977, 79-91.

5022     Rozsahegyi, Edit. "Dialectics and Phenomenology." (In Hungarian). *Magyar Filozof Szemle,* vol. 5, 1979, 681-714.

5023     Robert Candau, J. M. "La función de la filosofia el momento histórico actual. Un diálogo con Martin Heidegger." *Verdad y Vida* (Madrid), vol. 20, 1962, 433-446.

5024     Rubio Angulo, J. E. "El hombre en el pensamiento actual." *Universidad de Santo Tomas* (Bogota), vol. 3, 1970, 437-451.

5025     Rubio Angulo, J. E. "Filosofia y teologia en Martin Heidegger." *Publicacion cuadrimestral de investigacion e informacion* (Bogota) (Universidad de Santo Tomas), vol. 4, 1971, 587-591.

5026     Ruben Sanabria, J. "El concepto de libertad en Heidegger." *Revista de Filosofia* (Mexico), vol. 10, no. 28, 1977, 91-120.

5027     Rüfner, V. "Zur Methode der ontologischen Forschung." In *Sinn und Sein. Ein philosophisches Symposion.* Ed. R. Wisser. Tübingen, 1960, 209-229. [Martin Heideggers Zugang zur Ontologie, (specifically pages 216-221).]

5028     Rüfner, V. "Innere Zusammenhänge in den Denkmotiven bei Thomas von Aquin, Kant, Hegel und Heidegger." *Kant-Studien* (Köln), vol. 57, 1966, 90-99.

5029     Ruggemini, Mario. "La scomparsa del filosofo di 'Sein und Zeit': il commino di Martin Heidegger." *Vita e pensiero. Rassegna italiana di Cultura* (Milano), vol. 4, 1976, 141-147.

5029a    Ruggenini, Mario. *Il soggetto e la tecnica. Heidegger interprete inattuale dell'epoca presente.* (Biblioteca di cultura, 121). Roma: Bulzoni, 1978, 367 p.

5029b    Ruggenini, Mario. "Il pensiero dell'essere e il pensiero della separazione." *L'Uomo, un segno* (Milano), vol. 3, no. 1-2, 1979, 83-100.

5030     Ruggiero, G. de. "Note sulla piu recente filosofia europea." *La Critica* (Napoli), vol. 29, 1931, 100-109, (specifically pages 107-109).

5031     Ruggiero, G. de. *Filosofi del Novecento.* Bari, 1934, 90-101.

5032     Ruggiero, G. de. *Existentialisme.* London, 1946, 31-46.

5033     Ruggiero, G. de. *Filosofi del Novecento. Appendice a la filosofia contemporanea.* Bari, 1950, 285-292, passim.

5034     Ruiz de Elvira, A. "Humanismo y sobrehumanismo: Heidegger y San Pablo." *Revista de la Universidad de Madrid,* vol. 6, 1953, 165-193.

5035     Rukavina, Thomas F. "Being and Things in Heidegger's Philosophy: A Rejoinder." *New Scholasticism* (Washington), vol. 33, 1959, 184-201.

5036     Rukavina, Thomas F. Rev. of *An Introduction to Metaphysics,* by Martin Heidegger. New Haven, 1959; and *The Question of Being,* by Martin Heidegger. New York, 1958. *The New Scholasticism* (Washington), vol. 34, 1960, 367-369.

5037     Rukavinka, Thomas F. *Heidegger as Critic of Western Thinking.* Phil. Diss. Indiana Univ. Bloomington 1960 270 p. *Dissertation Abstracts International,* vol. 21/04, 928.

5038     Rukavina, Thomas F. Rev. of *Kant and the Problem of Metaphysics,* by Martin Heidegger. *The New Scholasticism* (Washington), vol. 39, 1965, 547-550.

5039     Rukavina, Thomas F. "Heidegger's Theory of Being." *The New Scholasticism* (Washington), vol. 40, 1966, 423-446.

5040 Rukavina, Thomas F. *Heidegger as Critic of Western Thinking.* Phil. Diss. Indiana Univ. 1960. Ann Arbor, Michigan: University Microfilms Inc., 1977, v-264.

5041 Rukser, U. "Ortega y Heidegger." *Humboldt* (Hamburg), vol. 45, 1971, 60-67.

5042 Runes, D. D. *Martin Heidegger. German Existentialism.* New York, 1965.

5043 Ruprecht, E. "Heideggers Bedeutung für die Literaturwissenschaft." In *Martin Heideggers Einfluss auf die Wissenschaften.* Bern, 1949, 122-133.

5044 Ruprecht, E. "Significación de Martin Heidegger en la ciencia literaria." *Revista de Literatura,* no. 21-22, 1957, 68-77.

5045 Russev, P. "Heidegger's Fundamental Ontology." (In Bulgarian). *Filosofska Misal* (Bulgaria), vol. 25, no. 12, 1969, 57-60.

5046 Russev, P. "Der Existentialismus und das menschliche Dasein." *Akten des XIV. Internationalen Kongresses für Philosophie [Wien. 2.-9.Sept. 1968]* (Wien), vol. V, 1970, XVI, 676 p.; darin: 66-68.

5047 Russev, P. "Einige Gesichtspunkte des deutschen Existentialismus." *Filosofska Misal* (Sofia), vol. 28, 1972, 55-60.

5048 Rydnin, I. V. "Kritika ekzistencialistskoj traktovki kategorii 'vozmoznost'" (The Criticism of the Existentialist Handling of the Category "Potentiality"). *V knoge 'Kritika antimarksistskich koncepcij v prepodavanii ovscestvennych nauk'* (Leningrad), 51-57.

5049 Ryffel, H. "Zu den neuen Veröffentlichungen von Martin Heidegger." *Studia Philosophica* (Basel), vol. 15, 1955, 176-202.

Rev. of these Heidegger works on pages 180-186:

[*Einfuhrung in die Metaphysik.* Tübingen, 1953, 186-192.]

[*Was heisst Denken?* Tübingen, 1954, 192-196.]

[*Vorträge und Aufsätze.* Pfullingen, 1954.]

5050 Ryle, E. Rev. of *Sein und Zeit,* by Martin Heidegger. *Mind* (London), vol. 38, 1929, 355-370.

5051 Ryle, G. "Martin Heidegger: 'Sein und Zeit'." *The Journal of the British Society for Phenomenology* (Manchester), vol. 1, 1970, 3-14. Rpt. in *Collected Papers,* by G. Ryle. London, 1971. In *Heidegger and Modern Philosophy. Critical Essays,* by Michael Murray (ed.). New Haven, Connecticut: Yale Univ. Press, 1978, 53-64.

5052 Sabatino, Charles Joseph. *World as a Context of Meaning: Heidegger's Gift.* Phil. Diss. Univ. of Chicago 1974.

5053 Sabatino, Charles Joseph. "Faith and Human Meaning." *Listening,* vol. 10, 1975, 51-58.

5054 Sacchi, Mario Enrique. "Santo Tomás de Aquino interpretado por Heidegger. Las referencias explicitas al Doctor Angélico en 'Sein und Zeit'." *Aquinas* (Roma), vol. 19, no. 1, 1976, 64-87.

5055    Sacco, Carmela. *Il luogo dello svelamento nel pensiero di Martin Heidegger.* (Pubblicazioni dell'Istituto universitario ni magistero di Cassino. Saggistica). Cassino: Editrice Garigliano, 1975, 83 p.

5056    Sachsse, Hans. "Die Technik in der Sicht Herbert Marcuses und Martin Heideggers." In *Proceedings of the XVth World Congress of Philosophy.* Vol. I: Philosophy and science. Morality and culture. Technology and man. Sofia: Sofia Press Production Centre, 1973, 371-375.

5057    Sachsse, Hans. "Was ist Metaphysik? Überlegungen zur Freiburger Antrittsvorlesung von Martin Heidegger und ein Exkurs über seine Frage nach der Technik." *Zeitschrift für Philosophische Forschung* (Schlehdorf am Kochelsee/Meisenheim/Glan), vol. 28, 1974, 67-93.

5058    Sacristán-Luzón, M. *Las ideas gnoseológicas de Heidegger.* (Barcelona, Instituto Luis Vives de Filosofia). Delegación de Barcelona, 1959, 281 p.

5059    Sadagane, Hiroshi. "Haideggâ ni okeru Kêre no Mondai" (The Problem of the "Turning" in Heidegger). *Tetsugaku* (Hiroshima Tetsugakukai, Hiroshima), vol. 17, 1965, 98-110.

5060    Sadagane, Hiroshi. "Haideggâni okeru Zettaiteki-Kyôiki" (The Realm of the Absolute in Heidegger). *Rinrigaku Nempô* (Nippon Rinrigakkai, Tôkyô), vol. 15, 1966, 91-99.

5061    Sadzik, J. *Esthétique de Martin Heidegger.* (Coll. 'Encyclopédie universitaire'). Paris, 1963, 213 p. Spanish trans. *La estética de Heidegger.* Trans. J. M. Garcia de la Mora. (Biblioteca Filosófica). Barcelona: Miracel, 1972, 235 p.

5062    Sáenz, R. G. "Reflexiones en torno al concepto Heideggeriano de verdad." *Revista de Filosofia* (Mexico), vol. 7, no. 21, 1974, 347-364.

5063    Sagave, P. P. "Martin Heidegger à Aix." *Cahiers du Sud* (Paris), Jg. 44, no. 344, 1957.

5064    Saheki, Mamoru. "Kibunron e no Shiten; Hitotsu no Haideggâ Hihan" (The Point of View to the Theory of the Mood; a Critique of Heidegger). In *Taiken to Seishin* (Experience and Spirit). Kôronsha, Kyôto, 1977, 132-169.

5065    Saitô, Shinji. "Jitsuzon to Shi, Haideggeru no Shiron ni tsuite" (Existence and Poetry. On Heidegger's Discussion of Poetry). *Risô* (Tôkyô), vol. 76, Oktober 1937.

5066    Saitô, Shinji. "Haideggâ to Yasupâsu" (Heidegger and Jaspers). *Tetsugakuzasshi* (Tôkyô), no. 623-625, Januar, Februar und März 1939.

5067    Saitô, Shinji. *Jitsuzon no Keijijôgaku* (Metaphysics of Existence). Tôkyô, 1947.

5068    Saitô, Shinji. "Haidegga no Tenkai o Megutte" (On Heidegger's Turning). *Risô* (Tôkyô), vol. 245, Oktober 1953.

5069    Saitô, Shinji. *Haideggâ no Hêgeru-Kaishaku* (Heidegger's Hegel-Interpretation). Chüôdaigaku-Bungakubu-Kiyô, Tôkyô, 1958.

5070    Saitô, Shinji. "Hêgeru to Haideggâ" (Hegel and Heidegger). *Jitsuzon no Shisô* (Kôbundô-Verlag, Tôkyô), 1960, 167-179.

5071    Saitô, Takeo. "Heideggâ ni okeru Sonzai to Jitsuzon" (Being and Existence in Heidegger). *Hirosaki Gakuin Daigaku, Hirosaki Gakuin Tanki-Daigaku Kiyô* (Hirosaki), vol. 13, 1977, 1-14.

5072    Saitô, Takeo. "Haideggâ ni okeru Nichijôteki-Hairyoteki-Kôshô to Jikansei" (The Everyday Providing Deal and the Temporality in Heidegger). *Tetsugaku-Ronsô* (Tôkyô), vol. 1, 1933, 179-221.

5073    Saitta, G. *La Libertà umana e l'esistenza.* Firenze, 1940, 48, 51-54, 189, 198-199, 242.

5074    Sáiz, B. *De Descartes a Heidegger.* Madrid, 1951.

5075    Sakabe, Megumi. "Haideggâ no Kanto Kaishaku no Kotonado" (On Heidegger's Interpretation of Kant. *Jitsuzonshugi* (Tôkyô), vol. 77, 1976, 105-107.

5076    Sakata, Chikanobu. "Kanjô ni tsuite" (On Feeling; Freud, Boss, Heidegger). *Kansai Daigaku Tetsugaku,* vol. 6, 1975, 45-62.

5077    Salaquarda, Jörg. Rev. of *Schellings Abhandlung über das Wesen der menschlichen Freiheit 1809,* by Martin Heidegger. Ed. Hildegard Feick. 1971, x-237. *Philosophy and History* (Tübingen), vol. 6, 1973, 139-142.

5078    Salaquarda, Jörg. Rev. of *Frühe Schriften,* by Martin Heidegger. 1972. *Philosophy and History* (Tübingen), vol. 7, 1974, 131-134.

5079    Sallis, John Cleveland. *The Concept of World: A Study in the Phenomenological Ontology of Martin Heidegger.* Phil. Diss. Tulane Univ. New Orleans 1964 256 p. *Dissertation Abstracts International,* vol. 25/07, 4193.

5080    Sallis, John Cleveland. "World, Finitude, Temporality in the Philosophy of Martin Heidegger." *Philosophy Today* (Celina, Ohio), vol. 9, 1965, 40-52.

5081    Sallis, John Cleveland. "La différence ontologique et l'unité de la pensée de Heidegger." *Revue Philosophique de Louvain* (Louvain), vol. 65, 1967, 192-206.

5082    Sallis, John Cleveland. "Language and Reversal." *Southern Journal of Philosophy,* vol. 8, 1970, 381-397.

5083    Sallis, John Cleveland. "Towards the Movement of Reversal: Science, Technology, and the Language of Homecoming." In *Heidegger and the Path of Thinking.* Ed. J. Sallis. Pittsburgh, 1970, 138-168.

5084    Sallis, John Cleveland, ed. and intr. *Heidegger and the Path of Thinking.* Pittsburgh, 1970, 236 p.

        [Rev. by G. Hoeffner in *Theologie und Philosophie* (Frankfurt/Pullach/Freiburg), vol. 47, no. 1, 1972, 151-152.]

        [Rev. by Robert L. Perkins in *Journal of the British Society for Phenomenology* (Manchester), vol. 1, 1973, 80-81.]

5086    Sallis, John Cleveland. "Language and Reversal." In *Martin Heidegger in Europe and America,* by Edward Goodwin Ballard and Charles E. Scott (eds.). The Hague, 1973, 129-145.

5087    Sallis, John Cleveland. "Towards the Showing of Language." In *The Southwestern Journal of Philosophy* (Norman), vol. 4, no. 3, 1973, 75-83.

5088    Sallis, John Cleveland. Rev. of *Die Grundprobleme der Phänomenologie*, by Martin Heidegger. Ed. Friedrich Wilhelm von Herrmann. 1975. *Research in Phenomenology* (Pittsburgh), vol. 6, 1976, 139-149.

5089    Sallis, John Cleveland. "Radical Phenomenology and Fundamental Ontology." *Research in Phenomenology* (Pittsburgh), vol. 6, 1976, 139-149.

5090    Sallis, John Cleveland. "The Origins of Heidegger's Thought." *Research in Phenomenology* (Pittsburgh), vol. 7, 1977, 43-57.

5091    Sallis, John Cleveland, ed. [Heidegger memorial issue.] *Research in Phenomenology* (Pittsburgh), vol. 7, 1977, 1-318.

5092    Sallis, John Cleveland. *The Concept of World. A Study in the Phenomenological Ontology of Martin Heidegger.* Authorized facsimile of the dissertation of the Tulane Univ. Phil. Diss. 1964. Ann Arbor, Michigan; London: University Microfilms International, 1977, iv-251.

5093    Sallis, John Cleveland. "Where Does 'Being and Time' Begin? Commentary on Section 1-4." In *Heidegger's Existential Analytic,* by Frederick Elliston (ed.). The Hague, New York: Mouton Pub., 1978, 21-43.

5094    Sallis, John Cleveland, ed. *Radical Phenomenology.* Essays in Honor of Martin Heidegger. Contributions by Jarava Lal Mehta, Werner Marx, Otto Pöggeler, et al. Atlantic Highlands: Humanities Press, 1979, 318 p.

5095    Sallis, John Cleveland. "Hades, Heraclitus, Fragment B 98." *Heraclitean Fragments.* Ed. John Sallis and Kenneth Maly. Univ. of Alabama Press, 1980, 61-67.

5096    Salmerón, F. "Lenguaje y significado en 'El ser y el tiempo' de Heidegger." *Diánoia* (Mexico), vol. 14, 1968, 96-121.

5097    Salaquarda, J., ed. *Philosophische Theologie im Schatten des Nihilismus.* Berlin, 1971, 205 p.

5098    Sanabria, José Rubén. "El concepto de libertad en Heidegger." *Revista de Filosofía* (Mexico), vol. 10, 1977, 91-120.

5099    Sanabria, José Rubén. "Ser, Persona, Dios." *Revista de Filosofía* (Mexico), vol. 12, 1979, 399-436.

5100    Sanada, Tadami. "'Sonzai to Jikan' to Ningengaku" ('Being and Time' and Anthropology). *Tetsugaku Ronshû (Ôtani Daigaku)* (Kyôto), vol. 23, 1977, 70-73.

5101    Sanborn, Patricia. *Existentialism.* New York, 1968, 192 p.

5102    Sánchez Arjona, A. "La medicina ante Heidegger." *Cuadernos Hispanoamericanos* (Madrid), vol. 43, 1960, 38-46.

5103    Sandin, B. T. "El giro radical de la filosofía de M. Heidegger." *Studium* (Madrid), vol. 19, no. 1, 1979, 121-129.

5104    Sánea, Raúl Gutierrez. "Reflexiones en torno al concepto Heideggeriano de Verdad." *Revista de Filosofía* (México), vol. 7, 1974, 347-364.

5105 Sangbaek, I. *Haidegkaûi chilliron* (On the Notion of Truth in Heidegger). M. A. Thesis, Kyôngbuk Univ., 1978.

5106 Sangdae, I. *Haidegkae issôsôûi hyôngisanghak munje* (The Problem of Metaphysics in Heidegger). M. A. Thesis, Tongguk Univ., 1972.

5107 Sangi, Kazuie. "Haideggâ no Puraton-Tetsugaku-Kan" (Heidegger's Opinion of Platon's Philosophy). *Jitsuzon* (Tôkyô), Mai 1955.

5108 Sangjin, An. *Haidegkaûi sigansông* (Temporality in Heidegger). M. A. Thesis, Sôul Univ., 1961.

5109 Sangjin, An. "Haidegkaûii siron" (Poetry in Heidegger). *Ch'ôrhak Yôngu* (Sôul), vol. 6, 1978, 7-30.

5110 Sangjin, An. *Haidegkae issôsôûi siljonjôk sayuwa chonjaeûi sayu* (Existential Thinking and Thinking of Being in Heidegger). Phil. Diss. Sôul Univ. 1979.

5110a Salien, Jean Marie. "Dialectique de lu raison et des passions dans la pensée de Jean-Jacques Rousseau." *International Studies in Philosophy,* vol. XII, no. 1, 1980, 55.

5110b Santaló, José Luis. "Sobre la teología de la existencia. Una neuva lectura de Heidegger." *Filosofia oggi* (Bologna), vol. 2, 1979, 410-415. [Summary, 402.]

5111 Santoro, F. *La ricerca dell'essere in Sein und Zeit di Martin Heidegger.* Salerno, 1969, 110 p.

5112 Santos, Delfim. "Heidegger e Hölderlin ou a essencia da poesia." *Revista de Portugal* (Porto), vol. 4, 1938, 532-539.

5113 Santos, M. I. "Busqueda de un nuevo espacio para la emergencia del hombre." *Stromata* (San Miguel/Argentinia), vol. 29, 1973, 215-239.

5114 Santos de Ihlan, R. H. *Der Begriff der Welt bei Heidegger und Sartre.* Tübingen, 1970, 172 p. [Phil. Diss. 17.9.1970.]

5115 Sanz Aleixandre, A. "Philosophie und Politik bei Heidegger, un libro de Otto Pöggeler." *Teorema* (Valencia), vol. 3, no. 4, 1973, 569-582.

5116 Sapontzis, S. F. "Community in 'Being and Time'." *Kant-Studien* (Bonn), vol. 69, no. 3, 1978, 330-340.

5117 Sarnowski, S. "Heidegger - przekraczanie metafizyki" (Heidegger - Passing Metaphysics). *Czlowiek i áwiatopoglad,* vol. 6, 1973.

5118 Sarr[, Ramon. "L'interprétation du mythe d'Oedipe chez Heidegger." *Acta psychotherapeutica et psychosomatica* (Basel/New York), vol. 8, 1960, 266-289.

5119 Sarr[, Ramon. "The Interpretation of the Oedipus Myth According to Freud and Heidegger." *Journal of Existentialism,* vol. 1, 1961, 478-500.

5120 Sartre, J.-P. *L'existentialisme est un humanisme.* Paris, 1946, 141 p.

5121 Sartre, J.-P. "Ein neuer Mystiker." *J.-P. Sartre, Situationen. Essais.* Hamburg, 1965, 59-88.

5122 Sasaki, Isao. "Existenzialismus to Ideal-Realismus" (Existentialism and Ideal-Realism). *Tetsugakukenkyû* (Kyôto), vol. 170, 1930, 41-76.

5123 Sasaki, Kazuyoshi. "Haidegga ni okeru Jitsuzon to Mu no Seikaku" (Existence and Non-Being in Heidegger's Philosophy). *Tetsugaku-Nempô* (Kyûshû Daigaku, Fukuoka), vol. 9, 1950, 77-104.

5124 Sasaki, Kazuyoshi. "Haidegga ni okeru Jitsuzon to Mu no Seikaku" (The Nature of Existence and the Non-Being in Heidegger). *Tetsugakunenpô* (Fukuoka), vol. 9, April 1951.

5125 Sasaki, Kazuyoshi. *Haidegga no Jitsuzonronteki Tetsugaku Josetsu* (Introduction Into the Existential Philosophy of Heidegger). Tôkyô, 1952.

5126 Sasaki, Kazuyoshi. "Haidegga no Jitsuzairon - Tetsugaku to Tetsugaku-teki-Ningengaku" (Heidegger's Existential Philosophy and the Philosophical Anthropology). *Tetsugaku-Mempô* (Fukuoka), vol. 14, 1953, 256-272.

5127 Sasaki, Kazuyoshi. "Haidegga no Jitsuzonrontetsugaku ni okeru Chôetsu to Mu" (The Transcendence and the Non-Being in the Existential Philosophy of Heidegger). *Rinrigakunenpô* (Tôkyô), June 1953.

5128 Sasaki, Kazuyoshi. "Haidegga no Jitsuzon Gainen ni tsuite no ichi-Kanken" (An Aspect in Heidegger's Notion of Existence). *Kyûshû Daigaku Tetsugaku-Nempô* (Fukuoka), vol. 15, 1954, 28-55.

5129 Sasaki, Kazuyoshi. "Haidegga ni okeru Gensonzai no Jitsuzonron-teki-Kôzô no Henka 1-2" (The Metamorphosis of the Existential Structure of the There-Being in Heidegger). *Kyûshû Daigaku Tetsugaku-Nempô* (Fukuoka), vol. 16, 19, 1954, 1956, 23-46, 87-108.

5130 Sasaki, Kazuyoshi. "Haidegga-Tetsugaku no 'Hiteki' Seikaku" (The 'Negatory' Nature of Heidegger's Philosophy). *Rinrigakunenpô* (Tôkyô), April 1957.

5131 Sasaki, Kazuyoshi. "Haidegga no Gensonzai no Jitsuzonronteki-Bunseki ni okeru Hititsu no Gimonten" (A Questionable Aspect in Heidegger's Existential Analysis of There-Being). *Theoria* (Fukuoka), 1957.

5132 Sasaki, Kazuyoshi. "Haidegga no Kûkan-ron ni kansuru ichi Kaishaku" (An Explication of Heidegger's 'Space'). *Theoria* (Kyûshû Daigaku, Fukuoka), vol. 2, 1958, 1-24.

5133 Sasaki, Kazuyoshi. "Haidegga no Jitsuzon-ron Tetsugaku" (The Existential Philosophy of Heidegger). *Jitsuzon Tetsugaku Yôron* (Sekishoin-Verlag, Tôkyô), Mai 1958, 136-192.

5134 Sasaki, Kazuyoshi. "Haidegga ni okeru 'Chôetsu' no Komponteki-Seikaku" (Basic Character of 'Transcendence' in Heidegger). *Theoria* (Kyûshû Daigaku, Fukuoka), vol. 4, 1960, 1-38.

5135 Sasaki, Kazuyoshi. "Haidegga ni okeru Jitsuzon no Kihonteki-Sonzaikôzô ni tsuite. I" (On the Basic Constitution of Existence Heidegger). *Theoria* (Kyûshû Daigaku, Fukuoka), vol. 5, 1961, 87-117.

5136 Sasaki, Kazuyoshi. "Haidegga ni okeru Chôetsu no Konpon-Seikaku" (The Basic Character of Transcendence in Heidegger). *Theoria* (Fukuoka), 1961.

5137 Sasaki, Kazuyoshi. "Haideggâ ni okeru Jitsuzon no Kihonteki Sonzai-Kôzô ni tsuite" (On the Fundamental Structure of Being of Existence in Heidegger). *Theoria* (Fukuoka), vol. 5-6, 8, 1962, 1963, 1965.

5138 Sasaki, Kazuyoshi. "Haideggâ ni okeru Jitsuzon no Kihonteki Sonzaikôzô ni tsuite - Chôetsu no Ichimensei Kokufuku e no Michi II" (On the Basic Constitution of Existence in Heidegger - One Way to Overcome the One-Sidedness of Transcendence). *Theoria* (Kyûshû Daigaku Kyôyôbu, Fukuoka), vol. 8, 1964, 29-65.

5139 Sasaki, Kazuyoshi. "Haideggâ ni okeru Mu to Jitsuzon-kôzô no Henka" (Heidegger's "Nothing" and the Metamorphosis of the Existential Structure). *Theoria* (Kyûshû Daigaku Kyôyôbu, Fukuoka), vol. 10, 1966, 37-62.

5140 Sasaki, Kazuyoshi. "Jitsuzon-Tetsugaku ni okeru Mu ni tsuite; Heideggâ o Chûshin to shite" (The "Nothing" in Existential Philosophy - Particularly in Heidegger). *Jitsuzonshugi* (Tôkyô), vol. 40, 1967,

5141 Sasaki, Kazuyoshi. *Haideggâ nô Ningensonzai no Tetsugaku* (The Philosophy of Human Being in Heidegger). Shôhakusha, Tôkyô, 1973, 372 p.

5142 Sasaki, Kazuyoshi. "Kôki Haideggâ no Ningenhonshitsukitei ni tsuite no ichi Kanken" (On the Definition of the Human Being in the Late Heidegger). *Theoria* (Kyûshû Daigaku Tetsugakukai), vol. 16, 1973, 1-26.

5143 Sasaki, Kazuyoshi. "Haideggâ ni okeru Jikoseisei no Mondai; kyôikugakuteki Ningengaku no tameno Hitotsu no Kokoromi" (The Problem of Self-Building in Heidegger; for a Pedagogical Anthropology). *Daitôbunka Daigaku Kiyô* (Tôkyô), vol. 14, 1976, 1-16.

5144 Sasaki, Tôru. "Haideggâ ni okeru Geijutsu no Honshitsu" (The Essence of Art in Heidegger's Thought). *Bungakubu Kiyô* (Oitemon Gakuin Daigaku) (Ôsaka), vol. 9, 1975, 115-123.

5144a Sasaki, Kazuyoshi. "Haideggâ ni okeru Jikoseisei no Mondai; kyôikugakuteki Ningengaku no tameno Hitotsu no Kokoromi" (The Problem of Self-Building in Heidegger; for a Pedagogical Anthropology). *Daitôbunka Daigaku Kiyô* (Tôkyô), vol. 14, 1976, 1-16.

5145 Sasamoto, Shunji. "Haideggâ no Shi" (Heidegger's Death). *Tosho* (Tôkyô), vol. 323, 1976, 47-49.

5146 Sass, Hans-Martin. *Heidegger-Bibliographie.* Meisenheim/Glan, 1968, 182 p.

[Rev. in *The Review of Metaphysics* (Haverford), September 1969.]

[Rev. in *Das Antiquariat* (Stammheim), vol. 20, no. 3, 1970.]

[Rev. in *Das Antiquariat* (Stammheim), vol. 20, no. 3, 1970.]

[Rev. by G. Haeffner in *Theologie und Philosophie* (Frankfurt/Pullach/Freiburg), vol. 44, 1969, 464-465.]

[Rev. by E. Landolt in *Teoresi* (Catania), vol. 24, 1969, 224-231.]

[Rev. by F. Vansina in *Tijdschrift voor Filosofie* (Leuven), vol. 31, 1969, 387.]

[Rev. in *Deutsche Literaturzeitung* (Berlin), vol. 90, 1969, 4733.]

[Rev. by Werner Flach in *Philosophy and History,* vol. 4, 1971, 42 f.]

5146a    Sass, Hans-Martin. *Materialien zur Heidegger Bibliographie 1917-1972.* Meisenheim/Glan, 1975, 225 p.

5147    Sass, Hans-Martin. "Heidegger's Konzept der Phänomenologie." *Allgemeine Zeitschrift für Philosophie* (Stuttgart), vol. 3, 1977, 70-75.

5148    Sasso, J. "La teoria de la culpabilidad en Heidegger." *Cuadernos uruguayos de Filosofia* (Montevideo), vol. 5, 1968, 83-119.

5149    Satô, Akio. "Haideggâ ni okeru 'Sonzai' to 'Shi'" ('Being' and 'Poetizing' in Heidegger). *Kônan Daigaku Bungakukai Ronshû* (Kôbe), vol. 16, 1961, 156-181.

5150    Satô, Keiji. "Haideggâ Hihan - sono Riron-Keitai ni tsuite" (A Critique on Heidegger's Philosophy - Its Theoretical Structure). *Risô* (Tôkyô), vol. 24, 1926, 84-95.

5151    Satô, Keiji. *Genshôgaku-Gaisetsu* (Introduction Into Phenomenology). Tôkyô, 1929, 293-340.

5152    Satô, Keiji. "Kiso-teki Sonzairon no Rikai" (The Impact of the Fundamental-Ontology). *Risô* (Tôkyô), vol. 16, 1930, 84-95.

5153    Satô, Keiji. "Haideggâ-Hihan, sono Rironkeitai ni tsuite" (Critic on Heidegger. On the Structure of His Theory). *Risô* (Tôkyô), vol. 24, April 1931.

5154    Satô, Keiji. *Haideggâ* (Heidegger). Tôkyô, 1943.

5155    Satô, Keiji. "Geijutsu no Honshitsu; Haideggâ no Geijutsuron" (The Nature of the Fine Arts; Heidegger's Theory of Art). *Waseda Daigaku Daigakuin Bungaku Kenkyû Kiyô* (Tôkyô), vol. 2, 1956, 1-17.

5156    Satô, Keiji. "Hanasu koto to Kiku koto; Haideggâ no Shii-ron" (Speaking, Hearing; Thinking in Heidegger). *Philosophia* (Tôkyô), vol. 35, 1958, 1-29.

5157    Satô, Keiji. "Haideggâ ni okeru 'Sonzai' ni tsuite" (On the Notion of 'Being' in Heidegger). *Risô* (Tôkyô), vol. 305, October 1958.

5158    Satô, Keiji. *Geijutsu no Honshitsu, Haideggâ no Geijutsu-Ron* (The Nature of Art. Heidegger's Discussion of Art). Wasedadaigaku-Daigakuin-Bungakukenkyuka-Kiyô, Tôkyô, 1959.

5159    Satô, Keiji. "Genshôgakuteki Hôhô, Fussâru to Haideggâ." (The Phenomenological Method. Husserl and Heidegger). *Risô* (Tôkyô), vol. 341, 1961.

5160    Satô, Keiji. *Haideggâ no Tetsugaku, Tenkai no Mondai o Chûsin ni shite* (The Philosophy of Heidegger. 'Turning' Regarded as a Fundamental Problem). Tôkyô, 1962.

5161    Satô, Keiji. "Zen ka Jôdo da - Haideggâ saikin no Kangaekata" ('Zen' or 'Jôdo' - Heidegger's Way of Thinking). *Risô* (Tôkyô), vol. 356, 1963, 49-57.

5162    Satô, Keiji. "Kyosei Chi ni otsu Haideggâ" (A Great Star Fell; Heidegger). *Jitsuzonshugi* (Tôkyô), vol. 77, 1976, 142-147.

5163    Satomi, Tatsurô. "Kami no Shi to Jinshin no Shi no atoni" (After the Death of God and the God of Mankind). *Risô* (Tôkyô), vol. 457, June 1971, 47-61.

5164    Savignano, Armando. "Il problema della salvezza nella filosofia dell'esistenza in Martin Heidegger." *Incontri Culturali* (Roma), vol. 9, 1976, 216-222.

5165    Savignano, Armando. *Psicologismo e giudizio filosofico in M. Heidegger - X. Zubiri - J. Maréchal.* (Centro internazionale di studi di filosofia della religione. Saggi, 11). Padova: La Garangola, 1976, 253 p.

5166    Savignano, Armando. Rev. of *La dottrina delle categorie e del significato in Duns Scoto,* by Martin Heidegger. Ed. Albino Babolin. 1974, xxvi-261. *Sapienza* (Roma), vol. 29, 1976, 237-245.

5167    Savioz, R. "Conférence de Martin Heidegger à Zürich 5. Nov.1951." *Revue de Theologie et de Philosophie* (Lausanne), vol. 1, 1951, 287-300.

5168    Savoini, G. "Studi sull'esistenzialismo in America." *Rivista di Filosofia* (Torino), vol. 61, 1970, 405-418.

5169    Sawicki, F. "Pojecie i zagadnienie nicoáci u Heideggera" (The Notion of Non-Being and Its Problem in Heidegger). *Roczniki Filozoficzne* (Lublin), vol. 4, 1954. (In Polish). [Summary: The Problem of Nothingness: Heidegger's View, 137.]

5170    Sawicki, F. "Pojecie i zagadnienie nicosci u Heidegger." (The Problem of Nothingness: Heidegger's View). *Rocznik filozoficzne* (Lublin), vol. 4, 1955, 125-137. (Poln. with English Summary).

5171    Scanlon, J. D. "The Epoche and Phenomenological Anthropology." *Research in Phenomenology* (Pittsburgh), vol. 2, 1972, 95-109.

5172    Scannone, J. C. "Un tercer Heidegger?" *Stomata. Ciencia y Fe* (San Miguel, Argentina), vol. 24, 1968, 15-21.
        [Rev. by E. Landolt in *Gelassenheit di Martin Heidegger.* Milano, 1967.]

5173    Scannone, J. C. "Dios en el pensamiento de Martin Heidegger." *Stromata, Ciencia y Fe* (San Miguel, Argentina), vol. 25, 1969, 63-77.

5174    Scannone, J. C. Rev. of *Zur Sache des Denkens,* by Martin Heidegger. Tübingen, 1969. *Stromata, Ciencia y Fe* (San Miguel, Argentina), vol. 9, 1970, 435-436.

5175    Scannone, J. C. "Ansencia y presencia de dios en el pensamiento de hoy." *Stromata* (San Miguel, Argentina), vol. 27, 1971, 207-215.

5176    Scannone, J. C. "Reflexiones acerca del tema 'Hegel y Heidegger'." *Stromata. Ciencia y Fe* (San Miguel, Argentina), vol. 27, 1971, 381-402.

5177    Scaravelli, L. "Il problema speculativo di Heidegger." *Studi Germanici* (Firenze), vol. 1, 1935, 178-199.

5178    Sciacca, M. F. *La filosofia oggi. Dalle origini romantiche della filosofia contemporanea ai problemi attuali.* Milano, 1945, (specifically pages 221-239).

5179    Schacht, Richard L. "Husserlian and Heideggerian Phenomenology." *Philosophical Studies* (Dordrecht), vol. 23, 1972, 293-314.

5180 Schadewaldt, Wolfgang. "Der neue deutsche Student." *Freiburger Studenten-Zeitung* 7.Semester (14), no. 6, July 1933, 1 f. Rpt. in *Nachlese zu Heidegger,* by G. Schneeberger. Bern, 1962, 94-97.

5181 Schadewaldt, Wolfgang. "Odysseus-Abenteuer. Aus einer gesprächsweisen homerischen Improvisation über Irrfahrer-Angelegenheiten." In *Martin Heideggers Einfluss auf die Wissenschaften. Aus Anlass seines sechzigsten Geburtstages verfasst.* Bern, 1949, 94-121.

5182 Schadewaldt, Wolfgang. "Pindars zehnte nemeische Ode." In *Martin Heidegger zum 70. Geburtstag.* Festschrift/Pfullingen, 1959, 252-263.

5183 Schadewaldt, Wolfgang. "Antikes Drama auf dem Theater heute." In *Martin Heidegger zum 80. Geburtstag am 26.September 1969.* Pfullingen, 1970, 48 p.

5184 Schadewaldt, Wolfgang. "Amphibolie des Worts." In *Erinnerung an Martin Heidegger,* by Günther Neske. Pfullingen: Verlag Günther Neske, 1977, 215-216.

5185 Schaeffler, Richard. "Martin Heidegger und die Frage nach der Technik." *Zeitschrift für philosophische Forschung* (Meisenheim/Glan), vol. 9, 1955, 116-127.

5186 Schaeffler, Richard. *Die Struktur der Geschichtszeit.* Frankfurt, 1963, 571 p., (specifically pages 295-353, passim).

5187 Schaeffler, Richard. *Wege zu einer Ersten Philosophie.* Frankfurt, 1964, 229 p., (specifically pages 99-111).

5188 Schaeffler, Richard. *Frömmigkeit des Denkens. Martin Heidegger und die katholische Theologie.* Darmstadt: Wissenschaftliche Buchgesellschaft, 1978, xiii-160 p.

5189 Schaerer, R. Rev. of *Qu'est-ce que la philosophie?* by Martin Heidegger. Paris, 1957. *Revue de Théologie et de Philosophie* (Lausanne), Ser.3, Bd 8, 1958, 74-75.

5190 Schain, Kathryn Ann. *Descriptive Ontology and Transcendental Philosophy: Heidegger and Kant.* Phil. Diss. Vanderbilt Univ. 465 p. *Dissertation Abstracts International,* vol. 39/06-A, 3637.

5191 Schajowicz, L. "La experiencia de la Sagrado Notas sobre Heidegger." *Dialogos* (Rio Pedras, Puerto Rico), vol. 13, no. 32, 1978, 7-18.

5192 Schapel, E. "Prolegomena zu einer triadischen Metaphysik." *Salzburger Jahrbuch für Philosophie* (Salzburg), vol. 21-22, 1976/77, 135-162.

5193 Schaper, E. "Saying and Showing in Heidegger and Wittgenstein." *The Journal of the British Society for Phenomenology* (New York), vol. 3, 1972, 36-41.

5194 Scharff, Robert Caesar. "On 'Existentialist' Readings of Heidegger." *Southwestern Journal of Philosophy* (West Lindsey/Norman), vol. 2, 1971, 7-20.

5195   Scharff, Robert Caesar. Rev. of *On Time and Being,* by Martin Heidegger. Trans. Jean Stambaugh. 1972, 84. *The Southwestern Journal of Philosophy* (Norman), vol. 4, no. 3, 1973, 191-195.

5196   Scharff, Robert Caesar. *'Erlebnis' and 'Existenz'. Dilthey and Heidegger on the Approach to Human Experience.* Phil. Diss. Northwestern Univ. 1970. Ann Arbor, Michigan: University Microfilms, 1977, viii-404. [Order No. 71-1964] *Dissertation Abstract International,* vol. 31/07-A, 3603.

5197   Scharff, Robert Caesar. "Heidegger's Path of Thinking." In *The Question of Being: East-West Perspectives.* Ed. M. Sprung. University Park, 1978, 67-92.

5198   Schefer, A. *Das Sein und die Geschichte.* Winterthur, 1961, 208 p.

5199   Scheler, Max. "Anmerkungen zu Heidegger und zur 'Sein un Zeit'." *Max Scheler, Gesammelte Werke* (Bern/München), vol. 9, 1976, 254-340.

5200   Scheler, Max. "Reality and Resistance: [On *Being and Time,* Section 43]." Trans. Thomas J. Sheehan. *Listening. Journal of Religion and Culture* (River Forest, Illinois), vol. 12, no. 3, 1977, 61-73.

5201   Scheler, Max. "Iz manjih rukopisa o *Bivstva i vremena* (1927)." Trans. Dragan Stojanovic. In *Rani Hajdeger - Recepcija i kritika Bivstva i vremena,* by Dragan Stojanovic and Danilo Basta (eds.). (Biblioteka Zodijak). Beograd, 1979, 25-38.

5202   Scheltens, G. "De middeleeuwse illuminatieleer en het denken van Heidegger." *Tijdschrift voor filosofie* (Leuven), vol. 31, 1969, 418-440.

5203   Scheltens, G. "Heidegger y la creecia en Dios." *Verdad y Vida* (Madrid), vol. 19, 1961, 145-150.

5204   Scheltens, G. "Sein und Denken. Ein Werk über Heidegger." *Franziskanische Studien* (Werl/Westf.), vol. 48, 1966, 166-176.

5205   Scheltens, G. "Heidegger und die thomistische Metaphysik." *Wissenschaft und Weisheit* (Düsseldorf), vol. 34, 1967, 158 ff.

5206   Scherer, G. "Der Begriff des Seins bei Martin Heidegger." *Die Kirche in der Welt* (Münster), vol. 6, 1953, 21-26.

5207   Scherer, M. "Martin Heidegger und der wahre Thomismus." *Wort und Wahrheit* (Wien), vol. 4, 1949, 680-686.

5208   Schérer, R. "Besuch bei Heidegger." *Wort und Wahrheit* (Wien), vol. 2, 1947, 780-781.

5209   Schérer, R. *Martin Heidegger.* Paris: Ed. Seghers, 1973.

5210   Schérer, R., and A. L. Kelkel. *Heidegger ou l'experience de la pensée-Présentation.* (Biographie, bibliographie). (Philosophes de tous les temps, 86). Paris: Ed. Seghers, 1973, 190 p. [Spanish trans. by Bartolomé Parera Galmes. Madrid: Edaf, 1975, 304 p.]

5211   Scherwatzky. "Philosophie und Theologie." Rev. of *Sein und Zeit,* by Martin Heidegger. 1927. *Monatsblätter für den evangelischen Religionsunterricht,* vol. 24, 1931, 81-89.

5212　　Schiavone, M. Rev. of *Was ist Metaphysik?* by Martin Heidegger. 1929. [Italian trans. 1953] *Rivista di filosofia neo-scolastica* (Milano), vol. 47, 1955, 86-88.

5213　　Schilling, K. Rev. of *Kant und das Problem der Metaphysik,* by Martin Heidegger. 1929. *Göttingische Gelehrte Anzeigen* (Göttingen), vol. 193, 1930, 337-352.

5214　　Schilling, K. Rev. of *Holzwege,* by Martin Heidegger. Frankfurt, 1950. *Archiv für Rechts und Sozialphilosophie* (Bern/München), vol. 38, 1950, 406-411.

5215　　Schilling, K. "Heideggers Interpretation der Philosophiegeschichte. Bemerkungen anlässlich des Erscheinens der 'Einführung in die Metaphysik' 1953." *Archiv für Rechts und Sozialphilosophie* (Meisenheim/Glan), vol. 41, 1955, 399-421.

5216　　Schimansky, St. "On Meeting a Philosopher." *Partisan Review* (New York), vol. 15, 1948, 506-509.

5217　　Schirbel, P. "Heidegger und die volkstümliche Bildung?" *Pädagogische Rundschau* (Ratingen), vol. 10, 1954/55, 433-441, 481-489.

5218　　Schirmacher, Wolfgang. "Heideggers Redikalkritik der Technik als gesellschaftlicher Handlungsentwurf." In *Proceedings of the XVth World Congress of Philosophy.* Vol. I: Philosophy and science. Morality and culture. Technology and man. Sofia: Sofia Press Production Centre, 1973, 383-387.

5219　　Schirmacher, Wolfgang. Rev. of *Revolution und Kehre,* by Reinhart Klemens Maurer. 1975. *Philosophischer Literaturanzeiger* (Meisenheim), vol. 30, 1977, 8-11.

5220　　Schirmacher, Wolfgang. "Uneinsichtige Menschen brauchen die Wahrheitsdroge Philosophie." *Deutsches Allgemeines Sonntagsblatt* (Hamburg), no. 38, 17 September 1978, 1978, 11.

5221　　Schirmacher, Wolfgang. "Heidegger sah sich als Vorläufer eines Grösseren." *Bremer Nachrichten* (Bremen), 25 September 1979, 9.

5222　　Schirmacher, Wolfgang. "Über das Ende hinaus zu einem anderen Anfang. Die zukunftweisende Bedeutung des Philosophen Martin Heidegger, der 90 Jahre alt geworden wäre." *Mannheimer Morgen* (Mannheim), no. 225, 28 September 1979, 38.

5223　　Schissler, Ingeborg. "The Methodological Significance of Anguish in Heidegger's Existential Analysis." (In Serbocroat). *Delo* (Beograd), vol. 23, no. 12, 1977, 151-162.

5224　　Schlawin, H. "Heideggers Überwindung der Metaphysik." *Zeitschrift für philosophische Forschung* (Meisenheim/Glan/Wien), vol. 8, 1954, 585-595.

5225　　Schlette, H. R. "Zwischen Respekt und Distanz. Zu Martin Heideggers Denken." *Publik,* no. 39, v.26.9.1969, 22.

5226　　Schlier, Heinrich. "Meditationen über den johannischen Begriff der Wahrheit." In *Martin Heidegger zum 70. Geburtstag.* Festschrift/Pfullingen, 1959, 195-203.

5227    Schlier, Heinrich. "Denken im Nachdenken." In *Erinnerung an Martin Heidegger,* by Günther Neske. Pfullingen: Verlag Günther Neske, 1977, 217-221.

5228    Schlüter, Jochen. *Heidegger und Parmenides.* Bonn, 1980, X, 397 p.

5229    Schmidt, Alfred. "Existential-Ontologie und historischer Materialismus bei Herbert Marcuse." *Antworten auf Herbert Marcuse.* Ed. J. Habermas. Frankfurt, 1968.

5230    Schmidt, Alfred. "Herrschaft des Subjekts. Über Heideggers Marx-Interpretation." In *Martin Heidegger. Fragen an sein Werk.* Ein Symposium. (Universal-Bibliothek, 9873). Stuttgart: Reclam, 1977, 54-65.

5231    Schmidt, Gerhardt. "Naturalismus und Realismus." In *Martin Heidegger zum 70. Geburtstag.* Festschrift/Pfullingen, 1959, 264-275.

5232    Schmidt, Gerhard. *The Concept of Being in Hegel and Heidegger.* (Abhandlungen zur Philosophie, Psychologie und Pädagogik, 116). Bonn: Bouvier Verlag Herbert Grundmann, 1977, x-192. *Dissertation Abstracts International,* vol. 36/06-A, 3773.

5233    Schmidt, H. "Der Existentialismus und Heideggers Frage nach dem Sein." *Zeitwende. Die neue Furche* (Hamburg), vol. 27, 1956, 542-547.

5234    Schmidt, Martin. "Die Zusammenarbeit von Martin Heidegger und Rudolf Bultmann unter konfessionskundlichem Gesichtspunkt." *Materialdienst des konfessionskundlichen Instituts Bensheim* (Darmstadt), vol. 28, no. 3, 1977, 45-51.

5235    Schmitt, Richard. "Phenomenology and Metaphysics." *Journal of Philosophy* (New York), vol. 59, 1962, 421-428.

5236    Schmitt, Richard. Rev. of *An Introduction to Metaphysics,* by Martin Heidegger. *The Philosophical Review* (Ithaca), vol. 69, 1960, 553-555.

5237    Schmitt, Richard. "Heidegger's Analysis of 'Tool'." *The Monist* (La Salle), vol. 49, 1965, 70-86.

5238    Schmitt, Richard. "Can Heidegger be Understood?" *Inquiry,* vol. 10, 1967, 53-73.

5239    Schmitt, Richard. *Martin Heidegger on Being Human. An Introduction to Sein und Zeit.* New York, 1969, 274 p.

        [Rev. by P. Emad in *Philosophischer Literaturanzeiger* (Meisenheim/Glan), vol. 23, 1970, 212-215.]

        [Rev. by St. A. Erickson in *Journal of the History of Philosophy* (Berkeley), vol. 10, no. 4, 1972, 491-492.]

        [Rev. by E. Feist Hirsch in *Journal of the History of Philosophy* (Berkeley), vol. 9, no. 3, 1971, 400-403.]

5240    Schmitt, Richard. "Martin Heidegger on Being Human. An Introduction to 'Sein und Zeit'." In *Studies in Philosophy.* Gloucester, Massachusetts: Peter Smith, 1976, 274 p.

5241    Schneeberger, Guido. *Ergänzungen zu einer Heidegger-Bibliographie.* Mit vier Beilagen und einer Bildtafel. Bern, 1959, 28 p. [Nachdruck Bern 1960]

5242    Schneeberger, Guido. *Nachlese zu Heidegger. Dokumente zu seinem Leben und Denken.* Mit zwei Bildtafeln. Bern, 1962, XVI, 288 p.

5243    Schneider, Herbert W. "Hegel, Heidegger, and 'Experience' - a Study in Translation." *Journal of the History of Philosophy* (La Jolla, California), vol. 10, no. 3, 1972, 347-350.

        [Rev. of *Hegel's Concept of Experience,* by Martin Heidegger. 1970; and *A Commentar on Heidegger's Being and Time,* by Gelven. 1970.]

5244    Schneider, Robert O. "Husserl and Heidegger: An Essay on the Question of Intentionality." *Philosophy Today* (Celina, Ohio), vol. 21, 1977, 368-375.

5245    Schöfer, Erasmus. *Die Sprache Heideggers.* Pfullingen, 1961, 312 p.

        [Rev. in *Foundations of Language.* 1967, 299.]

5246    Schöfer, Erasmus. "Heidegger's Language: Metalogical Forms of Thought and Grammatical Specialties." In *On Heidegger and Language.* Ed. J. J. Kockelmans. Evanston, Illinois, 1972, 281-301.

5247    Schöfer, Erasmus. "Un créateur de langue." *Magazine Littéraire* (Paris), no. 117, 1976, 21.

5248    Schoenborn, Alexander von. *Being, Man, and Questioning: An Ontological Prolegomena to Heidegger's Existentialism.* Phil. Diss. Tulan Univ. New Orleans 1971 329 p. *Dissertation Abstracts International,* vol. 32/05-A, 2750.

5249    Schoenborn, Alexander von. "Heideggerian Everydayness." *Southwestern Journal of Philosophy* (Norman, Oklahoma), vol. 3, 1972, 103-110.

5250    Schoenborn, Alexander von. "Heidegger's Question: An Exposition." In *Martin Heidegger: In Europe and America,* by Edward Goodwin Ballard and Charles E. Scott (eds.). The Hague, 1973, 47-54.

5251    Schoenborn, Alexander von. "More Heideggeriana: Whether and Whither." *Review of Existential Psychology and Psychiatry,* vol. 12, 1973, 169-183.

5252    Schoenborn, Alexander von. *Being, Man, and Questioning. An Ontological Prolegomenon to Heidegger's Existentialism.* Phil. Diss. Tulane Univ. 1971. Ann Arbor, Michigan; London: University Microfilms International, 1977, iv-251.

5253    Schoenborn, Alexander von. Rev. of *Die Grundprobleme der Phänomenologie,* by Martin Heidegger. *The Southwestern Journal of Philosophy* (Norman, Oklahoma), vol. 9, no. 3, 1978, 143-146.

5254    Schoeps, H.-J. "Tragische Existenz. Bemerkungen zu einem Buch über die Philosophie Martin Heideggers." *Philosophia* (Belgrad), vol. 2, 1937, 142-145.

        [Rev. of *Tragische Existenz,* by Delp. Freiburg, 1935.]

5255    Schoeps, H.-J. *Der Mensch in der Existenzphilosophie und Ontologie.* Heidegger, Jaspers, N. Hartmann). (Was ist der Mensch. Philosophische

Anthropologie als Geistesgeschichte der neuesten Zeit). Berlin/Frankfurt, 1960, 352 p.

5256 Scholler, Heinrich. "Interpretazione del diritto nello correnti contempurantee della filosofia." *Rivista Internazionale di Filosofia del Diritto* (Milano), vol. 50, 1973, 498-513.

5257 Schott, E. *Die Endlichkeit des Daseins nach Martin Heidegger.* Berlin, 1930, 20 p.

5258 Schottlaender, R. "Die Krise der Ethik als Wissenschaft." *Zeitschrift für philosophische Forschung* (Meisenheim/Glan), vol. 6, 1951/52, 17-41, (specifically pages 17-18, und passim).

5259 Schottlaender, R. "Heideggers Nietzsche-Buch." Rev. of *Nietzsche Bd I-II*, by Martin Heidegger. Pfullingen, 1961. *Deutsche Zeitschrift für Philosophie* (Berlin), vol. 11, 1963, 865-874.

5260 Schrader, George Alfred. "Heidegger's Ontology of Human Existence." *The Review of Metaphysics* (New Haven, Connecticut), vol. 10, 1956/57, 35-56.

5261 Schrag, Calvin Orville. *The Problem of Existence: Kierkegaard's Descriptive Analysis of the Self and Heidegger's Phenomenological Ontology of 'Dasein'.* Phil. Diss. Harvard Univ. 1957.

5262 Schrag, Calvin Orville. "Phenomenology, Ontology and History in the Philosophy of Heidegger." *Revue Internationale de Philosophie* (Bruxelles), vol. 12, 1958, 117-132.

5263 Schrag, Calvin Orville. "Whitehead and Heidegger: Process Philosophy Existential Philosophy." *Dialectica* (Neuchâtel), vol. 13, 1959, 42-54.

5264 Schrag, Calvin Orville. "Introduction." *The Phenomenology of Internal Time Consciousness,* by E. Husserl. Ed. Martin Heidegger. Trans. J. S. Churchill. Bloomington, Indiana Univ. Press, 1964.

5265 Schrag, Calvin Orville. "Heidegger and Cassirer on Kant." *Kant-Studien* (Bonn), vol. 58, 1967, 87-100.

5266 Schrag, Calvin Orville. "Re-Thinking Metaphysics." *Heidegger and the Quest for Truth.* Ed. M. S. Frings. Chicago, 1968, 106-125.

5267 Schrag, Calvin Orville. *Experience and Being.* Evanston, Illinois: Northwestern Univ. Press, 1969.

5268 Schrag, Calvin Orville. "Heidegger on Repetition and Historical Understanding." *Philosophy East and West* (Honolulu), vol. 20, 1970, 287-295.

5269 Schrag, Calvin Orville. "The Transvaluation of Aesthetics and the Work of Art." [Heidegger issue] *The Southwestern Journal of Philosophy* (Norman, Oklahoma), vol. 4, no. 3, 1973, 109-124.

5270 Schrey, H.-H. "Die Bedeutung der Philosophie Martin Heideggers für die Theologie." In *Martin Heideggers Einfluss auf die Wissenschaften.* Bern, 1949, 9-21.

5271    Schrey, H.-H. *Dialogisches Denken.* Darmstadt, 1970, 149 p., (specifically pages 30 ff, 47 ff, passim).

5272    Schrimpf, H. J. "Hölderlin, Heidegger und die Literaturwissenschaft." *Euphorion* (Heidelberg), vol. 51, 1957, 308-323.

5273    Schroeder, William Ralph. *Others: An Examination of Sartre and His Predecessors.* Volume I: Husserl, Hegel, Heidegger. Volume II: Sartre. Phil. Diss. Univ. of Michigan 1979 882 p. *Dissertation Abstracts International,* vol. 40/02-A, 906.

5274    Schühle, Siegfried. "Gedenkansprache." In *Gedenkschrift der Stadt Messkirch an ihren Sohn und Ehrenbürger Professor Martin Heidegger.* Foreword and postscript by Siegfried Schuhle. Messkirch: Stadt Messkirch, 1977, 10-12.

5275    Schühle, Siegfried. Foreword and postscript to *Gedenkschrift der Stadt Messkirch an ihren Sohn und Ehrenbürger Professor Martin Heidegger.* Messkirch: Stadt, Messkirch, 1977.

5276    Schülli, E. "Philosophie als Hermeneutik des Daseins." *Franziskanische Studien* (Paderborn), vol. 53, 1971, 59-71.

5277    Schürmann, Reiner. "La différence symbolique." *Cahiers Internationaux de Symbolisme,* vol. 211, 1972, 51-77.

5278    Schürmann, Reiner. "Heidegger and Meister Eckhart on Releasement." *Research in Phenomenology* (Pittsburgh), vol. 3, 1973, 95-119.

5279    Schürmann, Reiner. "Trois penseurs du délaissement: Maître Eckhart, Heidegger, Suzuki, I." *Journal of the History of Philosophy* (Claremont), vol. 12, 1974, 455-477.

5280    Schürmann, Reiner. "Il ya dans le poème..." (Hölderlin and René Char). *Cahiers Internationaux de Symbolisme,* vol. 25, 1974, 99-118.

5281    Schürmann, Reiner. "Trois penseurs du délaissement: Maître Eckhart, Heidegger, Suzuki, II." *Journal of the History of Philosophy* (Claremont), vol. 13, 1975, 43-60.

5282    Schürmann, Reiner. "Situating René Char. Hölderlin, Heidegger, Char, and the 'There Is'." *Boundary - 2* [Special issue on Heidegger and poetry], February 1976, 513-534.

5283    Schürmann, Reiner. "Political Thinking in Heidegger." *Social Research* (Albany), vol. 45, no. 1, 1978, 191-221.

5284    Schürmann, Reiner. "The Destruction of Metaphysics and Political Philosophy." *Philosophy and Phenomenological Research* (Buffalo, New York), 1979.

5285    Schürmann, Reiner. "Principles Precarious. The Origin of the Political in Heidegger." In *Heidegger. The Man and the Thinker,* by Thomas J. Sheehan (ed.). Chicago: Precendent Pub., 1979.

5286    Schürmann, Reiner. "Questioning the Foundation of Practical Philosophy." Followed by a debate with Prof. B. Dauenhauer. *Human Studies,* vol. I, 1979, 357-368.

5287    Schürmann, Reiner. "Anti-Humanism. Reflections on the Turn Towards the Post-Modern Epoch." *Man and World* (The Hague), vol. 12, no. 2, 1979, 160-177.

5288    Schürmann, Reiner. "Situating René Char: Hölderlin, Heidegger, Char and the 'There is'." In *Martin Heidegger and the Question of Literature*. Ed. William V. Spanos. Bloomington, Indiana/London: Indiana Univ. Press, 1979, 173-194.

5289    Schürmann, Reiner. "The Ontological Difference and Political Philosophy." *Philosophy and Phenomenological Research*, vol. 40, 1979, 99-122.

5289a   Schüssler, I. "Philosophie und Existenz bei Martin Heidegger." *Aquinas* (Roma), vol. 22, no. 2-3, 1979, 231-241.

5290    Schütz, Egon. "Didaktik als Besinnung. Anmerkungen zum Thema 'Sprach und Wirklichkeitsvergitterung' als Problem didaktischer Orientierung aus der Sicht Martin Heidegger." *Vierteljahresschrift für Wissenschaftliche Pädagogik* (Bochum), vol. 52, no. 4, 1976, 397-421.

5291    Schütz, P. "Was ist der Mensch? Bemerkungen zu Hölderlins und Heideggers Übersetzungen des grossen Antigonechores." *Neue deutsche Hefte. Beiträge zur europäischen Gegenwart* (Gütersloh), Hg. 3, 1956, 21-31.

5292    Schuhmann, Karl. "Zu Heidegger's Spiegel-Gespräch über Husserl." *Zeitschrift für Philosophische Forschung* (Schlehdorf/Kochelsee/Meisenheim/Glan), vol. 32, no. 4, 1978, 591-612.

5293    Schulmeister, Otto. "'Wach sein am Feuer der Nacht ' Zum Tod Martin Heideggers, des Denkers und Deuters." *Die Presse* (Wien), no. 8449, 29 May 1976, 7. (Jg. 3, 1976, Nr. 2).

5294    Schultz, U. *Das Problem des Schematismus bei Kant und Heidegger*. München, 1964, 195 p. [Phil. Diss. München v.26.3.1964.]

5295    Schulz, Walter. "Über den philosophiegeschichtlichen Ort Martin Heideggers." *Philosophische Rundschau* (Tübingen), vol. 1, Heft 1, 1953/54, 65-93, 211-232. Rpt. in *M. Heidegger*. Ed. O. Pöggeler. Köln/Berlin, 1969, 95-139.

Rev. of these Martin Heidegger Works:

[*Sein und Zeit*. 1927.]

[*Was ist Metaphysik?* 1929. 6th ed. 1951.]

[*Vom Wesen des Grundes*. 1929. 3rd ed. 1949.]

[*Die Selbstbehauptung des deutschen Universität*. 1933.]

[*Vom Wesen der Wahrheit*. 1st ed. 1943.]

[*Erläuterungen zu Hölderlins Dichtung*. 1st ed. 1944. 2nd enlarged ed. 1951.]

[*Über den Humanismus*. (1st ed in *Platons Lehre von der Wahrheit*. 1947). 2nd ed. 1949.]

[*Der Feldweg*. 1st ed. 1949. 3rd ed. 1953.]

[*Holzwege*. 1st ed. 1950. 2nd unaltered ed. 1952.]

[*Das Ding.* 1951.]

[*Bauen Wahnen Denken.* 1952.]

[*Was heisst Denken?* 1952.]

5296    Schulz, Walter. *Der Gott der neuzeitlichen Metaphysik.* Pfullingen, 1957, 119 p.

5297    Schulz, Walter. "Hegel und das Problem der Aufhebung der Metaphysik." In *Martin Heidegger zum 70. Geburtstag.* Festschrift/Pfullingen, 1959, 67-92.

5298    Schulz, Walter. "Heidegger, Martin." *Religion in Geschichte und Gegenwart.* (Handwörterbuch für Theologie und Religionswissenschaft). 3rd completely new revised ed. Tübingen, Bd III, 1959, 121-123.

5299    Schulz, Walter. *Philosophie in der veränderten Welt.* Pfullingen, 1972, 902 p., (specifically pages 292-301 und ff).

5300    Schulz, Walter. "God of the Philosophers in Modern Metaphysics." *Man and World* (The Hague), vol. 6, 1973, 353-371.

5301    Schulz, Walter. "... als ob Heraklit daneben steht." In *Erinnerung an Martin Heidegger,* by Günther Neske (ed.). Pfullingen: Verlag Günther Neske, 1977, 223-228.

5302    Schulz, Uwe. Rev. of *Logik. Die Frage nach der Wahrheit,* by Martin Heidegger. 1976. *Deutsche Zeitung- Christ und Welt* (Stuttgart), 20 August 1976.

5303    Schulze, F. "'Existenzphilosophie'. Zu Topographie von Heideggers Fundamentalontologie und Jaspers Transzendental-Philosophie." *Evangelisch-lutherische Kirchen-zeitung* (München), vol. 3, 1949, 155-157.

5304    Schulze, W. A. Rev. of *Einführung in die Metaphysik,* by Martin Heidegger. Tübingen, 1953. *Reformierte Kirchenzeitung* (Neukirchen), vol. 96, Heft 17/18, Theol. Lit. Beilage, 1955.

5305    Schulze, W. A. Rev. of *Was heisst Denken?* by Martin Heidegger. Tübingen, 1954. *Deutsches Pfarrerblatt* (Essen), vol. 55, 1955, 524-525.

5306    Schulze, W. A. Rev. of *Was heisst Denken?* by Martin Heidegger. Tübingen, 1954. *Zeitschrift für Religions und Geistesgeschichte* (Köln), vol. 8, 1956, 189.

5307    Schulz-Seitz, R.-E. "'Bevestigter Gesang'. Bemerkungen zu Heideggers Hölderlin-Auslegung." *Durchblicke.* Ed. V. Klostermann. Frankfurt, 1970, 63-96.

5308    Schuhmann, K. *Die Fundamentalbetrachtung der Phänomenologie. Zum Weltproblem in der Philosophie Edmund Husserls.* Den Haag, 1971, XLVII, 201 p.

5309    Schuurman, I. E. "Over anti-techniek en totale technokratie." *Philosophia Reformata* (Kampen), vol. 37, 1972, 156-173.

5310    Schuwer, André. "Prolegomena to Time and Being. Truth and Time." In *Heidegger and the Path of Thinking.* Ed. J. Sallis. Pittsburgh, 1970, 169-190.

5311    Schuwer, André. "Nature and the Holy: On Heidegger's Interpretation of Hölderlin's Hymn 'Wie wenn am Feiertage'." *Research in Phenomenology* (Pittsburgh), vol. 7, 1977, 225-237.

5312    Schuwer, André. "De zijnsleer van Martin Heidegger." *Studia Catholica* (Nijmegen), vol. 26, 1951, 78-87.

5313    Schuwer, André. "Intorno ai presupposti della demitizzazione 'Wie kommt der Gott in die Metaphysik'." (Heidegger). *Archives de Philosophie* (Paris), 1/2, 1961, 129-146.

5314    Schwan, Alexander. *Der Ort der Gegenwart in der Eschatologie des Seins. Eine Studie zur Ortsbestimmung der Gegenwart im 'neuen Denken' Heideggers.* Phil. Diss. Freiburg 1959 184 p.

5315    Schwan, Alexander. *Die politische Philosophie im Denken Heidegger.* (Ordo Politicus, 2). Köln/Opladen, 1965, 206 p.

5316    Schwan, Alexander. "Martin Heidegger, Politik und praktische Philosophie. Zur Problematik neuerer Heidegger-Literatur." *Philosophisches Jahrbuch* (München), vol. 81, 148-171.

5317    Schwarz, J. "Der Philosoph als Etymologe." *Philosophische Studien* (Berlin), vol. 1, 1949, 47-61, (specifically page 58 ff).

5318    Schwarz, T. "Der Existentialismus Martin Heideggers." *Filosofická Casopis* (Prag), vol. 18, 1970, 730-756.

5319    Schwarz, W. Rev. of *Die Frage nach dem Ding*, by Martin Heidegger. Tübingen, 1962. *Philosophy and Phenomenological Research* (Buffalo, New York), vol. 24, 1963/64, 449-451.

5320    Schweppenhäuser, H. "Studien über die Heideggersche Sprachtheorie." *Archiv für Philosophie* (Stuttgart), vol. 7, 1957, 279-324.

5321    Schweppenhäuser, H. "Studien über die Heideggersche Sprachtheorie III: Sprache und Sein." *Archiv für Philosophie* (Stuttgart), vol. 8, 1958, 116-144.

5322    Schwerner, Armand. "Three Poems." In *Martin Heidegger and the Question of Literature.* Ed. William V. Spanos. Bloomington, Indiana/London: Indiana Univ. Press, 1979, 149-153.

5323    Schyle, Hans Joachim. "Ein Denker in dürftiger Zeit. Nöte der Menschen als zentrales Thema." *Kölner Stadt-Anzeiger* (Köln), no. 114/9, 27 May 1976.

5324    Scott, Charles E. "Heidegger's Question About Thought." *Southern Journal of Philosophy,* vol. 2, Winter 1964, 174-179.

5325    Scott, Charles E. *Martin Heidegger's Concept of Man's Presence to Himself: Toward a Reconsideration of Religious Awareness.* Phil. Diss. Yale Univ. 1965 173 p. *Dissertation Abstracts International,* vol. 26/04, 2269.

5326    Scott, Charles E. "Heidegger, the Absence of God, and Faith." *The Journal of Religion* (Chicago), vol. 46, 1966, 365-373.

5327    Scott, Charles E. "Heidegger's Attempt to Communicate a Mystery." *Philosophy Today* (Celina, Ohio), vol. 10, 1966, 132-141.

5328    Scott, Charles E. "Notes and Observations. Heidegger Reconsidered. A Response to Professor Jonas." *The Harvard Theological Review* (Cambridge), vol. 59, 1966, 175-185. [vgl.Nr.1.1971.]

5329    Scott, Charles E. "Truth Without Dialectic." *Journal of the American Academy of Religion* (Philadelphia), vol. 38, 1970, 304-309.

5330    Scott, Charles E. "Heidegger and Consciousness." *The Southern Journal of Philosophy* (Memphis), 1970, 355-372. Rpt. in *Martin Heidegger: In Europe and America,* by Edward Goodwin Ballard and Charles E. Scott (eds.). The Hague, 1973, 91-108.

5331    Scott, Charles E. "Heidegger, Madness, and Well-Being." [Heidegger issue] *The Southwestern Journal of Philosophy* (Norman, Oklahoma), vol. 4, no. 3, 1973, 157-177.

5332    Scott, Charles E. "Daseinsanalysis: An Interpretation." *Philosophy Today,* vol. 19, Fall 1975, 182-197.

5333    Scott, Charles E. "Psychotherapy: Being and Being Many." *Review of Existential Psychology and Psychiatry* (Northwestern Univ., Evanston, Illinois), vol. 16, no. 1, 2, and 3, 1978/79.

5334    Seeberg, R. Rev. of *Die Kategorien- und Bedeutungslehre des Duns Scotus,* by Martin Heidegger. Tübingen, 1916. *Theologische Literaturzeitung* (Leipzig), vol. 43, 1918, 270.

5335    Seebohm, Thomas M. "Über die Möglichkeit konsequenzlogischer Kontrolle phänomenologischer Analysen." *Kant-Studien* (Bonn), vol. 63, 1972, 237-246.

5336    Seebohm, Thomas M. "The Problem of Hermeneutics in Recent Anglo-American Literature." (Part I and II). *Philosophy and Rhetoric* (Univ. Parc, Pennsylvania), vol. 10, no. 4, 1977, 263-275, 180-198.

5337    Seeburger, Francis Frey. *The Question of Being and the 'Reversal' of Thinking in the Works of Martin Heidegger.* Phil. Diss. Univ. of Colorado 1973. *Dissertation Abstracts International,* vol. 34/04-A, 1975.

5338    Seeburger, Francis Frey. "Heidegger and the Phenomenological Reduction." *Philosophy and Phenomenological Research* (Buffalo, New York), vol. 36, no. 2, 1975/76, 212-221.

5339    Sefler, George Francis. "Heidegger's Philosophy of Space." *Philosophy Today* (Celina, Ohio), vol. 17, 1973, 246-254.

5340    Sefler, George Francis. *Language and the World. A Methodological Structural Synthesis Within the Writings of Martin Heidegger and Ludwig Wittgenstein.* Atlantic Highlands, New Jersey: Humanities Press, 1974, xxxiii-228 p.

5341    Sefler, George Francis. *The Structure of Language and Its Relation to the World. A Methodological Study of the Writings of Martin Heidegger and Ludwig Wittgenstein.* Authorized facsimile of the dissertation of the Georgetown Univ. Phil. Diss. 1970 312. Ann Arbor, Michigan; London: University Microfilms International, 1978, viii-300. *Dissertation Abstracts International,* vol. 31/06-A, 2979.

5342    Seibert, Ch. H. *On Being and Space in Heidegger's Thinking.* Phil. Diss. De Paul Univ. Chicago 1972 308 p. *Dissertation Abstracts International,* vol. 33/07-A, 3718.

5343    Seidel, George J. *Martin Heidegger and the Pre-Socratics. An Introduction to His Thought.* Univ. of Nebraska Press, 1964, X-170.

5344    Seidel, George J. "Heidegger: Philosopher for Ecologists?" *Man and World* (Pittsburgh), vol. 4, 1971, 93-99.

5345    Seidel, George J. Rev. of *Schellings Abhandlung über das Wesen der menschlichen Freiheit,* by Martin Heidegger. 1971. *Studi Internazionali di Filosofia* (Torino), vol. 6, 1974, 170-173.

5346    Seidel, George J. "Heidegger on Schelling." *Studi Internazionali di Filosofia* (Torino), 1974, 170-174.

5347    Seidl, H. "Freiheit und Verantwortung aus heideggerscher Sicht." *Libertà e Responsibilità. XI. Convegno annuale di assistenti universitari di filosofia, promosso dal Centro di Studi Filosofici di Gallarate.* Padova, 1967, 147-150.

5348    Seidl, H. "Libertà e responsabilità in Heidegger." *Ethica* (Forli), vol. 6, 1967, 217-221.

5349    Seidle, Horst. "Zur Seinsfrage bei Aristoteles und Heidegger." *Zeitschrift für Philosophische Forschung* (Meisenheim/Glan), vol. 30, no. 2, 1976, 203-226.

5350    Seiffert, A. "Ernüchterung um das Nichts. Zur Besinnung auf den Realismus." *Zeitschrift für Philosophische Forschung,* vol. 5, 1950, 528-546.

5351    Seiffert, J. E. "Alienazione e dimenticanza dell'essere. Un Tentativo su Martin Heidegger." *Il Pensiero* (Milano), vol. 4, 1959, 360-377.

5352    Seiffert, J. E. "Entfremdung und Seinsvergessenheit. Ein Versuch über Martin Heidegger." *Il Pensiero* (Milano), vol. 4, 1959, 275-293.

5353    Seigfried, Hans. "Metaphysik un Seinvergessenheit." *Kant-Studien* (Bonn), vol. 61, 1970, 209-216.

5354    Seigfried, Hans. "Martin Heidegger - A Recollection." *Man and World* (Pittsburgh), vol. 3, 1970, 3-4.

5355    Seigfried, Hans. "Descriptive Phenomenology and Constructivism." *Philosophy and Phenomenological Research* (Buffalo, New York), vol. 37, 1976, 248-261.

5356    Seigfried, Hans. "Art and the Origin of Truth." *Man and World* (The Hague), vol. 11, no. 1-2, 1978, 45-58.

5357    Seigfried, Hans. "Heidegger's Longest Day: 'Being and Time' and the Sciences." *Philosophy Today* (Celina, Ohio), vol. 22, no. 4, 1978, 319-331.

5358    Seigfried, Hans. "Scientific Realism and Phenomenology." *Zeitschrift für Philosophische Forschung* (Schlehdorf/Kochelsee/Meisenheim/Glan), 1979.

5359    Seigfried, Hans. "Phenomenology, Hermeneutics and Poetry." *The Journal of the British Society for Phenomenology* (Manchester), vol. 16, 1979, 94-100.

5360 Sejima, Yutaka. "Haideggâ ni okeru U to Ningen no Honshitsu" (The Being and the Nature of Man in Heidegger). *Risô* (Tôkyô), vol. 319, Dezember 1959.

5361 Sekine, Nobuo. "Haideggâ 'Dôitsusei to Sabetsu'" (Heidegger's "Identität und Differenz"). *Philosophia* (Tôkyô), vol. 35, 1958, 151-154.

5362 Seligmann, R. "Sein oder Nichtsein? Zu Heidegger's Existenzphilosophie." *Sozialistische Monatshefte* (Berlin), Jg. 38, Bd 75, 1932, 432-441.

5363 Selle, Magr. H. de la. *Un duel à quatre. Saint Thomas, Kant, Bergson, Sartre.* (La Chapelle du Chêne). Vion, Sarthe, 1954, 62 p.

5364 Sellmair, J. "Menschenbild nach Blaise Pascal und Martin Heidegger." *Das Wort* (Regensburg), vol. 2, 1934, 10-19.

5365 Sendaydiego, Henry B. "Heideggerian Metaphysics, Logic and Emotionism." *Journal of the West Virginia Philosophical Society* (West Liberty), Fall 1973, 14-17.

5366 Sendaydiego, Henry B. "Applying Heidegger's 'Entschlossenheit' to a Political Matrix." *Journal of the West Virginia Philosophical Society* (West Liberty), Spring 1974, 15-17.

5367 Sendaydiego, Henry B. "Heidegger's Thoughts on the Aethetic." *Journal of the West Virginia Philosophical Society,* Spring 1976, 14-16.

5368 Sendaydiego, Henry B. "Heidegger on the Teaching-Learning Process." *Journal of the West Virginia Philosophical Society* (West Liberty), Fall 1976, 23-26.

5369 Sepich, J. R. "Existentialismo e historia." *Atti del congresso internazionale di filosofia, promosso dell'Istituto di Studi Filosofici, Roma 15-20 novembre 1946.* II. L'esistenzialismo. Milano, 1948, 437-451, (specifically pages 439-442 u.ö.).

5370 Sepich, J. R. "Situación de M. Heidegger en la filosofia." *Humanitas* (Tucumán), vol. 2, 1954, 15-113.

5371 Sepich, J. R. *La filosofia de ser y tiempo de M. Heidegger.* Buenos Aires, 1954, 528 p.

5372 Sera, Masuo. "Konkyo to Kongen; Raipunittsu, Haideggâ, Kôhen" (Ground and Origin; Leibniz, Heidegger, Cohen). *Tetsugaku-Ronshû* (Ôtani Daigaku, Kyôto), vol. 5, 1959, 1-17.

5373 Serra, Ordep. "Nota sobre o ensaio *Das Ding* de Martin Heidegger." *Revista brasileira de Filosofia* (Sao Paulo), vol. 27, no. 106, 1977, 185-188.

5374 Sessions, George. "Spinoza and Jeffers on Man in Nature." *Inquiry,* vol. 20, Winter 1977, 481-528.

5375 Seubert, K. Helen. *The Problem of Vision in Heidegger and Ancient Hindu Thought.* Phil. Diss. Pennsylvania State Univ. 1974. *Dissertation Abstracts International,* vol. 36/03-A, 1587.

5376 Seven, Friedrich. *Die Ewigkeit Gottes und die Zeitlichkeit des Menschen: e. Unters. d. Hermeneut. Funktion der. Zeit in Karl Barths Theologie der. Krisis u. im Seinsdenken Martin Heideggers.* (Göttinger theologische Arbeiten, 11). Göttingen: Vadenhoeck und Ruprecht, 1979, 126 p.

5377 Severino, Emanuele. *Heidegger e la metafisica.* Brescia, 1950, 437 p.

5378 Severino, Emanuele. "Recenti studi su Heidegger." *Rivista di filosofia neoscolastica* (Milano), vol. 45, 1953, 356-360.

5379 Severino, Emanuele. "Intervento." *Verifiche,* vol. 8, no. 1, 1979, 113-117.

5380 Seyppel, Joachim H. "A Comparative Study of Truth in Existentialism and Pragmatism." *The Journal of Philosophy* (Lancaster, Pennsylvania), vol. 50, 1953, 229-241, (specifically 232-236).

5381 Seyppel, Joachim H. Rev. of *Einführung in die Metaphysik,* by Martin Heidegger. 1953. *The Journal of Philosophy* (New York), vol. 51, 1954, 106-108.

5382 Seyppel, Joachim H. " A Criticism of Heidegger's Time Concept With Reference to Bergson's durée." *Revue Internationale de Philosophie* (Bruxelles), vol. 10, 1956, 503-508.

5383 Sezai, Yoshio. "Sonairon-teki Junkankôzô ni tsuite; 'Sein und Zeit' Kenkyû no ichi Shiron" (On the Ontological Circular Structure - Understanding Heidegger's 'Sein und Zeit'). *Nihon Daigaku Bungakubu Kenkyû-Nempô, Fukkan* (Tôkyô), vol. 1, 1951, 13-25.

5384 Sezai, Yoshio. "Sonzai no Bokujin, Haideggâ" (The Shepherd of Being, Heidegger). *Risô* (Tôkyô), vol. 247, Dezember 1953.

5385 Sezai, Yoshio. "Haideggâ, Tetsugaku to Shingaku tono Ketsugô wa Kanô de aruka" (Heidegger. Is it Possible that Philosophy and Theology Form an Alliance?) *Risô* (Tôkyô), vol. 250, März 1954.

5386 Sezai, Yoshio. "Haideggâ Tetsugaku no Gendaiteki Yûigisei to Muigisei" (The Significance and the Insignificance of Heidegger's Philosophy in the Present). *Risô* (Tôkyô), vol. 260, 1955, 59-61.

5387 Sezai, Yoshio. *Jitsuzon to Riron, Haideggâ no Jitsuzonron-Tetsugaku Josetsu* (Existence and Theory. Introduction Into Heidegger's Existential Philosophy). Tôkyô, 1955.

5388 Shahan, Robert W., ed. [Heidegger issue] *The Southwestern Journal of Philosophy* (Norman, Oklahoma), vol. 4, no. 3, 1973, 196 p.

5389 Shalom, A. Rev. of *The Question of Being,* by Martin Heidegger. 1959. *Les Etudes Philosophiques* (Paris), N.S. 15, 1960, 107.

5390 Shapiro, Gary. "The Owl of Minerva and the Colors of the Night." *Philosophy and Literature,* vol. 1, Fall 1977, 276-294.

5391 Shearson, William A. "The Common Assumptions of Existentialist Philosophy." *International Philosophical Quarterly,* vol. 15, July 1975, 131-147.

5392    Sheehan, Thomas J. "Heidegger: From Beingness to Time-Being." *Listening* (River Forest, Canada), vol. 8, 1973, 17-31.

5393    Sheehan, Thomas J. "Notes on a 'Lover's Quarrel': Heidegger and Aquinas." *Listening,* vol. 9, 1974, 137-143.

5394    Sheehan, Thomas J. "Heidegger, Aristotle and Phenomenology." *Philosophy Today* (Celina, Ohio), vol. 19, 1975, 87-94.

5395    Sheehan, Thomas J. Rev. of *M. Heidegger: In Europe and America.* Ed. E. G. Ballard and Charles E. Scott. 1973. *The Modern Schoolman* (St. Louis), vol. 53, 1975/76, 302-304.

5396    Sheehan, Thomas J. "Heidegger's Early Years. Fragments for a Philosophical Biography." *Listening. Journal of Religion and Culture* (River Forest, Illinois), vol. 12, no. 3, 1977, 3-20.

5397    Sheehan, Thomas J. "Getting to the Topic: The New Edition of *Wegmarken.* " *Research in Phenomenology* (Pittsburgh), vol. 7, 1977, 299-313.

5398    Sheehan, Thomas J. "Heidegger, the Man and the Thinker." [Foreword] *Listening. Journal of Religion and Culture* (River Forest, Illinois), vol. 12, no. 3, 1977, 1-2.

5399    Sheehan, Thomas J. "Heidegger's Interpretation of Aristotle: Dynamis and Ereignis." *Philosophy Research Archives,* vol. 4, no. 1253, 1978.

5400    Sheehan, Thomas J. "Tempo ed essere nelle lezioni di Heidegger del 1927." *Filosofia* (Torino), vol. 29, no. 3, 1978, 427-444.

5401    Sheehan, Thomas J. Rev. of *Vier Seminare,* by Martin Heidegger. *Review of Metaphysics* (Washington), vol. 32, 1978/79, 140-141.

5401a   Sheehan, Thomas J. Rev. of "Holzwege," by Martin Heidegger. Ed. Friedrich-Wilhelm von Herrmann. *Review of Metaphysics* (Washington), vol. 32, 1978/79, 546-548.

5402    Sheehan, Thomas J. "The 'Original Form' of Sein und Zeit: Heidegger's 'Der Begriff der Zeit' (1924)." *The Journal of the British Society for Phenomenology* (Manchester), vol. 10, no. 2, May 1979, 78-83.

5403    Sheehan, Thomas J. "Heidegger's Topic: Excess, Recess, Access." *Tijdschrift voor Filosofie* (Leuven), vol. 41, 1979, 615-635.

5404    Sheehan, Thomas J. "Heidegger's 'Introduction to the Phenomenology of Religion', 1920-21." *The Personalist,* vol. 55, 1979/80, 312-324.

5404a   Sheehan, Thomas J. "La stesura originale di *Sein und Zeit: Der Begriff der Zeit* (1924) di Heidegger." *L'Uomo, un segno* (Milano), vol. 3, no. 1-2, 1979, 111-121.

5405    Sheehan, Thomas J. "Cavear Lector: The New Heidegger." (Rev. of the first eight volumes of "Gesamtausgabe" in print). *The New York Review of Books,* 4 December 1980, 39-41.

5406    Shepard, L. A. "Verbal Victory and Existential Anguish." *The Philosophical Journal* (Edinburgh/London), vol. 6, 1969, 95-111.

5407   Sherover, Charles M. *The Kantian Source of Heidegger's Conception of Time.*
       Phil. Diss. New York 1966 435 p. *Dissertation Abstracts International,* vol.
       27/08-A, 2563.

5408   Sherover, Charles M. "Heidegger's Ontology and the Copernican
       Revolution." [Kant] *The Monist* (La Salle), vol. 51, 1967, 559-573.

5409   Sherover, Charles M. "Kant's Transcendental Object and Heidegger's
       Nichts." *Journal of the History of Philosophy* (Berkeley), vol. 7, 1969,
       413-422.

5410   Sherover, Charles M. *Heidegger, Kant and Time.* Bloomington, 1971, XVIII,
       322 p.

5411   Sherover, Charles M. Rev. of *What is a Thing,* by Martin Heidegger.
       *Philosophy and Rhetoric* (Univ. Park), vol. 5, 1972, 191-192.

5412   Sherry, Charles Evan. *The Poetics of Disclosure: Heidegger and Rilke.*
       Authorized facsimile of the dissertation of the Rutgers Univ. Phil. Diss.
       State Univ. of New Jersey 1972. Ann Arbor, Michigan; London: University
       Microfilms International, 1976, iv-222. *Dissertation Abstracts International,*
       vol. 33/08-A, 4432.

5413   Shida, Shôzô. "Haideggâ to Hêgeru" (Heidegger and Hegel). *Jitsuzonshugi*
       (Tôkyô), vol. 35, 1966, 39-47.

5414   Shimamoto, Kiyoshi. "Mu to Jitsuzon" (Non-Being and Existence). *Ryükoku
       Daigaku Ronshû* (Kyôto), vol. 348, 1954.

5415   Shimamoto, Kiyoshi. "Haideggâ no Tetsugaku ni okeru Niche no
       Keijijôgaku" (Nietzsche's Metaphysics in the Philosophy of Heidegger).
       *Ryûkoku Daigaku Ronshû* (Kyôto), vol. 352, 1956, 108-119.

5416   Shimamoto, Kiyoshi. "Haideggâ no Tetsugaku ni okeru Sonzai-ron-teki
       Sabetsu" ("Ontological Difference" in Heidegger's Philosophy). *Ryûkoku
       Daigaku Ronshû* (Kyôto), vol. 391, 1969, 63-80.

5417   Shimizu, Takichi. "Haideggâ to Marukûze." *Risshô Daigaku Bungakubu
       Ronsô* (Tôkyô), vol. 45, 1972, 69-85.

5418   Shimizu, Takichi. "Haideggâ to Marukûze" (Heidegger and Marcuse).
       *Gendai-Shisô* (Tôkyô), vol. 1, no. 2, 1973, 69-85.

5419   Shimizu, Takichi. "Haideggâ to Burohho" (Heidegger and Bloch).
       *Gendai-Shisô* (Tôkyô), vol. 2, no. 10, 1974, 194-205.

5420   Shimizu, Takichi. "Haideggâ to Furankufuruto Gakuha" (Heidegger and the
       Frankfurt School). *Gendai-Shisô* (Tôkyô), vol. 3, no. 5, 1975. Rpt. in *Risô*
       (Tôkyô), vol. 542, 1978, 155-171.

5422   Shimoyama, Tôkuji. "Haideggâ-Tetsugaku no Atarashii Tenkai" (New
       Developments in the Philosophy of Heidegger). *Sêki* (Tôkyô), Juni 1949.

5423   Shimoyama, Tôkuji. "Gensonzaibunseki to Genshogaku" (Analysis of
       There-Being and Phenomenology). *Risô* (Tôkyô), vol. 386, 1965.

5424   Shinoda, Shôzô. "Haideggâ to Hêgeru" (Heidegger and Hegel). *Jitsuzonshugi*
       (Tôkyô), April 1966.

5425 Shinozawa, Hideo. "Jikan no naka no Jikan no soto e; Buransho to Haideggâ" (Beyond the Time Within the Time; Blanchot and Heidegger). *Gendai-Shisô* (Tôkyô), vol. 2, no. 10, 1974, 56-59.

5426 Shioya, Takeo. "Haideggâ ni okeru Mu no Mondai" (The Problem of Non-Being in Heidegger). *Philosophia* (Tôkyô), vol. 22, Juni 1952.

5427 Shioya, Takeo. "Haideggâ ni okeru Tenkô no Mondai" (The Problem of the Turning in Heidegger). *Philosophia* (Tôkyô), vol. 27, 1955, 146-179.

5428 Shirai, Shigemichi. "Haideggâ no Chôetsu" (The Transcendence in the Philosophical Thinking of Heidegger). *Tetsugakukenkyû* (Kyôto), vol. 475, Juni 1961.

5429 Shirai, Shigemichi. "Haideggâ Shii no Michi; Dôkô to Kyoiki" (Heidegger's Way of Thinking). *Risô* (Tôkyô), vol. 507, 1975, 87-96; *Risô,* vol. 508, 1975, 81-92.

5430 Shmueli, Efraim. "Contemporary Philosophical Theories and Their Relation to Science and Technology." *Philosophy in Context* (Cleveland State Univ.), vol. 4, 1975, 37-60.

5431 Shouery, Emad. "Phenomenological Analysis of Waiting." *Southwestern Journal of Philosophy* (Norman, Oklahoma), vol. 3, 1972, 93-101.

5432 Shûta, Tatsuo. "Haideggâ ni okeru Sonzai - Dôitsusei no Meidai sonota ni tsuite" ("Being" in Heidegger - the Principle of Identity). *Theoria* (Kyûshû Daigaku Kyôyôbu, Fukuoka), vol. 9, 1965, 37-58.

5433 Shûta, Tatsuo. "Haideggâ Sonzai to Jikan ni okeru Shôkyokusei" (Negativity in Heidegger's "Sein und Zeit"). *Theoria* (Kyûshû Daigaku Kyôyôbu, Fukuoka), vol. 10, 1966, 63-86.

5434 Sieben, K. *Das Problem der Welt im Denken Martin Heideggers von "Sein und Zeit" bis zum Brief über den 'Humanismus'.* Phil. Diss. Fak. Mainz vom 17.9.1956 113 Bl.

5435 Siegmund, G. Rev. of *Holzwege,* by Martin Heidegger. Frankfurt, 1950. *Philosophisches Jahrbuch* (Fulda), vol. 60, 1950, 346.

5436 Siemianowshi, A. Rev. of *Budowaá, mieszkaá, myáleá. Eseje wybrane,* by Martin Heidegger. [Bauen, Wohnen, Denken] 1977. *W drodze,* vol. 12, 1977.

5437 Siewerth, G. *Das Schicksal der Metaphysik von Thomas zu Heidegger.* (Horizonte, 6). Einsiedeln, 1959, XXIV, 520 p.

5438 Siewerth, G. "Martin Heidegger und die Frage nach Gott." *Hochland* (München/Kempten), vol. 53, 1960/61, 516-526.

5439 Siewerth, G. "Martin Heidegger und die Frage nach Gott." In *Gustav Siewerth, Grundfragen der Philosophie im Horizont der Seinsdifferenz.* (Gesammelte Aufsätze zur Philosophie). Düsseldorf, 1963, 245-259, 301.

5440 Siewerth, G. *Gesammelte Werke.* [Bd III: Gott in der Geschichte. Zur Gottesfrage bei Hegel und Heidegger.] Ed. Alma von Stockhausen. Düsseldorf, 1971, 293 p.

5441 Sikora, Joseph J. "Articulation in Being and Consciousness." *Science et Esprit* (Montreal/Trois-Rivières), vol. 21, no. 2, 1969, 231-251.

5442 Silva, A. da. Rev. of *El ser y el tiempo,* by Martin Heidegger. 1951. *Revista Portuguesa di Filosofia* (Braga), vol. 9, 1953, 432-433.

5443 Silva, Carlos Henrique do Carmo. "O mesmo e a sua indiferença temporal. O parmenidianismo de Heidegger perspectivado a partir de *Zeit und Sein.* " *Revista Portuguesa de Filosofia* (Braga), vol. 33, no. 4, 1977, 299-349.

5444 Silva, Carlos Henrique do Carmo. "Nota bibliográfica. Martin Heidegger (26. 9. 1889 - 26. 5. 1976)." *Revista Portuguesa de Filosofia* (Braga), vol. 33, no. 4, 1977, 350-373.

5445 Silva, L. "El metafisico artista (Heidegger vs. La Ciencia)." *Cultura Universitaria* (Caracas), vol. 100, 1973, 181-188.

5446 Silva-Tarouca, A. *Die Logik der Angst.* Innsbruck, 1953, 251 p.

5447 Silveira Da Mota, W. "A consciência valorativa contemporânea sob uma nova perspectiva." *Revista brasileira de Filosofia* (Sao Paulo), vol. 25, no. 98, 1975, 230-243.

5448 Silverman, Hugh J. "Man and the Self as Identity of Difference." *Philosophy Today* (Celina, Ohio), vol. 19, 1975, 131-136.

5449 Silverman, Hugh J. "Heidegger and Merleau-Ponty: Interpreting Hegel." *Research in Phenomenology* (Pittsburgh), vol. 7, 1977, 209-224.

5450 Silverman, Hugh J. "Thinking and Being: The Essential Relation." *Philosophy Today* (Celina, Ohio), vol. 21, no. 3-4, 1977, 241-249.

5451 Silverman, Hugh J. "Dasein and Existential Ambiguity." In *Heidegger's Existential Analytic,* by Frederick Elliston (ed.). The Hague, New York: Mouton Pub., 1978, 97-108.

5452 Silverman, Hugh J. "Self-Decentering: Derrida Incorporated." *Research in Phenomenology,* vol. 8, 1978, 45-65.

5453 Sinari, Ramakanr. *Reason in Existentialism.* Bombay, India, 1967, 268; New York, 1969, 264 p.

5454 Sinari, Ramakanr. *Reason in Existentialism.* New York, 1969, 264 p.

5455 Sindelar, J. "Einleitung." *Antologie existencialismu* (Praha), vol. I, 1967, 5-22.

5456 Singevin, Charles. "De l'être a l'un." *Revue de Métaphysique et de Morale* (Paris), vol. 70, 1965, 1-34.

5457 Single, E. "Gespräch mit Heidegger." *Rheinischer Merkur* (Koblenz), Jg. 5, no. 16, 1950, 5.

5457a Sini, Carlo. "Heidegger e il problema del segno." *L'Uomo, un segno* (Milano), vol. 3, no. 1-2, 1979, 43-58.

5458 Sinn, Dieter. "Heideggers Spätphilosophie." *Philosophische Rundschau* (Tübingen), vol. 14, 1967, 81 ff.

5459 Sipowicz, K. "Neoplatonizm w hermeneutyce P. Ricoeura i M. Heideggera" (Newplatonism in P. Ricoeur's and M. Heidegger's Philosophy). *Studia Philosophiae Christianae,* vol. 1, 1978.

5460 Sipowicz, K. Rev. of *Budowaá, mieszkaá, myáleá. Eseje wybrane,* by Martin Heidegger. [Bauen, Wohnen, Denken] 1977. *Zycie i myál,* vol. 5, 1978.

5461 Sitter, Beat. "Zur Möglichkeit dezisionistischer Auslegung von Heideggers ersten Schriften." *Zeitschrift für Philosophische Forschung* (Meisenheim/Glan), vol. 24, 1970, 516-535.

5462 Sitter, Beat. "'Sein und Zeit' als Theorie der Ethik." *Philosophische Rundschau,* vol. 16, 1969, 273-281.

5463 Sitter, Beat. *Dasein und Ethik: Zu einer ethischen Theorie der Eksistenz.* München, 1975.

5464 Skirbekk, Gunnar. "Sirnes, Torgersen, Heidegger." *Tidsskrift for Den norske laegeforening* (Oslo), vol. 1962, 41-42.

  [Rev. of *Naturforskning og katedral,* by J. Torgersen. Oslo, 1960; and *Tidsskrift for Den norske laegeforening,* by T. Sirnes. Oslo, no. 20, 1961.]

5465 Skirbekk, Gunnar. "Sirnes, Torgerson, Heidegger." *Tidsskrift for Den norske lae geforening* (Oslo), 1962, 41-42.

5466 Skirbekk, Gunnar. *Tekstkommentar til 'Om sanninga sitt vesen'.* Bergen, 1964.

5467 Skirbekk, Gunnar. *Die filosofiske vilkar for sanning.* Oslo, 1966, (specifically 154-161).

5468 Skirbekk, Gunnar. *Reductio ad absurdum argument og filosofisk innsikt.* Bergen, 1966.

5469 Skirbekk, Gunnar. *Truth and Preconditions Approached Via an Analysis of Heidegger.* Bergen, 1972, 152 p.

5470 Skirbekk, Gunnar. "La vérité chez Heidegger. Esquisse d'une critique." *Annales de la Faculté des Lettres et Sciences Humaines de Nice* (Nice), no. 32, 1977, 73-81.

5471 Skjervheim, H. "Sanning og subjektivitet." In *Festskrift for A. H. Winsnes.* Oslo, 1959.

5472 Sladeczek, F.-M. *Ist das Dasein Gottes beweisbar? Wie steht die Existenzialphilosophie Martin Heideggers zu dieser Frage?* Würzburg, 1967, XVI, 127 p. 2nd ed. 1973, XVIII, 146 p.

5473 Slooten, J. van. "Inleiding tot het denken van Heidegger." *Hoofdfiguren van het menselijk denken* (Assen/Born), vol. 20, 1956, 47 p.

5474 Slooten, J. van. *Inleiding tot het denken van Heidegger.* (Bornpockets, 1). 2nd ed. Assen, 1965, 95 p.

5475 Slote, Michael A. "Existentialism and the Fear of Dying." *American Philosophical Quarterly* (Oxford), vol. 12, 1975, 17-28.

5476 Smith, F. Joseph. "The Meaning of the 'Way' in Heidegger." *The American Church Quarterly,* vol. 3, 1962, 89-102.

5477 Smith, F. Joseph. "Heidegger's Kant Interpretation." *Philosophy Today* (Celina, Ohio), vol. 11, no. 4, 1967, 257-264.

5478    Smith, F. Joseph. "In-the-World and On-the-Earth: A Heideggerian Interpretation." In *Heidegger and the Quest for Truth.* Ed. M. S. Frings. Chicago, 1968, 184-203.

5479    Smith, F. Joseph. "Being and Subjectivity: Heidegger and Husserl." In *Phenomenology in Perspective.* Ed. F. J. Smith. The Hague, 1970, 122-156.

5480    Smith, F. Joseph. "Two Heideggerian Analyses." *Southern Journal of Philosophy,* vol. 8, Winter 1970, 409-421. Rpt. in *Martin Heidegger: In Europe and America,* by Edward Goodwin Ballard and Charles E. Scott (eds.). The Hague, 1973, 171-182.

5481    Smith, F. Joseph. "A Critique of Martin Heidegger." [Heidegger issue] *The Southwestern Journal of Philosophy* (Norman, Oklahoma), vol. 4, no. 3, 1973, 137-156.

5482    Smith, James Leroy. "Nihilism and the Arts." *The Journal of Aesthetics and Art Criticism,* vol. 33, Spring 1975, 329-338.

5483    Smith, P. Christopher. *Das Sein und das Du. Bubers Philosophie im Leihte des Heideggerschen Denkens an das Sein.* Heidelberg, 1966, 129 p. [Phil. Diss. Heidelberg v.21. Juli 1966.]

5484    Smith, P. Christopher. "Heidegger, Hegel, and the Problem of das Nichts." *International Philosophical Quarterly* (New York/Heverlee-Leuven), vol. 8, 1968, 379-405.

5485    Smith, P. Christopher. "Heidegger's Critique of Absolute Knowledge." *The New Scholasticism* (Washington), vol. 45, 1971, 56-86.

5486    Smith, P. Christopher. "Heidegger's Break With Nietzsche and the Principle of Subjectivity." *The Modern Schoolman* (St. Louis), vol. 52, no. 3, 1974/75, 227-248.

5487    Smith, P. Christopher. "A Poem of Rilke: Evidence for the Later Heidegger." *Philosophy Today* (Celina, Ohio), vol. 21, no. 3-4, 1977, 250-262.

5487a   Smith, P. Christopher. "Heidegger's Misinterpretation of Rilke." *Philosophy and Literature* (Dearborn), vol. 3, 1979, 3-19.

5488    Smith, Vincent Edward. "Existentialism and Existence (part I and II)." *Thomist,* vol. 11, April 1948, 141-196; July 1948, 297-329.

5489    Smolko, John F. "Philosophy and Theology." *Proceedings of the American Catholic Philosophical Association,* vol. 44, 1970, 31-54.

5490    Smoot, William. "The Social Dimension of Death-Anxiety." *Philosophy Today,* vol. 21, Spring 1977, 84-89.

5491    Smoot, William. "The Future of Existentialism." *Philosophy Today* (Celina, Ohio), vol. 24, 1980, 3-10.

5491a   Snyder, L. Rev. of "Heidegger and Modern Philosophy." Ed. Michael Murray. *Philosophy and Phenomenological Research* (Buffalo), vol. 40, 1979/80, 147-148.

5492    Soaje Ramos, Guido. "Sobre Tópica Aristotélica Y Filosofia Práctica." *Ethos,* 1974/75, 147-185.

5493    Soaje Ramos, Guido. "La posición de Heidegger ante el tema del valor." *Ethos* (Buenos Aires), vol. 4-5, 1976/77, 117-161.

5494    Sobel, Jerry Edward. *Heidegger's Concept of the World.* Phil. Diss. Harvard Univ. 1974.

5495    Sôgyun, I. "Haidegkae issôsôûi chonjaeronjôk ch'ai" (Ontology in Heidegger). *Ch'ungnam Univ. Collection of Essays* (Ch'ungnam), vol. 1, part V, 1978, 121-136.

5496    Soler Grimma, F. "El origen de la obra de arte y la verdad en Heidegger." *Ideas y Valores* (Bogotà), vol. 2, 1952, 326-350.

5497    Soler Grimma, F. *El origen de la obra de arte y la verdad en Heidegger.* Bogota, 1953.

5498    Soleri, G. "M. Heidegger alla ricerca dell'essere." *Rassegna di scienze filosofiche* (Roma), vol. 8, 1955, 81-133, 238-276.

5499    Soll, Ivan. Rev. of *Heidegger und die Sprache,* by Hans Jaeger. 1971. *Monatshefte für Deutschen Unterricht, Deutsche Sprache und Literatur* (Madison, Wisconsin), vol. 65, 1973, 438-439.

5501    Solomon, Robert C. *From Rationalism to Existentialism; the Existentialist and Their Nineteenth-Century Backgrounds.* New York: Harper & Row, 1972.

5502    Solov'ëv, E. Ju. "Likvidacija filosofii pod vidom eë osoznanija (O nemeckom ekzistencializme)" (The Liquidation of Philosophy Under the Pretence of Its Realization (On German Existentialism)). *Voprosy filosofii,* vol. 6, 1962.

5503    Solov'ëv, E. Ju. *Ekzistencializm i naucnoe poznanie* (Existentialism and the Scientific Cognition). Moskva, 1966.

5504    Solov'ëv, E. Ju. "Ekzistencialism." *Voprosy filosofii.* Ed. Akademie der Wiss. Moskau, no. 12, 1966, 76-88; no. 1, 1967, 126-148.

5505    Soluguren López, Jaime. "Fin de la filosofia-comienzo del pensar." *Revista Venezolana de Filosofia,* vol. 8, 1978, 97-133.

5506    Sonnemann, Ulrich. *Existence and Therapy.* New York, 1954, 102-131, passim.

5507    Sonoda, Isao. "Haideggâ to Nîche no Sonzai no Toi o megutte" (On Heidegger and Nietzsche's Question About Being). *Gendai-Shisô* (Tôkyô), vol. 2, no. 11, 1974, 42-51.

5508    Sonoda, Isao. "Konkyo eno Toi, 1: Haideggâ no Kanto Kaishaku; Kanto 'Sonzai no Teidai ni tsuite'" (A Quest for Ground, 1: Heidegger's Interpretation of Kant; on Kant's Thesis About Being). *Joshi Êiyô Daigaku Kiyô* (Tôkyô), vol. 5, 1974, 89-109.

5509    Sonoda, Isao. "Konkyo e no Toi, 2; Haideggâ no kanto Kaishaku - Kanto 'Sonzai no Teidai' ni tsuite; Sonzai-Shikô-Chikaku" (A Quest for Ground, 2; Heidegger's Interpretation of Kant - On Kant's "Thesis About Being" and on Being, Thinking, Perception). *Joshi Eiyô Daigaku Kiyô* (Tôkyô), vol. 6, 1975, 83-101.

5510  Sonoda, Yoshimichi. "Mu ni tsuite, Haideggâ kara Sarutoru e" (On Non-Being. From Heidegger to Sartre). *Tôyôdaigaku-Kiyô* (Tôkyô), vol. 14, 1961.

5511  Sontag, Frederik. "Heidegger and the Problem of Metaphysics." *Philosophy and Phenomenological Research* (Buffalo, New York), vol. 24, 1963/64, 410-416.

5512  Sontag, Frederik. "Heidegger, Time and God." *The Journal of Religion* (Chicago), vol. 47, 1967, 279-294.

5513  Sontag, Frederik. *The existentialist prolegomena (To a Future Metaphysics).* Chicago/London, 1969, 223 p.

5514  Soriano, M. Rev. of *Kant et la métaphysique,* by Martin Heidegger. 1953. *Deutsche Zeitschrift für Philosophie* (Berlin), vol. 2, 1954, 739-740.

5515  Sotiello, G. de, and G. Zamora. "Heideggeriana, 1967." *Naturaleza y Gracia* (Madrid), vol. 17, 1970, 179-197.

    [Rev. of *Wegmarken* and *Der europäische Nihilismus,* by Martin Heidegger.]

5516  Soto Badilla, José Alberto. "Heidegger: el filósofo del *Dasein.*" *Revista de Filosofía de la Universidad de Costa Rica* (San José), vol. 14, no. 39, 1976, 191-194.

5517  Souche-Dagues, D. "Une exegèse heideggerienne: le temps chez Hegel d'après le section 82 de 'Sein und Zeit'." *Revue de Metaphysique et de Morale* (Paris), vol. 84, no. 1-3, 1979, 101-120.

5518  Soukup, L. "Sein oder Seiendes. Eine metaphysische Skizze über die Vorentscheidung zu jeder Ontologie. Zu Werken von Martin Heidegger und Caspar Nink." *Gloria Dei* (Graz), vol. 9, 1954, 120-122.

5519  "Sovremennaja filosofija i sociologija v stranach Zapadnoj Evropy i Ameriki (Istoriko-filosofskie ocerki)" (The Contemporary Philosophy and Sociology in the Countries of Western Europe and America (The Historical-Philosophical Outlines)). *Nauka.* Moskva, 1964.

5520  *Sovremennyi sub-ektivnyj idealizm* (Contemporary Subjective Idealism). Moskva, 1957, 428-436.

5521  Spagnolo, Salvatore. "Genesi e momenti dello 'assoluto realismo' di Vincenzo La Via." *Teoresi,* vol. 30, June-December 1975, 209-280.

5522  Spanos, William V., ed. *Martin Heidegger and the Question of Literature. Toward a Postmodern Literary Hermeneutics.* (Studies in Phenomenology and Existential Philosophy). Bloomington: Indiana Univ. Press, 1979.

5523  Spanos, William V. "Heidegger, Kierkegaard, and the Hermeneutic Circle. Towards a Postmodern Theory of Interpretation as Dis-Closure." In *Martin Heidegger and the Question of Literature.* Ed. William V. Spanos. Bloomington, Indiana/London: Indiana Univ. Press, 1979, 115-148.

5524  Spanos, William V. "Martin Heidegger and the Question of Truth. A Preface." In *Martin Heidegger and the Question of Literature.* Ed. William V. Spanos. Bloomington, Indiana/London: Indiana Univ. Press, 1979, ppix-xix.

5525　　Specht, E. K. *Sprache und Sein.* Berlin, 1967, 31 ff.

5526　　Speck, Josep. *Heideggers Philosophie in ihrem Verhältnis zur philosophischen Tradition.* Phil. Diss. Hamburg 1959 II 311 p.

5527　　Spiegelberg, Herbert. *The Phenomenological Movement. A Historical Introduction, I u. II.* The Hague, 1969, IX, 765 p.

5528　　Spiegelberg, Herbert. "On Some Human Uses of Phenomenology." In *Phenomenology in Perspective.* Ed. F. J. Smith. The Hague, 1970, 16-31.

5529　　Spiegelberg, Herbert, ed. "From Husserl to Heidegger. Excerpts From a 1928 Freiburg Diary by W. R. Boyce Gibson." *The Journal of the British Society for Phenomenology* (Manchester), vol. 2, no. 1, 1971, 58-83.

5530　　Spier, J. M. *Calvinisme en Existentie-philosophie.* Kampen, 1951.

5531　　Spiess, E. "Wege der neueren Philosophie zu Martin Heidegger." *Jahrbuch der Schweizerischen Philosophischen Gesellschaft* (Basel), vol. 2, 1942, 47-77.

5532　　Spiess, E. "Wege der neuen Philosophie zu Martin Heidegger." *Annalen der Philosophischen Gesellschaft Innerschweiz* (Schwyz), vol. 1, 1944, 45-66.

5533　　Spiess, E. "Der Ausgangspunkt der Existentialphilosophie Martin Heideggers." *Civitas* (Immensee), vol. 4, 1948, 161-166.

5534　　Spiess, E. "Die Entwicklung der Existenzialphilosophie Martin Heideggers." *Civitas* (Immensee), vol. 3, 1948, 481-487.

5535　　Splett, Jorg. Rev. of *Das Verhältnis von Philosophie und Theologie im Denken Martin Heideggers,* by Annemarie Gethmann-Sieffert. 1974. *Theologie und Philosophie* (Freiburg), vol. 51, 1976, 410-412.

5536　　Splett, Jorg. "Existenzial philosophie." In *Sacramentum Mundt.* Freiburg/Basel/Wien, 1968, 2-8.

5537　　Splett, Jorg. "Liberdaden nao livre." *Revista Portugesa de Filosofia* (Braga), vol. 29, 1973, 21-41.

5538　　Springer, J. L. "Hegel's phänomenolc̦ie en Heidegger's Ontologie." *Nederlands theologisch Tijdschrift* (Wageningen), vol. 17, 1962/63, 241-273.

5539　　Stack, George J. Rev. of *Heidegger and the Path of Thinking,* by J. Sallis (ed.). *The Modern Schoolman* (St. Louis), vol. 50, 1972/73, 100-103.

5540　　Stack, George J. Rev. of *Discourse on Thinking,* by Martin Heidegger. *The Modern Schoolman* (St. Louis), vol. 44, 1966/67, 397-399.

5541　　Stack, George J. "The Being of the Work of Art in Heidegger." *Philosophy Today* (Celina, Ohio), vol. 13, 1969, 159-173.

5542　　Stack, George J. "Concern in Kierkegaard and Heidegger." *Philosophy Today* (Celina, Ohio), vol. 13, 1969, 26-35.

5543　　Stack, George J. "Existence and Possibility." *Laval théologique et philosphique* (Quebec), vol. 28, 1972, 149-170.

5544　　Stack, George J. "The Language of Possibility and Existential Possibility." *The Modern Schoolman* (St. Louis), vol. 50, 1973, 159-182.

5545　　Stack, George J. "Heidegger's Concept of Meaning." *Philosophy Today* (Celina, Ohio), vol. 17, 1973, 255-266.

5546 Stack, George J. Rev. of *The End of Philosophy,* by Martin Heidegger. 1973. *Manuscripta* (St. Louis), vol. 51, 1973/74, 361-364.

5547 Stack, George J. "Heidegger: Significado y existencia, I-I." *Folia Humanistica* (Barcelona), vol. 13, 1975, 353-361, 431-438.

5548 Stack, George J. "Meaning and Existence." In *Heidegger's Existential Analytic,* by Frederick Elliston (ed.). The Hague, New York: Mouton Pub., 1978, 81-95.

5549 Stahl, Gerry. *Marxian Hermeneutics and Heideggerian Social Theory: Interpreting and Transforming Our World.* Phil. Diss. Northwestern Univ. 1975. *Dissertation Abstracts International,* vol. 36/07-A, 4567.

5550 Stahl, Gerry. "Attuned to Being. Heideggerian Music in Technological Society." In *Martin Heidegger and the Question of Literature.* Ed. William V. Spanos. Bloomington, Indiana/London: Indiana Univ Press, 297-324.

5551 Staiger, Emil. "Noch einmal Heidegger." *Neue Zürcher Zeitung,* 157.Jg., no. 125, 23 Januar 1936, 1.

5552 Staiger, Emil. "Die neuere Entwicklung Martin Heideggers." *Neue Zürcher Zeitung,* 30 Dezember 1944.

5553 Staiger, Emil. "Hölderlin-Forschung während des Krieges." *Trivium* (Zürich), vol. 4, 1946, 202-219.

5554 Staiger, Emil. "Martin Heidegger und der Humanismus." *Universitas* (Stuttgart), vol. 3, 1948, 237-239.

5555 Staiger, Emil. "Zu Klopstocks Ode 'Der Zürichersee'." In *Martin Heideggers Enfluss auf die Wissenschaften.* Aus Anlass seines sechzigsten Geburtstages verfasst. Bern, 1949, 145-164.

5556 Staiger, Emil. "Zu einem Vers von Mörike. Ein Briefwechsel mit Martin Heidegger." *Trivium* (Zürich), vol. 9, 1951, 1-16. Rpt. in "Ein Briefwechsel mit Martin Heidegger. Über das Gedicht 'Auf eine Lampe' von Eduard Mörike." In *Die Kunst der Interpretation. Studien zur deutschen Literaturgeschichte,* by E. Staiger. Zürich, 1955, 34-49. 4th ed. 1963.

5557 Staiger, Emil. *Grundbegriffe der Poetik.* 2nd ed. Zürich, 1951.

5558 Staiger, Emil. "Ein Rückblick. Martin Heidegger zum 70. Geburtstag/26 September." *Neue Zürcher Zeitung,* no. 2898/1 und 2 vom 27.9.1959. [Fernausgabe no. 264, 26 September 1959, 10.] Rpt. in "Ein Rückblick." In *Heidegger.* Ed. O. Pöggeler. Köln/Berlin, 1969, 242-245.

5559 Staiger, Emil. "Martin Heidegger. Eine Rede, gehalten in Amriswil an der Feier zum 80. Geburtstag des Philosophen." *Neue Zürcher Zeitung,* no. 606 v.5.10.1969, 51. [Fernausgabe, no. 273.]

5560 Staiger, Emil. "Martin Heidegger." *Martin Heidegger im Gespräch.* Ed. R. Wisser. Freiburg/München, 1970, 42-44.

5561 Staiger, Emil. "Streiflichter." In *Erinnerung an Martin Heidegger,* by Günther Neske (ed.). Pfullingen: Verlag Günther Neske, 1977, 229-232.

5562 Stallaert, L. *Waarheid en vrijheid.* (Bewerking van Martin Heidegger's voordracht 'Vom Wesen der Wahrheit'). Rotterdam, 1959, 82 p.

5563 Stallmach, Josef. "Seinsdenken bei Thomas von Aquin und Heidegger." *Hochland* (München), vol. 1, 1967/68, 1-13.

5564 Stambauch, Joan. "Commentary on T. Umehara's Heidegger and Buddhism." *Philosophy East and West* (Honolulu), vol. 20, 1970, 283-286.

5565 Stambaugh, Joan. "Time and Dialectic in Hegel and Heidegger." *Research in Phenomenology* (Pittsburgh), vol. 4, 1974, 87-97.

5566 Stambaugh, Joan. "Introduction." In *Identity and Difference,* by Martin Heidegger. New York: Harper & Row, 1974.

5567 Stambaugh, Joan. "Time, Finitude, and Finality." *Philosophy East and West,* vol. 24, 1974, 129-135.

5568 Stambaugh, Joan. "A Heidegger Primer." *Philosophy Today* (Celina, Ohio), vol. 19, 1975, 79-86.

5569 Stambaugh, Joan. "An Inquiry Into Authenticity and Inauthenticity in *Being and Time.*" *Research in Phenomenology* (Pittsburgh), vol. 7, 1977, 153-161.

5570 Stambaugh Joan. "On the Meaning of Ambivalence." *Philosophy Today,* vol. 24, 1980, 161-170.

5571 Stapleton, Timothy John. *Husserl and Heidegger: The Question of a Phenomenological Beginning.* Phil. Diss. Pennsylvania State Univ. 1978 235 p. *Dissertation Abstracts International,* vol. 39/10-A, 6176.

5572 Starr, David E. *Entity and Existence. An Ontological Investigation of Aristotle and Heidegger.* New York, 1975.

5573 Starr, David E. "Ousia and Dasein: An Ontological Investigation of Aristotle and Heidegger. Phil. Diss. Boston Univ. Graduate School Boston 1972 429 p. *Dissertation Abstracts International,* vol. 33/04-A, 1788.

5573a Starr, David E. *Entity and Existence. An Ontological Investigation of Aristotle and Heidegger.* New York: Burt Franklin & Co., 1975, xxi-336 p.

5574 Stassen, Manfred. *Heideggers Philosophie der Sprache in 'Sein und Zeit' und ihre philosophisch-theologischen Wurzeln.* Bonn, 1973, 180 p.

5575 Stavrides, Maria M. *The Concept of Existence in Kierkegaard and Heidegger.* Phil. Diss. Columbia Univ. New York 1952 205 p.

5576 Stefanini, L. *Il momento dell'educazione. Giudizio sull' esistenzialismo.* Padova, 1938, (specifically pages 119-159).

5577 Stefanini, L. "L'esistenzialismo nordico e italiano di fronte all'arte." In *Arte e Critica.* 2nd ed. Milano, 1943, passim.

5578 Stefanini, L. *L'esistenzialismo di M. Heidegger.* Padova, 1944.

5579 Stefanini, L. "Critica costruttiva dell'esistenzialismo teistico." *Giornale di metafisica* (Torino), vol. 5, 1950, 81-108, (specifically pages 81-86).

5580 Steffney, John. "Existentialism's Legacy of Nothingness." *Philosophy Today* (Celina, Ohio), vol. 21, 1977, 216-226.

5581    Steffney, John. "Non-Being-Being Versus the Non-Being of Being. Heidegger's
        Ontological Difference With Zen Buddhism." *The Eastern Buddhist*
        (Kyoto), vol. 10, no. 2, 1977, 65-75.

5582    Steffney, John. "Transmetaphysical Thinking and Zen Buddhism." *Philosophy
        East and West* (Honolulu, Hawaii), vol. 27, no. 3, 1977, 323-335.

5583    Stegmüller, W. *Hauptströmungen der Gegenwartsphilosophie. Eine
        historisch-kritische Einführung.* Wien/Stuttgart, 1952, 494 p., (specifically
        pages 117-220). [2.neubearbeitete und erweiterte Auflage Stuttgart 1960.]

5584    Stein, Ernildo. *Introducâo ao pensamento de Martin Heidegger.* Pôrto Alegre,
        Brasilien, 1966, 147 p.

5585    Stein, Ernildo. "Heidegger e a teologia natural." *Anuário Riograndense de
        Filosofia* (Pörto Alegre, Brasilien), Bd 1, 1967, 35-64.

5586    Stein, Ernildo. *Compreensâo e finitude - Estrutura e movimento da interrogaçâo
        heideggeriana.* Pôrto Alegre, Brasilien, 1967, 252 p. [Habilitationsschrift]

5587    Stein, Ernildo. "Possibilidades de uma nova ontologia." *Revista Organon*
        (Pôrto Alegre, Brasilien), vol. 12, 1968, 27-40.

5588    Stein, Ernildo. "Algumas consideraçôes sôbre o método fenomenológico em
        Ser e Tempo." *Revista Brasileira de Filosofia* (Sao Paulo), vol. 21, 1971.

5589    Stein, Ernildo. *A questño do método na filosofia (um estudo do modelo
        heideggeriano).* Sao Paulo: Livraria Duas Cidades, 1973, 170 p.

5590    Steiner, George. *Heidegger.* Hassocks, Sussex: The Harvester Press, 1978, 157
        p. Rpt. New York: The Viking Press, 1979.

5591    Steiner, Kenneth Mark. "Appropriation, Belonging Together and Being in the
        World." *The Journal of the British Society for Phenomenology,* vol. 10, no.
        2, 130-133.

5592    Steiner, Kenneth Mark. *Thinking, Being and Language in the Work of Martin
        Heidegger.* Authorized facsimile of the dissertation of the State Univ. of
        New York at Binghamton. Phil. Diss. 1976. Ann Arbor, Michigan; London:
        University Microfilms International, 1979, v-165. *Dissertation Abstracts
        International,* vol. 37/06-A, 3702.

5593    Stenström, Th. *Existentialismen, Studier i dess idétradition och litterära
        yttringar.* Stockholm, 1966, 346 p.

5594    Stern (Anders), G. "On the Pseudo-Concreteness of Heideggers Philosophy."
        *Philosophy and Phenomenological Research* (Buffalo, New York), vol. 8,
        1947/48, 337-371.

5595    Sternberger, Adolf. Rev. of *Kant und das Problem der Metaphysik,* by Martin
        Heidegger. 1929. *Frankfurter Zeitung,* 29.9.1929.

5596    Sternberger, Adolf. *Der verstandene Tod: eine Untersuchung zu Martin
        Heideggers Existenzialontologie.* Rpt. of the 1934 ed. pub. in Leipzig by S.
        Hirzel. (Phenomenology. Background, foreground, and influences). New
        York/London: Garland Pub., 1979, ix-155.

5597    Sternberger, Dolf. "Heidegger bleibt unverständlich." *Die Gegenwart* (Frankfurt), vol. 8, 1953, 639-642.

5598    Sternberger, Dolf. "In der Hut des Seins. Zu Heideggers 80. Geburtstag." *Frankfurter Allgemeine Zeitung,* no. 223, vom 26.9.1969, 32.

5599    Sternberger, Dolf. "Martin Heidegger." In *Martin Heidegger im Gespräch.* Ed. R. Wisser. Freiburg/München, 1970, 42-44.

5600    Sternberger, Dolf. "Am Ursprung? Ein Bericht über Heidegger aus dem Jahre 1936." *Frankfurter Allgemeine Zeitung* (Frankfurt/Main), 3./4.1.1975. 'Bilder und Zeiten', 2.

5601    Sternberger, Dolf. *Schriften. 1. Über den Tod.* Frankfurt, 1977.

5601a    Stevens, Jeffrey. "Nietzsche and Heidegger on Justice and Truth." *Nietzsche-Studien* (Berlin, New York), vol. 9, 1980, 224-238.

5602    Stewart, David. "Heidegger and the Greening of Philosophy." *Southwestern Journal of Philosophy* (Norman, Oklahoma), vol. 6, 1975, 15-19.

5603    Stewart, Roderick Milford. "Signification and Radical Subjectivity in Heidegger's *Habilitationsschrift.*" *Man and World,* vol. 12, 1979, 360-386.

5604    Stewart, Roderick Milford. "The Problem of Logical Psychologism for Husserl and the Early Heidegger." *The Journal of the British Society for Phenomenology,* vol. 10, 1979, 184-193.

5605    Stewart, Roderick Milford. *Psychologism, Sinn and Urteil in the Early Writings of Heidegger.* Authorized facsimile of the dissertation of the Syracuse Univ. Phil. Diss. 1977. Ann Arbor, Michigan; London: University Microfilms International, 1979, viii-502. *Dissertation Abstracts International,* vol. 39/02-A, 924.

5606    Stierlin, Helm. "Existentialism Meets Psychotherapy." *Philosophy and Phenomenological Research,* vol. 24, 1963, 215-239.

5607    Stoffer, H. "Die modernen Ansätze zu einer Logik der Denkformen." *Zeitschrift für philosophische Forschung* (Meisenheim/Glan), vol. 10, 1956, 442-466, 601-621, (specifically pages 611-616).

5608    Stohrer, Walter J. *The Role of Martin Heidegger's Doctrine of 'Dasein' in Karl Rahner's Metaphysics of Man.* Phil. Diss. Georgetown Univ. Washington 1967 213 p. *Dissertation Abstracts International,* vol. 29/03-A, 934.

5609    Stojanoviá, Dragan, and Danilo Basta. "Uvodne napomene o recepciji bivstva i vremena Martina Hajdegera." In *Rani Hajdeger - Recepcija i kritika Bivstva i vremena,* by Dragan Stojanovic and Danilo Basta (eds.). (Biblioteka, Zodijak). Beograd, 1979, 7-25.

5610    Stomps, M. "Heideggers Verhandeling over den Dood en de Theologie." *Vox Theologica* (Assen), vol. 9, 1938, 63-73.

5611    Stomps, M. "De philosophie van M. Heidegger." *Allgemeen Nederlands Tijdschrift voor Wijsbegeerte en Psychologie* (Assen), vol. 32, 1939, 267-280.

5612    Storch, A. Rev. of *Holzwege,* by Martin Heidegger. 1950. *Studia Philosophica* (Basel), vol. 12, 1952, 184-194.

5613     Storch, A. Rev. of *Was ist Metaphysik?* by Martin Heidegger. 1949. *Studia Philosophica* (Basel), vol. 13, 1953, 228-230.

5614     Strasser, Stephan. "The Concept of Dread in the Philosophy of Heidegger." *The Modern Schoolman* (St. Louis, Missouri), vol. 35, 1957/58, 1-20. Rpt. in *Bouwstenen voor een filosofische anthropologie.* Hilversum/Antwerpen, 1965, 271-292.

5615     Stratton, Jon David. "Identity and Difference as Austrag: Hegel and Heidegger." *Kinesis: Graduate Journal in Philosophy* (Carbondale, Illinois), vol. 3, 1971, 81-92.

5616     Stratton, Jon David. *The Hegelian Motif in Heidegger's Thought on Language.* Authorized facsimile of the dissertation of the Southern Illinois Univ. Phil. Diss. 1972. Ann Arbor, Michigan; London: University Microfilms International, 1977, iv-165. *Dissertation Abstracts International,* vol. 33/09-A, 5241.

5617     Strauss, Leo, and Hans-Georg Gadamer. "Correspondence Concerning *Wahrheit und Methode.*" *The Independent Journal of Philosophy,* vol. 2, 1978, 5-12.

5618     Strolz, Walter. "Der vergessene Ursprung." *Stimmen der Zeit* (Freiburg), vol. 158, 1955, 429-438.

5619     Strolz, Walter. "Heidegger und die Frage nach dem Wesen der Technik." *Orientierung. Katholische Blätter für weltanschauliche Information* (Zürich), vol. 21, 1957, 16-20.

5620     Strolz, Walter. Rev. of *Der Satz vom Grund,* by Martin Heidegger. *Orientierung. Katholische Blätter für weltanschauliche Information* (Zürich), vol. 22, 1958, 204-205.

5621     Strolz, Walter. "Der Denker des Seins. Zum 70. Geburtstag Martin Heideggers." *Wort und Wahrheit* (Freiburg), vol. 14, 1959, 502-510.

5622     Strolz, Walter. *Der vergessene Ursprung. Das moderne Weltbild, die neuzeitliche Denkbewegung und die Geschichtlichkeit des Menschen.* Freiburg, 1959, 168 p.

5623     Strolz, Walter. "Heideggers Nietzsche-Denkmal. - Der Philosoph am Scheideweg der Geschichte." *Wort und Wahrheit* (Freiburg), vol. 16, 1961, 821-828.

5624     Strolz, Walter. *Human Existence. Contradiction and Hope. Existential Reflections Past and Present.* Notre Dame, Indiana, 1967, 171 p.

5625     Strolz, Walter. "Der denkerische Weg Martin Heideggers (Zu seinem 80. Geburtstag am 26.9.69)." *Stimmen der Zeit* (Freiburg), vol. 184, no. 9, 1969, 172-185.

5626     Strolz, Walter. "Johann Peter Hebel im Denken Heideggers." *Montfort* (Zeitschrift für Geschichte, Heimat und Volkskunde Vorarlbergs), vol. 22, Bregenz 1970, 43-50.

5627     Strolz, Walter. *Heidegger als meditativer Denker.* St. Gallen: Erker-Verlag, 1974, 31 p.

5628    Strolz, Walter. "Ein Gedächtniswort zum Tode Martin Heideggers - gesprochen im Südwestfunk." In *Gedenkschrift der Stadt Messkirch an ihren Sohn und Ehrenbürger Professor Martin Heidegger.* Foreword and postscript by Siegfried Schürle. Messkirch: Stadt Messkirch, 1977, 18-21.

5629    Strolz, Walter. "Heidegger als besinnlicher Denker. Vortrag anlässlich der Gedenkfeier für Martin Heidegger." In *Gedenkschrift der Stadt Messkirch an ihren Sohn und Ehrenbürger Professor Martin Heidegger.* Foreword and postscript by Siegfried Schühle. Messkirch: Stadt Messkirch, 1977, 23-41.

5630    Strolz, Walter. Rev. of *Metaphysik. Grundfragen ihres Ursprungs und ihrer Vollendung,* by Fridolin Wiplinger. 1976. *Philosophischer Literaturanzeiger* (Meisenheim), vol. 30, 1977, 129-132.

5630a    Strube, C. Rev. of "Logik. Die Frage nach der Wahrheit," by Martin Heidegger. Ed. Walter Biemel. *Archiv für Geschichte der Philosophie* (Berlin), vol. 61, 1979, 237-245.

5631    Strunz, Adolf. "Die Frage nach der Wahrheit des Denkens. Einleitung in einen vorläufigen Weg durch das Denkwerk Heideggers zur denkenden Erfahrung." *Wissenschaft und Weltbild* (Wien), vol. 22, no. 3, 1969, 195-200.

5632    Struyker Boudier, C. E. M. "Genese, Struktur En Zin Van Het Verstaan." [Summary: Enstehen, Struktur und Sinn des Verstehens, 109.] *Tijdschr Filosof,* vol. 40, March 1978, 78-110.

5633    Stulberg, Robert B. "Heidegger and the Origin of the Work of Art: An Explication." *Journal of Aesthetics and Art Criticism* (Baltimore), vol. 32, no. 2, 1973, 257-265.

5634    Suchoá, J. "Chodzi o myálenie" (Concerning Thinking). *Punkt,* vol. 7, 1978.

5635    Suchy, V. "Martin Heideggers Einfluss auf die Wissenschaften." *Wissenschaft und Weltbild* (Wien), vol. 3, 1950, 228-230.

5636    Sugimori, Tamao. "Haideggâ no Chikara e no Ishi Ron no Hihan" (Criticism on Heidegger's Explication of "Wille zur Macht"). *Tetsugaku Ronsô* (Tôkyô Kyôiku Daigaku) (Tôkyô), vol. 23, 1965, 19-26.

5637    Sugio, Genyû. "Haideggâ saikin no Kyôgai to Dôgen-Zen" (Heidegger's Philosophical Position Today and Dôgen's Zen Buddhism). *Indogaku-Bukkyôgaku Kenkyû, Nihon-Indogaku-Bukkyô-Gakkai* (Tôkyô), XIX-2, März 1971, 220-223.

5638    Sugio, Genyû. "Der Zen des Dogen und die Erfahrung des 'Ereignisses' Heideggers." *Journal of Indian and Buddhist Studies* (Tokyo), vol. 19, 1971, 709-712.

5639    Sugio, Mamoru. "Ningenjiyû no Konkyo ni tsuite" (On the Origin of the Freedom of Man). *Rinrigakunenpô* (Tôkyô), März 1958.

5640    Sugio, Mamoru. "Haideggâ Tetsugaku to Hyümanizumu" (Heidegger's Philosophy and Humanism). *Yamaguchi Daigaku Kyôiku Gakubu Kenkyû Ronsô* (Yamaguchi), vol. 9, 1960, 27-38.

5641 Sugio, Mamoru. "Dôgen no Yûjiron to saikin no Haideggâ." *Yamaguchi Daigaku Kyôikugakubu Kenkyûronsô* (Yamaguchi), vol. 11, no. 1, 1961, 9-18.

5642 Sugio, Mamoru. "Dôgen no Uji-Ron to Saikin no Heideggâ" (Dôgen's Essay on 'Sein-Zeit' and the Later Heidegger). In *Yamaguchidaigaku-Kyôikugakubu-Kenkyûronsô.* Yamaguchi, 1962.

5643 Sugio, Mamoru. "Haideggâ to Konkyo no Mondai" (Heidegger and the Problem of Ground). In *Yamaguchidaigaku-Kyôikugakubu-Kenkâuronso.* Yamaguchi, 1963.

5644 Sugio, Mamoru. "Dôgen to Haideggâ" (Dôgen and Heidegger). *Risô* (Tôkyô), vol. 369, Februar 1964.

5645 Sugio, Mamoru. "Dôgen, Zeami, Bashô, oyobi Haideggâ" (Dôgen, Zeami, Bashô and Heidegger). *Yamaguchi Daigaku Kyôiku-gakubu Kenkyû Ronsô* (Yamaguchi), vol. 16, 1967, 1-46.

5646 Sugio, Mamoru. "Haideggâ Saikin no Kyôgai - Eruaikunisu to sono Keiken" (The Present Situation of Heidegger's Philosophy Event and Its Experience). *Tetsugaku Ronbunshû* (Kyûshû Daigaku Tetsugakukai) (Fukuoka), vol. 6, 1970, 79-99.

5647 Sugita, Yasuichi. "Haideggâ ni okeru Sonzai to Ningen-Sonzai tono Kakawari ni tsuite" (The Relationship Between Being and Human There-Being in Heidegger). *Tetsugaku* (Nippon Tetsugakukai) (Tôkyô), vol. 18, 1968, 209-220.

5648 Suhan, Ch'ae. *Pult'aûi konggwa Haidegkaûi muwaûi pikyoyôngu* (A Comparison Between the Vacancy in Buddha and the Non-Being in Heidegger). M. A. Thesis, Kyôngbuk Univ., 1959.

5649 Suhan, Ch'ae. "Buddahûi segan kaenyômgwa Haidegkaûi segye kaenyômûi pigyo yôngu" (The Notion of World in Buddha and Heidegger). *Yôngnam Univ. Collection of Essays* (Taegu), vol. 4, 1971, 125-154.

5650 Sûngdôk, Sô. "Haidegkae issôsôûi yôksasôngûi munje" (Historicity in Heidegger). *Ch'ôrhak Yôngu* (Taegu), vol. 18, 1974, 93-111.

5651 Sunggi, Paek. *Haidegkawa Yasûp'ôsûe issôssôûi ingangwa siljon* (Man and Existence in Heidegger and Jaspers). M. A. Thesis, Chônbuk Univ., 1960.

5652 Sruber, Jere Paul. "Heidegger's Critique of Hegel's Notion of Time." *Philosophy ad Phenomenological Research* (Buffalo, New York), vol. xxxix, no. 3, 1979, 358-377.

5653 Sutphin, Stanley T. *Options in Contemporary Theology.* Washington D. C.: Univ. Press of America, 1979.

5654 Suzuki, M. "Existential Philosophy and Philosophy of Buddhism." *Bunka* (Culture) (Tôhoku Univ.), vol. 21, 1957, 689-696.

5655 Suzuki, Saburô. "Jitsuzontetsugaku no Shisô-Dôki, Haideggâ to Yasupâsu" (The Motive for the Thinking of Existential Philosophy in Heidegger and Jaspers). *Tetsugakuzasshi* (Tôkyô), vol. 702, Januar 1949.

5656    Suzuki, Tôru. "Haideggâ to Watashi no Tachiba" (My Point of View on Heidegger). *Ôsaka Keizai Daigaku Ronshû* (Ôsaka), vol. 24, 1959.

5657    Suzuki, Tôru. "Haideggâ ni okeru Sonzaisha to Sonzai" (Being and Being-Process in Heidegger). *Ôsakakeidai-Ronshû* (Ôsaka), vol. 28, 1960.

5658    Svarc. *Ot Sopengaucra k Chejdeggeru.* Trans. from German by T. J. Oiserman. Moskva, 1964, 359 p.

5659    Svarcman, K. A. "Apologija individualizma V ékzistencialistskoj étike." *Voprosy Filosofii* (Moscow), vol. 10, 1959, 20-30.

5660    Switalski, B. W. Rev. of *Die Kategorien und Bedeutungslehre des Duns Scotus,* by Martin Heidegger. 1916. *Kant-Studien* (Berlin), vol. 30, 1925, 520-521.

5661    Synder, Roger David. *An Aproach to Some Philosophical Concepts of Marcel and Heidegger, Using Various Psychological Techniques.* Phil. Diss. 1972 353 p. Graduate Theological Union. *Dissertation Abstracts International,* vol. 33/10-B, 5040.

5662    Syski, J. "Heideggera pytanie o byt" (Heidegger's Being-Question). *Argumenty,* vol. 24, 1976.

5663    Szilasi, W. "Interpretation und Geschichte der Philosophie." In *Martin Heideggers Einfluss auf die Wissenschaften.* Bern, 1949, 73-87.

5664    Szilasi, W. "Ontologie et expérience." *Actas del primer Congreso nacional de Filosofia* (Mendoza), vol. 2, 1949, 847-853.

5665    Szilasi, W. "La philosophie allemande actuelle." *Actas del primer Congreso nacional de Filosofia* (Mendoza), vol. 1, 1949, 493-502.

5666    Szondi, P. "Hölderlins Brief an Böhlendorff." *Euphorion* (Heidelberg), vol. 58, 1964, 260-275.

5667    Tabackovskij, V. "Filosofija odinocestva. Bessi idej ekzistencializma" (The Philosophy of Loneliness. The Impotence of the Ideas of Existentialism). *Pod znamenem leninizma* (Kiev), vol. 15, 1970, 65-70.

5668    Tafforeau, J.-P. *Heidegger.* (Classiques du XXe siècle, 102). Paris, 1969, 128 p.

5669    Takahashi, Fumio. "Haideggâ no Shi no Kaishaku ni tsuite - Haideggâ no 'Sein und Zeit' o Kaimei shitsutsu Shi no Jitsuzon-ron-teki, Sonzai-ron-teki Kaishaku o Kyûmei Ronkô suru" (Heidegger's Exegesis of Death). *Hôgaku Kiyô* (Nihon Daigaku) (Tôkyô), vol. 9, 1967, 439-501.

5670    Takahashi, Nobukichi. "Haideggâ to Bukkyô to Shi" (Heidegger, Buddhism and Poetry). *Gendai-Shisô* (Tôkyô), vol. 2, no. 10, 1974, 48-52.

5671    Takahashi, Mitsuakj. "'Differenz' to 'Defférance'" (Differenz and Différance). *Gandai-Shisô* (Tôkyô), vol. 2, no. 10, 1974, 111-133.

5672    Takahashi, Satomi. "Haideggeru ni okeru Yugensi no Haaku ni tsuite" (On Heidegger's Concept of Finitude). *Risô* (Tôkyô), vol. 42, September 1933.

5673    Takashina, Junji. "Haideggâno Keijijôgaku" (Heidegger's Metaphysics). *Risô* (Tôkyô), März 1935.

5674    Takatsuka, Hiroshi. "Bashô to Haideggâ; Sonzaironteki Kôsatsu" (Basho and Heidegger; an Ontological Consideration). *Kiyo* (Ageto Gakuen Joshi Tanki Daigaku) (Kagawa), vol. 6, 1976.

5675    Takayanagi, Shun'ichi. "Haideggâ to Gendai Kirisutokyo Shisô" (Heidegger and the Modern Christian Thought). *Sophia* (Tôkyô), vol. 24, no. 2, 1975.

5676    Takechi, Tatehito. "Haideggâhihan to Yuibutsuron no Mondai" (Critique on Heidegger and the Problem of Materialism). Tôkyô, 1963.

5677    Takechi, Tatehito. "Haideggâ no Tenkai to sono Rekishite sugakuteki Igi" (Heidegger's Turning and Its Historic-Philosophical Relevance). *Shisô* (Tôkyô), Oktober 1952.

5678    Takechi, Tatehito. "Haideggâ ni yoru Tetsugaku no Henkaku" (Heidegger's Transformation of Philosophy). *Shisô* (Tôkyô), vol. 372, Juni 1955.

5679    Takechi, Takehito. "Haideggâ, Sarutoru, Marukusu no Hyûmanizumu - Haideggâ Tetsugaku no Hihan no Ichibu" (Humanism - Heidegger, Sartre, Marx). *Shisô* (Tôkyô), vol. 446, 1961, 75-84.

5680    Takeda, Munetoshi. "Haideggâ no Geijutsukan Bungeikan" (Heidegger's Opinion of Art and Literature). *Bunka* (Sendai), März 1942.

5681    Takeda, Sueo. *Sonzai to Snzaisha* (Being -Process and Being). Tôkyô, 1949.

5682    Takeichi, Akihiro. "Sei to Shi" (The Holy and the Death). *Risô* (Tôkyô), vol. 319, 1959, 67-76.

5683    Takeichi, Akihiro. "Haideggâ ni okeru Onaji Hitotsu no Mono" (The Self in Martin Heidegger's Thinking). *Kansaidaigaku-Bungakuronshu* (Ôsaka), November 1965.

5684    Takeichi, Akihiro. "Haideggâ to Nihirizumu no Mondai" (Heidegger and Nihilism). *Risô* (Tôkyô), vol. 444, 1970, 80-91.

5685    Takeichi, Akihiro. "Nihirizumu no Kongen ni tsuite" (On the Origin of Nihilism). *Risô* (Tôkyô), vol. 457, 1971, 37-46.

5686    Takeichi, Akihiro. "Alêtheia; U no Bôkyaku no Konpon-Keiken kara" (Alêtheia; From the Original Experience of the Forgotteness of Being). *Risô* (Tôkyô), vol. 500, 1975, 16-29.

5687    Takeichi, Akihiro. "Mu no genshôgkuteki Bunseki kara kongenteki Nichijôsei e" (From the Analysis of No-Thing to the Original Everydayness). *Shisô* (Tôkyô), vol. 652, 1978, 215-235.

5688    Takeichi, Akihiro. "Ein Weg zu *dem Selben* in Martin Heideggers Denken. Eine phänomenologische Analyse des Nichts." *Philosophisches Jahrbuch* (München), vol. 85, no. 1, 1978, 42-55.

5689    Takeshita, Keiji. "Haideggâ-Tetsugaku no ichi Kôsatsu, Riruke-Ron o Chûshin toshite" (A Contemplation on Heidegger's Philosophy, Particularly in Regard to His Essay on Rilke). *Risô* (Tôkyô), vol. 261, Februar 1955.

5690    Takeshita, Keiji. "Maruseru to Haideggâ" (Marcel and Heidegger). *Shisô* (Tôkyô), vol. 293, 1957.

5691 Takeshita, Naoyuki. "Haideggâ to Yasupâsu" (Heidegger and Jaspers). *Risô* (Tôkyô), März 1935.

5691 Takeshita, Keiji. "Maruseru to Haideggâ" (Marcel and Heidegger). *Shisô* (Tôkyô), vol. 293, 1957.

5692 Takeuchi, Gihan. "Jitsuzontetsugaku to Bukkyô" (Existential Philosophy and Buddhism). *Risô* (Tôkyô), vol. 319, Dezember 1959.

5693 Takeuchi, Toyoji. "Haideggâ no Riruke-Ron" (Heidegger's Essay on Rilke). *Jitsuzon* (Tôkyô), Dezember 1951.

5694 Takeuchi, Toyoji. "Haideggâ no Shi-Ron" (Heidegger's Discussion of Poetry). *Shigaku* (Tôkyô), Mai 1952.

5695 Takeuchi, Toyoji. "Heideggâ no Shiron - Tokuni Herudârin no ichi Shiku no Kaishaku o megutte" (Heidegger's Poetry; His Interpretation of Hölderlin's Poems). *Jitsuzonshugi* (Tôkyô), vol. 20, 1960, 50-61.

5696 Takizawa, Taketo. "Gunôshisu-shugi to Haideggâ no Shii" (Gnosticism and Heidegger's Way of Thinking). *Nihon Shûkyô Gakkai* (Tôkyô), vol. XLIV, no. 4, Juli 1971, 23-55.

5697 Taminiaux, Jacques. "Dialectique et différence." In *Durchblicke*. Ed. V. Klostermann. Frankfurt, 1970, 318-330.

5698 Taminiaux, Jacques. "Finitude et absolu. Remarques sur Hegel et Heidegger, interprètes de Kant." *Revue Philosophique de Louvain* (Louvain), vol. 69, 1971, 190-215.

5699 Taminiaux, Jaques. "Le regard et l'excédent. Remarques sur Heidegger et les *Recherches logiques* de Husserl." *Revue Philosophique de Louvain* (Louvain), vol. 75, 1977, 74-100. [Summary, 100] Rpt. in "Heidegger and Husserl's *Logical Investigations.*" *Research in Phenomenology* (Pittsburgh), vol. 75, no. 25, 1977, 58-83. [Trans. Jeffrey Stevens]

5700 Tanabe, Hajime. "Benshôgaku ni okeru atarashiki Tenkô-Haideggâ no Sei no Genshôgaku" (A New Turning-Point in Phenomenology - Heidegger's Phenomenology of Life). *Collected Works* (Tôkyô), vol. IV, 1924, 17-34.

5701 Tanabe, Hajime. "Ninshikiron to Genshôgaku." *Collected Works* (Tôkyô), vol. IV, 1925, 70-71.

5702 Tanabe, Hajime. "Sôgô to Chyoetsu" (Synthesis and Transcendence). *Collected Works* (Tôkyô), vol. IV, 1930, 329, 353.

5703 Tanabe, Hajime. "Zushiki 'Zikan' Kaya Zushiki 'Sekai' he" (From the Scheme of 'Time' to the Scheme of 'World'). *Collected Works* (Tôkyô), vol. VI, 1932, 1-49.

5704 Tanabe, Hajime. "Tetsugaku to Shi to Shukyo, Haidegga Riruke Herudarin" (Philosophy, Poetry, and Religion - Heidegger, Rilke, and Hölderlin). *Collected Works* (Tôkyô), vol. XIII, 1953, 305-524.

5705 Tanabe, Hajime. "Sûri no Rekishishugitenkai, Kôki" (Fatalistic Explication and Development of the Mathematical Historism). *Collected Works* (Tôkyô), vol. XII, 1954, 330-332.

5706 Tanabe, Hajime. "Sei-no-Sonzaigaku ka Shi-no; Benshôhô ka" (Ontology of Life and Dialectics of Death?) *Collected Works* (Tôkyô), vol. XIII, 1958, 525-641.

5707 Tanabe, Hajime. "Todesdialektik." *Martin Heidegger zum 70. Geburtstag.* Festschrift/Pfullingen, 1959, 93-133.

5708 Tanahashi, Minoru. "Haideggâ ni okeru Gijutsu no Imi" (Heidegger's Meaning of Technology). *Shibaura Kogyô Daigaku Kenkyû Hôkoku Jinbunkeihen* (Tôkyô), vol. 10, 1976, 34-40.

5709 Tanahashi, Minoru. "Haideggâ no Shiso ni okeru 'Mu' no Sobyo" (A Study of 'Nothing' in Heidegger's Thought). *Shibaura Kôgyo Daigaku Kenkyû Hôkoku; Jinbunkeihen.* Tôkyô, 1977, 96-105.

5710 Tanahashi, Minoru. "Haideggâ no Shiron" (Heidegger's Poetics). *Shibaura Kôgyo Daigaku Kenkyo Hôkoku; Jinbunkeihen* (Tôkyô), vol. 12, no. 1, 1978, 47-56.

5711 Tanahashi, Minoru. "Haideggâ ni okeru Hitei to Kôtei" (The Negative and the Positive in Heidegger's Thought). *Rinrigaku Nenpô* (Tôkyô), vol. 28, 1979, 131-143.

5712 Tanaka, Aiji. "M. Haideggâ ni okeru Mushin no Shikô to Shingaku" (Heidegger's Notion of 'Irreligion', and Theology). *Shôin Tanki Daigaku Kenkyû Kiyô* (Tôkyô), vol. 10, 1968, 16-27.

5713 Tanaka, Akira. "Ningen ni okeru Yûgensei to Zentaisei" (Finitude and Entity of Man). *Shisô* (Tôkyô), vol. 147, August 1934.

5714 Tanaka, Kôkô. "Jitsuzon ni okeru Chôetsu no Mondai" (The Problem of Transcendence in Existence). In *Yamagushidaigku-Bungakukaishi.* Yamaguchi, 1954-58.

5715 Tanaka, Masuo. "Haideggâ ni okeru Sonzai to Mu no Mondai" (The Problem of Being and Non-Being in Heidegger). *Tetsugakukenkyû* (Kyôto), vol. 419, September 1953.

5716 Tanaka, Masuo. "Genshoki-Girisha to Haidegga" (Early Greek Thinking and Heidegger). *Tetsugakukenkyu* (Kyôto), vol. 470, September 1960.

5717 Taniyama, Takao. "Jissenteki Jikan no Chôetsuteki Naizaiteki Kôzô" (The Transcendent - Immanent Stucture of Practice Time). *Tetsugakukenkya* (Kyôto), 219, 222, 225, Juni, September und Dezember 1934.

5718 Taniyama, Takao. *Kanto to Keijijôgaku* (Kant and Metaphysics). Tôkyô, 1935.

5719 Taniyama, Takao. *Haideggâ no Mu ni tsuite* (On the Non-Being in Heidegger). Ôsaka-furitsudaigaku-Kiyô, Ôsaka, 1957.

5720 Tank, K. L. "Nicht zu fassen. Martin Heidegger 80 Jahre." *Deutsches Allgemeines Sonntagsblatt,* no. 39, v.28.9.1969, 25.

5721 Tardy, V. "Nemecká filosofie mezi dvenma válkami." *Nová mysl* (Czechoslovakian), vol. 1, no. 1, 1947, 81-88.

5722 Tarnowski, K. "Heidegger i teologia" (Heidegger and Theology). *Znak,* 2 January 1979.

5723    Taroni, Alberto. "I limiti categoriali dell'ontologia Heideggeriana." *Hi dell'Istituto veneto di scienze lettere ed arti classe di scienze morali e lettere* (Venezia), vol. 130, 1972, 47-70.

5724    Tteno, Kiyotaka. *Haideggâ ni okeru Chôetsu no Mondai* (The Problem of Transcendence in Heidegger). Tetsugaku, Tôkyô, 1952, 1953.

5725    Tatsuno, Kiyotaka. "Haideggâ, Konkyo no Meidai" (Heidegger's 'Principle of Ground'). *Tetsugaku* (Mita Tetsugakukai) (Tôkyô), vol. 46, 1965, 125-141.

5726    Taubes, Jacob. "The Development of the Ontological Question in Recent German Philosophy." *Review of Metaphysics,* vol. 6, 1953, 651-664.

5727    Taubes, S. A. "The Gnostic Foundations of Heidegger's Nihilism." *The Journal of Religion* (Chicago), vol. 34, 1954, 155-172.

5728    Taureck, B. "Die Notwendigkeit der Kunst; Fragestellung und die Antwort Heideggers." *Wissenschaft und Weltbild* (Wien), vol. 1, 1972, 35-45.

5729    Taureck, Bernhard. Rev. of *Schellings Abhandlung über das Wesen der menschlichen Freiheit,* by Martin Heidegger. 1971. *Wiener Jahrbuch für Philosophie* (Wien), vol. 6, 1973, 399-405.

5730    Taureck, Bernhard. "Macht und nicht Gewalt. Ein anderer Weg zum Verständnis Nietzsches. Karl Ulmer zum sechzigsten Geburtstag." *Nietzsche-Studien* (Berlin/New York), vol. 5, 1976, 29-54.

5731    Taureck, Bernhard. "Perspektiven in Heideggers Nietzsche-Bild." *Wiener Jahrbuch für Philosophie* (Wien), vol. 9, 1976, 284-297.

5732    Tauxe, H.-Ch. *La notion de finitude dans la philosophie de Martin Heidegger.* (Dialectica). Lausanne, 1971, 253 p.

5733    Tavares de Miranda, M. C. "Caminho e experiência (Notas a propósito do 'Der Feldweg' e do 'Aus der Erfahrung des Denkens' de Martin Heidegger)." *Symposium. Revista da Universidad católica de Pernambuco* (Recife), vol. 2, no. 1, 1960, 1-9.

5734    Tavares De Miranda, M. C. "O pensar e o ser entre Heidegger." *Revista filosofia do Nordest* (Fortaleza, Brasil), vol. 2, 1961, 33-38.

5735    Tavares De Miranda, M. C. "Martin Heidegger, filósofo do Ser." *Revista brasileira de Filosofia* (Sao Paulo), vol. 26, no. 103, 267-274.

5736    Taverna, P. "Le basi della 'Daseinsanalyse': da Heidegger a Binswanger." [Teil 1] *Neuropsichiatria* (Italien), vol. 24, 1968, 37-49.

5737    Tavrizjan, G. M. "'Metatechniceskoe' obosnovanie suscosti techniki M. Chajdeggera" (The 'Meta-Technical' Explication of the Nature of Technology in M. Heidegger). *Voprosy filosofii,* vol. 12, 1971, 122-130.

5738    Tavrizjan, G. M. "Bourgeois Philosophy of Technics and Social Theories." (In Russian). *Voprosy Filosofii* (Moscow), no. 6, 1978, 147-159. [Summary in English]

5739 Tegawa, Seishirô. "30 Nendai no Kiki to Gakumon; Fussâru, Haideggâ, Horukuhaimâ o megutte" (A Crisis in the 1930's and Science; Around Husserl, Heidegger, Horkheimer). *Risô* (Tôkyô), vol. 468, 1972, 59-70.

5740 Tegawa, Seishirô. "Hyûmanizumu ni tsuite; J. Sarutoru, M. Haideggâ o megutte" (On Humanism; Around J. Sartre, M. Heidegger). *Risshô Daigaku Bungakubu Ronsô* (Tôkyô), vol. 46, 1973, 91-106.

5741 Tegawa, Seishirô. "30 Nendai ni okeru Haideggâ ni tsuite" (On Heidegger in the 1930's). *Risshô Daigaku Bungakubu Ronsô* (Tôkyô), vol. 49, 1974, 103-121.

5742 Tegawa, Seishirô. "30 Nendai ni okeru Haideggâ ni tsuite; sono Keijijôgaku-Hihan to Herudârin no Shi o megutte" (On Heidegger in the 1930's; Around the Criticism About Metaphysics and Hölderlin's Poetry). *Tetsugaku.* Tôkyô, 1975, 182-193.

5743 Tegawa, Seishirô. "Haideggâ no Jikansei ni tsuite, 1-2" (On Heidegger's Concept of Time, 1-2). *Risshô Daigaku Bungakubu Ronsô* (Tôkyô), vol. 55, 1976, 79-99; vol. 56, 1976, 76-94.

5744 Tegawa, Seishirô. "Kami no Shi to Ningen; Kerukegôru, Nîche, Haideggâ" (The Death of God and Man; Kierkegaard, Nietzsche, and Heidegger). *Dentô to Gendai* (Tôkyô), vol. 42, 1976, 105-113.

5745 Tegawa, Seishirô. "Haideggâ no 'Jikansei' ni tsuite, 1-2" (On Heidegger's 'Temporality', 1-2). *Risshô Daigaku Bungakubu Ronsô* (Tôkyô), vol. 55, 1976, 79-99; vol. 56, 1976, 76-94.

5746 Teo, Wesley K.-H. *Heidegger on Dasein and Whitehead on Actual Entities.* Phil. Diss. Southern Illinois Univ. 1969 112 p. *Dissertation Abstract International,* vol. 30/07-A, 3058.

5747 Teodorescu, St. "Von der denkenden Einkehr. Bemerkungen Anlässlich des 70. Geburtstages Martin Heideggers." *Christ und Welt* (Stuttgart), vol. 12, no. 3, 1959, 16.

5748 Terajima, Sanehito. "Jitsuzontetsugaku no Hôhô ni tsuite" (On the Method of Existential Philosophy). *Tetsugakuzasshi* (Tôkyô), vol. 602, April 1937.

5749 Teramura, Akinobu. "Haideggâ to Dentôtekironrigaku" (Heidegger and Traditional Logic). *Tetsugaku-Zasshi* (Tôkyô), vol. 92, no. 764, 1977, 161-181.

5750 Tewrizjan, A. "Fenomenologiczny antypsychologizm a problem intuicji w egzystencjalizmie" (Phenomenological Antipsychologism and the Problem of Intuition in Existentialism). Trans. from Russian. In *Filozofia marksizmu a egzystencjalizm* (Marxist Philosophy and Existentialism). Warszawa, 1974.

5751 Tewsadse, Guram. "Martin Heidegger's Critique of the Theory of Truth." *Acta Universitatis Lodziensis* (Uniwersytet Lódzki), Seria I, no. 61, 1979, 13-36.

5752 Tezuka, Tomio. "Haideggâ no Bundeikan" (Heidegger's Opinion on Literature). *Risô* (Tôkyô), vol. 223, Dezember 1951.

5753	Tezuka, Tomio. "Haideggâ tono ichi-Jikan" (An Hour With Prof. Heidegger). *Risô* (Tôkyô), vol. 264, 1955, 54-58.

5754	Theune, H.-J. "Vom eigentlichen Verstehen. Eine Interpretation der hermeneutischen Fragestellung R. Bultmanns auf dem Hintergrund der Existenzanalyse M. Heideggers." *Evangelische Theologie* (München), vol. 13, N.F.8, 1953, 171-188.

5755	Theunissen, Michael. "Intentionaler Gegenstand und ontologische Differenz. Ansätze zur Fragestellung Heideggers in der Phänomenologie Husserls." *Philosophisches Jahrbuch* (München), vol. 70, 1962/63, 344-362. "Objeto intencional y diferencia ontológica. Inicios del planteamiento de Heidegger en la fenomenologica de Husserl." Trans. Ramón Castilla Láaro. *Dialogos* (Rio Piedras, Puerto Rico), vol. 1, 1964, 35-59.

5756	Theunissen, Michael. *Der Andere. Studien zur Sozialontologie der Gegenwart.* Berlin, 1965, XV, 538 p.

5757	Theunissen, Michael. "Was heute ist. Über Not und Notwendigkeit des Umgangs mit Heidegger." In *Martin Heidegger. Fragen an sein Werk. Ein Symposium.* (Universal-Bibliothek, 9873). Stuttgart: Reclam, 1977, 21-27.

5758	Theunissen, Michael. "Was heute ist. Mit Heidegger gegen Heidegger denken." *Frankfurter Allgemeine Zeitung* (Frankfurt), no. 114, 17 May 1977, 21.

5759	Thévénaz, P. "Qu'est-ce que la phénoménologie? II. La phénoménologie de Heidegger." *Revue de théologie et de philosophie* (Lausanne), vol. 2, 1952, 126-140.

5760	Thévénaz, P. Rev. of *Kant et le problème de la métaphysique,* by Martin Heidegger. 1929. *Revue de Théologie et de Philosophie* (Lausanne), vol. 3, 1953, 301.

5761	Thévévaz, P. "Le dépassement de la métaphysique." *Revue internationale de philosophie* (Bruxelles), vol. 8, 1954, 189-217, (specifically pages 206-213).

5762	Thévenaz, P. *La fenomenologia. Husserl, Heidegger, Sartre, Merleau-Ponty.* Intr. J. Brun. Trans. G. Mura. Roma, 1969, 102 p.

5763	Thiel, Manfred. "Die Auflösung der Komödie und die Groteske des Mythos." *Studium Generale* (Heidelberg), vol. 8, 1955, 273-284, 328-348, 349-361, (specifically pages 328-348: Heidegger und die Groteskdynamik).

5764	Thiel, Manfred. "Der philosophische Stil." *Studium Generale* (Heidelberg), vol. 8, 1955, 169-194, (specifically pages 180-182).

5765	Thiel, Manfred. *Martin Heidegger. Sein Werk, Aufbau u. Durchblick.* Heidelberg: Elpis-Verlag, 1977, 509 p.

5766	Thielemans, H. "Existence tragique. La metaphysique du nazisme." *Nouvelle revue théologique* (Louvain), vol. 63, 1936, 561-579.

5767	Thielemans, H. "Een metaphysiek der existentie." *Streven* (Brugge), vol. 10, 1943, 332-339.

5768	Thiry, A. Rev. of *Introduction à la métaphysique,* by Martin Heidegger. 1958. *Nouvelle Revue Théologique* (Tournai), vol. 81, 1959, 1104.

5769 Thuijs, R. W. *Martin Heidegger als godsdienstwijsgeer.* Assen, 1956.

5770 Thuijs, R. W. "Het god-loze denken en de goddelijke god in de filosofie van M. Heidegger." In *Mens en God. Wijsgerige beschouwingen over het religieuze.* Utrecht, 1963, 189-220.

5771 Thyssen, J. "A priori, Unbewusstes und Heideggers Weltbegriff." *Archiv für Philosophie* (Stuttgart), vol. 3, 1949, 115-143.

5772 Thyssen, J. "Staat und Recht in der Existenzphilosophie." *Archiv für Rechts und Sozialphilosophie* (Neuwied), vol. 41, 1954, 1-18.

5773 Thyssen, J. "Heidegger und das 'ens et verum convertuntur'." In *Johannes Thyssen: Realismus und moderne Philosophie.* Bonn, 1959, 321-328.

5774 Thyssen, J. "Schopenhauer zwischen den Zeiten." *Kant-Studien* (Köln), vol. 52, 1960, 387-400, (specifically pages 388-393).

5775 Tiebout, H. M. "Subjectivity in Whitehead: A Comment on 'Whitehead and Heidegger'." *Dialectica* (Neuchâtel), vol. 13, 1959, 350-353.

5776 Til, C. van. "The Later Heidegger and Theology." *Westminster Theological Journal,* vol. 26, 1964, 121-161.

5777 Tillich, P. "Existential Philosophy." *Journal of the History of Ideas* (New York), vol. 5, 1944, 44-70.

5778 Tillich, P. *Systematic Theology.* Vol. I, Chicago, Illinois, 1951. 2nd ed. Stuttgart, 1956, 193-245, etc.

5779 Tillich, P. *Courage to be.* New Haven, 1952, (specifically pages 138-150, und passim).

5780 Tilliette, X. Rev. of *Essais et conférences,* by Martin Heidegger. 1958. *Etudes* (Paris), vol. 301, 1959, 127.

5781 Tilliette, X. "Argument ontologique et ontothéologie. Notes conjointes. Schelling et l'argument ontologique. La démarche des cinq voies d'aprés Gustav Siewerth." *Archives de Philosophie* (Paris), vol. 26, 1963, 90-116.

5782 Tilliette, X. Rev. of *L'être et le temps* and *Lettre sur l'humanisme,* by Martin Heidegger. 1964. *Etudes* (Paris), vol. 321, 1964, 304-305.

5783 Tint, H. "Heidegger and the 'Irrational'." *Proceedings of the Aristotelian Society* (London), vol. 57, 1956/57, 253-268.

5784 Tischner, J. "The Modifications of Primeval Structures in the Sphere of Consciousness." (In Polish). *Analecta Cracoviensia, Kraków,* vol. 2, 1970, 27-52. [Summary in French]

5785 Tischner, J. "Perspektywy hermeneutyki" (The Perspectives of Hermeneutics). *Znak,* 3 February 1971.

5786 Tischner, J. "Egzystencja i wartáá" (Existence and Value). *Znak,* 8 July 1972.

5787 Tischner, J. "Martina Heideggera milczenie o Bogu" (M. Heidegger's Silence Concerning God). *Znak,* vol. 6, 1973.

5788 Tischner, J. "M. Heidegger." *W drodze,* vol. 8, 1976.

5789 Tischner, J. Rev. of *Heidegger i filozofia wspóllczesna,* by Krzysztof Michalski. Warszawa, 1978. In *Tygodnik Powszechny,* vol. 31, 1978.

5790   Tlustá, M. [=Jetmarová, M.] "Existencialismus, Jeho filosofická podstata a funkce." *Nová mysl* (Czechoslovakian), no. 7, 1958, 638-653.

5791   Todisco, O. "Metafisica esistenziale e coscienza critica in Martin Heidegger." *Miscellanea Francescana* (Roma), vol. 70, 1970, 214-240.

5792   Todisco, O. "Orrizonte ermeneutico e razionalismo critico." *Miscellanea Francescana* (Roma), vol. 74, no. 1-2, 1974, 3-36.

5793   Todisco, O. "Ermeneutica storiografica, Couvergenza di tre ipotesi di lavoro." *Sapienza* (Roma), vol. 29, no. 4, 1976, 385-418.

5794   Toinet, P. "Vers un age théologique?" *Revue Thomiste,* vol. 75, 1975, 181-230.

5795   Tokawa, Kôji. "Haideggâ ni okeru Kyôsonzai ni tsuite" (On Being-With in Heidegger). *Senriyama Bungaku Ronshû* (Kansai Daigku Daigakuin Bungaku Kenkyûka Insei Kyôgikai) (Gappeigo, Suita), 11/12, 1974.

5796   Tolaba, W. A. "Heidegger y la lógica." *Universidad* (Argentina), no. 60, 95-104.

5797   Tolaba, W. A. "En torno a la pregunta 'Que es el Hombre?'" *Universidad* (Argentina), no. 76, 1968, 219-229.

5798   Tollenaere, M. de. "Immortality: A Reflective Exploration." *International Philosophical Quarterly* (New York/Heverlee/Leuven), vol. 10, 1970, 556-569, (specifically pages 559-561).

5799   Tomilov, V. G. "Kritika koncepcii licnosti M. Chajdeggera" (Criticism of M. Heidegger's Concept of Personality). *Ucenye zapiski Tomskogo universiteta* (Tomsk), vol. 89, 1973, 85-94. (In Russian).

5800   Tonggûn, Min. "Haidegkae issôsôûi singwa yulliûi munje" (God and Ethics in Heidegger). *Ch'ungnam Univ. Collection of Essays* (Ch'ungnam), vol. 1, 1978, 109-120.

5801   Topitsch, E. "Soziologie des Existenzialismus." *Merkur* (Stuttgart), vol. 7, 1953, 501-518, (specifically 511-512).

5802   Torgersen, J. *Naturforskning og katedral.* Oslo, 1960. Rev. of *Fra Homer til Heidegger,* by Wyller. Oslo, 1959.
       [Rev. by T. Sirnes in *Tidsskrits for Den norske laegeforening.* No. 20, 1961.]

5803   Torgersen, J. "Hitler er dod - leve Heidegger " *Verdens Gang* (Oslo), 12.4.1961.

5804   Torgersen, J. "Norsk filosofi og prosessen i Jerusalem." *Verdens Gang* (Oslo), 16.5.1961.

5806   Torii, Masao. "Jitsuzon Tetsugaku Kenkyû-Kirukegôru kara Haideggâ e" (Existential Philosophy - From Kierkegaard to Heidegger). *Gozen,* no. 1-5, September 1948-März 1949, insgesamt 56 p.

5807   Torrance, T. F. Rev. of *Being and Time,* by Martin Heidegger. *The Journal of the Theological Studies* (London), vol. 15, 1964, 471-486.

5808   Torres, J. V. "El primado de la temporalidad." *Actas del primer Congreso nacional de Filosofia* (Mendoza), vol. 2, 1942, 858-864, passim.

5809 Toussaint, Bernhard J. *The Interpretation of the 'Self' in the Early Heidegger.* Phil. Diss. De Paul Univ. Chicago 1971 326 p. *Dissertation Abstracts International,* vol. 33/01-A, 363.

5810 Towarnicki, A. De. "Visite à Martin Heidegger." *Les temps modernes* (Paris), vol. 1, no. 4, 1945/46, 717-724.

5811 Towarnicki, Frédéric de. "Conversación con Heidegger." *Ideas y Valores,* no. 35-37, 1970, 87-96.

5812 Towarnicki, Frédéric de. "Rencontres avec Heidegger." *Magazine Littéraire* (Paris), no. 117, 1976, 24-27.

5813 Tôyama, Taiken. "Pyusisu no jitsuzonteki-Kaishaku" (Existential Interpretation of Physis). *Risô* (Tôkyô), vol. 371, 1964, 71-83.

5814 Tôyama, Taiken. "Haideggâ no Dâzain no Kaijisei to Shûkyô" (Discloseness of Being-There in Heidegger's Philosophy and Religion). *Shûkyô Kenkyô* (Tôkyô), vol. 214, 1973, 73-74. Rpt. in *Jitsuzon no Chôetsu Konkyo* (The Transcendental Grounds of Existence). Nihon Gakujitsu Tsûshinsha, Tôkyô, 1979, 301-304.

5815 Tôyama, Taiken. "Naizai to Chôetsu oyobi Chôetsu-Konkyo" (Immanence, Transcendence, and the Ground of Transcendence). *Nihon Daigaku Rikôgakubu Ippankyôiku-Ihô* (Tôkyô), vol. 22, 1977, 1-6. Rpt. in *Jitsuzon no Chôetsukonkyo* (The Transcendental Grounds of Existence). Nihon Gakujitsu Tsûshinsha, Tôkyô, 1979, 1-20.

5816 Tôyama, Ikuyo. "Haideggâ ni okeru 'Mono' eno Toi" (Inquiry to 'Thing' in Heidegger). *Bukkyô Daigaku Kenkyû Kiyô* (Kyôto), vol. 62, 1978, 79-110.

5817 Tôyama, Yoshio. *Gendai Tetsugaku - Doitsu - Hussâru kara Haideggâ e* (Contemporary German Philosophy; From Husserl to Heidegger). Ed. S. Komatsu. Shisô no nagare (History of Philosophical Thought). Bunrin-Shoin, Tôkyô, 1967, (specifically pages 201-235).

5818 Tracy, David. "A Response and Commentary." *Listening,* vol. 10, Winter 1975, 73-77.

5819 Traub, F. "Heidegger und die Theologie." *Zeitschrift für systematische Theologie* (Güterloh), vol. 9, 1931/32, 686-743.

5820 Traugott, E. "Was ich begriffen habe ist grossartig..." Rev. of *Einführung in die Metaphysik,* by Martin Heidegger. 1953. *Kulturnachrichten in Oberösterreichische Nachrichten* (Linz), 25.9.1954.

5821 Trebolle, J. "El problema hermenéutico de la distancia temporal. Dilthey, Heidegger, Gadamer." *Augustinianum* (Roma), vol. 13, no. 1, 1973, 93-129.

5822 Trépanier, Emmanuel. "La signification du 'je suis' selon Martin Heidegger." *Sciences ecclésiastiques* (Montréal), vol. 10, 1958, 203-226.

5823 Trépanier, Emmanuel. "Phénoménologie et ontologie: Husserl et Heidegger." *Laval Théologique et Philosophique* (Québec), vol. 28, no. 3, 1972, 249-267.

5824 Tripp, Charles James. *The Comparative Study of Decision Making Methodologies: A Look at the Dicision Making Framework and Heidegger's*

*'Being and Time'.* Phil. Diss. Wayne State Univ. 1974. *Dissertation Abstracts International,* vol. 35/12-A, 7989.

5825    Tristani, J. L. "Machiavel ou le sytème indo-européen de la vertu." *Revue Philosophique de la France et de l'Etranger* (Paris), no. 3, 1974, 305-312.

5826    Trivers, Howard. "Heidegger's Misinterpretation of Hegel's Views on Spirit and Time." *Philosophy and Phenomenological Research* (Buffalo, New York), vol. 3, 1942/43, 162-168.

5827    Trotignon, P. "L'oeuvre de Heidegger." (Bibliographie). *Revue de l'Enseignement philosophique,* vol. 14, 1964, 10-18, 24-26.

5828    Trotignon, P. *Heidegger. Sa vie, son oeuvre avec un exposé de sa philosophie.* (Coll. 'Philosophies'). Paris, 1965, 124 p. 2nd ed. 1974, 128 p.

5829    Troutner, Leroy Franklin. *Educational Implications of Existentialism: An Analysis and Comparison of Martin Heidegger and John Dewey.* Phil. Diss. Stanford Univ. 1962. *Dissertation Abstracts International,* vol. 23/06, 2035, 347 p.

5830    Troutner, Leroy Franklin. "The Dewey-Heidegger Comparison Re-Visited: A Reply and Clarification." *Educational Theory* (Urbana), vol. 22, 1972, 212-220.

5831    Troutner, Leroy Franklin. "The Dewey-Heidegger Comparison Revisited: A Perspectival Partnership for Education." *Philosophy of Education Society* (Edwardsville), vol. 28, 1972, 28-44.

5832    Troutner, Leroy Franklin. "Toward a Phenomenology of Education: An Exercise in the Foundations." *Philosophy of Education: Proceedings,* vol. 30, 1974, 148-164.

5833    Tsujimura, Kôichi. "Haideggâ no Konponkeiken" (The Fundamental Experiences of Heidegger's Thinking). *Tetsugakukenkyû* (Kyôto), vol. 425, July 1954.

5834    Tsujimura, Kôichi. "Haideggâ to Rekishi no Mondai" (Heidegger and the Problem of History). *Tetsugakukenkyû* (Kyôto), 434, 437, August, November 1955.

5835    Tsujimura, Kôichi. "Benshôhô to Toki" (Dialectics and Time). *Tetsugakukenkyû* (Kyôto), vol. 489, April 1964.

5836    Tsujimura, Kôichi. "Burutoman to Haideggâ, Shinkô to Shii" (Bultmann and Heidegger. On the Problems of Belief and Thinking). *Tetsugakukenkyû* (Kyôto), vol. 493, Oktober 1964.

5837    Tsujimura, Kôichi. "Kanto to Haideggâ" (Kant and Heidegger). *Jitsuzonshugi* (Tôkyô), April 1966.

5838    Tsujimura, Kôichi. "Haideggâ ni okeru Sekai no Mondai - 'U to Toki' no Jiki ni okeru (1)" (The Problem of 'World' in Heidegger During the Genesis of 'Sein und Zeit'). *Tetsugaku Kenkyû* (Kyôto), vol. 44, no. 5, 1969, 21-48.

5839    Tsujimura, Kôichi. "Haideggâ ni okeru Sekai no Mondai - 'U to Toki' no Jiki ni okeru - (2)" (The Problem of 'World' in Heidegger - During the Genesis of 'Sein und Zeit' (2)). *Tetsugaku Kenkyû* (Kyôto), vol. 44, no. 6, 1969, 1-17.

5840 Tsujimura, Kôichi. "Martin Heidegger." In *Martin Heidegger im Gespräch.* Ed. R. Wisser. Freiburg/München, 1970, 27-30.

5841 Tsujimura, Kôichi. *Haideggâ Ronkô* (Research on Heidegger). Tôkyô, März, 1971, 278 p.

5842 Tsujimura, Kôichi. "Haideggâ Kyôju e no Henshin" (The Letter to Prof. Heidegger). *Risô* (Tôkyô), vol. 500, 1975, 7-15.

5843 Tsujimura, Kôichi. "Heimgang. Gedenkwort für Herrn Professor Martin Heidegger." In *Gedenkschrift der Stadt Messkirch an ihren Sohn und Ehrenbürger Professor Martin Heidegger.* Foreword and postscript by Siegfried Schuhle. Messkirch: Stadt Messkirch, 1977, 15-16.

5844 Tsujimura, Kôichi. "Eine Bemerkung zu Heideggers 'Aus der Erfahrung des Denkens'." In *Nachdenken über Heidegger.* Ed. Ute Guzzoni. Hildesheim: Gerstenberg Verlag, 1980, 275-286.

5845 Tsukagoshi, Satoshi. "Riruke Bungaku Kaimei ni okeru Haideggâ no Gobuâ" (Heidegger's Mistakes Concerning the Explication of Rilke's Poetry). *Geibun Kenkyu* (Tôkyô), vol. 6, 1957, 115-147.

5846 Tsumura, Yûzô. "Jitsuzon to Ryôshin - Haideggâ no Ryôshin-Ron" (Existence and Conscience - Heidegger's Theory of Conscience). *Jitsuzonshugi* (Tôkyô), vol. 58, Dezember 1971, 42-46.

5847 Tsunoda, Yukihiko. "Haideggâ no Kanto Kaishaku" (Heidegger's Interpretation of Kant). *Meiji Daigaku Kyoyô Ronshû* (Tôkyô), vol. 90, 1975.

5848 Tsunoda, Yukihiko. "Genshôgakuteki Sekai Gainen e no yobiteki Kôsatsu; Haideggâ to Meruro-Pontei" (Preparatory Consideration to the Phenomenological Concept of the World; Heidegger and Merleau-Ponty). *Meiji Daigaku Kyôyô Ronshû* (Tôkyô), vol. 105, 1976, 19-46.

5849 Tsuchida, Sadao. "Shizen no Henzai" (The Omnipresence of Nature). *Gendai-Shisô* (Tôkyô), vol. 2, no. 10, 1974, 53-55.

5850 Tsuchiya, Kenji. "Haideggâno Arisutoteresu-Kaishaku" (Heidegger's Interpretation on Aristotele). *Jitsuzonshugi,* vol. 69, 1974, 26-37.

5851 Tuedio, James Alan. "The Engagement in Lived Immediacy: A Phenomenological Uncovering of the Field of Human Freedom." *Auslegung,* vol. 6, Fall 1979, 97-113.

5852 Tugendhat, Ernst. *Der Wahrheitsbegriff bei Husserl und Heidegger.* Berlin, 1967, XII, 415 p. 2nd ed. 1970.

5853 Tugendhat, Ernst. "Heideggers Idee von Wahrheit." In *Heidegger.* Ed. O. Pöggeler. Köln/Berlin, 1969, 286-297.

5854 Tugendhat, Ernst. "Das Sein und das Nichts." In *Durchblicke.* Ed. V. Klostermann. Frankfurt, 1970, 132-161.

5855 Tuha, Chôn. "Haidegkaûi hugiûi chonjaewa Yulgokûi ujurone issôsôûi igiwaûi pigyo" (A Comparison Between the Being in the Late Heidegger and the Li in Yulgok's Cosmology). *Ch'ôrhak Yôngu* (Sôul), vol. 2, 1967, 26-48.

5856 Tuijie, Xiang. "Hai Dege de 'Cunyou yu shijian'" (Heidegger's 'Being and Time'). *Xiandai xueyuan* (Taibei), vol. 6, no. 10, 1969. (In Chinese).

5857 Tuijie, Xiang. "Hai Dege sixiang yu huangdi de shengfu" (Heidegger's Thinking and the Emperor's New Dress). *Zhexue yu wenhue yuekan* (Taibei), vol. 3, no. 7, 1976. (In Chinese).

5858 Tumarkin, A. "Heideggers Existenzialphilosophie." *Schweizerische Zeitschrift für Psychologie und ihre Anwendungen* (Bern), vol. 2, 1943, 145-159.

5859 Tuni, G. "Esistenzialismo e storia." *Atti del congresso internazionale di folosofia, promosso dall'Istitudi di Studi Filosofici, Roma 15-20 novembre 1946.* II.: L'esistenzialismo. Milano, 1948, 463-475, (specifically pages 466-468).

5860 Turnbull, Robert G. "Heidegger on the Nature of Truth." *The Journal of Philosophy* (Lancaster, Pennsylvania), vol. 54, 1957, 559-565.

5861 Tweedie, Donald F. *The Significance of Dread in the Thought of Kierkegaard and Heidegger.* Boston, 1954.

5862 Tymieniecka, Anna-Teresa. "Cosmos, Nature and Man and the Foundations of Psychiatry." In *Heidegger and the Path of Thinking.* Ed. J. Sallis. Pittsburgh, 1970, 191-220.

5863 Tzavaras, Johann. "Probleme der Übersetzung von Heideggers *Sein und Zeit* ins Neugriechische und Vorschläge zu ihrer Lösung." [Greek text with a summary in German.] *UIKOROUIA* (Athens), vol. 4, 1974, 449-457, 458.

5864 Uexküll, von. Rev. of *Was heisst Denken?* by Martin Heidegger. 1954. *Der Nervenarzt* (Berlin/Göttingen/Heidelberg), vol. 28, 1957, 39.

5865 Uffelmann, H. W. *Towards an Ontology of Social Relations.* Phil. Diss. Northwestern Univ. Evanston 1967 212 p.

5866 Ugazio, Ugo Maria. *Il problema della morte nella filosofia di Heidegger.* (Studi di filosofia, 14). Milano: Murisia, 1976, 191 p.

5867 Ugirashebuja, Octave. *Dialogue entre la poésie et la pensée d'après l'oeuvre de Heidegger.* Bruxelles: Editions Lumen Vitae, 1977, 236 p.

5868 Uhl, H., ed. *Hebeldank.* Bekenntnis zum alemannischen Geist in 7 Reden beim 'Schatzkästlein'. Freiburg, 1964, 154 p.

5869 Uhsadel, W. Rev. of *Unterwegs zur Sprache,* by Martin Heidegger. 1959. *Theologische Literaturzeitung* (Leipzig), vol. 86, 1961, 217-221.

5870 Ullmann, E. "Die 'gequantelte Zeit'." *Wissenschaft und Weltbild* (Wien), vol. 10, 1957, 132-137.

5871 Umehara, Takeshi. "Haideggâ no Jikan-Ron" (Heidegger's Discussion of Time). *Ritsumeikanbungaku* (Kyôto), vol. 110, 1954.

5872 Umehara, Takeshi, and Masahiro Oku. "Haideggâ to Bukkyô" (Heidegger and Buddhism - an Interview). *Risô* (Tôkyô), vol. 444, 1970, 105-118.

5873 Umehara, Takeshi. "Heidegger and Buddhism." *Philosophy East and West* (Honolulu), vol. 20, 1970, 271-281.

5874 Uña Juárez, A. "La cuestion heideggeriana." *La Ciudad de Dios* (Escorial/Madrid), vol. 181, 1968, 262-291.

5875 Uña Juárez, Octavio. "Fenomenologia del lenguaje como comunicación en Martin Heidegger." *Religion and Culture*, vol. 24, no. 104, 1978, 357-379.

5876 Uranga, E. "Heidegger, Kant y Santo Tomás en torno a la teoria de la verdad." *Filosofia y Letras* (Mexico), no. 55-56, 1954, 85-105.

5877 Urbach, O. "Sinnlose Existenz?" *Unsere Welt* (Leipzig), vol. 28, 1936, 138-141.

5878 Urbanáiá, Ivan. "A Marginal Note on the Question of the Origin and the Route." (In Serbocroat). *Delo* (Beograd), vol. 23, no. 12, 1977, 163-176.

5879 Urdanoz, J. "Heidegger y Sto. Tomás." *La Ciencia Tomista* (Salamanca), vol. 84, 1957, 674-681.

5880 Urdanoz, T. "Existencialismo y filosofia de la existencia humana." *Estudios Filosoficos* (Las Caldas de Besaya, Santander), vol. 9, 1960, 5-96, 199-263.

5881 Urdánoz, T. "El problema de la fundamentación del ser. Una confrontación de Heidegger con Sto. Tomás." *Estudios Filosóficos* (Las Caldas de Besaya, Santander), vol. 19, 1970, 203-218.

5882 Urmaneta, F. de. "Sobre estética heideggeriana." *Revista de Ideas Estéticas* (Madrid), vol. 26, 1968, 279-281.

5883 Uscatescu, G. "El humanismo de Martin Heidegger." *Revista de Filosofia* (Madrid), vol. 17, 1958, 459-470.

5884 Uscatescu, G. "L'umanésimo di Martin Heidegger." *Humanitas* (Brescia), vol. 13, 1958, 355-364.

5885 Uscatescu, G. "L'antropologia E I Suoi Problemi in San Tommaso D'Aquino." *Giornale di Metafisica*, vol. 32, 1977, 197-204.

5886 Uscatescu, Jorge. "Humanismo y tecnica en Martin Heidegger." *Crisis* (Madrid), vol. 7, 1960, 89-103.

5887 Uscatescu, Jorge. "Nuevos aspectos de la fenomenologia del lenguajâ." *Arbor* (Madrid), vol. 68, 1967, 199-211.

5888 Uscatescu, Jorge. "Los ochenta años de Martin Heidegger." Trans. by B. López-Riobóos. *Crisis* (Madrid), vol. 17, 1970, 287-293.

5889 Uscatescu, Jorge. *Symposion Heidegger.* Homenaje rumano a M. Heidegger, bajo la dirección de J. Uscatescu. Madrid, 1971, 87 p.

5890 Uscatescu, Jorge. "Platon et Aristote dans le 'système moderne du savoir'." *Diotima* (Athènes), vol. 4, 1976, 163-169.

5891 Usinger, F. "Denken und Sein." Rev. of *Was heisst Denken?* by Martin Heidegger. 1954. *Deutsche Rundschau* (Baden-Baden), vol. 81, 1955, 645-647.

5892 Uslar, D. von. *Vom Wesen der Begegnung. Eine Untersuchung am Phänomen des Gelübdes im Hinblick auf die Frage nach dem Selbstseinkönnen des Daseins bei Martin Heidegger.* Phil. Diss. Freiburg 1953 137 p.

5893 Uslar, D. von. "Vom Wesen der Begegnung im Hinblick auf die Unterscheidung von Selbstsein und Sein selbst bei Heidegger." *Zeitschrift für philosophische Forschung* (Meisenheim/Glan), vol. 13, 1959, 85-101.

5894 Uslar, D. von. *Die Wirklichkeit des Psychischen, Leiblichkeit - Zeitlichkeit.* Pfullingen, 1969, 108 p.

5895 Ussher, Arland. *Journey Through Dread.* (A study of Kierkegaard, Heidegger and Sartre). New York, 1955, 160 p. 2nd ed. 1968.

5896 [SSSR-Kollektiv] *Die deutsche Philosophie nach 1945.* 'Unser Weltbild', Bd 19, Ost-Berlin, 1961. [2. Die Existenzphilosophie: M. Heidegger, 15-20.]

5897 Utitz, E. "Bemerkungen zur deutschen Existenz-Philosophie." *Philosophische Studien* (Berlin), vol. 1, 1949, 392-402.

5898 Utsunomiya, Yoshiaki. "Nekuroröku" (Nekrolog). *Risô* (Tôkyô), vol. 517, 1976, 127-130.

5899 Utsunomiya, Yoshiaki. "Haideggâ to Kachi no Mondai" (Heidegger and the Problem of Value). *Risô* (Tôkyô), vol. 542, 1978, 61-75.

5900 V., E. Rev. of *Einführüng in die Metaphysik,* by Martin Heidegger. 1953. *Rheinische Post* (Düsseldorf), vom 22.8.1953.

5901 Vadakethala, Francis J. *Discovery of Being.* Bangalore: Dharmaram College, 1970, xii-148 p.

5902 Vail, Loy M. "Heidegger's Conception of Philosophy." *The New Scholasticism* (Washington), vol. 42, 1968, 470-496.

5903 Vail, Loy M. *Heidegger and Ontological Difference.* (A Rider College Pub.). Univ. Park/London: The Pennsylvania State Univ. Press, 1972, 224 p.

5904 Vandenberg, Donald. "Kneller, Heidegger, and Death." *Educational Theory,* vol. 17, 1967, 176-177. (15, July 1965, 217-221).

5905 Vander Gucht, R. Rev. of *L'ête et le temps; Heidegger, Lettre sur l'humanisme,* by Martin Heidegger. *La Revue Nouvelle* (Tournai), vol. 41, 1965, 440-441.

5906 Van der Wey, A. "De filosofische inslag van het National Socialisme." *Tijdschrift voor Filosofie* (Leuven), vol. 2, 1940, 21-110.

5907 Van de Water, Lambert. "Het 'Ding' in de metafysiek volgens Heidegger." *Tijdschrift voor Filosofie* (Leuven), vol. 30, 1968, 348-365.

5908 Van de Water, Lambert. "Being and Being Human: An Impasse in Heidegger's Thought." *International Philosophical Quarterly* (Bronx, New York), vol. 13, no. 3, 1973, 391-402.

5909 Van de Wiele, Joseph. "'Res' en 'Ding'. Bijdrage tot een vergelijkende studie van de zijnsopvatting in het thomisme en bij Heidegger." *Tijdschrift voor Philosophie* (Leuven), 1962, 427-506.

5910 Van de Wiele, Joseph. *Zijnswaarheid en onverborgenheid. Een vergelijkende studie over de ontologische waarheid in het thomisme en bij Heidegger.* (Leuvense universitaire uitgaven). Leuven, 1964, 448 p.

5911 Van de Wiele, Joseph. "Les structures fondamentales de la vie cognitive. Contribution à une anthropologie Philosophique." *Revue Philosophique de Louvain* (Louvain), vol. 64, 1966, 96-129.

5912 Van de Wiele, Joseph. "Heidegger et Nietzsche" (Le problème de la métaphysique). *Revue Philosophique de Louvain* (Louvain), vol. 66, 1968, 435-486.

5913 Van de Wiele, Joseph. "La dialectique chez Heidegger." *La Dialectique*. I; Actes du XIVe Congrès des Sociétés de Philosophie de Langue Française, Nice, 1-4 septembre 1969. Paris, 1969, 304 p; darin: 108-111.

5914 Van de Wiele, Joseph. "La métaphysique et le problème de Dieu. Un dialogue avec Martin Heidegger." In *Miscellanea Albert Dondeyne*. (Bibliotheca Ephemeridum Theologicarum Lovaniensium, 35). Leuven: Leuven Univ. Press; Gembloux: Ed. J. Duculot, 1974, 456 p.

5915 Van de Wiele, Jozeph. "Kant et Heidegger. Le sens d'une opposition." *Revue Philosophique de Louvain* (Louvain), vol. 76, no. 29, 1978, 29-52. (Abstract, 52-53).

5916 Van Doosselaere, E. "L'ouverture au mystère de l'Etre par l'angoisse et la Sérénité." (In Nederl). *Tijdschrift voor Filosofie* (Louvain), vol. 37, no. 3, 1975, 445-476.

5917 Van Doosselaere, E. "Angst en gelatenheid als openheid voor het zijns-mysterie." *Tijdschrift voor Filosofie* (Leuven), vol. 37, 1975, 445-474. [Résumé: *L'ouverture au mystère de l'Être par l'angoisse et la Sérénité*, 474-476.]

5918 Van Doosselaere, E. Rev. of *M. Heidegger: In Europe and America*. Ed. E. G. Ballard and Charles E. Scott. 1973, [1974]. *Tijdschrift voor Filosofie* (Leuven), vol. 38, 1976, 168-169.

5919 Van Dosselaere, E. Rev. of *Von der Existenzialontologie zur Seinsgeschichte: Eine Untersuchung über die Philosophie Martin Heideggers*, by Winfried Franzen. 1972. *Tijdschrift voor Filosofie* (Leuven), vol. 39, 1977, 347-348.

5920 Van Luijk, H. "De gelding van het woord. Een beschouwing rondom Heidegger." *Bijdragen. Tijdschrift voor Filosofie en Theologie* (Nijmegen/Leuven), vol. 30, 1969, 257-277. (Summary, Die Geltung des Wortes. Eine Darlegung mit Rücksicht auf Heidegger, 277-278).

5921 Van Nierop, M. *Martin Heideggers Ontologie van het Kunstwerk. Een kritische tekstanalyse van Sein und Zeit, 1. Abschnitt, en van Der Ursprung der Kunstwerkes*. (Filosofische reeks, no. 3 - 1977). Amsterdam: Centrale Interfaculteit, Univ. van Amsterdam, 1977, 47 p.

5922 Vanni-Rovighi, S. "Il valore della fenomenologia. A proposito di una discussione promossa dalla 'Société Thomiste'." *Rivista di filosofia neoscolastica* (Milano), vol. 25, 1933, 338-345.

5923 Vanni-Rovighi, S. "Un libro sulla filosofia di M. Heidegger." *Rivista di filosofia neoscolastica* (Milano), vol. 34, 1942, 286-302.

5924 Vanni-Rovighi, S. "L'interpretazione heideggeriana di Kant." *Esistenzialismo. Saggi di vari autori a cura di L. L. Pelloux.* Roma, 1943.

5925 Vanni-Rovighi, S. *Heidegger.* Brescia, 1945.

5926 Vassilie Lementy, S. T. "Le sens du néant." *Sapienza. Rivista Internazionale di Filosofia e di Teologie* (Napoli), vol. 25, no. 4, 1972, 419-429.

5927 Vásquez, E. *En torno al concepto de la alienación en Marx y Heidegger.* (Col. Avance, 17). Caracas, 1967, 144 p.

5928 Vater, Michael G. "Heidegger and Schelling: The Finitude of Being." *Idealistic Studies* (Worcester), vol. 5, 1975, 20-58.

5929 Vàttimo, Gianni. "Chi è il Nietzsche di Heidegger." *Filosofia* (Torino), vol. 14, 1963, 3-37.

5930 Vàttimo, Gianni. "Fondazione dell'ontologia in 'Sein und Zeit' di Heidegger." *Filosofia* (Torino), vol. 14, 1963, 745-782.

5931 Vàttimo, Gianni. *Essere, storia e linguaggio in Heidegger (Sguardi su la filosofia contemporanea, 50).* Filosofia, Torino, 1963, VIII, 202 p.

5932 Vàttimo, Gianni. "La riflessione sull'arte nel pensiero di Heidegger." *Rivista di Estetica* (Torino/Padova), vol. 8, 1963, 418-462.

5933 Vàttimo, Gianni. *Arte e verità nel pensiero di Martin Heidegger.* 1965/66. Torino, 1966, 146 p.

5934 Vàttimo, Gianni. "Arte, sentimento, originarietà nell'estetica de Heidegger." *Rivista di Estetica* (Torino/Padova), vol. 12, 1967, 267-288.

5935 Vàttimo, Gianni. *Introduzione a Heidegger.* Bari, 1971, 193 p.

5936 Vàttimo, Gianni. "Le aventure della differenza." *Verifiche,* vol. 8, no. 1, 1979, 63-79.

5937 Vàttimo, Gianni. "An-Denken. Denken und Grung." In *Nachdenken über Heidegger.* Ed. Ute Guszzoni. Hildesheim: Gerstenberg Verlag, 1980, 287-302.

5938 Vaya Menéndez, J. "La cuestión de la técnica en una doble 'meditación': Ortega y Heidegger." *Concivium* (Barcelona), vol. 5, no. 9-10, 1960, 69-91.

5939 Vaya Menéndez, J. "La cuestión de la técnica en una doble 'meditación': Ortega y Heidegger (continuación)." *Convivium* (Barcelona), vol. 6, no. 11-12, 1961, 75-97.

5940 Vázquez, Francisco. "Humanismo de la autenticidad esencial en Heidegger." *Estudios* (Merced), vol. 33, no. 116, 1977, 7-19.

5941 Veauthier, W. "Analogie des Seins und ontologische Differenz." *Symposion* (Stuttgart/Freiburg), vol. 4, 1955, 1-89.

5942 Vedaldi, A. *Esistenzialismo.* Verona, 1947, 63-76 und passim.

5943 Vedaldi, A. "Recenti studi sull'existenzialismo." *Rivista Critica di storia della filosofia* (Milano), vol. 7, 1952, 306-312.

5944 Vegas González, Serafin. "En torno a Martin Heidegger. Las contradicciones de la filosofia de lo extraordinario." *Arbor* (Madrid), vol. 94, no. 367-368, 1976, 353-362.

5945 Vélez, D. C. "Vicisitudes del yo en Husserl." *Man and World* (Pittsburgh), vol. 1, 1968, 540-562, (specifically pages 550-557).

5946 Vélez Sáenz, J. "La estructura ontológica del ser-ahi en Heidegger." *Ideas y Valores* (Bogotá), no. 48-49, 1977, 21-46.

5947 Veres, T. "The Last Days of Martin Heidegger." (In Serbocroat). *Obnovljeni Zivot* (Zagreb), vol. 32, no. 1, 1977, 53-59.

5948 Vergauwen, G. Rev. of *Schellings Abhandlung. Über das Wesen der menschlichen Freiheit,* by Martin Heidegger. 1971. *Tijdschrift voor Filosofie* (Leuven), vol. 34, 1972, 370-373.

5949 Vergote, A. "La philosophie de la religion." *Revue philosophique de Louvain,* vol. 68, 1970, 385-393.

5950 Vernaux, Roger. *Leçons sur l'existentialisme et ses formes principales.* Paris, 1948, (secifically pages 59-80).

5951 Vernaux, Roger. "Note sur la philosophie chretienne en marge de Heidegger." *Scripta Theologica* (Pamplona), vol. 11, 1979, 711-722.

5952 Verra, Valerio. "Heidegger, Schelling e l'idealismo tedesco." *Archivo di Filosofia* (Roma), no. 1, 1974. Padova: Cedam, 1974, 51-71.

5953 Versényi, Laszlo. *Heidegger, Being and Truth.* Yale Univ. Press, New Haven, 1965, 201 p.

5954 Versenyi, Laszlo. "The Quarrel Between Philosophy and Poetry." *The Philosophical Forum* (Boston), vol. 2, 1970/71, 200-212.

5955 Verweyen, H. *Ontologische Voraussetzungen des Glaubensaktes.* Düsseldorf, 1969, 236 p.

5956 Vetter, Helmuth. "Theologie und Philosophie. Zu Rudolf Bultmanns Ansatz einer existenzialen Interpretation der neutestamentlichen Verkündigung." *Wissenschaft und Weltbild* (München), vol. 24, 1971, 287-294.

5957 Vial Larrain, Juan de Dios. "Sobre el ser y la verdaad en Heidegger." *Anales de la Universidad de Chiles* (Santiago), vol. 102, 1956, 63-70.

5957a Vial Larrain, Juan de Dios. *Tres Ideas de la Filosofia y una Teoria.* Santiago, 1979.

5957b Vial Larrain, Juan de Dios. *Heidegger y la Filosofia.* Santiago, 1979.

5958 Vicente, L. de G. "Sobre la semática del ser en Martin Heidegger." *Estudios Filosóficos* (Valladolid), no. 65, 1975, 34-54.

5959 Vick, G. R. "Heidegger's Linguistic Rehabilitation of Parmenides 'Being'." *American Philosophical Quarterly* (Oxford), vol. 8, 1971, 139-150. Rpt. in *Heidegger and Modern Philosophy,* by M. Murray (ed.). Yale Univ. Press, 1978, 203-221.

5960 Vick, G. R. "A New 'Copernican Revolution' (Heideggerian Revolution Especially in His Work: 'Introduction to Metaphysics')." *The Personalist* (Los Angeles), vol. 52, 1971, 630-642.

5961 Vieillard-Baron, Jean-Louis. *Le temps. Platon, Hegel, Heidegger.* Paris: J. Vrin, 1978, 46 p.

5962    Vidal, Francisco Canals. "Teoria y Praxis en la Perspectiva de la Dignidad del ser Personal." *Espiritu,* vol. 25, 1976, 121-128.

5963    Vietta, Egon. "Martin Heidegger und die Situation der Jugend." *Die Neue Rundschau* (Berlin/Leipzig), vol. 2, 1931, 501-511.

5964    Vietta, Egon. "Martin Heidegger." *Die Literatur* (Monatsschrift für Literaturfreunde. Das Literarische Echo) (Stuttgart/Berlin), vol. 35, 1932/33, 585.

5965    Vietta, Egon. "Martin Heidegger." *Die Literarische Welt* (Berlin), vol. 12, 1936, 830-835.

5966    Vietta, Egon. *Theologie ohne Gott.* Zürich, 1946, 48 f.

5967    Vietta, Egon. "Der Wandel des Abendländischen Denkens. Heidegger und sein Brief an Jean Beaufret." *Die Zeit* (Hamburg), Jg. 3, no. 4, 1948, 4.

5968    Vietta, Egon. "Existentielles Philosophieren." *und liess ein Taube fliegen. Ein Almanach für Kunst und Dichtung.* Reinbek bei Hamburg, 1948, 78-91, passim.

5969    Vietta, Egon. *Die Seinsfrage bei Martin Heidegger.* Stuttgart, 1950, 146 p.

5970    Vietta, Egon. "Being, World and Understanding. A Commentary on Heidegger." *The Review of Metaphysics* (New Haven, Connecticut), vol. 5, 1951/52, 157-172.

5971    Vietta, Egon. "Die Vorträge Martin Heideggers 1949-1951." *Universitas* (Stuttgart), vol. 6, 1951, 1359-1361.

5972    Vietta, Egon. "Georg Trakl in Heideggers Sicht." *Die Pforte* (Stuttgart), vol. 5, 1953, 351-355.

5973    Vietta, Egon. Rev. of *Einführung in die Metaphysik,* by Martin Heidegger. 1953. *Süddeutsche Zeitung* (München), 7/8.11.1953.

5974    Vietta, Egon, and R. Krämer-Badoni. "Heideggers Sätze von 1935. Briefe an 'Die Zeit'." *Die Zeit* (Hamburg), no. 34, 20.8.1953.

5975    Vietta, Egon. Rev. of *Was heisst Denken?* and *Vorträge und Aufsätze,* by Martin Heidegger. 1954. *Universitas* (Stuttgart), vol. 10, 1955, 747-749.

5976    Vietta, Silvio. "Dialog mit den Dingen." In *Erinnerung an Martin Heidegger,* by Günther Neske (ed.). Pfullingen: Verlag Günther Neske, 1977, 233-237.

5977    Villani, A. "Heidegger e il 'problema' del diritto." *Annali d. Universitá di Macerata,* vol. 22, 1958, 251-312.

5978    Villani, A. *Heidegger e il problema del diritto.* Milano, 1958, 60 p. [deutsch: Heidegger und das 'Problem' des Rechts, in: Die ontologische Begründung des Rechts. Ed. A. Kaufmann. Darmstadt, 1965, 350-404.]

5978a   Villela-Petit, Maria. "Heidegger est-il 'idolàtre'?" In *Heidegger et la question de Dieu.* Ed. R. Kearney and J. S. O'Leary. Paris: B. Grasset, 1980, 75-102.

5979    Virasoro, M. *Introducción al existencialismo.* (Symposium sobre existencialismo 1). Rosario, 1955.

5980    Virasoro, R. "El problema moral en la filosofia de Heidegger." *Actas del primer Congreso nacional de Filosofia* (Mendoza), vol. 2, 1949, 1100-1105.

5981    Virasoro, R. "Existencia y dialectica." *Actas del primer Congreso nacional de Filosofía* (Mendoza), vol. 2, 1949, 1094-1099, passim.

5982    Virasoro, R. "Presencia de la muerte en la filosofia de nuestro tiempo." *Actes du XIe congrès international de philosophie, Bruxelles 20-26 Aoû 1953* (Amsterdam/Louvain), vol. 3, 1953, 237-242.

5983    Virasoro, R. "Existencia y mundo." *Actas du XIe congrès international de philosophie, Bruxelles 20-26 Août 1953* (Amsterdam/Louvain), vol. 3, 1953, 130-136.

5984    Virasoro, R. *Existencialismo y moral; Heidegger-Sartre.* Libreria y Editorial Castellvi. Santa Fé, 1957, 78 p.

5985    Vireillo, Domenico. "Il problema della metafisica in Heidegger." *Sapienza* (Roma), vol. 23, 1970, 377-401.

5986    Viti Cavaliere, Renata. Rev. of "In cammino verso il linguaggio," by Martin Heidegger. 1973. *Rivista di Studi Crociani* (Napoli), vol. 10, 1973, 478-480.

5987    Viti Cavaliere, Renata. Rev. of "La dottrina delle categorie e del significato in Duns Scoto," by Martin Heidegger. 1974. *Rivista di Studi Crociani* (Napoli), vol. 12, 1975, 220-224.

5988    Viti Cavaliere, Renata. "Martin Heidegger e la dottrina di Platone sulla verità." *Rivista di Studi Crociani* (Napoli), vol. 13, no. 3, 1976, 289-294.

5989    Viti Cavaliere, Renata. *Heidegger e la storia della filosofia.* (I principii, 16). Napoli: Giannini Editore, 1979, xii-200.

5990    Vitiello, Vincenzo. "Scienza e tecnica nel pensiero di Heidegger." *Il Pensiero* (Rom), vol. 18, 1973, 113-148.

5991    Vitiello, Vincenzo. *Heidegger. Il nulla e la fondazione della storicità. Dalla 'Überwindung der Metaphysik' alla 'Daseinsanalyse'.* (Studi filosofici). Urbino: Argalia Ed., 1976, 494 p.

5991a   Vitiello, Vincenzo. "Heidegger, Hegel e il problema del tempo." *L'Uomo, un segno* (Milano), vol. 3, no. 1-2, 1979, 59-82.

5992    Voelkel, Theodore Swallen. *Heidegger and the Problem of Circularity.* Authorized facsimile of the dissertation of the Yale Univ. Phil. Diss. 1971. Ann Arbor, Michigan; London: University Microfilms International, 1977, v-252. *Dissertation Abstracts International,* vol. 32/06-A, 3376.

5993    Vogl, G. *Das Problem des Todes bei Heidegger und Augustinus.* Phil. Diss. Wien 1966 131 Bl.

5994    Vogt, A. *Das Problem des Selbstseins bei Heidegger und Kierkegaard.* Emsdetten, 1936.

5995    Volkmann-Schluck, Karl-Heinz. "Zur Gottsfrage bei Nietzsche." *Anteile, Martin Heidegger zum 60. Geburtstag.* Frankfurt, 1950, 212-234.

5996    Volkmann-Schluck, Karl-Heinz. "Der Satz vom Widerspruch als Anfang der Philosophie." In *Martin Heidegger zum 70. Geburtstag.* Festschrift/Pfullingen, 1959, 134-150.

5997 Volkmann-Schluck, Karl-Heinz. *Einführung in das philosophische Denken.* Frankfurt, 1965, 143 p.

5998 Volkmann-Schluck, Karl-Heinz. *Mythos und Logos. Interpretationen zu Schellings Philosophie der Mythologie.* Berlin, 1969.

5999 Volkmann-Schluck, Karl-Heinz. "Das Problem der Sprache." In *Die Frage Martin Heideggers.* Eds. J. Beaufret, H.-G. Gadamer, K. Löwith, K.-H. Volkmann-Schluck. Heidelberg, 1969, 50-61.

6000 Volkmann-Schluck, Karl-Heinz. "Der Weg des Denkens in der modernen Welt." In *Weltaspekte der Philosophie. Rudolph Berlinger zum 26.Okt.1972.* Ed. Werner Beierwaltes und Wiebke Schrader. Amsterdam, 1972, 313-323.

6001 Volkmann-Schluck, Karl-Heinz. "The Problem of Language." In *Martin Heidegger: In Europe and America,* by Edward Goodwin Ballard and Charles E. Scott (eds). The Hague, 1973, 121-128.

6002 Volkmann-Schluck, Karl-Heinz. "Fügung und Geschick." *Frankfurter Allgemeine Zeitung* (Frankfurt), no. 118, 23 May 1977, 19.

6003 Volkmann-Schluck, Karl-Heinz. "The Existential Hermeneutic in Heidegger's *Being and Time* and *The Turn.*" (In Serbocroat). *Delo* (Beograd), vol. 23, no. 12, 1977, 21-32. Rpt. in *Rani Hajdeger - Recepcija i kritika Bivstva i vremena,* by Dragan Stojanovic and Danilo Basta (eds). (Biblioteka Zodijak). Beograd, 1979, 161-175.

6004 Volkmann-Schluck, Karl-Heinz. "Die technische Welt und das Geschick." In *Martin Heidegger. Fragen an sein Werk. Ein Symposium.* (Universal-Bibliothek, 9873). Stuttgart: Reclam, 1977, 33-36.

6005 Volkmann-Schluck, Karl-Heinz. "Il compito attuale della filosofia. L'essenza della tecnica alla luce del pensiero di Heidegger." *Humanitas* (Brescia), vol. 33, no. 4, 1978, 469-484.

6006 Vollrath, Ernst. "Platons Anamnesislehre und Heideggers These von der Erinnerung in die Metaphysik." *Zeitschrift für Philosophische Forschung* (Schlehdorf/Kochelsee/Meisenheim/Glan), vol. 23, 1969, 349-361.

6007 Vollrath, Ernst. *Die These der Metaphysik. Zur Gestalt der Metaphysik bei Aristoteles, Kant und Hegel.* Ratingen/Wuppertal, 1969, 292 p.

6008 Volpato, Annapaola. "Alcune interpretazioni italiane di Heidegger." *Aquinas* (Roma), vol. 21, 1978, 139-152.

6009 Volpi, Franco. Rev. of *Introduzione a Heidegger,* by Gianni Vàttimo. *Philosophischer Literaturanzeiger,* November-December 1973, 351.

6010 Volpi, Franco. Rev. of *Heidegger,* by Enrico Farulli. *Bollettino Filosofico* (Padova), vol. 9, 1975, 81-82.

6011 Volpi, Franco. Rev. of "La dottrina di Platone sulla verità. Lettera sull'umanesimo," by Martin Heidegger. 1975. *Bollettino filosofico* (Padova), vol. 9, 1975, 113-114.

6012 Volpi, Franco. *Heidegger e Brentano. L'aristotelismo e il problema dell'univocità dell'essere nella formazione filosofica del giovane Martin Heidegger.* (Pubblicazioni della Scuola di Perfezionamento in Filosofia dell'Università di Padova. Quaderni di Storia della Filosofia, 7). Padova: Cedam, 1976, 141 p.

6013 Volpi, Franco. "Ermeneutica." *Enciclopiedia Feltrinelli-Fischer: Letteratura* (Mailand), vol. 1, 1976, 115-144.

6014 Volpi, Franco. "Ontologia, teologia e antropologia in Heidegger in alcune recenti pubblicazioni su Heidegger." *Akwesasne Notes. Where the Partridge Drums,* vol. 10. Rpt. in *Bollettino filosofico* (Padova), vol. 10, no. 2, 1976, 17-21.

6015 Volpi, Franco. "Quello che Heidegger non ha detto." *Bollettino filosofico* (Padova), vol. 10, 1976, 97-99.

6016 Volpi, Franco, ed. *Martin Heidegger, Hegel e i greci.* Trans., intr., and commentary by Franco Volpi. Trento: Verifiche, 1977, 114 p.

6017 Volpi, Franco. Rev. of *Heidegger e la fine della filosofia,* by Pietro de Vitiis. *Philosophischer Literaturanzeiger* (Meisenheim/Glan), vol. 30, 1977, 48-50.

6018 Volpi, Franco. *Aristotele e Heidegger. La critica heideggeriana della concezione aristotelica del tempo.* Padova: Dispensa Univ., 1978, 36 p.

6019 Volpi, Franco. "Heideggers Verhältnis zu Brentanos Aristoteles Interpretation." *Zeitschrift für Philosophische Forschung* (Schlehdorf/Kochelsee/Meisenheim/Glan), vol. 32, 1978, 254-265.

6020 Volpi, Franco. "Nietzsche in Italien." [On Heidegger's Nietzsche interpretation.] *Philosophischer Literaturanzeiger* (Meisenheim/Glan), vol. 31, 1978, 170-184.

6021 Volpi, Franco. Rev. of *Denken und Metaphysik,* by G. Guzzoni. *Verifiche* (Trento), vol. VII, 1978, 134-135.

6022 Volpi, Franco. Rev. of *Grund und Allgemeinheit,* by G. Guzzoni. *Verifiche* (Trento), vol. VII, 1978, 511-513.

6023 Volpi, Franco. Rev. of *Vier Seminare,* by Martin Heidegger. *Bolletino filosofico* (Padova), vol. 12, 1978, 178-179.

6024 Volpi, Franco. Rev. of *Heidegger: il nulla e la fondazione della storicità,* by Vincenzo Vitiello. *Philosophischer Literaturanzeiger* (Meisenheim/Glan), vol. 31, 1978, 61-65.

6025 Volpi, Franco. *Martin Heidegger: la vita e l'opera.* Padova: Dispensa Univ., 1979, 37 p.

6026 Volpi, Franco. *Tempi e soggettività nella fenomenologia tedesca (Brentano, Husserl, Heidegger).* Padova: Dispensa Univ., 1979, 39 p.

6027 Volpi, Franco. "Heidegger e la 'legittimità filosofica' della Seinsfrage." *Bollettino filosofico* (Padova), vol. XIII, 1979, 49-55.

6028 Volpi, Franco. Rev. of *Heidegger and Modern Philosophy.* Ed Michael Murray. *Philosophischer Literaturanzeiger* (Meisenheim/Glan), vol. 32, 1979, 51-56.

6029 Volpi, Franco. "Nochmals Heidegger? Eine Bilanz der neuen internationalen Heidegger-Forschung." *Philosophischer Literaturanzeiger* (Meisenheim/Glan), vol. 33, 1980.

6029a    Volpi, Franco. "Alle origini della concezione heideggeriana dell'essere: il trattato *Vom Sein* di Carl Braig." *Rivista critica di Storia della Filosofia* (Milano), vol. 35, 1980, 184-195.

6030    Vonessen, F. *Das einzigartige Sein. Zur Frage der Seinsparadoxien bei Martin Heidegger.* Phil. Diss. Freiburg 1952 329 p. 26 Bl.

6031    Vonessen, H. *Die Angst und das menschliche Dasein Dargestellt an den Interpretationen der Angst bei Soren Kierkegaard, Sigmund Freud und Martin Heidegger.* Phil. Diss. Heidelberg 1960 240 p.

6032    Vorisek, R. *Existenciálni filosofie Martina Heideggera a Karla Jasperse.* 196 p. Phil. Diss. Prag 11.5.1934.

6033    Vorisek, R. "Tragika osamoceni a heroismus ztroskotáni ve filosofii M. Heideggera a K. Jasperse." *Rád* (Czechoslovakian), vol. 2, 1934/35, 436-451.

6034    Vos, A. De. "La théorie heidéggerienne de la vérité. Confrontation avec la doctrine traditionelle." *Analecta Gregoriana* (Romae), vol. 67, 1954: Studi filosofici intorno all 'Esistenza', al Mondo, al Trascendente, 35-43.

6035    Vries, B. de. Rev. of *Vom Wesen des Grundes,* by Martin Heidegger. 1929. *Scholastik* (Freiburg), vol. 6, 1931, 138.

6036    Vries, B. de. Rev. of *Kant und das Problem der Metaphysik,* by Martin Heidegger. 1929. *Scholastik* (Freiburg), vol. 5, 1930, 422-425.

6037    Vuillemin, J. *L'héritage Kantien et la révolution copernicienne. Fichte-Cohen-Heidegger.* Paris, 1954.

6038    Vuarnet, J.-N. "L'Artiste chargé de l'être." *Cahiers Internationaux du Symbolisme* (Genève), no. 29-30, 1976, 115-132.

6039    Vycinas, Vincent. *Earth and Gods. An Introduction to the Philosophy of Martin Heidegger.* The Hague, 1961, XII, 328 p.

6040    Vycinas, Vincent. "Lenguaje y poesia en la filosofia de Heidegger." *Diálogas, Revista del Departement de Filosofia, Universita de Puerto Rico* (Puerto Rico), vol. 3, 1966, 7-20.

6041    Vycinas, Vincent. *Search for Gods.* The Hague, 1972, (1973).

6042    Wach, J. *Das Problem des Todes in der Philosophie unserer Zeit.* Tübingen, 1934, (specifically pages 39-48).

6043    Waelhens, Alphonse de. "Existence concrète et nihilisme dans l'oeuvre de M. Heidegger." *La Cité Chrétienne* (Bruxelles), vol. 13, 1939, 264-269.

6044    Waelhens, Alphonse de. "Hedendaagsche wijsbegeerte." *Tijdschrift voor Philosofie* (Leuven), vol. 1, 1939, 475-479.

6045    Waelhens, Alphonse de. "L'existentialisme de M. Sartre est il un humanisme?" *Revue Philosophique de Louvain,* vol. 44, 1946, 291-300.

6046    Waelhens, Alphonse de. "Heidegger et J.-P. Sartre." *Deucalion* (Paris), vol. 1, 1946, 15-37.

6047    Waelhens, Alphonse de. "La philosophie de Heidegger et le nazisme." *Les temps modernes* (Paris), vol. 3, 1947/48, 115-127.

6048   Waelhens, Alphonse de. "De la phénomenologie à l'existentialisme." In *La Choix, Le Monde, L'Existence.* Paris, 1948, 37-82.

6049   Waelhens, Alphonse de. "Introduction et commentaire." Rev. of *De l'essence de la vérité,* by Martin Heidegger. Trans. in collaboration with W. Biemel. Louvain/Paris, 1948.

6050   Waelhens, Alphonse de. "Heidegger, Platon et l'humanisme." *Revue philosophique de Louvain* (Louvain), vol. 46, 1948, 490-496.

6051   Waelhens, Alphonse de. "Réponse à cette réponse." *Les temps modernes* (Paris), vol. 4, 1948, 374-377.

6052   Waelhens, Alphonse de. *Chemins et impasses de l'ontologie heideggérienne. A propos des 'Holzwege'.* Louvain/Paris, 1953, 52 p.

6053   Waelhens, Alphonse de. *Phénoménologie et vérité. Essai sur l'évolution de l'idée de vérité chez Husserl et Heidegger.* Paris, 1953, XIII, 167 p.

       [Rev. by J. Ecole in *Les études Philosophiques* (Paris), N.S. 9, 1954, 131.]

6054   Waelhens, Alphonse de. "Heidegger et le problème de la métaphysique." *Revue philosophique de Louvain* (Louvain), vol. 52, 1954, 110-119.

6055   Waelhens, Alphonse de. *Heidegger.* Trans. Carlos Fayard. (Colección 'Filosofos y Sistemas', II). Buenos Aires: Ediciones Losange, 1955, 77 p.

6056   Waelhens, Alphonse de. "Heidegger (1889)." *Les Philosophes célèbres.* Ouvrage publié sous la direction de Maurice Merleau-Ponty. (La Galerie des hommes célèbres. Collection créée et dirigée par lucien mazenod, Vol. X). Paris, 1956, 336-343.

6057   Waelhens, Alphonse de. "Identité et difference: Heidegger et Hegel." *Revue Internationale de Philosophie* (Bruxelles), vol. 14, no. 52, 1960, [Heidegger], 221-237.

6058   Waelhens, Alphonse de. "Pensee mythique et philosophie du mal." *Revue philosophique de Louvain,* vol. 59, 1961, 315-347.

6059   Waelhens, Alphonse de. "Nature humaine et compréhension de l'être." *Revue Philosophique de Louvain* (Leuven), vol. 59, 1961, 672-682.

6060   Waelhens, Alphonse de. "Ontologische problemen van de hermeneutica." *Tijdschrift voor Filosofie,* vol. 25, 1963, 688-705.

6061   Waelhens, Alphonse de. "Quelques problemes ontologiques de l'herméneutique." *Archivio di Filosofia* (Roma), 1963, 43-53.

6062   Waelhens, Alphonse de. "Reflexions on Heidegger's Development. A Propos of a Recent Book." *International Philosophical Quarterly* (New York/Heverlee-Louvain), vol. 5, 1965, 475-502.

6063   Waelhens, Alphonse de. *La philosophie de Martin Heidegger.* Louvain, 1942, XI, 379 p; Neudruck, 1946. 2nd ed. 1948. 4th ed. 1955. 5th ed. 1967. 6th ed. Paris, 1969, XII, 379 p.

6064   Waelhens, Alphonse de. "Note sur les notions d'historicité et d'histoire chez Martin Heidegger (Rivelazione e storia)." *Archivio di Filosofia* (Padova), no. 2, 1971, 117-124.

6065    Waelhens, Alphonse de. "La sécularisation dans la pensée de Heidegger." In *Herméneutique de la sécularisation,* by Enrico Castelli (ed.). (Actes du colloque organisé par le Centre International d'Etudes Humanistes et par l'Institut d'Etudes philosophiques de Rome. Rome, 3-8 Janvier 1976). Paris: Aubier-Montaigne, 1976, 287-296. Rpt. in *Archivio di Filosofia* (Roma), no. 2-3, 1976, 287-296.

6065a   Waelhens, Alphonse de. "Heidegger et le problème du sujet." Trans. Livia Bignami and Giuseppina Contiero. *Verifiche* (Trento), vol. 8, no. 1, 1975, 34-61.

6066    Wagner de Reyna, A. "La ontologia fundamental de Heidegger. Su motivo y significacion." *Revista de la Universidad Catolica del Peru* (Lima), vol. 5, 1937, 87-103, 198-213, 307-331.

6067    Wagner de Reyna, A. "La Ontologie fundamental de Heidegger." *Revista de la Universidad catholica del Peru* (Lima), 1938, 133-174.

6068    Wagner de Reyna, A. *La ontologia fundamental. Su motiv y significacion.* Buenos Aires, 1939.

6069    Wagner de Reyna, A. "La filosofia existencial de Heidegger." *Arch. de la Sociedad peruana de filosofia* (Lima), vol. 3, 1950, 33-42.

6070    Wagner de Reyna, A. "Die Enttäuschung." In *Martin Heidegger zum 70. Geburtstag.* Festschrift/Pfullingen, 1959, 151-156.

6071    Wahl, Jean. "Vers le concret." *Recherches philosophiques* (Paris), vol. 1, 1931, 1-16, passim.

6072    Wahl, Jean. "Heidegger et Kierkegaard; recherche des elements originaux de la philosophie de Heidegger." *Recherches philosophiques* (Paris), vol. II, 1932/33, 349-370.

6073    Wahl, Jean. "(Exposé et discussion) Subjectivité et Transcendance." *Bulletin de la Société française de Philosophie* (Paris), vol. 37, 1937, 161-211, passim.

6074    Wahl, Jean. *Etudes Kierkegaardiennes.* Paris, 1938, 455-476, passim.

6075    Wahl, Jean. *Esquisse pour une histoire de 'l'existentialisme'. Suivie de Kafka et Kierkegaard.* Paris, 1949, 155 p. [deutsch 1954]

6076    Wahl, Jean, and V. Jankáévitch. "Les philosophes et l'angoisse [Heidegger, Jaspers]." *Revue de Synthèse Historique* (Paris), vol. 25, 1949, 67-98.

6077    Wahl, Jean. "Sur les philosophies de l'existence." *L'Education nationale* (Paris), no. 33, 1950, 3-4 u.ö.

6078    Wahl, Jean. *L'idée d'être chez Heidegger.* Paris, 1951, 100 p.

6079    Wahl, Jean. *Esquisse pour un tableau des catégoris de la philosophie de l'existence.* Paris, 1951, passim.

6080    Wahl, Jean. *Sur l'interprétation de l'histoire de la métaphysique d'après Heidegger.* Paris, 1951.

6081    Wahl, Jean. *1848-1948. Cent années de l'histoire de l'idée d'existence. Heidegger.* Paris, 1951.

6082    Wahl, Jean. *La pensée de l'existence.* Paris, 1951, 290 p., (specifically page 239 f).

6083    Wahl, Jean. *La Philosophie de Heidegger.* Paris, 1952.

6084    Wahl, Jean. *La pensée de Heidegger et la poésie de Hölderlin.* (Les Cours de Sorbonne). Paris, 1953, 129 p.

6085    Wahl, Jean. "Sur l'interpretation de l'histoire de la métaphysique d'apres Heidegger." In *Les Cours de Sorbonne.* Paris, 1953, 105 p.

6086    Wahl, Jean. *Les Philosophies de l'Existence.* Paris, 1954, 35 ff und passim.

6087    Wahl, Jean. "Déclin ou floraison de la Métaphysique, Martin Heidegger: Einführung in die Metaphysik." *Critique* (Paris), no. 107, 1956, 353-361.

6088    Wahl, Jean. Rev. of *Einführung in die Metaphysik,* by Martin Heidegger. 1953. *Erasmus* (Darmstadt/Aarau), vol. 9, 1956, 707-713.

6089    Wahl, Jean. Rev. of *Einführung in die Metaphysik,* by Martin Heidegger. Tübingen, 1953. *Critique* (Paris), 9.Jg., Bd 14, no. 106, 1956, 354-361.

6090    Wahl, Jean. "Sur des écrits récents de Heidegger et de Fink." *Revue de Métaphysique et de Morale* (Paris), vol. 63, 1958, 474-482.

6091    Wahl, Jean. "Sein, Wahrheit, Welt. Zu: E. Fink, Sein, Wahrheit, Welt. 1959." *Revue de Métaphysique et de Morale* (Paris), vol. 65, 1960, 187-194.

6092    Wahl, Jean. *Mots, Mythes et réalité dans la philosophie de Heidegger (Les cours de Sorbonne).* Centre de documentation univ., Paris, 1961, 184 p.

6093    Wahl, Jean. Rev. of "Heidegger und die Tradition," by W. Marx. *Revue de Métaphysique et de Morale* (Paris), vol. 68, 1963, 229-233.

6094    Wahl, Jean. "Nietzsche et la pensée contemporaine." *Bulletin de la Société française d'Etudes nietzschéennes* (Paris), Mars 1963, 1-5.

6095    Wahl, Jean. *Philosophies of Existence. An Introduction to the Basic Thought of Kierkegaard, Heidegger, Jaspers, Marcel, Sartre.* Trans. F. M. Lory. London, 1969, 126 p.

6096    Wahl, Jean. *Verso la fine dell'ontologia. Studio sull'introduzione alla metafisica di Heidegger.* Trans. and intr. G. Masi. Milano, 1971, 456 p.

6097    Wakayama, Hideo. "Haideggâ-cho 'Genshôgaku to Shingaku'" (On Heidegger's Work "Phänomenologie und Theologie"). *Shisaku* (Tôkyô), vol. 4, October 1971, 114-117.

6098    Wakisaka, Kôji. "'Junsui-Risei-Hihan' no Bonzaironteki Kaishaku ni tsuite; Kôsôryoku no Bunseki ni Kansuru hitotsu no Junbiteki-Kôsatsu" (Ontological Exegesis of the "Kritik der reinen Vernunft"). *Tetsugaku-Kenkyû* (Kyôto), vol. 16, 1931, 25-52.

6099    Walsh, J. H. "Heidegger's Understanding of No-Thingness." *Cross Currents* (West Nyack), vol. 13, 1963, 305-323.

6100    Walsh, J. H. *A Fundamental Ontology of Play and Leisure.* Phil. Diss. Georgetown Univ. Washington 1968 388 p.

6101    Wandel, F. *Bewusstsein und Wille.* Bonn, 1972, 243 p., (specifically pages 37-52).

6102    Warnock, G. J. Rev. of *An Introduction to Metaphysics*, by Martin Heidegger. *Mind* (London), vol. 71, 1962, 135-136.

6103    Warnock, Mary. *Existentialist Ethics*. New York: St. Martin's Press, 1967.

6104    Warnock, Mary. *Existentialism (Kierkegaard, Nietzsche, Heidegger, Sartre, Marcel, Merleau-Ponty)*. London/Oxford/New York, 1970, 145 p.

6105    Watabe, Kiyoshi. "Sonzai to Ryôshin - Haideggâ to Editto Shutain o megutte" (Being and Conscience - Heidegger and Edith Stein). *Sophia* (Tôkyô), vol. 20, no. 3, November 1971, 60-72.

6106    Watanabe, Jirô. "Haideggâ no Sonzai no Shisaku o megutte" (On the Thinking of Being in Heidegger). *Tetsugaku-Zasshi* (Tôkyô), vol. 733, 1956, 47-91.

6107    Watanabe, Jirô. "Haideggâ no Sonzai no Shisaku o megutte" (On Heideggerian Thinking on Being). *Tetsugaku-Zasshi* (Tôkyô), vol. 733, 1957.

6108    Watanabe, Jirô. "Shoki no Haideggâ" (The Early Heidegger). *Risô* (Tôkyô), vol. 305, Oktober 1958.

6109    Watanabe, Jirô. *Haideggâ no Jitsuzonshisô* (Heidegger's Concept of Existence). Tôkyô, 1962.

6110    Watanabe, Jirô. *Haideggâno Sonzaishisô* (Heidegger's Concept of Being). Tôkyô, 1962.

6111    Watanabe, Jirô, and Arêteia Shôkô. "Furidorendâ no Haideggâ no Bakuron ni kanren shite" (On "Aletheia" - in Regard to Friedländer's Refutation of Heidegger). *Tetsugaku-Zasshi* (Tôkyô), vol. 752, 1965, 64-92.

6112    Watanabe, Jirô. "Haideggâ no ichi Shokan ni tsuite" (On a Paper by Heidegger). *Jitsuzonshugi* (Tôkyô), vol. 35, 1966, 86-93.

6113    Watanabe, Jirô. "Haideggâ no Shogaku e no Eikyô" (Heidegger's Influence on the Sciences). *Risô* (Tôkyô), vol. 444, 1970, 55-68.

6114    Watanabe, Jirô. "Nihirizumu no Mondai Genshô" (The Basic Problems of Nihilism). *Gendai-Shisô* (Tôkyô), vol. 1, no. 4, 1973, 103-121.

6115    Watanabe, Jirô. "Sonzai to Jikan kara Jikan to Sonzai e" (From 'Being and Time' to 'Time and Being'). *Gendai-Shisô* (Tôkyô), vol. 2, no. 10, 1974, 74-95.

6116    Watanabe, Jirô. "Honshitsu, Kangen, Genshô; Hussâru, Haideggâ, Meruro-Ponti" (Essence, Reduction, Phenomen; Husserl, Heidegger and Merleau-Ponty). *Gendai-Shisô* (Tôkyô), vol. 2, no. 8, 1974, 38-59.

6117    Watanabe, Jirô. *Heideggâ no Jirsuzon-Shisô* (Heidegger's Thought on the Existence, 2nd ed.). Keisô-Shobô, Tôkyô, 1974, 705.

6118    Watanabe, Jirô. *Nihiruzumu* (Nihilism). Tôkyô Daigaku Shuppankai, Tôkyô, 1975, 304.

6119    Watanabe, Jirô. "Haideggâ to Genshogaku" (Heidegger and Phenomenology). *Jôkyo* (Tôkyô), vol. 85, 1975, 67-89.

6120    Watanabe, Jirô. "Ruiji" (A Requiem). *Misuzu* (Tôkyô), vol. 198, 1976, 32-40.

6121 Watanabe, Jirô. "Mominoki no Ura" (The Song of "Tannenbaum"). *Gendai-Shisô* (Tôkyô), vol. 4, no. 7, 1976, 48-54.

6122 Watanabe, Jirô. "Kasutânien no Kokage de" (Under the Tree of 'Kastanien'). *Risô* (Tôkyô), vol. 517, 1976, 122-126.

6123 Watanabe, Jirô. "Shisaku koso mottomo takai Kôkô" (The Thinking is the Highest Action). In *Shisô to Shâyû* (Thought and Stream). Ed. Asahi-Journal. Tôkyô, 1977, 109-115.

6124 Watanabe, Jirô, and Akihiro Takeichi. "Taidan 'Haideggâ Tetsugaku wa Nani de attaka?'" *Conversation: What was Heidegger's Philosophy?) Risô* (Tôkyô), vol. 542, 1978, 43-60.

6125 Watanabe, Jirô. *Naimensei no Genshogaku* (The Phenomenology of the Inner Life). Keiso-Shobo, Tôkyô, 1978, 279 p.

6126 Watanabe, Jirô. "Haideggâ Jishin ni yoru 'Sonzai to Jikan' no Rangai Chûki" (On the Marginal Notes of 'Being and Time'). *Gendai-Shisô* (Seidosha, Tôkyô), vol. 1979, 251-261.

6127 Watanabe, Jirô. "Wahrheit und Unwahrheit oder Eigentlichkeit und Uneigentlichkeit, eine Bemerkung zu Heideggers Sein und Zeit." *Analecta Husserliana* (Japanese Phenomenology). Vol. VIII. Ed. Tymienieeka. Dordrecht, Holland: Reidel Pub. Co., 1979, 131-203.

6128 Water, Lambert van de. "The Work of Art, Man, and Being: A Heideggerian Theme." *International Philosophical Quarterly* (New York/Heverlee-Leuven), vol. 9, 1969, 214-235.

6129 Water, Lambert van de. "Being and Being Human: An Impasse in Heidegger's Thought." *International Philosophical Quarterly* (New York), vol. 13, no. 3, 1973, 391-417.

6130 Watson, James Raymond. "Heidegger's Hermeneutic Phenomenology." *Philosophy Today* (Celina, Ohio), vol. 15, 1971, 30-43.

6131 Watson, James Raymond. *Martin Heidegger's Attempt to Ground Metaphysics: The Time-Character of Being.* Phil. Diss. Southern Illinois Univ. 1973. *Dissertation Abstracts International,* vol. 34/09-A, 6053.

6132 Watson, James Raymond. "Being...There: The Neighbourhood of Being." *Philosophy Today* (Celina, Ohio), vol. 19, 1975, 118-130.

6133 Watson, James Raymond. "The Ego and the Other." *Tijdschrift voor Filosofie* (Leuven), vol. 38, 1976, 574-601.

6134 Wawrzyniak, A. "O wlaáciwe rozumienie Heideggera" (Genuinely Understanding Heidegger). *Znak,* vol. 4, 1965.

6135 Wawrzyniak, A. "Filozofia M. Heideggera w áwietle nowszych opracowan" (New Essays on M. Heidegger's Philosophy). *Roczniki Filozoficzne KUL,* vol. 1, 1965.

6136 Wawrzejniak, A. "Filozofia M. Heideggera v swietle nowszych opracowan" (Heidegger's Philosophy Illuminated by His Recent Work). *Roczniky filozoficzne.* Ed. Towarystwo Naukowe Katolickiego Univ. Lubelskiego

(Scientific Society at the Catholic Univ. of Lublin). Bd XIII, no. 1, 1965, 119-128.

6137    Weber, René. "A Critique of Heidegger's Concept of 'solicitude'." *The New Scholasticism* (Washington), vol. 42, 1968, 537-560.

6138    Weber, Renée Oppenheimer. *Individual and Social Being in Heidegger's 'Being and Time'.* Phil. Diss. Columbia Univ. 1966. Ann Arbor, Michigan: University Microfilms, 1977, 248 p. *Dissertation Abstracts International,* vol. 28/02-A, 735.

6139    Weier, W. "Die Vorläufigkeit der nihilistischen Selbstreflexion." *Theologie und Philosophie* (Freiburg), vol. 47, 1972, 77-89.

6140    Weier, Winfried. "Die nihilistischen Wurzeln der Existenz- Philosophie." *Sophia* (Padua), vol. 41, 1973, 93-106.

6141    Weier, Winfried. "Menschliches Fragen als Zeugnis für objektiven Sinn." *Freiburger Zeitschrift für Philosophie und Theologie* (Freiburg), vol. 20, 1973, 168-197.

6142    Weier, Winfried. "Die definitorischen Urspruenge des Nihilismus." *Studia Philosophica* (Switzerland), vol. 34, 1974, 162-198.

6143    Weier, Winfried. "Die Überhöhung der Endlickheit im existentiellen Sprung." *Salzburger Jahrbuch für Philosophie* (Salzburg), vol. 20, 1975, 21-46.

6144    Weier, Winfried. "Die Wende im existentiellen Bewusstsein von Zeit und Tod." *Salzburger Jahrbuch für Philosophie* (Salzburg), vol. 21-22, 1976/77, 163-182.

6145    Weigl, L. *Kosmos und Arche. Eine philosophische Untersuchung vom Anfang der griechischen Philosophie bis Platon. Mit einem Nachwort über die Beziehung dieses Themas zur Existentialphilosophie M. Heideggers.* Phil. Diss. Würzburg 1949 206 Bl.

6146    Wei-Hsunfu, C. "The Trans-Onto-Theo-Logical Foundation of Language in Heidegger and Taoism." *Journal of Chinese Philosophy* (Honolulu, Hawai), vol. 5, no. 3, 1978, 301-333.

6147    Weil, E. "Le cas Heidegger." *Les temps modernes* (Paris), vol. 3, 1947/48, 128-138.

6148    Weiland, J. Sp. "Sprong in het Zijn." *Vox Theologica* (Rotterdam), 1957, 180-187.

6149    Weiler, G. "On Heidegger's Notion of Philosophy." *Hermathena. A Series of Papers by Members of Trinity College Dublin* (Dublin), vol. 93, 1959, 16-25.

6150    Wein, Hermann. "Der wahre cartesianische Dualismus." *Zeitschrift für philosophische Forschung* (Meisenheim/Glan), vol. 10, 1956, 3-28, (specifically pages 23-27).

6151    Weinberger, David. *Heidegger's Ontology of Things.* Phil. Diss. Univ. of Toronto 1979. *Dissertations Abstracts International,* vol. 40/08-A, 4632.

6152    Weinstein, Michael A., and Deena Weinstein. "An Existential Approach to Society: Active Transcendence." *Human Studies,* vol. 1, 1978, 38-47.

6153    Weischedel, Wilhelm. "Wesen und Grenzen der Existenzphilosophie."
        *Frankfurter Hefte* (Frankfurt), vol. 3, 1948, 726-735, 804-813, passim.

6154    Weischedel, Wilhelm. Rev. of *Holzwege*, by Martin Heidegger. Frankfurt,
        1950. *Philosophischer Literaturanzeitger* (Schlehdorf, Obb.), vol. 2, 1950,
        49-56.

6155    Weischedel, Wilhelm. "Weg und Irrweg im abendländischen Denken."
        *Zeitschrift für philosophische Forschung* (Meisenheim/Glan), vol. 7, 1953,
        3-19, (specifically pages 17-19).

6156    Weischedel, Wilhelm. "Denker zwischen den Zeiten. Zum 80. Geburtstag von
        Martin Heidegger." *Christ und Welt*, no. 39, vom 26.9.1969, 14.

6157    Weischedel, Wilhelm. *Der Gott der Philosophen. Grundlegung einer
        philosophischen Theologie im Zeitalter des Nihilismus.* 2 Bde. Darmstadt,
        1971/72, 516 u. 277 p. 2nd ed. 1972.

6158    Weischedel, Wilhelm. "El tiempo de un pensador. Martin Heidegger a los 80
        años." Trans. A. O. Publiese. *Cuadernos de Filosofia* (Buenos Aires), vol.
        11, no. 15-16, 1971, 7-10.

6159    Weischedel, Wilhelm. "Der Wille und die Willen. Zur Auseinandersetzung
        Wolfgang Müller-Lauters mit Martin Heidegger." *Zeitschrift für
        Philosophische Forschung* (Schlehdorf/Kochelsee/Meisenheim/Glan), vol.
        27, 1973, 71-76.

6160    Weischedel, Wilhelm. "Heidegger oder die Sage vom Sein. (Aus dem
        Nachlass)." *Der Tagesspiegel* (Berlin), Ausgabe A, vol. 32, no. 9324, 27 May
        1976, 4. (Jg. 3, 1976, Nr. 2).

6161    Weiss, Helene. "The Greek Conceptions of Time and Being in the Light of
        Heidegger's Philosophy." *Philosophy and Phenomenological Research* (New
        York), vol. 2, 1941/42, 173-187.

6162    Weiss, Th. *Angst vor dem Tode und Freiheit zum Tode in M. Heideggers 'Sein
        und Zeit'.* Innsbruck, 1947, 16 p.

6163    Weizsäcker, Carl Friedrich von. "Beziehungen der theoretischen Physik zum
        Denken Heideggers." *Martin Heideggers Einfluss auf die Wissenschaften.*
        Bern, 1949, 172-174.

6164    Weizsäcker, Carl Friedrich von. "Allgemeinheit und Geneigtheit." In *Martin
        Heidegger zum 70. Geburtstag.* Festschrift/Pfullingen, 1959, 157-171.

6165    Weizsäcker, Carl Friedrich von. "Martin Heidegger." In *Martin Heidegger im
        Gespräch.* Ed. R. Wisser. Freiburg/München, 1970, 13-15.

6166    Weizsäcker, Carl Friedrich von. "Begegnungen in vier Jahrzehnten." In
        *Erinnerung an Martin Heidegger,* by Günther Neske (ed.). Pfullingen:
        Verlag Günther Neske, 1977, 239-247.

6167    Welch, Cyril. Rev. of *What is Called Thinking?* by Martin Heidegger. *Dialogue*
        (Montreal/Kingston), vol. 7, 1968/69, 646-652. Rpt. in *Man and World*
        (Pittsburgh), vol. 2, 1969, 467-473.

6168    Welch, Cyril. Rev. of "Frühe Schriften," by Martin Heidegger. 1972. *Man and
        World* (The Hague), vol. 7, no. 1, 1974, 87-91.

6169    Welch, Cyril. "In Memoriam Martin Heidegger." *Man and World* (The Hague), vol. 9, 1976, 321-322.

6170    Welch, L., and C. Welch. Rev. of *Poetry, Language, Thought*, by Martin Heidegger. *Journal of Aesthetics and Art Criticism* (Baltimore), vol. 31, 1972/73, 117-123.

6171    Weldhen, Margaret. "The Existentialists and Problems of Moral and Religious Education 1, Bultmann and Heidegger." *Journal of Moral Education* (London), vol. 1, 1971, 19-26.

6172    Welte, Bernhard. "Remarques sur l'ontologie de Heidegger." *Revue des sciences philosophiques et théologiques* (Paris), vol. 31, 1947, 379-393.

6173    Welte, Bernhard. "Die Lichtung des Seins. Bemerkungen zur Ontologie Martin Heideggers." *Wort und Wahrheit* (Wien), vol. 3, 1948, 401-412.

6174    Welte, Bernhard. "La question de Dieu dans la pensée de Heidegger." *Les Etudes Philosophiques* (Paris), N.S. 19, 1964, 69-84.

6175    Welte, Bernhard. "La métaphysique de S. Thomas d'Aquin et la pensée de l'histoire de l'être chez Heidegger." *Revue des Sciences Philosophiques et Théologiques* (Le Soulchoir), vol. 50, 1966, 601-661.

6176    Welte, Bernhard. "La question de Dieu dans la pensée de Heidegger." *Revista Portuguesa de Filosofia* (Braga), vol. 26, 1970, 147-165.

6177    Welte, Bernhard. "Preface." In *F. Couturier, Monde et être chez Heidegger.* Montreal, 1971.

6178    Welte, Bernhard. "Denken und Sein. Gedanken zu Martin Heideggers Werk und Wirkung." *Herderkorrespondenz* (Freiburg), vol. 30, no. 7, 1976, 373-377. Sebocroation trans. in *Obnovljeni Zivot* (Zabreb), vol. 32, no. 1, 1977, 60-68.

6179    Welte, Bernhard. "*Suchen und Finden.* Grabrede für Martin Heidegger." In *Gedenkschrift der Stadt Messkirch an ihren Sohn und Ehrenbürger Professor Martin Heidegger.* Foreword and postscript by Siegfried Schühle. Messkirch: Stact Messkirch, 1977, 6-9. English trans. "Seeking and Finding. The Speech at Heidegger's Burial." Trans. Thomas J. Sheehan. *Listening. Journal of Religion and Culture* (River Forest, Illinois), vol. 12, no. 3, 1977, 106-109.

6180    Welte, Bernhard. "Erinnerung an ein spätes Gespräch." In *Erinnerung an Martin Heidegger,* by Günther Neske (ed.). Pfullingen: Verlag Günther Neske, 1977, 249-252.

6181    Welte, Bernhard. "Discorso alla sepotura di Martin Heidegger. Cercare e trovare." *Humanitas* (Brescia), vol. 33, no. 4, 1978, 423-426.

6182    Wenzl, A. "Fundamentalontologie - Metaphysik oder Ende der Metaphysik?" *Sitzungsberichte der Bayerischen Akademie der Wissenschaften* (München), Philos.-hist. Kl., 6, 1950, 19 p.

6183    Werkmeister, William H. "An Introduction to Heidegger's 'Existenzialphilosophy'." *Philosophy and Phenomenological Research* (Buffalo, New York), vol. 2, 1941/42, 79-87.

6184 Werkmeister, William H. Rev. of *An Introduction to Metaphysics,* " *by Martin Heidegger. The Personalist* (Los Angeles), vol. 41, 1960, 213.

6185 Werkmeister, William H. Rev. of *Essays in Metaphysics,* by Martin Heidegger. *The Personalist* (Los Angeles), vol. 42, 1961, 399-400.

6186 Werkmeister, William H. Rev. of *Kant and the Problem of Metaphysics,* by Martin Heidegger. *The Personalist* (Los Angeles), vol. 43, 1962, 551.

6187 Werkmeister, William H. Rev. of *Being and Time,* by Martin Heidegger. *The Personalist* (Los Angeles), vol. 44, 1963, 244.

6188 Werkmeister, William H. Rev. of *Discourse on Thinking,* by Martin Heidegger. *The Personalist* (Los Angeles), vol. 47, 1966, 559-560.

6189 Werkmeister, William H. "Heidegger and the Poets." *The Personalist* (Los Angeles), vol. 52, 1971, 5-22.

6190 Werkmeister, William H. "Hegel and Heidegger." In *New Studies in Hegel's Philosophy.* Ed. W. E. Steinkraus. New York/Toronto/Holt, 1971, 142-155.

6191 Werkmeister, William H. "From Kant to Nietzsche: The Ontology of Martin Heidegger." *The Personalist,* vol. 60, 1979, 397-401.

6192 Werner, M. *Der religiöse. Gehalt der Existenzphilosophie.* Bern/Leipzig, 1943, passim.

6193 Weyenbergh, M. "Heidegger en de taalproblematik." *Dialoog* (Brussel), vol. 6, 1965/66, 253-272.

6194 Weyembergh, M. "Heidegger en de taalproblematik, II." *Dialoog* (Amsterdam), vol. 7, 1966/67, 98-111.

6195 White, Carol Jean. *Time and Temporality in the Existential Thought of Kierkegaard and Heidegger.* Phil. Diss. Univ. of California Berkeley 1976 369 p. Ann Arbor, Michigan: University Microfilm International. [HGK77-15912] *Dissertation Abstracts International,* vol. 38/02-A, 853.

6196 White, David Allen. "World and Earth in Heidegger's Aesthetics." *Philosophy Today* (Celina, Ohio), vol. 12, 1968, 282-286.

6197 White, David Allen. "Revealment: A Meeting of Extremes in Aesthetics." *The Journal of Aesthetics and Art Criticism* (Baltimore), vol. 28, 1970, 515-520.

6198 White, David Allen. *Heidegger and the Language of Poetry.* German Literature. Phil. Diss. Univ. of Toronto Canada 1973. *Dissertation Abstracts International,* vol. 36/05-A, 2869.

6199 White, David Allen. "Truth and Being: A Critique of Heidegger on Plato." *Man and World* (The Hague), vol. 7, 1974, 118-134.

6200 White, David Allen. "A Refutation of Heidegger as Nihilist." *The Personalist* (Los Angelos), vol. 56, 1975, 276-288.

6201 White, David Allen. "Two Premises in Heidegger's Analysis of Identity ." *Southwestern Journal of Philosophy,* vol. 9, Fall 1978, 51-63.

6202 White, David Allen. *Heidegger and the Language of Poetry.* Lincoln: Univ. of Nebraska Press, 1979, xv-245.

6203    Wichmann, Ottomar. "Existenziale Platondeutung." *Kant-Studien* (Bonn),
        vol. 53, 1961, 441-489.

6204    Wiedmann, F. "Heidegger heute." *Philosophische Strömungen der Gegenwart.*
        Zürich/Einsiedeln/Köln, 1972, 21-33.

6205    Wienpahl, P. D. "Philosophy and Nothing." *Chicago Review,* vol. 13, 1959,
        59-74.

6206    Wild, John. "The New Empirism and Human Time." *The Review of
        Metaphysics* (New Haven, Connecticut), vol. 7, 1953/54, 537-557.

6207    Wild, John. "An English Version of Martin Heidegger's 'Being and Time'."
        *Review of Metaphysics* (New Haven, Connecticut), vol. 16, 1962/63,
        296-315.

6208    Wild, John. "The Philosophy of Martin Heidegger." *The Journal of Philosophy*
        (New York), vol. 60, 1963, 664-667.
        [Rev. by Hubert L. Dreyfus in *The Journal of Philosophy,* vol. 60, 1963,
        677-679.]

6209    Wild, John. "Being and Time: A Reply." *Review of Metaphysics* (New Haven,
        Connecticut), vol. 17, 1963/64, 610-616.

6210    Wild, John. "William James and Existential Authenticity [James-Heidegger]."
        *Journal of Existentialism,* vol. 5, 1964/65, 243-256.

6211    Wild, John. "Heidegger and the Existential a priori." In *Heidegger and the
        Path of Thinking.* Ed. J. Sallis. Pittsburgh, 1970, 221-234.

6212    Wild, John. "Being, Meaning, and World." *The Review of Metaphysics*
        (Haverford), vol. 18, 1964/65, 411-429.

6213    Will, Frederic. "Heidegger and the Gods of Poetry." *The Personalist* (Los
        Angeles), vol. 43, 1962, 157-167.

6214    Williams, John R. "Heidegger and the Theologians." *The Heythrop Journal.
        A Quarterly Review of Philosophy and Theology* (London/Oxford), vol. 12,
        1971, 258-280.

6215    Williams, John R. "Heidegger, Death, and God." *Studies in Religion*
        (Toronto), vol. 1, 1972, 298-320.

6216    Williams, John R. Rev. of *The End of Philosophy,* by Martin Heidegger. 1975.
        *Heythrop Journal,* vol. 17, 1976, 199-200.

6217    Williams, John R. *Martin Heidegger's Philosophy of Religion.* Waterloo,
        Ontario: Wilfred Laurier Univ. Press, 1977, 188 p.

6218    Willms, Bernhard. "Erwartung des Geniestreichs? Politik - Martin Heidegger
        als Zeitgenosse." *Frankfurter Allgemeine Zeitung* (Frankfurt), no. 112, 14
        May 1977, 23.

6219    Willms, Bernhard. "Politik als Geniestreich? Bemerkung zu Heideggers
        Politikverständnis." In *Martin Heidegger. Fragen an sein Werk.* (Ein
        Symposium, Universal-Bibliothek, 9873). Stuttgart: Reclam, 1977, 16-20.

6220    Wilmsen, A. "Zur Kritik der Phänomenologischen 'Seins' Philosophie."
        *Philosophisches Jahrbuch* (München), vol. 57, 242-255.

6221 Wilshire, Bruce. "James and Heidegger on Truth and Reality." *Man and World* (The Hague), vol. 10, no. 1, 1977, 79-94.

6222 Wimmer, Hans. "Die Maske." In *Erinnerung an Martin Heidegger,* by Günther Neske (ed.). Pfullingen: Verlag Günther Neske, 1977, 8-9.

6223 Wind, H. C. *Erkendelse of eksistens. Hovedlinjer: Heideggers filosofi.* Kopenhagen, 1974.

6224 Wind, H. C. *Historicitet og ontologie: en undersogelse af sammenhaengen hellem synet pa erkendelsen og eksistensforstaelsen i Heideggers eksistensforstaelsen i Heideggers eksistential-ontologi.* Arhus, 1974.

6225 Windischer, H. Rev. of *Platons Lehre von der Wahrheit mit einem Brief über den Humanismus,* by Martin Heidegger. 1947. *Erasmus* (Basel), vol. 3, 1950, 198-200.

6226 Winkler, R. "Martin Heidegger." *Zeitschrift für systematische Theologie* (Gütersloh), vol. 9, 1931/32, 290-294.

6227 Winquist, Charles E. Rev. of *The End of Philosophy,* by Martin Heidegger. Trans. Joan Stambaugh. New York, 1973. *Anglican Theological Review* (Evanston, Illinois), vol. 57, 1975, 362-363.

6228 Winter, G. "Human Science and Ethics in a Creative Society." *Cultural Hermeneutics* (Chestnut Hill), vol. 2, 1973, 145-174.

6229 Wiplinger, F. *Wahrheit und Geschichtlichkeit. Eine Untersuchung über die Frage nach dem Wesen der Wahrheit im Denken Martin Heideggers.* Phil. Diss. Wien 1959 vii and 447 p.

6230 Wiplinger, F. *Wahrheit und Geschichtlichkeit. Eine Untersuchung über die Frage nach dem Wesen der Wahrheit im Denken Martin Heideggers.* Freiburg/München, 1961, 386 p.

6231 Wiplinger, F. "Würdigung eines Denkens? Martin Heideggers 80. Geburtstag." *Wissenschaft und Weltbild* (Wien), vol. 22, no. 3, 1969, 175-194.

6232 Wiplinger, F. "Heidegger: integriert." *Wort und Wahrheit* (Freiburg), vol. 2, 1970, 160-163.

6233 Wisser, Richard. "La voix qui pense et sa pensée, Martin Heidegger." *Les Etudes Philosophiques* (Paris), N.S. 13, 1958, 495-500.

6234 Wisser, Richard. "Humanismus und Wissenschaft in der Sicht Martin Heideggers." Eds. D. Stolte and R. Wisser. In *Integritas. Geistige Wandlung und Menschliche Wirklichkeit.* Tübingen, 1966, 141-159.

6235 Wisser, Richard. "Humanismo y ciencia en la perspectiva de Martin Heidegger." *Folia Humanistica* (Barcelona), vol. 4, 1966, 441-454.

6236 Wisser, Richard. "Der zu sich kommende Mensch und das Sein. Abschnitt III: Martin Heidegger. Der Mensch als Da des Seins." In *Menschliche Existenz und moderne Welt. Ein internationales Symposium zum Selbstverständnis des heutigen Menschen.* Ed. R. Schwarz. Berlin, 1967, 274-295.

6237 Wisser, Richard. *Verantwortung im Wandel der Zeit. Jaspers, Buber, v. Weizsäcker, Guardini, Heidegger.* Mainz, 1967, 280 p.

6238 Wisser, Richard. "Martin Heidegger und der Wandel der Wirklichkeit." *Areopag* (Mainz), vol. 5, 1970, 79-90.

6239 Wisser, Richard. "Einfärung." In *Martin Heidegger im Gespräch.* Ed. R. Wisser. Freiburg/München, 1970, 9-11.

6240 Wisser, Richard, ed. *Martin Heidegger im Gespräch.* Freiburg/München, 1970, 77 p.

[Rev. by H. Jansohn in *Philosophischer Literaturanzeiger* (Meisenheim/Glan), vol. 23, 1970, 132-134.]

[Rev. by H. Kimmel in *Hochland* (München), vol. 62, 1970, 368-370.]

[Rev. by H. Ogiermann in *Theologie und Philosophie* (Frankfurt), vol. 46, 1971, 141-142.]

[Rev. by M. T. Presas in *Revista de Filosofia* (La Plata), vol. 22, 1971, 90-95.]

[Rev. by P. Emad in *Thought* (New York), vol. 46, 1971, 146-148.]

[Rev. by Br. Romano in *Rivista di internazionale di Filosofia del Diritto* (Milano), vol. 48, 1971, 377-378.]

[Rev. by T. Sampaio Ferroz in *Revista brasileiro de Filosofia* (Sao Paulo), vol. 21, 1971, 206-207.]

6241 Wisser, Richard. "Zur Verantwortung des Denkens." In *Martin Heidegger im Gespräch.* Ed. R. Wisser. Freiburg/München, 1970, 51-56.

6242 Wisser, Richard. "Martin Heidegger y el cambio de la realidad de lo real." *Revista de Filosofia de la Univ. de Costa Rica* (San José), vol. 9, 1971, 1-7.

6243 Wisser, Richard. "Martin Heidegger y el cambiode la realidad da lo real." *Folia Humanistica* (Barcelona), vol. 12, 1974, 305-315.

6244 Wisser, Richard. "Das Fernseh-Interview." In *Erinnerung an Martin Heidegger,* by Günther Neske (ed.). Pfullingen: Verlag Günther Neske, 1977, 257-287.

6245 Wittenkemper, K. "Existentialismus und moderne protestantische Theologie." *Theologie und Glaube. Zeitschrift für den katholischen Klerus* (Paderborn), vol. 30, 1938, 641-655.

6246 Wittgenstein, Ludwig. "On Heidegger on Being and Dread." Trans. and commentary by Michael Murray. In *Heidegger and Modern Philosophy. Critical Essays,* by Michael Murray (ed.). New Haven, Connecticut: Yale Univ. Press, 1978, 80-83.

6247 Wohlgenannt, Rudolf. *Der Philosophiebegriff. Seine Entwicklung von den Anfängen bis zur Gegenwart.* (Linzer Univ. Monographien. 1). Wien/New York, 1977. (Martin Heidegger, 90-100).

6248 Wolf, E. "Aner Dikaios." In *Anteile, Martin Heidegger zum 60. Geburtstag.* Frankfurt, 1950, 80-105.

6249 Wolff, Georg. "Haus und Hütte. Eindrücke bei einem Spiegel-Gespräch." In *Erinnerung an Martin Heidegger,* by Günther Neske (ed.). Pfullingen: Verlag Günther Neske, 1977, 289-291.

6250 Wolz, Henry G. "The Paradox of Piety in Plato's *Euthyphro* in the Light of Heidegger's Conception of Authenticity." *The Southern Journal of Philosophy* (Memphis), vol. 12, no. 4, 1974, 493-511.

6251 Wood, Allen W. Rev. of *Discourse on Thinking,* by Martin Heidegger. *Review of Metaphysics* (Haverford), vol. 20, 1966/67, 543.

6252 Woznicki, A. "In Search of the Meaning of Human Existence." *Zeszyty Naukowe Katolickiego Uniwersytetu Lubels-kiego* (Lublin), vol. 21, no. 1, 1978, 25-33. (Summary in English).

6253 Wren, Thomas E. "Heidegger's Philosophy of History." *The Journal of the British Society for Phenomenology* (Manchester), vol. 3, 1972, 111-125.

6254 Wucherer-Hildenfeld, K. "Zu M. Heideggers Analytik der Alltäglichkeit." *Wissenschaft und Weltbild* (Wien), vol. 7, 1954, 458-464.

6255 Würzbach, F. Rev. of *Einführung in die Metaphysik,* by Martin Heidegger. 1953. *Welt und Wort* (Tübingen), vol. 9, 1954, 282.

6256 Wust, P. *Der Mensch und die Philosophie. Einführung in die Haupfragen der Existenzphilosophie.* Münster, 1946, 151 p.

6257 Wurzer, William Stefan. "Nietzsche's Dialectic of Intellectual Integrity: A Propaedeutic Study." *Southern Journal of Philosophy,* vol. 13, Summer 1975, 235-245.

6258 Wurzer, William. "Heidegger's Problem of the 'Hermeneutic Who'." *Dialogos,* vol. 15, 1980, 121-137.

6259 Wyller, E. A. *Fra Homer til Heidegger.* Oslo, 1959.

6260 Wyller, E. A. *Tidsproblemet hos Olaf Bull. Et eksistensfilosofisk bidrag.* Oslo, 1959.

6261 Wyschogrod, Michael. *Kierkegaard and Heidegger. The Ontology of Existence.* London, 1954, XII, 156 p. 2nd ed. New York, 1969.

6262 Wyschogrod, Michael. "Heidegger's Ontology an Human Existence." *Diseases of the Nervous System* (New York), vol. 22, no. 4, Suppl., 1961, 50-56.

6263 Yagi, Tadesaburô. "Jitsuzon ni oderu Shinri no Haaku, Haideggâ to Kierukegôru" (The Concept of Truth in Existence. Heidegger and Kierkegaard). *Fukushimadaigaku-Gakudeigakubu-Ronshû* (Fukushima), April 1950.

6264 Yagüe, Joaquin. "El concepto de mundo en Heidegger." *Mayéutica,* vol. 3, no. 8, 1977, 204-236.

6265 Yamado, Teruo. "Haideggâ 'Sonzai to Jikan' o meguru Shomondai" (The Problems on Heidegger's 'Being and Time'). *Shimonoseki Shôkei Ronshû* (Shimonoseki), vol. 16, no. 2, 1973, 285-301.

6266 Yamado, Taruo. "Haideggâ ni okeru Sonzaibôkyaku to Sonzai no Akarumi ni tsuite" (The Being-Forgottenness and the Being-Lighting in Heidegger). *Shimonoseki Shôkei Ronsyû* (Shimonoseki), vol. 18, no. 2, 1974, 67-85.

6267 Yamada, Masanori. "Haideggâ to 'Mu' eno Toi" (Heidegger and the Question of 'Nothingness'). *Tôkyô Daigaku Daigakuin Kiyô* (Tôkyô), vol. 11, 1974, 71-82.

6268 Yamamoto, Eiichi. "Haideggâ on Kanto-Kaishaku" (Heidegger's Kant-Exegesis). *Risô* (Tôkyô), vol. 23, 1931, 14-36.

6269 Yamamoto, Eiichi. *Haideggâ no Ninshikiron* (Heidegger's Theory of Cognition). *Risô* (Tôkyô), März 1935.

6270 Yamanouchi, Tokuryû. "Haideggâ no Kincho" (Heidegger's Recent Writings). *Tetsugakukenkyû* (Kyôto), vol. 34, no. 4, 1950, 58-63.

6271 Yamazaki, Shôichi. "Haideggetutetsugaku no Kiso" (The Basis of Heidegger's Philosophy). *Tetsugakuzasshi* (Tôkyô), vol. 6-8, Oktober 1937.

6272 Yamazaki, Shôichi. "Tetsugakuhihan no Rinen. Haideggerutetsugaku no Hihan" (The Idea of the Criticism of Philosophy. Criticism of Heidegger's Philosophy). *Tetsugakuzasshi* (Tôkyô), vol. 600-601, Februar und März 1937.

6273 Yamazaki, Shôichi. "Jitsuzonshugi-Hihan, Haideggâ ni tsuite" (Criticism of Existentialism. On Heidegger). *Tetsugakuhyôron* (Tôkyô), Dezember 1948.

6274 Yamazaki, Syôiti. "The Basis of Heidegger's Philosophy." (In Japanese). *Tetuga-ku-Zassi,* vol. 608, 1938, 23-42.

6275 Yamazaki, Yôsuke. "Niche to Haideggâ" (Nietzsche and Heidegger). *Gendaitetsugaku no Kadai* (Tôkyô), Oktober 1963.

6276 Yanaibara, Isaku. "Kirukegôru, Sarutoru, Haideggâ, Yasupâsu" (Kierkegaard, Sartre, Heidegger, Jaspers). *Gendai-Shisô* (Naukasha-Verlag) (Tôkyô), 12 Juni 1951, 57-70.

6277 Yangbu, Ch'oe. *Hugi Haidegkaûi chonjaesasang t'amgu* (A Contemplation on Being in the Late Heidegger). M. A. Thesis, Ch'ungnam Univ., 1969.

6278 Yaoxum, Hong. *Shizaizhexue lunping* (Critique of Existential Philosophy). Taibei: Shuiniu wenku, 1970. (In Chinese).

6279 Yannaras, Ch. *Der ontologische Gehalt des theologischen Begriffs von der 'Person'.* Phil. Diss. Univ. Thessaloniki Athen 1970 96 p.

6280 Yannaras, Ch. *De l'absence et de l'inconnaissance de Dieu, d'après les écrits aréopagitiques et Martin Heidegger.* (Théologie sans frontière, 21). Paris, 1971, 135 p.

6281 Yasui, Genji. "Haideggâ to Sarutoru ni okeru Shi no Mondai - Gendai-Shisô no Ugoki" (The Problem of Death in Heidegger and Sartre). *Risô* (Tôkyô), vol. 223, 1951, 71-73.

6282 Yassa, S. *Die existenziale Grundlage der Philosophie Pascals.* Würzburg, 1934.

6283 Yasui, Genji. "Haideggâ to Sarutoru ni okeru Shi no Mondai" (The Problem of Death in Heidegger and Sartre). *Risô* (Tôkyô), vol. 223, Dezember 1950.

6284 Yela, J. F. "El tema de la verdad en la metafisica de Heidegger." *Revista de Filosofia* (Madrid), vol. 8, 1948, 659-672.

6285 Yoneda, Shigeo. "Haideggâ no Kanto Kaishaku ni tsuite" (On Heidegger's Interpretation of Kant). *Ôita Daigaku Kytôiku Gakubu Kenkyû Kiyô* (Ôita) (Jinbun-Shakai Kagaku B), vol. 5, no. 2, 1977, 27-35.

6286 Yoneda, Shôtarô. "Haideggâ no Kanshinron" (The 'Care' in Heidegger). *Keizaironso* (Kyôto), vol. 26, no. 1, 1928, 22-55.

6287 Yonekura, Mitsuru. "Haideggâ ni okeru 'Kami no Shi' no Mondai" (The Problem of the Death of the God in Heidegger). *Jinbun Ronkyû* (Nishinomiya) (Kansai Gakuin Daigaku), vol. 22, no. 3, 1972, 1-22.

6288 Yonekura, Mitsuru. "Shoki Haideggâ to Burutoman" (The Early Heidegger and Bultmann). *Jinbun Ronkyû* (Nishinomiya) (Kansai Gakuin Jinbun Gakkai), vol. 24, no. 3, 1974.

6289 Yonezawa, Aritsune. "Die *Kunst* Philosophie Heideggers." (In Japanese). *Bigaku,* vol. 26, 1975, 16-26.

6290 Yonezawa, Aritsune. "Critical Thoughts on the 'Vergangenheit-Charakter' of Art: Hegel and Heidegger." (In Japanese). *Bigaku. The Japanese Journal of Aesthetics* (Tokyo), vol. 27, 1976, 43.

6291 Yôngeh'un, I. "Haidegkaûi chonjaee kwanhan yôngu - yusillronjôk ipjangesô" (Being in Heidegger - in Regard to Theism). *Ch'ungnam University Collection of Essays* (Ch'ungnam), vol. 3, 1963, 151-207.

6292 Yôngeh'un, I. "Haidegkaûi sinûi munje - Hölderingwaûi gwangyee issôsô" (The Problem of God in Heidegger With Respect to Hölderlin). *Ch'ungnam University Collection of Essays* (Ch'ungnam), vol. 4, 1965, 103-145.

6293 Yôngch'un, I. *Haidegkaûi sinûi munje* (The Problem of God in Heidegger). Phil. Diss. Ch'ungnam Univ. 1966. (In Korean).

6294 Yôngch'un, I. "Haidegkae issôsôûi chonjaewa siwa sin" (Being, Poetry, and God in Heidegger). *Ch'ôrhak Yôngu.* Ed. Philosophers' Society. Sôul, vol. 1, 1966, 7-33.

6295 Yônggu, I. *Haidegkae issôsôûi yôksaûi kûnwônûrosôûi si* (Poetry as a Source of History in Heidegger). M. A. Thesis, Sôul Univ., 1960.

6296 Yônggu, I. "Muûi kaenyôme taihan haemyông" (Explanation of the Notion on Non-Being." *Ch'ungbuk Univ. Collection of Essays* (Ch'ungbuk), vol. 6, 1972, 227-238.

6297 Yongmu, Kim. *Haidegkaûi chilli munje* (The Problem of Truth in Heidegger). M. A. Thesis, Sôul Univ., 1965.

6298 Yôngmyông, Kim. *Haidegkaûi chonjaeûi t'op' orogi* (Topology of Being in Heidegger). M. A. Thesis, Yônse Univ., 1966.

6299 Yoshizawa, Denzaburô. "Haideggâ no Niche-Kaishaku" (Heidegger's Nietzsche-Exegesis). *Jitsuzonshugi* (Tôkyô), April 1966.

6300 Yoshizawa, Denzaburô. "Haideggâ no Nîcheron" (On Nietzsche in Heidegger). *Jitsuzonshugi* (Tôkyô), vol. 77, 1976, 122-128.

6301 Yovel, Yirmiahu. "Existentialism and Historical Dialectic." *Philosophy and Phenomenological Research* (Buffalo, New York), vol. xxxix, no. 4, 1979, 480-497.

6302 Yuasa, Seinosuke. "Kanto Hêgeru Haideggâ - Hêgeru ni okeru Genshô no Imi" (Kant, Hegel, Heidegger - The Meaning of the Phenomenon in Hegel). *Risô* (Tôkyô), vol. 22, 1931, 106-115.

6303 Yuasa, Seinosuke. "Kyôjô ni okeru Haideggâ" (Heidegger in His Seminars). *Risô* (Tôkyô), vol. 16, 1930, 62-83.

6304 Yuasa, Seinosuke. "Doitsu no Konogoro; Haideggâ no Daigakuron o chûshin toshite" (Germany Today and the Idea of Univ. in Heidegger). *Risô* (Tôkyô), vol. 43, 1933, 113-116.

6305 Yuasa, Shin-ishi B. *Recht und Sein nach Heidegges Fundamentalontologie. Der Weg zur Phänomenologie des Rechts.* Köln, 1969, 110 p. Phil. Diss. Köln 16.6.1969.

6306 Yuasa, Yasuo. "Sei no Rinri to Shi no Shinri - Watsuji-Rinrigaku to Haideggâ no Gensonzai Bunseki o megutte" (The Ethics of Life and the Sensation of Death - Ethics of Watsuji and Heidegger's Analysis of There-Being). *Jitsuzonshugi* (Tôkyô), vol. 32, 1965, 35-45.

6307 Yuasa, Yasuo. "Mu to Kû no Aida; Watsuji, Nishida, Sarutoru, Haideggâ" (In Between Nothing and 'Kû': Watsuji, Nichida, Sartre, Heidegger). *Jitsuzonshugi* (Tôkyô), vol. 40, 1967, 47-64.

6308 Yuasa, Yasuo. "Shi ni okeru Sonzai" (Being in Death). *Jitsusonshugi Kozâ* (Rishôsha, Tôkyô), vol. 3, 1972, 179-198.

6309 Yuasa, Yasuo. "Haideggâ to Kindai Nippon Tetsugaku no Deai" (Meeting of Heidegger and Modern Japanese Philosophy). *Jitsuzonshugi* (Tôkyô), vol. 77, 1976, 43-56.

6310 Yûki, Gen'ichi. "Nihon ni okeru Haideggâ Kaishaku" (Exegesis of Heidegger in Japan). (Yuibutsuron-Kenkyû (Tôkyô), vol. 15, 1934, 58-73.

6311 Yura, Tetsuji. "Haideggâ to Kasshirâ tono Ronso" (A Dispute Between Heidegger and Cassirer). *Shisô* (Tôkyô), vol. 90, November 1929.

6312 Yura, Tetsuji. "Haideggâ no Rekishi-Kagaku ni okeru Jikan-Gainen 1-3" (The Notion of Time in the Heideggerian Concept of History). *Kyôikugakujutsukai,* LXVIII-6, LXIX-1, 2. 1934, 2-16, 19-32, 38-53.

6313 Zabielskis, P. "Martin Heidegger on Guilt." *The Undergraduate Journal of Philosophy* (Oberlin, Ohio), vol. 7, no. 2, 1976, 32-44.

6314 Zajceva, Z. M. "Filosofskij jazyk M. Chajdeggera na sluzbe ego sistemy" (Heidegger's Philosophical Language as Function Within His System). *Filosofskie nauki* (Moskva), vol. 6, 1966, 105-112.

6315 Zajceva, Z. "Kritika ekzistencialistskoj koncepcii jazyka M. Chajdeggera" (The Criticism of Heidegger's Existentialist Conception of Language). *Avtoreferat dissertacii na soiskanie ucënoj stepeni kandidata filosofskich nauk.* Moskva, 1968.

6316    Zaluska, A. Rev. of *Heidegger i filozofia wspólczesna,* by Krzysztof Michalski. 1978. *Studia Filozoficzne,* vol. 7, 1979.

6317    Zanardo, A. "Heidegger e il naturalismo di Löwith." *Rivista critica di Storia della Filosofia* (Milano), vol. 24, 1969, 312-324.

6318    Zboril, B. "'Being and Time' by Martin Heidegger." (In Czechoslovakian). *Sbornik Praci Filosofické Fakulty Brnenské University, Rada Literárnevedná* (Brno), no. 21-22, 1975, 75-96.

6319    Zehm, Günther. "Auf der Lichtung des Seins. 'Zur Sache des Denkens' oder Die letzte Standortbestimmung. Zu Martin Heideggers 80. Geburtstag." *Die Welt,* no. 224, 1969, 31.

6320    Zehm, Günther. "Der Alleszermalmer aus Messkirch auf der Lichtung des Seins. Der Philosoph Martin Heidegger ist im Alter von 86 Jahren Gestorben." *Die Welt* (Hamburg), Ausgabe D, no. 123, 28 May 1976, 23. (Jg. 3, 1976, Nr. 2).

6321    Zelená, Jindrich. "Heidegger's Criticism of Metaphysics." (In Czechoslovakian). *Filosoficky Casopis CSAV,* vol. 27, 1979, 205-218.

6322    Zelnov, M. V. "Sovremennaja neotomistskaja koncepcija licnosti" (The Contemporary Neo-Thomist Conception of Personality). *V knige 'Problema celoveka v sovremennoj filosofii', Izdatel'stvo 'Nauka'* (Moskva), 1969, 405-408.

6323    Zeltner, H. "Universitas Litterarum? Zu Heideggers Kritik der modernen Wissenschaft." *Die Erlanger Universität* (Erlangen), Jg. 4, no. 4, 1; no. 5, 1-2; no. 6, 3, 1950. (Univ. des Erlanger Tagblattes).

6324    Zeltner, H. Rev. of *Holzwege,* by Martin Heidegger. 1950. *Philosophisches Jahrbuch* (Fulda), vol. 60, 1950, 346-347.

6325    Zeltner, H. Rev. of *Platons Lehre von der Wahrheit. Mit einem Brief über den 'Humanismus'.* 1947. *The Times Literary Supplement* (London), 2.6.1950.

6326    Zeltner, H. "Eine Betrachtung zu Heideggers 'Holzwege'." *Die Gegenwart* (Freiburg), vol. 5, 1950, 19.

6327    Zeltner, H. "Martin Heidegger." In *Gestalter unserer Zeit. Denker und Deuter im heutigen Europa.* Oldenburg, 1954, 90-101.

6328    Zeltova, V. "Ekzistencializm i krizis burzuaznoj filosofii prava" (Existentialism and the Crisis of the Bourgeois Philosophy of Law). *Voprosy filosofii,* vol. 12, 1969, 73-84.

6329    Zeltova, V. "Ekzistencialistskaja filosofija prava" (The Existentialist Philosophy of Law). *Avtoreferat dissertacii na soiskanie ucenoj stepeni kandidata filosofskich nauk* (Moskva), 1969.

6330    Zenzen, M. J. "The Suggestive Power of Color." *Journal of Aesthetics and Art Criticism* (Baltimore), vol. 36, no. 2, 1977, 185-190.

6331    Zimmerman, Michael E. *The Concept of Self in Martin Heidegger's 'Being and Time'.* Phil. Diss. Tulane Univ. 1974. *Dissertation Abstracts International,* vol. 35/04-A, 2344.

6332  Zimmerman, Michael E. "Heidegger, Ethics, and National Socialism." *The Southwestern Journal of Philosophy* (Norman, Oklahoma), vol. 5, no. 1, 1974, 97-106.

6333  Zimmerman, Michael E. "On Discriminating Everydayness, Unownedness, and Falling in 'Being and Time'." *Research in Phenomenology* (Pittsburgh), vol. 5, 1975, 109-127.

6334  Zimmerman, Michael E. "A Door to a New Way of Thinking. The Foundering of Being and Time." *Philosophy Today* (Celina, Ohio), vol. 19, no. 2-4, 1975, 100-107.

6335  Zimmerman, Michael E. "Heidegger on Nihilism and Technique." *Man and World* (The Hague), vol. 8, no. 4, 1975, 394-414.

6336  Zimmerman, Michael E. "The Unity and Sameness of the Self as Depicted in *Being and Time*." *The Journal of the British Society for Phenomenology* (Manchester), vol. 6, 1975, 157-167.

6337  Zimmerman, Michael E. "The Foundering of *Being ad Time*." *Philosophy Today* (Celina, Ohio), vol. 19, 1975, 100-107.

6338  Zimmerman, Michael E. Rev. of *The End of Philosophy,* by Martin Heidegger. 1973. *International Philosophical Quarterly,* vol. 15, 1975, 501-504.

6339  Zimmerman, Michael E. Rev. of *Heidegger on the Divine. The Thinker, the Poet, and God,* by James L. Perotti. Athens, 1974. *Philosophy and Phenomenological Research* (Buffalo, New York), vol. 36, 1975, 285-286.

6340  Zimmerman, Michael E. "A Comparison of Nietzsche's Overman and Heidegger's Authentic Self." *The Southern Journal of Philosophy* (Memphis), vol. 14, no. 2, 1976, 213-231.

6341  Zimmerman, Michael E. "Heidegger's New Concept of Authentic Selfhood." *The Personalist* (Los Angelos), vol. 57, no. 2, 1976, 198-212.

6342  Zimmerman, Michael E. "Heidegger and Nietzsche on Authentic Time." *Cultural Hermeneutics* (Dordrecht/Boston), vol. 4, no. 3, 1977, 239-264.

6343  Zimmerman, Michael E. Rev. of *Die Grundprobleme der Phänomenologie,* by Martin Heidegger. 1975. *International Philosophical Quarterly* (New York/Herverlee-Louvain), vol. 17, 1977, 235-237.

6344  Zimmerman, Michael E. "Some Important Themes in Current Heidegger Research." *Research in Phenomenology* (Pittsburgh), vol. 7, 1977, 259-281.

6345  Zimmerman, Michael E. "Beyond *Humanism.* Heidegger's Understanding of Technology." *Listening. Journal of Relgion and Culture* (River Forest, Illinois), vol. 12, no. 3, 1977, 74-83.

6346  Zimmerman, Michael E. Rev. of *The Piety of Thinking,* by Martin Heidegger. 1976. *The Modern Schoolman* (Saint Louis), vol. 54, 1977, 393-396.

6347  Zimmerman, Michael E. "Dewey, Heidegger, and the Quest for Certainty." *The Southwestern Journal of Philosophy* (Norman, Oklahoma), vol. 9, no. 1, 1978, 87-95.

6348     Zimmerman, Michael E. Rev. of *Die Grundprobleme der Phänomenologie,* by Martin Heidegger. 1976. *Journal of the History of Philosophy* (Claremont, California), vol. 16, 1978, 244-246.

6349     Zimmerman, Michael E. "Marx and Heidegger on the Technological Domination of Nature." *Philosophy Today,* vol. 23, no. 2-4, 99-112.

6350     Zimmerman, Michael E. "Heidegger's 'Completion' of 'Sein und Zeit'." *Philosophy and Phenomenological Research* (Buffalo, New York), vol. xxxix, no. 4, 1979, 537-560.

6350a     Zimmerman, Michael E. "Heidegger and Bultmann: Egoism, Sinfulness, and Inauthenticity." *The Modern Schoolman* (Saint Louis), vol. 57, 1979/80, 1-20.

6351     Zingari, Guido. "L'interpretazione della possibilita in Heidegger." *Aquinas. Rivista de Filosofia* (Roma), vol. 20, no. 2, 1977, 255-280.

6352     Zivotiá, M. "Die Metaphysikkritik Martin Heideggers." (Roumanian). *Revista de Filozofie* (Bucuresti), vol. 16, no. 5, 1969, 575-584.

6353     Zivotiá, Miladin. "The Significance of the Fundamental-Ontological Point of View." (In Serbocroat). *Delo* (Beograd), vol. 23, no. 12, 1977, 110-126.

6354     Zongsan, Mou. *Zhi de zhijue yu zhongguo zhexue* (Intellektuelle Anschauung and Chinese Philosophy). Taibei: Shangwu yin shu guan, 1971. (In Chinese).

6355     Zuidema, J. M. "Heideggers Wijsbegeerte van het zijn." *Wetenschappelijke Bijdragen door Leerlingen von Dr. D. H. Vollenhoven. Aangeboden ter gelegenheid van zijn 25-jarig.-Franeker-Potchefstrom 1951.* 1951.

6356     Zuidema, S. U. "De dood bij Heidegger." *Philosophia reformata* (Kampen), vol. 12, 1947, 49-66.

6357     Zuidema, S. U. *De mensch als historie.* [Rede gehouden bij de aanvaarding van het ambt van buitengewoon hoogleeraar in de faculteit der letteren en wijsbegeerte aan de voije Univ. te Amsterdam. Op woensday 9.Juni 1948.]

6358     Zuidema, S. U. "De plaats der theologie in het denken van Martin Heidegger." *Vox Theologica* (Amsterdam), vol. 25, 1955, 184-193.

6359     Zuidema, S. U. "Heidegger." *Denkers van deze tijd.* 2: Heidegger; Dostojewski; Jaspers; Toynbee. (Franeker), 1955.

6360     Zuidema, S. U. "The Idea of Revelation With Karl Barth and With Martin Heidegger. The Comparability of Their Patterns of Thought." *Free Univ. Quarterly* (Amsterdam), vol. 4, 1955/56, 71-84. [In Netherlands: De openbaringsideen van Karl Barth en Martin Heidegger. De vergelijkbaarheid van beider denkstructuur *Philosophia Reformata* (Kampern), vol. 20, 1955, 162-175.]

6361     Zuidema, S. U. "Kontemporain situationisme." *Philosophia reformata* (Kampen), vol. 23, 1958, 85-94.

6362     Zyciáski, J. Rev. of *M. Heidegger and the Nazi Party,* by K. G. Moehling. *Znak,* vol. 9, 1978.

# PART V
# HEIDEGGER CONFERENCES

## 1966

Heidegger Symposium - DePaul Univ. - Nov. 11-12
Convener: Manfred S. Frings

Papers:

John M. Anderson: "Truth, the Metaphysical Tradition, and Creation in the Thought of Martin Heidegger."

Albert Borgmann: "Heidegger and Symbolic Logic."

Alphonso F. Lingis: "The Essence of Technique and Its Relationship to Metaphysics."

Paul Ricoeur: "The Critique of Subjectivity and Cogito in the Philosophy of Heidegger."

Joseph J. Kockelmans: "Thanks-giving: The Completion of Thinking."

Bernard J. Boelen: "The Question of Ethics in the Thought of Martin Heidegger."

Clavin O. Schrag: "Re-Thinking Metaphysics."

## 1967

The Pennsylvania State Univ. - May 12-13
Convener: Joseph J. Kockelmans

Papers:

Cyril Welch: "Heidegger's Contribution to the Idea of Phenomenology."

Joseph Smith: "Being and Subjectivity: Heidegger and Husserl."

Stanley Rosen: "Identification of Being as Historicity."

Bernard Boelen: "Heidegger and the Question of Ethics."

## 1968

Univ. of Pittsburgh - April 26-27
Convener: Joseph J. Kockelmans

Papers:

Richard Palmer: "The Meaning and Scope of Hermeneutics."

Thomas Langan: "Historicity in Hegel and Heidegger."

Theodore Kisiel: "The Happening of Tradition in Gadamer's Hermeneutics."

John M. Anderson: "The Language of Being."

## 1969

Heidegger Circle Meeting - DePaul Univ. - April 18-19
Convener: Manfred S. Frings

Papers:

F. J. Smith: "Being and Time and Being."

Rev. Schuwer: "Reflections and Comments on 'Zeit und Sein'."

Hans-Georg Gadamer: "Empty Time and Filled Time."

J. D. Bailiff: "Art, Opposition and the Advent of Truth."

## 1970

Heidegger Conference - Trinity College - April 24-25
Convener: Drew A. Hyland

Papers:

James Morrison: "Heidegger's Interpretation of Kant in regard to the Question of Being."

Michael Gelven: "Kant's Transcendentalism and Heidegger's Ontological Difference."

Robert Goff: "Heidegger and Language."

Joseph J. Kockelmans: "Language and Hermeneutics."

## 1971

Heidegger Conference - Victoria College, Univ. of Toronto - April 16-17
Convener: James C. Morrison

Papers: John Sallis: "Nietzsche and the Problem of Metaphysics."

Manfred S. Frings: "Heidegger's Interpretaiton and Explication of Protagoras' Fragmant 1."

Graeme Nicholson: "The Futural Character of Thought."

B. Toussaint: "The Interpretation of the 'Self' in Heidegger."

## 1972

6th Annual Heidegger Conference - DePaul Univ. - March 24-25
Convener: Manfred S. Frings

Papers:

Joan Stambough: "Time and Dialectic in Hegel and Heidegger."

Alexander von Schoenborn: "Heidegger's Concept of Everydayness: Some Steps Toward Its Elucidation."

Theodore Kisiel: "The Mathematical and the Hermeneutical: A Discourse on Method in Heidegger."

Dieter Misgelt: "Heidegger and Understanding."

## 1973

Heidegger Conference - Hunter College CUNY - April 6-7
Convener: Charles M. Sherover

Papers:

Rudolf Grew: "Heidegger and Xavier Zubiri."

Elisabeth Hirsch: "Heidegger's View on Language Compared With Those of Chomsky and Wittgenstein."

Don Ihde: "Heidegger and Phenomenology."

Bruce Wilshire: "Heidegger, James and Dewey."

William Barrett: "Heidegger and Me."

Manfred S. Frings: "On Heidegger's Essay on Heraclitus."

Joan Stambough: "On Heidegger's Book an Schelling."

Glen Gray: "Some Considerations on Translating Heidegger."

## 1974

The Heidegger Conference - Duquesne Univ.
Convener: Andre Schuwer

Papers:

Don Ihde: "The Experience of Technology: A Phenomenological Analysis."

Christopher Smith: "Language as the Ground of Self-Conscious: H. G. Gadamer's Heideggerian Critique of Hegel's Dialectical Method."

Jose Huertas-Jourda: "A Husserlian Foundaton for Heidegger's *Sein und Zeit.*"

## 1975

9th Annuel Heidegger Circle Meeting - Wilfrid Laurier Univ., Waterloo, Ontario - May 16-18
Convener: Jose Huertas-Jourda

Papers:

Zygmunt Adamczewski: "The Queston of Being."

Thomas J. Sheehan: "Heidegger's Interpretation of Aristotle."

F. Joseph Smith: "Heidegger's Copula, or the Wedding Between Time and Being."

Theodore Kisiel: "Heidegger (1912-1927) the Transformation of the Categorial."

Richard Palmer: "Heidegger's Contribution to a Post-Modern Interpretive Self-Awareness."

Graeme Nicholson: "Truth, Practice and Perception Notes on 'Vom Wesen der Wahrheit'."

Joan Stambough: "Authenticity and Inauthenticity in 'Being and Time'."

Hans Seigfried: "Descriptive Phenomenology and Constructivism."

Walter Biemel: "Heidegger und die Phänomenologie."

## 1976

10th Heidegger Conference - DePaul Univ. - May 14-16
Convener: Manfred S. Frings

Papers:

John Caputo: "Mysticism, Metaphysics and Thought: A Reading of 'Der Satz vom Grund'."

Parvis Emad: "The 'Mathematical Project' in Heidegger's Criticism of Metaphysics."

André Schuwer: "Remarks on Heidegger's Interpretation of Hölderlin's Hymn 'Wie wenn am Feiertage'."

Walter Biemel: "The Structure of Heidegger's Logic Lecture 1925/26."

Alexander von Schoenborn: "Heidegger's Concept of 'Falling'."

Michael Zimmermann: "On Discriminating Everydayness Unownedness, and

P. Christopher Smith: "A Poem of Rilke's as Substantiation of Heidegger's Philosophy After the Kehre."

Eugene Gendlin: "Two Phenomenologists do not Disagree."

Charles Seibert: "On the Body Phenomenon in 'Being and Time'."

John Sallis: Rev. of 'Die Grundprobleme der Phänomenologie'," by Martin Heidegger.

## 1977

11th Heidegger Conference - Tulane Univ. - May 26-28
Convener: Michael E. Zimmermann

Papers:

Edward G. Ballard: "Opening Remarks on Heidegger and Technology."

David Kolb: "Heidegger on the Limits of Science."

P. Christopher Smith: "Pre-Scientific Truth and *Aletheia.*"

Elisabeth F. Hirsch: "In Memory of Martin Heidegger: Observations on Heidegger as Teacher and Scholar."

Walter Biemel: "Zur Komposition und Einheit der 'Holzwege'."

Reiner Schürmann: "Ontological Difference and Political Philosophy."

Kenneth Maly: "The Philosophical Significance of the New Edition of *Sein und Zeit.*"

Eugene Gendlin: "Eternal Return and Experiental Meaning."

Theodore Kisiel: "Heidegger and the New Images of Science."

Michael E. Zimmermann: "Closing Remarks and Future Prospects."

## 1978

12th Heidegger Conference - Villanova Univ.
Convener: John Caputo

Papers:

P. Christopher Smith: "Heidegger's Misinterpretation of Rilke."

Joan Stambough: "The Question of God in Heidegger's Thought."

Translator's Panel: Keith Hoeller, Thomas Sheehan, Joan Stambough: "Problems and Issues in Translating the Works of the *Sein und Zeit* Period."

Theodore Kisiel: "A Diagrammatical Approach to Heidegger's Schematism of Existence."

Thomas Sheehan: "Time and Being, 1925-27."

Michael E. Zimmermann: "Bridging the Gap: The Critique of Everydayness by Heidegger and the Critical Marxists."

Don Ihde: "Heidegger's Philosophy of Technology."

Parvis Emad: "Heidegger's Value-Criticism and Its Bearing Upon the Phenomenology of Values."

## 1979

13th Heidegger Conference - Duquesne Univ. - May 18-20
Convener: John Sallis

Papers:

Graeme Nicholson: "The One True Circle of Interpretation."

Hans-Martin Sass: "Heidegger's Post-Phenomenological Experiences."

Jeffner Allen: "Madness and the Poet."

Keith Hoeller: "Is Heidegger Really a Poet?"

James R. Watson: "Marxian Theory and the Movement of Heidegger's Detotalization of Technological-Scientific Rationality."

Reiner Schürmann: "Heidegger's Deconstruction of Action."

William J. Richardson: "Phenomenology and Psychoanalysis."

Wilhelm S. Wurzer: "Heidegger's Geviert, ...an Entirely Different Difficulty..."

## 1980

14th Heidegger Conference - Univ. of Toronto - May 16-18
Convener: Graeme Nicholson

Papers:

Thomas Langan: "Personal Responsibility and the Fostering of Truth."

John Caputo: "Heidegger and Aquinas: An Essay on Overcoming Metaphysics."

David Michael Levin: "Hearing and the End of Metaphysics."

Keith Hoeller: "The Repetition of the First Beginning as Prelude to Another Beginning: The Role of the Early Greeks in Heidegger's Turning."

Walter Biemel: "The Development of Heidegger's Concept of the Thing."

Charles Scott: "Heidegger and Fantasy."

Hans-Martin Sass: "Report on the Heidegger-Glossary."

Parvis Emad: "Heidegger and Pain: Focussing on a Recurring Theme of His Thought."

James R. Watson: "Thinking and Tradition."

# PART VI
# INDEXES

## Name Index

# Subject Index

Logik 1538, 1542, 1675, 1923, 2198, 2201, 2203, 2204, 2796, 4142, 4537, 5305, 5749, 5796

-symboliche 1463, 1464

Logos 1192, 2588, 3732, 4811


Marburg 2335, 2384, 2396, 2843, 4230

Marxismus 1143, 1179, 1499, 1500, 1780, 1947, 2977, 3020, 3785, 3788, 4560

Mateialismus 5676

Mathematik 1296, 1298

Medizin 1481

Mensch 3363, 3424

Menschheit 3393

Menschwerdung Gottes 3498

Messkirch 2477, 2618

Metaphysik 1051, 1052, 1062, 1082, 1101, 1119, 1123, 1260, 1360, 1420, 1427, 1514, 1572, 1627, 1667, 1675, 1684, 1847, 1934, 2143, 2146, 2161, 2179, 2222, 2230, 2300, 2306, 2333, 2372, 2388, 2484, 2590, 2821, 2909, 3390, 3432, 3526, 3592, 3779, 3889, 3914, 4026, 4073, 4107, 4148, 4149, 4604, 4666, 4686, 4729, 4756, 4823, 4878, 4909, 4954, 4955, 5106, 5224, 5235, 5297, 5353, 5365, 5377, 5437, 5511, 5673, 5718, 5768, 5914, 5985, 6007, 6054, 6131, 6352

-interpretative 1923

-neoscholatische 3924

-thomistische 5205

Metaphysikkritik 1578

Methode 4800, 4811, 4823

Mit-Dasein 3523, 4695

Mitmensch 3699, 4556

Mit-sein 3364, 5795

Mord 1988

Musik 2229, 2263

Mystik 1656, 2349, 3428, 3663, 4374

Mystizismus 3514, 3516, 4202, 4700, 5000


Nachrufe 1088, 1174, 1284, 1359, 1362, 1414, 1487, 1545, 1598, 1746, 1749, 1975, 2024, 2027, 2042, 2313, 2654, 2724, 2746, 2775, 2798, 2848, 2888, 2918, 2934, 3084, 3130, 3150, 3156, 3244, 3266, 3307, 3426, 3470, 3621, 3637, 3856, 3879, 3880, 4232, 4237, 4270, 4535, 4701, 4733, 4845, 4869, 4870, 4905, 5145, 5162, 5274, 5275, 5293, 5444, 5628, 5843, 5898, 5947, 6120, 6169, 6179, 6320

Optimismus 1634

Pädagogik 2097, 2539, 2907, 3922, 4078, 4654, 4890, 5143, 5144, 5217, 5368

Phänomenologie 1190, 1200, 1248, 1364, 1418, 1485, 1508, 1520, 1612, 1646, 1679, 1802, 1961, 2071, 2104, 2106, 2142, 2186, 2190, 2239, 2297, 2318, 2860, 2921, 2954, 2955, 2966, 2981, 2995, 3162, 3202, 3316, 3376, 3536, 3565, 3503, 3700, 3954, 3900, 3945, 4007, 4300, 4525, 4548, 4688, 4772, 4785, 4852, 4896, 4906, 4908, 4939, 4970, 5022, 5151, 5159, 5179, 5236, 5262, 5308, 5335, 5359, 5358, 5394, 5423, 5527, 5528, 5538, 5571, 5700, 5759, 5762, 5823, 5875, 6048, 6053, 6119

    -deskriptive 5355

    -existentialistische 3588

    -existentielle 3782, 4098

    -hermeneutische 4715, 6130

    -radikale 5089, 5094

    -transzendentale 1653, 3286, 4092

Philosophie

    -anthropologische 2450

    -chinesische 1910, 1944, 6354

    -indische 3960

    -japanische 3011

    -klassische 2356

    -marxistisch - leninistische 2876

    -östliche 2840

    -praktische 3918

    -spätbürgerliche 2499

    -sprachanalytische 4758

    -transzendentale 4012

    -zeitgenössische 3269

Physik 2778

Politik 1070, 1434, 1451, 1568, 1919, 2734, 2783, 3704, 3857, 3858, 4233, 4465, 4512, 4528, 4721, 4723, 5115, 5283, 5284, 5285, 5289, 5315, 5316, 5366, 6218, 6219

Positivismus 1419, 1539

    -logischer 4197

Pragmatismus 3689

Praxis 2778

## Index of Editors and Translators of Works by Heidegger

## Review Index

G = German
E = English
F = French
I = Italian
D = Dutch
Sp = Spanish
IA = Ibero-American
Ch = Chinese
J = Japanese
Cor = Corean
Pl = Polish
Cz = Czechoslovakian
R = Russian
You = Yougoslavian

Aus der Erfahrung des Denkens (*See* 72) 5844 (G); 1862, 1865, 1974, 3643, 4780, 4849
    (F); 3569 (I); 2449 (Sp); 4810, 5733 (IA)
Aus einer Erörterung der Wahrheitsfrage (*See* 116) 4820, 4821 (G)

Bauen Wohnen Denken (*See* 67) 2114 (G); 1872, 2841, 3471, 4125, 6170, 4700A (E);
    2067, 2626 (Pl); 1900, 5436 (Cz); 1108 (R); 5460 (You)
Brief über den Humanismus (*See* 50, 52) 1253, 1318 (G); 3471, 4700A (E); 1819, 1850,
    1862, 1864, 1974, 2756, 3643, 4780, 4849, 5019, 5782, 5905 (F); 2659 (I); 2292,
    4687 (IA); 2242 (Pl)

Colloque Cassirer - Heidegger (*See* 163) 1690, 1691 (F)

...Dichterisch wohnet der Mensch... (*See* 73) 1872, 2114, 2841, 3893, 4125, 6170 (E);
    3242 (You)
Das Ding (*See* 66) 2114 (G); 1250, 1872, 2841, 3471, 4125, 6170 (E); 5573 (IA)

Identität und Differenz (*See* 88) 1241, 4706 (G); 3973 (E); 2602, 4849 (F); 5361 (You)

Kant und das Problem der Metaphysik (*See* 22, 61) 1506, 1514, 1576, 1692, 1703, 2134, 2615, 3662, 3673, 3792, 4137, 4311, 4313, 4393, 5213, 5514, 5595, 6036 (G); 1289, 3792, 5038, 6186 (E); 1691, 1852, 2490, 5760 (F); 1664, 2580, 3570 (I); 1957, 3414 (D); 4089 (Sp); 2292 (IA); 4345

Kants These über das Sein (*See* 114, 119) 3120, 3223, 4415 (G); 3345 (E); 1752, 3602 (F); 1081, 2076 (Sp); 4953 (IA)

Die Kategorien- und Bedeutungslehre des Duns Scotus (*See* 11) 2220, 3099, 3344, 4040, 4305, 4309, 5334, 5660 (G); 5603 (E); 1458, 1614, 2008, 4025, 4310, 4844, 5166, 5987 (I); 2068 (D); 3842 (Sp)

Die Kunst und der Raum (*See* 144) 2676, 2811, 3054 (G)

Die Lehre vom Urteil im Psychologismus (*See* 6) 2003, 2428, 5005 (I)

Logik. Die Frage nach der Wahrheit (*See* 171) 4731, 5302 (G); 2738, 3467, 5630A (E); 1930, 2997 (D); 4775 (IA) 4018 (Pl)

Logos (*See* 65) 2123 (G); 1656A, 2842, 3282 (E)

Metaphysische Anfangsgründe der Logik im Ausgang von Leibniz (*See* 182) 2123A (E)

Nietzsche Vol. I (*See* 106) 4682 (IA); 3262 (You)

Nietzsche Vol. I - II (*See* 106 and 107) 1523, 2216, 3640, 3994, 5259 (G); 2319 (E); 3545, 4805 (I); 1081, 3087 (Sp)

Nietzsche's Wort 'Gott ist tot' (*See* 46) 1814 (I); 4400 (You)

Nur noch ein Gott kann uns retten (*See* 170) 1194 (D)

Phänomenologie und Theologie (*See* 152) 6346 (E); 1249, 3803A, 4814 (I); 4000, 4002 (Pl); 6097 (You)

Phänomenologische Interpretation von Kants Kritik der reinen Vernunft (*See* 176) 3792A (E); 1933 (D)

Platons Lehre von der Wahrheit (*See* 42) 2845 (G); 1752, 3602 (F); 3114 (D); 1158, 2292 (IA)

Platons Lehre von der Wahrheit. Mit einem Brief über den Humanismus (*See* 52) 1220, 2100, 2708, 3488, 3744, 3831, 3916, 4334, 4409, 6225 (G); 2183, 4362, 6325 (E); 1768, 2489, 6011 (I); 1219, 4338 (D); 1708 (Sp)

Was ist das - die Philosophie? (*See* 81) 4710 (G); 2189 (E); 1752, 2150 (F); 2228, 3577, 3840, 4765 (I); 3055, 4989 (IA)

Was ist Metaphysik? (*See* 21, 44, 55) 1232, 1577, 2866, 2882, 3609, 3674, 3744, 4314, 5057, 5613 (G); 1534, 3471, 4531, 4700A (E); 1838, 1850, 3438 (F); 2298, 4577, 5212 (I); 1063, 2060, 3115, 4227 (D); 1708 (Sp); 2292 (IA); 4109, 4394 (You)

Wegmarken (*See* 130, 172) 2784 (G); 4397 (E); 1932 (D); 5515 (Sp); 4774 (IA)


Zeit und Sein (*See* 135) 2115 (G); 3827, 3939, 4974, 5195 (E); 3613 (F); 2998 (D); 4986 (IA)

Zur Sache des Denkens (*See* 139) 3121, 3123, 4417 (G); 1818, 2108, 4161, 5540, 6188, 6251, 6346 (E); 2577 (F); 1999 (D); 5174 (IA)

Zur Seinsfrage ( *See* 82) 1836, 3263, 3264, 5036 (E); 2455, 4847 (F); 1608 (I)

# PART VII
# GLOSSARY

prepared by

## Keith Hoeller, Wei Hsiung, Tadashi Kouzuma,
## Eduard Landolt, Orlando Pugliese, Dominique Saatdjian

arranged by

## Hans-Martin Sass

The international Heidegger Glossary, representing for the first time 100 technical terms in seven different languages is an adventurous enterprise. It does not at all aim to serve as a translators dictionary or to uniformize the art of translating; it is not a prescription of définitions constructives. The most fundamental question which led to the idea of pragmatically compiling such glossary is a Heideggarian as well as a very basic human question: what is language? What does it mean to say: Language is the House of Being? This very question breaks down into a couple of questions still under discussion or even not yet addressed in contemporary philosophy of language: Is language essentially rooted in hearing or in seeing, is it reproducing or representing ideas or experiences or things, is it phonems or graphems? Having included Chinese and Japanese characters in our Glossary only underlines the importance of the questions raised. Answering those questions one way or another is the precondition for approaching the more specific questions of philosophy of translation, to the disposal of which this Glossary wants to present material and information on so far existing translations of works of Martin Heidegger.

Heidegger's own approach to words and terms was a translative one, i.e., thoughtfully transforming, translating and transfigurating original ideas attached to words into an actual dialogue context, digging deep to the foundation, to the Grund. "Grund" in German according to Heidegger reads as the translation of the Latin ratio, which itself is the translation of the Greek Logos. Ratio had become a technical term in academic philosophy, onedimensional and forgetting almost about its rich original meaning of logos. Rationalization is just a small aspect of ratio in its original use which also meant Rechnung, i.e., billing or totalling what had happened, or Sagen, i.e., logos or legein, speak out what is, what is inquired or demanded (Auskunft). Grund and Vernunft on one hand, and Being on the other hand belong to each other, this is Heidegger's final result of entertaining the question of how to translate ratio into German: Grund is the dwelling, the Haus for Being.

Eduard Landolt, who together with Anna Maria Salmeri and Silvana Cirrone prepared the Italian part of the Glossary, stresses the fact that the chronological order of the translations presents different steps or schools of interpreting Heidegger in Italy. Pietro Chiodi's translations as well as Enzo Pozi's and Armando Carliri's follow a more existentialist Daseins interpretation, while Mario Manno's and Eduard Landolt's mode of interpretative translations is influenced by Vincenzo La Via's position of absolute realism which is close to the late Heidegger. It would be worthwhile to have more elaborated studies in the field of analyzing philosophical translations under such aspects as Landolt mentioned. It would be especially a valuable contribution to comparative philosophy and crosscultural dialoguing, including dialogues between Eastern and Western traditions. While many translations as well as books on Heidegger contain bilingual glossaries, Krzysztof Michalski attaches a small essay on Polish terminology to his translation of selected texts into Polish, talking about different connotations of terms like Wesen, Existence, Dasein, Geschick, Stellen, Ereignis in German and in the Polish language.

Due to its purpose to serve as a paradigm and as an instrument to present material for future philosophy and practice of translations, as well as due to limited space, the Glossary presents the English, Chinese, French, Italian, Japanese and Spanish translations of just one hundred (100) words, fundamental to Heidegger's thinking. Selecting these terms and excluding others has been done in part as a result of many discussions, including discussions with those colleagues who devoted hours and hours of scholarly work in finding and collecting the translation terms.

The Glossary, finally, is not just a scholarly contribution to Heidegger translation and to the philosophy of translation, it is an eminent documentation of international cooperation among Heidegger scholars around the world: Eduard Landolt (Catania, Italy), Keith Hoeller (Seattle, USA), Tadashi Kouzuma (Tokyo, Japan), Orlando Pugliese (Buenos Aires, Argentina and Berlin, Federal Republic of Germany), Dominique Saatdjian (Paris, France), and Hsiung Wei (Peking, China). The role of the editor was just a coordinating and compiling one.

H. M. S.

ABWESEN (1) -heit absence; (2) Abwesende what does not come to presence, Abwesung negatived coming-to-presence, going-from-presence, dis-
appearing; (5) -heit absence; (6) -heit absence; chin.: (7) 不在场
187(51), (8) 19(103); (9) 无所有 39(356); franz.: (13) se-déployer
-en-éloi, gnement, ab-sence; (15) ab-sence; ital.: (24) 343,12-13
irrealtà 498,6; (27) -heit 39,10 non-essenza 98; (28) 39,10 in-
esistenza 29; (34) 250 non-presenza 249; 320 ab-senza 323; 327
assenza 331; (35) (-end) 135 assenza 89; (36) 41,9 assenza 93,21;
(43) 21,27 assenza 34,36; (44) 139,284-6; 288-9 assenza 243; 389-91;
393-5; jap.: (51), (84) 不现前 Fugenzen; (48), (50), (51), (59), (75),
(77), (81), (47), (84) 不 在 Fuzai; (58) 現にないこと Genninaikoto;
(66) 離 坑 Rigen; span.: (89) (Abwesenheit) ausencia, 394; (93) (Abwesenheit:) ausencia, 146; (94) (Abwesenheit) ausencia, 109; (107)
(abwesen) retirarse, 185; (108) (abwesen) ausentarse, 27; (113)
au-sencia, 228; ausencia, 228; (das Abwesende) lo ausente, 99; (114)
(Abwesenheit) ausencia, 44; (117) ausencia, 60; (118) estar ausente, 92.

ALLTÄGLICHKEIT (1) everydayness; alle Tage every day; (2) everydayness; chin.: (7) 日常情况 66(25); (7) 日常生活 128(39), 175(42); (7)
日常状态 43(19), 129(41); franz.: (12) banalité quotidienne; quoti-
dienneté; (16) banalité quotidienne; ital.: (24) Par. 51 quotidianità; (25) 34 quotidianità 656; (26) 211,26 quotidianità 307; (27) esistenza quotidiana (I); 11,14;12,12; (29) 40,17 l'ogni giorno 14,35;
(35) (-lich) 27 quotidiano 15; 157 d'ogni giorno 104; 255 abituale 174;
(37) (quotidianità 74); (43) (-lich) 31 quotidianità 42; jap.: (61),
(71), (73), (77), (78), (79), (81), (85) 日常性 Nichijōsei; span.: (89)
cotidianidad (52ff. u. passim); (89) cotidianidad; (90) "cotidianidad"
(195), cotidianidad (195); (93) (alltäglich) cotidiano (135) (adjektiviert); (94) (alltäglich) a diario (94); (98) (alltäglich) cotidiano
(74); (99) (alltäglich) cotidiano (19); (112) (alltäglich) cotidiano
(114); (117) vida cotidiana (48); (118) vida cotidiana (83).

ANDENKEN (2) re-collection -d recollective; (5) remember, recall,
recollect; chin.: (8) 思念 42(128), 45(132); franz.: (11) la pensée
qui se souvient; (14) la pensée dirigée vers; (16) mémorial; (23)
le mémorial-pensé-dans-l'Etre; ital.: (28) 9E pensamento 67; 17 ri-

flessione 78; (29) 38,8 "Ricordo" 12,16; (32) 23 ripensamento 107;
42 rifarsi a... 127; 45 ricordo 128; 47,4 riflettere 133-5; (33) 81
rimemorazione 101; u. ff.; (-end) 118 pensare 133; (34) 245 capacità
rimemo ravita 244; (35) 79; 107; 130 pensiero rammemorante, rimemo-
rante 51; 70; 86; 40 rimemorare 25; (36) 1,23 ricordo 38,3; 7,23 il
pensiero voltato all'indietro 67,17; (37) (rammentare 20; rievosazio-
ne 70); (38) 6 richiamare alla memoria 7; (39) rammentare 376; (40) 18
... 19; (41) 62 pensare a..., ricordare, II,28; (42) 65,10 pensare
a... II 231,10; (43) 85;102 ricordo 83; 94; 206 memoria 186; jap.:
(66), (84)回 忠 Kaishi; (46), (48), (51), (58), (76), (81)回 想
Kaiso; (72)追 思 Tsuishi; (46), (48), (58), (67), (70), (81) 追 想
Tsuiso; (67)追 憶 Tsuioku; span.: (95) pensamiento (209), recuerdo
(215); (102) "Andenken" ("Conmemoración") (172) (Hölderlin-Zitat);
(103) "En memoria" (27) (Hölderlin-Zitat); (104) En memoria (Andenken) (137) (Hölderlin-Zitat); (107) recuerdo (Andenken) (191), re-
cordar (= pensar) (223), recuerdo (= pensar) (228); (108) el pensar-en
(32,58,63) )Vgl. Anm. 41); (113) recuerdo (9, passim), remembranza
(16 f.), recordación (145), recordar (151), (An-denken:) pensar-en
(55,138), re-cordar (136).

ANGST (1) anxiety, dread; (2) anxiety; chin.: (7), (9)畏; franz.: (12)
angoisse; (16) angoisse; ital.: (24) Par. 40 angoscia; (26) 214-5 angoscia 311-313; (27) 31 angoscia 81; 37 (-lich) angustiato 95; (28)
31 angoscia 18; (34) 66 angoscia 63; (35) 164 angoscia 110; 229 paura
157; jap.: (61), (57), (73), (78), (79), (85) 不 安 Fuan; span.: (89)
angustia (§§ 40,68 b); (89) angustia; (90) angustia (230f.); (93) angustia (137ff., 141f. u. passim); (94) angustia (97ff., 101f. u. passim);
(95) angustia (211, 218); (96) angustia (Angst) (76), angustia (76f.,
78, 82); (109) angustia (35()); (110) temor (120); (111) miedo (65);
(112) (temor) angustioso (115) (paraphrastische Üb.); (114) angustia
(33), miedo (34); (115) angustia (4); (116) angustia (137); (119) miedo
(55); (120) angustia (57); (121) angustia (66).

ANKÜNFTIG come along, come on, oncoming, Ankunft arrival; (5) Ankunft
advent, arrival; (6) Ankunft advent, arrival; chin.: --; franz.: (16)
Ankunft: l'arrivée; ital.: (24) 341,21 sopravviente 495,29 (avveniente);
(28) 50N (nft) annunciante 54; (29) 80,1 "an" das K.; (32) 45(ank...end)
arrivante 128; 46 (künftig) d'ora in anvanti 129; veniente 133; (33) 75

avveniente 95; (36) 5,26 veniente, 42,23; (39) (Ankunft) avveniente
(avvento); (40) arrivante (arrivo); (41) (Ankunft) 45 avvento (-iente)
II 14; (42) (Ankunft) 62,20 arrivo (-ante) II 229,26; (43) (Ankunft)
169 avvento, avveniente 135; jap.: (81) 到米する tōrai-suru; span.: (89)
(das Ankünftige) lo por venir (392); (89) (ankünftig) por venir; (95)
(Ankunft) revelación (210); (96) (Ankunft) anuncio (81); (100) (künftig)
en el futuro (157); (101) (künftig) en lo futuro (57); (107) (künftig)
en lo venidero (229), (Ankunft) llegada (179,218,230), arrivo (185);
(108) (künftig) en el porvenir (63), (Ankunft) advenimiento (22,27),
venida (54,64); (109) (künftig) en adelante (354); (110) (künftig) en
el futuro (117); (111) (künftig) futuro (63) (adjektiviert); (113) futuro (141); (119) (künftig) venidero (54); (120) (künftig) futuro (57);
(121) (künftig) futuro (66).

ANSCHAUEN  (1) behold, intuit, Anschauung intuition; (4) looking at, in-
tuiting, Anschauung intuition; chin.:  (7) 直观 193(59); franz.: (12) das
Anschauen l'intuition théorique; la contemplation; (16) (S.u.Z., § 82a,
S.431, keine Übersetzung); ital.: (24) intuire, intuizione fattuale,
procedimento intuitivo; (25) intuire; (26) intuire; (29) 40,35 (schauen)
contemplare 15,12; (34) 22 vedere 18; 111 intuire 109; 133 contemplare
131; (35) 53 guardare 33; (43) fissare, contemplare, guardare 45-51;
61-64; 69-70; (45) (-ung) 26 intuire 27; jap.: (61), (71), (79), (81)
直観する chokkansuru; (78) 観 るmiru; (85) (Anschauen) 直 観 Chokkan;
span.: (89) intuir (247), (das Anschauen) intuición (157), el intuir (170);
(90) intuir (29, 39, 84); (91) (Anschauen) intuición (64); (92) (Anschauen)
el intuir, intuición (17); (107) (Anschauung) visión (198); (108) (Anschauung) visión (37); (109) intuir (263) (Anschauung) visión (14);
(110) mirar (75) (Anschauung) visión (55); (111) contemplar (35) (Anschauung) visión (22); (113) ("Anschaun") "mirada" (144, N.) (Trakl-Zitat);
(114) intuir (174) (Anschauen) el intuir (172f.) intuición (173); (117)
contemplar (41); (118) contemplar (80).

AN-SICH-SEIN  (1) Being-in-itself, Being-in-themselves; chin.: (7) 自 在
118(27); franz.: (12) l'être-en-soi; ital.: (24) 75 "essere in sé", essere-in-sé, Essere in-sé 150; (34) 154 essere-in-sé 151; (35) (84 "essente in sé") 55; 175 "in sé" 117; jap.: (79), (81) 自体存在 Jitaisonzai;

(73) 自体に－於いて－有ること Jitaini-oite-arukoto; (85) 即自的存在 Sokujitekisonzai; (78) それ自体であること Sorejitaidearukoto; span.: (89) el "ser en sí" (8, 136 u. passim); (89) "ser en sí"; (93) (an sich) en sí (136); (94) (an sich) en sí (95); (96) (an sich) en sí (75); (98) ("an sich") "en sí" (69); (99) ("an sich") "en sí" (12); (109) (an sich) en sí (6); (110) (an sich) en sí (42); (111) (an sich) en sí (14); (114) (an sich) en sí (174); (115) (das "An-sich") en-sí (14); (116) (das "An-sich") el en-sí (148); (119) (Ansichhalten) el detenerse (51); (120) (Ansichhalten) el detenerse (54); (121) (Ansichhalten) contenerse (65).

ANWESEN (1) -d having presence, -heit presence; (2) come(ing)-to-presence, -de that which comes-, gesammeltes (logos) gathered-together, coming-to-presence, -heit presence, -ung come(ing)-to-presence; (4) -de present, -heit presence; (5) to come to presence, presencing (éón), -de éonta) what is present, -heit presence; (6) presencing, becoming present, -heit presence; chin.: (7) 25(14), (8) 18(102), 41(127) 在场 ; franz.: (11) la présence; (13) Se-déployer-en-présence, Approche-de-l'être; (15) L'ad-estance; la présence; (16) a-: être-présent; (22) présence; être en présence; ital.: (24) Esser-presente; 25 (-heit) presenzialità 83; (26) presenza; (28) 17E esser presente 79; (29) (-heit) 127; 136; (30) 11 "essere presente 22; 16 presenza 32; (31) 26 esser presente 49; (32) 20 presenza, essere presente in essenza 105; 41 farsi presente; (33) 74 presenza, esser presente 94; 76 ciò che è presente 96; (34) 15 presenza 11; 18 esser presente 14; 31 esser presente 27; 120 esser presente 120; (-nde) 319, 20 u.ff. l'essente presente 322,-6-7; 322,13; (35) presenza 8; 164 esser presente 110; (36) 5,29; 36,28; 47,37 esser presente 42,27; 87, 17; 101,23; 41,3; 47,37 presenza 93,13; 101,23 (u.144ff.); (37) presenza 20; (42) 23,2; 65,20 presenza I 23,2; II 231,22 (An-wesen, presenza a...); (43) 19 essere reale 33; 22 presenza 35; 21 esse-represente 33; 64 essere (esistere), operante presenza 66; (44) presentarsi, presenza 259; 280 presentazione 386; (45) 28 presenza 29; jap: (59), (77), (81) 現 在 Genzai; (47), (48), (49), (50), (54), (59), (67), (69), (70), (78) 現 仔 Genzon; (51), (74), (85), (84), (86), (88),

(71)現 前 Genzen; (87), (88)現前すること Genzensurukoto; (55)現前存在 Genzensonzai; (57)本質的にあるということ Honshitsutekini-arutoūkoto; (65)本質の実現 Honshitsu no Jitsugen; (66)前 現 Zengen; (61), (68) 臨 在 Rinzai; span.: (89) (das Anwesende) lo presente (479); (89) (Anwesenheit) presencia; (90) "presente" (199) (Anwesendes) lo que está presente (156), (algo) presente (147); (95) presencia (215), (Anwesenheit) afincamiento (215); (98) lo que surge como presente (aufgehendes Anwesen) (72); (99) presencia (13); (100) (Anwesung) presencialización (151) apresentación; (101) (Anwesung) esencializa- ción (54); (107) (anwesen) presentarse (185) (das Anwesende) lo pre- sente (183); (108) (anwesen) presentarse (27) (das Anwesende) lo pre- sente (26); (109) presencia (10, 261) el presenciarse (265) presen- cialidad (270); (110) presencia (48, 71, 78, 87); (111) presencia (18, 37) el estar-presente (42) (S. 33: Satz fehlt); (113) presencia (96,99 f., 193) el estar-presente (100,107) el asistir (115,225) el a-sistir (136,224,227); (114) presencia (171,193) (An-wesen) el pre- senciarse-de-la-esencia (An-wesen) (166); (115) el presentar (15) (das Anwesende) lo-que-se-presenta (13); (116) el pre-senciarse (149) (das Anwesende) lo pre-sente (147); (117) presencia (41,60 f.) pre- sentarse (64); (118) lo presente (80) estar presente (92) presencia (92 ff.).

AUFBRUCH  chin.: (9) 344 动作起来; (8) 348来临; franz.: (15) départ; (17) éclosion (I.); ital.: (25) 46 aprirsi 669; 48 sorgere 671; (27) 26 rivelarsi 61; 30,34 (-en) invadere 79,11; (28) 26 rivelare 7; 30 affiorare 16; (29) 40,30 partenza 15,7; (35) 19 movimento iniziale, (-en) schiudersi 9; jap.: (75)勃 興 Bokkō; (82) 破 開 Hakai; (62) 綻 び Hokorobi; (62) 打ち開き Uchihiraki; span.: (90) (Einbruch) irrupción (190,201); (91) irrumpir, irrupción (124); (92) irrupción (50); (93) (aufbrechender Einbruch) irrupción desplegadora (130); (94) (aufbre- chender Einbruch) descubridora irrupción (88); (114) (aufbrechen) ini- ciar (91).

AUFHEBUNG  (4) being lifted up; chin.: (7) 15扬弃; franz.: (11) en- gloutissement; (14) affranchissement; (22) dépassement; ital.: (24) 430,18 superamento 610,15; (32) 28 risolvenza 110; (33) 89 superamento; (38) (-en) 6 custodire in ...7; (42) 45,9 u.ff sussunsione II 219,27 u.ff.; (-hoben) 44,7 sussunto, conservato II 219,7; jap.: (55), (64),

(75), (79) 止 揚 Shiyō; span.: (89) "levantamiento" (494); (96)
(aufgehoben) superado (75); (107) (aufheben) recoger (191,215);
(108) (aufheben) absorber (32) levantar (52); (113) disolución
(101); (114) superación (109).

AUSLEGUNG (1) interpretation, laying out; (2) laying out in full
view; chin.: (7) 120 (29), 44 (20) 下定义; (7) 194 (60) 景象; (9)
39 (357) 讲法; (7) 25 (14) 解说 ; (7) 20 (8) 处境; (7) 129 (40) 意义;
franz.: (11) interprétation; (12) explication; (15) interprétation;
ital.: Par. 32;148 interpretazione; (25) interpretazione; (26) interpretazione; (27) 32 caratteristica 82; 39 concetto 98; (28) 32
significato 18; 39 concezione 29; 47N esposizione 50; 7E interpretazione 64; (29) 32,22 interpretare 6,27; 43,8 esegesi 17,25; 43,
13 spiegazione 17,30; (30) 9 interpretazione 15; (31) 25 interpretazione 48; 37,2 spiegazione 59,6; (32) 21 interpretazione 105;
36 esporre 120; (33) 55 interpretazione 76; 80 chiarificazione 76;
(34) 12 interpretazione 8; 57 visione 54; 183 spieganzione 181;
(35) 39 interpretazione 24; 78 modo incuisi interpreta 50; (36) 41,
31-2 interpretazione 94,11-2; (37) 16;17;21;20;28 interpretazione
11;117;132; (42) 24,9 predicazione I 15,30;65,12 interpretazione II
231,12; (43) interpretazione; (44) 131,24 interpretazione 235,23;
132 esplicazione 236;279 spiegazione 385; (45) (-en) 16 intendere
17; 18 enunciazione 19; 30 esposizione 31; 34 tema 35; 36 dottrina
37; 38concezione 39; 44 trattazione 45; jap.: (61), (73) 解 意 Kaii;
(47), (50), (54), (56), (63), (67), (68), (71) (75), (78), (79),
(81), (85), (86), (87), (88) 解 釈 Kaishaku; span.: (89) interpretación (§ 32 u.passim); (89) interprecatión; (90) interpretación (7
ff., 41, passim); (91) explicación (106), interpretación (114), exposición (126), ser explicado (131); (92) interpretación (41 u. passim);
(93) expresión (138), interpretación (147); (94) expresión (98), interpretación (110); (96) interpretación (79); (98) interpretación (65);
(99) interpretación (8); (100) explicación (114,154), interpretación
(126,141,151), exposición (127); (101) exégesis (35), interpretación
42,49,54 f.); (102) interpretación (178); (103) explanación (35);
(104) interpretación (145); (107) interpretación (163,172,188,213);
(108) interpretación (9,16,30,50); (109) interpretación (8 ff., 15,
348 f.); (110) interpretación (45,47,49,57,108); (111) interpretación (17 f., 24,56 f.); (113) interpretación (55 f., 99 f., passim);
(114) interpretación (30,42,51, passim); (115) interpretación (14);

(116) interpretación (148); (117) interpretación (18 f., 27,40,53);
(118) interpretación (68,73,79,87); (119) interpretación (21,27,37,
59); (121) interpretación (50 f., 54,58,67).

AUSSTEHEN  (1) outstanding, has yet to be given; (2) with-stand;
chin.: (8) 16(100) 忍受; franz.: (16) être-en-sursis; (17) soutenir
l'épreuve (D.3); (23) soutenir; ital.: Par.48 (-stand); 241 Mancanza
366,144,16; 242,26 mancare 238,19 ; 367,31; (28) 47N affrontare 49;
15 sostenere 75; (32) 20 sostenere 105; (33) 74 assumere 93; 77 sostenere 97; (34) 56 esposizione 52; 311,-2 (steht dasEkst. ... aus) sop-
porta 315,12; (35) 141 sostenere 94; 158,7 sostenere e abbracciare
105; 198 percorrere 133; jap.: (61) 未済分があるmisaibun ga aru; (79)
未済である misaide aru; (73)未済になるmisaini naru; (76) 耐える taeru;
(61) (Ausstand) 未 済 misai; span.: (89) faltar (278 f.), no haber
aportado (260); (89) "faltar" (Ausstand) "lo que falta"; (95) estar
ausente (213) (Anm. 1: faltar, ausentarse); (105) sufrir (151); (106)
soportar (34); (107) soportar (180,183,187); (108) soportar (23,25,29);
(109) soportar (347) (Ausstehen) el soportar (347); (110) soportar
(105) (Ausstehen) el soportar (106); (111) exteriorizar (55) (Ausstehen) exposición (55).

BEDEUTEN  (1) signify, -ung signification, significance; (2) -ung
meaning, -samkeit (Total) Meaningfulness; chin.: (7) 175(42), (8)
24(108) 意思是; (8) 27(211)重要;(7) 43(18), (8) 35(120)意味; (7)
324(72) 指; franz.: (12) be-deuten: signi-fication; ital.: (24) significare; (25) significare; (26) significare, vuol dire, designare,
equivalere; (28) 9E significare 67; (30) 9 significare 16; 9 voler
dire 17; 12 importare 23,5; (31) 22 significare 46; (32) significare;
(33) 90 significare 108; (34) 7 significare 3; 298 far riferimento
301; (35) significare; (37) 14;21;32;41 significare 94;111; (41) 46
significare II,15; (43) 97 significare 91; (44) 135 significare 239;
271 dire 379; (45) 38 significare 39; jap.: (79) 意義づける igizukeru;
(71), (73), (78), (81), (85), (86), (87), (88) 意味する imisuru; (61)
指意する siisuru; span.: (89) significar (102 f.) (be-deuten) "signi-
-ficar" (102); (89) "significar"; (90) significar (9); (91) significar (85,102) (gibt sich zu bedeuten) se da a sí a entender (106);

(92) significar (40) (gibt sich zu bedeuten) indicar (42); (95) significar (214); (97) significar (10); (98) significar (63,68,82); (99) significar (7,10,21); (100) (el) significado (es) (119) significar (141); (101) significar (39,49); (102) significar (167); (103) significar (21); (104) significar (130); (105) significar (146); (106) significar (29); (107) significar (193,205) querer decir (193); (108) significar (33 f., 44); (113) querer decir (134) significar (145,174,195,211); (114) significar (185,189); (115) significar (10,13); (116) significar (144); (117) significar (21,54,63); (118) significar (69,82,88) ser el significado (94); (119) significar (24,27,32,45); (120) significar (18,21,27,44); (121) significar (49,51,54,61).

BEFINDLICHKEIT  (1) state-of-mind Befund: findings, datum; (2) (ontological) disposition; chin.: (7) 189(54), (9) 31(348) 现身状态; (7) 188(53)现身情况; (7) 179(46)现场; franz.: (12) sentiment de la situation; (16) situation-affective; ital.: (24) 123,33 situazione emotiva 224,24; (25) 13;36 situazione emotiva 633;658; (26) situazione affettiva 311,3 (214); (27) tono fondamentale 80; (28) 31 disposizione d'animo 17; (29) 113; jap.: (73) 情状性 Jōjōsei; (78), (85) 情態性 Jōtaisei; (46) 感受性 Kanjusei; (79) 感存性 Kanzonsei; (61) 心 情 Shinjyō; span.: (89) el "encontrarse", el encontrarse (§§ 29,30,40, 68b); (89) el encontrarse; (90) el encontrarse (Befindlichkeit) (196); (91) el encontrarse con que estamos en el ente (129); (92) el "encontrarse" (17,41) el encontrarse (52); (93) posibilidad de darse (en nosotros) (136); (94) el encontrarse (96); (114) (sich befinden) encontrarse (174).

BEGEGNEN  (1) encounter, Begegnisart way of encountering, Begegnis mishap; (4) -lassen letting encounter; chin.: (8) 9(92)遭遇; (9) 34(351)露面; (7) 44(20), 186(50)碰到 ; (7) 324(72)对; (7) 185(50) 照面 ; (7) 387(86) 应付 ; (7) 264(69) 看一看，看一眼 ; (9) 29(347)遇到; franz.: (15) das Begegnen: le donné; ital.: (24) Par.15;66 incontrarsi 138;31,4;119,1 incontrare 90,13;205,22;86,21 venire incontro 164,13; (26) 70,1 farsi incontro 95,25;86,25,27 incontrare 120,23,25;

(27) 29 incontrare 75; 33 presentarsi 86; 34(es) arrivare 87;
(28) 29 incontrare 13; 29 venire incontro 14; (29) 59,141; (34)
22 incontrare 19; 30 venire incontro 26; (35) 35 incontrare 21;
42 ovviare 26; 192 venire incontro 128; (38) (sich) 10,16 incontrarsi 11,16; (43) 47 incontrare 53; 74 accostarsi 74; (44) venire incontro 241 u. passim; jap.: (61), (66), (71), (73), (75),
(78), (81), (85) 出会う deau; (69), (85) 出会はれる deawareru; (48)
まみえる mamieru; (79) 出会する shukkaisuru; span.: (89) hacer frente
(103,139 u. passim); (89) hacer frente los entes intramundanos al
"ser ahí" y éste a ellos; (90) salir al encuentro (32,65,106),
hacer frente (48) encontrar(se con) (45,78); (93) encontrarse con
(134) venir al encuentro (135) concurrir (140) hallarse presente (140);
(94) encontrar (93) tropezar con (94) salirnos al paso (100 f.);
(98) (als Partizip Präsens) encontrado (71); (99) (als Partizip Präsens) presente (12); (100) presentarse (129) ofrecerse (129); (101)
salir al encuentro (43) venir al encuentro (44); (105) (sich begegnen) encontrarse (148); (106) (sich begegnen) encontrarse (33); (109)
encontrar (260,270) (Begegnenlassen) encuentro (10); (110) enfrentarse (69) encontrar (69) hacer frente (86) (Begegnenlassen) encuentro (48); (111) encontrar (31, 42) presentarse (32) (Begegnenlassen) el dejarse encontrar con (18); (113) encontrarse con (54,114)
salir al encuentro (126); (114) encontrar (19,178,180) salir al encuentro (19,161,175,212 u. passim); (117) (das Begegnende) lo que en-
cuentra (24); (118) (das Begegnende) lo que se encuentre (71).

BEHAUSUNG (2) taking up lodging; chin.: (8) 为家 13(97); (8) 住处
1o(92); (8) 居家情况 21 (1o5); (8) 住家之所 45 (131); franz.: (11) demeure; (23) abri; ital.: (31) 7 dimora 38; (32) dimora; (33) dimora;
(35) 159 dimora 1o6; (-en) 145 albergare 96; 159 dare ricetto 1o6;
(41) 7o dimora II 33; jap.: (48), (67), (76) 住 居 Jūkyo; (67) 住み家
Sumika; span.: (1oo) "mansión" (114) (Platon-Zitat) morada (118, 12o);
(1o1) "recinto" (35) (Platon-Zitat) morada (38 f.); (1o7) morada (161,
169, 175, 189, 227 f.); (1o8) vivienda (7, 14, 19, 62) habitación (3o)

BODEN (2) -nehmen take-possession; (3) foundation, ground, soil,
-ständig rooted, autochthonic, -ständigkeit rootedness, autochthony;
chin.: (7)基地 24 (13), 261 (64); (7)基础 25 (14); (7)立足之地 119 (28);
(7)根基 177 (43); franz.: (12) fondement, plan, base; (16) base; ital.:
(24) 144, 3 terreno 238, 4; 25, 15 basi 83, 6; (25) 45 base 668; 5o ba-
samento 673; (26) 192 base 28o, 1; 194, 9 terreno 282, 2; (28) 7E fondamento 63; 8E terreno 64; (29) 28, 29, 5o, 1o3; (3o) 5 terreno 7; (32)
fondamento; (33) fondamento; (34) 13 base 9; 58 terreno 55; 233 campo
232; (35) 164 fondo 11o u. passim; (36) 8, 12 terreno 46, 5; 16, 42
suolo 59, 15; (41) 15 terreno I 7; 16 suolo, terra I 8; (42) 21, 19
terreno I 14, 12; (43) 2o5 (ständig) radici (radicamento) 162; (45) 12
terreno 19; jap.: (48) 地 Chi; (78) 土 台 Dodai; (5o), (61),(71),(73),(78),(85)
地 盤 Jiban; (Boden-ständigkeit) (54), (61), (73), (85) 土着性
Dochakusei; span.: (89) terreno (21, pas.) base (22o, pas.) suelo (438)
capa (13o) campo (191); (9o) base (119) terreno (192) (Grund und Boden:)
base (1oo, 182); (91) tierra (121, 124, 134) base (132); (92) apoyo
(49 f., 55) base (54); (95) terreno (2o7) suelo (2o8); (1o7) base (222);
(1o8) fundamento (58); (1o9) base (349); (11o) terreno (1o9); (111)
terreno (57); (113) terreno (23) suelo (44, 89); (114) sostén (17) base
(5o, 89, 112) suelo (113 f.) fondo (54, 89) posibilidad (74); (115)
fondo (5, 7); (116) fondo (137, 14o); (117) terreno (43); (118) terreno
(81).

DA-HABEN (4) having-there; chin.: (7)亲有 265 (69); franz.: --; ital.:
(24) 265, 21 "detenere" 397, 7; jap.: (85) 現に－もつ Genni-motsu; span.:
(89) ("da-haben":) "estar-ahí" (3o4); (114) el tener-aquí (Da-haben)
(19o).

DASEIN, DA-SEIN (1) Dasein, Being-there; (2) There-being; (4) existence;
chin.: (7)亲在 265 (70), 382(81), 13o(41); (8) 44(13o); (9)具体存在 30; franz:(12)
être-là, être-"là"; (15) être-Là, existence, être-le-là; (16) réalité-
humaine; (21) être-là, être-le-là; (22) être-le-là; ital.: (24) Esserci,
esser-Ci / Par. 29; 134 L'Esserci, Esser-Ci; (25) 16 Esserci 636 / 2o
Esser-ci 641; (26) 211, 15 Esserci 3o6, 18 / 212, 31 Esser-ci 3o8, 19;
(27) 24 l'essere presente; 36, 7 esistenza; 36, 15 il nostro essere di
uomini; 37 l'esistere umano; l'essere esistenziale dell' uomo; 41 essere
dell' uomo / 26 esserci; 34 essere; (28) 24 esistere, essere esistenziale;

3o esistenza 16; 35 Esserci 23 / 26 essere eistenziale 8; u. 34 ... 23;
35 Esserci 23, 11; (29) 34, 26 esistenza 8, 34; (3o) 15, -8 esserci 32, 4;
21, 22 essere esistenziale 45, 47 / 15, -1o "esser-ci" 31, -0:22 essere
esistenziale 47; (32) 36 esistenza 119 / 29 essere-esistenziale 111; (33)
1o1 Esserci 119; 71 l'Esserci 91; 1o1 esistenza 1o8 / 71 Esser-ci 91;
(34) 4o Esserci 36 / 56 Esser-ci 52; (35) 13 esserci 5; 47 esistenza
29 / 63 e-sistere 4o; (37) 18, 7, 13; l'esistere 29; la vita 74; Esser-
ci 96; (41) 21 esistere I 12; (43) 1o6 esistere 96; 237 esistenza 186;
(45) 6 esistenza 7; 12 esserci 13; jap.: (46), (48), (52), (54), (55),
(56), (61), (62), (63), (67), (71), (73), (78), (79), (81) 現存在
Gensonzai; (66), (71), (85)現 有 Genyū; (57), (7o)生 存 Seizon;
(Da-sein) (46), (49), (55), (61), (68), (69), (71), (79), (81) 現-存在
Gen-sonzai; (66), (85)現-有 Gen-yū; (71)現に-有ること Genni-arukoto;
span.: (89) (Dasein:) "ser ahí" (14, 5o f. u. passim) (Da-sein:) "ser
ahí" (154 f.) "ser ahí" (165) "ser ahí" (185); (89) "ser ahí"; (9o)
ser-ahí (9, 188) existencia (66, 78) (Da-sein:) ser-ahí (189, 192);
(91) Realidad-de-verdad (64, 68, 74, 8o) "realidad"-ser real, Dasein
(97) Realidad óntica (179) (Da-sein:) darse una Realidad-de-verdad (77);
(92) el Dasein (17, 2o u. passim) (auch für Da-sein, vgl. 24); (93)
(Dasein:) existencia (136, 139, 144 u. passim) ( auch für Existenz, vgl.
13o, 15o) (Da-sein:) "presencia" (Da-sein) (13o) "existencia" (137, 141)
"existir" (Da-sein) (138 f., 141); (94) (Dasein:) existencia (85, 1o2,
113 u. passim) (auch für Existenz, vgl. 87 f., 114) (Da-sein:) el
existir (88, 96, 99, 1o2) el puro existir (1oo) existir (ex-sistir) (1o2);
(95) ("Dasein":) "estar-en-algo" (212) "existencia" (212) .(Anm. 1:
Estar abierto, Patentizar); (96) (Dasein:) el Dasein (81); (97) (Dasein:) el Dasein (el estar presente) (17) el Dasein (18, 2o ff. u.
passim) (auch für Da-sein, vgl. 2o - 23); (98) (Dasein:) el Dasein
(7o, 77) (auch für Da-sein, z.B. 78 f.) (Da-sein:) el Da-sein (71) el
Da-sein (72, 75 f., 79, 83); (99) hombre (Dasein) (12) el Dasein (17 f.)
(auch für Da-sein, vgl. 18, 22) (Da-sein:) el Da-sein (13, 16, 19, 22);
(1o2) (Dasein:) existencia (167, 17o, 173, 175 f.); (1o3) (Dasein:)
realidad-de-verdad (Dasein) (21) realidad-de-verdad ( 25, 29, 31, 34)
(Dasein d. Menschen:) realidad de Hombre (21); (1o4) (Dasein:) existencia
(13o, 138 f., 14o, 143) existencia (Dasein) (134); (1o5) (Dasein:)en-ser
(146) (vgl. Anm. S. 156); (1o6) (Dasein:) existencia (Dasein) (29);

(1o7) (Dasein:) el existir (177, 213, 126) (auch für Da-sein: 183,
192 f.) (Da-sein:) el existir (= el estar-allí) (18o, 191, 226); (1o8)
(Dasein:) En-ser (21) Enser (35, 5o, 61) (Da-sein:) En-ser (23, 25, 33)
(Vgl. Anm. 22); (1o9) (Dasein:) el Dasein (353, 355 f.) (Da-sein:) el
Da-sein (347); (11o) (Dasein:) el existente (Dasein) (115 f.) existencia
(118, 121) (Da-sein:) el existente (Da-sein) (1o6); ;111) (Dasein:)
existencia (62 f., 65) (Da-sein:) existencia (65); (113) ("Dasein")
"existencia" (173) (Kant-Zitat); (114) (Dasein:) existencia (44, 195 ff.,
2o2, passim) (auch Kant-Zitate) mundo (1o6) (Da-sein:) el ser-ahí
(Da-sein) (5o); (117) ("Da-sein":) el existir (54) (Da-sein:) el existir
(estar-ahí) (69); (118) ("Da-sein":) "ser-ahí" (88) (Da-sein:) el estar-
ahí (98); (119) (Dasein:) ser-ahí (Dasein) (28); (12o) (Dasein:) el
Dasein (23 f.); (121) (Dasein:) existencia (Dasein) (52).

DASS-SEIN  (2) that being(s) is(are); chin.: (7)然 14 (6); franz.:
(22) existence; ital.: (24) 134, 38 II "che-c'è" 226, 33; (25) 7
"che-è" 625; (26) 2o2, il "che è" 293; 2o5, 1o l'essere di fatto 297, 21;
(44) 15o, 4 che ... è 254, 3; jap.: (63), (78) 在ること(あ) Arukoto; (85)
が−有ること Ga-arukoto; (63), (81) 事実−什在 Jijitsu-sonzai; (66)事実・什
Jijitsu・u; (54) 事−什在 Koto-Sonzai; (68), (79) 什在事実 Sonzaijijitsu;
(89) el "que es" (6, 8, 17, 156) hecho de "que es" (156); (89) "que es";
(9o) el "que-es" (186, 189) el "que" (que es algo) (187); (91) el por qué
es en realidad (la cosa tal o cual) (51); (92) lo-que-es (11); (113) el
que... es, el hecho de que es (155); (114) el hecho d- que algo sea (198).

DAS DASS  (1) the "that-it-is"; chin.:--; franz.: (12) le "qu'il est";
ital.: (24) 135, 4, 15,22, Il "che" (c'è) 226, 2o, 35; 227, 5; 136, 4; 276,
2o Il ;che" 227, 33; 411, 25; (28) 47 che... è 49; (34) 53 il che 49; (37)
(il fatto che 23); jap.: (85) が有ること gaarukoto; (61), (73), (78), (79),
(81) 事 実 Jijitsu; span.: el "que es" (156f.) ese "que" (326) el que (317)
hecho de "que" se es (318); (1o9) el "que" (345f.); (11o) el "que es" (1o2f.);
(111) el "de que" (53).

DENKEN  (2) think(ing), thought; (5) thinking; chin.: (8)思维 5(87);
(7)思想 261(65), 31(349); (9) 思 30(347); (8)想 21(105); (8)设想 35(120);
franz.: (11) penser; ital.: (24) pensare; (26) pensare; (27) pensare;
(28) pensare; (29) 7;92;95;108;110;112;114;117;131;134-6;143;147;20;

(30) 9 pensare 17; 14 intendere 29; (31) 26;37 pensare 49;59? (32) pensare 26 intendere 108; (33) pensare; (34) 11 alludere 7; 12 pensare 8; 25 riflettere 21; 32 procedere 28; 47 intendere 43; 178 concepire 176; (35) pensare (9-195); (36) pensare; (38) pensare; (39) pensare; (40) pensare; (41) 12 memorare, pensare I 5; 43 pensare II 13 u. passim; (42) pensare; (43) 11 pensare 27; 13 riflettere 29; 172 portare alla mente 136; por mente; (44) 147 pensare 251; (45) pensare; jap.: (70) 考える kangaeru; (48); (58); (70); (71); (79); (81) 思惟する shiisuru; (52); (65); (67); (78) 思考する shikōsuru; (47); (59); (68); (69); (72);(86); (87); (88) 思索する shisakusuru; (72) 思 う omou; (Denken)(51); (66); (75); (77); (83), (85) 思 惟 Shii; (46); (50); (54); (55); (57); (58) 思 考 Shikō; (49); (68); (83); (82); (85) 思 索 Shisaku; span.: (89) pensar (247,367 u. passim); (90) pensar (74 u. passim); (93) pensar (135); (94) pensar (94); (95) pensar (207, 211); (96) pensar (80); (98) pensar (79, 83); (99) pensar (19, 22); (100) concebir (141) pensar (157) repensar (157); (101) pensar (49, 57); (105) pensar (146); (106) pensar (29); (107) pensar (161, 192, 199, 222, 227); (108) pensar (8,33,39,57,61); (109) pensar (15,21,268,354,356); (110) pensar (57,83,118,120) concebir (67); (111) pensar (24,30,40,63,65) concebir (40); (113) pensar (passim); (114) pensar (61,94 f. u. passim); (115) pensar (6); (116) pensar (139,157).

EK-SISTENZ (2) ek-sistence; chin.: (8) 存在 14(97), 21(105); franz.: (16) ex-sistance; ital.: (25) (Existenz) 42, 17 Fußnote 59 esistenza 664 a, 14; (26) 2o5, 218 (Existenz, esistenza) 298, 316; (27) 41 (Existenz, esistenza) 1o2, 42 esistere 1o3; (28) siehe (27); (3o) ex-sistenza; (32) ex-sistenza; (33) ex-sistenza; (34) 311 ex-sistenza 315; (35) 35, 63 (-en) ek-sistere 21, 41; (37) (Existenz) 12,-3 esistenza 1o6,-3; (44) 151 (ek-sistent) e-sistente 255; jap.: (56) 脱自的実存 Datsujitekijitsuzon; (82) 脱 存 Datsu-zon; (76) 明 在 Meizai; (55) 実－存 Zitsu-zon; (67) 脱自－存在 Datsuji-Sonzai; span.: (89) (Existenz:) existencia (15 u. passim); (89) (Existenz:) existencia; (9o) (Existenz:) existencia (195); (93) (Existenz:) existencia (13o, 15o) (auch für Dasein, vgl. 136 pas.); (94) (Existenz:) existencia (87 f., 114) (auch für Dasein, vgl. 85 pas.); (95) (Existenz:) existencia (221 f.); (97) Existencia (17) ec-sistencia (21) existencia (21 ff.); (98) ex-sistencia (72, 78 ff.); (99) existencia (13) ex-sistencia (14, 18 ff.); (1o7) ec-sistencia (175, 177, 2o1, 215); (1o8) ec-sistencia (19, 2o, 41, 52); (114) (Existenz:) existencia (185); (119)(Existenz:)

existencia (22); (12o) (Existenz:) existencia (16); (121) (Existenz:) existencia (48).

ENTBERGEN (2) reveal, revealing, -ung revealment; (5) disclosure; chin.: --; franz.: (11) dévoilement, das E-: le dé-couvrement; (15) dé-celer; (17) déclor (19), -ung: désabritement (2o); ital.: (28) 8E rivelare 65, 2oE manifestare 82, 12; (29) 1o9; (3o) 15 svelare, rivelare 3o, 15, 16 disvelare 31, 33; (31) 32 disvelare 55; (34) 28 svelare 25; 278 disvelare 278; (35) 21 disvelare 1o; (37) (svelare 84); (41) 61 svelare II 26; (42) 54, 17; 62, 19 svelare II 224, 44; II 229, 15; 65, 15; 66, 19 rivelare II 231, 16; II 232, 8; (43) 62 disvelare 64; 62 lasciare inviolato 65 ( non violare); 134 disoccultare 112; (44) 272 disoccultare, disoccultare 379; 289 schiudere 394; (45) 28 disvelare 29; jap.: (62) 露わに発く arawanihiraku; (48) 暴露する bakurosuru; (62) 発露する hatsurosuru; (58) 蓋をとる ooi wo toru; (51), (83)露現する rogensuru; (81)露呈する roteisuru; (Entbergen, -ung) (88)顕わにすること Arawanisurukoto; (87), (86)顕わし Arawashi; (7o) 顕 現 Kengen; (66)露 顕 Roken; (54) 露 呈 Rotei; (57) おおいを取り去る ooi wo torisaru; span.: (95) desvelar (2o7) (sich entbergen:) engendrar (sic!) (217); (97) desocultar, poner de manifiesto (17) revelar (18) descubrir (19) poner al descubierto (19); (98) des-velar (72, 74 f.); (99) develar (14 ff.) desechar (sic!) (16); (1oo) (Entbergung:) desencubimiento (151); (1o1) (Entbergung:) rescate (54); (112) abrirse (116); (113) desocultar (2o1); (117) (Sich-entbergen:) le des-cubrirse (64); (118) (Sich-entbergen:) el desnudarse (94).

ENTGEGENSTEHEN (4) standing over against, -lassen allowing to stand against; chin.: (1o)対立 264 (374); franz.: (11) -de: ce qui est en face; (15) -de: l'ob-posé; ital.: (26) 7o, 7 obiettarsi 96, 4; (3o) 11 star di contro 21; (34) 3o star dinnanzi 26, 84 contrapposto 92; (35) 74 star di fronte 47; (36) porre (posto) di fronte 26, 16 (J); (41) 43 star di fronte II 13; (45) 36 stare in contrapposizione 37; jap.: (63), (85) 対立する tairitsusuru; span.: (9o) ob-jetarse (65 ff., 72, 78) enfrentarse (34); (98) contraponerse ( 67); (99) surgir ante nosotros (Entgegenstehenlassen) (9 f.); (1o9) enfrentarse (26o) (Entgegenstehen:) el estar frente (26o); (11o) estar frente (69) (Entgegenstehen:) el oponersénos (7o); (111) encontrar (+Ak.) (32) (Entgegen-

stehen:) si se nos presentan (32); (114) contraponerse (31) oponerse (entgegenstehen) (126) enfrentarse (159) estar en frente (178) (tener) en
frente (21o); (117) (Entgegenstehendes:) (1o) opuesto (42); (118) (Entgegenstehendes:) un opuesto (8o).

ENTSCHLOSSENHEIT  (1) resoluteness, entschließen resolve, Entschluß re-
solution; (2) re-solve; (3) resolve; (6) resolute openness; <u>chin.</u>:
(7) 决断  323 (72); <u>franz.</u>: (15) résolution, déclosion déterminée, ré-
solvance déterminée, ouverture déterminée; (16) décision résolue; <u>ital.</u>:
(24) II, 2 Kap. 267 decisione 4oo; (27) decisione (J) 16; (3o) 23 dischiu-
sura 5o; 24 risolutezza 54; (34) 321 decisione 325; (41) 6o, 61 risolutezza, decisione II 26; 61 l'aprirsi a ..., il risolversi, il de-
cidersi per ... II, 26;  (43) 134 esser deciso, decisione 112; <u>jap.</u>:
(49) 脱出領性 Datsu-heisasei; (68) 覚 悟 Kakugo; (61), (78), (79), (85)
覚悟性 Kakugosei; (54) 决 意 Ketsui; (66), (73) 决意性 Ketsuisei; (57)
决 断 Ketsudan; <u>span.</u>: (89) "estado de resuelto" (341, 354 f.); (89)
"estado de resuelto"; (97) el mantenerse abierto (?) (22); (98) (Ent-
schlossenheit:) abierta decisión (Ent-schlossenheit) (79 f.); (99)
(Ent-schlossenheit:) aceptación resuelta (19) re-solución (2o); (1o9)
existencia resuelta (Entschlossenheit) (347) (Ent-schlossenheit:) re-solución (347); (11o) estado de resolución (Entschlossenheit)(1o5)
(Ent-schlossenheit:) estado de resolución (1o5); (111) resolución (55)
(Ent-schlossenheit:) resolución (55).

ER-LEBEN  (1) living through, erleben, Erlebnis Experience; (2) Er-lebnis
living experience, Erlebnis esthetic experience; (6) Erlebnis lived
experience; <u>chin.</u>: (8) 体验  4o (126), 14 (97); <u>franz.</u>: (16) le fait
d'éprouver, l'expérience vécue; <u>ital.</u>: (24) 13o, 24 (-bnis) esperienza vissuta 22o, 16; (26) (-nisse) 211, 29 esperienze vissute 3o7, 13;
(28) 21 (Erleben) esperienza vissuta 84; (3o) (Erlebnis) 18 intuizione
vissuta, asperimentare 37; (32) 4o (vivere) 124; (33) 67 esperienza
vissuta 87; 1o7 "fare esperienza" 124; (34) 86,-5 vivere, esperienza
vissuta 99, 1; (35) (Erleben) 157 esperienza 1o4, 177 fatto di esser
vivo 199; (36) 8, 19 vivere 47, 7; (43) (-bnis) esperienza vissuta
.129 - 1o9; <u>jap.</u>: (61), (65), (67), (68), (73), (78), (85) 体 験 Taiken
(Er-lebnis); <u>span.</u>: (89) (Erleben:) vivecia (335) el "vivir" (288) vivir
las vivencias (56) viviendo (284); (89) (Leben) vida, viv-r; (9o) (Er-

lebnisse:) "vivencias" (195); (95) (Erleben:) vivencia (218); (98)
("erleben":) "vivenciar" (74) ("Erlebnis":) "vivencia" (74); (99) ("erleben":) "vivir" (15) ("Erlebnis":) "vivencia" ("Erlebnis") (15); (1o7)
("erleben":) "vivir" (219); (1o8) ("erleben":) "vivir" (55); (1o9) (Erleben:) le vivenciarse (347) tener vivencias (356); (11o) (Erleben:)
vivencias (1o5) vivencia (12o); (111) (Erleben:) vivencia (55, 65); (113)
(Erleben:) vivencia (34); (117) (er-lebt:) vivido (46) (Erleben:) vi-
vencia(s) (16, 18); (118) (er-lebt:) vivivo (82) (Erleben:) vivencia
(67).

EREIGNIS  (1) event; (2) e-vent; (5) event; (6) event; chin.: --;
franz.: --; ital.: (24) 284, 18 evento 422, 5; (27) 38, 1 avvenimento
96, 12; (28) 38, 1 avvenimento 27, 21, 49N (-nen) verificarsi 53, 51N
accadimento 57, 11E fatto 7o, 13E (-nen) originare 72; (29) 35, 3o, 38
accadere 1o, 1, 37, 1 evento 11, 11; (32) 21 fatto 1o6; (33) 57 fatto
come avvenimento 78, 65 accadimento 86, 81 (-net) istituito 1o1; (34)
evento, (sich -en) realizzarsi, attuarsi; (35) 4o evento, accadimento
24, 148 fatto 98, 151 avvenimeto 1oo (sich -en) darsi (-en) 179 il
far-avvenire-traspropriante 12o; (36) 4, 1o evento 4o, 37, 6o, 18 evento
12o, 8 u. passim; (37) ("evento", accadimento risultare) 65, 9o, evento
dell' essere e l'esse come evento 15o; (41) 48 accadimento II, 16 u.
passim; (42) 28, 28 appropriamento fontale, originario I 18, 32, 3o, 12
accadimento I 19, 32; (43) 12, 3o evento 28, 41, 14 avvenimento 24, 132, 3
fatto 111, 16 (sich ereignen) farsi apparire, realizzarsi, generararsi,
evenire, divenire, avvenire; jap.: (68), (71), (78) 出来事 Dekigoto; (7o)
本有化生起 Honyūka-seiki; (66) 自性発起 Jiseihokki; (7o), (71), (86),
(88) 生起 Seiki; (51), (66) 性起 Shoki; (62) 出現 Shutsugen; (55)
(62) 出来 Shutsurai; span.: (89) suceso (326, 334) sucesos (435, pas.)
accidente (29o); (93) acaecimiento (145); (94) suceso (1o7); (95) re-
sultado (21o); (96) acaecimiento (Ereignis) (78) lo que acontece (81);
(1o2) acontecimiento (171) (paraphrastische Übersetzung: 169); (1o3)
todo un acontecimiento histórico (24) fasto (27); (1o4) acontecimiento
(133, 136);  (1o9) lance (345); (11o) acontecimiento (1o2); (111) acontecimiento (1o2); (113) acontecimiento (12, 14, 47); (117) acontecimiento
(67); (118) acaecimiento (97).

GEDACHTES  (4) What is thought; chin.: (8)ǀ 所思 44(130), 46(132);
franz.: (11) le déjà-pensé; (23) ce qui est pensé; ital.: (28) 13E il ensato
72; (30) 8 conzetto 14; (32) 44 pensato 132; (33) 82 pensato 101,113 fatto
del pensiero 129; (34) 118 ciò che (1'uomo) pensa 116, 133 pensato 131,
245 pensabile 244, 334 pensiero 338; (35) 48 ciò che èstato pensato 30,
114 il pensato 75, 247 pensiero 169, 253 ciò che 1'uomo pensa 173; (36)
11,21,36,14 pensato 52,17,86,37,71,26 pensieri 133,41; (37) 21,16 pensato
117,13; (42) 44,46,9 ciò che èstato pensato, il pensato II, 219, II 220,
10-11; (43) 123,0 pensiero 106; jap.: (67), (76)考えられたもの Kangaerare-
tamono; (79)思惟内実 Shiinaijitsu; (69), (72)思索されたもの Shisakusaretamono;
span.: (89) algo pensado (103,497) (Gedachtheit:) el ser-pensado (494);
(95) lo pensado (211); (96) (das Gedachte:) lo pensado (76); (107) algo
pensado (225); (108) un pensado (sig!) (60); (113) pensamientos (76) algo
pensado (33, 90) lo pensado (124, 128, 134, 176, vgl. 74) pensamiento
(74); (114) (das Gedachte:) lo pensado (126).

GEGENSTEHEN (1) Gegenstand object; (2) Gegenstand object, being-as-op-
posed, Gegenständlichkeit objectiveness, -lassen let stand opposed, objec-
tivate; (4) standing before, -lassen permitting a standing against, Gegen-
uns-stehenden what stands-over-against, Gegenstand object, Gegenständlichkeit objectivity; chin.: -; franz.: (11) -de: ce qui s'op-pose; ital.:
(26) 109, 171 obijettare 155, 248; (35) 165 lo star di fronte 111; (43)
132 star di contro 111; (45) 26 stare di fronte 27, 36 (-keit) stare come
opposto 37; jap.: (63), (70)対 立 Tairitsu; 対して立つTaishitetatsu;
(64), (71), (85) (-こと) (-koto); span.: (89) (Gegenüberstehen:) el enfrentarse (204); (90) ob-jeción (71,107) (auch für gegenstehend, vgl. 81);
(107) (gegenüberstehen:) estar frente (230); (108) (gegenüberstehen:)
estar ante (64); (113) (Gegenständigkeit:) objetividad (233); (114) estar
enfrente (194,210) (Gegen-stehen:) estar-enfrente (159,209); (115) el
obstar (5); (116) el ser objeto (Gegenstehen) (138).

GELASSENHEIT  (2) release; chin.: -; franz.: (11) la sérénité; (13) le
savoir laisser; (17) désinvolture; (23) le calme; ital.: (28) 44N tran-
quillità 45; ( 29) 40,33 (-ener Hand) sciolta mano 15,11; (35) 68 tran-
quillo abbandono 43; (37) (fiducioso abbandono); (42) 25 rilassamento I
15 u. passim; (43) 169 calmo abbandono 134-5; jap.: (66) おちつき Ochitsuki;

(69) 平静さ Heiseisa; (60), (66) 故 下 Hōge; (52) 従容 Shojō; (55) 従容性 Shōjōsei; span.: (96) serenidad (76); (97) moderación (23); (98) serenidad (80); (99) dulzor (20).

GEREDE (1) idle talk, Geredete what is said in the talk; (2) loquacity; chin.: 空谈 UH30(115) 闲谈 SuZ175(42) 言谈 WiM29(347) franz.: (12) bavardage; (16) parlerie; ital.: (24) Par. 35,167 chiacchera 269; (27) 29 discorsi 76; (28) 29 discorsi 14; (32) 40 discorsi 124; (33) 92 serie di chiacchere 110,107 chiacchere 124; (43) 152 chiacchera 123; (45) 4 chiacchera 5; (35) 76 parlare 49; jap.: (73), (79) 空 以 Kūdan; (85) 空 品 Kūwa; (78) おしゃべり Oshaberi; (61) 世間品 Sekenbanashi; span.: (89) "habladurías" (§ 35); (89) habladurías; (93) lenguaje (sic!) (135); (94) conversaciones (94); (107) charla (203, 219); (108) charla (42, 55).

GESCHICK (1) destiny, vicissitude; (2) common fortune, mittence; (5) destiny, destining, Fate; (6) destiny; chin.: 命运 Hw267(377) 273(383) 式样 UH11(94) franz.: (11) dispensation, destin; (12) destin; (13) destination, destinement; (15) pro-de-stin; (16) destinée; (17) destin (D.3.); (22) destin; ital.: (24) 384, 31 destino comune 551,19; (28) 51N senso 57, 12E destino 71, 12E sorte 71; (29) 14, 84, 1o8, 1o9, 117-9, 122, 13o; (31) 31 storia 54; (32) 23 destinazione 1o6, 24 ragione interna 1o7, 27 destino 1o9; (33) 63 destino 83 u.ff.; (42) 66, 1 destino II 231, 26, (-lich) 47, 17 secondo un cammino storicamente destinato II 22o-21, 52, 2-II 223, 17 u.passim, 65, 7, 9 darsi, destinarsi II 231; (43) 71 destino 72, 8o destnazione 79; (34) 31 destino 27, 244 struttura-destino 243 u.ff.; (35) 32 destino 18, 217 dono 148; (36) 8, 26, 26, 14 destino 47, 16, 71, 27; (37) "fatalità" comestori città 53, 18 (-lich) fatale storico 114, 1 (fato da fari); (39) sorte 374; (4o) destino 9; jap.: (61) 共同運命 Kyōdōmunmei; (49), (54), (62), (66), (75), (85) 命 運 Meiun; (86), (87), (88) 送り定め Okurisadame; (48), (81) 歴 運 Rekiun; (48) 摂 理 Setsuri; (46) 宿 命 Shukumei; (57), (59), (65), (67), (69), (7o), (73), (78), (79) 運 命 Unmei; (66) 爾 道 Zōken; (47) 歴史的運命 Rekishitekiunmei; span.: (89) destino colectivo (442 ff.) "destino" (66); (89) destino colectivo (Schicksal:) destino individual; (95) destino (211); (96) destino (Geschick) (82); (1oo) caso (sic!) (134); (1o1) destino (46); (1o7) destino (171, 182 u.pas.); (1o8) destinación (16,25,32 u.pas.); (1o9) suerte (261), destino (266 f.); (11o) destino (71, 8of.);

天命 SuZ384(83) UH14(97)

(111) habilidad (sic!) (33), destino (38f.) ;(113) destino (22, 24, 61, 66, 83, 132, 159f.); (116) destino (157); (117) destino (67); (118) destino (97).

GESTELL   (2) -ung taking (a) place; (6) frame;

franz.: (11) Arraisonnement; (13) le Dis-positif; (22) Gestell; ital.: (34) 52 costituzione 48; (35) 27 imposizione 14, 184 im-posizione 123; (36) im-posizione 3o, 2o (J); (42) supporto 28, 8 il porre-insieme fondamentale 18, 16, 29, 1o struttura fondamentale dell rapporto technologico essere-uomo, costellazione technologico di essere-uomo I 19, 3; (43) 263 (Ge-stell) 2o7; jap.: (&1), (57), (62), (66), (74) 組 立 Kumitate; (75) せき立て Seki-tate; (55), (59) 仕組み Shikumi; (51) 朱 立 Shūritsu; (69) 立て構え Tatekamae; (62) 立て-組み Tate-gumi; (81) 枠-組み Waku-gumi; span.: (1o9) (Ge-stell:) esbozo estructurador (344); (11o) (Ge-stell:) composición (1oo); (111) (Ge-stell:) el armar (52); (116) armazón aducido (Gestell) (157,184).

GEWESENHEIT   (1) having been, the character of having been, Gewesen the "been", gewesend in the process of having been; (2) past (what is-as-having-been),having-been-ness; chin.: 曾在 SuZ386(85)   326(75)
franz.: (13) Le recueil de s'être-déployé; (16) Etre-ayant-été;ital.: (24) 326, 7, 328, 3o L'esser stato, Il passato 475, 3o, 478, 18; (25) 46 esser-stato 669; (26) 165, 22 il passato 24o, 1; (34) 295 essere stato 297; (35) 71 esser-stato 45; (37) 15 (das Gewesene) ciò che è stato 1o9; (39) (das Gewesene) l'essuto (?) 376; (4o) il passato 19; (42) 65, 18 il passato come pienezza II 231, 19, 21; (43) 27, 213 essere stato 39, 168; jap.: (66) 本現性 Hongensei; (69) 既住性 Kiōsei; (85) 既有性 Kiyūsei; (63), (7o) 既 在 Kizai; (73), (78), (79) 既在性 Kizaisei; (81) 既存性 Kizonsei; span.: (89) el sido (§§ 65, 68, 74 u.passim) "sido" (444); (89) el "sido"; (9o) el "sido" (154) el sido (154, 165) el pasado (155); (91) lo pasado (124); (92) el pasado (5o); (1o9) (die Gewesenen:) lo sido (26o); (11o) (die Gewesenen:) las (obras) pasadas (69); (111) (die Gewesenen:) ya no son: fueron (32); (114) (das Gewesene:) lo sido (45); (119) (das Gewesene:) lo que ha sido (25); (12o) (das Gewesene:) lo sido (Gewesenes) (19); (121) (das Gewesene:) lo sido (5o).

GEWORFENHEIT   (1) throwness; (2) thrown-ness; <u>chin.:</u> 被抛入的境界
　　　被抛入的处境
<u>franz.:</u> (12) déréliction, l'être-jeté; (16) déréliction; (17) être jeté (I);
(23) situation d'être jeté; <u>ital.:</u> (24) Par. 38, 175 L'esser-getatto 279;
(25) 36, 54 esser-getatto 658, 669; (26) 2o6, 13, 2t2 essere getatto 299, 9,
3o8; (27) 37, 15 caduta 95, 1o, deiezione, l'esser getatti 95 nota 65; (28)
37, 15 essere getatto nel mondo 26; (32) 29 essere getatto nel mondo 111,
essere getatto; (33) 9o l'essere getatto 1o8, s.71-91, s.84-1o3; (34) 59
esser-getatto 66; (36) gettatezza 18, 33 (J); <u>jap.:</u> (66) 被投入性  Hitōn-
yūsei; (61), (67), (73), (78), (79), (85) 被投性 Hitōsei; (57) 投げかけられて
いること Nagekakerareteirukoto; <u>span.:</u> (89) "estado de yecto" (§§ 29, 31, 38,
58, 68b); (89) "estado de yecto" (Geworfensein:) ser yecto; (9o) "estado de
yecto" (196); (91) aplanamiento (14o, 177); (92) el estar arrojado (41,58);
(93) "abandono" (Geworfenheit) (144); (94) el hallarse arrojado (1o6); (1o7)
lanzamiento (2-of.); (1o8) arrojamiento (4o); (1o9) el estar arrojado (35o);
(11o) estado de proyección (11o); (111) condición de ser-lanzado (58).


GRUND   (1) ground, base, basis, reason, bottom; (2) essence, gründen
ground, -ing-process, coming-to-pass-of; (3) ground; (4) basis,principle;
(5) ground, reason (for); (6) ground(s); <u>chin.:</u> 根据     基础
割怔詳印   理由　深处　底层
<u>franz.:</u> (12) fondement; (15) fond, fondement, base, raison; (16) raison,
fondement, fond, base; <u>ital.:</u> (24) fondamento; (25) 7 fondamento 625, 9
ragion sufficiente 629, 36 ragione 658; (26) fondamento; (27) base, 24
il profondo 56, 25 fondamento 57, 41 ragione 1o1, 41 fondo 1o2; (28) 25
fondamento 5, 41 motivo 33, 41 profondità 33, 44N ragione fondamentale 44,
7E terreno, fondo 63; (29) 36, 11, 4o, 22 fondamento 1o, 19, 14, 36, 37,
35 principio 12, 7, 39, 4 base 13, 17, 39, 22 fondo 14, 3; (3o) 14 fondamento 29; (31) 23 fondo 46, 25 fondamento 48; (32) 19 ragione 1o4, 28 fondamento 111; (33) 6o fondamento 81, 86 ragione 1o6; (34) fondamento, suolo,
base, ragione, 112 presupposto 11o, 161 causa  159, 298 fatto 3o1; (35)
fondamento, ragione, base, causa 178 ragione fondante 12o; (36) ragione
sufficiente 35,11 (J), 4, 31 ragione 41, 23, 31, 16 fondamento 8o, 14;
(37) 26, 27 fondamento, origine 8o, principio 128; (41) terreno, causa,
fondamento; (42) fondamento; (43) 13 abisso 28, 13 basi di appoggio 29,
13 fondamento 29, 44 fondo 51, 51 ragione 86; (44) 133 base 237, 134
ragione 238, 135 fondamento 239, 279 "motivo" 385, 287 radice 392; (45)

6 motivo 7, 8 fundamento 9; jap.: (57), (69) 地 盤 Jiban; (63) 基 健
Kiso; (47), (48), (52), (54), (55), (61), (66), (68), (69), (7o), (71),
(73), (75), (77), (78), (79), (8o), (81), (83) 根 拠 Konkyo; (83), (85)
根 本 Konpon; (5o), (81), (83), (85) 根 底 Kontei; span.: (89) fundamento (326 f., 4o9 u. passim) razón (39, 213) razón de ser (37, 39) base
(4o9, 456); (89) razón (Grundsein:) ser el fundamento; (9o) fundamento
(4o, 11o u. passim) origen (15) base (23, 25) razón suficiente (1o5);
(91) fundamento (51, pass.) Fundamento (55, 111) Fundamento o razón
(52) Fundamento racional (54, 57 f.) razón suficiente (54) (+ mehr. a.
Formen); (92) fundamento (11, 49 u. passim) razón (Grund) (13 f., 57)
"fundamento" (Grund) (11, 16) razón (16, 55); (93) base (13o, 145, 149)
(im Grunde:) en el fondo (129, 149) fundamentalmente (138) ( Gründe:)
principios (149) (abgründiger Grund:) profundidades abismales (149 f.);
(94) fondo (86) fundamento (88) (im Grunde:) en realidad (99, 113) (auf
dem Grunde:) apoyado en (1o8) (Gründe:) fundamentos (113) (abgründiger
Gründ:) abismos insondables (114); (95) fundamento (2o3, 2o8, 214, 219)
suelo (2o7 f.) terreno (2o8) base (21o) fundamentos (2o7) principio
(2o7); (96) fundamento (75); (97) fundamento (21); (98) fundamento (7o,
76, 78, 81, 83); (99) fundamento (12, 16, 21 f.) el asiento (18); (1oo)
"fondo" (126) (Platon-Zitat) fundamento (143) fondo (151); (1o1) "fundamento" (42) (Platon-Zitat) fundamento (5o, 54); (1o2) fundamento (171,
175 f.) base (173) fondo (173 f.); (1o3) fondo (27 f., 3o) fundamento
(29 f., 31) fundamento y fondo (34); (1o4) fundamento (136, 139 f.)
razón de ser (138 f.) base (143); (1o5) fundamento (147); (1o6) fundamento (32); (1o7) fundamento (1o6); (1o8) cimiento (45) fundamento (5o);
(1o9) terreno (261) el fundamentarse (349) fundamento (353); (11o) suelo
(72) fundamento (1o9, 115 f.) fondo (115); (111) suelo (33) fondo (58,
62); (113) fundamento (98, 1o3) razón (13, 1o2, 172) causa (29) fondo
(83 f., 213, 215) base (192) cimientos básicos (134) fundamentos (197);
(114) fundamento (17 f., 47, 89 passim) fundamento ( Grund) (95 f., 125
passim) fondo (13, 57) razón (19, 95, 13o, 167) base (35, 85, 11o) principio (77, 96) principio-fundamento (Grund) (85) razón suficiente (98,
1o6, 117) (+ mehr. a. Formen); (117) fundamento (16, 54, 56) causa (31)
fondo (34, 62); (118) fundamento (67, 76, 88 f., 93); (119) "principio"
(37) (auf dem Grund:) por razón (39) en virtud de (48); (12o) "fundamento"
(Grund) (35) (auf dem Grund:) sobre la base (36, 48); (121) "principio"
(57 f.) (auf dem Grund:) por (57) sobre la base (62).

HEIMISCHWERDEN (2) becoming at home; chin.: 内行　　在家之感
franz.: (11) se sentir chez soi; ital.: (28) 47N essere come in casa sua
49, 5o trovarsi come di casa; (29) 42, 13 essere a casa nostra 16, 3o, 83
u. ff.; (32) 32 diventar di casa 113; (33) 95 essere di casa 113; (34)
118 ... a casa propria 116, 121 immede simarsi 119; (35) 98 stabilirsi
come nelle propria casa 64, 259 prendere dimestichezza 172; (38) 12
diventare familiari 13; (39) diventar famil. 373; (4o) esser di case 19;
(43) 13 esser di casa 29, 61 trovarsi nella naturale di mora 64; (44)
264, 27 dimestichezza 39o, 18; jap.: (54) 土着的になる Dochakuteki-ninaru;
(48) 故郷に住み馴れる Kokyoni suninareru; (48) 親しんで住むこと Shitashinde-
sumukoto; (48) 住み馴れる Suminareru; (48) 住みつくこと Sumitsukukoto;
span.: (96) (heimisch:) arraigado (heimisch) (78) (heimisch sein:) morar
(81); (1o2) (heimisch:) en la propia casa (177); (1o3) (heimisch:) en
casa popia (34); (1o4) (heimisch:) en casa (143); (1o7) (heimisch sein:)
tener por hogar (2o3); (1o8) (heimisch sein:) asentarse en (42); (1o9)
(heimisch:) en casa (263) como "en casa" (271) (einheimisch wird:) es
nativo en (347); (11o) (heimisch:) en casa (75) como en casa (88) (einheimisch wird:) se naturalizar (1o5); (111) (heimisch:) estar aclimatado
(35, 42)(einheimisch wird:) se aclimata en (55); (113) (heimisch sein:)
ser familiar, estar familiarizado con, habituado a (115 f.); (114)
(heimisch:) sentirse familiar en (184).

HERGESTELLTHEIT (2) com-position; chin.: 在家之感　　内行
franz.: (13) l'avoir-été-produit; ital.: (24) 24, 39 ciò che prodotto
82, 26, (-stellen) 67 manipolare 139; (34) 16o il fatto di esser prodotto 119, 184 l'esser prodotto 123; (35) 34 l'esser fatto 3o; (44)
14o essere (stato) prodotto 245; jap.: (81) 被製作性 Hiseisakusei; (81)
こちらへ向けて立てられていること Kochiraemuketetaterareteirukoto; (83),
(85) 作り立てられてあること Tsukuritaterareteaarukoto; span.: (89) el
"ser producido" (29); (9o) (Herstellung:) produción (113); (96) (Herstellen:) construir (74); (1o7) (Herstellen:) el producir (228); (1o8)
(Herstellen:) el establecer (62); (1o9) (hergestellt:) (estar) hecho
(264); (11o) (hergestellt:) (estar) hecho (76); (111) (hergestellt:)
(estar) elaborado (36); (114) (Herstellen:) producción (28, 68); (115)
lo establecido (6) (auch für das Hergestellte: vgl. 5); (116) producen-
cia (sic!) (139, 157).

HERVORBRINGEN (2) bring-forth, lead forth;

franz(11Her-vor-bringen: la pro-duction; (15) pro-duire; (17) mise au jour
(2o); ital.: (24) 3o, 21-4 produrre 89, 28-3o; (25) 43 pro-durre 666; (34)
25 produrre 22, 59 idem 55, 58 trare fuori 54; (35) 19 pro-duzione 9, 42
produrre 26u.ff.; (41) 16 suscitare I 8; (42) 51, 12 edurre, tirar fuori,
produrre II 223,4,66,21 portare fuori, ricavare II 232, 11; (43) 143, 153
rigenerare 117, 123, 2o7 attingere 163; jap.: (62) 出で米たらし  idetitarashi;
(77) きわだたせる kibadataseru; (83) 此方へ前にもたらす kochirahe maenimotarasu;
(71) もたらす motarasu; (57) ひき出す hikidasu; (57) つくる tsukuru; (69)
持ち米たり・持ち－出す mochi-kitari-mochi-dasu; (69), (81) 産出する sansgut-
susuru; (66) 惹 起 Jakki; span.: (89) (Hervorbringung:) producción (35)
(Hervorbringendes:) productor (35); (9o) producir (33, 66); (91)abrontar
(118); (92) producir (48); (1o9) producir (19), crear (19), hacer (264);
(11o) crear (63, 76); (111) producir (28, 36); (112) (Hervorbringen:)
creación (119); (115) (Sichhervorbringen:) un producirse (6); (116) (Sichhervorbringen:) un brotar (139).

HÖREN (1) hear, listen; (2) attend, bloßes mere listening, -auf listening
to others; chin.:  | 听从  ; 听
franz.: (12) ovïr; (15) entendre; ital.: (24 udire (-ig): attento a sentire e pronto ad ubbidire 12(I); (25) sentire 678; (29) 31,12 ascoltare
6,28; 42,22 sentire 17,5; u. 36, 74; 117; 119; (30) aver orecchio 53;
(32) 37 intendere 127; 40 udire 124; 44 appartenere 132; (33) 57 dare ascolto 78; 102 ascoltare 119; (-ig) essere inascolto a disposizione 113-
5:129, 12; (34) 15 udire 11; 245 ascoltare 244; 246 avere orecchie per
intendere 245-6; (35) udire, ascoltare, sentire; 238 porsi in ascolto 162;
(36) 19,32 udire,2; 19,180 obbedire 62,17; ascoltare u. passim; (37)
12,15, 20,4, 14, 22, 33-6, 42 ascoltare 136; stare a sentire 150; (Ohr
öffnen) aprire l'orecchio 34,4-136,11; (38) 8 sentire 9; (39) prestare
ascolto; (40) ascoltare 9; (41) 49 ascoltare II,17; 69 sentire II 32;
(42) 10,7; 22, 65, 17 ascoltare I6,1, 14,36, II 231,18; (43) percepire,
ascoltare, cogliere, intendere, sentire, pogere ascolto, avventire;
(44) 137 sentire 241; (45) 6 rivolgersi a 7; 10;58 prestare ascolto 11;59;
jap.: (52) 聴取する chöshusuru; (79), (83), (85), (88) 聴 く kiku;

(48), (54), (61), (71), (73), (75), (77), (78) 聞 く kiku; (48); (52)
耳を傾ける mimiokatamukeru; (65) 聞きつける kikitsukeru; (Hören) (66) 聴 従 Chōju; span.: (89) oír (189 f. u. passim); (89) oír; (98) oír (80); (99)
prestar atención (20); (102) "oír"(163,170) (Hölderlin-Zitat) oír(170) escuchar(172); (103) "oir"(15,25)(Hölderlin-Zitat) oir(sic!)(25,27); (104)"oír"
(126, 134) (Hölderlin-Zitat) oír (134, 137); (105) oír (145, 147 f.)
escuchar (147); (106) escuchar (29, 32) oír (32 f.); (107) escuchar (hören) (165) oír (214); (108) oír (10,51) (Vgl. Anm. 8); (109) oír (10);
(110) oír (49); (111) oír (19); (112) percibir (116); (113) escuchar
(25,50,77,126,169,181,222 f.,225) percibir (114) oír (126) llegere escuchar (21,217); (119) oír (21,46) escuchar (25,31,45) (hören auf:) escuchar, obedecer (44) escuchar (54); (120) oír (14,19,26,29,46) escuchar
(44) (hören auf:) escuchar y obedecer (42) escuchar (57); (121) oír
(hören) (48,62) escuchar (50,53 f., 61) (hören auf:) prestar oídos a
(60) / oír (66).

HÜTEN -; chin.: (8) 看护 19(103); (7) 提防 184(48); franz.: (11) veiller;
ital.: (28) 50N proteggere; (be-) custodire 55; (29) 22-3, 25, 28, 50-1,
95, 101, 104; (33) 75 custodire 75; (34) 23 custodire 19; (35) 22 vegliare 11, 40, 53 custodire 25, 33; (36) 1,17 custodire 37,20; (38) 6 custodire; (43) 31 guardarsi 42; 55 custodire 58; 171 star a custodia 135;
jap.: (48), (85) 守 る mamoru; (85) 護 る mamoru; (62) 看守る mimaroru;
(48) 守護する shugosuru; span.: (89) (sich hüten:) guardarse de (213);
(96) custodiar (81); (105) guardar (150); (106) proteger (34); (109)
custodiar (272); (110) resguardar (90); (111) cobijar (44); (113) custodiar (9) (sich hüten:) cuidarse de (105,20).

ICHHEIT (1) "I"-hood; (4) I-ness; chin.: (7) 我之为我 323 (72); franz.:
(11) égoïté; (12) ipséité; (21) égoïté; ital.: (24) 38, 54 Iità 66o, 678;
(25) 38, 54 Iità 66o, 678; (34) 241 iità 24o; (35) 74 egoità 47; (41)
57, 12 egoità II 23, 15; jap.: (66) 我 性 Gasei; (7o), (71), (73), (78)
自我性 Jigasei; (58) わたしであること Watashidearukoto; span.: (89)
el "ser yo" (134, 366) (Ich-heit:) el "yo" (372); (9o) (Ich:) yo (129,
134 f.); (91) 'yo' (141); (92) yoidad (58); (114) yoidad (95); (117)
"yoidad" (59 f., 67); (118) yoidad (91, 97).

IN-SEIN (1) Being-in; (2) In-being; chin.: (7) 在中 176 (43); (8) (128); (7) 在内的在 118 (27); (7) 其中的在 119 (28); franz.: (12) être-à ...; ital.: (24) Par. 13, 59, par. 28, 13o in-essere; (33) 111 "in-essere" 127; jap.: (73) 内存在 Naisonzai; (61), (67), (78), (79) 内-存在 Nai-sonzai; (76) 内・在 Nai-zai; (85) 内に-有ること Uchini-arukoto; span.: (89) (In-Sein:) el "ser en" (§ 28 u. passim); (89) (In-sein:) "ser en".

KEHRE (2) reversal; chin.: --; franz.: (22) tournant; (23) renversement; ital.: (24) "svolta" 1o(J); (29) 21, 23, 33, 67, 7o, 92, 93, 1oo, 11o, 112-3, 131-3; (3o) 26 svolta 57; (32) 17 ....; (33) 72 svolta 92; (35) 182 rovesciamento 122; (36) svolta (conversione) 23, 31-2(J); (37) (ritorno 13, svolta 56); (38) (-en) 1o, 25 ritorno 11, 26; (42) (-en) 28, 28 (ritorno), pervenire con una svolta I 18, 31; (43) (Um...ung) 176 inversione 14o; jap.: (67) 転向 Kikō; (66) 戻り Modori; (76) 転回 Tenkai; span.: (89) (Umkehrung:) convertir (292) (sich kehren:) vertirse (157); (89) vuelta; (95) (sich kehren:) volverse (2o7); (98) vuelta (Kehre) (82); (99) fin interno (21); (1o7) vuelta (181); (1o8) vuelta (24); (116) viraje (155, 157).

LICHTEN (1) clear, Gelichtetheit cleared-ness; (5) to clear, lighten, illuminate; chin.: (8) 恬然澄明 24 (1o9), 45 (131); (8) 照明 36 (121); (8) 照亮 119 (28); franz.: (15) sich -: se luminer; (17) il-luminer; (21) ouvrir en clairière; ital.: (24) 133, 4 illuminare 21o, (147, 2-23o); (28) 47N introdurre spazi luminosi, illuminare 49, 7E tralucere 64; (29) 97; (3o) 26 tralucere 57; (32) 35 illuminare 119, 43 tralucere 13o, 36 dar luce 119; (33) 65 illuminare 86, 7o manifestare 9o, 83, aprire, aprirsi 1o3; (34) 31,-7 illuminare 27, o, (sich) 67 prender luce 64; (35) 33 illuminare 19, 258 aprire-illuminare 176, (sich) 99 farsilargo 65, 247 farsiluce 169, 178 portare alla luce 119; (37) 36 rischiarare 139; (41) 68 irradiare II 31; (42) 66, 18 far luce, manifestare II 332, 7; (43) 6o illuminare 63, 6o rischiarare 63, 7o portare alla luce 71; (45) 6o, 7 discoprire 61, 8, 62 rischiarare 63; jap.: (7o) 明らめる akarameru; (48), (52), (67), (78), (86) 明るくする akarukusuru; (81) 空るみに出す

akaruminidasu; (46) 明るみを與える akarumi o ataeru; (51), (57), (84) 空ける akeru; (51), (84) 開 く hiraku; (79) 明開する meikaisuru; (81) 朏明する shōmeisuru; (62) 透かし開く sukashihiraku; <u>span.:</u> (89) iluminar (154, 4o3); (95) (sich lichten:) transparentarse (2o7); (96) despejar (78) (sich lichten:) despejarse (78); (98) (lichtendes Bergen:) un cobijar que despeja (lichtendes Bergen) (82); (99) (lichtendes Bergen:) ocultante develamiento (lichtendes Bergen) (21); (1o7) despejar (179, 212) (sich lichten:) despejarse (224, 228); (1o8) ilumniar (22, 49) (sich lichten:) iluminarse (59, 63); (1o9) iluminar (351, 272) (sich lichten:) iluminarse (262, 357); (11o) iluminar (111) alumbrar (9o) (sich lichten:) iluminarse (74) alumbrarse (121); (111) iluminar (59) aclarar (45) (sich lichten:) esclarecerse (34) iluminarse (66); (113) (sich lichten:) esclarecerse (189, 193); (115) iluminar (9, 16); (116) lucir (142, 151); (119) iluminar (47); (12o) aclarar (47); (121) iluminar (62).

LICHTUNG  (1) clearing; (2) lighting-process; (4) illumination; (5) clearing, lighting; <u>chin.:</u> (8) 澄明 19 (1o3); (8) 光亮 24 (1o9); <u>franz.:</u> (11) éclairci; (12) lumière; (13) éclairci; (15) lumination; (17) clairière (19); (21) lumination, clairière; (23) éclairci; <u>ital.:</u> (24) illuminazione; (28) 47N tralucere 49; (29) 18, 55-8, 114; (3o) 26 Tralucere 52; (32) 2o tralucere 1o4, 35 luce 118, 3 (apertura) 118; (33) 67 apertura della luce 87, 69 apertura 89, s. 76, 77-96; (34) 41 illuminazione 38; (35) 33 apertura 19, 241 illuminazione-apertura, luminosità 1o4, 247 apertura illuminata, luce 169, 251 apertura-illuminazione 171, 258 "slargo" 177; (36) illuminazione-apertura 26, 34(J); (37) (tralucere 81); (42) 23, 7 radura, adito I 15, 5, 47, 13 apertura illuminante II 22o, 37, 63, 5, 68, 8 apertura II 229, 34, II 232, 5, 65, 4-6 irradiamento II 231, 3-5; (43) 11o radura luminosa 98, 126 chiarità 1o7; <u>jap.:</u> (7o) 明らめ Akarame; (56) 明かり Akari; (57), (59), (65), (86), (87) 明るめ Akarume; (48), (52), (61), (66), (67), (76), (78), (73), (87), (68) 明るみ Akarumi; (85) 明け開け Akehirake; (51), (57) 空 地 Akichi; (51), (71) 開 け Hirake; (79) 明開作用 Meikaidayō; (54) 朏 明 Shōmei; <u>span.:</u> (89) iluminación (154, 197); (96) luminidad (Lichtung) (78); (98) despejamiento (Lichtung) (82); (99) develamiento (21); (1o7) despejo (Lichtung) (175, 179, 186, 193, 211, 228); (1o8) iluminación (19, 22, 34, 62) luz (28, 48); (1o9) iluminción (27o ff., 341 f., 347, 35o, 352) esclarecimiento (342); (11o) un claro (86) luz (86, 88) iluminación (87 f., 1o5) campo luminoso (87) alumbra-

miento (89, 96 f., 11o, 114); (111) un claro (42 ff., 49) iluminación
(44, 49, 58, 61) esclarecimiento (49); (114) el claro (Lichtung) (96).

DAS MAN (1) the "they", -selbst the they-self; (2) "people"; chin.:
(7) 普通人 126(36); (8) 8(91); franz.: (12) le "on"; ital.: (24) Par.
27,126 il "Si"; (27) Il si 58 (nota 5); (33) 59 il Si 80; jap.: (67),
(78), (79), (85) ひ と Hitho; (73) 世 人 Sejin; (61) 世 間 Seken;
span.: (89) el "uno" (§ 27 u.passim) el uno (353); (89) ((das) MAN (selbst):)
(el) uno (mismo) (man:) se; (91) Don Nadie (Man) (153, Anm. 9); (107)
(das "man":) el "uno" (man) (167); (108) (das "man":) el "se" (man) (12).

MITSEIN (1) Being-with; (2) with-being; chin.: (7) 共在 118(27);
franz.: (12) être-avec-autrui; (16) réalité-interhumaine; ital.: (24)
43,54 con-essere 666, 678; (25) 43, 54 con-essere 666, 678; (36) con-essere
19,35 (J); (37) (con-essere 74); jap.: (61), (78), (79) 共同存在 Kyōdosonzai;
(73) 共存在 Kyosonzai; (71), (85) 共に有ること Tomoni arukoto; span.: (89)
el "ser con" (132, 137, 139 f. u. passim); (89) "ser con"; (91) 'ser junto'
(118) el estar con (141); (92) el ser-con (47) el ser-con (Mit-sein) (58).

DAS NICHTENDE (2) negativing element, Nichten des Nichts Non-being in
its very assence; chin.: (8) 能不者 44 (130); franz.: (23) le néantisant;
ital.: (24) Par. 58, 285, 25 (nichten) il nullificante 423, 29; (25) 5
Il nullificante 623; (27) 34-4, 37,7,14 l'annullante 89,7, l'annullare
95,1,8; (28) 34 il nientificante 23; (32) 43 (ciò che nientifica), il
nientificante 130; (33) 112-4 il nullificante 128; (35) (das Nichtige)
117 il nulla 77; (43) (das Nichtige) 190 insignivicanze 150; jap.: (76)
無化するところのもの Mukasuru tokonoro mono; (82) 無にするもの Munisuru
mono; (67) 無化するもの Mukasurumono; span.: (89) (Nichtigkeit:) "no ser"
(325 f.) (nichtig:) afectado de no ser (330); (89) (Nichtigkeit:) "no ser"
(Nichtheit:) (carácter) de "no"; (93) (das Nichten:) el anular (142 f.)
(nichtend:) anulador (141, 143); (94) (das Nichten:) el anonadar (102 ff.)
(nichtend:) anonadante (102, 105); (107) lo anonadante (227); (108) lo
anonadador (61); (115) (etwas Nichtiges:) algo inútil (8); (116) (etwas
Nichtiges:) una nonada (141).

NOCH-NICHT (1) the "not-yet", vorläufig noch nicht not right away;

chin.: (7) 还不 327 (76); franz.: (13) le pas encore; ital.: (24) 242, 15
non-ancora 367,18; (26) non-ancora; (29) 43, 3 ciò che non è ancora 17, 2o,
44, 2o non-ancora 19, 9; (34) 167 il non-ancora 165; (35) 13o l'ancora non
86, 182 il non-essere-ancora 122; (36) 2, 8 ancora non 38, 23, 12, 12 "non
ancora" 53, 19, u.passim, 59, 5 non-ancora 118, 2o; (37) (non-ancora 45);
(42) 24, 1 ... I 15; (44) 278 non ancora 384; jap.: (79), (85) 未だ－ない
imada-nai; (78) まだ－ない mada-nai; (73) 未 了 miryo̅; (61) 未 然 mizen;
span.: (89) el "aún no" (278, 28o, 287); (1o2) (das Nochnicht:) el "aún
no" (179); (1o3) (das Nochnicht:) el aún no (37); (1o4) (das Nochnicht:)
el todavía no (147); (113) todavía-no (179) el todavía-no (38f.); (114)
(ein "noch nicht":) un "todavía no" (127); (116) no-ser-todavía (155) el
aún-no (156).

DAS OFFENBARE (1) Offenbar, offenbaren manifest, open up (2) that which
is open, Offenbar revealed, Offenbarkeit manifestation; (4) what is manifest; chin.: (9) 启示出来的 35 (353); (8) 发乎外的 5 (87); franz.: (12)
le manifeste, ce qui se manifeste; (13) le manifeste, l'ouvert; (17) le
manifeste (19); ital.: (24) 28, 33 il manifesto 87, 19, il manifestabile
8-, 27 (3o, 21); (25) 12 il mostrante, il manifestante 632; (26) 2o1, 34
l'ente che ci è manifesto 292, 26; (27) 25, 3 (-en) il rivelante 6o, 7,
31, 19, 22 Il rivelante 81, ..., 14, 34 (-keit) il rivelarsi 89; (28) 25
il rivelante 7; (29) 34,25 manifestazione dell'essere 32, 33; (3o) 11
ciò che si rivela, si manifesta 22, 24 il rivelato 53; (32) 27 il rivelato 1o9; (33) 88 l'aperto 1o7, 12; (34) 12 l'evidente 8, 6o ciò che è
già rivelato 57; (35) 25 (l'evidente) 13, 197 (il manifestato) 132; (45)
14, 2o l'evidente 15, 17; jap.: (78) 明らさまなもの Akarasamanamono; (56),
(85) 顕わなもの Arawanamono; (61). (73) あらわなものArawanamono; (48)
顕わなるものArawanarumono; (54) 開けて明らかなもの Hirakete-akiraka-naru-
mono; (82) 開示されうるもの Kaijisareurumono; (82) 顕示され得るもの Kenji-
sareurumono; span.: (89) lo patente (33, 35) ; (89) (Offenheit u. verw.
Termini:) patencia, franquía, revelación; (9o) (offenbaren:) hacer patente
(65); (93) (Offenbarkeit:) manifestación (142, 144, 149); (94) (Offenbarkeit:) patencia (1o2, 1o6, 113); (97) lo manifiesto (?) (13); (98) lo
patente (67f.) lo abierto (68) lo manifiesto (7o) ... manifestarsi (7o);
(99) aquello (1o) que se manifiesta (1of.) lo que es manifiesto (1o) lo
revelado (12) lo que se revela (12); (1o2) revelación (167); (1o3) campo
abierto (22) (auch für offenbare Stätte: vgl. ib.); (1o4) un Revelado
(sic!) (131); (1o9) lo abierto (351); (11o) lo patente (112); (111) lo

abierto (59); (112) (das Offene:) lo abierto (116); (114) lo patente (127).

SACHE (1) thing, matter, affair, die Sachen selbst the things themselves;
(4) fact, a something; chin.: (8) 事 7 (9o); (8) 事物 4o (126); (7) 事情
26 (16); (7) 事业 122 (32); (8) 堂奥 3o (115); (1o) 东西 269 (379); franz.:
(11) cause, affair, cas, propos, chose; (12) chose, oject; (16) chose; (17)
question (D.2), affair, chose (18), chose, cause à débattre (19); (21)
chose, affair, cause (res); ital.: (24) 27, 21, 38, 122, 31 "cose", cosa
85, 32 / 86,16, 21o, 21 (affare, causa); (25) 34 cosa 655; (26) 2o2 cosa
292; (27) 25, 28 cosa 6o,2; (28) 25 cosa 6; (3o) 7 cosa 12; (31) 36
contenuto 58; (32) 24 cosa 1o7, 42 ciò che, questo che 127, 47 missione
133; (33) 57 cosa 78, 91 oggetto 11o; (34) cosa, 117 compito 115, 139
affare 137, 197 senso 195; (35) cosa, 183 qual cosa 123, 223 cosa stessa
153, 229 le cose 157; (36) 2, 27, 4o, 37 cosa 38, 7, 93, 9,u.passim; (37)
9, 13 espressione, qual cosa, cosa 1o1, 1o7; (39) cosa; (4o) cosa, 7
faccenda9; (42) cosa u.passim, 62, 1, 63, 12, 22 faccenda II 229, 6, II
23o, 1, 12; (43) 99 cosa 91, 1o9 ragione oggettiva 97, 173-6 compito 137, o;
(44) 135 cosa 239; (45) 6 compito 7, 14 cosa 15; jap.: (51), (61), (69),
(73), (78), (79), (85) ❀ ❀ Jishō; (75), (77), (81), (82) ❀ 柄 Kotogara; span.: (89) cosa (2oof., 275) (auch für Ding); (9o) (Sachen:) cosas
(116, 136) (der Sache nach:) en el fondo (14o); (91) (Übers. aus d. 1.
Ausg.: Beleg (in Vorwort z. 3. Aufl.) fehlt!); (92) asunto (7); (93) cosas
(13o); (94) cosa (87); (95) cosa (212, 219); (97) cosa (9f.); (98) cosa
(63, 65f.); (99) cosa (6f., 8); (1oo) cosa (147) ("Sachen":) "cosas" (144);
(1o1) cosa (52) ("Sachen":) "cosas" (51); (1o5) cosa (147); (1o6) cosa (32);
(1o7) cosa (2o3, 222f.) cosa (=terreno) (222) cosa (=función) (23o); (1o8)
cosa (42, 58, 64) cuestión (58); (1o9) cosa (268); (11o) cosa (84); (111)
asunto (41) cosa (41); (113) cosa (1o, 19, 86, 165, 188, 2o1, 21o) asunto
(18, 29f., 36, 1o5, 12o, 181, 188, 197f.) estado de cosas (99) objetivo
(19) fondo de la cuestión (88) causa (142) algo (195); (114) contenido
(65) problema (141, 195) cosa (113, 124, 184f.) (auch f. Ding: passim)
cuestión (139) asunto (135) algo (135) cosa objetiva (147); (115) cosa
(13) (auch für Ding: vgl. pas.); (116) cosa (147) (auch für Ding: vgl.
passim); (119) asunto (18, 2o) cosa (31); (12o) cosa (11f., 26) (auch für
Ding: vgl. 2o); (121) cosa (46f., 53) (auch für Ding: vgl. 5o).

SCHEIN (1) thing, matter, affair, die Sachen selbst the things themselves;
(4) fact, a something; (6) matter; <u>chin.:</u> (7)假象 195 (61); (1o) 273 (383);
(1o) 似是而非 268 (378); <u>franz.:</u> (12) apparence; (15) apparence, parence;
<u>ital.:</u> (24) 29, 3 parvenza 87, 26; (26) 221 illusione 321; (28) 48N appa-
renza 5o 17E apparire 77; (29) 35, 12 apparenza 9, 18; (3o) 6 apparenza 11;
(31) 21 chiarore 44, 28 luce 51, 34 risplendere 56, 39 splendore 61; (34)
2o evidenza 16, 36 apparenza 32, 117 parvenza 115,129 apparire 127; (35)
31 apparenza 17, 276 il risplendere 189; (38) (-en) 1o, 14 sembianza 11, 14;
(43) 51 apparenza 56, 115 bagliore 1o1; (44) 156 apparenza 26o; (45) 64, 15
apparenza 65, 16; <u>jap.:</u> (61), (63), (69), (7o), (73), (79), (81), (85)
仮 象 Kashō; (78) 仮 相 Kasō; (62) 幻 し Maboroshi; (77) 出 現 Shutsugen; 存在せしめる sonzaiseshimeru; (57) 見せかけ Misekake ; <u>span.:</u> (89)
el "parecer" (254) el "parecer ser" (33f., 35) ilusión (2o2) apariencia (235);
(89) (Schein, scheinen:) parecer ser; (90) apariencia (34, 12o, 2o4); (97)
apariencia (?) (1o); (98) apariencia (62, 69, 73f.); (99) apariencia (6, 11,
14) aparentemente... (15); (1oo) resplandor (122, 13of., 133, 143); (1o1)
respandor (4o, 44, 47, 5o); (1o2) apareincia (168, 177); (103) aparencias
(23, 34); (104) apariencia (132, 143); (1o9) lo aparente (15) el paricer
(265) apariencia (27o); (11o) lo falso (56) apariencia (78) falsa apariencia
(87); (111) ilusión (23) apariencia (37, 43); (113) aureola (92) apariencia
(92) resplandor (18) apariencias (192); (114) apariencia (2o, 131, 134,
171, 186) "ilusion" (113) (Kant-Zitat).

SEIEND (1) being, entity, is, are -es entity, entities, that which is,
what is; (2) being (verb adj.) -e being (noun) -e im Ganzen beings-in-the-
ensemble, totality of beings; (6) -es being(s); <u>chin.:</u> (7) 在着的 12o (29)
(9) 39 (356); (7)存在着 1 (3); (9)有所有的 3o (348); <u>franz.:</u> (11) étant;
(15) das S-: le "étant"; <u>ital.:</u> (24) essente; (26) 2o4 ente 296; (27) 7,
39, 5 essente, essere 98, 18; (28) 39, 5 essente 29, 14, 2oE essente 83;
(29) 34, 19... ciò che esiste, esistente, ciò che è esistente 8, 26...;
(34) essente, 54 (s. werden) sussistere 51; (36) 4o, 22 essente 92, 2o ;
(37) 27, 3, 46 essente 74, 117, 128; (43) 165 essente 132, 171 esistente
136; (44) 132 essente 236; <u>jap.:</u> (82), (85)有るもので有る arumonodearu; (54)
存在者的 sonzaishateki; (73)存在しつつある sonzaishitsutsuaru; (78)存在する
sonzaisuru; (58), (79), (81)存在的 sonzaiteki; (61)存在するもの Sonzai-
surumono; <u>span.:</u> (89) "ente" (2) siendo (326) "entes" (8) ser (15) "es"

(472); (9o) siendo (194) ente en el grado más alto posible (199); (93) ente (146); (94) ente (1o9); (95) ente (217); (96) (als Adjektiv:) entitativo (77); (1o7) (als Adjektiv:) siente (225) (vgl. Anm.72); (1o8) (als Adjektiv:) que es ente (6o); (1o9) (seiend wird:) es (355) (paraphrastische Übers.); (11o) (seiend wird:) Ilega a ser (118); (111) (seiend wird:) Ilega a ser existente (64); (113) ente (75, 91) siendo (99, 215f., 218) entitativo (seiend) (98f.); (114) existente (94, 192) siendo (21o); (117) ente (35) (considerado como) siendo (4o) siendo (41, 59, 65) ser siendo (46); (118) existente (77, 79f., 82, 96) (S. 91: fehlt ein Satz); (119) "ente" (58) (Aristoteles-Zitat); (12o) "ente" (61) (Aristoteles-Zitat); (121) "siendo" (68) (Aritoteles-Zitat).

SEIENDER (2) -heit (ousia) being-ness; (4) one that is; chin.: (7)在者 122 (31); (9) 32 (35o); franz.: (11) l'étant; (12) les étants, l'étant; (13) l'étant; (15) l'étant; ital.: (25) 39, 22 "essente" 661, 35; (32) 43 più essente 131; (33) 13 più essente 129; (34) 33, 279 più essente 3o, 28o; (36) 41, 4 più essente 92, 14; (42) 28, 4-5 più reale I 18,1o; jap.: (Seiendes) (57), (85)有るもの Arumono; (49), (62), (67), (78)存在するもの Sonzai-surumono; (59), (61), (65), (68), (7o), (72), (73), (76), (79), (81)存在者 Sonzaisha; span.: (89) (seiender:) "es" más (482); (91) ("seiender":) "más ser" (111); (92)("seiender":) "más ente" (44); (1oo) ("Seienderes":) lo que es más ser (146) ("seiender":) "más ser" (146); (1o1) ("Seienderes":) lo que "es más ente" (52) ("seiender":) "es más" (51);(1o7) (seiender:) más siente (225); (1o8) (seiender:) un más en ser (6o) (Vgl. Anm.53); (1o9) (seiender:) más ente (263, 27o, 272); (110) (seiender:) más existente (74, 86) más ente (9o); (111) (seiender:) más existente (35, 42, 45); (114) (seiender:) más existente (163).

SEIN (1) Being; (2) Being (-process); (5) Being; (6) Being; chin.: (7)在 1 (3); (9) 35 (353); franz.: (11) être; (12) êtu; (13) êtu; (14) êtu; (15) êtu; (16) être; (17) êtu; (21) êtu; (22) êtu; (23) Etre; ital.: (24) Essere; (25) 14 essere 634-35; (26) 2o4 essere 296; (27) 36 essere 94; (28) essere; (29) 34,24 essere 8, 31 u.ff. l'Essere come tale, Essere, Essere dell'ente, -dell'ente come ente sommo, -dell'essente, -dell'ente, dell'ente in generale, Essere come presenza; (3o) 25 essere 55; (31) 25 essere 48, 35 Essere 57; (32) Essere, essere, "Essere", "essere"; (33) 53 Essere 75, u.passim; (34) essere, 273 insieme 273; (35) essere (71-45); (36) 74, 25 essere 137, 22 (27); (37) essere; (39) (Seyo) essere; (4o) essere; (42) 59,

14 "Essere" II 227, 19; (43) 13 essere 29, u. passim, 173 Essere 138, 165 esistenza 131, 21; (44) 132 "essere" 236, 148 essere 252, 149 essere 253; jap.: (47), (48), (49), (50), (52), (54), (56), (59), (61), (62), (55), (65), (66), (68), (70), (71), (72), (73), (75), (77), (78), (79), (81), (85), (86), (87) 存 在 Sonzai; (71), (85) 有ること Arukoto; (57), (65), (66), (73) 有 U; span.: (89) ser (passim); (89) (sein, Sein:) ser; (90) ser (15 u. passim); (91) Ser (65, 68, 112 u. passim); (92) ser (18, 44 f. u. passim); (93) ser (142, 144, 147 f.); (94) ser (103, 105, 110 f.); (95) ser (207, 209); (96) ser (75 ff. u. passim); (97) ser (22); (98) ser (79, 81 ff.); (99) Ser (19, 21 f.); (100) ser (138, 152, 154, 158) (auch für das Seiende: 149, 151, 153) Ser (149, 151, 153 f.,158); (101) ser (48, 53 ff.,57); (102) ser (172, 177 u. passim); (103) ser (28) Ser (29, 34 f. u. passim); (104) ser (137, 144 u. passim); (107) ser (161, 165, 185 f.); (108) ser (7, 10, 28); (109) ser (10, 21 u. passim); (110) ser (48, 67 u. passim); (111) ser (18, 30 u. passim); (112) modo de ser (115) ser (120);(113) ser (100, 205, 214) "ser" (173, Kant-Zitat); (114) ser (28, 60, 78 f.,91, 94, 96, 116, 208 f.); (115) ser (16); (116) ser (150); (117) ser (39, 54); (118) ser (79, 88); (119) ser (32 f., 35 f., 43, 45, 52, 55, 58); (120) ser (28 f., 32, 41, 45, 52, 55, 61); (121) Ser (54, 56, 60 f. 65, 67 f.).

SEIN-BEI   (1) Being alongside; (2) be immersed in;   chin.: (7) 在于 120 (29); (7) 寄于…的在   192 (58); (7) 寓于…的在 327 (76); franz.: (12) être auprès de...; ital.: (24) 141, 26-7 esser-presso 234, 34, 36; (25) 43 esser-presso 665; jap.: (61), (79) 許での存在   Motodeno Sonzai; (85) 許に‥有ること Motoni-Arukoto; (73) 何かのもとでの存在   Nanika no motodeno Sonzai; (78) ラ つ ヲ サ ? ラ ヲ の… Motoni-Arukoto; span.: (89) "ser cabe..." (289, 420) el "ser cabe" (64 f., 139); (89) (sein bei (der Welt:)) "ser cabe (el mundo)"; (91) ser (110, 112) ser del ente (65) "ser entre"(118); (92) el ser junto a (47).

SEIN-KÖNNEN   (1) potentiality-for-Being; (2) drive-toward-Being, power-to-be; chin.: (7) 能在 122 (31) 179 (46); (7) 能够在的情况 186 (50); franz.: (12) savoir-être, pouvoir-être; (16) pouvoir-être; ital.: (24) Par. 60 poter-essere; (25) 48 poter essere 671; (37) (poter-essere 74);, jap.: (85) 有り−得る Ari-uru; (61), (78), (79) 存在−可能   Sonzai-kano; (73) 存在可能性 Sonzaikanōsei; span.: (89) "poder ser" (166, 340, 221: mit Art.) (auch für Seinkönnen, z.B. 166f.); (89) (seinkönnen:) poder ser; (91) (Seinkönnen:) el 'poder de ser' (129, 139f.); (92) (Seinkönnen:) el poder-ser (42).

SEINSFRAGE (2) Being-question; <u>chin.</u>: (8) 在的问题 3o (115); <u>franz.</u>: (14) question de l'être; (17) question enquête de l'être; (22) question de l'être; <u>ital.</u>: (24) problema dell'essere; (25) 42 problema dell'essere 664; (26) 211, 11 problema dell'essere 3o6, 12; (28) 12E questione dell'essere 7o; (31) 52 (S. fragwürdig) l'essere... come problema 72; (32) 2o, 5 il problema dell'essere 1o4, 1o; (33) 76 "problema dell'essere" 96; (34) 84 domanda all'essere 55; (35) 84 domanda dell'essere 55; (37) (problema dell'essere 45, ricerca dell'essere, l'essere come problema, come ulteriore ricerca, come sempre rinnovante domanda 52, 1o4 Fußnote); (45) 66 problema dell'essere 67; <u>jap.</u>: (61), (67), (78), (79) 存在問題 Sonzaimondai; (73) 存在に対する問い Sonzainitaisurutoi; (54), (81) 存在の問い Sonzai no toi; (66), (85) 有の問い U-no-toi; <u>span.</u>: (89) pregunta que interroga por el ser (§§ 1-5) (auch für Frage nach dem Sein) questión del ser (5o1); (89) (Frage nach dem Sein, Seinsfrage:) pregunta que interroga por el ser, pregunta por el ser, questión del ser; (9o) pregunta que interroga por el ser (185, 194f., 2o4) pregunta por el ser (187, 199) pregunta del ser (188); (91) el que pueda ser "su" ser (1o6) questión acerca del Ser (179); (92) pregunta por el ser (46); (95) pregunta por el sér (21o); (1o7) "pregunta del ser" (185f.); (1o8) "pregunta del ser" (28).

SEINSGESCHICHTE (2) Being-as-history; <u>chin.</u>: (8) 在的历史 3o (115); <u>franz.</u>: (11) histoire de l'être; <u>ital.</u>: (24) Par. 1 storia dell'essere; (32) 47 storia dell'essere 134; (33) 11o storia dell'essere 134; (34) 3o2 storia dell'essere 3o5 (-lich) 254 storico-ontologico; (35) 71 storia dell'essere 45; <u>jap.</u>: (5o), (52), (67), (76), (81) 存在の歴史 Sonzai no rekishi; (51), (64), (66), (67), (84) 有の歴史 U-no-rekishi; <u>span.</u>: (1o7) "historia del ser" (2o3 historia del ser (231); (1o8) historia del ser (65) (auf S.42 unübersetzt).

SEIN-ZU (1) Being towards; (2) Being-unto; <u>chin.</u>: (7) 对···的在 177 (43); <u>franz.</u>: (12) être-á-l'égard-de... être-"relatif"-á...; (16) l'être-pour; <u>ital.</u>: (24) 124, 29, 32 essere per... 213, 1, 4; (25) 43 essere in rappoto con 666; <u>jap.</u>: (78), (79) への存在 eno-sonzai; (73) へとかかわる存在 etokakawarusonzai; (85) へ有ること he-arukoto; (85) 際にあること kiwani-arukoto; (61) 臨む存在 nozomu-sonzai; <u>span.</u>: (89) "ser relativamente a" (288, 285, 298, 365); (89) ("sein zu":) "ser realtivamente a"; (91) 'ser para' (118); (92) el ser para (47); (95) ser para (213); (1o7) ser-hacia- (213); (1o8) ser para (5o).

SELBSTSEIN (1) Being-one's-Self, Being-its-Self; chin.: (7) 自己的在 126
(36); (7)自己在 184 (48); (9) 自我存在 35 (353); franz.: (12) être-soi-même,
ipséité; (16) l'être soi-même, l'être personnel; ital.: (24) Par. 27, 126
esser se-Stesso 214; (26) 145 esser se stesso 211; (27) 35 essere noi Stessi
91; (28) 35 essere se stesso 23, 16E essere un Selbst 77; (29) 42, 17
essere se stessi 16 (nota 2); (33) 59 esser se stesso 8o; (37) (essere se
stesso 74); jap.: (85)自己で有ること Jikodearukoto; (61), (73), (78), (79),
(81)自己存在 Jikosonzai; span.: (89) el "ser si mismo" (169, 213, 326f.)
(auch für Selbstheit, z.B. §64); (89) (Selbstsein, Selbstheit:) "ser si
mismo"; (9o) ser-mismo (136) (auch für "Selbst-sein, vgl. 137); (91) (Selbstheit:) mismidad o asimisma miento (76, 1o6ff.) (Selbst:) ser 'mismo' y un
'mismo' (119); (92) (Selbstheit:) mismidad (Selbstheit) (24, 42, 48, 58)
(Selbst:) un Mismo (48); (93) ser por si mismo (Selbstsein) (142); (94)
mismidad (1o3); (95) el ser si mismo (214); (97) ipseidad (?) (23); (1o7)
en cuanto es ella (la persona) misma (Selbstsein der Person) (167); (1o8)
el ser-mismo (12); (117) (Selbstheit:) "mismidad" (59); (118) (Selbstheit:)
autidad (59).

SINN (1) meaning, sense; (2) sense; chin.: (7) 意义 324 (72) 326 (75); (7)
意思 326 (75); franz.: (12) sens; (16) sens; ital.: (24) Par.83 senso 617;
(25) 25 significato 646, 26, 28 senso 648, 3; (26) senso; (28) 18, 22E
senso 8o, 11 (senso dell'essere); (29) 136; (3o) 25,-3 "senso" 56,5; (32)
senso, significato; (33) senso; (34) senso, 83 modo 88; (35) senso; (37)
16, 18, 27 senso 115; (41) senso; (42) 2o, 3 senso I, 13, 11; (43) 44
senso 51 u.passim, 167 significato 133; (44) 135 senso 233; (45) 18 senso,
significato 19; jap.: (81)意 義 Igi; (48), (52), (54), (59), (61), (65),
(66), (71), (73), (78), (79), (81), (85), (87), (88)意 味 Imi; span.: (89)
sentido (175f. u.passim); (89) sentido; (93) sentido (14o, 143, 148); (94)
sentido (1oo, 1o4, 111); (95) sentido (2o7, 216); (96) sentido (75); (1o2)
sentido (166 u.passim); (1o3) sentido (2o u.passim) (im Sinne:) cual si
fuera (37); (1o4) sentido (13o u.passim); (1o5) sentido (148, 153); (1o6)
sentido (32, 35); (1o7) sentido (188, 191, 199); (1o8) sentido (3o, 35, 39);
(113) sentido (65, 122, 125, 171, 182, 197) órgano sensitivo (194) mente
(198, 211); (114) sentido (14, 116, 174, 194, passim) intención (112);
(117) sentido (19, 25, 32, 4o, 44, 54f.); (118) sentido (68, 75, 79, 81,
88); (119) sentido (27f., 32, 35f., 42, 45, 49); (12o) sentido (21ff., 27,
31, 33, 4o, 44, 51); (121) sentido (5off., 54ff., 59, 61, 63).

SORGE  (1) care besorgen concern (with things) Fürsorge solicitude vor-
sorgen take precautions;  (2) concern besorgen be preoccupied with;  (6) care;
<u>chin.</u>:  (7)烦  192  (58)  1o  (92);  <u>franz.</u>:  (12) souci;  (16) Souci;  <u>ital.</u>:  (24)
Par. 41 Cura 299;  (25) 36 Cura 658;  (26) 196 Cura 285;  (28) 15E "aver cura
per" 75;  (29) 13, 25-8, 95;  (32) 35 cura 118;  (33) 71 "cura" 91, s.61-82
u.passim;  (34) 332 cura 336;  <u>jap.</u>:  (46)配 慮 Haii;  (48),  (49)配 慮  Hai-
ryo;  (61),  (66),  (67),  (78),  (85)関 心 Kanshin;  (66)懸 念 Kenen;  (73)
気遣い Kizukai;  (46)思い煩い Omoiwazurai;  (79)慮 Ryo;  (79)憂 慮 Yūryo;
<u>span.</u>:  (89) cura (§§39, 63, 65) "cura" (67);  (89) cura;  (9o) cura (196ff.);
(91) apuro (Sorge) (177) preocupación (134);  (92) Sorge (cura) (41) cuidado
(55);  (95) cura (213);  (96) cuidado (Sorge) (82);  (1o7) cuidado (169, 18o,
185) cuidado de (=por) (2o2);  (1o8) cuidado (14, 23, 27, 41);  (114) cura
(33).

TUN  (2) dynamic accomplishment;  (4) doing;  <u>chin.</u>:  (8)行为 35 (12o);  (8)
行动 41 (127);  (1o)作 27o (38o);  <u>franz.</u>:  (11) le faire, l'activité, l'acte;
(22) l'entreprise;  <u>ital.</u>:  (26) 217 operare 315;  (27) 25 fare 59;  (28) 25
agire 6;  (3o) 15 fare 31;  (32) 35 attività 117, 41 azione 125, 45 agire
128;  (33) 54 fare 76, 96 posizione 114, 99 attività 117;  (34) fare, agire
19 oprare 15, 24 procedimento 21, 48 attività 44, 159 intervento 157, 21o
azione 2o9;  (35) fare, agire, attività 22 opera 11, 26 operare 14, 255 com-
portamento 173;  (38) 1o operare 1;  (41) 25 attività I 15;  (43) 254 operare
199;  <u>jap.</u>:  (69)沾 動 Katsudo;  (76)行 動 Kōdō;  (75),  (81)行 為 Koi;
<u>span.</u>:  (9o) el hacer (Tun) (173) hacer (2oo);  (93) el actuar (13o);  (94)
el hacer (87);  (97) el hacer (2o);  (98) (Tun und Lassen:) acción (76);  (99)
(Tun und Lassen:) actividad (17);  (1o5) hacer (154);  (1o6 hacer (35);  (1o7)
el hacer (162) el proceder (2o7) el actuar (211) el actuar (22o, 228f.);
(1o8)el que hacer (8, 45, 48, 56, 62f.);  (1o9) el hacer (13, 34of., 346);
(11o) el hacer (54) acción (94f., 1o4);  (111) accion (22) faena (47) el
hacer (48) lo que hace (el artista) (48) obrar (54);  (113) obrar (1o, 13,
2o, 188) actividad (28, 63) hacer (36, 141, 218) acción (61, 184, 193)
(paraphrast.: 63);  (114) acción (28) hacer (66, 181);  (117) quehacer (17)
el hacer (56);  (118) el obrar (67) el hacer (89).

ÜBERLASSEN  (1) abandon;  (3) released; <u>chin.</u>:  (8) 一任 2o (1o4);  (1o) 264
(374);  (7) 交付 193 (59);  (7)交托 286 (85);  (7) 听天由命 384 (83);  <u>franz.:</u>--
<u>ital.</u>:  (24) 138, 2, 141, 21 affidare (-to) abbandonare, essere abbandonato

23o, 15, 234, 28; (25) 49 (.......) 672; (34) 15 abbondonarsi 11, 257
essere rimesso 257; (35) 73 abbandonato 47 (abbandonare); (44) 131, 2o
lasciare (-to) 235, 2o; jap.: (73), (78)引渡す hikiwatasu; (61), (85)委ねる
yudaneru; span.: (89) abandonar a (16o) abandonado a (475) (sich überlassen:)
abandonarse (475); (89) (Überlassen, Überlassenheit, Verlassenheit:) estar
abandonado, estado de abandono; (91) quedar al arbitrio de (131); (92)
quedar confiado a (54); (1o9) (sich überlassen:) entregarse a (1o); (11o)
(sich überlassen:) abandonarse a (48); (111) (sich überlassen:) entregarse
a (18); (113) abandonar (38) (sich selbst überlassen:) dejar que vayan
corriendo su suerte (78).

ÜBERLIEFERN　(1) hand down, come down traditional; chin.: (7)流传 21 (1o);
(8) 14 (98); (7)传递　383 (82); (7)遗传 3C4 (82); franz.: (16) transmettre,
la mission; (17) transmettre, livrer, "délivrer" sagt Heidegger in "Was ist
das, die Philosophie?"; ital.: (24) 21, 22, 27, 11 tramandare 78, 85; (25)
28 tradere 649; (26) 15 tradere (tradizionale) 15; (3o) 9 tradere, tramandare 17; (32) 28 tradere, tramandare 111; (33) 68, 74 tradere 88, 93, 1o9
tramandare 125; (34) (-ung) 3o, 88 tradere 26, 1o1; (35) trasmettere, tramandare; (37) 14, 15 tradere 1o8, 33, 4o tramandare 135; (41) 17 tramandare, tradere  I 9; (42) 22, 11 tradere I 14, 24, 44, 12, 21 tramandare
(tradizione) II 219, 11, 2o; (43) 164 avere tradizionalmente, per tradizione
131; (44) 133 tramandare 237; (45) 6 (-ung) tradere 7; jap.: (52), (61),
(66(, (73), (75), (78), (79), (85)伝承する denshōsuru; (61)付託する huta-
kusuru; span.: (89) (sich überliefern:) hacerse tradición (441, 443, 448)
(überliefert:) tradicional, trasmitida (443 bzw. 492); (89) (überliefern,
Überlieferung, überliefert:) (hacer) tradición, tradicional; (91) (überliefert:) tradicional (137); (92) (überliefert:) tradicional (56); (1oo) (überliefert:) tradicional (151); (1o1) (überliefert:) tradicional (54); (1o2)
ilegar (178) (in paraphrasistischer Übersetzung); (1o3)conservar (35);
(1o4) trasmitir (145); (113) (Überlieferung:) tradición (222); (114) (überliefert:) que han quedado (135); (119) entregar (25) entregar la tradición
(Subjekt) (44); (12o) transmitir (überliefern) (19) transmitir por tradición (überliefern) (43); (121) transmitir (5o, 61).

ÜBERSTIEG　(2) transcendence; (4) passing over; chin.: --; franz.: (14)
transcendance; (16) transcendance, dépassemente; ital.: (25) 18 u.ff. oltrepassamento 639 e sgg.; (26) (212)(Transzendenz); (27) il sorpassare 13 (J),
l'andar oltre 9o (nota 61), 38 il superamento 97; (28) 38 superamento 28;

(32) 37 sorpassare in una sfera superiore 122; (33) 83 oltre passamento 1o3, 1o3 superamento 12o; (34) (-en) 216 oltre passamento 215, 218 supera-mento 217; (35) (-en) 153 superamento 1o2, 178 innalzarsi (innalzamento) oltre 12o, 192 andare aldi la 128; jap.: (66), (81)趀 越 Chōetsu; (71) 趀 丼 Chōshō; (82)乗り越え Norikoe; span.: (89) (übersteigern:) superar (177); (9o) (sich übersteigern zu:) ir tan lejos que (1o8); (91) sobre-pujamiento o traspaso (73f., 76f.) sobrepujamiento o trascendencia (77) trascendencia (118) sobre pujar (139) "subirse a Mundo" (154, Anm.11 d.Ü.); (92) sobrepasar (Überstieg:) (22, 41) el sobrepasar (22, 45, 47f., 57) ascenso (22ff., 42); (93) (das Übersteigen:) superación (145); (94) (das Übersteigen:) el sobrepasar (1o8); (1o2) (Übersteigerung:) redundancia, superfetación (165) (paraphrastisch); (1o3) (Übersteigerung:) exageración (18); (1o4) (Übersteigerung:) exceso (128); (1o7) (Übersteigen:) el sobre-pasar (193); (1o8) (Übersteigen:) el sobrepasar (34); (113) trascendencia (214); (114) el trascender (156) (auch f. Hinübersteigen:vgl. ib.); (115) (übersteigen:) sobrepasar (17); (116) (übersteigen:) aobrepasar (152).

ÜBERWINDUNG (1) overcome, surmount, conquest; (2) overcoming; chin.: (7) 克服 266 (7o); (8) 26 (111); (1o) 268 (378); franz.: (11) dépassement; (14) dépassement; ital.: (28) 43N su peramento 41, 9E sorpassamento 67; (3o) 27 superamento 58; (31) 31 superamento 53; (32) 26 superamento 108; (33) 86 superamento 1o5; (34) 214 oltrepassamento 212; (35) (s. Inhalt) 9 oltrepassamento 195 (cfr. Indice), 71-45, 164 superamento 11o; (37) (super-amento 57); (43) 1o9 superamento 97; (44) 289 superamento 394; jap.: (7o), (71), (82)趀 克 Chōkoku; (62), (75), (77), (78), (81)克 服 Kokufuku; span.: (89) superración (498); (95) superación (2o8); (96) superación (74); (98) transformación (83); (99) superación (22); (1oo) vencimiento (133); (1o1) superación (45f.); (1o7) (überwinden:) superar (215); (1o8) (über-winden:) superar (52); (113) superación (86); (114) superación (9o,176); (115) (Überwinden:) superación (4); (116) (Überwinden:) el vencer (137); (117) superación (54, 59); (118) superación (87f., 91).

UMWELT (1) environment; (2) World-about; chin.: (7) 周围世界 66 (25); franz.: (12) monde ambiant; (15) monde environmant; (16) milieu; ital.: (24) Par. 15, 66, 136, 32 mondo-ambiente, mondo ambiente 138, 228, 29; (25) 36 mondo-ambiente 658; jap.: (79) 環境界 Kankyōkai; (61), (73), (78) 環境世界 Kankyōsekai; (85)廻りの世界 Mawarinosekai; span.: (89) mundo circundante (77f., 83ff., 93f.) "mundo" (68); (89) mundo circundante .

UNHEIMLICH (1) uncanny; (2) Un-heimlich not "at home" Unheimische condition
of expatriation Unheimisch (sein) alien-to-home; (3) uncanny; (4) -er more
uncanny; chin.: (9)茫然失措 32 (35o); (7) 茫然失据 189 (53); franz.: (11)
-ste: la chose la moins rassurante; (12) étranger; (13) U-: l'inhabituel,
l'inquiétant; (15) inquiétant; ital.: (24) 188, 27 spaesante, spaesati,
sentirsi spaesati 296, 23, 25; (27) 32 opprimente, sentirsi oppressi 82;
(28) 32 sgomento 18, 32 vaga inquietudine 19, 48N (-keit) straneità 52;
(29) 122; (34) 235 inquietante 234; (35) 14 straordinariamente 6, 88 inquietante 57, 1o1 in strano modo 66; (36) 11, 28 inquietante 52, 26, 22,
24 sconcertante 66, 16; (41) 22 sinistro, incredibile I 12, 26 inverosimile
(non-familiare) I 15; (43) (-isch) 18 sperduti 32; jap.: (54), (66), (75),
(81), (85)無気味な bukimina; (46), (79)気味が悪い kimi ga warui; (78)気味悪く
kimiwaruku; (73)不気味 bukimi; (61)無気味さ bukimisa; span.: (89) "inhóspitamente" (217) inhóspitamente (218) (als Adjektiv:) inhóspito (318); (89)
(unheimlich, Unheimlichkeit:) inhóspito, inhospitalidad; (93) "estar uno
con zozobra" (es ist einem unheimlich), Wörtlich: "ello es a uno insólito"
(138); (94) ("es ist einem unheimlich":) "estar uno desazonado" (98), Ib.:
venirle a uno la desazón, desazonado (99); (96) (Unheimlichkeit:) carácter
desasosegante (Unheimlichkeit) (79); (1o5) (als Adjektiv:) inquietante
(153); (1o6) (als Adjektiv:) inquietante (35); (113) (als Adjektiv:) inquietante (33, 52) aciago (83); (114) (als Adjektiv:) inquietante (45);
(115) inquietante (8); (116) inquietante (141).

UNVERBORGEN (2) un-concealed -heit non-concealment; chin.: --; franz.:
(12) dé-voilé; ital.: (24) 33, 18 non- nascosto 93, 15; (25) (-heit) 12
non-esser-nascosto 633, 19 non-più-nascosto 64o; (26) 115 non-occultato
163; (28) 8E (heit) non-ascoso 64, 2oE rivelato 83; (29) 114, 139; (3o)
15 non-nascosto 3o, 16 non-ascoso 32; (31) 9 disvelato 39; (34) 41 non-
nascosto 37; (35) (-heit) 19 disvelato 9; (36) 126, 29, 144, 7; (41) 61
non- ascoso II 26; (42) 62, 13 non-ascoso II 229, 2o; (43) 29 disvelato
36, 134 non esser nascosto 112; (44) 146 disocculto 25o, 156 inocculto
26o; jap.: (57)あからさま akarasama; (51)隠蔽されていない fukurosareteinai;
(81) 隠蔽されない inpeisarenai; (69), (73) 非秘匿性（的） hihitoku(teki);
(56) 隠れない kakurenai; (Unverborgenheit) (51), (66)不機嫌 Fufukozō; (57),
(65) 非秘匿性 Hihitokusei; (5o)非隠蔽性 Hiinpeisei; (54), (74), (77)非－隠蔽
Hi-inpei; (61)隠れなきありさま Kakurenakiarisama; (61), (78)隠れなさ Kakurenasa; (49)隠れていないこと Kakureteinaikoto; span.: (89) (Unverborgenes:)

no-oculto (38) (Unverborgenheit:) estado de no oculto (252); (89) s.u.
verbergen; (9o) (Unverborgenheit:) manifestación (1o8); (91) descubierto
(76); (92) desoculto (24); (97) desoculto (16) que estár a descubierto (?)
(16); (98) (das Unverborgene:) lo desoculto (71); (99) (das Unverborgene:)
lo no-revelado (das Unverborgene:) (13); (1oo) desencubierto (131, 148)
("unverborgener":) "más desencubierto" (116) (Platon-Zitat); (1o1) desoculto (45, 53) ("unverborgener":) "más desoculto" (37) (Platon-Zitat);
(1o9) estar desvelado (269) ser desvelado (27o) (Unverborgenheit:) desve-
lamiento (13f., 269); (11o) estar descubierto (85f.) (Unverborgenheit:)
desocultación (54, 85); (111) desnudado (41) desnudo (42) (Unverborgenheit:)
nitidez (22) desnudez (41f.); (113) patente (227) (das Unverborgene:) lo
revelado (2o1); (115) no-oculto (11); (116) declarado  (145).

UR-SACHE   (2) ultimate Source; chin.: --; franz.: (11) cause, Chose pri-
mordiale; (19) cause;(18) cause première, cause; (23) cause ultime; ital.:
(25) (Ursache) 7 causa 625; (28) 22 (Ursache) cosa 85; (31) 4o fondamento
originario, "causa" 61, 62; (32) 35 (causa prima) 118; (33) (1oo causa
prima 117); (34) 138 (causa prima) 136, 2o4 (causa originaria) 2o3; (35)
15 (causa) 6, 34 (causalità) 2o; (37) (Ursache) 26, 38 causa 128; (42)
(Ur-Sache) 57, 7 causa prima, originaria II 226, 18, (Ursache) 68, 11
causasuprema II 233, 8; (43) (Ursache) 258 causa 2o3; (44) 136 "ur-cosa"
24o; jap.: (71), (81)原－因 Gen-in; (71)（元－事象） (Gen-jisho); (51)原－事柄
Gen-Kotogara; span.: (89) (Ursache:) causa (324); (91) ("Ursache":) "causa"
(52, 131); (92) ("Ursache":) "causas" (11) "causa" (53); (95) (Ursache:)
causas (219); (1oo) "originaria causa"/causa originaria (144) (auch für
Ursache: vgl. 154) original causa (148); (1o1) "causa"/cosa-primaria (51)
causa (Ur-sache = proto-cosa) (52) (Ursache:) causa (55); (1o7) (Ursache:)
causa (211); (1o8) (Ursache:) causa (49); (113) (Ursachen:) causas (174);
(114) causa (125) (auch für Ursache: vgl. 8o, 86, 124, 126, 164, 182); (115)
(Ursache:) causa (13); (116) (Ursache:) causa (146f.); (117) (Ursache:)
causa (4o); (118) (Ursache:) causa (79); (119) (Ursache:) causa (37, 5o);
(12o) (Ursache:) causa (35, 52); (121) (Ursache:) causa (57, 64).

VERBERGEN   (2) conceal, -ing; chin.: (8)蔽而不明 2o (1o4); franz.: (11)
cacher; (12) cacher; (13) celer; (15) garder latent, celer; ital.: (24) 3o,
35 nascondere 9o, 2, celare, velare; (25) 17 celare 638, 45 nascondere
668/; (26) 2o9, 3, 212 esser segreto 3o3, 4, 3o8, 215, 9 nascondere 311,
3o/; (27) 31 nascondere 81, 34 celare 88/; (28) 31 nascondere 17, 51N

coprire nel mistero 57, 18 ascondere 8o; (29) 34, 33, 97, 1o9, 113, 3-4; (3o) 14 nascondere 29, 19 velare 39, 24 oscurare 54; (31) 25 occultare 48, 32 nascondere 54; (32) 2o nascondere 1o4, 27, celare 1o9, chiudersi; (33) 59 celare 8o, 86 nascondere 1o5, 114 occultare 13o; (34) nascondere, celare, occultare; (35) nascondere, calare; (36) 144, 16; (37) 45 nascondere 84; (38) 8 celare 9; (41) 2o, 26, 59 ascondere I 11, 15, II 25; (42) 66, 12 nascondere II, 232, 2; (43) celare, occultare, nascondere 52 custodire 56, 65 esser se segreto 67; (44) 133 occultare 237 134 nascondere 238; (45) 4 nascondere 5; jap.: (52), (69)體藏する fukuzōsuru; (51), (66), (85)秘めかくす himekakusu; (52), (69)秘匿する hitokusuru; (46), (48), (54), (61), (62), (71), (77)隠蔽する inpeisuru; (5o), (57), (59), (67), (87)隠 す kakusu; (81) 身を隠す mio kakusu; (78) おおい隠す ooi kakusu; span.: (89) ocultar (259) (sich verbergen:) ocultarse (35, 2o6); (89) (verbergen, (Un)Verborgenheit:) ocultar, "estado de (no) oculto"; (9o) esconder (35); (91) (sich verbergen:) ocultar (65) estar latente (71); (92) (sich verbergen:) ocultarse (18, 22); (93) encubrir (137); (94) ocultar (97); (95) (sich verbergen:) ocultarse (213, 217) estado de oculto (21o); (96) ocultar (81) (sich verbergen:) ocultarse (76); (97) ocultar (19); (98) ocultar (75, 82) (sich verbergen:) ocultarse (76, 81) (auch für verbergen: 75); (99) disimular (16) (verbergend:) interno (21) (sich verbergen:) esconderse (17); (1o5) (sich verbergen:) encubrirse (15o); (1o6) (sich verbergen:) ocultarse (34); (1o7) esconder (174) (sich verbergen:) ocultarse (19o) esconderse (224); (1o8) ocultar (2o) (sich verbergen:) ocultarse (31, 59); (1o9) (sich verbergen:) ocultarse (8, 354, 357); (11o) (sich verbergen:) ocultarse (45, 117, 122); (111) (sich verbergen:) esconderse (16, 63, 66); (112) (sich verbergen:) encerrarse (116); (113) ocultar (145, 199)ocultarse (17) (sich verbergen:) ocultarse (1o9, 147) esconderse (186) estar oculto (187); (114) (sich verbergen:) ocultarse (24, 1oo); (115) (sich verbergen:) ocultarse (4, 15); (116) (sich verbergen:) ocultarse (137, 149).

VERBORGENHEIT (2) hidden-ness; (5) concealment; chin.: (7)悔莫如深 2o (8); (7) 不知情 126 (36); franz.: (12) dissimulation, être-couvert; (15) la tence; ital.: (24) 33, 17 nascondimento 93. 15, velamento; (26) 2o6, 34 nascondimento 3oo, 2; (27) 36 oscurità 93; (28) 36 oscurità 25, 11E ascosità 69; (29) 34, 33 realtà segreta 9, 3; (3o) 19 oscurità 41, 19, 24 oscuramento 41, 54; (31) 32 nascondimento, occultamento 54; (32) 2o nascondimento 1o4; (33) 77 nascondimento 96; (34) nascondimento, 4o esser-nascosto 36; (35) 19 nascondimento 9; (36)144, 31; (37) (ascosità 81); (43) 134

(Un-) nascondimento 122; (44) 289 (Un-) occultezza (nascondimento) 395;
<u>jap.:</u> (66) 櫃 蔵. Fukuzō; (51) 櫃蔵性 Fukuzōsei; (54), (62), (71), (79), (81)
隱蔽性 Inpeisei; (56) 隠れなさ Kakurenasa; (61) 隠れたありさま Kakuretaarisama;
(57), (61) 隠れたところ Kakuretatokoro; (58), (78) 隠されくいること Kakusaretei-
rukoto; <u>span.:</u> (89) "estado de oculto" (35ff., 252-255) el estar oculto (42)
ocultos (242); (89) s.u. verbergen; (9o) (verborgen:) oculto (192, passim);
(93) ocultación (143); (94) latencia (1o5); (96) (verborgen:) oculto (81f.)
secreto (8of.); (97) encubrimiento (2o, 23) el estar oculto (2o); (98)
ocultamiento (75, 8o); (99) obnubilación (Verborgenheit) (16, 2o); (1oo)
encubrimiento (135) (auch für Verbergung: vgl. ib.); (1o1) ocultación (46)
(Verbergung:) disimulación (46); (1o5) encubrimiento (15o); (1o6) ocultamiento (34); (1o7) ocultamiento (186); (1o8) ocultación (28); (1o9) vela-
miento (268, 341) ocultamiento (27o) (auch für Verbergung: vgl. ib.); (11o)
ocultación (84, 87, 95) (auch für Verbergung: vgl. 87); (111) envoltura (41)
ocultación (42, 48) (auch für Verbergung: vgl. 48); (112) (Unverborgenheit:)
no ocultamiento (12o); (113) lo latente (228); (117) cobertura (6o); (118)
ocultación (92) desnudez (sic!) (92).

VERENDLICHUNG  (1) verenden perish; (2) way-of-being-finite; <u>chin.:</u> --;
<u>franz.:</u> (16) verenden: le fait "d'être acheré"; <u>ital.:</u> (27) 38, 1o  ciò
che c'è di finito 97, 5; (28) 38 la tendenzaa limitare 28; <u>jap.:</u> (82) 有限化
Yūgenka; <u>span.:</u> (89) (Verenden:)  "finalizar" (276); (89) (enden, verenden:)
finar, finalizar; (93) limitación (145); (94) finitud (1o8) (auch für Endlichkeit, vgl. ib.); (113) (verenden:) perecer (64); (115) (verenden:) perecer (16); (116) (verenden:) acabar (15o).

VERFALLEN  (1) fall, deteriorate; <u>chin.:</u> (7) 沆沦 21 (9); (8) 21 (1o5); (8)
陷于 46 (132); (7) 沆溺于 21 (9); <u>franz.:</u> (12) succomber, déchoir; (13) Verfall: pente; (17) le déclin (D.3) la chute (I) Verfall: la pente; <u>ital.:</u>
(24) 21 cadere 79, deietto, abbandonato, par.38 Deiezione; (26) 212, 32
deietto, deiezione 3o8, 2o, 21; (33) 78 (deiezione) 97; (35) 38 perire 23;
(36) deietto, deiezione (J); (43) 57 andare in ruvina 61, 1o9 cadere 97;
<u>jap.:</u> (61), (73), (79), (85) 頹落する tairakusuru; (78) 転落する tenraku-suru;
<u>span.:</u> (89) caer (2o7, 473) (Adj.:) caido (2o3); (89) caer en; (9o) (Ver-
fallen:) "caida" 196; (1o7) caer en (229); (1o8) caer en (64); (113) (ver-
fallend:) decadente (4o); (114) (als Verb:) caer en (86).

VERFALLENHEIT (2) fallen-ness; <u>chin.:</u> (7) 沉沦 175 (42); (7)沉沦状态 177 (44); <u>franz.:</u> (12) Verfallen: la déchéance; (16) Verfallen: déchéance, dé-gradation; <u>ital.:</u> (24) 175 stato di deiezione 279, 16, 33; (35) 2o6 deca-denza 2o4; (43) 64 decadimento 66, 65 (deiettità) disfacimento 67, 74 ro-vina 74, 112 caduta 99; <u>jap.:</u> (61), (73) 頽 落 Tairaku; (75) 退落性 Taira-kusei; 転 落 Tenraku; (78) (ーしていること ) (-shiteirukoto); (79), (85) 頽落性 Tairakusei; <u>span.:</u> (89) "estado de caido" (2o2ff., 221) caida (364); (89) "estado de caido"; (1o2) (Verfall:) depravación (169); (1o3) (Verfall:) caidas (23); (1o4) (Verfall:) caida (133); (1o7) ("Verfallen":) "decadencia" (187); (1o8) ("Verfallen":) el "decaer" (29); (1o9) (Verfall:) decadencia (261); (11o) (Verfall:) ruina (71); (111) (Verfall:) lo caduco (33); (113) (Verfall:) decadencia (178).

VERNEHMEN (1) perceive, be aware; (2) (no-in) accept, receive, contain, bring to containment, concentrate; (5) apprehension, perception; <u>chin.:</u> (7) 听取 21 (9); (8) 1o (93); (7)知觉 25 (15); (8)了解 13 (96); <u>franz.:</u> (12) V-: l'apprêhension; (15) apprêhender; (21) l'entente; (23) le percevoir; <u>ital.:</u> (24) apprensione, 147, 5 visione 242, 4, 25, 39 percezione 83, 35; (25) 41 apprensione 664; (27) 37 (un... lich) percepire 95; (28) 37 (un-) avvertire, percepire 27; (29) 55, 68; (31) 35 percepire 57; (32) 2o appre-(he)ndere 1o5; (33) 65 apprensione 88, 77 percepire 96; (34) percepire, appre(he)ndere, 14 penetrare 11, 295 conoscere 296; (35) percepere, appren-dere 2o7 intendere 141, 148 trovare 98; (36) 27, 27, 47, 36 apprendere, apprendimento 73, 9, 1o1, 2o u.pass.; (37) (rappresentazione essenziale 2o); (38) 6, -8 sentire distintamente 7; (42) 18, 6 intendere I 12, 6; (43) (-bar) 137 percepire 114, 228 riuscire a cogliere 179; (44) 288 percepire 394; (45) 62 intendere 63; <u>jap.:</u> (57), (67) 知覚する chikakusuru; (54), (87) 会得する etokusuru; (47), (61)覚知する kakuchisuru; (71)覚取する kakushusuru; (55)観取する kanshusuru; (62), (85) 聴き取る kikitoru; (75)聞きとる kikitoru; (81), (78)認知する ninchisuru; (85)認取する ninshusuru; (47) さとる, satoru; (66)認 知 Ninchi; (77) 理 解 Rikai; <u>span.:</u> (89) percibir (39, 198, 257) por via de simple aprehensión (244); (9o) (Vernehmen:) percepción (148); (91) (Vernehmen:) percepción (115); (92) (Vernehmen:) el percibir (46); (1oo) (Vernehmen:) precepción (115); (1o1) (Vernehmen:) el percibir (Ver-nehmen) (46); (1o5) (Vernehmen:) un aprehender (151); (1o6) (Vernehmen:) el percibir (34); (1o7) escuchar (17o) entender (195) (Vernehmen:) cap-tación (174) intelección (186); (1o8) experimentar (15) tomar de (35) (Ver-nehmen:) aprehensión (18) el percibir (28); (1o9) percibir (1o, 15, 34o)

(vernehmender:) más captador (1o); (11o) percibir (49, 57, 94) (vernehmender:) más percipiente (48); (111) percibir (18, 48) advertir (24) (ver-
nahmender:) más perceptivo (18); (113) percibir (63f., 193f., 198) percatarse
de (134) recibir (135); (114) percibir (68) captar (182f., 188) (164:
falsch übers.) (das Vernehmen:) captación (19o); (117) inteligir (41) "inteligir" (6o) (Protagoras-Zitat); (118) percibir (8o) "percibir" (92)
(Protagoras-Zitat).

VERWEILEN (1) tarry; (2) while (verb); (3) abide, endure; <u>chin.</u>: (7) 滯留
12o (29); <u>franz.</u>: (12) la demeure; (16) s'arrêter; <u>ital.</u>: (24) 12o, 14
sovvermarsi 2o7, 13; (25) 18 mantenersi 639; (29) 141; (34) 54 soggiornare
51, (319, 31-323, 2); (35) 52 sostare 33, 172 trattenere 115, 176 far permanere 118, 2o4 permanere 138, 247 sostare con attenzione 169, trattenersi,
soffermarsi, soggiornare; (36) 144, 18; (38) 8 soggiornare; (41) 16 sostare I 88, 11, 66 muoversi II 3o; (43) 22 trattenere 35, 29 fermare 4o,
242 dimorare 189, 253 rimanere 198; (44) 155 sostare 259; <u>jap.</u>: (85)
立ち留まっている tachitodomatteiru; (61) 立ちどまっている tachidomatteiru; (48)
ただよう tadayou; (48), (73) 滯留する tairyūsuru; (54), (81) 滯在する taizai-
suru; (78) 留まる todomaru; (83) 逗留する tōryūsuru; <u>span.</u>: (89) demorarse
(72) permanecer (398); (89) (verweilen, Verweilen, verweilend:) demorarse,
demora, morosidad, moroso; (91) estar demorándose (73); (92) perdurar (22);
(1oo) estar demorándose (73); (1o1) perdurar (22); (1o5) "posarse" (154)
(Hölderlin-Zitat); (1o6) "permanecer" (36) (Hölderlin-Zitat); (1o9) quedarse (346) (auch für Verweilen: vgl. ib.); (11o) demorarse (1o4) (auch
für Verweilen: vgl. ib.); (111) permanecer (54) (auch für Verweilen: vgl.
ib.); (112) (Verweilen:) presencia en el instante (118) permanencia (12o);
(113) permanecer (227) (das Verweilen:) morada (182); (115) fincar (11)
afincar (11, 15); (116) perdurar (145, 149); (117) permanecer (59) "quedar" (5o) (Hölderlin-Zitat); (118) permanecer (91) "quedarse" (84) (Hölderlin-Zitat).

VERWIRKLICHEN (1) actualize; <u>chin.</u>: (7) 實現 261 (64); <u>franz.</u>: (11) Verwirklichung: l'accomplissement; (13) Verwirklichung: réalisation; (16) ré-
aliser; (19) Verwirklichung: réalisation; <u>ital.</u>: (24) 261, 3o ralizzare
392, 11; (29) 31, 2o realizzare, essere realizzato 5, 15; (32) 11 realizzare 95; (33) 63 realizzare 83; (34) (sich) 246 realizzarsi 245; (35) 91
realizzare 59; (44) (-ung) 289 realizzare 395; <u>jap.</u>: (81) 現實化する

genjitsukasuru; (71), (75), (85)実現する jitsugensuru; span.: (89) (sich
verwirklichen:) realizarse (3oo, 498); (89) (Wirklichkeit:) realidad; (9o)
(sich verwirklichen:) realizarse (192); (1o2) realizar (164); (1o3) realizar (17) realizarse en (18); (1o4) realizar (127f.); (114) (sich verwirklichen:)  realizarse (55) (Verwirklichung:) realización (1o4f.).

VOLLENDUNG  (1) vollenden fulfill, complete; (2) consummation; chin.: (8)
完成 25 (11o); (1o) 268 (378); franz.: (11) achèrement; (15) accomplissement, achèrement; (19) achèrement; (2o) accomplissement; ital.: (27) 24
(-en) conclusione 51; (28) 24 (-en) termine 3, 43, 7N (...) 45, 15, 51N
compimento 57, 11E fine 7o; (29) (en) 137; (31) 5o compimento 7o; (32) 33
conclusione 115; (33) 85 rendere definitiva 1o4, 97 conpimento 115; (34)
121 conpimento 119, 187 fine 185; (35) 72 conpimento 46, 12o conclusione
78; (36) 23, 28 conpimento 67, 24; (37) 42 conpimento, fine 145; (42) 66,
2 conpimento (ultimazione) II 231, 27; (43) 16 realizzarsi 3o, 57 conpimento 6o; (44) 133 conpimento 237; jap.: (7o), (77)完 結 Kanketsu; (51)
完 了 Kanryō; (68), (69), (78), (79), (81) 完 成 Kansei; (52)終 結 Shu-
ketsu; span.: (89) el ilegar a la plenitud (28of., 287ff.); (89) ((Un)Voll-
endung:) (no)ilegar a la plenitud; (95) consumación (21o); (96) "consumación" (82) (Sophokles-Zitat); (1oo) plenitud (133) consumación (15o, 156)
remate (156); (1o1) perfección (45) culminación (54, 56) acabamiento (56);
(1o7) perfección (195); (1o8) plenitud (35); (113) consumación (55) acabamiento (57); (114) haber ilenado (el cometido) (16o) (paraphrasistisch)
(das Vollendete:) lo perfecto (78); (117) perfeccionamiento (34) perfección
(53) plenitud (68); (118) carácter decisivo (76) consumarse (87) consumación (87, 98); (119) pleno acabamiento (53f.); (12o) consumación (Vollendung) (56); (121) acabamiento (Vollendung) (66).

VORGÄNGIG  (1) previous, preliminary, prior, beforehand, first; (2) ante-
cedent; chin.: (7) 先行 2o (9) 123 (32); (7) 事先 119 (27); (9) 35 (352);
(9) 事前 36 (354); (7) 首 14 (7); franz.: (12) préalable (ment), apriori-
quement; ital.: (24) 2o, 35 preliminarmente 77, 19, 24, 5 preliminare 81,
23; (25) 14 presupposto, preliminare 634, 23 dall'inizio 644; (26) 177
preliminare 256; (27) 34 precedente 89, 36 in conseguenza di 94, 4; (28)
34 precedente 23 36 precedente 25; (34) 222 precedente 221; (35) (preceden-
temente); jap.: (81)先立つ sakidatsu; (73) (79), (81), (85) 先行的 senkōteki;
span.: (89) previamente (97, pas.) desde un principio (143) en principio

(1o9) desde luego (159) provisionalmente (24) por adelantado (153) desde el primer momento (126) (als Adjektiv:) previo (6f., pas.); (9o) previamente (81, 1o4) de antemano (81) (als Adjektiv:) previo (18, 7o, 96); (91) previamente (135) que precede a (65) de antemano (84) (als Adjektiv:) previo (85, 11o) preliminar (66, 127) (als Superlativ:) primero de todos (13o); (92) previamente (18, 28, 55) (als Adjektiv:) previo (18, 28, 43, 52) (als Superlativ:) que antecede a todo otro (53); (93) previamente (143) (Adverbialisierung des Adjektivs:) previamente (141); (94) (Adjektivierung:) previo (1o5) (Adverbialisierung eines Adjektivs:) previamente (1o2); (1o7) (vorläufig:) provisorio (232); (1o8) (vorläufig:) provisorio (66); (114) (als Adjektiv:) previo (1o1, 148) (das Vorgängige:) lo que precede (147).

VORGESTELLTHEIT (2) presented-ness; chin.: (1o) 被意象到的 266 (376); franz.: (19) l'être-représenté; (21) représentéité; ital.: (3o) 11 appresentazione 2o, 11 posizione 21; (34) 1o2, 9, 11, 13 esserrappresentato 96, 32, 34, 36; jap.: (7o), (81)被表象性 Hihyoshosei; (58), (83)表象されてあること Hyoshosaretearukoto; (81) 前に立てられていること Maenitaterareteirukoto; (83) 前立されてあること Zenritsusaretearukoto; span.: (89) (Vorstellen:) el representarse (179, 25o, 368); (117) el estar representado (39f.) representamiento (43) lo que está representado (64) representación (66); (118) condición de representado (79, 81) lo representado (95f.).

VORGRIFF, VOR-GRIFF (1) fore-conception, something we grasp in advance; (4) enticipation, reaching before; chin.: --; franz.: (12) anticipation; ital.: (24) 15o, 28 pre-cognizione 247, 2; (25) (-end) 17 anticipazione 637, 37 precomprensione 659; (28) (-end) 48N anticipazione 51; (34) 29 preconcetti 25; jap.: (78)予め捉えられること Arakajime toraerarerukoto; (85) 先 掣 Sen aku; (71)先把掘 Senhaaku; (61), (85)先 收 Sensyu; (73), (78), (79)予 掴 Yoaku; span.: (89) (Vorgriff:) el "concebir previo" (174f., 266); (89) concebir previo; (9o) (vorgreifen:) concebir previamente (7o); (96) (vorgreifend:) anticipadamente (79); (1o9) (Vorgriff:) marco previo (259) (Vorgriffe:) anticipación conceptual (15); (11o) (Vorgriff:) preconcepto (68) (Vorgriffe:) prejuicios (56); (111) (Vorgriff:) anticipación (31) (Vorgriffe:) los anticipos (23); (114) (Vorgriff:) antelación (192) preaprehensión (198, 211) (Vor-griff:) pre-aprehensión (211) presencia fáctica (196).

VORHANDENSEIN (1) being present-at-hand; (2) being a (mere) entity; (4) being-present-at-hand; (5) being something at hand; (6) being at hand; chin.: (7) 现成的在 121 (31); (9) 现成存在 29 (347); (7) 现成状态 128 (39); (7) 现成的事 179 (46); franz.: (12) subsistance,être subsistant; (15) existence, présence, subsistance; (16) chose donnée, chose qui subsiste, chose in-sistante; ital.: (24) essere semplicemente presente, (-heit) semplice-presenza 128, 13 essere presente, 217, 21; (25) 13 esser semplicemente-presente 633, 21 semplice presencoza intramondana 642; (26) 7o essere già presente 95, 24, 171 semplice presenza 248; (27) 29 realtà dell'aggetto 75, 31 realtà di fatto 81; (28) 29 aver sotto mano 13; (29) 38, 13 ciò che è già esistente 12, 22, 38, 32 quanto c'è 13, 8; (3o) 15 presenza 32; (31) (vorhanden) 37 esistente 59; (34) 9 trovarsi nella semplice presenza 5; (35) 23 (essere disponibile) 11, 236 (essere presente) 161, 172 (semplice-presenza) 115; (44) 143, 35 trovarsi 248, 8; jap.: (85) 直前に有ること Chokuzenniarukoto; (71) 直前者 Chokuzensha; (73) 事物的存在 Jibutsuteki sonzai; (61) 客体性 Kyakutaisei; (78) 目の前にあること Menomae ni arukoto; (63) 目の前に既にあるもの Me-no-mae-ni-sudeni-Arumono; (79) 前在存在 Zenzaisonzai; span.: (89) "ser ante los ojos" (5o, 183) (auch für Vorhandenheit, z.B. 234, 112); (89) (Vorhandensein, Vorhandenheit:) "ser ante los pjos"; (9o) "ser-ante-jos-ojos" (66) ser ante los ojos (122); (91) (das Vorhandene:) lo que está de cuerto presente (63, 79f., vgl. 66) entes que 'hay de presente' (118); (92) (das Vorhandene:) lo presente-fác-tico (Vorhandenes) (17) lo presente fáctico (26, 47) lo fácticamente presente (25, 31, vgl.18); (93) el "estar presente" (134); (94) estar ahî (93); (98) presencia fáctica (71); (99) ente simplemente dado (Vorhandensein) (13); (1o2) (das Vorhandene:) lo que existe (172) lo preexistente (172); (1o3) (das Vorhandene:) lo presente (28) lo que está simplemente ahî, a la mano (29); (1o4) (das Vorhandene:) lo existente (136, 138); (1o9) (das Vorhandene:) lo existente-presente (35o) el (") existente (-) presente (") (35o, 353); (11o) (das Vorhandene:) lo existente (11o, 115) el existente (11o); (111) (das Vorhandene:) lo presente (58) lo existente (61); (113) (vorhanden:) existente (52) (vorhanden sein:) existir (163); (114) (vorhanden sein:) existir (9o, 94); (115) (Vorhandenes:) lo-que-está-ante-los-ojos (11); (116) (Vorhandenes:) algo ante uno (145).

VORSICHT, VOR-SICHT (1) fore-sight, something we see in advance; chin.: (8) 小心 22 (1o6); franz.: (12) vue préalable, pré-voyance; (21) présaisi,

anticipation; <u>ital.</u>: (24) 15o, 19 pre-visione 236, 12; (34) 161 prudenza
159; (36) 16, 28 timore 59, 3; <u>jap.</u>: (78) 予め眺められること Arakajime-nagame-
rarerukoto; (51), (85) 先 見 Senken; (51), (61), (81), (85) 先 視 Senshi;
(73), (78), (79) 予 視 Yoshi; <u>span.</u>: (89) "ver previo" (174f., 266f) (Vor-
sicht:) "ver previo" (266f.) v. p. que se fija en, se dirige a (266, 364);
(89) (Vorsicht:) ver previo.

VORSTELLEN (1) represent, lay before, put before; (2) pro-pose, (render)
present; (3) to re-present; (4) -ung conception, representation; (5) repre-
sentational thought; (6) represent; <u>chin.</u>: (8) 摆出来 12 (95); (8) 设想 28
(113); (1o) 265 (375); (9) 介绍 24 (343); <u>franz.</u>: (11) représentation; (12)
-ung: représentation; (15) pro-poser, re-présenter; (2o) représentation;
(21) représenter, proposer; <u>ital.</u>: (24) 139, 1o conoscere 231, 32, 368
rappresentare 531, 3; (25) (-ung) 9 rappresentazione 629; (26) 166 attività
-appresentativa 241; (27) 24, 6 presentare 51, 8-9, 31, 2o porre in presenza di 81, 1o-11; (28) 24 presentare 3, 31 porre innanzi 17, 8-9E posizione
66, 3, 11, 1o, -5 pensare 68, -2, 11E rappresentare 69 u.ff.; (29) 65, 13;
(3o) 11, 4, 5 porre innanzi 21, 2, 11, 13 "presentare innanzi" 21, 16, 15,
1o appresentare 31, 3, 27, 2 (rappresentazione) 58, -3; (31) 26 rappresentare,
-zione 49; (32) rappresentare 42 mettersi innanzi 127, 42 considerare 127,
19; (33) rappresentare 78 intendere 98, 91 attività intellettuale 1o9, -4;
(34) rappresentare 21 modo di vedere 17, 39 raffigurare 35, 12o cogliere
118, 127 immaginare 125; (35) rappresentare 2o concipire 9, 25o immaginare
17o 251 considerare 17; (36) rappresentare; (37) 14, 28, 3o, 32, 39 rappresentare 19, 81, 13o, (ung) 25 rappresentazione 126; (41) 43 rappresentare I
13 u.passim; (42) rappresentare, concepire, conoscere, pensare rappresenta-
tivo; (43) 11 fare presente 27, 14 dare presenza 29, 38 pensare presentativo
46, 43 capacità immaginativa 5o, 57 concepire 61, 77 identificarsi 76, 115
rappresentare 1o1, 126 raffigurarsi 1oo, 145 pro-porre 118, 242 oggettivare
19o; (44) 154 concepire 258, 141 rappresentare 245; (45) rappresentare;
<u>jap.</u>: (47), (52), (54), (58), (63), (67), (69), (71), (72), (78), (79),
(81), (86), (87), (88) 表象する hyoshosuru; (47), (63) 前に置く maenioku; (62)
目前に立てる mokuzennitateru; (83) 前立する zenritsusuru; <u>span.</u>: (89) representarse (25o, 367); (9o) representar (59, 98) representarse (85); (91) representar (93) presentar (95); (92) representar (33) presentar (34); (93)
(sich vorstellen:) presentarse (128); (94) (sich vorstellen:) ponerse de

manifiesto (85); (95) representar (2o7, 21o, 214) representarse (2o8f.);
(96) representar (77); (98) representar (64f., 68ff.); (99) representar (8)
explicitar (8) presentar (11f.); (1oo) (Vorstellen:) representación (149f.,
157); (1o1) (Vorstellen:) el representar (53f.) pensamiento (57); (1o5)
(vorstellen:) imaginar (145) presentar (148) concebir (149) representarse
(151); (1o6) (vorstellen:) concebir (29, 32f.); (1o7) (vorstellen:) representar (objetivante) (18o) representarse (188, 19o) representar (2oo); (1o8)
(vorstellen:) representar (23, 27, 29, 4o) representarse (31); (1o9) (vorstellen:) representarse (13) representar (13, 268, 348); (11o) (vorstellen:)
representar (54, 82, 1o7) (unübersetzt: 54); (111) (vorstellen:) representarse (22) presentar (22) representar (4o, 56); (113) (vorstellen:) presentar
(44, 117, 143, 158) representar (61, 63, 159, 163) (auch representarse, representar: vgl. 96); (114) representar (19, 122, 124, 138f., 143f.) representarse (44, 86, 123) presentar (56); (115) (vorstellen:) representar (5,
6, 8) (Vgl. Anm. S.22f. =anteponer); (116) (vorstellen:) representarse (138,
142) representar (139); (117) (vorstellen:) representar (26, 28, 43, 61);
(118) (vorstellen:) representar (72f., 81, 92); (119) (vorstellen:) representar (24, 38f., 41); (12o) (vorstellen:) representar (39) representarse
(18, 36, 42, 53) (auch für sich vorstellen: vgl. 42); (121) (vorstellen:)
presentar (57) conceptuar (59) representarse (57, 64).

VOR-STELLEN  (1) -ung representation, ideation; (2) -d present-ative -ung
(re)presentation; (4) pre-senting, representing -d pre-senting; chin.: (1o)
意象 265 (375); franz.: --; ital.: (26) 173 pro-porre 251; (3o) 11, 3, 6
"presentare innanzi", "appresentare" 2o, -2, -o, 21, 5, 11, 6 porre 21, 4,
11, -o appresentazione 23, 2, 23,17 appresentare 5o, 1o-11; (34) 84, 14
porre-innanzi 92, 1; (35) 113 rap-presentare 73; (36) porre-dinnanzi (porre
innanzi; (37) (v. Denken) conoscere ogettivante 73; (42) (porre davanti al
soggetto); jap.: (83) 表 － 象 する hyō-shōsuru; (58), (7o), (81) 前に－立てる
maeni-tateru; (Vorstellen) (48), (59), (61), (62), (65), (68), (77) 表 象
Hyōshō; (66), (67) 表象作用 Hyōshōsayō; (62) 対象的に立たせること Taishōtekini-
tataserukoto; (Vor-stellen) (54) 表 － 象 Hyō-shō; span.: (9o) (vor-stellen)
re-presentar (73, 161); (98) re-presentar (vor-stellen) (67) re-presentar
(67f.); (99) pre-sentar (vor-stellen) (9) (auch für vorstellen: 1o); (114)
(vor-stellen) re-presentar (vor-stellen) (122f., 127, 166); (116) (vor-stellen:) re-presentar (155); (117) (vor-stellen:) (re)presentar (42) re-presentar (63) (sich vor-stellen:) re-presentarse (42); (118) (vor-stellen:)
re-presentar (8o, 94) (sich vor-stellen:) re-presentarse (8o); (119) (sich
vorstellen:) representarse (43) (auch für vorstellen: vgl. 51); (121) (sich

vorstellen:) representar (6o).

WAS-SEIN  (2) what being(s) is (are); chin.: (7)是什么 42 (17); franz.:
(12) quiddité; (22) l'essence; ital.: (24) 27, 3o L'essere-che cosa 86, 7,
42, 4 "essenza" 1o6, 13; (25) 7 "Che cos'è" 625, 48 esser-che-cosa 672, 3;
(26) 2o2 il "cos'è dell'ente" 292, 2o5, 1 ciò che l'ente è 297, 12, 2o5, 1o
l'essere quidditativo 297, 21; (31) 3o, 5 il "che cosa" (le quiddità) 52,
-4, 35, quiddità, quidditas 57; (35) 73 il che cosa dell'essere 47, 271 il
"che cosa" delle cose 185; (37) 15 (was -ist das) l'essere del "che cosa",
quiddità, essenza; (43) 2o1 il quid che costituisce ciò che è 158, 247
quidditas 194; jap.: (63), (68) 本質－存在 Honshitsu-sonzai; (66) 実体有
Jittai-u; (63), (73), (79)何であるか Nandearuka; (85) 何で－有るかということ
Nand--arukatoifukoto; (78)ナ二－であること Nani-dearukoto; (54), (81)何－存在
Nani-sonzai; span.: (89) el "qué es" (5o) (Was:) un "qué" (15) el "qué es"
(5o); (89) "qué es"; (9o) el qué es (186) (auch für Wassein) el "qué" (qué
es algo) (187); (91) el por qué es la cosa tal o cual (51) el "qué-es" (65,
13o, vgl. 66, 137) (auch für Wassein, 97) 'qué es ser' (129); (92) el qué-
es (11) quididad (17f., +(Was-sein)(53)) quiddidad (53, 56) (Wassein:) el
ser-qué (35); (93) (Wasinhalt:) el contenido (13o); (94) (Wasinhalt:) el
"qué de las cosas (87); (1oo) el qué-es (132) el "qué es" (138) el "qué-es"
(138); (1o1) el qué es o esencia (45, 48); (113) (was etwas ist:)lo que es
155, 166, 172, 197); (114) (Was:) un Quid (186) (Was-seiendes:) lo que es,
como quid (193); (119) (das Was:) el "qué" (27) (Washeit:) quididad (sic!)
(27); (12o) (das Was:) el qué (Was) (21) (Washeit:) la Washeit (lit.:
quidditas) (21); (121) (das Was:) el "qué" (5of.) (Washeit:) quidditas
(5of.).

WELTLICHKEIT  (1) worldhood; (2) Being of World; chin.: (7) 世界之为世界
63 (21); (7)世界性 65 (25); (7)成为世界 187 (51); franz.: (12) mondanéité;
ital.: (24) Par. 14, 63 mondità; (35) (Welt) 92 "mondo" 6o; jap.: (61),
(73), (78), (79), (85)世界性 Sekaisei; span.: (89) "mundanidad" (63) mundanidad (§ 14 u.passim); (89) mundanidad.

WELTVERTRAUTHEIT  (2) familiarity with World; chin.: --; franz.: (12)
familiarisation avec le monde; ital.: (24) 86, 33 intimità col mondo 164,
22; jap.: (79)世界昵懇性 Sekaijikkonsei; (85)世界に慣れ親しんでいること Se-

kaininareshitashindeirukoto;  (78) 世界の親近さ, Sekainoshinkinsa;  (73) 世界親密性 Sekaishinmitsusei;  (61) 世界との親しみ Sekaitonoshitashimi;  span.: (89) (Vertrautheit:) familiaridad.

WESEN, wesen  (1) essence -haft, -tlich essential Essenz Essence; (2) essence (noun and verb) presence (verb), (come-to-) -tlich foundational, essential; (5) essence, essential being, occur essentially, presence; (6) essence; chin.: (7) 本质 42 (17); (1o) 万物 27o (38o); (1o) 东西 27o (38o); (8) 成其本质 7 (9o); (1o) 264 (374); franz.: (12) essence; (13) déploiement, manière d'être, existence; (14) maintien; (15) essence, estance, ester; (18) l'essence; (19) le but; (21) le déploiement essentiel; (22) essence, être, merveille, mesure; ital.: (24) 12, 22 essenza 66, 2o; (25) 7 essenza 625, 36 (Fussnote): esistenza 658; (26) 28, 193 essenza 37, 281; (27) 27 essenza 67, 3o, 2... 77, 9; (28) Essenza, Essere, 3o, 2 esseri 15, 41 specie 4o, 17E, 34 senso 79, 13 44N valere 44, 45N comportari 46, 46N aver realtà 47, 8E allignare 65, 15E presentarsi 75, 17E costituire l'essenza 78, 23E comparire 86; (29) 31, 16 essenza 5, 12 u.ff. 137, 141, 99 (das Wesende); (3o) 5 Essenza 7, 16 realizzarsi 33; (31) 5 essenza 37, 35, 4 rendersi presente 57, 13-14; (32) Essenza, essere, 21 realizzarsi 105, 4o esser presente 124; (33) 56 essenza 78, u.passim, 57 portare all'essenza 78, 66, 69 essere 87, 89, 71 (das W.-nde) essenza propria dell'esistenza 91, 78, 81, 3 aprirsi nella propria essenza 98, 1o1, 8, 112 instaurarsi 128; (34) essenza, essere, natura 274 "esseri" 274, 3o9 significato essenziale 311, esser presente, essere, 264 sussitere 264, 41 dominare 39, 6o aver luogo 57; (35) essenza, essere, essere essenziale, modo di essere, 7o dispiegare il proprio essere 118; (36) essenza, 7, 25 sussistere, essere essente 45, 9-1o, essenzializzarsi, essere in senso essenziale, darsi 15, 1 (J), eventualizzarsi, 17, 29 (J); (37) essere, essenza, (porre in essere 3o); (38) 6 essere7; (39) essenza 37; (4o) essenza 21, 23; (41) Essenza, essere, (-nd) attuare, attuante (61, 1o -II 26, 7) in atto; (42) essenza, struttura, natura, essere, 23, 8-15, 6, 32, 15-21, 8, 3o, 1o-19, 29, 23, 2 essere presente I 15, 1; (43) essenza, essere, natura, 46 vero essere, figura, modo di essere 52, 48 realtà vera 54, 61 internità 64, 69 presenza 64, 1o8 realtà 97, 12 operare 28, 26 essere 36, raggiungere la propria vera essenza 46-52; (44) 131, 14 essere 235, 14, 133, 151 Wesen 237, 254, 135, 19 presenza 239, 21, 136 presentarsi 239; (45) essenza; jap.: (62) 本 性 Honsei (Honshō); (62) 成 存

Seizon; (47), (48), (5o), (56), (57), (59), (61), (63), (65), (66), (67), (68), (7o), (71), (72), (75), (78), (79), (81), (83), (86), (87) (88) 本 質 Honshitsu; (69), (7o), (72) 存在（する）Sonzai(-suru); (71) 存在者 Sonzaisha; (48), (54), (59), (81) 現成する genjōsuru; (83) 現留する genryūsuru; (86), (87), (88) 現成する genseisuru; (48), (7o) 現存する genzonsuru; (66) 現ずる genzuru; (83) 本質を現ずる honschitsuogenzuru; (76) 本当に存在する hontōni sonzaisuru; (57) 本質的にある honshitsutekiniaru; (76) 成在する seizaisuru; (62) 本性として存する Honshōtoshitesonsuru; (62) 成存する seizonsuru; span.: (89) (Wesen:) esencia (passim); (89) esencia; (9o) (Wesen:) esencia (1o u.passim); (91) (Wesen:) esencia (54f., 18o u.passim); (92) (Wesen:) esencia (13, 47 u.passim); (93) (Wesen:) esencia (132f., 135, 141f., 149); (94) (Wesen:) esencia (9of., 1o1ff., 113) (Mehrzahl:) seres (94); (95) (Wesen:) esencia (21o u.passim) (wesen:) ser esencialmente (2o8, 213ff., 219); (96) (Wesen:) esencia (74, 76 u.passim) (wesen:) presentarse (wesen) (75) estar presente (wesen) (77); (97) (Wesen:) esencia (8, 15 u.passim); (98) (Wesen:) esencia (61, 81 u.passim) (wesen:) cobrar presencia (wesen) (72f., 82) esenciar (7o) hacer presente (76); (99) (Wesen:) esencia (11, 21 u.passim) (wesen:) producirse (14) estar presente (14) existir (16) esencia originante (21); (1oo) (Wesen:) esencia (113, 138 u.passim); (1o1) (Wesen:) esencia (35, 48 u.passim); (1o2) (Wesen:) esencia (164f.u.passim); (1o3) (Wesen:) esencia (17f. u.passim) Esencia (29); (1o4) (Wesen:) esencia (127 u.passim); (1o5) (Wesen:) (e)sencia (146f., 15o-154) esencia (149, 153) (Vgl. Anm. S.157) (wesen:) (e)senciar (15o) (e)senciar (verbo) (153); (1o6) (Wesen:) esencia (29, 32-36) (wesen:) desplegar su esencia (wesen) (33); (1o7) (Wesen:) esencia (161, 168 u.passim) (wesen:) ser esencialmente (165, 175, 177, 188, 212, 224, 226); (1o8) (Wesen:) esencia (7,13 u.passim) (wesen:) hacer ser (dejarse ser) (11) dejarse ser (19, 21, 29, 49, 59, 61); (1o9) (Wesen:) esencia (3, 266 u.passim) (wesen:) ser esencialmente (26o, 271 f., 339, 241, 344, 348, 351) esenciar (261, 265, esenciarse (263, 27o); (11o) (Wesen:) esencia (7, 8off. u.passim) (wesen:) existir (7o, 79, 86, 112) ser (72, 75, 88, 9o, 1oo, 1o7) estar (92, 96); (111) (Wesen:) esencia (11, 39f. u.pas.) (wesen:) tener como esencia (32) estar presente (33, 45f., 49) hacerse presente (35, 38, 52, 56) allarse (35) morar (42) presentarse (44); (113) (Wesen:) esencia (9, 56, 143, 149, 179, 2o5, 225) ser (143) ente (143, 169, 225) (wesen:) ser (17, 121, 143, 213) ilegar a tener esencia (186) realizar su esencia (197); (114) (Wesen:) esencia (77, 164) Esencia (26) "seres" (174) (Kant-Zitat) (wesen:) estar presente (wesen) (45); (115) (Wesen:)

esencia (4) (wesen:) ser-esencialmente (8f.); (116) (Wesen:) esencia (137)
(wesen:) esenciar (142, 145, 15o); (117) (Wesen:) esencia (16, 31, 34);
(118) (Wesen:) esencia (67, 76); (119) (Wesen:) propio ser (Wesen) (18, 2o,
32, 45, 56) esencia (22f., 29, 36, 39, 41, 52) ser (32); (12o) (Wesen:) ser
(Wesen) (11, 27) esencia (Wesen) (13, 17, 24, ?3, 36, 39, 45, 54, 59); (121)
(Wesen:) ser (46f., 49) esencia (49, 52, 54, 56f., 59, 61, 65).

DAS WOHIN   (1) the 'whither'; <u>chin.</u>: --; <u>franz.</u>: (12) endroit, adhésion;
(14) le "vers-où"; (19) le but; <u>ital.</u>: (24) 135, 9 "Il dove" 226, 28, 28o,
29 II verso dove 417, 11; (28) 16 la direzione 76; (34) 32o, 33 verso che?
324; (35) 1o8 Il "verso dove", "verso dove" 7o; (37) (wohin) 24 verso cui
122; (43) 5o Il verso dove 55, 99 Il dove 92; (44) 135 Il Dove 239, 271 Il
verso dove 378, 282 Il verso cui? 388, 283-389; (45) 4 ciò a cui 5; <u>jap.</u>:
(78) どこへ Dokoe; (73)どこへと帰属するのか Doko e to kizokusurunoka; (85)
何処へということ Doko he to ihukoto; (61) 帰 趨 Kisuu; (79) 帰属先 Kizokusaki;
<u>span.</u>: (89) el "adónde" (156f., 424) el "adonde" (119, 126ff.) el lugar
adonde (322); (91) (woraufhin:) lo que (65); (92) (woraufhin:) sobre lo que
(18); (95) (wohin:) hacia dónde (214); (1o9) (wohin:) a qué (26o); (11o)
(wohin:) adónde (7o); (111) (wohin:) de dónde (sic!) (32); (112) dirección
(117); (113) a dónde (2o1); (114) (wohin (?):) dónde (4o) dentro de qué
(66); (115) (wohin:) sitio a que (3); (116) (wohin:) a donde (136); (119)
(wohin:) aquello hacia lo cual (que) (43f.); (12o) (wohin:) aquello hacia
lo cual (donde) (41f.); (121) (wohin:) aquello hacia lo que (donde) (6o).

WOHNEN   (1) reside, accustom; (2) dwell(ing); <u>chin.</u>: (8) 居住43 (129);
<u>franz.</u>: habiter; <u>ital.</u>: (27) 41, 25 risiedere 1o2, 15; (28) 41 abitare 33,
47N stare 49; (29) abitare; (32) 26 abitare 1o8u.ff.; (33) 66 abitare 87,
u.passim; (34) abitare; (35) abitare; (41) 17 abitare, dimorare I 9; (43)
38 dimorare 46, 77 abitare 76; (45) 58, 23 risiedere 59, 23; <u>jap.</u>: (66)
居 住 kyojū; (59), (67), (76), (88) 住まう sumau; (48), (57), (59), (67),
(79), (81), (85) 住 む sumu; <u>span.</u>: (89) "habitar" (64f.) (auch für Wohnen,
217); (93) habitar (149); (94) habitar (113); (96) habitar "morar" (82)
(Hölderlin-Zitat); (1o2) "morar" (163, 173f., 179) "habitar" (166) (Hölderlin-Zitate); (1o3) "hacer su morada" (15, 3o, 36) "morar" (2o, 3o) (Hölderlin-Zitate); (1o4) "habitar" (126, 139, 146) "vivir" (129) (Hölderlin-Zitate); (1o5) "habitar" (145u.passim) (Hölderlin-Zitate) habitar (145f.u.
passim); (1o6) "habitar" (29u.passim) (Hölderlin-Zitate) habitar (29u.passim);

(1o7) habitar (161, 175, 2o1, 223: Zitat) morar (218); (1o8) morar (19, 4o, 54, 59) habitar (59: Hölderlin-Zitat) (Vgl. Anm.3); (1o9) "habitar" (355) (Hölderlin-Zitat); (11o) "morar" (119) (Hölderlin-Zitat); (111) "estar" (64) (Hölderlin-Zitat); (112) existir (116) (Wohnen:) el habitar (116); (113) habitar (129, 142, 145, 226); (119) "habitar" (57) (Hölderlin-Zitat); (12o) "habitar" (Hölderlin-Zitat); (121) "vivir" (Hölderlin-Zitat).

ZEIGEN (1) show, indicate Zeiger pointer; (2) show-forth -de sign; chin.: (7) 表現出来 26 (15); (7) 表示 261 (65); (9) 显示出 33 (351); (8) 出现 45 (132); (7)指出 42 (17); franz.: (12) signaliser, montrer; (13) montrer; ital.: (24) 313, 2o manifestare 328, 12, 22o, 21 mettere a nudo 336, 3o; (25) 11 mostrare 631, 16 far vedere 636, 42 dimostrare 665, (sich) 25 presentarsi 644, 24 farsi luce 644; (28) 17E far vedere 78; (29) indicare; (3o) 25 indicare 56; (31) 21 (sich) mostrare 45; (32) 28 mostrare 11o u.passim; (33) 94 mostrare 112 u.ff.; (34) mostrare, rivelare, manifestare, 27, 12 constatare 23, 21; (35) mostrare, manifestare, indicare; (36) 6, 6 segnalare 43, 11, 6, 8 indicare 43, 13; (37) (indicare 94, manifestare, significare 149); (39) (sich) manifestarsi 377; (4o) apparire 2; (43) 49 indicare 54, 168 mostrare 134; (44) 14o mostrare 245; (45) 6 indicare 7, 12 mostrare 13, 46 presentare 47; jap.: (61), (79) 表示する hyojisuru; (48), (67) 指示する shijisuru; (78) ( 指し )示す (sashi)shimesu; (71), (72), (85) 示 す shimesu; (das Zeigende) (48) 指示者 Shijisha; span.: (89) mostrar (253) señalar (91, 95) (sich zeigen:) mostrarse (34f.u.passim); (89) ((sich) zeigen:) 1. mostrar(se) 2. señalar; (9o) mostrar (7o, 84) demostrar (92, 124) (sich zeigen:) mostrarse (33, 83) manifestarse (43, 124); (91) mostrar (69, 124) (sich zeigen:) quedar al descubierto (7o) mostrarse (122); (92) mostrar (2o, 5o) (sich zeigen:) mostrarse (21, 49); (93) señalar (147) (als zeigte sich:) de tal modo que se revele (14o); (94) mostrar (11o) (als zeigte sich:) como si estuviese (1oo); (95) (sich zeigen:) mostrarse (217); (1oo) mostrar (148) poner de manifiesto (128) (sich zeigen:) dar muestras (144) "mostrar" (116) (Platon-Zitat); (1o1) mostrar (43, 53) exhibir (54) (sich zeigen:) mostrarse (51) "mostrar" (37) (Platon-Zitat); (1o2) mostrar (164); (1o3) mostrar (17); (1o4) mostrar (127); (1o5) (sich zeigen:) mostrarse (15o); (1o6) (sich zeigen:) mostrarse (34); (1o7) mostrar (2o5) presentar (2o6); (1o8) mostrar (43, 45); (1o9) mostrar (271) (sich zeigen:) mostrarse (268); (11o) mostrar (89) (sich zeigen:) mostrarse (84); (111) mostrar (44) (sich zeigen:) mostrarse (41); (112) mostrar (119) (sich zeigen:) mostrarse (115); (113) señalar (15, 23, 48, 143f.) manifestar (213); (114) mostrar (2o, 36,

127 u.passim) señalar (3o) indicar (67) (sich zeigen:) mostrarse (6o, 76, 84 f.); (115) indicar (6) (sich zeigen:) mostrarse (4); (116) mostrar (139) (sich zeigen:) mostrarse (137); (117) ("sich zeigen") "presentarse" (58) (Platon-Zitat); (118) ("sich zeigen":) "mostrarse" (91) (Platon-Zitat); (119) indicar (35); (12o) señalar hacia (31); (121) apuntar a (55).

ZEUG (1) equipment, item of equipment -ganze, -ganzheit equipmental totality, totality of equipment; (2) instrument -haftigkeit instrumentalness; chin.: (9)见证 37 (354); (7) 工具 117 (26); (7) 东西 261 (64); (7) 家伙 118 (27); franz.: (12) outil; ital.: (24) 118, 12 mezzo 2o4, 23; (25) 36 mezzo 657; (31) 7 cose 38; (34) 18 mezzo 14; (35) 14 mezzo 5; (42) 3o, 13 materiale I 19, 34; jap.: (57), (61), (73), (78), (79), (81), (85) 道 具 Dōgu; span.: (89) el útil (§§ 15-18) el "útil" (8o); (89) (Zeug, Zeughaftigkeit:) útil, "ser útil"; (91) instrumento (176); (92) el útil (4o) utensilio (4o); (1o2) (Werkzeug:) instrumento (169); (1o3) (Werkzeug:) instrumento (23); (1o4) (Werkzeug:) instrumento (133); (1o9) instrumento (12 ff., 263, 344) utensilio (341); (11o) el útil (53, 55, 58 f.,75, 95, 1o1); (111) instrumento (21 f., 24 f., 35, 48, 52); (114) útiles (27) utensilio (27).

ZU-FALL (1) be-fall; (4) to occur in addition; chin.: --; franz.: (S.u.Z. §6o, s.3oo. Keine Übersetzung); ital.: (25) (Zufall) 24 caso 645; (27) (Zu-fall) 26, 26 caso 66, 2; (28) (Zufall) 26 caso 8; (45) (-ig) 18 accidentale 19 (Ad-cadimento); jap.: (59), (73), (78), (85) 偶 然 Gūzen; (79) 偶然事 Gūzenji; (85) 降りかかる Furikakaru; span.: (89) (Zu-fälle:) a-caecimientos (471) (Zufall:) el acaso (191 f.) (Zufälle:) accidentes (345); (89) (zufallen:) acaecer (Zufall:) accidente (Fall:) caso; (93) (Zufall:) casu alidad (131); (94) (Zufall:) azar (89); (113) (zu-fallen:) ad-venir (61); (114) (zu-fallen:) acontecer (2o4).

ZUHANDEN (1) ready-to-hand -heit readiness-to-hand; (2) -es instrument (being ready-at-hand) -heit instrumentality;chin.: 在手边 117 (26); (7) 在手头 186 (5o); franz.: (12) disponible, l'étant disponible; (16) Z-: l'ustensile, l'instrumente, l'objet d'usage; ital.: (24) 118, 12 utilizzabi-le 2o4, 23; (27) maneggiabile (J) 11; (37) utilizzabile 74; jap.: (73) 道具的 dōguteki; (71), (85) 手許に temotoni; (78) 手もとにある temotoni aru; (61) 用具的 yōguteki; (79) 用在する yōzaisuru; span.: (89) "a la mano" (81 f., 85, 123, 147); (89) "a la mano" (Zuhandensein, Zuhandenheit:) "ser a la mano";

ZUSPRUCH (2) address, intimation, appeal; chin.: --; franz.: (11) appel;
(13) la parole adressée; (18) l'appel; ital.: (29) 115, -o; (34) 341 parola
rivolta 345; (35) appello, parola, 129-3o il rivolgere la parola 85, 89
parola rivolta 127; (37) 34-7, 43, 46 appello 136-7, 14o, 148; (38) 8, -8,
1o, 7 voc 9, 27, 11, 8, -8 15, 1o, o, 12, 5 allocuzione 9, 18, 11, 13, 5;
(42) 34, 3 allocuzione I 22, 8, 33, 3 parola I 21, 21; (43) 7o invito 71,
79 comando 78, 11o volgersia noi della parola 98, 122 parola 1o5, 175 la
parola solletatrice 138, 257 parteciparsi a... 2o2; jap.: (48) 話しかけ
Hanashikake; (52) 言いかけ Iikake; (69) 語り勧め Katari-susume; (51) 呼び掛け
Yobikake; (59)勧 告 Kankoku; (65) 要 請 Yōsei; span.: (1o5) re-clamación
(146) (Vgl. Anm. S.156); (1o6) requerimiento (Zuspruch) (32); (113) atri-
bución (2o) exhortación (2o9) (palabras de) un habla que se dirige a (169);
(119) asignación (45) ilamado (Zuspruch) (46 f., 49, 55, 58); (12o) ilama-
miento-asignación (Zuspruch) (44-47, 5o); (121) comunicación (61) ilamada
(61 ff., 67 f.).

## GLOSSARY REFERENCES

engl.:

(1) John Macquarrie & Edward Robinson; Being and Time (Sein und Zeit), 1962 New York: Harper & Row

(2) William J. Richardson (Author); Heidegger: Through Phenomenology to Thought, 1963 The Hague: Martinus Nijhoff

(3) John M. Anderson & E. Hans Freund; Discourse on Thinking (Gelassenheit), 1966 New York: Harper & Row

(4) W.B.Barton & Vera Deutsch; What is a Thing? (Die Frage nach dem Ding), 1967 Chicago: Regnery

(5) David Farrell Krell & Frank A. Capuzzi; Early Greek Thinking ("Der Spruch des Anaximander", Holzwege; "Logos", "Moira", & "Aletheia", Vorträge und Aufsätze), 1975 New York: Harper & Row

(6) David Farrell Krell; Nietzsche, Vol. I: The Will to Power as Art, 1980 New York: Harper & Row


chin.:

(7) Wei Hsiung; Sein und Zeit 存在与时间 (Tsun dsai yü schi djiän), Peking 1963

(8) Wei Hsiung; Über den Humanismus 论人道主义 (Lun ren dau dschou yi), Peking 1963

(9) Wei Hsiung: Was ist Metaphysik? 形而上学是什么? (Hsing erh schang hsüa schi schi mo?), Peking 1964

(1o) Wei Hsiung; Holzwege 林中路 (Lin dschong lu), Peking 1964


franz.:

(11) André Préau; Essais et Conférences, Identité et Difference (Questions I) Gallimard, 1958, 1968; Sérénité (Questions III) Gallimard, 1966

(12) Rudolf Boehm und Alphonse de Waelhens; L'être et le temps, Gallimard 1964

(13) Francois Fédier; La Physis (Questions II), Gallimard 1968; Temps et Etre, (Questions IV) Gallimard, 1976; Acheminement vers la parole, Gallimard, 1976

(14) Gérard Granel; Qu'appelle-t-on penser?, Presses Universitaires de France, 1959; Contribution à la question de l'être. (Questions I), Gallimard, 1968

(15) Gilbert Kahn; Introduction â la métaphysique, P.U.F., 1958; Gallimard, 1967

(16) Henri Corbin; Qu'est-ce que la métaphysique? (jetzt in Questions I), Gallimard, 1937; Gallimard, 1968

(17) Jean Beauffret; Introduction aux philosophes de l'existence. (I), Denoel-Gonthier, 1971; Dialogue avec Heidegger I, II, III, (D1; D2; D3), Editions de Minuit, 1973, 1973, 1974

(18) mit Kostas Axelos; Qu'est-ce que la philosophie? (Questions II), Gallimard, 1968

(19) mit Francois Fédier; La fin de la philosophie et la tâche de la pensée. (Question IV), Gallimard, 1976

(2o) mit D. Janicaud; Hegel et les Grecs. (Qu. II) Gallimard 1968

(21) Jean-Francois Courtine; Schelling, Gallimard, 1977

(22) Claude Roels und Jean Lauxerois; Protocole d'un séminaire sur la conférence Temps et Etre; Le tournant. (Question (IV), Gallimard, 1976

(23) Roger Munier; Lettre sur l'humanisme, Aubier, 1964; Qu'est-ce que la métaphysique (Introduction et Postface) Questions I, Gallimard, 1964

ital.:

(24) Chiodi, Pietro; Essere e tempo. L'essenza del fondamento. 1969 (1961) Turin

(25) Chiodi, Pietro; Essere e tempo. L'essenza del fondamento. (M.H. Sein und Zeit. 7.Auflage. Tübingen 1953. Vom Wesen des Grundes. 5.Auflage. Frankfurt a.M. 1965), 1969, Turin

(26) Reina, Maria Elena; Kant e il problema della metafisica. (M.H. Kant und das Problem der Metaphysik. 3.Auflage. Frankfurt a.M. 1965), 1962, Mailand

(27) Paci, Enzo; Che cos'é la metafisica? (ohne Nachwort und Einleitung) 1946, Mailand

(28) Carlini, Armado; Che cos'é la metafisica? (Con estratti della "Lettera su l'Umanesimo") (M.H. Was ist Metaphysik? 9.Auflage. Frankfurt a.M. 1965), 1953, Florenz

(29) Cantoni, Carlo; Hölderlin e l'essenza della poesia, in "Studi Germanici", 2(1), Heft 1 (M.H. Hölderlin und das Wesen der Dichtung, in "Erläuterungen ...". 2.Aufl. Frankfurt a.M. 1951) Mit Seitenangaben. 1937 Florenz

(3o) Carlini, Armado; Dell'essenza della verità (M.H. Vom Wesen der Wahrheit. 2.Aufl. Frankfurt a.M. 1949), 1952, Mailand

(31) Vattimo, Gianni - Bixio, Andrea; La dottrina di Platone. Lettera sull' umanesimo. (M.H. Platons Lehre von der Wahrheit. Mit einem Brief über den "Humanismus", Bern, 1947), 1978, Turin

(32) Carlini, Armado; Che cos'é la metafisica? (Con estratti della "Lettera su l'Umanesimo") (M.H. Über den Humanismus. Frankfurt a.M. 1949), 1953 Florenz

(33) Vattimo, Gianni - Bixio, Andrea; La dottrina di Platone sulla verità.
     Lettere sull'umanesimo. (M.H. Platons Lehre von der Wahrheit. Mit einem
     Brief über den "Humanismus". Francke Verlag Bern 1947), 1978 Turin

(34) Chiodi, Pietro; Sentieri interotti. (M.H. Holzwege. Frankfurt a.M. 195o),
     1968 Florenz

(35) Vattimo, Gianni; Saggi e Discorsi. (M.H. Vorträge und Aufsätze. Pfullin-
     gen 1954), 1976 Mailand

(36) Vattimo, Gianni - Ugazzi, Ugo; Che cosa significa pensare? (I.Parte)
     (M.H. Was heißt Denken? Tübingen 1954), 1978 Mailand

(37) Manno Mario; Che cos'é la filosofia? in "Heidegger e la filosofia", SS.
     99-152 (M.H. Was ist das-die Philosophie? Pfullingen 1956), 1962 Rom

(38) Landolt, Eduard; Il sentiero di campagna, in "Teoresi", 16, SS. 3-27
     (M.H. Der Feldweg. Frankfurt a.M. 1953 (1949)), 1961 Catania

(39) Favino, Francesco; Dall'esperienza del pensare, in "Filosofia", 8, SS.
     373-378, 1957 Turin

(4o) Landolt, Eduard; Dall'esperienza del pensare, in"Teoresi", 2o, SS. 3-28
     (M.H. Aus der Erfahrung des Denkens. Pfullingen 1954 (1947)),1965
     Catania

(41) Landolt, Eduard; Rilassamento, I. in "Teoresi", 24, SS.3-17; 1969 Ca-
     tania; II.in "Teoresi",27, SS.3-35 (M.H. Gelassenheit. Pfullingen 1959),
     1972 catania

(42) Landolt, Eduard - Cristaldi, Mariano; Identità e Differenza, I. "Teoresi"
     21, SS.3-22; 1966 Catania; II. "Teoresi", 22, SS.213-235 (M.H. Identität
     und Differenz. Pfullingen 1957), 1967 Catania

(43) Caracciolo, Alberto; In cammino verso il linguaggio. (M.H. Unterwegs
     zur Sprache. Pfullingen 1957), 1973 Mailand

(44) Guzzoni, Giorgio; Dell'essere e del concetto della PHYSIS. Aristotele
     Fisica B 1, in "Il Pensiero",2, SS.235-26o u. 3, SS.372-395 (M.H. Vom
     Wesen und Begriff der PHYSIS. Aristoteles Physik B 1, in "Il Pensiero",
     2, SS.129-156 u. 3,SS. 265-29o), 1958 Mailand

(45) Lacorte, Carmelo; La tesi kntiana sull'essere, in "Studi Urbinati di
     Storia, Filosofia e Letteratura", 42, SS. 4-67 (M.H. Kants These über
     das Sein. Frankfurt a.M. 1963 (1962)), 1968 Urbino


jap.:
(46) Keijijōgaku towa Nani ka (Was ist Metaphysik?), translated by Ōe Sei-
     shiro, 1952, 9oP.

(47) Niche no Kotoba "Kami wa Shiseri" (Nietzsches Wort "Gott ist tot"),

translated by Hosoya Sadao. 1954, PP.1-76.

Hegeru no "Keiken" Gainen (Hegels Begriff der Erfahrung), translated by Hsoya Sadao, 1954. PP.76-195.

(48) Herudārin no Shi no Kamei (Erläuterungen zu Hölderlins Dichtung), translated by Tezuka Tomio, Saito Shinji, Tsuchida Sadao, Takeuchi Toyoji. 1955, 234P.

(49) Anakushimandorosu no Kotoba (Der Spruch des Anaximander, in Holzwege), translated by Tanaka Masuo. 1957. 129P.

(5o) Toboshiki Jidai no Shijin (Wozu Dichter?, in Holzwege), translated by Tezuka Tomio and Takahashi Hideo. 1958. 118P.

(51) Shii no Keiken yori (Aus der Erfahrung des Denkens), translated by Tsujimura Kōichi. 196o. 71P.

(52) Tetsugaku towa Nanika (Was ist das-die Philosophie?), translated by Hara Tasuku. 196o. 75P.

(53) No no Michi (Feldweg), Heberu - Ie no Tomo (Hebel , der Hausfreund), translated by Kōsaka Masaaki and Tsujimura Kōichi. 196o. 84P.

(54) Keijijōgaku-Nyūmon (Einführung in die Metaphysik), translated by Kawahara Eihō. 196o. 279P.

(55) Dōchisei to Saisei (Identität und Differenz), translated by Oe Seishirō. 196o. 86P.

(56) Shinri no Honshitsu nitsuite (Vom Wesen der Wahrheit), Puraton no Shinri-Ron (Platons Lehre von der Wahrheit), translated by Kiba Shinjō. 1961. 168P.

(57) Geijutsusakuhin no Hajimari (Der Ursprung des Kunstwerks), translated by Kikuchi Eiichi. 1962. 137P.

(58) Sekaizō no Jidai (Die Zeit des Weltbildes), translated by Kuwaki Tsutomo. 1962. 93P.

(59) Shi to Kotoba (Die Sprache im Gedicht, in Unterwegs zur Sprache), translated by Miki Masayuki. 1963. 124P.

(6o) Hōge (Gelassenheit), translated by Tsujimura Kōichi. 1963. 154P.

(61) Sonzai to Jikan (Sein und Zeit), translated by Hosoya Sadao, Kamei Yutaka and Funabashi Hiroshi. 1963. XVI,42oP., XVII,395P.

(62) Gijutsu-Ron (Die Technik und die Kehre), translated by Kojima Takahiko and Armbruster. 1965. 1o6P.

(63) Kanto to Keijijōgaku no Mondai (Kant und das Problem der Metaphysik), translated by Kiba Shinjō. 1967. 273P.

(64) U ni tsuite no Kanto no Teze (Kants These über das Sein), translated by Tsujimura Kōichi. 1972. 1o4P.

(65) Kotoba ni tsuite no Taiwa (Aus einem Gespräch von der Sprache, in

Unterwegs zur Sprache), translated by Tezuka Tomio. 1968. 166P.

(66) U no Toi e (Zur Seinsfrage), translated by Kakihara Tokuya. 197o. 281P.

(67) Hyūmanizumu ni tsuite (Brief über den Humanismus & Der Weg zur Sprache), translated by Sasaki Kazuyoshi. 1974. 2o7P.

(68) Niche (Nietzsche), translated by Hosoya Sadao. 1975. 534P.; 1977. 528P. XXIV,534P., XXV,528P.

(69) Kagaku to Chinshi (Wissenschaft und Besinnung, in Vorträage und Aufsätze.), translated by Arai Shigeo. Risō, 518, Tōkyō, 1976. PP. 129-14o; Risō, 519, 1956. PP. 134-144.

(7o) Keijijōgaku no Chōkoku (Überwindung der Metaphysik, in Vorträge und Aufsätze), translated by Arai Shigeo. Risō, 522, Tōkyō, 1976, PP. 151-165; Risō, 523, 1976, PP. 143-155.

(71) Mono e no Toi (Die Frage nach dem Ding), translated by Arifuku Kōgaku. Kōyoshobō, Kyōto, 1978. 342P.

(72) Niche no Tsuaratosutora wa dare ka (Wer ist Nietzsches Zarathustra, in Vorträge und Aufsätze), translated by Arai Shigeo, Risō, 524, Tōkyō, 1977, PP. 18o-191: Risō, 525, 19z7, PP. 15o-162.

(73) Sonzai to Jikan (Sein und Zeit), translated by Hara Tasuku and Watanabe Jirō. Chūōkoronsha. Tōkyō. 1971. 686P.

(74) Haideggā wa Kataru (Martin Heidegger im Gespräch im Richard Wisser in TV), translated by Kawahara Eihō. Risōsha, Tōkyō, 1973, 94P.

(75) Haideggā no Benmei (Heidegger/Spiegel Dialogue), translated by Kawahara Eihō. Risō, 52o Tōkyō , 1976, PP. 2-38.

(76) Hyūmanizumu ni tsuite (Brief über den Humanismus), translated by Kuwaki Tsutomo. Kadokawa. Tōkyō. 1958. 11oP.

(77) Tetsugaku no Owari to Shii no Shimei (Ende der Philosophie und die Aufgabe des Denkens), translated by Kawaharw Eihō. Ikeru Kierkegaard (Jinbun-senscho 3) Jinbun-Schoin, Tōkyō, 1967, PP. 129-155.

(78) Sonzai to Jikan (Sein und Zeit), translated by Kuwaki Tsutomo. 3 Vols. Iwanami Tōkyō. 196o, 1963. I 3o5P., II 373P., III 335P.

(79) Sonzai to Jikan (Sein und Zeit), translated by Matsuo Keikichi. 2 Vols. Keiso-Shobō, Tōkyō, 196o. I 467P. 1966. II 536P.

(8o) Konkyo no Honshitsu (Vom Wesen des Grundes), translated by Saitō Shinji. Risōsha, Tōkyō. 1939. 87P.

(81) Niche (Nietzsche), translated by Sonoda Muneto. Hakusuisha. Tōkyō, 1976. 5o2P., 1977. 3ooP.

(82) Shisaku no Kotogara e (Zur Sache des Denkens), translated by Tsujimura Kōichi and Hartmut Buchner. Chikuma-Shobō. Tōkyō, 1973. 224P.

(83) Konkyoritsu (Der Satz vom Grund), translated by Tsujimura Kōichi and Hartmut Buchner. Sōbunsha, Tōkyō, 1962. 335P.

(84) Shii no Shimei (Zur Frage nach der Bestimmung der Sache des Denkens), translated by Tsujimura Kōichi. Kōza Zen 8, Chikuma-Shobō, Tōkyō. 1968. PP. 321-365.

(85) U to Toki (Sein und Zeit), translated by Tsujimura Kōichi. Kawade-shobō-shinsha, Tōkyō. 1967. 527P.

(86) Arēteia (Aletheia, in Vorträge und Aufsätze), translated by Utsunomiya Yoshiaki. Risō 516, Tōkyō, 1976, PP. 2o2-214; Risō, 517, 1976, PP. 1o6-12o.

(87) Moira (Moira, in Vorträge und Aufsätze), translated by Utsunomiya Yoshiaki. Risō 514, Tōkyō, 1976, PP. 143-155; Risō 515, 1976, PP. 147-16o.

(88) Rogos (Logos, in Vorträge und Aufsätze), translated by Utsunomiya Yoshiaki. Risō 512, Tōkyō, 1976, PP. 172-184; Risō 513, 1976, PP. 164-176.


span.:

(89) José Gaos; El Ser y el Tiempo (Sein und Zeit, 1927), [1]1951, México

(9o) Gred Ibscher Roth ("Revisión": El Cecilia Frost); Kant y el problema de la metafisica (Kant und das Problem der Metaphysik, 1929), [1]1954, México

(91) Juan David Garcia Bacca; Esencia del fundamento (Vom Wesen des Grundes, 1929), 1944, México

(92) Eduardo García Belsunce; "De la esencia del fundamento" (Vom Wesen des Grundes, Wegmarken, 1967). In: Ser, verdad y fundamento, [1]1968, Caracas

(93) Raimundo Lida; Qué es metafísica? (Was ist Metaphysik? , 1929), 1932, Buenos Aires

(94) Xavier Zubiri; Qué es metafísica? (Was ist Metaphysik?, 1929), 1933, Madrid

(95) Rafael Gutiérrez Girardot; El retorno al fundamento de la metafísica ("Einleitung"von 1949 zu Was ist Metaphysik?), 1952, Bogotá

(96) Eduardo García Belsunce; Qué es metafísica? Epílogo ("Nachwort" von 1949 zu Was ist Metaphysik?), 1964, La Plata (Argentinien)

(97) (Carlos Astrada); De la esencia de la verdad (aus einer stenographi-schen Fassung des Vortrages von Heidegger, 193o), 1948, Buenos Aires

(98) Eduardo García Belsunce; De la esencia de la verdad (Vom Wesen der Wahrheit, Wegmarken, 1967). In: Ser, verdad y fundamento, 1968, caracas

(99) Humberto Piñera Llera; De la esencia de la verdad (Vom Wesen der Wahr-

heit, [2]1949), 1952, La Habana

(1oo) Juan David García Bacca; Doctrina de la verdad según Platón (Platons Lehre von der Wahrheit, 1947), s.d. (1958?), Santiago de Chile

(1o1) Noberto V. Silvetti ("supervisada": Carlos Astrada); La doctrina de Platón acerca de la verdad (Platons Lehre von der Wahrheit, 1947), 1953, Buenos Aires

(1o2) G. F.; Hölderlin y la esencia de la poesía (Hölderlin und das Wesen der Dichtung, 1936). In: Escorial. Revista de cultura y letras. 1943 Madrid

(1o3) Juan David García Bacca; Hölderlin y la esencia de la poesía (Hölderlin und das Wesen der Dichtung, 1936, 1943). Verbesserte, kommentierte Ausgabe der Übersetzung-Ausgaben von 1944 und 1955. [3]1969, Mérida (Venezuela)

(1o4) Samuel Ramos; Hölderlin y la esencia de la poesía (Hölderlin und das Wesen der Dichtung, 1943), 1958, México

(1o5) Rafael Gutiérrez Girardot; En poema habita el hombre ("... dichterisch wohnet der Mensch...", 1954), 1955, Caracas

(1o6) Ruth Fischer de Walker; "... poéticamente habita el hombre ..." "... dichterisch wohnet der Mensch ..." ("... dichterisch wohnet der Mensch ...", 1954), 196o, Santiago de Chile; 1963, Hamburg

(1o7) Alberto Wagner de Reyna; Carta sobre el humanismo (Brief über den "Humanismus"), s.d. (1958), Santiago de Chile

(1o8) Rafael Gutiérrez Girardot; Carta sobre el humanismo (Brief über den "Humanismus"), 1959, [3]197o, Madrid

(1o9) Francisco Soler Grima; El origen de la obra de arte (Der Ursprung des Kunstwerks), 1949), 1952, Madrid

(11o) Samuel Ramos; El origen de la obra de arte (Der Ursprung des Kunstwerks), 1958, [3]1978, México

(111) José Rovira Armengol; El origen de la obra de arte (Der Ursprung des Kunstwerks), 196o, Buenos Aires

(112) Tulia de Dross; El arte y el espacio (Die Kunst und der Raum), 197o, Bogotá

(113) Haraldo Kahnemann; Qué significa pensar? (Was heißt Denken?), s.d. (1958), Buenos Aires

(114) Eduardo García Belsunce - Zoltan Szankay; La pregunta por la cosa (Die Frage nach dem Ding), 1962, [2]1975, Buenos Aires

(115) Rafael Gutiérrez Girardot; La cosa (Das Ding, Gestalt und Gedanke, 1951), 1953, Córdoba (Argentinien)

(116) Víctor Sánchez de Zavala; La cosa (Das Ding, Vorträge und Aufsätze, 1954), 1958, Madrid

(117) Alberto Wagner de Reyna; La época de la imagen del mundo (Die Zeit des Weltbildes, Holzwege, 1950), 1958, Santiago de Chile

(118) José Rovira Armengol; La época de la imagen del mundo (Die Zeit des Weltbildes, Holzwege, 1950). In: Sendas perdidas, [1]1960 Buenos Aires

(119) Víctor Li Carrillo; Qué es esto, la filosofía? (Was ist das - die Philosophie?), 1958, Lima

(120) Adolfo P. Carpio; Qué es eso de filosofía? (Was ist das - die Philosophie?), 1960, Buenos Aires

(121) José Luis Molinuevo; Qué es filosofía? (Was ist das - die Philosophie?) 1978, Madrid